OCR Anthology for Classical Greek AS and A Level: 2021–2023

The following titles are available from Bloomsbury for the OCR specifications in Latin and Greek for examinations from June 2021 to June 2023

Catullus: A Selection of Poems, with introduction, commentary notes and vocabulary by John Godwin

Cicero *Pro Cluentio*: A Selection, with introduction, commentary notes and vocabulary by Matthew Barr

Livy *History of Rome* I: A Selection, with introduction, commentary notes and vocabulary by John Storey

Ovid *Heroides*: A Selection, with introduction, commentary notes and vocabulary by Christina Tsaknaki

Tacitus *Annals* IV: A Selection, with introduction, commentary notes and vocabulary by Robert Cromarty

Virgil *Aeneid* XII: A Selection, with introduction, commentary notes and vocabulary by James Burbidge

OCR Anthology for Classical Greek AS and A Level, covering the prescribed texts by Aristophanes, Homer, Plato, Plutarch, Sophocles and Thucydides, with introduction, commentary notes and vocabulary by Simon Allcock, Sam Baddeley, John Claughton, Alastair Harden, Sarah Harden, Carl Hope and Jo Lashly

Supplementary resources for these volumes can be found at
www.bloomsbury.com/OCR-editions-2021-2023

Please type the URL into your web browser and follow the instructions to access the Companion Website. If you experience any problems, please contact Bloomsbury at academicwebsite@bloomsbury.com

OCR Anthology for Classical Greek AS and A Level: 2021–2023

Selections from

Thucydides, *Histories*, Book 6

Plato, *Symposium*

Plutarch, *Alcibiades*

Homer, *Odyssey*, Books 1 and 6

Sophocles, *Ajax*

Aristophanes, *Clouds*

With introduction, commentary notes and vocabulary by
Simon Allcock, Sam Baddeley, John Claughton,
Alastair Harden, Sarah Harden, Carl Hope
and Jo Lashly

BLOOMSBURY ACADEMIC
LONDON • NEW YORK • OXFORD • NEW DELHI • SYDNEY

BLOOMSBURY ACADEMIC
Bloomsbury Publishing Plc
50 Bedford Square, London, WC1B 3DP, UK
1385 Broadway, New York, NY 10018, USA

BLOOMSBURY, BLOOMSBURY ACADEMIC and the Diana logo are trademarks of Bloomsbury
Publishing Plc

First published in Great Britain 2020

Cover design: Terry Woodley
Cover image © Hoika Mikhail/Shutterstock

A catalogue record for this book is available from the British Library.

A catalog record for this book is available from the Library of Congress.

ISBN: PB: 978-1-3500-6042-5
       ePDF: 978-1-3500-6044-9
       eBook: 978-1-3500-6043-2

Typeset by RefineCatch Limited, Bungay, Suffolk
Printed and bound in India

To find out more about our authors and books visit www.bloomsbury.com and sign up for our
newsletters.

CONTENTS

The teaching content of this resource is endorsed by OCR for use with specification AS Level Classical Greek (H044) and specification A Level Classical Greek (H444). In order to gain OCR endorsement, this resource has been reviewed against OCR's endorsement criteria.

This resource was designed using the most up to date information from the specification. Specifications are updated over time which means there may be contradictions between the resource and the specification, therefore please use the information on the latest specification and Sample Assessment Materials at all times when ensuring students are fully prepared for their assessments.

Any references to assessment and/or assessment preparation are the publisher's interpretation of the specification requirements and are not endorsed by OCR. OCR recommends that teachers consider using a range of teaching and learning resources in preparing learners for assessment, based on their own professional judgement for their students' needs. OCR has not paid for the production of this resource, nor does OCR receive any royalties from its sale. For more information about the endorsement process, please visit the OCR website, www.ocr.org.uk.

GENERAL PREFACE

The text and notes found in this volume are designed to guide any student who has mastered Greek up to GCSE level and wishes to read these selections in the original.

The editions are, however, particularly designed to support students who are reading the set text in preparation for OCR's AS and A-level Greek examination from June 2021–June 2023. (Please note this edition uses AS to refer indiscriminately to AS and the first year of A level, i.e. Group 1.)

Thucydides, *Histories*
Introduction, commentary notes and vocabulary by John Claughton
AS: Book 6: 19–32
A Level: Book 6: 47–50.1, 53–61

Plato, *Symposium*
Introduction, commentary notes and vocabulary by Simon Allcock
AS: 189c2–194e2
A Level: 201d–206b

Plutarch, *Alcibiades*
Introduction, commentary notes and vocabulary by Carl Hope
A Level: 10.1.1–16.5

Homer, *Odyssey*
Introduction and vocabulary by Sarah Harden and Alastair Harden
Commentary notes to Book 1 by Sarah Harden
Commentary notes to Book 6 by Alastair Harden
AS: Book 1: 213–444
A Level: Book 6: 85–331

Sophocles, *Ajax*
Introduction, commentary notes and vocabulary by Sam Baddeley
AS: 1–133, 284–347, 748–783
A Level: 430–582, 646–692, 815–865

Aristophanes, *Clouds*
Introduction, commentary notes and vocabulary by Jo Lashly
A Level: 1–242

Each edition contains a detailed introduction to the context of the ancient work. The notes aim to help students bridge the gap between GCSE and AS level or A-level Greek, and focus therefore on the harder points of grammar, word order and idiom. At the end of the book is a full vocabulary list for all the words contained in the prescribed sections, with words in OCR's Defined Vocabulary List for AS Level Greek flagged by means of an asterisk.

Thucydides, *Histories* Book 6

Introduction, Commentary Notes and Vocabulary by John Claughton

AS: 19–32

A Level: 47–50.1, 53–61

Introduction

Thucydides the historian

In front of the Royal Palace in Syntagma Square, Athens, the Evzones, with their tasselled clogs and wondrous choreography, guard the Tomb of the Unknown Soldier. Inscribed on the wall behind them are two inscriptions from Thucydides, both taken from his account of the public funeral which took place in 430 BCE, at the end of the first year of the Peloponnesian War. The inscription on the left quotes Thucydides' narrative of the funeral, 'There is one empty, decorated bier for the missing.' (2.34.2). The inscription on the right quotes the speech which Thucydides gives to Pericles, the Funeral Oration, perhaps the most important statement of a people's values in history: 'For brave men, the whole earth is their tomb.' (2.43.3)

In 1.22.4 Thucydides writes that his purpose in writing the history of the Peloponnesian War is to produce 'a possession for all time'. Whether he achieves that, only time will tell, but it has survived for more than 2,400 years and, in Syntagma Square and elsewhere, his words are read every day around the world. In recent years his name has even had something of a revival: the Thucydides Trap, a dominant state going to war in fear of losing that dominance, has become a potent way of thinking about global politics.

> Thucydides the Athenian wrote the history of the war fought between Athens and Sparta, beginning the account at the very outbreak of the war, in the belief that it was going to be a great war and more worth writing about than any of those which had taken place in the past. (1.1.1–2)

So begins Thucydides' work and his work as a historian is striking in a number of ways. The first is that he is writing as a contemporary historian: he tells us that he lives as an adult through this war which lasted, on and off, from 431 BCE to 404 BCE (5.26.4). Although we have no exact date of his birth, the best use of the evidence is that he was born about 460 BCE: if he was a general in 424 BCE (see below p. 4), he would have had to be born before 454 BCE. Although Thucydides writes as a historian who has seen and analysed the end of the war in 404 BCE, (cf. 2.65) his narrative comes to an abrupt end in 411 BCE: 'Tissaphernes went first to Ephesus where he made a sacrifice to Artemis. . . .' This is not some failure of survival of the manuscript because Xenophon, whose *Hellenica* survives, and two other authors whose works are lost, all took up Thucydides' narrative, starting where he left off. It must be assumed that, although he lived to see the end of the war, he did not live to see the end of his writing about that war.

The second striking aspect is that he was actually a participant in the war. Indeed, such was his closeness to events that he even caught the plague which attacked Athens – and killed Pericles – in the early years of the war (2.48.3). More importantly, he was one the ten generals elected annually by the Athenians in 424 BCE. Perhaps this is no surprise in that Thucydides, son of Olorus, clearly came from an aristocratic family: in Herodotus 6.39.2, we hear of a Thracian king, Olorus, whose daughter married Miltiades, the victor of Marathon. And he was related to another Thucydides, son of Melesias, the rival of Pericles in the middle years of the fifth century. Thucydides tells us (4.104–108) that, in 424 BCE, he was in command in northern Greece of an Athenian force that failed to defend the strategically important town of Amphipolis from the Spartan general Brasidas. After such a failure, he was, like other Athenian generals during the war, sent into exile so that, between 424 BCE and Athens' defeat in 404 BCE, he lived in exile. It must have been a bitter exile as he watched from a distance the Athenian slide towards defeat, but, as he tells us (5.26.5), that distance did enable him to gain evidence from all sides that would have been impossible for him as an Athenian fighting for Athens.

The third important element is that Thucydides is writing in full awareness of, and reaction to, Herodotus, his older contemporary who had written a work of similar scale about the Persian Wars and their origins. Thucydides' opening words, quoted above, echo Herodotus' first sentence.

> This is the publication of the enquiry of Herodotus of Halicarnassus, written so that the achievements of men should not be rubbed out by time and so that the great and remarkable deeds of men, some performed by Greeks, some by non-Greeks, should not be without glory. And, in particular it is an explanation of why they waged war against each other.

Herodotus was probably in Athens and his work was certainly known there by the mid-420s BCE. The whole of the first chapter is an introduction in which Thucydides proves, to his own satisfaction, that nothing of any great significance occurred before the Peloponnesian War, thus putting the Persian Wars, and Herodotus in their place. When Thucydides comes to define his own, meticulous methodology in 1.20, he deliberately doesn't name Herodotus, but that doesn't stop it being obvious that he has Herodotus on his mind:

> People are inclined to accept all stories of ancient times in an uncritical way.

He then gives, as examples of the lack of rigorous method, two 'errors' that are to be found in Herodotus, about the killing of Hipparchus whom Herodotus falsely names as the tyrant of Athens (5.55), and about the voting rights of the Spartan kings. And it is to the first of these errors that Thucydides returns at greater length in 6.53–59.

In 1.21 Thucydides once again sets himself apart by emphasizing the difference between his use of evidence and those of 'the prose-chroniclers, who are less interested in telling the truth than in catching the attention of their public'. And his most striking statement about his work's purpose, that it is 'a possession for all time' is set against 'a piece of work designed to meet the taste of an immediate public'.

Perhaps the greatest difference lies in the tightness of narrative and structure adopted by Thucydides compared with the world-wandering of Herodotus. Both historians are committed to the central purpose of history, to explain 'why' as well as 'what', but their methods are very different. Herodotus' account of the conflict between Greeks and Persians ranges across time and space, going back to the land of myth, jumping across generations to offer explanations, and describing Scythia and Egypt in great detail. Thucydides locks himself, with a few exceptions into the period of the fifth century BCE and to the sites of conflict, proceeding deliberately and explicitly in an annalistic way: the war is divided up year by year by year.

So ended the second year of this war recorded by Thucydides. (2.71)

Herodotus' work has the whole of human life in it: Thucydides is about war and politics and power, and not much else.

The fourth aspect is the most important of all. Thucydides sets himself a most serious task and then undertakes it in the most serious of ways. His purpose is to enable future generations to understand the world better and thereby, he hopes, make better judgements:

It will be enough for me if these words are judged useful by those who want to understand clearly the events which happened in the past and which, human nature being what it is, will, at some time or other and in much the same ways be repeated in the future. (1.22.5)

The seriousness of his method has two distinct characteristics. The first is that he lays out a clear, explicit methodology about the importance of accuracy, whilst acknowledging the difficulty of the task:

With regard to my factual reporting of the events of the war, I have made it a principle not to write down the first story that came my way, and not even to be guided by my own general impressions; either I was present myself at the events which I have described or else I heard them from eye-witnesses whose reports I have checked with as much thoroughness as possible. Not that even so the truth was easy to discover; different eyewitnesses give different accounts of the same events, speaking out or partiality for one side or the other or else from imperfect memories. (1.22)

In his mind, it is clearly the case that his history cannot be of use to his future readers if it is not accurate. However, he knows that accuracy is not enough: getting the number of ships or casualties might be necessary but it is not sufficient. Thucydides also engages in a deep analysis of events and their causes. Throughout his work, he is searching for the fundamental truths about politics and power, human character and human nature to find the reasons why events happened and why, in the end, the greatness of Athens should be brought low. So, in his accounts of events before our prescription begins – the Plague in Athens (2.47–54), the Civil War in Corcyra (3.82–

85) and the Melian Dialogue (5.84–115) – he charts the collapse of human morality. In his narratives of the revolt on Lesbos (3.36–49) and the Athenian success at Pylos (4.1–41), he shows us the inconsistency of a direct democracy and the destructive power of rhetoric in the hands of demagogues. At Pylos again, and in the expedition to Sicily which occupies books 6 and 7, he represents the dangers of rule by emotion, not reason, the risk of over-confidence bred of good fortune.

Thucydides explores all this through a variety of different methods. Sometimes he tells us directly what his conclusions are, about events and people. The most obvious example of that is in 2.65 where he gives his overarching explanation of the final defeat of Athens. More often, he uses speeches to explore the issues and to set words spoken against the events that ensue. In the passages prescribed in English and Greek, you will read speeches by Nicias (6.9–15, 20–23), Alcibiades (6.16–18) in Athens and Hermocrates (6.33–34) and Athenagoras (6.36–40) which offer predictions about and analysis of future events. These speeches then face the reality of what happens.

As we have seen above in Thucydides' own account of his methods, he accepts that the speeches he records cannot be as 'accurate' as his narrative of events, but, whatever their accuracy, they serve a critical purpose in his work.

The power of Thucydides' thinking and the seriousness of his questions and his answers have brought him the reputation of greatness, if not infallibility. And it is not always easy to gainsay Thucydides when other sources are limited. However, in the succeeding decades a more balanced and critical view of his writing has developed. It has become acceptable to question, if not his commitment to accuracy, at least his judgement and analysis of events and characters. Perhaps, in the end, this just shows that a historian who is not only writing about but participating in contemporary events cannot entirely find the necessary distance to write an objective narrative. Even so, it's hard not to think that Thucydides' work is one of the greatest and most intelligent ever written and that his purpose of creating 'a possession for all time' will be fulfilled.

Book 6: The Sicilian Expedition: its context and its consequences

The setting out of the expedition (6.1–32)

The prescribed passages in Book 6 describe the beginning of the Athenians' expedition to Sicily in 415 BCE, sixteen years after the beginning of the war and six after the Peace of Nicias, which brought the first phase of the war to an end.

This expedition sets out with high hopes and big ambitions but it ends in 413 BCE with a defeat that, in the eyes of Thucydides, was very significant in the final defeat of Athens. Thucydides marks out the significance of the moment and the decision to undertake the expedition in three different ways. So, firstly, Book 6 begins with a detailed historical account of the history of Sicily and the different peoples that have occupied and colonized the islands (6.1–6). Then, secondly, Thucydides gives an extensive presentation of the debate in the Athenian assembly about the decision to launch the expedition (8–25). That debate presents two speeches by the reluctant Nicias (6.9–14, 6.20–23) and the ambitious Alcibiades (6.16–18), the two key figures in the whole ensuing narrative, as the Athenian people are led in different directions by different arguments and different characters. Thirdly, Thucydides gives a detailed account of the scale and magnificence of the expedition as it sets out (6.30–32). It is as if this is the equivalent of the Homeric and heroic expedition against Troy.

However, there is a cloud that comes to overshadow the departure of the expedition, acts of sacrilege in Athens: in chapters 27–29 Thucydides describes the evidence that is brought forward about abuse of the Eleusinian Mysteries, the most sacred and significant rites enacted in the city state of Athens, and about acts of vandalism against the Herms, stone statues of Hermes visible throughout the city. Alcibiades is implicated in these activities and there is a dispute as to whether he should lead the expedition in such circumstances.

Reaction in Syracuse (6.32–41)

At this point, Thucydides turns his focus from Athens to Sicily in general and Syracuse in particular. Syracuse is the main objective of the expedition and he presents a debate there which is a mirror of the debate in Athens, reflecting the differing opinions and adversarial nature of debate. Just as in Athens, there are two speakers at odds with each other: Hermocrates (6.33–34), who urges the Syracusans to take seriously the imminent threat of the Athenians; and Athenagoras (6.36–40), who dismisses the whole notion and uses the moment to attack his political opponents.

The arrival of the Athenians in Sicily (6.42–52)

Chapters 42–46 describe – once again – the scale of the Athenian expeditionary force as it sets out from Corcyra but also show the reality of the situation in southern Italy and Sicily where the Athenians do not receive the welcome and support which they had anticipated: in particular, the funds promised by Egesta (see p. 4 below) did not exist. So, Thucydides represents the three different tactical proposals of the three Athenian generals: Nicias, who wants to go home; Alcibiades, who proposes a gradual progress along the coast of Sicily; and Lamachus, who urges an immediate attack on Syracuse (47–50). Alcibiades' plan is adopted to no great effect but this is his last act as a general on the expedition because at this point the Athenians summon him home to face trial (6.53).

A digression: Harmodius and Aristogeiton (6.53–59)

At this point, Thucydides turns aside from his narrative to account for the high state of anxiety in Athens at the acts of sacrilege. It is associated with the threat of tyranny imposed by the aristocracy and he now tells the story of the murder of Hippocrates, the brother of the tyrant Hippias, by Harmodius and Aristogeiton.

The escape of Alcibiades (6.60–61)

Thucydides describes events in Athens after the departure of the expedition and the decision to recall Alcibiades. However, Alcibiades never does return, jumping ship at Thurii and escaping to Sparta.

The wider context

It is not possible to join in with the Sicilian Expedition, to be thrust in medias res, into the later books of Thucydides without some wider historical, even ethnological and geographical, context. The following sections attempt to provide that context in a variety of different ways and from different angles.

Ionians and Dorians, the Greek diaspora and Sicily

We live round the sea like ants or frogs around a pond.

So says Socrates in Plato's *Phaedo* (109b), the account of his final conversations before he drinks the hemlock that kills him.

The Greeks did not only or always live in mainland Greece. The received narrative amongst the Greeks (as told, for example, by Thucydides himself at 1.12) was that the Ionians, of whom the Athenians were part, were the original, autochthonous inhabitants of Greece and the Dorians came from the north to settle in the Peloponnese and Boeotia in the centuries around 1000 BCE. That difference, in dialect, in myth, cult and sympathy, was a fault-line in Greek history and is still at play in the Peloponnesian War.

At the same time as the Dorian invasions from the north, some Ionian Greeks migrated from the mainland to the islands of the Aegean and its eastern coast, an area which the Greeks called Ionia and which is now the coast of Turkey. There cities such as Smyrna, Ephesus and Miletus grew up to be as rich and powerful as the cities of the Greek mainland. And it was these strong ties of Ionian ancestry which were the basis of much that happened in the Greek world in the early fifth century BCE, long before the Peloponnesian War: it was the Athenians who went to the help of the Ionian cities in their revolt against Persia in 499 BCE, which led to the Persian attack on Athens in 490 BCE; after the Persian Wars, Athens formed the largely Ionian cities into the Delian League as a defence against future Persian incursions and that Delian League became the Athenian Empire from the middle of the fifth century [see below p. 4].

Both the Dorian invasion of mainland Greece and the Ionian migration eastwards from mainland Greece would have taken place gradually over a long period of time so that dating is necessarily imprecise. However, the next phase of migration has more specific and dateable events, starting in the second half of the eighth century BCE and ending by the beginning of the sixth century. These migrations included colonization of Sicily, a key background event in the prescription you will read.

Mainland Greece is not a naturally productive country: it is mountainous, jagged and has few rich fertile plains: Plato in *Critias* laments that it was more fertile in the past but now, 'there are remaining only the bones of the wasted body'. As trade and travel developed in the Mediterranean and even into the Black Sea, the communities of the Greek mainland began to see the opportunities elsewhere. This colonization was not a Panhellenic strategy. It was something that individual Greek city states undertook for their own reasons, in their own way, at different times and in different directions, to the north of the Aegean, into the Black Sea, to the coast of North Africa, to southern Italy, to Sicily and even to southern France and Spain.

In 733 BCE settlers from Corinth travelled to Sicily and founded Syracuse on the south-eastern coast, a city with a great natural harbour and a fertile hinterland. At about the same time, people from Chalcis, an Ionian city on the island of Euboea, founded three cities which have significance in the narrative of Book 6, Naxos, Leontini and Catana, and people from Megara founded Megara Hyblaea. All of these foundations were on the east coast of Sicily and were neighbours of Syracuse. Thereafter, colonies themselves became founders of colonies; for example, Megara Hyblaea founded Selinus, and Gela, itself founded in 688 BCE on the south coast of Sicily by Cretans and Rhodians, founded Acragas. So, the only city that is of significance in Thucydides' narrative that is not a Greek colony is Egesta in the west of Sicily, a neighbour of but no friend to Selinus. Egesta had been founded by one of the indigenous peoples of Sicily.

These colonies, throughout the Mediterranean and beyond, were occupied because they offered major advantages and opportunities in trade or natural resources, including fertile land. Although they remained close in kinship and culture to their mother city, their 'metropolis', they were independent and autonomous states. They often became city states of great significance in their time and throughout history. Naples (Neapolis), Marseilles (Massilia), even Monaco, Nice and Antibes are all Greek colonies or colonies of Greek colonies. The southern Italian mainland and Sicily were given a name that reflected this close connection with their mother cities: Magna Graecia. It is an indication of their prosperity that perhaps the greatest and best-preserved Greek temples are found at Paestum (Poseidonia) in southern Italy, and at Selinus, Acragas, Egesta and elsewhere in Sicily.

Another indication of the power of these cities can be found in the work of Pindar, who, in the first half of the fifth century BCE, wrote odes (songs) to celebrate athletic victories at the great sporting festivals at Olympia, Delphi, Nemea and Corinth. A very high density of his odes to celebrate victories in the chariot races, the most expensive and aristocratic of all the events, were written for the tyrants of Sicilian cities, such as Theron of Acragas and Hieron of Syracuse. In one of the prescribed chapters, Alcibiades himself is very keen to emphasize in his speech to the Athenians that he can compete in this Panhellenic sport of the very wealthiest (6.16).

This Ionian/Dorian dichotomy is of material significance during the Peloponnesian War in the relations between the cities of mainland Greece and Sicily. On the first occasion during the war that Athens is drawn into action in Sicily, the people of Leontini, a city colonized by Chalcis, appeal to 'their ancient alliance and to their Ionian origin' against the Syracusans who are in alliance with the other Dorian cities of Sicily and Sparta (3.86). It is a key element in the alliances and actions of the Sicilian Expedition. In 6.34, Hermocrates urges the Syracusans to seek help from

Sparta and Corinth. In a later debate in 415 BCE, he says 'the Ionians, who are always our enemies, are plotting against us, whilst we, being Dorians, are betrayed by you, who are Dorians, too'. (6.80.3) The Athenian speaker at the same debate doesn't disagree: 'The Syracusan representative said that the Ionians are always the enemies of the Dorians. That's true.' (6.82.2) In the same way, Thucydides' catalogue of forces at the final battle at Syracuse (7.57–58) is detailed and specific in his categorization by the Dorian/Ionian divide.

The history of the fifth century BCE and the Peloponnesian War (431–404 BCE)

Events in 415 BCE also need to be set in the context of the relations between the two key city states, Athens and Sparta, of the fifth century and the enmity which led to the Peloponnesian War and the defeat of Athens in 404 BCE.

Athens and Sparta in the fifth century BCE: the causes of the Peloponnesian War

In 480 and 479 BCE, the Persian invasion of Greece, led by Xerxes, was turned back by the Greeks at two key battles, the sea battle in the bay of Salamis in 480 BCE and the land battle at Plataea in Boeotia in 479 BCE. The Spartans had been the nominal leaders of the Greek states that won those victories, but it was perhaps Athens which came out with its reputation enhanced.

Although the Persians had retreated from the Aegean, the Greeks could not trust that this retreat was permanent, so they needed a means to secure their safety and that meant a strong, allied force in the Aegean to protect the islands and the Ionian coast. So, they formed a defensive alliance, the Delian League, led by Athens. Her claim to be a better leader of that alliance than Sparta was based on the fact that, whereas the Spartans were Dorians – land-based, defensive and cautious – the Athenians were Ionians, confident after their victories and equipped with a strong fleet.

In the beginning, the Delian League was based on the tiny and sacred island of Delos, the birthplace of Apollo and Artemis in the very centre of the Aegean. And, in the beginning, the allies contributed ships and men to the defensive alliance. However, as time went by, Athenian influence and power grew, not least because the allies increasingly contributed money, not ships, and the Athenians used that money to grow their own fleet.

So, as time went by, what had started as the Delian League became an Athenian empire and there were certain key indicators of this: in 454 BCE, the funds for the alliance on Delos were transferred to Athens; the language of inscriptions changed from 'Athens and her allies' to 'Athens and the cities over which it rules'; and the freedom to leave the empire disappeared.

In the decades that followed 480 BCE, there was no physical return of the Persian threat and, as time went by, Athens grew in power and wealth from her dominance of the Aegean. That is most clearly still to be seen by the great architectural achievements on the Acropolis, the Parthenon and the Erectheum, and elsewhere, which were built with the funds that came into the treasury in Athens. The key figure in the growth to greatness of Athens was Pericles, who was the dominant political figure from 460 BCE until his death in 430 BCE.

During these years and these developments, Sparta was for a long time content to preserve what it had and work alongside its existing mainland allies. However, there were occasional confrontations in mainland Greece, often centred upon the tension between Athens and Corinth, and in 446 BCE, the Athenians and the Spartans negotiated the Thirty Years' Peace. This was never going to last as the Spartans watched the continued growth of Athenian power and confidence.

In Book 1 Thucydides presents the events that led to the Peloponnesian War in a dual way. On the one hand, he narrates the incidents that were the specific triggers that led to the war: incidents on the west coast of Greece, at Epidamnus (1.24–30) and Corcyra (1.31–55) and in the north of the Aegean, at Epidamnus (1.56–65), where Athens finds itself in conflict with Corinth (see below p. 4). He also records the debates that took place in Sparta between Sparta and her allies (1.66–88, 118–125). On the other hand, he also makes clear that these events do not represent the ultimate cause: the 'truest cause' (1.23.6) was Sparta's fear of the growing power of Athens. The significance of that 'truest cause' is conveyed in Thucydides' narrative of the Pentecontaetia (1.89–117), the 50-year period from 480 BCE to the outbreak of war in 431 BCE.

The Peloponnesian War Phase 1:
The Archidamian War: 431–421 BCE

The Archidamian War, named after Archidamus, who was the king of Sparta during this decade, was an asymmetric war which did not follow any traditional pattern. It was asymmetric in that the strengths of both sides were very different. The Athenians were largely dependent on their sea power and their empire, consisting of the islands and coastlines of the Aegean. The Spartans were land-based and strong in their land force, so that they embarked on the traditional approach, invading and ravaging the enemy's territory in the expectation that they would come out and fight. Pericles and the Athenians were having none of this. Instead, safely behind the walls that encompassed the city and the Piraeus and joined the two together, Athens pretended it was an island and, even under great pressure, did not oblige the Spartans by confronting them in a land battle. In the same way, there was no chance that the Spartans were going to put out to sea for a naval engagement with the large, richly experienced and well-trained Athenian fleet.

In such circumstances, there were only a certain number of devices available to each side. The Spartans would keep on with their annual invasions, but, apart from that, they could strive to undermine the solidarity of the Athenian Empire, and they were most successful in that under Brasidas in the later years of this first phase of the war. The Athenians could use their control of the sea to inflict damage and casualties on the Peloponnesian coast and to attack island territories that were not part of their empire. Later in the war, they also tried to attack Boeotia, Sparta's key ally and Athens' worst neighbour.

During this period, the Athenians also became engaged in military activities in Sicily, which must be a sign of their desire to find an advantage. In 427 BCE, the Athenians came to the aid of the Ionian city of Leontini which was at war with Syracuse and other Dorian colonies. Athens sent 20 ships, ostensibly to keep its side of an ancient alliance, but, according to Thucydides, the real reason was to prevent corn coming from fertile Sicily to Sparta and to conduct a reconnaissance mission about a possible invasion of the island (3.86). At the end of the following year, the Athenians decided to send out a further 40 ships to try to quell the growing power of Syracuse (3.115) and in the spring of 425 BCE they set out (4.2). However, that fleet never got as far as Sicily because it was used by Demosthenes in perhaps the most striking single incident in the Peloponnesian War, the capture and surrender of the Spartans on the island of Sphacteria, off Pylos (4.2–41).

The Athenian intervention in Sicily in the years 427–424 BCE was not decisive: such an outcome was unlikely when there was so much rivalry and tension between the cities of Sicily and suspicion of the Athenians themselves. Hermocrates of Syracuse, a key figure in the debates and actions of the expedition of 415–413 BCE, convinces the cities of Sicily to lay aside their Dorian/Ionian differences as a means of restoring peace and keeping the Athenians at bay (4.59–64). So, in 424 BCE, the cities of Sicily came to a truce which the Athenians had little choice but to accept. However, the Athenians, carried away by their recent triumph at Pylos, blamed their own generals for not bringing back victory, exiling two of them and fining a third (4.65).

In the course of this decade of fighting, there were key, and unexpected, moments, the plague in Athens, the remarkable surrender of the Spartans at Pylos, the great success of Brasidas at Delium and in the north of the Aegean, but, in the end, neither side could secure a significant advantage. So, Nicias gave his name to a peace treaty which enabled Athens to keep the empire which had been so significant in her prosperity and Pericles would have seen that as a victory.

The Peloponnesian War Phase 2: The Peace of Nicias to the failure of the Sicilian Expedition: 421–413 BCE

The signing of a 50-year peace treaty between Athens and Sparta did not bring the end of hostilities in the Greek world. Instead, other tensions emerged and the Athenians, in particular, tried to use the moment to strengthen their position in a variety of ways.

The first area of activity was in the north-east of the Peloponnese. The cities in that area, Argos, Corinth, Elis and Mantinea formed themselves into an alliance in opposition to their previous ally, Sparta, and Athens itself then joined that alliance. All of this activity culminated in the largest land battle of the war, at Mantinea in 418 BCE, a battle which the Spartans won decisively. Thereafter, the Argives and the Spartans agreed to a five-year peace treaty.

The second area was in the Aegean. There the Athenians, to assert their power, forced the neutral island of Melos into surrender and, in the most dreadful act of the war, killed all adult males and enslaved the rest of the population.

The third was Sicily, which is where this prescription from Book 6 takes its place. At a time when the Athenians seemed confident of the situation on mainland Greece and the Aegean, Sicily offered them the chance to extend their power. Selinus and Egesta, two rival cities in the west of Sicily, were at war over disputed territory. Selinus, itself a colony of Megara Hyblaea on the east coast of Sicily, had got help from Syracuse and the people of Egesta, a more ancient non-Greek settlement, were under military pressure and came to Athens for support. As has been described, the Athenians had helped the people of Leontini ten years previously and there were also exiles from Leontini there during the Athenians' deliberations (6.19.1). Their arguments in the Athenian assembly were that Syracuse should not be allowed to intervene in the affairs of other cities – as it had with its neighbour Leontini – lest it grow so strong that it might join with the Spartans and become a threat to Athens itself (6.6).

Because of the political machinations of Nicias and Alcibiades, whose speeches comprise the first passages of your prescribed texts in English and Greek, the expedition was much greater than had been originally proposed and this made logistics more difficult and the risks greater. The expedition was also beset by problems that were, in many cases, foreseeable. The Athenian leadership was fragmented and, for long periods of time, indecisive. On the arrival of the expedition, the three generals, Nicias, Alcibiades and Lamachus could not agree on the right strategy (6.47–50), as described above. The situation was made worse when Alcibiades was recalled to Athens (6.53) and Lamachus was killed (6.103), leaving Nicias, naturally cautious and an opponent of the whole enterprise, in sole command. Secondly, the cities in Sicily were not as welcoming and supportive as the Athenians had hoped, so they did not find it easy to find a foothold in Sicily. Thirdly, the expedition lacked the cavalry which could have been decisive in winning victory. Even so, the Athenians did manage to win a military victory outside Syracuse and to besiege the city itself.

In the end, however, the Athenians were not able to force final victory for three reasons. The first was the arrival of Gylippus, a Spartan general, with Spartan forces to support the Syracusans. The second was the growing weakness of Nicias as a leader, through illness and a fear of how the Athenians might judge the expedition's failure. And, thirdly, Demosthenes, the Athenian general sent to work alongside Nicias, took reckless decisions which led to final and catastrophic defeat (7.85–87).

The endgame: 413–404 BCE

Thucydides presents the disaster in Sicily in remarkable language, as if it were the end of the war (7.87.6):

[The Athenians] had been completely and utterly defeated, having suffered the greatest of misfortunes, "utter destruction" as the saying goes. The infantry, the navy was gone and there was nothing that was not destroyed. Few out of many returned home. This is what happened in Sicily.

And yet, final defeat and surrender, the end of the democracy and the ensuing rule of the Thirty Tyrants were nine years away. In this phase of the war, as in the Archidamian

War, two key centres of activity were the land of Attica and Athens' Aegean empire. However, the strategy and the dramatis personae were different. Instead of annual invasions, the Spartans set up a permanent base at Decelea, which did much more long-term damage to Athens and its sources of revenue. In the Aegean, there was a new key player, the Persians, and the Spartans were dependent on their intervention to make real headway. Another key player, Alcibiades, was not new, but his presence, on either side, became critical. For a time, when he was taken back by Athens, her fortunes were restored, but, in the end, after a serious naval defeat at Aegospotami, Athens was blockaded and forced into submission. The walls were demolished and a Spartan puppet government, the Thirty Tyrants, was installed with the connivance of a number of Athenian aristocratic fellow-travellers. Of these final years, Thucydides' narrative goes only so far as the Athenian sea victory at Cynossema in 411 BCE.

Nicias and Alcibiades

Nicias and Alcibiades, the two key figures of the prescription and the entire account of the Sicilian Expedition came to violent, but very different, ends. After the final catastrophic defeat of the Athenians on their retreat from Syracuse in 413 BCE, Nicias surrendered to the Spartan leader, Gylippus, in the hope that his previous acts of good will towards them might save him. Instead, he was executed by some Syracusans along with his fellow general, Demosthenes:

> So, Nicias died, of all the Greeks of my time the least deserving to come to such a misfortune because of his total commitment to the practice of virtue. (7.86)

Alcibiades, on the other hand, survived ten years longer than Nicias, until after the final defeat and surrender of Athens. He, too, was executed, in Phrygia, now central Turkey, where he was living with a courtesan, Timandra. Plutarch, who wrote the lives of great Greek and Athenian leaders in the second century AD, offers a range of alternatives for Alcibiades's fate: he could have been killed on the orders of Pharnabazus, the Persian satrap, or Lysander, the Spartan king, or the Spartans themselves. Or, it might even have been an honour killing by the brothers of a girl from a noble Phrygian family whom Alcibiades had seduced (Plutarch, *Alcibiades* 39).

These ends, noble and ignoble, show the fundamental difference between these two rivals for power in Athens. Alcibiades comes from the very heartland of the ancient Athenian aristocracy. Plutarch's account of his life begins significantly with his ancestry, which goes back to the heroes of the Trojan War:

> Tradition has it that Alcibiades' family was founded by Eurysaces, the son of Ajax. His mother was Deinomache, the daughter of Megacles, and on her side was descended from Alcmaeon. His father Cleinias fitted out a warship at his own expense and fought brilliantly at the sea battle at Artemision.
> (Plutarch, *Alcibiades* 1)

The Alcmaeonids, the family of Alcmaeon who was the son of one of the Seven who attacked Thebes, were the most significant family in Athens from the middle of the sixth century BCE: a later Alcmaeon became very rich in the sixth century BCE by his association with Croesus, the king of Lydia. His son, Megacles, married the daughter of Cleisthenes, the tyrant of Sicyon (Herodotus 6.125–131, the funniest of all Herodotus' stories). His son, Cleisthenes, was the key figure in the fall of the Peisistratid tyranny and the introduction of democracy, and the grandfather of Pericles, the most important Athenian leader from 460 BCE until his death in 430 BCE. Indeed, Pericles was Alcibiades' uncle and guardian.

We know, not only from Thucydides and Plutarch, but, above all, from Plato that Alcibiades was both famous and notorious for living the life of the wild, extravagant young aristocrat. That is visible in his late and drunken arrival, conversation and behaviour in Plato's *Symposium,* but also in Thucydides' references to his horse-racing exploits, then as now the sport of the cosmopolitan élite. This behaviour did not stop him being popular, but it did make the Athenians suspicious of him and his ambitions and doubtful about his loyalty to the democracy (6.16.2).

Alcibiades' background, character, ambition and connections with other city states, particularly Sparta, meant that he was active in Athenian public life from a young age. Born in 451/0 BCE, he first appears in in Thucydides in 420 BCE, at a time when there is discontent in Athens after the signing of the Peace of Nicias and a move towards forming an alliance with Argos. He is described then as 'young and honoured for the reputation of his ancestors' and motivated partly by resentment that the Spartans had not negotiated the peace of 421 BCE through him (5.43.2).

Between this date and the Sicilian Expedition of 415 BCE, Alcibiades was largely engaged in a strategy to work with Argos and other cities in the Peloponnese to undermine the Spartans. He could present those machinations as a success (6.16.6), but the truth of the matter was that the Spartans won the key battle of this period, at Mantinea in 418 BCE.

Thucydides' account of Alcibiades' role in the disaster that is the Sicilian Expedition is very clear. Alcibiades is motivated by personal ambition for honour, glory and money and by a personal antipathy towards Nicias. His grand plans of conquest, stretching even as far as Carthage (6.15), are not rooted in any realistic account of the challenges of the campaign and the fundamental distrust of his way of being destroys him when the sacrilegious crimes around the Herms and the Eleusinian Mysteries emerge. On the other hand, he has the power to persuade the people (cf. 6.19.1) and Thucydides also attributes blame to Alcibiades' enemies for their eagerness to bring him down. This is Thucydides overarching judgement of the man and his impact:

> He had a big name with the citizens and he tended to have ambitions beyond his financial means with regard to his breeding of horses and other kinds of expenditure. And it was this quality which was contributed in no small degree to the downfall of the city of the Athenians. For the most people were scared by the scale of his lawless way of life and behaviour and by his attitudes of mind in each and every circumstance. So, his enemies put it about that his ambition was to become a tyrant. In the public sphere his conduct of the war was excellent, but everyone was deeply offended by his way of life. For that reason they

entrusted then conduct of the war to others and, not long after, they brought the city down. (6.15)

Alcibiades is one of the three generals, along with Nicias and Lamachus, to lead the expedition out towards Sicily. However, there is no chance to see how his proposed strategy works out because he is recalled to Athens to face his trial. From this point, the treachery of Alcibiades' life after his escape on his way back to Athens (6.61) does not burnish his reputation. He escapes to Sparta and there gives them strategic advice about involvement in Sicily and occupation of Attica which are critical in Athens' final defeat (6.88–93). Then, discredited and disgraced in Sparta, he crosses over to the Persian side of the satrap Tissaphernes. He nearly secures a coup in and a return to Athens through promising Persian support to the Athenians and, even when that fails, he is appointed general of the Athenian fleet at Samos for several years. In 407 BCE he even gets back to Athens, but, after the defeat at Notium in 406 BCE, he withdrew, first to Thrace and then to Pharnabazus and then to his ignoble and uncertain end.

Nicias is otherwise in almost every respect. His public standing didn't come from an ancient family but from his wealth, made from the silver mines of Laurium in Attica (Plutarch *Nicias* 4). He used this wealth to engage in public acts of generosity, funding offerings to the gods, choruses and the purification of Delos (Plutarch *Nicias* 3, Thucydides 3.104). Despite the scale of expenditure, this was perceived as piety rather than self-aggrandizement. Indeed, Nicias' strict attention to matters of religion was one of the most striking of his qualities, in direct contrast to the παρανομία, lawlessness of Alcibiades, and, at a crucial, tragic moment in Sicily, he refuses to retreat after an eclipse of the moon (7.51).

Nicias was about 20 years older than Alcibiades and he gained his public status not by youthful extravagance and ambition, but by a reputation for caution, reliability and integrity. He was engaged in several major expeditions in the Aegean from 427 BCE onwards (3.51, 3.92, 4.42–45, 53, 129) and he was the key figure in the armistice (4.119) and treaty (5.16–19) that brought an end to the first phase of the Peloponnesian War.

In all of this, it might be perceived that Nicias was the true heir to Pericles, who had led Athens to its greatness in the years before the war (cf. 2.65). However, Nicias, for all his qualities, lacked the authority and confidence in the assembly to direct policy as he would have wanted, not least in the face of other leaders, 'demagogues', who were more popular and persuasive. For example in 425 BCE, the Athenians had trapped the Spartan soldiers on the island of Sphacteria but had failed to bring the situation to its conclusion. Nicias, under attack from Cleon, the most powerful figure in the assembly, foolishly handed over his command to him and Cleon quickly forced the Spartans to surrender (4.27–41). The people were quick to condemn him for his dithering and Plutarch (*Nicias* 8) and Thucydides blame him for giving Cleon his moment of triumph.

In the same way, the early chapters of Book 6 show Nicias being outdone by the high hopes and grand designs of Alcibiades. Nicias criticises Alcibiades for his youthful over-confidence and personal ambition (6.12) but Alcibiades manages to deflect such accusations (6.16) to such good effect that the Athenians are keener than ever to take on the challenge. Nicias then tries to deter them by emphasizing the need for an expedition of great scale, but this merely leads to them agreeing to something even bigger, so that he not only does not win the argument, but actually ends up generating an even bigger force (6.19, 24).

The failure of the Sicilian Expedition and the death of Nicias are presented in tragic terms. Nicias, leading an expedition he doesn't believe in, loses his two fellow generals, Alcibiades through treachery, Lamachus in battle. As he is left in sole command, his natural caution leads him to miss opportunities (7.42) and he is slow to realize the significance of the arrival of the Spartan forces with Gylippus. When Demosthenes arrives to share that command, his haste makes matters worse and from then on the two generals cannot agree (7.47–49). And throughout all this Nicias is beset with illness (7.15) and a fear of how the Athenians might treat him (7.48). In the end, this noblest Athenian of them all can be seen and heard organizing his troops and encouraging them to hope and endure:

> It is now reasonable for us to hope that the gods will be kinder to us, since by now we deserve their pity rather than their jealousy. (7.77)

Thucydides may be most famous for his search for facts and accuracy, for ἀκρίβεια, but in his account of Alcibiades and Nicias he presents us with a deeply human and intellectual analysis of character and its impact on events.

Thucydides and rhetoric

> Speech is a powerful ruler. Its substance is minute and invisible, but its achievements are superhuman; for it is able to stop fear and to remove sorrow and to create joy and to increase pity . . . Into those who hear it come fearful fright and tearful pity and mournful longing.

So writes Gorgias in his *Encomium of Helen*, a brief defence of the indefensible in which he aims to prove that, if Helen was seduced by Paris, she was not to be blamed for being unable to resist the irresistible powers of words. It is itself a showcase of the tricks and devices of rhetoric, which are largely, but perhaps not entirely lost in translation.

Rhetoric, the power to speak and to persuade, mattered in fifth-century Athens' participatory and direct democracy. It was vital to be able to speak in public, in front of the Assembly on the Pnyx, in order to gain influence and power. The law courts mattered, too, and in those law courts each citizen had to make his own speech of act or defence, just as Socrates himself did unsuccessfully in 399 BCE. L. B. Carter wrote a book called *The Quiet Athenian*, an account of those who were not engaged in Athenian political life. It was impossible to be quiet and successful. That's why so much of the prose that has survived from the fifth and fourth centuries comes from the law courts, the works of Lysias, Aeschines, Isocrates and, most famously, Demosthenes. Thucydides himself, as a general and a public figure, would have needed these rhetorical skills and the significance of debate, of the power of rhetoric to influence decision-making are central to Thucydides' work in general, and in Book 6 in particular. That's why, for example, there are eight speeches in Book 1 about the decision to go to war.

Gorgias, who is quoted above, is a key figure in the power of rhetoric and, remarkably, although unnamed, he is a participant in Thucydides' narrative: in 3.86, Thucydides describes the arrival from Sicily of a delegation from Leontini whose purpose is to persuade the Athenians to come to their aid. Gorgias, a native of the city, was part of that delegation, as we are told by Socrates in Plato's *Hippias Major* (282b).

> Gorgias, the famous sophist of Leontini came here on public business as the representative of his native city, because he was thought to be the most competent of the Leontinians to conduct their state affairs; and not only was he popularly regarded as the best speaker ever to have addressed the Assembly, but he also gave lectures as a private individual and met with our young men, and earned and received a lot of money from our city.

It is not only here that Gorgias appears in Plato. In the dialogue called *Gorgias*, Socrates engages in discussion with Gorgias, Polus, another teacher from Sicily, and Callicles, a young Athenian aristocrat about the nature, purpose and moral value of rhetoric. Early in the dialogue (453a) Socrates calls rhetoric 'the manufacturer of persuasion' and that dialogue grows naturally from a dialogue about the art of words into a dialogue about the art of government: the very word 'rhetor' comes to mean politician as well as speaker.

For all the power of rhetoric, it was considered to be a deeply ambivalent skill. As the quotation from Gorgias above shows, words have the power to stir emotions, but are they equally effective in ensuring that reason, intelligence and good judgement prevail? And, if rhetoric can be taught for high fees by Gorgias, and other highly paid itinerant sophists, what does that do to the whole edifice of a democracy designed to be equal and open to all? Nor was this an entirely academic debate: the Athenian people had a deep suspicion that these clever, rhetorically-trained aristocrats were a threat to democracy itself and the oligarchic coup of 411 BCE and the collusion of some Athenians, often closely linked to Socrates, with the Spartans in 404 BCE, merely confirmed those dark suspicions.

Since speeches and the ability to persuade were such a central part of Athenian, and Greek, politics, it is no surprise that Thucydides make extensive use of them. And there are other obvious forces at work, too: both Homer and Herodotus presented their narratives as a combination of deeds and words and in their works speeches convey character, conflict, debate and causality. Thucydides would also have spent a good deal of time in the Theatre of Dionysus.

Whereas Herodotus gives no account of his method with speeches and simply pretends that what he writes is what people said, Thucydides is, as ever, more explicit in his method, contrasting his reporting of words with his reporting of deeds.

> In this history I have made use of set speeches some of which were delivered just before and others during the war. I have found it difficult to remember the precise words used in the speeches which I listened to myself and my various informants have experienced the same difficulty; so, my method has been, whilst keeping as closely as possible to the general sense of the words that were actually used to

make the speakers say what, in my opinion, was necessary for each situation. (1.22)

It is striking that Thucydides in the phrase 'speaking what is necessary' uses the same Greek, 'τὰ δέοντα', to describe what he is doing as Gorgias himself does at the beginning of the *Encomium of Helen*, where he notes that the task of the speaker is to speak 'τὸ δέον'. There is much scholarly debate about what Thucydides actually means in his account of his speeches and it cannot be clear how much of the speeches is the speaker and how much is Thucydides. However, it is clear that the speeches are absolutely central to Thucydides' historical purpose. He makes use of them throughout his work at critical moments of decision. In the course of Book 6 alone, we hear the voices of Nicias and Alcibiades in Athens, (6.16–23), of Hermocrates and Athenagoras in Syracuse (6.33–40), of Nicias before the first engagement with the Syracusans (6.68), of the Syracusan Hermocrates and the Athenian Euphemus at Camarina (6.76–88), and of Alcibiades in Sparta (6.89–92). And, in addition to these speeches presented in direct speech, he can present the content of speeches in indirect speech, as he does with the three alternative tactics advised by Nicias, Lamachus and Alcibiades on their arrival in Sicily (6.47–49). Elsewhere in his work, Pericles' Funeral Oration (2.35–46) is Thucydides' truly remarkable representation of the greatness of Athens which this war would tragically end, and in the Melian Dialogue (5.85–113) he goes beyond set speeches into the Socratic form of dialectic to show the Athenians' refusal to accept traditional morality and their trust that might is right.

All of these speeches serve a variety of functions: they can enable Thucydides to present the character and methods of key figures, and the reaction of the different audiences; they make explicit and dramatic the issues of the moment and the underlying issues of strategy and morality; they can place the reader inside the action, so that she can, as if in real time, evaluate the quality, or dishonesty, of the argument and make a choice between the differing sides of the argument. The speeches, their arguments and their predictions can then also be set against the reality of events, so that we can come to see who was right and who was wrong, and why decisions, good and bad were made. As Colin Macleod wrote:

> In the speeches Thucydides does what any artist and any historian must do: he refashions his subject in order to draw out its significance.

In his introduction to his work, Thucydides says that his purpose is to make his history useful for future generations: by understanding the past, we can better judge our own present and future. However, there is little to be learnt from a simple narrative with numbers of ships or hoplites. For Thucydides, the speeches are the best way for him to bring out those issues which resonate throughout history in times of war, that 'violent teacher'.

As Macleod also wrote:

> The relation of words to deeds is at the heart of Thucydides' thinking; for the whole work is a passionate, though often gloomy, enquiry into the possibility of rational behaviour in politics and war.

Thucydides' style

R. G. Collingwood once wrote in *The Idea of History*, 'In reading Thucydides I ask myself, what is the matter with the man that he writes like that?' You might ask the same question about Marcel Proust.

However we answer that question, there is no doubt that Thucydides' way of writing is unique and very different from the works of his close contemporaries, Herodotus, Xenophon, Plato, Lysias. He is capable of writing in a clear, direct way in narrative passages about events, whether that be in the Pentecontaetia or the history of Sicily or in accounts of military operations. However, in his accounts of speeches or in his analysis of events, he creates a style of writing of extraordinary density and complexity. There is nothing to compare anywhere in Greek literature with Pericles' Funeral Oration or Thucydides' analysis of the impact of civil war on Corcyra. It is as if he is forging a new way of writing in an attempt to convey the deep historical truths which are the central purpose of his whole work.

If Thucydides' style is unique, what are the ingredients that make it so? There are several in Book 6:

- the frequent use, even the invention, of abstract nouns: ἀπραγμοσύνη (18.7), τῆς ἀπούσης πόθῳ ὄψεως καὶ θεωρίας (24.3), ἐπὶ ξυνωμοσίᾳ ... δήμου καταλύσεως (27.3, cf. 28.2), τόλμης τὲ θάμβει καὶ ὄψεως λαμπρότητι (31.6), τὸ γὰρ Ἀριστογείτονος καὶ Ἁρμοδίου τολμημα δι' ἐρωτικὴν ξυντυχίαν (54.1).

- the formation of abstract concepts from prepositions and nouns and neuter adjectives: τὸ μὲν ἐπιθυμοῦν τοῦ πλοῦ (24.2), διὰ τὴν ἄγαν τῶν πλεόνων ἐπιθυμίαν (24.3), ἐς τὸ ἀγριώτερόν (60.1).

- the use of compound verbs : ξυγκατέβη (6.30.1), προετετελέκει (6.31.5) ξυνεπηύχοντο (6.32.2).

- the use of balance in the style of Gorgias and other authors: πολλὰ μεν ἡμᾶς δέον εὖ βουλεύσασθαι, ἔτι δὲ πλείω εὐτυχῆσαι (23.3), πολλοὶ μὲν γὰρ ὁπλῖταί ... πολλαὶ δε τριήρεις (20.4).

- the deliberate disruption of the expected balance in sentence structure: chapter 22, 31.3 31.5 are examples of sentences which just keep on going; ὡς ἄν μάλιστα δὶ ὀργῆς ὁ μὲν ἐρωτικῆς, ὁ δὲ ὑβρισμένος (57.3) has two balanced, but also unbalanced clauses.

- the use of short sentences at key moments to contrast with the complexity elsewhere: καὶ ἔδοξε πλεῖν τὸν Ἀλκιβιάδην (29.3), Ἁρμόδιος δὲ αὐτου παρταχρῆμα ἀπόλλυται (57.4).

- striking word order: e.g. words placed emphatically at the beginning of sentences: (24.3), ξυγκατέβη (6.30.1), ξυνεπηύχοντο (6.32.2), αἰφνίδιοι (49.2).

- choice/creation of powerful vocabulary: καὶ ἔρως ἐνέπεσε (24.3), εὐέλπιδες (24.3), πολυτελεστάτη δὴ καὶ εὐπρεπεστάτη (31.1), ταχυναυτεῖν (31.3), ἀσκέπτως (21.2) and ἀπερισκέπτως (57.3).

- deliberate repetition: ὁρμάομαι (6.19.1, 20.1); Lamachus uses the word ὄψις three times in 49.1.

- alliteration: οἱ πλεῖστοι περιεκόπησαν τὰ πρόσωπα(27.1), ἀπερισκέπτως προσπεσόντες (57.3), τὴν πόλιν τῆς παρούσης ὑποψίας παῦσαι (60.3), ἡ μέντοι ἄλλη πόλις ἐν τῷ παρόντι περιφανῶς ὠφέλητο (60.5).

All of this means that Thucydides' writing, more than that of any other prose author of the period, is dense, difficult, complex, hard to understand and even harder to translate. However, le style, c'est l'homme, or perhaps le style, c'est l'histoire. It reflects the restless creativity and energy of Thucydides as he fights to find the words that will convey the truth about events that his high purpose demands. Collingwood is wrong to think there is something wrong with Thucydides. There is something right: Thucydides is one of the cleverest people ever to write.

Further Reading

Cawkwell G. *Thucydides and the Peloponnesian War*. Routledge 1997.
Dover K. J. *Thucydides Book VI*. OUP 1965.
Hornblower S. *A Commentary on Thucydides, Volume III*. OUP 2010.
MacDowell D. M. *Gorgias: Encomiun of Helen*. Bristol Classical Press, 1982.
Macleod C. *Collected Essays*. OUP 1983.
Pelling C. and Wyke M. Twelve Voices from Greece and Rome. OUP 2014.
Plato: Gorgias. Penguin.
Plutarch: The Rise and Fall of Athens. Penguin.
Rusten J. S. *Thucydides*. Oxford Readings in Classical Studies, OUP 2009.
The Greek Sophists. Penguin 2003.

FIGURE 1 *Map of Sicily and Southern Italy.*

Text

Book 6 begins with a history of Sicily and the settlement of the island by the Greeks. Thucydides then presents two speeches by Nicias and Alcibiades in the Assembly at Athens in response to the decision to send 60 ships to Sicily. Alcibiades has just finished speaking in support of the expedition as the selection starts.

19

τοιαῦτα μὲν ὁ Ἀλκιβιάδης εἶπεν· οἱ δ᾽ Ἀθηναῖοι ἀκούσαντες ἐκείνου τε καὶ τῶν Ἐγεσταίων καὶ Λεοντίνων φυγάδων, οἳ παρελθόντες ἐδέοντό τε καὶ τῶν ὁρκίων ὑπομιμνήσκοντες ἱκέτευον βοηθῆσαι σφίσι, πολλῷ μᾶλλον ἢ πρότερον ὥρμηντο στρατεύειν. [2] καὶ ὁ Νικίας γνοὺς ὅτι ἀπὸ μὲν τῶν αὐτῶν λόγων οὐκ ἂν ἔτι ἀποτρέψειε, παρασκευῆς δὲ πλήθει, εἰ πολλὴν ἐπιτάξειε, τάχ᾽ ἂν μεταστήσειεν αὐτούς, παρελθὼν αὐτοῖς αὖθις ἔλεγε τοιάδε.

20

᾽ἐπειδὴ πάντως ὁρῶ ὑμᾶς, ὦ Ἀθηναῖοι, ὡρμημένους στρατεύειν, ξυνενέγκοι μὲν ταῦτα ὡς βουλόμεθα, ἐπὶ δὲ τῷ παρόντι ἃ γιγνώσκω σημανῶ. [2] ἐπὶ γὰρ πόλεις, ὡς ἐγὼ ἀκοῇ αἰσθάνομαι, μέλλομεν ἰέναι μεγάλας καὶ οὔθ᾽ ὑπηκόους ἀλλήλων οὔτε δεομένας μεταβολῆς, ᾗ ἂν ἐκ βιαίου τις δουλείας ἄσμενος ἐς ῥᾴω μετάστασιν χωροίη, οὐδ᾽ ἂν τὴν ἀρχὴν τὴν ἡμετέραν εἰκότως ἀντ᾽ ἐλευθερίας προσδεξαμένας, τό τε πλῆθος ὡς ἐν μιᾷ νήσῳ πολλὰς τὰς Ἑλληνίδας. [3] πλὴν γὰρ Νάξου καὶ Κατάνης, ἃς ἐλπίζω ἡμῖν κατὰ τὸ Λεοντίνων ξυγγενὲς προσέσεσθαι, ἄλλαι εἰσὶν ἑπτά, καὶ παρεσκευασμέναι τοῖς πᾶσιν ὁμοιοτρόπως μάλιστα τῇ ἡμετέρᾳ δυνάμει, καὶ οὐχ ἥκιστα ἐπὶ ἃς μᾶλλον πλέομεν, Σελινοῦς καὶ Συράκουσαι. [4] πολλοὶ μὲν γὰρ ὁπλῖται ἔνεισι καὶ τοξόται καὶ ἀκοντισταί, πολλαὶ δὲ τριήρεις καὶ ὄχλος ὁ πληρώσων αὐτάς. χρήματά τ᾽ ἔχουσι τὰ μὲν ἴδια, τὰ δὲ καὶ ἐν τοῖς ἱεροῖς ἐστι Σελινουντίοις, Συρακοσίοις δὲ καὶ ἀπὸ βαρβάρων τινῶν ἀπαρχὴ ἐσφέρεται· ᾧ δὲ μάλιστα ἡμῶν προύχουσιν, ἵππους τε πολλοὺς κέκτηνται καὶ σίτῳ οἰκείῳ καὶ οὐκ ἐπακτῷ χρῶνται.

21

'πρὸς οὖν τοιαύτην δύναμιν οὐ ναυτικῆς καὶ φαύλου στρατιᾶς μόνον δεῖ, ἀλλὰ καὶ πεζὸν πολὺν ξυμπλεῖν, εἴπερ βουλόμεθα ἄξιον τῆς διανοίας δρᾶν καὶ μὴ ὑπὸ ἱππέων πολλῶν εἴργεσθαι τῆς γῆς, ἄλλως τε καὶ εἰ ξυστῶσιν αἱ πόλεις φοβηθεῖσαι καὶ μὴ ἀντιπαράσχωσιν ἡμῖν φίλοι τινὲς γενόμενοι ἄλλοι ἢ Ἐγεσταῖοι ᾧ ἀμυνούμεθα ἱππικόν [2] (αἰσχρὸν δὲ βιασθέντας ἀπελθεῖν ἢ ὕστερον ἐπιμεταπέμπεσθαι, τὸ πρῶτον ἀσκέπτως βουλευσαμένους): αὐτόθεν δὲ παρασκευῇ ἀξιόχρεῳ ἐπιέναι, γνόντας ὅτι πολύ τε ἀπὸ τῆς ἡμετέρας αὐτῶν μέλλομεν πλεῖν καὶ οὐκ ἐν τῷ ὁμοίῳ στρατευσόμενοι καὶ ὅτε ἐν τοῖς τῇδε ὑπηκόοις ξύμμαχοι ἤλθετε ἐπί τινα, ὅθεν ῥᾴδιαι αἱ κομιδαὶ ἐκ τῆς φιλίας ὧν προσέδει, ἀλλ᾽ ἐς ἀλλοτρίαν πᾶσαν ἀπαρτήσοντες, ἐξ ἧς μηνῶν οὐδὲ τεσσάρων τῶν χειμερινῶν ἄγγελον ῥᾴδιον ἐλθεῖν.

22

ὁπλίτας τε οὖν πολλούς μοι δοκεῖ χρῆναι ἡμᾶς ἄγειν καὶ ἡμῶν αὐτῶν καὶ τῶν ξυμμάχων, τῶν τε ὑπηκόων καὶ ἤν τινα ἐκ Πελοποννήσου δυνώμεθα ἢ πεῖσαι ἢ μισθῷ προσαγαγέσθαι, καὶ τοξότας πολλοὺς καὶ σφενδονήτας, ὅπως πρὸς τὸ ἐκείνων ἱππικὸν ἀντέχωσι, ναυσί τε καὶ πολὺ περιεῖναι, ἵνα καὶ τὰ ἐπιτήδεια ῥᾷον ἐσκομιζώμεθα, τὸν δὲ καὶ αὐτόθεν σῖτον ἐν ὁλκάσι, πυροὺς καὶ πεφρυγμένας κριθάς, ἄγειν, καὶ σιτοποιοὺς ἐκ τῶν μυλώνων πρὸς μέρος ἠναγκασμένους ἐμμίσθους, ἵνα, ἤν που ὑπὸ ἀπλοίας ἀπολαμβανώμεθα, ἔχῃ ἡ στρατιὰ τὰ ἐπιτήδεια (πολλὴ γὰρ οὖσα οὐ πάσης ἔσται πόλεως ὑποδέξασθαι), τά τε ἄλλα ὅσον δυνατὸν ἑτοιμάσασθαι, καὶ μὴ ἐπὶ ἑτέροις γίγνεσθαι, μάλιστα δὲ χρήματα αὐτόθεν ὡς πλεῖστα ἔχειν. τὰ δὲ παρ᾽ Ἐγεσταίων, ἃ λέγεται ἐκεῖ ἕτοιμα, νομίσατε καὶ λόγῳ ἂν μάλιστα ἕτοιμα εἶναι.

23

ἢν γὰρ αὐτοὶ ἔλθωμεν ἐνθένδε μὴ ἀντίπαλον μόνον παρασκευασάμενοι, πλήν γε πρὸς τὸ μάχιμον αὐτῶν, τὸ ὁπλιτικόν, ἀλλὰ καὶ ὑπερβάλλοντες τοῖς πᾶσι, μόλις οὕτως οἷοί τε ἐσόμεθα τῶν μὲν κρατεῖν, τὰ δὲ καὶ διασῶσαι. [2] πόλιν τε νομίσαι χρὴ ἐν ἀλλοφύλοις καὶ πολεμίοις οἰκιοῦντας ἰέναι, οὓς πρέπει τῇ πρώτῃ ἡμέρᾳ ᾗ ἂν κατάσχωσιν εὐθὺς κρατεῖν τῆς γῆς, ἢ εἰδέναι ὅτι, ἢν σφάλλωνται, πάντα πολέμια ἕξουσιν. [3] ὅπερ ἐγὼ φοβούμενος, καὶ εἰδὼς πολλὰ μὲν ἡμᾶς δέον εὖ βουλεύσασθαι, ἔτι δὲ πλείω εὐτυχῆσαι (χαλεπὸν δὲ ἀνθρώπους ὄντας), ὅτι ἐλάχιστα τῇ τύχῃ παραδοὺς ἐμαυτὸν βούλομαι ἐκπλεῖν, παρασκευῇ δὲ ἀπὸ τῶν εἰκότων ἀσφαλὴς ἐκπλεῦσαι. ταῦτα γὰρ τῇ τε ξυμπάσῃ πόλει βεβαιότατα ἡγοῦμαι καὶ ἡμῖν τοῖς στρατευσομένοις σωτήρια. εἰ δέ τῳ ἄλλως δοκεῖ, παρίημι αὐτῷ τὴν ἀρχήν.'

24

ὁ μὲν Νικίας τοσαῦτα εἶπε νομίζων τοὺς Ἀθηναίους τῷ πλήθει τῶν πραγμάτων ἢ ἀποτρέψειν ἤ, εἰ ἀναγκάζοιτο στρατεύεσθαι, μάλιστ᾽ <ἂν> οὕτως ἀσφαλῶς ἐκπλεῦσαι: [2] οἱ δὲ τὸ μὲν ἐπιθυμοῦν τοῦ πλοῦ οὐκ ἐξῃρέθησαν ὑπὸ τοῦ ὀχλώδους τῆς παρασκευῆς, πολὺ δὲ μᾶλλον ὥρμηντο, καὶ τοὐναντίον περιέστη αὐτῷ: εὖ τε γὰρ παραινέσαι ἔδοξε καὶ ἀσφάλεια νῦν δὴ καὶ πολλὴ ἔσεσθαι. [3] καὶ ἔρως ἐνέπεσε τοῖς πᾶσιν ὁμοίως ἐκπλεῦσαι: τοῖς μὲν γὰρ πρεσβυτέροις ὡς ἢ καταστρεψομένοις ἐφ᾽ ἃ ἔπλεον ἢ οὐδὲν ἂν σφαλεῖσαν μεγάλην δύναμιν, τοῖς δ᾽ ἐν τῇ ἡλικίᾳ τῆς τε ἀπούσης πόθῳ ὄψεως καὶ θεωρίας, καὶ εὐέλπιδες ὄντες σωθήσεσθαι: ὁ δὲ πολὺς ὅμιλος καὶ στρατιώτης ἔν τε τῷ παρόντι ἀργύριον οἴσειν καὶ προσκτήσεσθαι δύναμιν ὅθεν ἀίδιον μισθοφορὰν ὑπάρξειν. [4] ὥστε διὰ τὴν ἄγαν τῶν πλεόνων ἐπιθυμίαν, εἴ τῳ ἄρα καὶ μὴ ἤρεσκε, δεδιὼς μὴ ἀντιχειροτονῶν κακόνους δόξειεν εἶναι τῇ πόλει ἡσυχίαν ἦγεν.

25

καὶ τέλος παρελθών τις τῶν Ἀθηναίων καὶ παρακαλέσας τὸν Νικίαν οὐκ ἔφη χρῆναι προφασίζεσθαι οὐδὲ διαμέλλειν, ἀλλ᾽ ἐναντίον ἁπάντων ἤδη λέγειν ἥντινα αὐτῷ παρασκευὴν Ἀθηναῖοι ψηφίσωνται. [2] ὁ δὲ ἄκων μὲν εἶπεν ὅτι καὶ μετὰ τῶν ξυναρχόντων καθ᾽ ἡσυχίαν μᾶλλον βουλεύσοιτο, ὅσα μέντοι ἤδη δοκεῖν αὐτῷ, τριήρεσι μὲν οὐκ ἔλασσον ἢ ἑκατὸν πλευστέα εἶναι (αὐτῶν δ᾽ Ἀθηναίων ἔσεσθαι ὁπλιταγωγοὺς ὅσαι ἂν δοκῶσι, καὶ ἄλλας ἐκ τῶν ξυμμάχων μεταπεμπτέας εἶναι), ὁπλίταις δὲ τοῖς ξύμπασιν Ἀθηναίων καὶ τῶν ξυμμάχων πεντακισχιλίων μὲν οὐκ ἐλάσσοσιν, ἢν δέ τι δύνωνται, καὶ πλέοσιν: τὴν δὲ ἄλλην παρασκευὴν ὡς κατὰ λόγον, καὶ τοξοτῶν τῶν αὐτόθεν καὶ ἐκ Κρήτης καὶ σφενδονητῶν, καὶ ἤν τι ἄλλο πρέπον δοκῇ εἶναι, ἑτοιμασάμενοι ἄξειν.

26

ἀκούσαντες δ᾽ οἱ Ἀθηναῖοι ἐψηφίσαντο εὐθὺς αὐτοκράτορας εἶναι καὶ περὶ στρατιᾶς πλήθους καὶ περὶ τοῦ παντὸς πλοῦ τοὺς στρατηγοὺς πράσσειν ᾗ ἂν αὐτοῖς δοκῇ ἄριστα εἶναι [Ἀθηναίοις]. [2] καὶ μετὰ ταῦτα ἡ παρασκευὴ ἐγίγνετο, καὶ ἔς τε τοὺς ξυμμάχους ἔπεμπον καὶ αὐτόθεν καταλόγους ἐποιοῦντο, ἄρτι δ᾽ ἀνειλήφει ἡ πόλις ἑαυτὴν ἀπὸ τῆς νόσου καὶ τοῦ ξυνεχοῦς πολέμου ἔς τε ἡλικίας πλῆθος ἐπιγεγενημένης καὶ ἐς χρημάτων ἄθροισιν διὰ τὴν ἐκεχειρίαν, ὥστε ῥᾷον πάντα ἐπορίζετο. καὶ οἱ μὲν ἐν παρασκευῇ ἦσαν.

27

ἐν δὲ τούτῳ, ὅσοι Ἑρμαῖ ἦσαν λίθινοι ἐν τῇ πόλει τῇ Ἀθηναίων (εἰσὶ δὲ κατὰ τὸ ἐπιχώριον, ἡ τετράγωνος ἐργασία, πολλοὶ καὶ ἐν ἰδίοις προθύροις καὶ ἐν ἱεροῖς), μιᾷ νυκτὶ οἱ πλεῖστοι περιεκόπησαν τὰ πρόσωπα. [2] καὶ τοὺς δράσαντας ᾔδει οὐδείς, ἀλλὰ μεγάλοις μηνύτροις δημοσίᾳ οὗτοί τε ἐζητοῦντο καὶ προσέτι ἐψηφίσαντο, καὶ εἴ τις ἄλλο τι οἶδεν ἀσέβημα γεγενημένον, μηνύειν ἀδεῶς τὸν βουλόμενον καὶ ἀστῶν καὶ ξένων καὶ δούλων. [3] καὶ τὸ πρᾶγμα μειζόνως ἐλάμβανον: τοῦ τε γὰρ ἔκπλου οἰωνὸς ἐδόκει εἶναι καὶ ἐπὶ ξυνωμοσίᾳ ἅμα νεωτέρων πραγμάτων καὶ δήμου καταλύσεως γεγενῆσθαι.

28

μηνύεται οὖν ἀπὸ μετοίκων τέ τινων καὶ ἀκολούθων περὶ μὲν τῶν Ἑρμῶν οὐδέν, ἄλλων δὲ ἀγαλμάτων περικοπαί τινες πρότερον ὑπὸ νεωτέρων μετὰ παιδιᾶς καὶ οἴνου γεγενημέναι, καὶ τὰ μυστήρια ἅμα ὡς ποιεῖται ἐν οἰκίαις ἐφ᾽ ὕβρει: ὧν καὶ τὸν Ἀλκιβιάδην ἐπῃτιῶντο. [2] καὶ αὐτὰ ὑπολαμβάνοντες οἱ μάλιστα τῷ Ἀλκιβιάδῃ ἀχθόμενοι ἐμποδὼν ὄντι σφίσι μὴ αὐτοῖς τοῦ δήμου βεβαίως προεστάναι, καὶ νομίσαντες, εἰ αὐτὸν ἐξελάσειαν, πρῶτοι ἂν εἶναι, ἐμεγάλυνον καὶ ἐβόων ὡς ἐπὶ δήμου καταλύσει τά τε μυστικὰ καὶ ἡ τῶν Ἑρμῶν περικοπὴ γένοιτο καὶ οὐδὲν εἴη αὐτῶν ὅτι οὐ μετ᾽ ἐκείνου ἐπράχθη, ἐπιλέγοντες τεκμήρια τὴν ἄλλην αὐτοῦ ἐς τὰ ἐπιτηδεύματα οὐ δημοτικὴν παρανομίαν.

29

ὁ δ᾽ ἔν τε τῷ παρόντι πρὸς τὰ μηνύματα ἀπελογεῖτο καὶ ἕτοιμος ἦν πρὶν ἐκπλεῖν κρίνεσθαι, εἴ τι τούτων εἰργασμένος ἦν (ἤδη γὰρ καὶ τὰ τῆς παρασκευῆς ἐπεπόριστο), καὶ εἰ μὲν τούτων τι εἴργαστο, δίκην δοῦναι, εἰ δ᾽ ἀπολυθείη, ἄρχειν. [2] καὶ ἐπεμαρτύρετο μὴ ἀπόντος πέρι αὐτοῦ διαβολὰς ἀποδέχεσθαι, ἀλλ᾽ ἤδη ἀποκτείνειν, εἰ ἀδικεῖ, καὶ ὅτι σωφρονέστερον εἴη μὴ μετὰ τοιαύτης αἰτίας, πρὶν διαγνῶσι, πέμπειν αὐτὸν ἐπὶ τοσούτῳ στρατεύματι. [3] οἱ δ᾽ ἐχθροὶ δεδιότες τό τε στράτευμα μὴ εὔνουν ἔχῃ, ἢν ἤδη ἀγωνίζηται, ὅ τε δῆμος μὴ μαλακίζηται θεραπεύων ὅτι δι᾽ ἐκεῖνον οἵ τ᾽ Ἀργεῖοι ξυνεστράτευον καὶ τῶν Μαντινέων τινές, ἀπέτρεπον καὶ ἀπέσπευδον, ἄλλους ῥήτορας ἐνιέντες οἳ ἔλεγον νῦν μὲν πλεῖν αὐτὸν καὶ μὴ κατασχεῖν τὴν ἀναγωγήν, ἐλθόντα δὲ κρίνεσθαι ἐν ἡμέραις ῥηταῖς, βουλόμενοι ἐκ μείζονος διαβολῆς, ἣν ἔμελλον ῥᾷον αὐτοῦ ἀπόντος ποριεῖν, μετάπεμπτον κομισθέντα αὐτὸν ἀγωνίσασθαι. καὶ ἔδοξε πλεῖν τὸν Ἀλκιβιάδην.

30

μετὰ δὲ ταῦτα θέρους μεσοῦντος ἤδη ἡ ἀναγωγὴ ἐγίγνετο ἐς τὴν Σικελίαν. τῶν μὲν οὖν ξυμμάχων τοῖς πλείστοις καὶ ταῖς σιταγωγοῖς ὁλκάσι καὶ τοῖς πλοίοις καὶ ὅση ἄλλη παρασκευὴ ξυνείπετο πρότερον εἴρητο ἐς Κέρκυραν ξυλλέγεσθαι ὡς ἐκεῖθεν ἀθρόοις ἐπ᾽ ἄκραν Ἰαπυγίαν τὸν Ἰόνιον διαβαλοῦσιν: αὐτοὶ δ᾽ Ἀθηναῖοι καὶ εἴ τινες τῶν ξυμμάχων παρῆσαν, ἐς τὸν Πειραιᾶ καταβάντες ἐν ἡμέρᾳ ῥητῇ ἅμα ἕῳ ἐπλήρουν τὰς ναῦς ὡς ἀναξόμενοι. [2] ξυγκατέβη δὲ καὶ ὁ ἄλλος ὅμιλος ἅπας ὡς εἰπεῖν ὁ ἐν τῇ πόλει καὶ ἀστῶν καὶ ξένων, οἱ μὲν ἐπιχώριοι τοὺς σφετέρους αὐτῶν ἕκαστοι προπέμποντες, οἱ μὲν ἑταίρους, οἱ δὲ ξυγγενεῖς, οἱ δὲ υἱεῖς, καὶ μετ᾽ ἐλπίδος τε ἅμα ἰόντες καὶ ὀλοφυρμῶν, τὰ μὲν ὡς κτήσοιντο, τοὺς δ᾽ εἴ ποτε ὄψοιντο, ἐνθυμούμενοι ὅσον πλοῦν ἐκ τῆς σφετέρας ἀπεστέλλοντο.

31

καὶ ἐν τῷ παρόντι καιρῷ, ὡς ἤδη ἔμελλον μετὰ κινδύνων ἀλλήλους ἀπολιπεῖν, μᾶλλον αὐτοὺς ἐσῄει τὰ δεινὰ ἢ ὅτε ἐψηφίζοντο πλεῖν· ὅμως δὲ τῇ παρούσῃ ῥώμῃ, διὰ τὸ πλῆθος ἑκάστων ὧν ἑώρων, τῇ ὄψει ἀνεθάρσουν. οἱ δὲ ξένοι καὶ ὁ ἄλλος ὄχλος κατὰ θέαν ἧκεν ὡς ἐπ᾽ ἀξιόχρεων καὶ ἄπιστον διάνοιαν. παρασκευὴ γὰρ αὕτη πρώτη ἐκπλεύσασα μιᾶς πόλεως δυνάμει Ἑλληνικῇ πολυτελεστάτη δὴ καὶ εὐπρεπεστάτη τῶν ἐς ἐκεῖνον τὸν χρόνον ἐγένετο. [2] ἀριθμῷ δὲ νεῶν καὶ ὁπλιτῶν καὶ ἡ ἐς Ἐπίδαυρον μετὰ Περικλέους καὶ ἡ αὐτὴ ἐς Ποτείδαιαν μετὰ Ἅγνωνος οὐκ ἐλάσσων ἦν· τετράκις γὰρ χίλιοι ὁπλῖται αὐτῶν Ἀθηναίων καὶ τριακόσιοι ἱππῆς καὶ τριήρεις ἑκατόν, καὶ Λεσβίων καὶ Χίων πεντήκοντα, καὶ ξύμμαχοι ἔτι πολλοὶ ξυνέπλευσαν. [3] ἀλλὰ ἐπί τε βραχεῖ πλῷ ὡρμήθησαν καὶ παρασκευῇ φαύλῃ, οὗτος δὲ ὁ στόλος ὡς χρόνιός τε ἐσόμενος καὶ κατ᾽ ἀμφότερα, οὗ ἂν δέῃ, καὶ ναυσὶ καὶ πεζῷ ἅμα ἐξαρτυθείς, τὸ μὲν ναυτικὸν μεγάλαις δαπάναις τῶν τε τριηράρχων καὶ τῆς πόλεως ἐκπονηθέν, τοῦ μὲν δημοσίου δραχμὴν τῆς ἡμέρας τῷ ναύτῃ ἑκάστῳ διδόντος καὶ ναῦς παρασχόντος κενὰς ἑξήκοντα μὲν ταχείας, τεσσαράκοντα δὲ ὁπλιταγωγοὺς καὶ ὑπηρεσίας ταύταις τὰς κρατίστας, τῶν <δὲ> τριηράρχων ἐπιφοράς τε πρὸς τῷ ἐκ δημοσίου μισθῷ διδόντων τοῖς θρανίταις τῶν ναυτῶν καὶ ταῖς ὑπηρεσίαις καὶ τἆλλα σημείοις καὶ κατασκευαῖς πολυτελέσι χρησαμένων, καὶ ἐς τὰ μακρότατα προθυμηθέντος ἑνὸς ἑκάστου ὅπως αὐτῷ τινι εὐπρεπείᾳ τε ἡ ναῦς μάλιστα προέξει καὶ τῷ ταχυναυτεῖν, τὸ δὲ πεζὸν καταλόγοις τε χρηστοῖς ἐκκριθὲν καὶ ὅπλων καὶ τῶν περὶ τὸ σῶμα σκευῶν μεγάλῃ σπουδῇ πρὸς ἀλλήλους ἁμιλληθέν. [4] ξυνέβη δὲ πρός τε σφᾶς αὐτοὺς ἅμα ἔριν γενέσθαι, ᾧ τις ἕκαστος προσετάχθη, καὶ ἐς τοὺς ἄλλους Ἕλληνας ἐπίδειξιν μᾶλλον εἰκασθῆναι τῆς δυνάμεως καὶ ἐξουσίας ἢ ἐπὶ πολεμίους παρασκευήν. [5] εἰ γάρ τις ἐλογίσατο τήν τε τῆς πόλεως ἀνάλωσιν δημοσίαν καὶ τῶν στρατευομένων τὴν ἰδίαν, τῆς μὲν πόλεως ὅσα τε ἤδη προετετελέκει καὶ ἃ ἔχοντας τοὺς στρατηγοὺς ἀπέστελλε, τῶν δὲ ἰδιωτῶν ἅ τε περὶ τὸ σῶμά τις καὶ τριήραρχος ἐς τὴν ναῦν ἀνηλώκει καὶ ὅσα ἔτι ἔμελλεν ἀναλώσειν, χωρὶς δ᾽ ἃ εἰκὸς ἦν καὶ ἄνευ τοῦ ἐκ τοῦ δημοσίου μισθοῦ πάντα τινὰ παρασκευάσασθαι ἐφόδιον ὡς ἐπὶ χρόνιον στρατείαν, καὶ ὅσα ἐπὶ μεταβολῇ τις ἢ στρατιώτης ἢ ἔμπορος ἔχων ἔπλει, πολλὰ ἂν τάλαντα ηὑρέθη ἐκ τῆς πόλεως τὰ πάντα ἐξαγόμενα. [6] καὶ ὁ στόλος οὐχ ἧσσον τόλμης τε θάμβει καὶ ὄψεως λαμπρότητι περιβόητος ἐγένετο ἢ στρατιᾶς πρὸς οὓς ἐπῇσαν ὑπερβολῇ, καὶ ὅτι μέγιστος ἤδη δίάπλους ἀπὸ τῆς οἰκείας καὶ ἐπὶ μεγίστῃ ἐλπίδι τῶν μελλόντων πρὸς τὰ ὑπάρχοντα ἐπεχειρήθη.

32

ἐπειδὴ δὲ αἱ νῆες πλήρεις ἦσαν καὶ ἐσέκειτο πάντα ἤδη ὅσα ἔχοντες ἔμελλον ἀνάξεσθαι, τῇ μὲν σάλπιγγι σιωπῇ ὑπεσημάνθη, εὐχὰς δὲ τὰς νομιζομένας πρὸ τῆς ἀναγωγῆς οὐ κατὰ ναῦν ἑκάστην, ξύμπαντες δὲ ὑπὸ κήρυκος ἐποιοῦντο, κρατῆράς τε κεράσαντες παρ᾽ ἅπαν τὸ στράτευμα καὶ ἐκπώμασι χρυσοῖς τε καὶ ἀργυροῖς οἵ τε ἐπιβάται καὶ οἱ ἄρχοντες σπένδοντες. [2] ξυνεπηύχοντο δὲ καὶ ὁ ἄλλος ὅμιλος ὁ ἐκ τῆς γῆς τῶν τε πολιτῶν καὶ εἴ τις ἄλλος εὔνους παρῆν σφίσιν. παιανίσαντες δὲ καὶ τελεώσαντες τὰς σπονδὰς ἀνήγοντο, καὶ ἐπὶ κέρως τὸ πρῶτον ἐκπλεύσαντες ἅμιλλαν ἤδη μέχρι Αἰγίνης ἐποιοῦντο. καὶ οἱ μὲν ἐς τὴν Κέρκυραν, ἔνθαπερ καὶ τὸ ἄλλο στράτευμα τῶν ξυμμάχων ξυνελέγετο, ἠπείγοντο ἀφικέσθαι. [3] ἐς δὲ τὰς Συρακούσας ἠγγέλλετο μὲν πολλαχόθεν τὰ περὶ τοῦ ἐπίπλου, οὐ μέντοι ἐπιστεύετο ἐπὶ πολὺν χρόνον οὐδέν, ἀλλὰ καὶ γενομένης ἐκκλησίας ἐλέχθησαν τοιοίδε λόγοι ἀπό τε ἄλλων, τῶν μὲν πιστευόντων τὰ περὶ τῆς στρατείας τῆς τῶν Ἀθηναίων, τῶν δὲ τὰ ἐναντία λεγόντων, καὶ Ἑρμοκράτης ὁ Ἕρμωνος παρελθὼν αὐτοῖς, ὡς σαφῶς οἰόμενος εἰδέναι τὰ περὶ αὐτῶν, ἔλεγε καὶ παρῄνει τοιάδε.

33–46: In the intervening chapters, Thucydides recounts the debate at Syracuse as the people decide how to respond to the news of the imminent expedition (chapters 33–41) and the journey – and scale – of that expedition from Athens to Sicily via Corcyra. On arrival they discover that the promised financial support of Egesta does not exist. The three generals consult on the next step.

47

καὶ Νικίου μὲν ἦν γνώμη πλεῖν ἐπὶ Σελινοῦντα πάσῃ τῇ στρατιᾷ, ἐφ᾽ ὅπερ μάλιστα ἐπέμφθησαν, καὶ ἢν μὲν παρέχωσι χρήματα παντὶ τῷ στρατεύματι Ἐγεσταῖοι, πρὸς ταῦτα βουλεύεσθαι, εἰ δὲ μή, ταῖς ἑξήκοντα ναυσίν, ὅσασπερ ᾐτήσαντο, ἀξιοῦν διδόναι αὐτοὺς τροφήν, καὶ παραμείναντας Σελινουντίους ἢ βίᾳ ἢ ξυμβάσει διαλλάξαι αὐτοῖς, καὶ οὕτω παραπλεύσαντας τὰς ἄλλας πόλεις καὶ ἐπιδείξαντας μὲν τὴν δύναμιν τῆς Ἀθηναίων πόλεως, δηλώσαντας δὲ τὴν ἐς τοὺς φίλους καὶ ξυμμάχους προθυμίαν, ἀποπλεῖν οἴκαδε, ἢν μή τι δι᾽ ὀλίγου καὶ ἀπὸ τοῦ ἀδοκήτου ἢ Λεοντίνους οἷοί τε ὦσιν ὠφελῆσαι ἢ τῶν ἄλλων τινὰ πόλεων προσαγαγέσθαι, καὶ τῇ πόλει δαπανῶντας τὰ οἰκεῖα μὴ κινδυνεύειν.

48

Ἀλκιβιάδης δὲ οὐκ ἔφη χρῆναι τοσαύτῃ δυνάμει ἐκπλεύσαντας αἰσχρῶς καὶ ἀπράκτους ἀπελθεῖν, ἀλλ᾽ ἔς τε τὰς πόλεις ἐπικηρυκεύεσθαι πλὴν Σελινοῦντος καὶ Συρακουσῶν τὰς ἄλλας, καὶ πειρᾶσθαι καὶ τοὺς Σικελοὺς τοὺς μὲν ἀφιστάναι ἀπὸ τῶν Συρακοσίων, τοὺς δὲ φίλους ποιεῖσθαι, ἵνα σῖτον καὶ στρατιὰν ἔχωσι, πρῶτον δὲ πείθειν Μεσσηνίους (ἐν πόρῳ γὰρ μάλιστα καὶ προσβολῇ εἶναι αὐτοὺς τῆς Σικελίας, καὶ λιμένα καὶ ἐφόρμησιν τῇ στρατιᾷ ἱκανωτάτην ἔσεσθαι): προσαγαγομένους δὲ τὰς πόλεις, εἰδότας μεθ᾽ ὧν τις πολεμήσει, οὕτως ἤδη Συρακούσαις καὶ Σελινοῦντι ἐπιχειρεῖν, ἢν μὴ οἱ μὲν Ἐγεσταίοις ξυμβαίνωσιν, οἱ δὲ Λεοντίνους ἐῶσι κατοικίζειν.

49

Λάμαχος δὲ ἄντικρυς ἔφη χρῆναι πλεῖν ἐπὶ Συρακούσας καὶ πρὸς τῇ πόλει ὡς τάχιστα τὴν μάχην ποιεῖσθαι, ἕως ἔτι ἀπαράσκευοί τε εἰσὶ καὶ μάλιστα ἐκπεπληγμένοι. [2] τὸ γὰρ πρῶτον πᾶν στράτευμα δεινότατον εἶναι: ἢν δὲ χρονίσῃ πρὶν ἐς ὄψιν ἐλθεῖν, τῇ γνώμῃ ἀναθαρσοῦντας ἀνθρώπους καὶ τῇ ὄψει καταφρονεῖν μᾶλλον. αἰφνίδιοι δὲ ἢν προσπέσωσιν, ἕως ἔτι περιδεεῖς προσδέχονται, μάλιστ᾽ ἂν σφεῖς περιγενέσθαι καὶ κατὰ πάντα ἂν αὐτοὺς ἐκφοβῆσαι, τῇ τε ὄψει (πλεῖστοι γὰρ ἂν νῦν φανῆναι) καὶ τῇ προσδοκίᾳ ὧν πείσονται, μάλιστα δ᾽ ἂν τῷ αὐτίκα κινδύνῳ τῆς μάχης. [3] εἰκὸς δὲ εἶναι καὶ ἐν τοῖς ἀγροῖς πολλοὺς ἀποληφθῆναι ἔξω διὰ τὸ ἀπιστεῖν σφᾶς μὴ ἥξειν, καὶ ἐσκομιζομένων αὐτῶν τὴν στρατιὰν οὐκ ἀπορήσειν χρημάτων, ἢν πρὸς τῇ πόλει κρατοῦσα καθέζηται. [4] τούς τε ἄλλους Σικελιώτας οὕτως ἤδη μᾶλλον καὶ ἐκείνοις οὐ ξυμμαχήσειν καὶ σφίσι προσιέναι καὶ οὐ διαμελλήσειν περισκοποῦντας ὁπότεροι κρατήσουσιν. ναύσταθμον δὲ ἐπαναχωρήσαντας καὶ ἐφορμηθέντας Μέγαρα ἔφη χρῆναι ποιεῖσθαι, ἃ ἦν ἐρῆμα, ἀπέχοντα Συρακουσῶν οὔτε πλοῦν πολὺν οὔτε ὁδόν.

50

Λάμαχος μὲν ταῦτα εἰπὼν ὅμως προσέθετο καὶ αὐτὸς τῇ Ἀλκιβιάδου γνώμῃ. μετὰ δὲ τοῦτο Ἀλκιβιάδης τῇ αὑτοῦ νηὶ διαπλεύσας ἐς Μεσσήνην καὶ λόγους ποιησάμενος περὶ ξυμμαχίας πρὸς αὐτούς, ὡς οὐκ ἔπειθεν, ἀλλ᾽ ἀπεκρίναντο πόλει μὲν ἂν οὐ δέξασθαι, ἀγορὰν δ᾽ ἔξω παρέξειν, ἀπέπλει ἐς τὸ Ῥήγιον.

51–52: The Athenians enact Alcibiades' proposal and sail 60 ships down the east coast of Sicily as far as Syracuse and then back to Catana, meeting with mixed levels of support.

53

καὶ καταλαμβάνουσι τὴν Σαλαμινίαν ναῦν ἐκ τῶν Ἀθηνῶν ἥκουσαν ἐπί τε Ἀλκιβιάδην ὡς κελεύσοντας ἀποπλεῖν ἐς ἀπολογίαν ὧν ἡ πόλις ἐνεκάλει, καὶ ἐπ᾽ ἄλλους τινὰς τῶν στρατιωτῶν τῶν μετ᾽ αὐτοῦ μεμηνυμένων περὶ τῶν μυστηρίων ὡς ἀσεβούντων, τῶν δὲ καὶ περὶ τῶν Ἑρμῶν. [2] οἱ γὰρ Ἀθηναῖοι, ἐπειδὴ ἡ στρατιὰ ἀπέπλευσεν, οὐδὲν ἧσσον ζήτησιν ἐποιοῦντο τῶν περὶ τὰ μυστήρια καὶ τῶν περὶ τοὺς Ἑρμᾶς δρασθέντων, καὶ οὐ δοκιμάζοντες τοὺς μηνυτάς, ἀλλὰ πάντα ὑπόπτως ἀποδεχόμενοι, διὰ πονηρῶν ἀνθρώπων πίστιν πάνυ χρηστοὺς τῶν πολιτῶν ξυλλαμβάνοντες κατέδουν, χρησιμώτερον ἡγούμενοι εἶναι βασανίσαι τὸ πρᾶγμα καὶ εὑρεῖν ἢ διὰ μηνυτοῦ πονηρίαν τινὰ καὶ χρηστὸν δοκοῦντα εἶναι αἰτιαθέντα ἀνέλεγκτον διαφυγεῖν. [3] ἐπιστάμενος γὰρ ὁ δῆμος ἀκοῇ τὴν Πεισιστράτου καὶ τῶν παίδων τυραννίδα χαλεπὴν τελευτῶσαν γενομένην καὶ προσέτι οὐδ᾽ ὑφ᾽ ἑαυτῶν καὶ Ἁρμοδίου καταλυθεῖσαν, ἀλλ᾽ ὑπὸ τῶν Λακεδαιμονίων, ἐφοβεῖτο αἰεὶ καὶ πάντα ὑπόπτως ἐλάμβανεν.

54

τὸ γὰρ Ἀριστογείτονος καὶ Ἁρμοδίου τόλμημα δι᾽ ἐρωτικὴν ξυντυχίαν ἐπεχειρήθη, ἣν ἐγὼ ἐπὶ πλέον διηγησάμενος ἀποφανῶ οὔτε τοὺς ἄλλους οὔτε αὐτοὺς Ἀθηναίους περὶ τῶν σφετέρων τυράννων οὐδὲ περὶ τοῦ γενομένου ἀκριβὲς οὐδὲν λέγοντας. [2] Πεισιστράτου γὰρ γηραιοῦ τελευτήσαντος ἐν τῇ τυραννίδι οὐχ Ἵππαρχος, ὥσπερ οἱ πολλοὶ οἴονται, ἀλλ᾽ Ἱππίας πρεσβύτατος ὢν ἔσχε τὴν ἀρχήν. γενομένου δὲ Ἁρμοδίου ὥρᾳ ἡλικίας λαμπροῦ Ἀριστογείτων ἀνὴρ τῶν ἀστῶν, μέσος πολίτης, ἐραστὴς ὢν εἶχεν αὐτόν. [3] πειραθεὶς δὲ ὁ Ἁρμόδιος ὑπὸ Ἱππάρχου τοῦ Πεισιστράτου καὶ οὐ πεισθεὶς καταγορεύει τῷ Ἀριστογείτονι. ὁ δὲ ἐρωτικῶς περιαλγήσας καὶ φοβηθεὶς τὴν Ἱππάρχου δύναμιν μὴ βίᾳ προσαγάγηται αὐτόν, ἐπιβουλεύει εὐθὺς ὡς ἀπὸ τῆς

**A
Level**

ὑπαρχούσης ἀξιώσεως κατάλυσιν τῇ τυραννίδι. [4] καὶ ἐν τούτῳ ὁ Ἵππαρχος
ὡς αὖθις πειράσας οὐδὲν μᾶλλον ἔπειθε τὸν Ἁρμόδιον, βίαιον μὲν οὐδὲν
ἐβούλετο δρᾶν, ἐν τρόπῳ δέ τινι ἀφανεῖ ὡς οὐ διὰ τοῦτο δὴ παρεσκευάζετο
προπηλακιῶν αὐτόν. [5] οὐδὲ γὰρ τὴν ἄλλην ἀρχὴν ἐπαχθὴς ἦν ἐς τοὺς
πολλούς, ἀλλ᾽ ἀνεπιφθόνως κατεστήσατο· καὶ ἐπετήδευσαν ἐπὶ πλεῖστον δὴ
τύραννοι οὗτοι ἀρετὴν καὶ ξύνεσιν, καὶ Ἀθηναίους εἰκοστὴν μόνον
πρασσόμενοι τῶν γιγνομένων τήν τε πόλιν αὐτῶν καλῶς διεκόσμησαν καὶ
τοὺς πολέμους διέφερον καὶ ἐς τὰ ἱερὰ ἔθυον. [6] τὰ δὲ ἄλλα αὐτὴ ἡ πόλις τοῖς
πρὶν κειμένοις νόμοις ἐχρῆτο, πλὴν καθ᾽ ὅσον αἰεί τινα ἐπεμέλοντο σφῶν
αὐτῶν ἐν ταῖς ἀρχαῖς εἶναι. καὶ ἄλλοι τε αὐτῶν ἦρξαν τὴν ἐνιαύσιον Ἀθηναίοις
ἀρχὴν καὶ Πεισίστρατος ὁ Ἱππίου τοῦ τυραννεύσαντος υἱός, τοῦ πάππου ἔχων
τοὔνομα, ὃς τῶν δώδεκα θεῶν βωμὸν τὸν ἐν τῇ ἀγορᾷ ἄρχων ἀνέθηκε καὶ τὸν
τοῦ Ἀπόλλωνος ἐν Πυθίου. [7] καὶ τῷ μὲν ἐν τῇ ἀγορᾷ προσοικοδομήσας
ὕστερον ὁ δῆμος Ἀθηναίων μεῖζον μῆκος τοῦ βωμοῦ ἠφάνισε τοὐπίγραμμα·
τοῦ δ᾽ ἐν Πυθίου ἔτι καὶ νῦν δῆλόν ἐστιν ἀμυδροῖς γράμμασι λέγον τάδε·
"μνῆμα τόδ᾽ ἧς ἀρχῆς Πεισίστρατος Ἱππίου υἱὸς θῆκεν Ἀπόλλωνος Πυθίου ἐν
τεμένει."

55

ὅτι δὲ πρεσβύτατος ὢν Ἱππίας ἦρξεν, εἰδὼς μὲν καὶ ἀκοῇ ἀκριβέστερον ἄλλων
ἰσχυρίζομαι, γνοίη δ᾽ ἄν τις καὶ αὐτῷ τούτῳ· παῖδες γὰρ αὐτῷ μόνῳ φαίνονται
τῶν γνησίων ἀδελφῶν γενόμενοι, ὡς ὅ τε βωμὸς σημαίνει καὶ ἡ στήλη περὶ τῆς
τῶν τυράννων ἀδικίας ἡ ἐν τῇ Ἀθηναίων ἀκροπόλει σταθεῖσα, ἐν ᾗ Θεσσαλοῦ
μὲν οὐδ᾽ Ἱππάρχου οὐδεὶς παῖς γέγραπται, Ἱππίου δὲ πέντε, οἳ αὐτῷ ἐκ
Μυρρίνης τῆς Καλλίου τοῦ Ὑπεροχίδου θυγατρὸς ἐγένοντο· εἰκὸς γὰρ ἦν τὸν
πρεσβύτατον πρῶτον γῆμαι. [2] καὶ ἐν τῇ αὐτῇ στήλῃ πρῶτος γέγραπται μετὰ
τὸν πατέρα, οὐδὲ τοῦτο ἀπεοικότως διὰ τὸ πρεσβεύειν τε ἀπ᾽ αὐτοῦ καὶ
τυραννεῦσαι. [3] οὐ μὴν οὐδ᾽ ἂν κατασχεῖν μοι δοκεῖ ποτὲ Ἱππίας τὸ παραχρῆμα
ῥᾳδίως τὴν τυραννίδα, εἰ Ἵππαρχος μὲν ἐν τῇ ἀρχῇ ὢν ἀπέθανεν, αὐτὸς δὲ
αὐθημερὸν καθίστατο· ἀλλὰ καὶ διὰ τὸ πρότερον ξύνηθες τοῖς μὲν πολίταις
φοβερόν, ἐς δὲ τοὺς ἐπικούρους ἀκριβές, πολλῷ τῷ περιόντι τοῦ ἀσφαλοῦς
κατεκράτησε, καὶ οὐχ ὡς ἀδελφὸς νεώτερος ὢν ἠπόρησεν, ἐν ᾧ οὐ πρότερον
ξυνεχῶς ὡμιλήκει τῇ ἀρχῇ. [4] Ἱππάρχῳ δὲ ξυνέβη τοῦ πάθους τῇ δυστυχίᾳ
ὀνομασθέντα καὶ τὴν δόξαν τῆς τυραννίδος ἐς τὰ ἔπειτα προσλαβεῖν.

56

τὸν δ᾽ οὖν Ἁρμόδιον ἀπαρνηθέντα τὴν πείρασιν, ὥσπερ διενοεῖτο,
προυπηλάκισεν· ἀδελφὴν γὰρ αὐτοῦ κόρην ἐπαγγείλαντες ἥκειν κανοῦν
οἴσουσαν ἐν πομπῇ τινι, ἀπήλασαν λέγοντες οὐδὲ ἐπαγγεῖλαι τὴν ἀρχὴν διὰ
τὸ μὴ ἀξίαν εἶναι. [2] χαλεπῶς δὲ ἐνεγκόντος τοῦ Ἁρμοδίου πολλῷ δὴ μᾶλλον
δι᾽ ἐκεῖνον καὶ ὁ Ἀριστογείτων παρωξύνετο. καὶ αὐτοῖς τὰ μὲν ἄλλα πρὸς τοὺς

A
Level

ξυνεπιθησομένους τῷ ἔργῳ ἐπέπρακτο, περιέμενον δὲ Παναθήναια τὰ μεγάλα, ἐν ᾗ μόνον ἡμέρᾳ οὐχ ὕποπτον ἐγίγνετο ἐν ὅπλοις τῶν πολιτῶν τοὺς τὴν πομπὴν πέμψοντας ἀθρόους γενέσθαι: καὶ ἔδει ἄρξαι μὲν αὐτούς, ξυνεπαμύνειν δὲ εὐθὺς τὰ πρὸς τοὺς δορυφόρους ἐκείνους. [3] ἦσαν δὲ οὐ πολλοὶ οἱ ξυνομωμοκότες ἀσφαλείας ἕνεκα: ἤλπιζον γὰρ καὶ τοὺς μὴ προειδότας, εἰ καὶ ὁποσοιοῦν τολμήσειαν, ἐκ τοῦ παραχρῆμα ἔχοντάς γε ὅπλα ἐθελήσειν σφᾶς αὐτοὺς ξυνελευθεροῦν.

57

καὶ ὡς ἐπῆλθεν ἡ ἑορτή, Ἱππίας μὲν ἔξω ἐν τῷ Κεραμεικῷ καλουμένῳ μετὰ τῶν δορυφόρων διεκόσμει ὡς ἕκαστα ἐχρῆν τῆς πομπῆς προϊέναι, ὁ δὲ Ἁρμόδιος καὶ ὁ Ἀριστογείτων ἔχοντες ἤδη τὰ ἐγχειρίδια ἐς τὸ ἔργον προῇσαν. [2] καὶ ὡς εἶδόν τινα τῶν ξυνωμοτῶν σφίσι διαλεγόμενον οἰκείως τῷ Ἱππίᾳ (ἦν δὲ πᾶσιν εὐπρόσοδος ὁ Ἱππίας), ἔδεισαν καὶ ἐνόμισαν μεμηνῦσθαί τε καὶ ὅσον οὐκ ἤδη ξυλληφθήσεσθαι. [3] τὸν λυπήσαντα οὖν σφᾶς καὶ δι᾽ ὅνπερ πάντα ἐκινδύνευον ἐβούλοντο πρότερον, εἰ δύναιντο, προτιμωρήσασθαι, καὶ ὥσπερ εἶχον ὥρμησαν ἔσω τῶν πυλῶν, καὶ περιέτυχον τῷ Ἱππάρχῳ παρὰ τὸ Λεωκόρειον καλούμενον, καὶ εὐθὺς ἀπερισκέπτως προσπεσόντες καὶ ὡς ἂν μάλιστα δι᾽ ὀργῆς ὁ μὲν ἐρωτικῆς, ὁ δὲ ὑβρισμένος, ἔτυπτον καὶ ἀποκτείνουσιν αὐτόν. [4] καὶ ὁ μὲν τοὺς δορυφόρους τὸ αὐτίκα διαφεύγει ὁ Ἀριστογείτων, ξυνδραμόντος τοῦ ὄχλου, καὶ ὕστερον ληφθεὶς οὐ ῥᾳδίως διετέθη: Ἁρμόδιος δὲ αὐτοῦ παραχρῆμα ἀπόλλυται.

58

ἀγγελθέντος δὲ Ἱππίᾳ ἐς τὸν Κεραμεικόν, οὐκ ἐπὶ τὸ γενόμενον, ἀλλ᾽ ἐπὶ τοὺς πομπέας τοὺς ὁπλίτας, πρότερον ἢ αἰσθέσθαι αὐτοὺς ἄπωθεν ὄντας, εὐθὺς ἐχώρησε, καὶ ἀδήλως τῇ ὄψει πλασάμενος πρὸς τὴν ξυμφορὰν ἐκέλευσεν αὐτούς, δείξας τι χωρίον, ἀπελθεῖν ἐς αὐτὸ ἄνευ τῶν ὅπλων. [2] καὶ οἱ μὲν ἀνεχώρησαν οἰόμενοί τι ἐρεῖν αὐτόν, ὁ δὲ τοῖς ἐπικούροις φράσας τὰ ὅπλα ὑπολαβεῖν ἐξελέγετο εὐθὺς οὓς ἐπῃτιᾶτο καὶ εἴ τις ηὑρέθη ἐγχειρίδιον ἔχων: μετὰ γὰρ ἀσπίδος καὶ δόρατος εἰώθεσαν τὰς πομπὰς ποιεῖν.

59

τοιούτῳ μὲν τρόπῳ δι᾽ ἐρωτικὴν λύπην ἥ τε ἀρχὴ τῆς ἐπιβουλῆς καὶ ἡ ἀλόγιστος τόλμα ἐκ τοῦ παραχρῆμα περιδεοῦς Ἁρμοδίῳ καὶ Ἀριστογείτονι ἐγένετο. [2] τοῖς δ᾽ Ἀθηναίοις χαλεπωτέρα μετὰ τοῦτο ἡ τυραννὶς κατέστη, καὶ ὁ Ἱππίας διὰ φόβου ἤδη μᾶλλον ὢν τῶν τε πολιτῶν πολλοὺς ἔκτεινε καὶ πρὸς τὰ ἔξω ἅμα διεσκοπεῖτο, εἴ ποθεν ἀσφάλειάν τινα ὁρῴη μεταβολῆς γενομένης ὑπάρχουσάν οἱ. [3] Ἱππόκλου γοῦν τοῦ Λαμψακηνοῦ τυράννου Αἰαντίδῃ τῷ παιδὶ θυγατέρα ἑαυτοῦ μετὰ ταῦτα Ἀρχεδίκην Ἀθηναῖος ὢν Λαμψακηνῷ ἔδωκεν, αἰσθανόμενος αὐτοὺς μέγα παρὰ βασιλεῖ Δαρείῳ δύνασθαι. καὶ αὐτῆς

A
Level

σῆμα ἐν Λαμψάκῳ ἐστὶν ἐπίγραμμα ἔχον τόδε: "ἀνδρὸς ἀριστεύσαντος ἐν Ἑλλάδι τῶν ἐφ᾽ ἑαυτοῦ

Ἱππίου Ἀρχεδίκην ἥδε κέκευθε κόνις,

ἣ πατρός τε καὶ ἀνδρὸς ἀδελφῶν τ᾽ οὖσα τυράννων

παίδων τ᾽ οὐκ ἤρθη νοῦν ἐς ἀτασθαλίην."

[4] τυραννεύσας δὲ ἔτη τρία Ἱππίας ἔτι Ἀθηναίων καὶ παυθεὶς ἐν τῷ τετάρτῳ ὑπὸ Λακεδαιμονίων καὶ Ἀλκμεωνιδῶν τῶν φευγόντων, ἐχώρει ὑπόσπονδος ἔς τε Σίγειον καὶ παρ᾽ Αἰαντίδην ἐς Λάμψακον, ἐκεῖθεν δὲ ὡς βασιλέα Δαρεῖον, ὅθεν καὶ ὁρμώμενος ἐς Μαραθῶνα ὕστερον ἔτει εἰκοστῷ ἤδη γέρων ὢν μετὰ Μήδων ἐστράτευσεν.

60

ὧν ἐνθυμούμενος ὁ δῆμος ὁ τῶν Ἀθηναίων, καὶ μιμνησκόμενος ὅσα ἀκοῇ περὶ αὐτῶν ἠπίστατο, χαλεπὸς ἦν τότε καὶ ὑπόπτης ἐς τοὺς περὶ τῶν μυστικῶν τὴν αἰτίαν λαβόντας, καὶ πάντα αὐτοῖς ἐδόκει ἐπὶ ξυνωμοσίᾳ ὀλιγαρχικῇ καὶ τυραννικῇ πεπρᾶχθαι. [2] καὶ ὡς αὐτῶν διὰ τὸ τοιοῦτον ὀργιζομένων πολλοί τε καὶ ἀξιόλογοι ἄνθρωποι ἤδη ἐν τῷ δεσμωτηρίῳ ἦσαν καὶ οὐκ ἐν παύλῃ ἐφαίνετο, ἀλλὰ καθ᾽ ἡμέραν ἐπεδίδοσαν μᾶλλον ἐς τὸ ἀγριώτερόν τε καὶ πλείους ἔτι ξυλλαμβάνειν, ἐνταῦθα ἀναπείθεται εἷς τῶν δεδεμένων, ὅσπερ ἐδόκει αἰτιώτατος εἶναι, ὑπὸ τῶν ξυνδεσμωτῶν τινὸς εἴτε ἄρα καὶ τὰ ὄντα μηνῦσαι εἴτε καὶ οὔ: ἐπ᾽ ἀμφότερα γὰρ εἰκάζεται, τὸ δὲ σαφὲς οὐδεὶς οὔτε τότε οὔτε ὕστερον ἔχει εἰπεῖν περὶ τῶν δρασάντων τὸ ἔργον. [3] λέγων δὲ ἔπεισεν αὐτὸν ὡς χρή, εἰ μὴ καὶ δέδρακεν, αὑτόν τε ἄδειαν ποιησάμενον σῶσαι καὶ τὴν πόλιν τῆς παρούσης ὑποψίας παῦσαι: βεβαιοτέραν γὰρ αὐτῷ σωτηρίαν εἶναι ὁμολογήσαντι μετ᾽ ἀδείας ἢ ἀρνηθέντι διὰ δίκης ἐλθεῖν. [4] καὶ ὁ μὲν αὐτός τε καθ᾽ ἑαυτοῦ καὶ κατ᾽ ἄλλων μηνύει τὸ τῶν Ἑρμῶν: ὁ δὲ δῆμος ὁ τῶν Ἀθηναίων ἄσμενος λαβών, ὡς ᾤετο, τὸ σαφὲς καὶ δεινὸν ποιούμενοι πρότερον εἰ τοὺς ἐπιβουλεύοντας σφῶν τῷ πλήθει μὴ εἴσονται, τὸν μὲν μηνυτὴν εὐθὺς καὶ τοὺς ἄλλους μετ᾽ αὐτοῦ ὅσων μὴ κατηγορήκει ἔλυσαν, τοὺς δὲ καταιτιαθέντας κρίσεις ποιήσαντες τοὺς μὲν ἀπέκτειναν, ὅσοι ξυνελήφθησαν, τῶν δὲ διαφυγόντων θάνατον καταγνόντες ἐπανεῖπον ἀργύριον τῷ ἀποκτείναντι. [5] κἀν τούτῳ οἱ μὲν παθόντες ἄδηλον ἦν εἰ ἀδίκως ἐτετιμώρηντο, ἡ μέντοι ἄλλη πόλις ἐν τῷ παρόντι περιφανῶς ὠφέλητο.

61

περὶ δὲ τοῦ Ἀλκιβιάδου ἐναγόντων τῶν ἐχθρῶν, οἵπερ καὶ πρὶν ἐκπλεῖν αὐτὸν ἐπέθεντο, χαλεπῶς οἱ Ἀθηναῖοι ἐλάμβανον: καὶ ἐπειδὴ τὸ τῶν Ἑρμῶν ᾤοντο

A
Level

σαφὲς ἔχειν, πολὺ δὴ μᾶλλον καὶ τὰ μυστικά, ὧν ἐπαίτιος ἦν, μετὰ τοῦ αὐτοῦ λόγου καὶ τῆς ξυνωμοσίας ἐπὶ τῷ δήμῳ ἀπ᾽ ἐκείνου ἐδόκει πραχθῆναι. [2] καὶ γάρ τις καὶ στρατιὰ Λακεδαιμονίων οὐ πολλὴ ἔτυχε κατὰ τὸν καιρὸν τοῦτον ἐν ᾧ περὶ ταῦτα ἐθορυβοῦντο μέχρι Ἰσθμοῦ παρελθοῦσα, πρὸς Βοιωτούς τι πράσσοντες. ἐδόκει οὖν ἐκείνου πράξαντος καὶ οὐ Βοιωτῶν ἕνεκα ἀπὸ ξυνθήματος ἥκειν, καὶ εἰ μὴ ἔφθασαν δὴ αὐτοὶ κατὰ τὸ μήνυμα ξυλλαβόντες τοὺς ἄνδρας, προδοθῆναι ἂν ἡ πόλις. καί τινα μίαν νύκτα καὶ κατέδαρθον ἐν Θησείῳ τῷ ἐν πόλει ἐν ὅπλοις. [3] οἵ τε ξένοι τοῦ Ἀλκιβιάδου οἱ ἐν Ἄργει κατὰ τὸν αὐτὸν χρόνον ὑπωπτεύθησαν τῷ δήμῳ ἐπιτίθεσθαι, καὶ τοὺς ὁμήρους τῶν Ἀργείων τοὺς ἐν ταῖς νήσοις κειμένους οἱ Ἀθηναῖοι τότε παρέδοσαν τῷ Ἀργείων δήμῳ διὰ ταῦτα διαχρήσασθαι. [4] πανταχόθεν τε περιειστήκει ὑποψία ἐς τὸν Ἀλκιβιάδην. ὥστε βουλόμενοι αὐτὸν ἐς κρίσιν ἀγαγόντες ἀποκτεῖναι, πέμπουσιν οὕτω τὴν Σαλαμινίαν ναῦν ἐς τὴν Σικελίαν ἐπί τε ἐκεῖνον καὶ ὧν πέρι ἄλλων ἐμεμήνυτο. [5] εἴρητο δὲ προειπεῖν αὐτῷ ἀπολογησομένῳ ἀκολουθεῖν, ξυλλαμβάνειν δὲ μή, θεραπεύοντες τό τε πρὸς τοὺς ἐν τῇ Σικελίᾳ στρατιώτας τε σφετέρους καὶ πολεμίους μὴ θορυβεῖν καὶ οὐχ ἥκιστα τοὺς Μαντινέας καὶ Ἀργείους βουλόμενοι παραμεῖναι, δι᾽ ἐκείνου νομίζοντες πεισθῆναι σφίσι ξυστρατεύειν. [6] καὶ ὁ μὲν ἔχων τὴν ἑαυτοῦ ναῦν καὶ οἱ ξυνδιαβεβλημένοι ἀπέπλεον μετὰ τῆς Σαλαμινίας ἐκ τῆς Σικελίας ὡς ἐς τὰς Ἀθήνας: καὶ ἐπειδὴ ἐγένοντο ἐν Θουρίοις, οὐκέτι ξυνείποντο, ἀλλ᾽ ἀπελθόντες ἀπὸ τῆς νεὼς οὐ φανεροὶ ἦσαν, δείσαντες τὸ ἐπὶ διαβολῇ ἐς δίκην καταπλεῦσαι. [7] οἱ δ᾽ ἐκ τῆς Σαλαμινίας τέως μὲν ἐζήτουν τὸν Ἀλκιβιάδην καὶ τοὺς μετ᾽ αὐτοῦ: ὡς δ᾽ οὐδαμοῦ φανεροὶ ἦσαν, ᾤχοντο ἀποπλέοντες. ὁ δὲ Ἀλκιβιάδης ἤδη φυγὰς ὢν οὐ πολὺ ὕστερον ἐπὶ πλοίου ἐπεραιώθη ἐς Πελοπόννησον ἐκ τῆς Θουρίας: οἱ δ᾽ Ἀθηναῖοι ἐρήμη δίκῃ θάνατον κατέγνωσαν αὐτοῦ τε καὶ τῶν μετ᾽ ἐκείνου.

Commentary Notes

1

The Athenians decide to invade Sicily with a larger force than previously, with the intention of conquest, despite the fact that, according to Thucydides they are unaware of the scale of the island or the challenge.

2–3: The History of Sicily before the arrival of the Greeks

Thucydides goes back to the monsters of Homer, the Cyclopes and the Laestrygonians, and then proceeds through the original settlers. Sicanians from Spain, survivors from the Trojan War who settled Eryx and Egesta in the west of the island, Sicels from southern Italy and Phoenicians, who founded modern-day Palermo.

3–5: Colonization by the Greeks

Thucydides lists with great precision and chronological accuracy the founding of Greek colonies:

> 734 BCE: *Naxos founded by Thucles from Chalcis on Euboea*
> 733 BCE: *Syracuse founded by Archias from Corinth*
> 729 BCE: *Leontini founded by people from Naxos*
>   *Catana also founded by people from Naxos*
> 728 BCE: *Megara Hyblaea founded by colonists from Megara*
>   – 628 BCE: *Selinus founded by people from Megara Hyblaea*
> 689 BCE: *Gela founded by settlers from Rhodes and Crete*
>   – 580 BCE: *Acragas founded by settlers from Gela*
> Eighth/seventh century: *Zancle founded by people from Euboeans but later it was called Messana (modern-day Messina)*
> 648 BCE: *Himera founded by settlers from Zancle with some Syracusan exiles*
> 598 BCE: *Camarina founded by settlers from Syracuse.*

6

The people of Egesta, with whom the Athenians had an alliance since 424 BCE (4.65), were in dispute with the neighbouring city of Selinus and Selinus had called in the Syracusans as their allies. So, the people of Egesta had sent a delegation to Athens seeking support from a naval expedition. Their argument was that only then would they check the growing power of Syracuse, who could become increasingly powerful allies of the Spartans. In response to these requests, the Athenians sent a delegation to Egesta to probe the military and financial situation.

7

Thucydides gives accounts of contemporary military activity which is not relevant to the Sicilian Expedition, in Argos and in Thrace, to ensure that he keeps his chronological approach at the end of the sixteenth year of the war.

8

In spring 415 BCE, the Athenian delegation returned from Sicily with some Egestaeans and 60 talents of silver, a month's pay for 60 ships. The Athenians, although, according to Thucydides, misinformed about the financial strength of Egesta, voted in the Assembly to send 60 ships to Egesta under the command of Nicias and Lamachus. Their mission was to help Egesta against Selinus, to re-establish Leontini, another ally, and, more vaguely, to secure Athenian interests on the island.

Five days after this decision, there was another Assembly to confirm the timetable and preparation for the expedition. At that Assembly, Nicias, who was against the expedition as being too ambitious, attempted to change the assembly's mind.

9–14 The Speech of Nicias

9

Nicias argues that this debate should not be about the preparations for the expedition, but about the very purpose of the expedition itself. Nicias defends his right to raise this fundamental question: the decision has been made in haste on unreliable evidence; although he gains honour from his appointment, he must speak according to his convictions and express his concerns at the risk. However, he has to concede that it is no easy task to stand in the way of the Athenians' desire for ambition and risk, so he will argue that this is too big a challenge undertaken at the wrong time.

10

Nicias' first argument is that the peace treaty with Sparta, for which he was responsible in 422/421 BCE, is too fragile to be relied upon so this is no time to be taking on new enemies. The treaty certainly will not hold if their enemies see that the Athenians have been defeated elsewhere. The treaty is weak for a variety of reasons: the Spartans only accepted it because of their military failures, particularly on Sphacteria; the treaty has unresolved issues; a number of states – Corinth and Megara – had not accepted the treaty and are only working on short-term renewable truces; these same states have long-term links with cities in Sicily and would gladly join forces with them against Athens; not even Athens' control of its own empire is secure with uncertainties in Thrace and unreliable support elsewhere. In such circumstances there is no need to rush to the aid of Egesta.

11

Nicias turns away from Athens' own situation on mainland Greece and in the Aegean, to the scale of the challenge in Sicily. He has plenty of reasons for not taking on Sicily:

AS

- *Sicily is a very populous and distant island so that, even if Athens were to be successful, they would not be easy to govern. So, success would not bring any benefit and failure would be very damaging.*

- *Sicily is not a current threat to Athens, and would be no more of a threat if, as the Egestaeans warn, it came under the control of Syracuse. As things are, individual cities sympathetic to Sparta might come against Athens. However, if they all formed a Syracusan empire, it is highly unlikely that that empire would move against Athens in alliance with Sparta. The Syracusans would be concerned that they, in turn would suffer the same fate as Athens at the hands of the Spartans.*

- *The best way to be feared is to keep a distance or, at least, make a show of force and depart. Any failure in action would reduce Athens' reputation and thereby increase the likelihood of attack from their enemies.*

Nicias then turns to the state of mind of the Athenians themselves and the Spartans. The Athenians, after their unexpected successes on Sphacteria, have come to despise the Spartans and think about new challenges. On the other hand, the Spartans, after their defeat and disgrace, are only waiting for the moment to regain their honour, since military success is the centre of their existence.

So, the Athenians should forget about the remote peoples of Sicily and concentrate on the threat from Sparta.

12
Nicias' argument moves to the situation in Athens. The city is only just recovering after the losses from the plague of 430/429 BCE and the war itself, so that any recovery should be concentrated on development at home. On the other hand, these people from Egesta are not worthy of help: they have speeches to make and tales to tell but nothing to contribute. However, it is the Athenians who will take the risks. If they succeed, the Egestaeans won't be duly grateful. If they fail, they will merely take everyone else down.

He then turns on Alcibiades, although he does not name him. He says that he only wants the command for his own selfish glory. He is too young and too extravagant – with his fine horses – and he hopes to make a profit from the adventure. So, there is a risk that the state's fortunes will be put at risk for an individual's glorification.

13
Nicias describes a generational split in the Assembly: Nicias' older supporters run the risk of being bullied or brow-beaten into silence, as if their plan was an act of cowardice. Nicias argues the importance of reason and forethought at a time of the greatest danger for Athens. He urges his supporters to vote so that Sicily, separated from Greece by the Ionian Gulf, should be left to itself and the Egestaeans should be told that the Athenians are unwilling to come to their aid in a conflict which they started without consultation.

14
Nicias ends his speech by turning to the president of the Assembly and demanding that he should, as a good citizen, allow the decision about the expedition to be

debated again. He urges the president to accept that his duty is to act as the city's physician and ensure that to care for the city's best interests.

15

After Nicias' speech, the majority of other speakers were in favour of the original decision to make the expedition to Sicily. Alcibiades was the strongest advocate of this position for a range of reasons: he was a political enemy of Nicias who had just made a personal attack; he was ambitious to lead the expedition against Sicily, and even Carthage, because it would bring him wealth and honour.

Thucydides now turns to a wider analysis of Alcibiades and his role in Athens' downfall. He describes his public visibility and the unsustainable extravagance of his lifestyle. These qualities, enacted in a wild and lawless way of living in public and private, created a suspicion amongst the people that he was aiming to become a tyrant. So, even though his conduct of the war was excellent, he lost the support of the people and thereby power was put in the hands of others who led Athens to defeat.

16–18 The speech of Alcibiades

16

Alcibiades starts his speech with a defence of his own personal contribution to Athens and of his right to command the expedition – even though he was not one of the original generals appointed. This defence is remarkable in its emphasis on his personal status. It starts with the glory that came to Athens, at a time of hardship, with his entry of seven chariot teams and victory at the Olympic Games – almost certainly in 416 BCE. Such glory brings honour and is a symbol of power.

He then accepts that the scale and extravagance of his public generosity, in the provision of choruses for the dramatic festivals and other liturgies, breeds envy amongst Athenians but it also wins respect of Athens' strength in the wider world.

He then argues that it is entirely reasonable that a man with such a high opinion of himself and such success should be placed above others. He accepts that hostility for such people from contemporaries is inevitable but in the future they will get due honour.

Finally, he claims that, even though his private life is criticized, he is the best man for being in charge of public matters, citing his success in bringing together a coalition of Peloponnesian forces against Sparta at the Battle of Mantinea in 418 BCE, even though they lost.

17

Alcibiades concludes the first part of his argument by emphasizing the success of his youthful ability and energy in winning over the Peloponnesians and insisting that his youth and Nicias' reputation for good luck are the perfect combination.

He now turns to the situation in Sicily and argues that they are a disparate and fragmented bunch who will be no match for the Athenians. The cities have mixed, swollen and transitory populations which have no sense of loyalty to their own city, are always looking out for personal gain and are subject to internal strife. They lack the necessary military forces, equipment and infrastructure, and their numbers are always an overestimation. For all these reasons, they are not capable of a consistent policy or concerted action and are likely to come to separate agreements. His final point about Sicily is that there are large numbers of native Sicels who, out of hatred, will side with Athens against Syracuse.

Alcibiades then turns to the situation at home. They should not be concerned about leaving enemies at home because the Athenians had done the same thing earlier in the century in securing the empire in the Aegean after the Persian Wars. The Spartans are no greater threat if they go to Sicily: they could invade by land, whether the Athenians go to Sicily or not, and they have no fleet to take on the fleet that would be left behind.

18
Alcibiades now argues for the value of intervention in Sicily:

- *The Athenians have a sworn duty to help their allies in Sicily.*
- *These alliances were put in place to cause difficulty to Athens' enemies in Sicily and thereby prevent them from coming to mainland Greece.*
- *Such engagement is the way in which the Athenians, and others, have won an empire, by intervention and offering help to allies. An empire must not only defend itself against attacks but act to prevent any such attack happening.*
- *Our empire has reached such a state that continued expansion is inevitable to ward of the threat of being overcome by others. Inactivity is no longer an option.*

So, going to Sicily will depress the Spartans when they see that the Athenians are never going to settle for a quiet life. The likely outcome is that Athens will conquer Sicily and thereafter become the ruler of all Hellas or, at the very least do the Syracusans harm and our allies some good. Naval superiority will always allow the Athenians to decide whether to stay or return.

Alcibiades ends his speech by arguing for the unity between the old and the young which has brought Athens' greatness. Such greatness will only be enhanced by bringing together all elements of Athenian society. Any state will wear out and become obsolete by inactivity and that kind of inactivity is completely alien to the Athenian way of being. Only action and conflict generate the experience that leads to success and this is particularly true of Athens which must remain true to its own particular character and institutions.

Chapter 19

After Alcibiades' speech supporting the expedition to Sicily, the Athenians are further encouraged in this direction by an embassy from Egesta and some exiles from Leontini. Nicias, realizing that his previous arguments have now failed, decides to deter the Athenian people by exaggerating the scale of the challenge.

AS

19.1

Ἐγεσταίων καὶ Λεοντίνων φυγάδων: Leontini is a city 20 miles north-west of Syracuse. In 427 BCE Athens had sent a fleet to support the Ionian city of Leontini in its war against Syracuse (3.86.1). In 422 BCE, the Syracusans took control of the city (5.4) and some of the democrats left the city and came to Athens as exiles (5.4.3). Nicias has already referred to these exiles as unreliable witnesses in his speech (6.12.1) Egesta (today Segesta), a city founded by Greeks at the western end of Sicily, was also being put under pressure by Syracuse and had sent envoys to Athens to seek support (6.6.2). The Athenians, in response to this request, had sent delegates to Egesta to assess the situation (6.6.3).

τῶν ὁρκίων . . . ἱκέτευον: there survive inscriptions of a treaty between Athens and Egesta (Meiggs and Lewis 37) and of one between Athens and Leontini (Meiggs and Lewis 64), both from the period before the Peloponnesian War. The embassy from Egesta and the exiles from Leontini appeal to oaths taken in the past and engage in an act of supplication. In the minds of the Greeks, failure to stand by oaths or accept supplication would bring down the divine wrath of Ζευς ὁρκιος and/or Ζευς ἱκεσιος.

ὥρμηντο: pluperfect indicative of ὁρμάομαι with an imperfect meaning: 'they had come to be eager', i.e. 'they were eager'.

γνοὺς: nominative, aorist participle of γιγνώσκω. This is the key – and tragic – moment. Nicias now knows he cannot win the rhetorical battle against Alcibiades and the other voices. But, in his attempt to deter the Athenians by exaggerating the scale of the challenge, he merely makes the expedition bigger and thereby matters worse.

ἀποτρέψειε, ἐπιτάξειε, μεταστήσειεν are all aorist optatives as future remote conditionals from ἀποτρέπω, ἐπιτάσσω and μεθίστημι.

ἀπὸ . . . τῶν αὐτῶν λόγων: 'by means of the same arguments', which is balanced by παρασκευῆς . . . πλήθει, 'by the size of the commitment' as the μὲν and δὲ show. It's typical of Thucydides' style that he does not balance the ἀπὸ with another ἀπὸ but with a dative (πλήθει).

ἀποτρέψειε . . . μεταστήσειεν: in these clauses there is a high density of alliteration with strong consonants, π, τ, σ as if to mark out the strength of his exasperation.

πολλὴν sc. παρασκευήν: from the line above.

Chapter 20

Nicias' speech, Part 1, emphasizes the size and strength of the island against which they intend to make their expedition. Sicily has many stable cities with no desire for constitutional change, with substantial financial and military resources, especially in the provision of cavalry. This argument is a direct rebuttal, point by point, of Alcibiades' argument for involvement in his speech in 6.17.2 ff.

20.1

πάντως: a word emphatically, and plosively, placed up front: Nicias has to accept the overwhelming tide of feeling in this debate.

AS

ὡρμημένους: acc. pl. perfect participle of ὁρμάομαι (see ὥρμηντο above in 6.19.1). This verb conveys the urgency and energy which is typical of the Athenians, a quality celebrated in Alcibiades' speech (6.18.6).

ξυνενέγκοι: aorist optative of the impersonal verb ξυμφέρει, conveying a wish: 'may it all turn out . . .'

ξυνενέγκοι μὲν ... ἐπὶ δε τῷ παρόντι: Nicias starkly contrasts the wish, ξυνενέγκοι μὲν, or wishful thinking, with the reality, ἐπὶ δε τῷ παρόντι.

σημανῶ: future indicative of σημαινω, formed by shortening the penultimate vowel and making it into an epsilon contraction: cf. φαίνω, future φανῶ, μένω, future μενῶ.

20.2

ἐπὶ γὰρ πόλεις: 'as for the cities we intend to go against'. Nicias gets the topic of the sentence to the front: what kinds of cities are we going against?

ὡς ἐγὼ ἀκοῇ αἰσθάνομαι: Alcibiades has used exactly this phrase in his speech (6.17.6) but Nicias finds himself having to give an account of Sicily's stability that is directly contrary to Alcibiades' picture of fickle and unstable cities and citizens (6. 17.4). According to Thucydides' later narrative, Nicias is right (7.15.1).

μεγάλας, οὔθ' ὑπηκόους, δεομένας, προσδεξαμένας, πολλὰς τὰς Ἑλληνίδας all agree with πόλεις and then there are subordinate clauses each of which brings into doubt the outcome of the expedition. Nicias piles on the factors that make the expedition so difficult, one after the other, their size, their lack of need for change or desire to be under the Athenian Empire – and there are lots of them.

δεομένας: present participle + genitive (μεταβολὴς): 'in need of change'. Nicias is arguing that the cities of Sicily have no need of Athens to help them throw off an unpopular regime. If the Athenians are bringing change, μεταβολὴς, μετάστασιν, it's not going to be popular.

ᾗ: dative singular feminine relative of which μεταβολὴς is the antecedent: 'in need of change by which . . . .'

ἐκ βιαίου τις δουλείας ἄσμενος ἐς ῥᾴω μετάστασιν χωροίη: 'anyone would gladly make a move from a repressive slavery to an easier new regime.' βιαίου agrees with δουλείας, being sometimes, and for no fathomable reason, a two-termination adjective. χωροίη is optative with the ἂν which precedes it, making this the main clause of a remote conditional.

ῥᾴω: accusative feminine singular: comparative of ῥᾴδιος; a contraction of ῥᾴδιονα.

οὐδ' ἂν τὴν ἀρχὴν ... προσδεξαμένας: another clause which foresees further difficulties: the cities of Sicily aren't likely to swap their independence for being part of the Athenian Empire. The ἂν in the clause once again make this a remote conditional, even if there is no optative verb: 'nor would they welcome our rule . . . .'

Τό ... πλῆθος: accusative of respect: 'as for the number of them'. Whereas we might have thought that Nicias' sentence had run its course, in fact there is this final point: it's not that they are big and have no reason to welcome, but also there are lots of them, and they aren't just a bunch of foreigners. Ἑλληνίδας is emphatically placed at the very end of this crushing sentence, in direct response to Alcibiades' insistence that there are lots of non-Greeks who will come to their aid.

20.3

Νάξου καὶ Κατάνης: two Greek cities on the east coast of Sicily. Naxos was the first Greek city founded in Sicily in 734 BCE, by Ionian settlers from Euboea, and it is from there that Leontini was founded in 729 BCE. Catana was founded soon after: hence, κατὰ τὸ Λεοντίνων ξυγγενές in the next clause.

προσέσεσθαι: future infinitive of πρόσειμι (sum) with the dative (ἡμῖν): 'will be on our side'.

ἑπτά: an ancient commentator has a go at naming the seven: Syracuse, Selinus, Gela, Acragas, Messana, Himera, Camarina. However, Nicias may have just used a specific number for rhetorical effect.

παρασκευασμέναι: nominative feminine plural perfect middle participle of παρασκευάζω: 'equipped . . . .'

τοῖς πᾶσιν: 'in all respects'. This clause is strongly alliterative, perhaps conveying Nicias' urgency to convey his point.

ὁμοιοτρόπως and μάλιστα go together: 'most like'.

ἐπὶ ἅς: sc. πόλεις: 'the cities against which . . . .'

Σελινοῦς: Selinus (today Selinunte) is a city in the west of Sicily, allied to Syracuse, close to and an enemy of Egesta. It was founded from Megara Hyblaea, another Sicilian colony, probably in 628 BCE (6.4.2) Selinus and Egesta vied for control of the western plain of Sicily and in 415 BCE they were in dispute. Selinus called in the help of Syracuse and the Egestaeans sent to Athens for assistance (6.6.2). There remain remarkable sixth/fifth century temples on both sites, indicative of the prosperity of these cities: see ἐν τοῖς ἱεροῖς below (6.6.4).

20.4

ὁπλῖται, τοξόται, ἀκοντισταί: in simple, direct language, with repetition of πολλοί/πολλαί starting each clause, Nicias describes the resources of the Athenians' enemies: the three human component elements of land warfare, heavily-armed hoplites who engaged in direct, hand-to-hand fighting, and the archers and javelin-throwers whose job was to do damage from a distance.

πληρώσων: future participle of πληρόω: triremes required a lot of men to row them, as many as 170 in each crew, and, unlike the Roman galleys depicted in the great cinematic epic *Ben Hur*, they were rowed by citizens.

χρήματα: the irony is that, when the Athenians reach Egesta, they discover that the Egestaeans have conned the Athenians about the amount of money they had and are unable to provide the necessary resources (6.46). At that moment, Nicias isn't surprised, but Alcibiades and Lamachus are, viewing it as ἀλογώτερα. The story there about the deception has echoes of the story of Oroetes who cons the secretary of Polycrates, the tyrant of Samos, with some jars full of stones and topped with gold (Herodotus 3.123).

Σελινουντίοις, Συρακοσίοις: a chiasmus which throws together the names of their two key enemies and gives further chance for dramatic alliteration.

ἀπὸ βαρβάρων τινῶν ἀπαρχή: just as Athens received tribute from the islands and cities of the Aegean, so according to Nicias, Syracuse receives tribute from the non-Greek inhabitants of Sicily.

ᾧ δὲ μάλιστα προύχουσιν: 'in the matter in which they most excel us.'

ἵππους: the cities of Sicily were particularly strong in cavalry because Sicily, unlike mainland Greece, has large, fertile plains on which to rear horses. That is one of the reasons why the tyrants of Sicily dominated the chariot races at Olympia and Delphi, and elsewhere, and why many of Pindar's victory odes in the first half of the fifth century are written for Sicilian victors.

Here, and at 6.21.1 and 6.22.1, Nicias raises the issue of the need for cavalry. In 6.43.1 the Athenians set out with 30 horses in one ship, whereas the Syracusans have 1,200 cavalry (6.67.2). As the narrative of the war proceeds this supremacy is significant (6.63.3, 70.3, 71.2, 74.2). So, once again Thucydides' narrative supports Nicias' prognosis.

οὐκ ἐπακτῷ: unlike the Athenians. Attica is a barren land so the Athenians were dependent on grain imported from their Aegean empire but also Sicily and even Egypt. This close attention to the logistical realities of the campaign is typical of the experienced and cautious Nicias, and alien to the approach of Alcibiades.

Chapter 21

Nicias' speech, Part 2, concentrates on the demands that the expedition will place on the Athenians. There will be the need not only of a large fleet but also of a substantial land force and all of this will be made difficult by the problems of distance, logistics, even climatic conditions. Nicias' analysis may not manage to persuade the Athenian Assembly, but they are the realistic ideas of an experienced general.

21.1

πρὸς . . . τοιαύτην δύναμιν: 'against such forces'. Thucydides sums up the content of the previous chapter.

δεῖ + genitive means 'there is a need of' and it is followed by ναυτικῆς καὶ φαύλου στρατιᾶς. φαύλος can be a two-termination adjective.

πεζὸν πολὺν ξυμπλεῖν: the syntax shifts from a genitive after δεῖ into accusative (πεζὸν πολὺν) with infinitive (ξυμπλεῖν): 'it is necessary that a large land force should sail out together'. With powerful alliteration Nicias tries to show the reality of such an expedition.

διανοίας: genitive after ἄξιον: 'worthy of our purpose/ambition'.

μὴ . . . εἴργεσθαι τῆς γῆς: 'not to be cut off from the land.' This, in fact, is what does happen (6.70.3, where the language is very similar and 7.4.6).

ἄλλως τε καὶ: 'especially': once again this sentence spins off into a complexity which reflects the enormity of the challenge.

εἰ: the two verbs dependent on the εἰ are subjunctive in an open conditional: ξυστῶσιν (3rd plural aorist subjunctive (intransitive) of ξυνίστημι: 'stand together, unite') and ἀντιπαράσχωσιν (see below). However, in that case the εἰ ought to be ἐαν and that has led some to amend the text.

αἱ πόλεις: Nicias envisages the possibility that no city other than Egesta will become their ally, once again challenging Alcibiades' much more optimistic analysis of the situation in his speech (6.17.4). The later narrative suggests that Nicias is right.

φοβηθεῖσαι: 'in a state of fear': nominative feminine plural aorist participle of φοβέομαι.

ἀντιπαράσχωσιν: 3rd plural aorist subjunctive of ἀντιπαρέχω, to provide (cavalry) in return. The subject of the verb is the phrase that runs from φίλοι to Ἐγεσταῖοι. 'some people other than the Egestaeans having become our friends.' and the object is ἱππικόν.

ᾧ ... ἱππικόν: 'cavalry with which we might keep them at bay.' The antecedent is ἱππικόν, which actually comes after the relative.

21.2

αἰσχρὸν: sc. ἐστὶ and ἡμᾶς: 'It would be disgraceful for us.' which is then followed by two infinitives (ἀπελθεῖν and ἐπιμεταπέμπεσθαι) of which (the non-existent) ἡμᾶς is the subject. The ἐπὶ in ἐπιμεταπέμπεσθαι adds the sense of 'after'. A striking feature of Thucydides' style is the constant use of compound forms of a verb to enhance its force and accuracy. Nicias is presenting the two consequences of failing to go with the correct forces in the first place, the need either to return home or to send for reinforcements.

βιασθέντας: 'under duress, by necessity': accusative plural aorist passive participle from βιάζω.

ἀσκέπτως βουλευσαμένους: another aorist participle agreeing with (the non-existent) ἡμᾶς. Nicias continues to warn against agreeing to the expedition with too little planning and forethought. He warns against the very quality of restless energy which Alcibiades celebrates.

ἐπιέναι: another infinitive (of ἐπέρχομαι) dependent on the δεῖ several lines back.

παρασκευῇ ἀξιόχρεῳ: 'with an adequate level of preparation'

πολύ ... ἀπὸ τῆς ἡμετέρας: sc. γῆς: 'a very long way from our own country.'

γνόντας: accusative aorist participle of γιγνώσκω, another participle agreeing with (the non-existent) ἡμᾶς. Nicias is trying to emphasize the things that are known, as opposed to hope and speculation, and in this (complex) sentence, he is drawing a contrast between an expedition to a distant and hostile land and fighting closer at hand in their own empire in the Aegean, where they have allies and logistical support.

μέλλομεν πλεῖν ... στρατευσόμενοι: as is typical of Thucydides the two verbs after ὅτι are different in form, one an infinitive, the other a future participle.

Μέλλομεν .... ἤλθετε: it is striking that, all of a sudden, Nicias moves from the first person plural to the second person plural, as if distancing himself from his audience.

οὐκ ἐν τῷ ὁμοίῳ ... καὶ ὅτε: 'not in the same circumstances as when ...'

ἐν τοῖς τῇδε ὑπηκόοις: 'amongst our subjects in this part of the world.'

ὧν προσέδει: 'of the things for which there was an additional need'.

ἐς ἀλλοτρίαν πᾶσαν: sc. γῆν: 'to a completely foreign country'.

ἀπαρτήσοντες: 'about to go away': this meaning of the verb is very unusual, found for the first time here. It is another future participle parallel with στρατευσόμενοι.

ἐξ ἧς: 'from which (country)'.

μηνῶν οὐδὲ τεσσάρων τῶν χειμερινῶν: genitive of time within which. For all the pictures of the blue sea and cloudless skies, the winter months are very dangerous for sailing in the Aegean and, even in the sixteenth century, there was a clear sailing – and non-sailing – season. cf. Braudel's *The Mediterranean and the Mediterranean World in the Age of Philip II*: 'The sea becomes hostile in winter, so much so that in the past it brought shipping to a standstill. In Roman times ships were laid up by order between October and April.'

ἄγγελον ῥάδιον: sc. ἐστί: ἄγγελον is the subject of the infinitive ἐλθεῖν.

Chapter 22

Nicias' speech, Part 3, gets down to the details of land forces from Athens and elsewhere, provisions, control of the sea and the need for self-sufficiency.

In this chapter Nicias constructs a mighty list of all the things that the expedition will need in one sentence of thirteen lines, hoping that this shopping list without a full stop will scare the people off the whole idea. The sentence has six infinitives, starting with ἄγειν, dependent on μοι δοκεῖ χρῆναι ἡμᾶς, 'it seems to me that we must . . . .' Each item on his list is followed by a purpose clause to explain the reason for its importance.

22.1

ὁπλίτας τε ... πολλούς: Greek warfare was centred upon heavily-armed foot soldiers, the victors of Marathon in 490 BCE and Plataea in 479 BCE, who formed up in phalanxes to face the enemy. Alcibiades argues that the cities of Sicily are under-equipped in terms of hoplites (6.17.5), but Nicias is addressing the more significant issue of the Sicilian strength in cavalry (cf. 6.20.4).

καὶ ἡμῶν αὐτῶν ... προσαγαγέσθαι: Nicias' first item is lots of hoplites and these words identify the sources from which he will get those hoplites, from their own people, from allies, from subjects and even mercenaries from the Peloponnese.

ἤν ... δυνώμεθα: future open conditional clause with a subjunctive verb.

τοξότας ... σφενδονήτας: item 2 in Greek warfare, light-armed troops that can do damage from a distance.

ὅπως ... ἀντέχωσι: purpose clause with a subjunctive: one of Nicias' problems is that the enemy has cavalry, the third key ingredient of ancient warfare, and he hasn't. Each item on Nicias' list is followed by the reason for that specific need.

περιεῖναι: the second infinitive dependent on χρῆναι: 'to be superior in ships'.

ἵνα ... ἐσκομιζώμεθα: another purpose clause with a subjunctive.

ἄγειν: infinitive number 3 and now we are into supplies (σῖτον) and the catering corps (καὶ σιτοποιούς).

πυροὺς καὶ πεφρυγμένας κριθας: 'wheat and roasted barley'.

πρὸς μέρος: 'in proportion'.

ἠναγκασμένους: accusative plural perfect passive participle from ἀναγκάζω.

ἵνα ... ἔχῃ: another purpose clause to explain why with a conditional clause (ἤν ... ἀπολαμβανώμεθα) embedded within it.

ὑπὸ ἀπλοίας: 'in case sailing becomes impossible.'

πολλὴ γὰρ οὖσα οὐ πάσης ἔσται πόλεως ὑποδέξασθαι: 'since it (the force) is large, not every city will be able to receive us.'

ἑτοιμάσασθαι ... γίγνεσθαι ... ἔχειν: the fourth, fifth and sixth infinitives dependent on χρῆναι.

ἐπὶ ἑτέροις: 'dependent on others.'

πλεῖστα: In this big sentence, Thucydides has used some part of πολύς four times before he ends with this superlative. It's going to take a lot of stuff.

τὰ δὲ παρ' Ἐγεσταίων: after one sentence of thirteen lines listing the needs of the Athenians, the capacity of the people of Egesta to support them is dismissed in one short sentence. Nicias' scepticism about the reality of these funds matches Thucydides' earlier account (6.6.2).

νομίσατε: aorist imperative.

λόγῳ ἄν: the whole weight of the sentence falls on these two words: it's all talk from the people of Egesta and the ἄν conveys the unreality of it all in contrast to all the hard facts of the previous sentence. And Nicias is right, as 6.46 shows.

Chapter 23

The reader, or the citizen in the Assembly, might have thought that chapter 22 was enough. However, Nicias hasn't finished. He concludes his speech by insisting that the Athenians will need superiority over their opponents as if they were about to set up a colony in enemy territory. Only with such a force could Nicias envisage the safety and success of the expedition.

23.1

μὴ ἀντίπαλον μόνον παρασκευασάμενοι … ἀλλὰ καὶ ὑπερβάλλοντες: Nicias puts two participles in parallel: arriving with matching forces (ἀντίπαλον παρασκευασάμενο) will not be enough but they will need to be superior (ὑπερβάλλοντες).

πλήν γε πρὸς τὸ μάχιμον αὐτῶν, τὸ ὁπλιτικόν: 'apart from with regard to the fighting force, the hoplites.' Nicias has to accept that it will not be possible to ship enough hoplites to match the enemy.

τῶν μὲν κρατεῖν, τὰ δὲ καὶ διασῶσαι: 'to take control of some things and even to preserve others' (i.e. what is ours already).

23.2

πόλιν: Nicias presents the expedition as if Athens intended to found a colony in Sicily, as many had done before in the previous centuries. So πόλιν is emphatically placed at the front of the sentence, even though it is the object of οἰκιοῦντας.

οἰκιοῦντας: accusative plural future participle of οἰκίζω, conveying purpose. It agrees with a supplied ἡμᾶς, which is the antecedent for the relative οὓς which goes with πρέπει. This is then followed by the infinitives κρατεῖν and then εἰδέναι.

ᾗ ἂν κατάσχωσιν: 'on whatever (day) they land'. κατάσχωσιν is the 3rd plural aorist subjunctive of κατέχω, subjunctive because it is in an indefinite clause.

23.3

φοβούμενος … εἰδὼς: these two nominative participles are waiting for the first person main verb βούλομαι.

εἰδὼς πολλὰ μὲν ἡμᾶς δέον εὖ βουλεύσασθαι, ἔτι δὲ πλείω εὐτυχῆσαι: 'knowing that we must make a lot of good plans, and need even more good luck.'

AS

δέον is the accusative neuter participle of δεῖ following εἰδώς. Nicias states explicitly one of the key themes of Thucydides' narrative, the significance in history, and in particular in times of war, of luck and chance, τύχη, in relation to people's intelligence and capacity for forethought and preparation, παρασκευή. Over time, the Athenians have become too inclined to believe that their success is a proof that all will continue to go well in the future. Alcibiades' speech has none of Nicias's expressions of uncertainty or anxiety.

εὖ βουλεύσασθαι, ἔτι δὲ πλείω εὐτυχῆσαι: this balance and repetition of εὖ is an echo of the high style of Gorgias of Leontini in Sicily whose rhetorical skills made a massive impact in Athens in the 420's BCE. Hence the existence of Plato's *Gorgias*.

χαλεπὸν δὲ ἀνθρώπους ὄντας: 'which is hard since we are humans'. The sentiment reminds us of Herodotus' thoughts on the fragility of human existence (πᾶν ἐστ' ἄνθρωπος συμφορὴ as Solon is made to say in 1.32.4), but the compressed style is Thucydidean: the accusative neuter of the present participle is to be supplied: ἀνθρώπους ὄντας is accusative as the subject of the preceding infinitives.

ὅτι ἐλάχιστα: 'as little as possible', a variation on ὡς ἐλάχιστα.

παραδοὺς: nominative singular aorist participle of παραδίδωμι.

ἐκπλεῖν ... ἐκπλεῦσαι: another rhetorical repetition, again reminiscent of Gorgias.

ἀπὸ τῶν εἰκότων: 'according to what is probable.' Thucydides' historical method often makes use of the idea that something is probable and Nicias' generalship follows the same principle.

τῇ ξυμπάσῃ πόλει: Nicias emphasizes that he is trying to think what is best for the whole city, as well as the expedition itself.

σωτήρια: 'a source of safety', a word emphatically placed at the end of the sentence.

τῳ is the dative of τις, a variant on τινι: 'to anyone'.

παρίημι αὐτῷ ἀρχήν: 'I pass on the command to him.' This might seem a somewhat reckless end to a speech full of technical analysis and logistical demands. At the time of Pylos, Nicias similarly volunteered to step down from his command to enable Cleon to be in charge. On that occasion, Cleon was, according to Thucydides, bullied into taking command and he was then successful (4.28).

Chapter 24

Thucydides tells us that Nicias had a twin purpose, either to discourage the expedition altogether or to ensure that, if it went, it had the scale to be secure. Tragically, that speech, instead of deterring the Athenian people, merely encourages them to greater enthusiasm for the enterprise, not least because Nicias' demands make them feel that all will be well. So the expedition's opponents are cowed into silence and Nicias ends up inadvertently encouraging confidence in something he opposes.

24.1

ὁ μὲν Νικίας ... οἱ δὲ: disastrously, Nicias' speech has the exact opposite effect from the one he intended. He meant to deter them, but he merely stirred their enthusiasm for the whole thing.

τῷ πλήθει τῶν πραγμάτων ἢ ἀποτρέψειν: striking alliteration of π.

AS

ἀποτρέψειν . . . ἐκπλεῦσαι: both infinitives dependent on νομίζων: 'thinking that he would either turn them away or he would sail out in this way with the greatest safety'.

εἰ ἀναγκάζοιτο: a remote future conditional with the optative: 'if he were forced to take the expedition'.

ἀσφαλῶς ἐκπλεῦσαι: this picks up the words in the penultimate sentence of Nicias' speech.

24.2

τὸ μὲν ἐπιθυμοῦν . . . ὥρμηντο . . . ἔρως: after Nicias' voice of reason and calculation, the people are carried along by emotion. And ὁρμάομαι makes another appearance (6.19.1, 20.1). Powerful, emotional vocabulary continues throughout this chapter: πόθῳ, εὐέλπιδες, ἐπιθυμίαν. Nicias' voice of reason and list of requirements have achieved nothing, or rather the wrong thing. Instead the people's hopes and desires match those of Alcibiades (6.15.2), although he is also driven by the chance of money and glory. The use of ἔρως echoes Nicias' earlier warnings that the Athenians are δυσέρωτας . . . τῶν ἀπόντων, 'sick with love for that which isn't there' (6.13.1).

τὸ μὲν ἐπιθυμοῦν: accusative present participle of ἐπιθυμέω, 'the desire'. Once again, the key word is put at a key place in the sentence.

ἐξῃρέθησαν: 3rd plural aorist passive of ἐξαιρέω: 'they were not taken out of . . .'

ὀχλώδους: this is a very rare word and is unusual in its usage here. ὄχλος means the mob, the rabble, the people at their worst. So this adjective must mean 'the troublesome nature (of the preparation)', conveying the scale and the complexity – and the potential chaos – of the expedition.

περιέστη: 3rd singular aorist (intransitive) of περιίστημι: 'turned out, happened'.

ἀσφάλεια . . . πολλὴ: the people pick up two key words from Nicias' speech but that was not what he meant to happen. ἔδοξε seems to be doing two different jobs, one with παραινέσαι, 'Nicias seemed to have offered good advice', one with ἀσφάλεια as its subject, 'there seemed to be a great chance of safety.'

24.3

ἔρως ἐνέπεσε: this is quite remarkable language to describe an assembly's process of decision-making: reason and argument are nowhere and the same passion falls upon everyone equally: that is what happens to an ὄχλος.

τοῖς μὲν γὰρ πρεσβυτέροις . . . τοῖς δ' ἐν τῇ ἡλικίᾳ: Thucydides separates out the different attitudes of the different generations. Both are in the dative to follow on from the previous sentence. This picks up on words from previous speeches: in 6.13.1 Nicias encourages the old men not to be cowed by their younger fellow citizens; in 6.18.6 Alcibiades argues that young and old should work together. Now the city is united, but for the wrong thing and the wrong reasons.

ἢ καταστρεψομένοις ἐφ' ἃ ἔπλεον ἢ οὐδὲν ἂν σφαλεῖσαν μεγάλην δύναμιν: Thucydides presents the alternatives in the minds of the old through two participles, one dative plural future to agree with τοῖς . . . πρεσβυτέροις, 'that they would complete . . .', the other aorist passive based on an understood verb of thinking, 'that a great force would not fail.'

AS

τῆς τε ἀπούσης πόθῳ ὄψεως καὶ θεωρίας: 'in longing for absent/far-off sights and sight-seeing.' The Athenians see the expedition as if they were on a cruise to the splendours and wealth of Sicily, 2,500 years before such things became big business.

εὐέλπιδες ὄντες σωθήσεσθαι: Thucydides takes this sentence out of the dative into the nominative. σωθήσεσθαι is a future passive infinitive, dependent on εὐέλπιδες: 'with high hopes that they would be safe', as if it were following a part of the verb ἐλπίζω.

ὁ δὲ πολὺς ὅμιλος … οἴσειν … προσκτήσεσθαι … ὑπάρξειν: there is no indicative verb in this sentence. Instead, there are three future infinitives all dependent on an understood verb of thinking: 'the mass of the people thought they would get … and would obtain … from which there would be …' The Athenians clearly felt that Sicily was a land of wealth and plenty.

ὁ δὲ πολὺς ὅμιλος καὶ στρατιώτης: Nicias wanted to do the right thing for the city and the expedition, but all he has achieved is unity between people and army in wild hopes. στρατιώτης in the singular is striking, as if every single soldier felt this way. The mood here is in direct contrast to Thucydides' account of the reaction in Athens to the news of the final defeat (8.1.1-2).

24.4

διὰ τὴν ἄγαν τῶν πλεόνων ἐπιθυμίαν: 'on account of their excessive desire for more.' Thucydides identifies one of the key elements of ultimate defeat, πλεονεξία, excessive ambition. This is a key word in the Athenians' response to their success at Pylos: cf. 4.21.2, 4.41.4, 4.65.4, situations where success leads the Athenians to want more.

τῳ is the dative of τις, a variant on τινι: 'to anyone', dependent on the impersonal verb, ἤρεσκε.

ἀντιχειροτονῶν: 'voting against', a word used for the first time by Thucydides.

δεδιὼς μὴ … δόξειεν: a fear clause in historic sequence with an optative verb: 'fearing lest he might seem to be disloyal to the city.' Another danger identified in this passage is the tyranny of the majority and the fear of the dissenter to speak against the crowd. The behaviour of the Athenians here is also to be compared with their behaviour in relation to events at Pylos in 425 BCE. There Nicias found himself facing not Alcibiades but Cleon, another politician with popular – populist? – appeal (4.27–28).

Nicias' speech of caution and detail can also be compared with the words of Archidamus, King of Sparta, in the debate in Sparta before the war (1.80–85).

Chapter 25

An unnamed Athenian forces Nicias, against his better judgement, to give exact details of the expedition's requirement.

25.1

τις τῶν Ἀθηναίων: it is striking that Thucydides attributes this critical intervention to an anonymous Athenian, an ordinary citizen. Plutarch names him

AS

as Demostratus in his life of Nicias (12.6). Thucydides shows that in Athens an ordinary citizen can tell the leaders to get on with it and there is no place for Nicias to hide at this moment.

ἐναντίον ἁπάντων: 'in front of everyone'. Once again, the context of the Assembly is important: this is, with all its faults, direct democracy at work. Nicias might want to work with his fellow generals in peace and quiet (καθ' ἡσυχίαν, 25.2) but he is not going to get what he wants.

ψηφίσωνται: aorist subjunctive: but why? Some manuscripts just have the future, changing the omega to an omicron.

25.2

ἄκων: now Nicias is being bounced into making statements on the hoof.

μετὰ τῶν ξυναρχόντων: 'with his fellow commanders'. The Athenians elected ten generals each year.

μᾶλλον βουλεύσοιτο: future optative: 'he would rather plan'.

ὅσα μέντοι ἤδη δοκεῖν αὐτῷ: a typically dense Thucydidean clause with an infinitive which is not immediately explicable: 'however, as far as he could see at the moment.' Thucydides starts this sentence with an indirect statement using a ὅτι clause, but then he goes into an accusative and infinitive with δοκεῖν and εἶναι.

τριήρεσι μὲν οὐκ ἔλασσον ἢ ἑκατὸν: dative plural: 'with not less than 100 triremes'. The μὲν is picked up by ὁπλίταις δὲ, also in the dative.

πλευστέα: neuter plural gerundive: 'they must sail'.

αὐτῶν ... Ἀθηναίων ... ὁπλιταγωγοὺς: there would be a need for triremes adapted to carry troops and they would be supplied by the Athenians.

ὅσαι ἂν δοκῶσι: indefinite with subjunctive + ἂν: 'as many as they think right.'

μεταπεμπτέας: feminine accusative plural gerundive: 'must be sent for'.

ἢν δύνωνται: subjunctive: 'if they could'. Nicias is piling on the demands and the numbers and the 'not less than' and the 'if' clauses: οὐκ ἐλάσσοσι ... καὶ πλέοσιν.

τὴν δὲ ἄλλην παρασκευὴν: this accusative is the object of ἑτοιμασάμενοι and ἄξειν: ἄξειν is infinitive because this is still an indirect statement going back to the εἶπεν at the beginning of the sentence.

ὡς κατὰ λόγον: 'in proportion': this is the fourth time in the sentence that Nicias qualifies his demands, as if he doesn't want to be tied down to exact details.

ἢν τι ἄλλο πρέπον δοκῇ εἶναι: another qualification by Nicias.

τοξοτῶν ... σφενδονητῶν: this takes us back to Nicias' list in 22.1. They even have to go as far as Crete to get archers, although Crete has had no previous engagement in the war. Nicias has tried to make his shopping list as open-ended and difficult to achieve as possible.

Chapter 26

The Athenians vote immediately for full powers to be given to the generals and swift preparations begin in the city and amongst Athens' allies.

AS

26.1

ἐψηφίσαντο εὐθὺς αὐτοκράτορας: Nicias achieves the exact opposite of what he wants, immediate and complete authority and the provision of all the resources that he asked for.

περὶ στρατιᾶς πλήθους καὶ περὶ τοῦ παντὸς πλοῦ τοὺς στρατηγοὺς πράσσειν: very striking and forceful alliteration, as there was in Nicias' speech in 6.9.1.

ᾗ ἂν αὐτοῖς δοκῇ: 'in whatever way in might seem best to them.'

ἐγίγνετο: 'began to take place': the imperfect is important.

ἀνειλήφει: 3rd singular pluperfect of ἀναλαμβάνω: 'the city had recovered itself.'

ἀπὸ τῆς νόσου: In 2.47–54 Thucydides describes the impact of the plague which came on Athens in 430 BCE as a result of the confined living conditions in which the besieged Athenians were living. Pericles was one of its victims.

τοῦ συνεχοῦς πολέμου: the Athenians had been fighting constantly from 431 BCE until the Peace of Nicias in 421 BCE (ἐκεχειρίαν).

ἔς τε ἡλικίας πλῆθος ἐπιγεγενημένης: 'with regard to the number of men of fighting age who had come after.' ἐπιγεγενημένης is the genitive feminine singular perfect participle of ἐπιγίγνομαι.

Chapters 27–29: the mutilation of the Herms

The next three chapters deal with the strange, but highly significant tale of the mutilation of the Herms, the profanation of the Eleusinian Mysteries and the (alleged) implication of Alcibiades in what happened. These events, which struck at the very heart of religious belief in Athens and the wellbeing of the city were significant in creating confusion and dissension in Athens at a critical moment in the plans to invade Sicily.

Chapter 27

Whilst preparations for departure are taking place, the Herms, a common feature of the streets and houses of Athens, are mutilated by persons unknown. During the investigation, further accusations are brought about the profanation of the Eleusinian Mysteries, the most secret and sacred of rites in Athens.

27.1

ἐν δὲ τούτῳ: K. J. Dover worked out that this took place on 25 May 415 BCE!

Ἑρμαῖ: these were stone statues of Hermes, sculptured heads on square bases with the added feature of an erect phallus. Hermes was the god of travel so that they were originally found as road-markers. They were particularly common in Athens, not only at crossroads but outside homes and sacred places. A number of Herms still survive, some of them damaged in the mutilation described here.

ὅσοι... πολλοὶ... οἱ πλεῖστοι: 'As for all those of the Herms that were made of stone – there are lots of them in porches and sacred places, very many of them were mutilated.'

κατὰ τὸ ἐπιχώριον: 'according to the local custom'.

ἡ τετράγωνος ἐργασία: 'a four-square piece of work'.

οἱ πλεῖστοι περιεκόπησαν τὰ πρόσωπα: powerful alliteration reflects the violence and the strangeness of the action.

περιεκόπησαν: 3rd plural aorist passive of περικόπτω.

τὰ πρόσωπα: accusative of respect.

27.2

τοὺς δράσαντας: accusative plural participle of δράω, the topic of the sentence given the key position.

ᾔδει: 3rd singular imperfect of οἶδα.

οὗτοί τε ἐζητοῦντο ... καὶ ἐψηφίσαντο: the two things the Athenians did, one in the continuous imperfect, the other in the aorist. ἐψηφίσαντο: this is followed by an accusative (τὸν βουλόμενον) and infinitive (μηνύειν).

τὸν βουλόμενον: 'anyone who wanted'.

εἰ τις ἄλλο τι οἶδεν ἀσέβημα γεγενημένον: accusative (ἄλλο τι ἀσέβημα) and participle construction (γεγενημένον) after οἶδεν. γεγενημένον is the accusative neuter perfect participle of γίγνομαι.

καὶ ἀστῶν καὶ ξένων καὶ δούλων: this tricolon and repetition of ending at the end of the sentence shows the range and urgency of the enquiry: any evidence from anyone will do. And so it turns out.

27.3

τὸ πρᾶγμα μειζόνως ἐλάμβανον: 'they took the matter rather seriously/too seriously', a very simple, direct statement. μειζόνως is the comparative adverb of μέγας.

οἰωνὸς: 'an omen', originally 'a large bird' and thereafter a bird of omen, and then an omen. This is the word's only appearance in Thucydides. Damage to Hermes, the god of travel, was likely to be interpreted as a bad sign, running the risk of divine displeasure, as would the damage to divine images that were so central to Athenian life.

γεγενῆσθαι: perfect infinitive of γίγνομαι, dependent on ἐδόκει.

ἐπὶ ξυνωμοσίᾳ ἅμα νεωτέρων πραγμάτων καὶ δήμου καταλύσεως: 'with the purpose of a revolutionary conspiracy aimed at the destruction of the democracy'. This is a typically Thucydidean form of expression, using two abstract nouns of which the first is a very unusual word, first used by Thucydides. The people are constantly concerned that the aristocratic élite, with their long family histories and their connections outside Athens, want the end of democracy and a return to a system of narrower participation. That concern was turned into reality in 411 BCE with an oligarchic coup and in 404 BCE some aristocrats sided with the victorious Spartans.

Chapter 28

Further information is brought forward about the Mysteries and the misbehaviour of the young, including Alcibiades. His opponents take advantage of the moment to suggest that this is all an anti-democratic plot.

AS

28.1

μηνύεται: the first subject of this passive verb is οὐδέν, but then in the second clause, the subject is περικοπαί with which γεγενημέναι agrees and the verb μηνύεται has to be supplied in the plural.

ἀπὸ μετοίκων τέ τινων καὶ ἀκολούθων: 'metics' are resident aliens, non-Athenians who are long-term residents in Athens who have certain rights and fiscal responsibilities. Metics were numerous in Athens because of its prosperity and wide-ranging trading activity.

περὶ μὲν τῶν Ἑρμῶν οὐδέν, ἄλλων δὲ ἀγαλμάτων περικοπαί ... γεγενημέναι: this sentence is shaped by the balance between the μὲν and δὲ clauses, but the δὲ clause is much longer and then spins out into a third clause about the Mysteries (καὶ τὰ μυστήρια) which becomes a ὡς clause with an indicative (ποιεῖται).

ὑπὸ νεωτέρων μετὰ παιδιᾶς καὶ οἴνου: as ever, the drunken revelry of youth, particularly upper-class youth, causes unease amongst the elders: cf. the Bullingdon Club in Oxford. This concern about the young reflects the rift between young and old in the earlier speeches of Nicias and Alcibiades and such behaviour would seem to fit in with Alcibiades' wild ways.

τὰ μυστήρια: the Mysteries were a major, Panhellenic religious festival based at Eleusis, a coastal town on the western edge of Attica, 12 miles from Athens. The secret ritual was sacred to Demeter and Persephone and was open to all (male, female, free and slave) and was associated with the idea of rebirth.

ἐν οἰκίαις: the performance of these sacred and secret rites in private houses would be perceived as particularly insulting to the gods and sacrilegious.

ἐφ' ὕβρει: 'as an act of deliberate contempt'.

ὧν καὶ τον Ἀλκιβιαδην ἐπῃτιῶντο: 'and they accused Alcibiades, too, of these activities.' This last clause appended to the sentence drops the bombshell of Alcibiades' involvement.

28.2

καὶ αὐτὰ ὑπολαμβάνοντες ... δημοτικὴν παρανομίαν: a typically complex and very long Thucydidean sentence which strives to convey both the motivation and the actions of those who are the enemies of Alcibiades. The subject is οἱ μάλιστα τῷ Ἀλκιβιάδη ἀχθόμενοι: 'those who most hated Alcibiades'.

Thucydides now tells us two things about the attitude of Alcibiades' enemies, his blocking of their leadership of the people and their hopes of gaining supremacy. The first is conveyed by a participle clause in the dative case (ἐμποδὼν ὄντι), agreeing with Alcibiades. μὴ ... προεστάναι depends on ἐμποδὼν ὄντι: 'preventing them from securing leadership of the people'. The second is conveyed by a nominative aorist participle (νομίσαντες), agreeing with the enemies, followed by a nominative and infinitive (πρῶτοι ἂν εἶναι).

εἰ αὐτὸν ἐξελάσειαν, πρῶτοι ἂν εἶναι: this is a remote conditional in future time: hence the aorist optative in the subordinate clause (from ἐξελαύνω) and the ἂν in the main clause: 'if they were to drive him out.'

ἐμεγάλυνον καὶ ἐβόων: two imperfect verbs to convey the continuous nature of their efforts to cause trouble for Alcibiades by insisting that these acts were part of an anti-democracy plot.

AS

ἐπὶ δήμου καταλύσει: 'with the purpose of doing down the democracy'. Once again, the key element of the clause is put in the prominent and emphatic position.

ὡς ... γένοιτο ... εἴη: an indirect statement in historic sequence: hence the optative verbs.

γένοιτο: the subjects of the verb are τά τε μύστικα καὶ ἡ τῶν Ἑρμῶν περικοπὴ.

ἐπράχθη: 3rd singular perfect passive of πράσσω.

ἐπιλέγοντες: Thucydides once again disturbs the symmetry of his sentence by ending with a participle clause: 'bringing forward as evidence . . .'.

τὴν ἀλλὴν ... παρανομίαν: 'the other signs of undemocratic lawlessness with regard to his behaviour.' This reflects Thucydides' judgement of Alcibiades in 6.15.4: his behaviour is indicative of a lack of respect for the people and democracy.

Chapter 29

In response to these charges, Alcibiades declared himself willing to stand trial at once, thereby hoping to take advantage of his current popularity. His opponents, on the other hand, strove to delay the trial, in the hope that more charges would come to light, and it was agreed that Alcibiades and the expedition should set out without further delay.

29.1

In this chapter, we see a complex political situation in which each side is doing the opposite of what you would expect: Alcibiades is calling for his own prosecution to take place at once whilst his enemies are trying to delay it. As ever, it is the mood of the people – and the army – that is the critical factor.

πρὶν ἐκπλεῖν: 'before setting sail': πρὶν followed by the infinitive.

εἰργασμένος ἦν: 'he had done': middle pluperfect passive, which means exactly the same as εἴργαστο two lines later.

τὰ τῆς παρασκευῆς: this neuter plural phrase with a definite article is typical of Thucydides and just means 'the preparations'.

ἐπεπόριστο: 3rd singular pluperfect passive of πορίζω.

δίκην δοῦναι ... ἄρχειν: δοῦναι is aorist infinitive of δίδωμι. Both of these infinitives are dependent on ἕτοιμος. Alcibiades' position is very simple and simply expressed: try me. If I am guilty, convict and punish me. If not, let me take up my command. The next sentence in 29.2 merely develops this simple argument in greater detail.

ἀπολυθείη: 3rd person singular aorist passive optative.

29.2

ἐπεμαρτύρετο μὴ: 'he appealed to them not to . . . .'

ἀπόντος πέρι αὐτοῦ: 'about him in his absence.'

σωφρονέστερον εἴη μὴ ... πέμπειν αὐτὸν: 'it would be more sensible not to send him'.

πρὶν διαγνῶσι: 3rd plural aorist subjunctive of διαγιγνώσκω: subjunctive because it's an indefinite clause in primary sequence.

AS

29.3

δεδιότες: perfect participle of δείδω with present sense which controls two fear clauses, μὴ εὐνοῦν ἔχῃ and μὴ μαλακίζηται.

μὴ εὐνοῦν ἔχῃ: 'that he would have the army on his side.'

ἢν ἀγωνίζηται: ἢν plus subjunctive: conditional in future time: 'if he should come trial'.

ὅ τε δῆμος μὴ μαλακίζηται: 'that the people should go soft on him.'

θεραπεύων: 'supporting, siding with him'.

οἵ τ' Ἀργεῖοι . . .. καὶ τῶν Μαντινέων τινές: Argos and Mantinea are two cities in the north-eastern Peloponnese who provided 500 and 250 soldiers to the expedition (6.43). In his earlier speech, Alcibiades had made play with the fact that he had persuaded the Argives and Mantineans to join with the Athenians at the Battle of Mantinea (6.16.6).

ξυνεστράτευον: 'were joining the expedition.'

ἀπέτρεπον καὶ ἀπέσπευδον: the repetition of compounds with ἀπό and the imperfect tenses show how hard Alcibiades' enemies are trying to avert a trial. ἀπέσπευδον is an unusual word, meaning to be enthusiastically *against* something.

ἐνιέντες: present participle of ἐνίημι, 'introducing, sending in . . .'.

ἀναγωγήν: 'departure' (of the expedition): the verb ἀνάγομαι means 'I set sail.'

νῦν μὲν πλεῖν . . . ἐλθόντα δὲ κρίνεσθαι: 'that he should sail now . . . but that he should come [i.e. be brought] to trial after he had gone.'

πλεῖν, κατασχεῖν and κρίνεσθαι are all infinitives dependent on ἔλεγον, 'telling him to . . .'. Once again the imperfect is significant.

βουλόμενοι: 'with the intention of bringing him to trial' with the infinitive ἀγωνίσασθαι.

ἐκ μείζονος διαβολῆς: 'as a result of some even greater accusation'.

ῥᾷον: 'more easily', comparative adverb of ῥᾴδιος.

ποριεῖν: future infinitive of πορίζω.

αὐτοῦ ἀπόντος: genitive absolute: 'while he was absent.'

κομισθέντα: accusative aorist passive participle of κομίζω.

μετάπεμπτον κομισθέντα . . . ἀγωνίσασθαι: Thucydides uses a verbal adjective, a participle and then an infinite, whereas we would say 'that he should be sent for, brought back and put on trial.'

καὶ ἔδοξε πλεῖν τὸν Ἀλκιβιάδην: after long and complex sentences about the states of mind and the intentions of Alcibiades and his enemies, the decision is presented in the shortest and simplest possible way. Indeed, Athenian inscriptions often begin with the word ἔδοξε, 'it was decided . . .'.

Chapter 30

The expedition sets forth from the Piraeus, the harbour of Athens, and all the people go down from the city to see the departure. After all the confusion and machinations of the previous chapter, Thucydides now describes at great length the scale of the expedition and the splendour of its departure, a splendour which will, in the end, be brought low. The description emphasizes the engagement of the whole city in the enterprise. As Nicias said earlier (6.23.2), it is as if the Athenians are setting out to found a new city.

30.1

ἐγίγνετο: the imperfect is important, reflecting that this is the start of something.

τῶν μὲν οὖν ξυμμάχων: this sentence tells us about the plans for the allies and their naval forces in contrast with the activities of αὐτοὶ δ' Ἀθηναῖοι in the next. The two sentences are carefully balanced against each other, perhaps suggesting the scale and order of the preparations.

τῶν μὲν οὖν ξυμμάχων τοῖς πλείστοις . . . ξυνείπετο: all of this is dependent on εἴρητο, 3rd singular pluperfect passive of λέγω: literally 'most of the allies and the grain-bearing cargo ships . . . had been told to . . .'.

ὅση ἄλλη παρασκευὴ: 'all the rest of the equipment': this really ought to be in the dative, too, but the antecedent has been taken inside the relative clause. but we know what he means.

ἐς Κέρκυραν: Corcyra (modern-day Corfu), the largest island in the Ionian sea and an ally of Athens throughout the war, is the obvious place for an expeditionary force against Sicily to gather.

ὡς . . . διαβαλοῦσιν: ὡς plus dative plural future participle: 'so they could make the crossing'.

ἐπὶ ἄκραν Ἰαπυγίαν: 'the promontory of Iapygia' which is on the heel of Italy.

τὸν Ἰόνιον: sc. κόλπον: the Ionian Gulf.

ἐς τὸν Πειραιᾶ: the Piraeus is the harbour of Athens, five miles from the city and joined to it by the Long Walls. (Plato's *Republic* starts with Socrates going down to the Piraeus: κατέβην χθὲς εἰς Πειραιᾶ).

ὡς ἀναξόμενοι: future participle of purpose in exactly the same place in the sentence as ὡς . . . διαβαλοῦσιν above. ἀναξόμενοι picks up and echoes ἀναγωγὴ at the beginning of the chapter.

30.2

ξυγκατέβη: an unusual word, strikingly placed: 'they all went down together'. Thucydides emphasizes throughout these chapters the sense that this is an expedition that involves, and thereby imperils, the whole city and the city's empire. The first words of Plato's *Republic* are κατέβην χθὲς εἰς Πειραιᾶ, perhaps echoing this sentence.

ἅπας ὡς εἰπεῖν: Thucydides uses the emphatic ἅπας and then qualifies it, 'so to speak'.

This long sentence is awash with μὲν . . . δὲ to show the different groups and the different partings and the different emotions. The clause that balances οἱ μὲν ἐπιχώριοι is οἱ δὲ ξένοι in the middle of 31.1.

μετ' ἐλπίδος . . . καὶ ὀλοφυρμῶν: Thucydides shows the mixture of emotions in those who were present. 'Hope, that comforter in danger' (ἐλπὶς δὲ κινδύνῳ παραμύθιον οὖσα), as the Athenians say to the people of Melos in the Melian Dialogue (5.103.1), is one of the things that carries the expedition forward (cf. 6.24.3 and 31.6). Lamentation (7.71.3 and 7.75.2) is where the expedition ends two years later.

AS

τὰ μὲν ὡς κτήσοιντο, τοὺς δ' εἴ ποτε ὄψοιντο: the first clause is matched up with μετ' ἐλπίδος, the second with ὀλοφυρμῶν: 'the hope at what they might gain ... the lamentations/fear if they would ever see them again.' The two verbs are future optatives.

ἐνθυμούμενοι: the sentence ends with a participle phrase introducing an indirect question summing up the people's realization of the scale and significance of what they were undertaking.

Chapter 31

At the moment of departure, those watching, Athenian and non-Athenian, are stirred by different emotions as they confront the reality of their decision. Then there is a detailed account of the scale, daring and significance of the expedition, comparing it with other military expeditions. Nothing can compare with this, according to Thucydides, and the whole thing is described as more a display of greatness than a military expedition. By the end, there is a strong sense of the hubris of it all, the massive outflow of resources and the attendant risk. This expedition is out of proportion to its purpose.

31.1

These sentences sum up the confusion and mixed emotions of the people, both excited and troubled by the size and the sight of what they had agreed to undertake. The non-Athenians have just come for the display of it all.

ἐν τῷ παρόντι καιρῷ .... τῇ παρούσῃ ῥώμῃ: Thucydides balances the two reasons for different reactions in parallel participial phrases but it is the very size of the expedition that brings both confidence and a sense of crisis.

τὰ δεινά: this is the subject of ἐσήει, a plural neuter noun with a singular verb: 'the risks came upon them.'

ἑκάστων ὧν ἑώρων: 'of each of the things which they saw': ὧν is attracted into agreeing with the genitive antecedent when it would logically be accusative into the genitive when it should be accusative; ἑώρων (ὁράω) is imperfect, like all the verbs around it.

διάνοιαν: a remarkable word to end this sentence: 'idea', 'plan'. The very idea is a wonder.

πολυτελεστάτη δὴ καὶ εὐπρεπεστάτη: these two superlatives, emphasized by δὴ, are very striking, and more reminiscent of Herodotus' hyperbole (cf. the description of Adrastus in Herodotus 1.45.3) or the splendour of Venice's celebration of its maritime wealth. There is a sense not only of expense but also of display and extravagance.

31.2

After these striking sentences Thucydides returns to his usual meticulous attention to detail to prove his point.

ἡ ἐς Ἐπίδαυρον μετὰ Περικλέους καὶ ἡ αὐτὴ ἐς Ποτείδαιαν μετὰ Ἅγνωνος οὐκ ἐλάσσων ἦν: this refers to two expeditions undertaken in the summer of

AS

430 BCE, one to the north-east coast of the Peloponnese (2.56), the other to the Chersonese in the north of the Aegean (2.58).

Λεσβίων καὶ Χίων: Lesbos and Chios are two of the three largest islands in the Aegean, along with Samos. From the foundation of the Delian League in 478 BCE through its metamorphosis into the Athenian Empire they were the biggest contributors to Athens' resources.

31.3

ὡρμήθησαν: 'they set out': 3rd plural aorist indicative of ὁρμάομαι, a key word in these chapters.

οὗτος δὲ . . . στόλος: this is a truly wondrous Thucydidean sentence. It grows and grows to reflect the scale of the expedition itself. No one other than Thucydides could have written it. It starts with a participial phrase (ὡς . . . ἐσόμενος) and an aorist passive participle (ἐξαρτυθείς) but then it divides in two in the description of the fleet (τὸ μὲν ναυτικὸν) which goes on for ten lines and then, finally, the land forces (τὸ δὲ πεζὸν). As the sentence grows, it is worth exploring how much of it is about money, show, extravagance and internal competition.

ἐκπονηθέν: neuter singular aorist passive participle, agreeing with τὸ . . . ναυτικὸν.

τῶν τε τριηράρχων καὶ τῆς πόλεως: funds for the expedition come from two sources, the public purse and from the contribution of wealthy individual citizens. Under the system of liturgies, wealthy citizens were required to fund major aspects of Athenian life, whether triremes as here or choruses for tragedy and comedy In the case of triremes, the state provided the ship, the basic equipment and the sailor's pay, whereas the trierarch covered all provisions, repairs and additional equipment and ornamentation. This canny form of wealth tax encouraged competition between these individuals to outshine each other, and thereby extravagance: cf. Alcibiades' pride in such extravagance for civic glory (6.16.3).

τοῦ μὲν δημοσίου . . . τῶν δὲ τριηράρχων: this sentence is now shaped around two massive genitive absolutes: τοῦ μὲν δημοσίου picks up τῆς πόλεως from the previous clause and has two participles attached to it, διδόντος and παρασχόντος and τῶν δὲ τριηράρχων has two, διδόντων and χρησαμένων.

δραχμὴν: a drachma is a decent day's pay: surviving accounts from the building of the Erectheum show that a skilled workman on that building got the same amount.

ταχείας . . . ὁπλιταγωγοὺς: the swift ships are the triremes, the fighting ships, whereas there was also a need for slower ships to carry the land forces.

ὑπηρεσίας: 'petty officers', the 30 members of the crew who oversaw the rowers.

θρανίταις: the rowers on the top level of the trireme had to work harder and be more skilful which is why they get a bonus.

σημείοις: 'figureheads'.

προθυμηθέντος ἑνὸς ἑκάστου: after the two long genitive absolutes, Thucydides introduces a third in the singular to tell of the individual competitiveness of the trierarchs (see note above).

προέξει: future of προέχω with ὅπως: each man wants his ship to excel in appearance (εὐπρεπείᾳ) and speed (τῷ ταχυναυτεῖν): ταχυναυτεῖν is a very rare verb which makes its first appearance in Greek literature here.

AS

τὸ δὲ πεζὸν has two aorist passive participles attached to it: ἐκκριθὲν (from ἐκκρίνω) and ἁμιλληθέν.

καταλόγοις τε χρηστοῖς: 'from good lists', i.e. lists of hoplites which have fit and able soldiers rather than those who were unfit for service.

31.4

ξυνέβη: not to be confused with ξυγκατέβη in 30.2. This just means 'it happened that' plus accusative and an infinitive, ἔριν γενεσθαι, and then ἐπίδειξιν ... εἰκασθῆναι.

ἔριν: Hesiod (*Works and Days* line 11) famously tells us that there are two kinds of strife, good strife and bad strife. Such competitiveness lies at the heart of the Athenians' way of being but it undoubtedly has ominous overtones for the future.

ᾧ τις ἕκαστος προσετάχθη: 'in the activity to which each individual had been assigned.'

ἐπίδειξιν ... εἰκασθῆναι: 'it were more that a show was being presented than preparation against an enemy.' ἐπίδειξις is also the word that is used of the rhetorical displays enacted by sophists like Gorgias.

31.5

Another sentence, long and straggling, about cost and expenditure and once again there is the distinction between public and private funds.

τήν τε τῆς πόλεως ἀναλωσιν δημοσίαν ... τὴν ἰδίαν: is picked up by τῆς μεν πόλεως and τὴν ἰδίαν is picked up by τῶν δὲ ἰδιωτῶν. The piling up of three examples of ὅσα shows the constant piling up of resources.

εἰ γάρ τις ἐλογίσατο: the 'if' clause stretches as far as ἔπλει, and the main verb is ηὑρέθη, a long way away.

προετετελέκει: 'it had expended in advance': the subject is πόλις and has to be supplied: the verb is pluperfect. It is the protasis of an unfulfilled past conditional and ἂν ... ηὑρεθη is the apodosis – quite a few lines later.

ἃ ἔχοντας τοὺς στρατηγοὺς ἀπέστελλε: 'the funds which the city was sending the generals off with'.

τῶν δὲ ἰδιωτῶν: 'as for the private citizens'.

ἀνηλώκει ... ἀναλώσειν: the former is the pluperfect, and the latter is the future infinitive of ἀναλίσκω, I spend. The repetition emphasizes – again –the scale of expense.

χωρὶς δ' ἅ εἰκὸς ἦν ... πάντα τινὰ παρασκευάσασθαι: 'apart from what it was reasonable that every man should have prepared'.

ἐφόδιον: 'provisions for the journey'.

ηὑρέθη: 3rd singular aorist passive of εὑρίσκω: it has a plural subject, πολλὰ τάλαντα.

πολλὰ τάλαντα: a talent is 6,000 drachmas and a drachma was a day's pay for a skilled worker (see above in 31.3). In the years of the Athenian Empire, the subject cities contributed 600 talents a year to Athens.

31.6

τόλμης τε θάμβει καὶ ὄψεως λαμπρότητι: Thucydides uses unusual, striking abstract vocabulary to convey the strangeness of the expedition's appearance.

στρατιᾶς πρὸς οὕς ἐπῆσαν ὑπερβολῇ: this phrase is parallel to τόλμης τε
θάμβει καὶ ὄψεως λαμπρότητι above: 'for the superiority of forces compared
with those against whom they are going'.

καὶ ὅτι μέγιστος διάπλους ... ἐπεχειρήθη: this clause is also dependent on
περιβόητος.

ἐπεχειρήθη: 3rd singular aorist passive from ἐπιχειρέω.

ἐπὶ μεγίστῃ ἐλπίδι τῶν μελλόντων πρὸς τὰ ὑπάρχοντα: 'with the greatest
expectations for the future compared with the current situation.' Once again we
return to the emotion of hope, cf. ἐλπὶς in 6.15.3, εὐέλπιδες in 6.24.3.

Chapter 32

The moment of departure. That moment is celebrated with prayer, hymns, libations
and a race to Aegina. After all the economics, the numbers and the costs, here comes
the pomp and circumstance and ritual. Another long sentence conveys all of the scale
and detail of the moment of setting sail and the sense of unity of action and purpose.

32.1

ὑπερσημάνθη: 3rd singular aorist passive of ὑπερσημαίνω.

εὐχὰς ... τὰς νομιζομένας: 'the customary prayers', cf. νόμος. Perhaps the
religious aspects of the departure are emphasized to contrast with the acts of
sacrilege which have been recently committed. Sadly, none of this piety did the
Athenians any good.

ὑπὸ κήρυκος: 'at the instruction of a herald.'

κρατῆρας τε κεράσαντες: 'having mixed their mixing bowls'. Both words come
from the same basic stem and mixing bowls, for mixing water and wine, become
craters in our sense because of their shape. It is ironic that in 6.46 the Athenians
are tricked by the Egestaeans with the gold and silver bowls which are passed
from dinner party to dinner party to suggest great wealth.

ἐπιβάται: these are the marines, the fighting soldiers on the decks of the ships.

ξυνεπηύχοντο: a rare word – this is its first known appearance in Greek literature
– emphatically placed, emphasizing once again the communal aspect of what is
going on.

παιανίσαντες δὲ καὶ τελεώσαντες τὰς σπονδὰς: a paean is a sacred choral
song sung at key moments, to celebrate a victory or to mark the beginning or end
of any undertaking. Libations were poured as an offering to the gods at key
moments, whether at a dinner party or on a more public occasion. Hence, σπονδαί
comes to mean truce.

ἐπὶ κέρως: 'in a wing shape', in single file.

ἅμιλλαν: once again, the sense of competition and rivalry against each other, but
there is also perhaps a sense that it's all a game.

Αἰγίνης: the island of Aegina is an island facing the Piraeus, seven miles away.
Pericles once described it as 'the eyesore of the Piraeus' because it was a long-term
rival/enemy.

ἠπείγοντο: once again, the sense of eagerness and competition: they can't wait to
get there.

AS

32.3

ἐς δὲ τὰς Συρακούσας: at this point, after three chapters about the preparations and departure from Athens there is a very swift change of focus to Syracuse.

τὰ περὶ ἐπίπλου: 'news of the invasion' is the subject of ἠγγέλλετο.

οὐ . . . ἐπιστεύετο . . . οὐδέν: 'was completely misbelieved'. The double negative at either end of the sentence is striking. It's important that, whereas the Athenians think that the expedition is the best of ideas, the rest of the world can't quite believe it.

ἐκκλησίας: the people of Syracuse have a democratic assembly in the same way as the Athenians. The Athenians think they are going somewhere distant and different whereas it turns out to be all too similar to Athens. As is typical of such an assembly, they can't agree on the big issue.

AS

33–41

33–34: The speech of Hermocrates
Hermocrates is the most important figure in Syracuse and has already made a speech
at the time of the peace agreement with Athens in 424 BCE (4.59–64). In his speech
he urges the Syracusans to believe that the expedition is coming from Athens and is
coming to conquer Sicily. He encourages the Syracusans to be confident in final
victory because the very scale of the Athenian of the expedition will stir the other
cities of Sicily to action and will be hard to sustain because of the demands of
logistics.

He goes on to encourage the Syracusans to seek help from all possible sources, the
indigenous Sicels, the other Greek cities in Sicily, Carthage, Sparta and Corinth. His
proposed strategy is to put together a large fleet from all of the cities and sail out to
meet the Athenians at Tarentum, on the east coast of Italy, so that the Athenians
would face opposition even before they got across the Ionian sea.

34–40
The Syracusans are not inclined to take seriously Hermocrates' warning or advice
and Athenagoras, the leader of the democratic party, speaks against him. He first
argues that there is no danger that the Athenians will come against Sicily and these
rumours are merely designed to cause panic. He then argues that, even if the Athenians
were to come, they would not have the cavalry, the hoplites, the base or provisions
to be an effective threat. He then turns his attention on those people in Syracuse
whom he accuses of trying to stir up civil strife and to undermine the power of the
people. His speech ends with the contrast between democracy and oligarchy and an
attack on those who are inventing the Athenian invasion as a means of destabilizing
the city.

41
The debate ends with the call from an anonymous speaker to put an end to such
personal and political attacks and to make preparations by preparing military forces
and contacting neighbouring cities.

42–46: The Athenians arrive in Sicily

These chapters show the problems that the expedition, for all its scale, faces in reality;
the difficulty of making an expedition of such size; the lack of enthusiasm and support
for the Athenians in Italy and Sicily: the capacity of the Syracusans to prepare themselves
against attack, the duplicity of the people of Egesta and their lack of financial support.
The great ambitions of the departure are soon brought low.

42
The Athenians are at Corcyra, the largest island in the Ionian sea, an ally of Athens
and the base from which to cross to Sicily. The three generals divide the fleet in three
so that the force could go forward more effectively: the fleet is too big altogether to

**A
Level**

find suitable harbours and provisions and to sail effectively. This shows the unprecedented scale of the expedition and the difficulties that will lie ahead.

They also sent three ships in advance to find out which cities would be willing to receive them. They would sail back after their enquiries to inform the rest of the fleet of the situation.

43
This chapter is Thucydides' small version of the Catalogue of Ships, listing the forces as they set forth from Corcyra to Sicily. Thucydides' attention to detail is striking:

- 134 triremes and 2 ships from Rhodes.
- 100 of the triremes were from Athens – 60 for fighting and 40 for troop transport – and the rest from the other cities in the Athenian Empire.
- 5,100 hoplites, of which 1,500 are Athenian citizens and 700 from the lowest citizen class who served as marines. The rest of the troops came from their allies plus 500 Argives and 250 Mantineans (cf. 6.29.3).
- 480 archers, of whom 80 were from Crete.
- 700 slingers from Rhodes.
- 120 light-armed troops from Megara.
- 1 horse transport carrying 30 horses.

44
The catalogue now turns to the logistics of the expedition:

- 30 merchant ships carrying corn, equipment for building fortifications, bakers, masons and carpenters.
- 100 smaller craft.
- merchant ships and small boats which followed the expedition to trade with them.

The expedition crosses the Ionian Gulf and makes land at the promontory of Iapygia and Tarentum. They make their way down the coast of southern Italy, but the Greek cities are unwilling to provide a market or to let them into the city. So, they have to settle for water and a place to moor.

All three parts of the expedition are reunited at Rhegion, at the very toe of Sicily, where they are not forced to make camp outside the city walls. The Athenians enter into negotiations with the people of Rhegium, encouraging them to help the people of Leontini because both of the two cities were founded from Chalcis on Euboea. However, the people of Rhegion refuse to take sides and await a decision from all the Greek cities in Italy.

In this situation, the Athenians await the return of the three ships from Sicily.

45
The people of Syracuse finally accept from reports that the Athenians are at Rhegion so that they make preparation for their arrival, putting garrisons into Sicel towns, sending troops to forts in the country, reviewing all of their military resources.

A
Level

46

The three ships that had been sent ahead to Egesta return to Rhegion. It turns out that Egesta has only 30 talents, not 60, to offer the Athenians, something which surprised Alcibiades and Lamachus, but not Nicias. The combination of this news with the lack of support from Rhegion discourages the generals: Rhegion, because of its ancient connection with Leontini, was their best hope of an ally.

The people of Egesta had tricked the original Athenian ambassadors (6.6.3, 6.8.1) with a method that bears a close resemblance to a story told by Herodotus of Oroetes in 3.123. The people of Egesta set about proving their wealth by showing them a temple to Aphrodite at Eryx, which was full of treasure – but wasn't theirs. Then they gather together all the most expensive dinner ware they can muster from Egesta and neighbouring cities and then they pass it round to entertain the Athenians. So, the Athenians think that everywhere they are entertained is equally and splendidly rich.

Those who fall for this device are much blamed by everyone else.

Chapter 47–50: The debate at Rhegion

The Athenians had used Rhegion, on the tip of the toe of Italy, as a base earlier in the war (3.86.5). These chapters convey the different opinions of the three generals, Nicias, Alcibiades and Lamachus, now that they face the reality of the situation in Sicily. Commentators cannot decide which of the three proposals Thucydides would have supported, although there is a tendency towards Lamachus' position. Perhaps it is not Thucydides' intention to make that clear and he may be showing, by the diversity of options, the uncertainty and confusion that beset such an expedition from the start. However, in 7.42.3, Thucydides does say that the Athenians missed their chance by not acting swiftly on their arrival. One question that might be asked is about Thucydides' sources for this debate: Lamachus died in 414 BCE, Nicias in 413 BCE.

Chapter 47

Nicias' proposal is limited and cautious, as befits a general who didn't want to go in the first place. He proposes an attack on Selinus and says that any further involvement will depend on the willingness and capacity of the people of Egesta to support the force. If that support is not forthcoming, he suggests a show of strength to the cities of Sicily and a return to Athens.

47.1

At this point Thucydides could have given each of the generals a speech, as he does throughout his work. Instead, he presents their arguments through indirect speech. Nicias' ideas are presented indirectly through γνώμη, his opinion, followed by a succession of infinitives (πλεῖν, βουλεύεσθαι, ἀξιοῦν, διαλλάξαι, ἀποπλεῖν, μὴ κινδυνεύειν). This may seem difficult to us but the greater part of Plato's *Symposium* is all in indirect speech.

A
Level

Σελινοῦντα: In 6.20.3, Nicias stated that Selinus and Syracuse were the two central objectives of the expedition.

ἐφ' ὅπερ: 'for which purpose'.

Ἐγεσταῖοι: In early spring 415 BCE, the Egestaeans came to Athens with the Athenian embassy, bringing 60 talents of silver to fund, for a month, the 60 ships for which they were asking (6.8.1). In 6. 19.1 it was the Egestaeans' pleas for help which persuaded the Athenian people and that decision was predicated on Egestaean wealth. In 6.46, we learn, as Nicias suspected, that such wealth does not exist and the Athenians have been duped.

πρὸς ταῦτα βουλεύεσθαι: this infinitive is dependent on γνώμη: 'to make plans in the light of this.'

ὅσασπερ ἠτήσαντο: 'as many as they had asked for' (6.19.1).

παραμείναντας ... παραπλεύσαντας ... ἐπιδείξαντας ... δηλώσαντας: all of these accusative aorist participles agree with an understood Ἀθηναίους.

παραμείναντας: as mentioned above, this participle agrees with the Athenians, not with Σελινουντίους, despite being next to it.

Σελινουντίους ... διαλλάξαι αὐτοῖς: 'having waited for the people of Selinus to make an agreement with them' (i.e. the people of Egesta).

ἐπιδείξαντας ... δηλώσαντας: it's not easy to see the difference in meaning between these two verbs. This repetition does suggest that Nicias' tactic is more form than substance.

ἢν μή τι δι' ὀλίγου ... οἷοί τε ὦσιν ὠφελῆσαι: just when there was hope that this sentence – and Nicias' proposal – might have come to an end, it launches into some more possibilities. What does this tell us about the clarity of Nicias' thinking?

οἷοί τε ὦσιν: this verb controls three infinitive verbs, ὠφελῆσαι, προσαγαγέσθαι and μὴ κινδυνεύειν. The last of these infinitives seems like an appendage even to a clause which is itself an appendage.

Chapter 48

Alcibiades proposal is dependent on the Athenians' capacity to win over the cities of Sicily and the native Sicels. His plan is that, only when such support has been won, they should attack Selinus and Syracuse. It might be typical of Alcibiades that he sees the way forward through persuasion and is motivated by a danger of losing face.

48.1

τοσαύτῃ δυνάμει ... αἰσχρῶς: Alcibiades is driven by a sense of shame. It is ironic that the very size of the force, which Nicias argued for, now becomes a reason for doing the wrong thing.

ἐκπλεύσαντας: an accusative participle which agrees with an understood Ἀθηναίους. This sentence thereby follows exactly the same pattern as chapter 47.

αἰσχρῶς καὶ ἀπράκτους ἀπελθεῖν: the alliteration and the harsh consonants convey Alcibiades' disgust at the very notion of retreat.

ἀπελθεῖν ... πειρᾶσθαι ... πείθειν ... ἐπιχειρεῖν: these are infinitives dependent to οὐκ ἔφη χρῆναι.

τοὺς Σικελούς: the Sicels are some of the indigenous inhabitants of Sicily who were there before the colonization of the island by the Greeks.

ἀφιστάναι: this is the transitive form of the verb, 'to make to revolt'.

τοὺς μὲν ... τοὺς δὲ: the plan is to get some of the Sicels to revolt, others to become friends with them.

Μεσσηνίους: the Messanians lived on the Sicilian side of the narrow straits between Sicily and Italy, which are today the straits of Messina.

ἐν πόρῳ ... εἶναι αὐτοὺς ... ἔσεσθαι: the bracket is an accusative subject with two infinitives because this is all part of Alcibiades' indirect statement.

ἐν πόρῳ ... καὶ προσβολῇ ... τῆς Σικελίας: 'in the crossing and approach to Sicily.'

προσαγαγομένους ... εἰδότας: these accusative plural participles all agree, like ἐκπλεύσαντας in the first line of the sentence, with an understood Ἀθηναίους.

Chapter 49

Lamachus, although less significant in Thucydides' work than Nicias or Alcibiades, gets the longest account of his plan. He is an Athenian general with a long career, stretching back into the 430s. In 425 BCE he is sufficiently famous to be the object of Aristophanes' comic attacks in *Acharnians*.

Lamachus' approach is more direct and practical than those of Nicias and Alcibiades, as might be expected. He proposes an immediate assault on the city of Syracuse, which will catch them unawares and strike fear into the cities of Sicily. His proposal is that they should use Megara as their naval base.

49.2

τὸ γὰρ πρῶτον πᾶν στράτευμα δεινότατον εἶναι: this is meant to be a simple truth, conveyed with brevity and strong alliteration for emphasis. It is an opinion expressed earlier by the Spartan general Brasidas (5.9.8).

ἀνθρώπους ... καταφρονεῖν: as with Alcibiades, Lamachus' opinion is presented through the accusative and infinitive construction, dependent on ἔφη χρῆναι.

ἐς ὄψιν ... τῇ ὄψει ... τῇ ὄψει: Lamachus insists that appearances and the shock of the new is vital to their success. This picks up the arguments from the debate in Athens (6.31.2).

αἰφνίδιοι δὲ ἢν προσπέσωσιν ... περιδεεῖς προσδέχονται: once again Lamachus' language is strongly alliterative, conveying the force of argument.

τῇ τε ὄψει ... καὶ τῇ προσδοκίᾳ ... τῷ αὐτίκα κινδύνῳ: these three nouns develop what he means by ἐκφοβῆσαι.

πλεῖστοι γὰρ ἂν νῦν φανῆναι: 'for they would now appear to be at their greatest in number.' This has an infinitive verb because it is all in Lamachus' indirect speech. The ἂν here and the ἂν in the final clause of the sentence all make this into a remote conditional, as if Lamachus doesn't really think his plan is going to be accepted. After all, he supports Alcibiades immediately after he has finished what he has to say. Once again, this is a very alliterative piece of writing.

**A
Level**

49.3

εἰκὸς δὲ εἶναι: [He said that] 'it was reasonable'.

διὰ τὸ ἀπιστεῖν σφᾶς μὴ ἥξειν: 'on account of not believing that they would come.' The μὴ seems superfluous after the negative verb ἀπιστεῖν but must add emphasis. Lamachus is right that the Sicilians didn't expect the Athenians to come, despite all of the reports (6.32.3).

ἐσκομιζομένων αὐτῶν: 'while they (the Syracusans) were bringing them in.'

καθέζηται: 'sets up a siege.'

49.4

τούς τε ἄλλους Σικελιώτας: Lamachus here answers what Alcibiades says, arguing that this is a much better and immediate route to winning the support of the Sicels.

οὐ διαμελλήσειν ... ὁπότεροι κρατήσουσιν: 'they will not delay (in deciding) who would win.'

ναύσταθμον: this is placed emphatically. The final question for Lamachus is where the fleet can anchor. This is his answer.

ἔφη χρῆναι: Thucydides repeats the introductory words of the chapter to clarify the final sentence.

Μέγαρα: Megara Hyblaea is a city 12 miles from Syracuse. It was originally colonized from Megara, the city state which lies between Athens and Corinth.

ἀπέχοντα οὔτε πλοῦν πολὺν οὔτε ὁδόν: 'being not far from Syracuse whether on land or sea.' The accusatives are accusatives of distant travelled after ἀπέχοντα.

Chapter 50

In a single, simple sentence, Lamachus gives up on his proposal and supports Alcibiades, perhaps showing the thrall in which Alcibiades has his fellow general. It almost makes a mockery of the previous chapters and, immediately, Alcibiades' plan to win over the cities fails at Messana. Then the fleet sails down the east coast of Sicily. Catana is unwilling to receive the fleet and their overtures to the people of Leontini at Syracuse are equally ineffectual. So they return to Catana.

50.1

τῇ αὑτοῦ νηὶ: this means what it says: Alcibiades sails in the warship he owns. Alcibiades' great-grandfather had his own ship at the Battle of Artemision in 480 BCE, as described by Herodotus. This little detail adds to the sense of self-advertisement on which Alcibiades' whole approach depends.

Ῥήγιον: a city across the straits from Messana, on the very toecap of Italy.

50.2–52

The Athenians now set about enacting Alcibiades' proposal by taking 60 ships and sailing down the east coast of Sicily from their base at Rhegion. They are welcomed at Naxos, turned away at Catana and at Syracuse they engaged in reconnaissance of the city, its harbours and its forces.

A Level

They then sail back to Catana where the Athenian generals are allowed into the city to present their case. During the Assembly, the Athenian soldiers break into the city and the people of Catana, realizing what had happened, invite the Athenians to bring their forces from Rhegion to Catana. So, they do.

Then news comes that Camarina, a city on the south-west coast of Sicily is willing to come over to the Athenians and that the Syracusans are manning a fleet. They sail first to Syracuse and find no activity and go on to Camarina where the promise of Camarina is not enacted. The Athenians return to Catana.

Chapter 53

On their return to Catana, the Athenians find that the Athenian state trireme, the *Salaminia*, has arrived with orders that Alcibiades should return to Athens to face trial. Thucydides describes the febrile atmosphere in Athens which led the people to listen to unreliable witnesses. He attributes this to the people's constant concern about the threat of a return to the days of tyranny a century before.

53.1

Σαλαμινίαν: the Athenian state has two state triremes, the *Salaminia* and the *Paralos*. The former is obviously named after Athens' great naval victory against the Persians in 480 BCE.

ὡς κελεύσοντας: this future participle hasn't got anything in the accusative plural to agree with but we need to understand that it is the Athenians who came on the *Salaminia*.

53.2

ὧν ἡ πόλις ἐνεκάλει: 'for the charges the city was bringing against him.'

μεμηνυμένων: 'those who had been denounced': perfect passive participle of μηνύω. Thucydides describes what he believes to be the witch-hunt that had taken place after the fleet had left. There are two main verbs in the sentence, ἐποιοῦντο and κατέδουν (from καταδέω) and four participles describing the behaviour of the Athenians (δοκιμάζοντες, ἀποδεχόμενοι, ξυλλαμβάνοντες, ἡγούμενοι). Once again, there is a considerable amount of alliteration in the sentence, e.g. διὰ πονηρῶν ἀνθρώπων πίστιν πάνυ χρηστοὺς τῶν πολιτῶν. All of this conveys the frantic activity in Athens at the time.

τῶν ... δρασθέντων: genitive plural aorist passive participle of δράω.

πάντα ὑπόπτως ἀποδεχόμενοι: 'accepting every accusation in a state of suspicion'.

χρησιμώτερον ... ἤ: 'more useful ... than that ...': the clause after the ἤ is an accusative, τινὰ καὶ χρηστὸν δοκοῦντα 'someone who had been accused, even if he seemed to be a good man', followed by an infinitive, διαφυγεῖν.

53.3

Πεισιστράτου: Peisistratus first took power in Athens in 560 BCE but was ousted twice and returned in 546 BCE. He ruled until his death in 527 BCE and the tyranny was taken over by his sons.

A Level

ὑφ' ἑαυτῶν καὶ Ἁρμοδίου ... ἀλλ' ὑπὸ τῶν Λακεδαιμονίων: the accepted
Athenian narrative was that the tyrannicides had been two Athenians, Harmodius
and Aristogeiton, whose statues stood in the Agora, whereas, in fact, it had
been effected by Spartan intervention, not what the Athenians wanted to hear or
believe.

τελευτῶσαν γενομένην: these participles are dependent on the verb of knowing:
'it had become harsh when near its end.'.

Chapters 54–59: The end of the tyranny in Athens, 514–510 BCE

At this point, something remarkable happens. In 1.20.1-2 Thucydides has already
referred at some length to the end of the tyranny of Peisistratus and his family,
complaining of the inaccuracy of the prevailing narrative. Now, he turns aside from
events in Athens and Sicily to expend six chapters on the story of Harmodius and
Aristogeiton, the two men to whom the Athenians attributed the killing of the tyrant
and the ending of the tyranny. The reason for this digression, that the problems
associated with the end of the tyranny nearly a century before created fear and
suspicion in the body politic in 415 BCE, does not really justify the detail or scale of
these chapters.

These chapters are very striking. On the one hand, they are like Herodotus in that
they concern events from the sixth century and have a strong human and emotional
content. On the other hand, they are a direct rebuttal of Herodotus' own account of
events. Thucydides has a point to prove, that the killing of Hipparchus, who was not
even the tyrant, was not simply a political act, but an act born of sexual jealousy and
this act was not the end of the tyranny. And that rebuttal is conducted by a very
careful, analytical use of evidence, as if to show Herodotus how history should really
be done.

Chapter 54

Thucydides tells the story of Aristogeiton's love for the younger Harmodius and his
fear that Hipparchus might seduce him. Thucydides also explains that, until this
time, the Peisistratid tyranny had been law-abiding and beneficial for Athens.

54.1

τὸ ... τόλμημα: this daring act is the killing of Hipparchus, Hippias' brother.
Thucydides is arguing that this was not a political act but an affair of the heart,
caused by Hipparchus' rejection by Harmodius and his jealousy of Aristogeiton.

ἀποφανῶ: this sounds Herodotean: whereas Thucydides tends to limit his own
personal interventions, Herodotus is very often the visible narrator.

λέγοντας: this accusative participle is dependent on ἀποφανῶ.

ἀκριβὲς: In 1.22.1 and 1.22.2 Thucydides refers to ἀκρίβεια as a key element of his
method.

**A
Level**

54.2

Πεισιστράτου γὰρ γηραιοῦ τελευτήσαντος: he died in 527 BCE.

Ἁρμοδίου ὥρᾳ ἡλικίας λαμροῦ: Greek society, from the sixth century BCE onwards, was bisexual, in that a man could have erotic feelings for males and females. The homosexuality element of this was constructed on the love of an older man for a younger man 'in the first bloom of youth'. cf. Socrates and Alcibiades in Plato's *Symposium*.

μέσος πολίτης: a citizen of the middle class. Athens was a city which, despite its democracy, had a strong sense of class with aristocrats like Pericles and Alcibiades still holding immense influence.

54.3

ὡς ἀπὸ τῆς ὑπαρχούσης ἀξιώσεως: 'as far as his standing allowed.'

54.4

παρεσκευάζετο προπηλακιῶν αὐτόν: παρασκευάζομαι is usually followed by ὡς plus a future participle. In this case, the ὡς is understood.

54.5

ἀνεπιφθόνως κατεστήσατο: 'he was not the subject of envy/hostility.'

ἀρετὴν καὶ ξύνεσιν: Thucydides' narrative is concerned with the qualities that make for successful leadership and these words are high praise from him, however you translate the first of them. In these lines Thucydides is making clear that a tyranny can be an effective and fair regime, not exacting high taxes, protecting and developing the city, doing the right thing in relation to the gods, and not changing the constitution. Perhaps this is no surprise when much of his History shows the failings of an open democracy.

πρασσομένοι: 'exacting (taxes)'.

καλῶς διεκόσμησαν: the Peisistratids did engage in a substantial building programme in Athens.

54.6

ἐν ταῖς ἀρχαῖς: there is evidence from an inscription (Meiggs and Lewis 6) that they ensured, when possible, that one of the Peisistratid family was the eponymous archon, the highest magistracy in Athens.

τῶν δώδεκα θεῶν βωμὸν: the remains of the Altar of the Twelve Gods are still to be seen in the Agora. The 12 Olympian gods are Zeus, Hera, Hephaestus, Poseidon, Apollo, Artemis, Athena, Dionysus, Hermes, Ares, Aphrodite and Demeter.

τὸν τοῦ Ἀπόλλωνος ἐν Πυθίου: 'the altar of Apollo at the shrine of Pythian Apollo.' This lay in the south-east of the city. A dative noun is supplied.

54.7

ἀμυδροῖς γράμμασι: the lettering of this inscription is still visible today. This kind of quotation of a written source may show Thucydides' pursuit of accuracy, but Herodotus did the same thing, for example with the memorials at Marathon and Thermopylae.

A Level

Πεισίστρατος Ἱππίου υἱός: the Athenians tended to alternate names between generations, calling male children after their grandfathers. So this Peisistratus who set up the memorial is the grandson of the tyrant Peisistratus.

Chapter 55

This chapter is given over to Thucydides' proof by various means that it was Hippias, not Hipparchus, who was the tyrant at the time of the death of Hipparchus.

55.1
Thucydides goes back onto the offensive to show that he is right in his account of the tyranny with strong vocabulary: εἰδὼς ... ἀκριβέστερον ... ἰσχυρίζομαι. This is proof by written evidence and by logical deduction and probability (εἰκὸς at the end of 55.1 and ἀπεοικότως in 55.2).

γνοίη δ᾽ ἄν τις: 'anyone would know': aorist optative of γιγνώσκω.

φαίνονται ... γενόμενοι: φαίνομαι plus a participle means 'it is clear that.'

τῶν γνησίων ἀδελφῶν: Peisistratus had three legitimate sons, Hippias, Hipparchus and Thessalus.

ἡ στήλη περὶ τῆς τῶν τυράννων ἀδικίας: this stele does not survive but it must have decreed a ban on the family of Peisistratus and thereby given names. The inscription on the altar which Thucydides quotes does not necessarily prove his point that Hippias was the only son of Peisistratus to have legitimate offspring.

σταθεῖσα: feminine nominative aorist passive participle of ἵστημι.

Μυρρίνης τῆς Καλλίου τοῦ Ὑπεροχίδου θυγατρὸς: it is rare in Thucydides to have the name of a woman mentioned, even though her family is then described through the names of her father and grandfather. This Callias is unknown but the most famous Callias was a key figure in Athens in the middle of the fifth century, the eponymous negotiator of the Peace of Callias with Persia – if that peace was ever formally made.

55.2
διὰ τὸ πρεσβεύειν τε ἀπ᾽ αὐτοῦ καὶ τυραννεῦσαι: 'on account of being the oldest after him and having been tyrant.'

55.3
οὐ μὴν οὐδ᾽ ἂν κατασχεῖν μοι δοκεῖ . . .. τὴν τυραννίδα: 'it seems to me that he would not have taken possession of absolute power . . . .'

Ἵππαρχος μὲν: this μὲν is picked up by Ἱππάρχῳ δὲ at the beginning of 55.4.

διὰ τὸ πρότερον ξύνηθες ... φοβερόν ... ἀκριβές: this is a typical Thucydidean phrase, a form of expression that did not exist before him, a prepositional phrase with a neuter noun made from an adjective followed by two clauses, organized by μὲν and δὲ: 'on account of his previous habitual way of being an object of fear to the citizens and strict in his attitude to his bodyguard.'

ἐπικούρους: tyrants were perceived as being very dependent on their bodyguards. It is interesting that Hippias is as ἀκριβής with his bodyguard as Thucydides with his facts.

A Level

πολλῷ τῷ περιόντι τοῦ ἀσφαλοῦς: another very Thucydidean phrase: 'with a superabundance of security.'

ἐν ᾧ: 'at a time when . . .': supplying χρόνῳ, as often.

Ἱππάρχῳ δὲ ξυνέβη ... ὀνομασθέντα ... προσλαβεῖν: this sentence has Hipparchus appears both in the dative and (invisibly) in the accusative with which ὀνομασθέντα agrees, as the sentence slips naturally into accusative and infinitive. 'It happened that Hipparchus gained his reputation from the misfortune of his fate and thereafter got the reputation of being the tyrant.'

Chapter 56

Hipparchus, having been rejected by Harmodius, takes his revenge by insulting Harmodius' sister. Incensed by this, Harmodius, Aristogeiton and their fellow conspirators plan to attack Hipparchus at the Great Panathenaea.

56.1

After a chapter of deduction based on probability about the relative seniority of Hippias/Hipparchus, Thucydides returns to his more Herodotean narrative. That return is marked by striking alliteration, culminating in προυπηλάκισεν, repeated from 54.4, which shows us the point from which the tale is being picked up.

τὴν πείρασιν: 'in respect of his approach': an accusative of respect.

ἐν πομπῇ: as we can see from the Parthenon frieze, which represents the Panathenaea (see 56.2), young girls played a key part in religious festivals as carriers of sacred objects. To be excluded from such a ceremony would have been deeply insulting to the family.

οἴσουσαν: future participle of φέρω expressing purpose.

τὴν ἀρχὴν: 'in the first place'.

56.2

πρὸς τοὺς ξυνεπιθησομένους: future middle participle of ξυνεπιτίθημι, 'those who were going to join them in the attack.'

ἐπέπρακτο: 3rd person singular pluperfect passive of πράσσω.

Παναθήναια τὰ μεγάλα: the Great Panathenaea is represented on the frieze of the Parthenon, of which substantial parts are, at the moment, in the British Museum. The Panathenaea was the greatest of all Athenian festivals, doing honour to Athena Parthenos. The festival was annual but the Great Panathenaea, like the Olympics, took place every fourth year. At that festival the small wooden statue of Athena was dressed in a new robe.

τοὺς τὴν πομπὴν πέμψοντας: 'those about to participate in the procession.' Here we can see the relationship between the verb with an epsilon and the noun with an omicron: cf. λέγω and λόγος.

ἔδει ἄρξαι αὐτούς, ξυνεπαμύνειν δὲ ... ἐκείνους: 'it was necessary that they (Harmodius and Aristogeiton) should start and that they (the supporters) should help out with defence against the bodyguards.'

A
Level

ξυνεπαμύνειν ... ξυνομωμοκότες ... ξυνελευθεροῦν: the repetition of ξυν in
    these compounds emphasizes the hope of Harmodius and Aristogeiton that they
    will succeed through wider support.

56.3
εἰ ... τολμήσειαν: this conditional clause has an aorist optative verb because it is
    in historic sequence. If it were in direct speech it would be a future open conditional.
καὶ ὁποσοιοῦν: 'even as many (or as few) as they were.'
ἤλπιζον ... τοὺς μὴ προειδότας ... ἐθελήσειν ... ξυνελευθεροῦν: this is an
    accusative and infinitive dependent on ἤλπιζον: 'They hoped that those not in the
    know would be willing to . . . .'

Chapter 57

On the day of the festival and the assassination, Harmodius and Aristogeiton are
ready to act, but fearing that the plot is being betrayed, they attack prematurely and
kill Hipparchus. Both men are killed.

57.1
ἔξω ἐν τῷ Κεραμεικῷ: the Kerameikos, the Potters' Quarter, was close to the
    Agora and the Acropolis to the north-west but it was separated from it by the city
    wall.
ἕκαστα ... τῆς πομπῆς: 'the different parts of the procession.'

57.2
ὅσον οὐκ ... ξυλληφθήσεσθαι: 'they were on the point of being captured.' This
    is a future passive infinitive.

57.3
τὸν λυπήσαντα ... σφᾶς: 'the man who had caused their grief', i.e. Hipparchus.
    This accusative is the object of προτιμωρήσασθαι which is dependent on
    ἐβούλοντο.
δι' ὅνπερ πάντα ἐκινδύνευον: 'on account of whom they were risking everything'.
εἰ δύναιντο: an optative verb in a subordinate clause in indirect speech: cf. εἰ ...
    τολμήσειαν in 56.3. As there, in direct speech it would be an open future
    conditional.
ὥσπερ εἶχον: 'just as they were.'
παρὰ τὸ Λεωκόρειον καλούμενον: a shrine in the Agora, although its exact site
    has not been discovered, dedicated to the daughters of a mythical Athenian hero,
    Leos, who were sacrificed to secure the city's safety.
ἀπερισκέπτως προσπεσόντες: as often, Thucydides marks a dramatic moment
    with powerful, plosive alliteration and an unusual word ἀπερισκέπτως.
ὡς ἂν μάλιστα: 'certainly'.
δι' ὀργῆς ὁ μὲν ἐρωτικῆς, ὁ δὲ ὑβρισμένος: 'the one (Aristogeiton) driven
    through a lover's anger, the other (Harmodius) the victim of a personal insult.'

**A
Level**

This is typically Thucydidean *variatio* in that the second clause hasn't got another prepositional phrase, but is a passive participle.

ἔτυπτον καὶ ἀποκτείνουσιν αὐτόν: a striking use of tenses, an imperfect emphasizing the rain of blows followed by a vivid historic present. Several of the following verbs are also in the present tense.

57.4

ληφθείς: aorist passive participle of λαμβάνω.

οὐ ῥαδίως διετέθη: aorist passive of διατίθημι: 'he was disposed of not in an easy way'. An ugly euphemism for summary killing.

ἐπὶ τὸ γενόμενον: dependent on ἐχώρησε: 'to the place where it had happened.'

Chapter 58

Hippias responds to the crisis by rounding up the potential conspirators and arresting those in possession of knives. Thucydides narrates these moments of high drama with pace and urgency in a manner worthy of a movie.

58.1

πρότερον ἢ αἰσθέσθαι αὐτούς: 'before they found out': πρότερον ἤ is followed by an infinitive, αἰσθέσθαι, and αὐτούς is its accusative subject of the infinitive.

ἀδήλως τῇ ὄψει πλάσμενος: literally: 'having moulded himself in his face unclearly', i.e. with a façade of inscrutability.

58.2

ἐρεῖν: future infinitive of λέγω.

εἴ τις ηὑρέθη: 3rd singular aorist passive of εὑρίσκω: 'if anyone who was found'.

Chapter 59

So the conspiracy came to an end but Hippias' response was to turn towards a more oppressive and violent form of rule, killing his opponents. At this stage he started to look for an exit strategy and three years later, having been deposed by the Spartans and the Athenian noble family of the Alcmaeonids, went into exile. He returned with the Persians in 490 BCE and was present at the battle of Marathon.

59.1

ἐκ τοῦ παραχρῆμα περιδεοῦς: 'from momentary panic.' A typical Thucydidean phrase, conveying a complex concept with a neuter adjective and an adverb.

59.2

διὰ φόβου ἤδη μᾶλλον ὢν: 'being now more in a state of fear.'

ὁρῴη: 3rd person present optative of ὁράω: an indefinite clause in historic sequence.

μεταβολῆς γενομένης: a genitive absolute doing the job of a conditional clause: 'if there were a revolution.'

A Level

59.3

Ἱππόκλου γοῦν τοῦ Λαμψακηνοῦ τυράννου Αἰαντίδη τῷ παιδὶ θυγατέρα ἑαυτοῦ μετὰ ταῦτα Ἀρχεδίκην Ἀθηναῖος ὢν Λαμψακηνῷ ἔδωκεν: this sentence is a wondrous example of the way in which an inflected language can use word order to give emphasis to certain words. The most obvious word order for us would be Ἀθηναῖος ὢν θυγατέρα ἑαυτοῦ ἔδωκεν Αἰαντίδη τῷ παιδὶ Ἱππόκλου τοῦ Λαμψακηνοῦ τυράννου.

Thucydides' choice gives him chance to emphasize the strangeness of involvement with a family from Lampsacus by an Athenian tyrant. Lampsacus is a city on the east coast of the Dardanelles, by the entrance to the Sea of Marmara. It is particularly odd of Hippias to be forming a marital link with this small city because in the past there had been enmity between the Peisistratids and the city (Herodotus 6.37ff).

παρὰ βασιλεῖ Δαρείῳ: Herodotus tells us that Hippoclus was with Darius in his expedition beyond the Danube (Herodotus 4.138). Tyrants in Greek cities within the Persian Empire like Hippoclos were likely to be puppet rulers, imposed by the Persian King.

ἐπίγραμμα: it is remarkable that Thucydides can quote an inscription from Lampsacus. Aristotle attributes this epigram (Rhetoric 1367b19) to Simonides, the most famous writer of epigrams of the late sixth century and early fifth century BCE. He composed many of the funeral epigrams of the Persian Wars, including, most famously, the epigram for the Spartan dead at Thermopylae: Herodotus 7.228.2.

ἀνδρὸς ἀριστεύσαντος: although the tomb is that of the tyrant's daughter, it is her father who appears first in the epigram.

ἤρθη: 3rd single aorist passive of αἴρω.

νοῦν: accusative of respect.

ἀτασθαλίην: Archedike avoids the folly that might beset someone of such a remarkably family. ἀτασθαλία is a common word in Homer, conveying the folly and recklessness that destroys men.

59.4

ἐν τῷ τετάρτῳ: 511/10 BCE

ὑπὸ Λακεδαιμονίων καὶ Ἀλκμεωνιδῶν τῶν φευγόντων: Herodotus tells the tale of the end of the tyranny in much greater detail in 5.63–65. The Peisistratids were besieged on the Acropolis. The Alcmeonids were a rival family to the Peisistratids, who were said to have gone into exile during the tyranny. The first major figure of the Alcmaeonids was Megacles who married the daughter of Cleisthenes, the tyrant of Sicyon and from that marriage was born Cleisthenes, the founder of the Athenian democracy. The story of Megacles' successful courtship is one of the best and funniest in Herodotus (6.126–130). The Alcmaeonids were said to have gone into exile during the tyranny, but this is somewhat undermined by an inscription (Meiggs and Lewis 6) which almost certainly has Cleisthenes as eponymous archon in 525/524 BCE.

Σίγειον: a small city on the east side of the Dardanelles.

ἐς Μαραθῶνα: the end of the story is very striking: Hippias, having 'defected' to the Persian King, returns in 490 BCE in the hope of restoration: the story is told in full by Herodotus 6.102, 107–108.

A Level

Chapter 60

Thucydides gets back on track with events in 415 BCE. Athens is in a state of confusion and fear of an oligarchic coup. The situation is brought to a crisis when one of the prisoners comes forward and, with the promise of impunity, incriminates a number of his fellow prisoners who are put to death.

60.1

Ὧν ἐνθυμούμενος: this provides the link back to events in 415 BCE, even though it's not entirely obvious in what way events in the late sixth century really could have had such an impact on the attitudes of the Athenians in 415 BCE.

ξυνωμοσία ὀλιγαρχικῇ καὶ τυραννικῇ: 'with the intention of a conspiracy for an oligarchy and tyranny'. The Athenians were always conscious of the threat to their democracy from an aristocratic coup, whether that led to rule by a few or by a tyrant. Indeed, such oligarchic coups did come to pass in 411 BCE and 404 BCE.

60.2

ἐς τὸ ἀγριώτερον τε καὶ πλείους ἔτι ξυλλαμβάνειν: ἐς controls a comparative adjective turned into a neuter noun and then an infinitive.

εἷς τῶν δεδεμένων: 'one of those who had been imprisoned', from δέω, I bind. By wondrous chance we not only know the name of this person, Andocides, but also have the speech, '*On the Mysteries*', he gave in his defence against the charge of involvement in the mutilation of the Herms in a trial 15 years later. Andocides 1.48ff gives the details of this moment.

εἴτε ἄρα καὶ τὰ ὄντα . . . εἴτε καὶ οὔ: 'whether it was true or not.'

ἐπ' ἀμφότερα γὰρ εἰκάζεται: 'it's a matter of conjecture on both sides.'

60.3

τὴν πόλιν τῆς παρούσης ὑποψίας παῦσαι: Thucydides presents the urgency of the argument in the prison with more powerful alliteration.

βεβαιοτέραν . . . σωτηρίαν. . . εἶναι: this accusative and infinitive continues to represent what one prisoner was saying to the other. Thucydides vividly represents the drama of the prison with prisoner persuading and pressurising prisoner.

60.4

ὁ δὲ δῆμος . . . ἄσμενος: Thucydides now represents the speed – and relief – with which the people seized upon this confession, whether true or not. His narrative is constantly questioning the rationality and reliability of the people under the pressures of war. He suggests that the people are almost paranoid about the threat of a coup and then they jump with rare haste to release a number of prisoners and execute those who have been named.

εἴσονται: 3rd plural future of οἶδα.

ἔλυσαν . . . τῷ ἀποκτείναντι: the speed of the decisions and the actions is conveyed by the remarkable density of verbs conveying vigorous action. The trials are dealt with in two words and the executions and death sentences and offering of money

A Level

are done with similar haste. This is made the more striking by the fact that many chapters have intervened since anything happened in Athens about this crisis.

60.5

οἱ μὲν παθόντες: although this is the topic of the sentence and therefore comes first, it belongs syntactically in the εἰ clause.

ἐτετιμώρηντο: 3rd plural pluperfect middle of τιμωρέω.

περιφανῶς ὠφέλητο: 'had been helped.' It's hard to see how the Athenians have been helped by making such a hasty and bad decision. Are they cheered up because they think they don't have to worry anymore? Is Thucydides being grimly ironic?

Chapter 61

The fate of Alcibiades. The resolution of the mutilation of the Herms merely increases suspicion of Alcibiades and the sacrilege associated with the Mysteries. The people believe that Alcibiades is already in secret alliance with the enemy. Alcibiades is brought home, but at Thurii, on the instep of Italy, he and others escape and, in the end, he turns up in Sparta. He is condemned to death in absentia.

61.1

καὶ πρὶν ἐκπλεῖν αὐτὸν ἐπέθεντο: αὐτὸν is the accusative subject of the infinitive, not the object of ἐπέθεντο, the aorist middle of ἐπιτίθημι.

τὰ μυστικά . . . ἀπ' ἐκείνου ἐδόκει πραχθῆναι: 'it seemed that the mysteries had been performed by him.' τὰ μυστικά is the nominative subject of ἐδόκει.

τῆς ξυνωμοσίας ἐπὶ τῷ δήμῳ: this echoes the vocabulary of 60.1 and the proximity of a Spartan force must have increased suspicion. Alcibiades was the proxenos of Sparta in Athens, which meant that he represented Spartan interests, and this made him particularly a figure of suspicion.

61.2

ἐθορυβοῦντο: 'they were making a noise/fuss.' The word shows that Thucydides didn't have a great regard for the quality of democratic debate at this point.

μέχρι Ἰσθμοῦ ... πρὸς Βοιωτούς: the cities of Boeotia, Athens' immediate neighbour to the north-west, were natural allies of Sparta, and to get there the Spartans would have to lead their force over the Isthmus of Corinth.

ἐδόκει: the subject is the Spartan military force.

ἐκείνου πράξαντος: 'by his (i.e. Alcibiades') agency.

εἰ μὴ ἔφθασαν ... ξυλλαβόντες: 'if they hadn't arrested them beforehand.' φθάνω + participle conveys the sense of doing something first: cf. λανθάνω, I escape notice, which takes a dependent participle in the same way.

προδοθῆναι ἄν ἡ πόλις: 'the city would have been betrayed'. This clause is also dependent on ἐδόκει: προδοθῆναι is the aorist passive infinitive of προδίδωμι.

ἐν Θησείῳ τῷ ἐν πόλει: this is not the well-preserved temple, commonly called the Theseion, but actually a temple to Hephaistos. This Theseion, a temple to the founding hero of Athens, lies south-east of the Agora. Earlier in the century the bones of Theseus had been brought back to Athens from Scyros by Cimon and

A Level

deposited here. These bones, and therefore this shrine, were meant to have powers to support and defend the city so this is the obvious place to go for the night. It is interesting that the Athenians have no standing army so it is ordinary citizens who keep guard under arms.

61.3

οἵ τε ξένοι τοῦ Ἀλκιβιάδου οἱ ἐν Ἄργει: Argos was one of the most ancient and famous of Greek cities, already powerful and famous in the Mycenaean age and the kingdom of Agamemnon. It is in the north-east corner of the Peloponnese, not far from the Isthmus of Corinth. One thing that worried the Athenian people about aristocrats like Alcibiades was that they had connections and loyalties that lay beyond the city state of Athens, even though earlier in the book Alcibiades had support precisely because he had these strong connections (6.17, 6.29.3).

τοὺς ὁμήρους τῶν Ἀργείων τοὺς ἐν ταῖς νήσοις κειμένους: 'the Argive hostages who had been deposited on the islands'. In 5.84.1 Thucydides tells us that in 416 BCE there had been a democratic uprising in Argos against the regime imposed by Sparta and the Athenians had taken 300 pro-Spartan hostages and placed them on some Aegean islands which were under their control.

61.4

πανταχόθεν τε περιειστήκει ὑποψία ἐς τὸν Ἀλκιβιάδην: this brief, alliterative sentence sums up the overwhelming sense of suspicion in Athens. Everything is about suspicion and seeming, without any solid fact on which to act. On such evidence and in such uncertainty, 300 Argive hostages are summarily despatched.

βουλόμενοι ... ἀποκτεῖναι: 'wishing to kill him.' Thucydides is starkly honest about the motivation of the Athenians. The trial is merely a means to the end of getting rid of Alcibiades: so much for the rule of law.

τὴν Σαλαμινίαν ναῦν: the narrative gets back – finally – to 6.53 and the arrival of the *Salaminia* at Catana.

61.5

εἴρητο δὲ προσειπεῖν αὐτῷ ἀπολογησομένῳ ἀκολουθεῖν: 'the instructions were to tell him to accompany them to make his defence'. ἀπολογησομένῳ is a future participle expressing purpose.

θεραπεύοντες τό ... μὴ θορυβεῖν: 'taking care not to upset ...'. The object of θεραπεύοντες is the phrase formed by the neuter definite article with the infinitive enclosing two objects.

Μαντινέας καὶ Ἀργείους: Mantinea is another city state in Arcadia, the central part of the Peloponnese. Once again we see that Alcibiades' has influence and connections beyond Athens.

61.6

οἱ ξυνδιαβεβλημένοι: 'his fellow accused/victims of slander': perfect passive participle of διαβάλλω.

ἐν Θουρίοις: Thurii was a colony on the instep of the foot of Italy, founded in 444/443 BCE on the site of Sybaris. It was largely an Athenian foundation but Herodotus was said to have been one of the founding colonists.

A Level

τὸ ἐπὶ διαβολῇ ἐς δίκην καταπλεῦσαι: 'sailing back home to face trial in the face of prejudice.'

61.7

ἐς Πελοπόννησον: the people's suspicions about Alcibiades are confirmed because he can so easily escape and defect to the enemy.

ἐρήμῃ δίκῃ: 'condemnation *in absentia*.'

Vocabulary

An asterisk * denotes a word in OCR's Defined Vocabulary List for AS.

ἄγαλμα - ατος τό — statue
*ἄγαν — too much
*ἀγγέλλω - aor. pass. — announce
  ἠγγέλθην
*ἄγγελος - ου ὁ — messenger
Ἅγνων - ωνος ὁ — Hagnon
ἀγριός - ά - όν — wild
*ἀγρός - οῦ ὁ — field
*ἄγω - fut. ἄξω - aor. — lead
  ἤγαγον
ἀγωνίζομαι — contend in a lawsuit
*ἀδελφός - οῦ ὁ — brother
ἀδεῶς — fearlessly
ἀδήλως — unclearly
*ἀδικέω — do wrong
*ἀδικία - ας ή — injustice
*Ἀθηναῖοι - ῶν οἱ — Athenians
ἄθροισις - εως ή — gathering, collection
ἀθρόος - η - ον — in crowds, densely
  packed
ἀΐδιος - ον — everlasting
*αἰεί — always
*αἴρω - aor. ἦρα - aor. — raise
  pass. ἤρθην
*αἰσθάνομαι — perceive, learn
*αἰτέω - aor. mid. — ask for
  ἠτήσάμην
*αἰσχρός - ά - όν — shameful, disgraceful
*αἰτία - ας ή — cause
*αἰτιάομαι — blame, acccuse
*αἰτιός - ά - όν — responsible
αιφνίδιος - ον — unexpected
ἀκοή - ῆς ή — hearing, hearsay
ἀκολουθέω — accompany
ἀκόλουθος - ου ὁ — attendant
ἀκοντιστής - οῦ ὁ — javelin-thrower
*ἀκούω - aor. ἤκουσα — hear

ἄκρα - ας ή — promontory
ἀκριβής - ές — accurate, strict
ἀκροπόλις - εως ή — acropolis
*ἄκων -ἄκουσα - — unwilling
  ἄκον
*ἀλλά — but
*ἀλλήλους — each other
*ἄλλος - η - ο — other
ἀλλότριος - α - ον — someone else's
ἀλλοφύλος - η - ον — of a different tribe
ἄλλως — otherwise
ἄλλως τε καί — especially
ἀλόγιστος - ον — illogical
*ἅμα — at the same time as
  (+ dat.)
ἅμιλλα - ης ή — race
ἁμιλλάομαι - aor. — compete
  ἡμιλλήθην
ἀμυδρός - ά - όν — indistinct
*ἀμύνομαι — protect
*ἄν — indefinite particle
*ἀναγκάζω - perf. — compel
  pass. ἠνάγκασμαι
*ἀνάγομαι - fut. — set out to sea
  ἀνάξομαι
ἀναγωγή ἦς ή — setting out to sea, launch
ἀναθαρσέω — be enthused, cheered up
ἀναλίσκω - fut. — spend
  ἀναλώσω - perf.
  ἀνήλωκα
ἀνάλωσις - εως ή — expenditure
ἀναπείθομαι — obey
ἀνατίθημι - aor. — set up
  ἀνέθηκα
ἀνέλεγκτος - ον — unexamined
ἀνεπιφθόνως — generously
*ἄνευ — without (+ gen.)

*ἀνήρ - ἀνδρός ὁ	man
*ἄνθρωπος - ου ὁ	man
ἀντέχω	resist
*ἀντί	instead of (+ gen.)
ἄντικρυς	opposite
ἀντίπαλος - ον	hostile
ἀντιπαρέχω - aor. ἀντιπαρέσχον	resist
ἀντιχειροτονέω	vote against
*ἀξιόλογος - ον	worthwhile
*ἄξιος - α - ον	worthy
ἀξιόχρεως - ἀξιόχρεων	adequate, sufficient
*ἀξιόω	deem worthy
ἀξίωσις - εως ἡ	reputation
ἀπαράσκευος - ον	unprepared
ἀπαρνέομαι - aor. ἠπαρνήθην	refuse, reject
ἀπαρτάω - fut. ἀπαρτήσω	remove
ἀπαρχή - ῆς ἡ	tribute
*ἄπειμι	be absent
ἀπεοικότως	unreasonably
*ἀπέχω	be distant
ἀπιστέω	distrust
ἄπιστος - ον	unbelievable
ἄπλοια - ας ἡ	not fit for sailing
*ἀπό	from (+ gen.)
ἀπὸ τοῦ ἀδοκήτου	unexpectedly
ἀποδέχομαι	accept
*ἀποθνήσκω - aor. ἀπέθανον	die
*ἀποκρίνομαι - aor. ἀπεκρινάμην	reply
*ἀποκτείνω - aor. ἀπέκτεινα	kill
ἀπολαμβάνω - aor. pass. ἀπελήφθην	remove
ἀπολείπω - aor. ἀπέλιπον	leave behind
*ἀπόλλυμαι	die
Ἀπόλλων - ωνος ὁ	Apollo
ἀπολογία - ας ἡ	defence
ἀπολύω - aor. pass. ἀπελύθην	acquit
*ἀπορέω	be at a loss
ἀποσπεύδω	dissuade earnestly
ἀποστέλλω	send out
ἀποτρέπω - aor. ἀπέτρεψα	turn away
ἀποφαίνω - fut. ἀποφανῶ	show
ἄπρακτος - ον	undone
ἄπωθεν	from afar
ἀργυρέος - η - ον	of silver

*ἀργύριον - ου τό	silver
ἀρέσκω	please
*ἀρετή - ῆς ἡ	virtue, excellence
*ἀριθμός - οῦ ὁ	number
ἀριστεύω	be the best
Ἀριστογείτων - ονος ὁ	Aristogeiton
*ἄριστος - η - ον	best
Ἁρμοδίος - οῦ ὁ	Harmodius
ἀρνέομαι - aor. ἠρνήθην	deny
*ἀρχή - ῆς ἡ	rule
*ἄρχω	take command
ἀσεβέω	commit sacrilege
ἀσέβημα - ατος τό	act of sacrilege
ἀσκέπτως	without forethought
*ἀσπίς - ίδος ἡ	shield
ἀστός - οῦ ὁ	town dweller
*ἀσφάλεια - ας ἡ	safety
*ἀσφαλής - ές	safe
ἀτασθαλία - ας ἡ	folly, arrogance
αὐθημερόν	this very day
*αὖθις	again
αὐλίζομαι - aor. ηὐλισάμην	pitch camp
αὐτόθεν	from here
αὐτοκράτωρ - ορος	with full authority
*αὐτός - αὐτή - αὐτό	himself/herself/itself or him/her/it
ἀφανής - ές	unclear
ἀφανίζω - aor. ἠφάνισα	make invisible
*ἀφικνέομαι - aor. ἀφικόμην	arrive
*ἀφίστημι - pres. inf. ἀφιστάναι	cause to revolt
ἄχθομαι	be hostile to (+ dat.)
*βάρβαρος - ου ὁ	non-Greek
βασανίζω	put to the test
*βασιλεύς - έως ὁ	king
*βέβαιος - α - ον	secure
*βία - ας ἡ	force
βιάζω - aor. pass. ἐβιάσθην	compel
βίαιος - α - ον	by force
*βοηθέω	help (+ dative)
Βοιωτός - οῦ ὁ	Boeotian
*βουλεύω - aor. mid. ἐβουλευσάμην	plan
βούλημα - ατος τό	wish
βραχύς - εῖα - ύ	short
*βωμός - οῦ ὁ	altar
*γέρων - οντος ὁ	old man
*γῆ - γῆς ἡ	land

γηραιός - ά - όν — old
*γίγνομαι - aor. — become, happen
  ἐγενόμην - perf.
  γεγένημαι
*γιγνώσκω - aor. — get to know, learn
  ἔγνων
γνήσιος - α - ον — legitimate
*γνώμη - ης ἡ — opinion
γράμμα - ατος τό — piece of writing
*γράφω - perf. pass. — write
  γέγραμμαι

δαπανάω — spend
δαπάνη - ης ἡ — expense
*δεῖ — there is a need of (+ gen.)
*δείνος - ή - ον — dangerous
*δέομαι — ask
*δεσμωτήριον - ου τό — prison
δέω - aor. ἔδησα - perf. — bind, imprison
  pass. δέδεμαι
*δηλόω — show
*δῆμος - ου ὁ — people
δημοσία — at public expense
δημοτικός - ή - όν — of the people, democratic
δι' ὀλίγου — in a short time
*διά — on account of (+ acc.)
διαβάλλω - fut. — insult, abuse, cross
  διαβαλῶ - perf. pass. — (intrans.)
  διαβέβλημαι
διαβολή - ῆς ἡ — abuse, insult
διακοσμέω — arrange, decorate
*διαλέγομαι — converse
διαλλάσσω — exchange
διαμέλλω - fut. — delay
  διαμελλήσω
διανοέομαι — think
διάνοια - ας ἡ — opinion, plan, enterprise
διάπλους - ου ὁ — crossing, journey
διασκοπέω — consider
διασώζω - aor. — save
  διέσωσα
διατίθημι - aor. pass. — manage, sort, handle,
  διετέθην — arrange
διαφέρω — carry through
διαφεύγω - aor. — flee
  διέφυγον
διαχράομαι — use, meet with
*δίδωμι - aor. ἔδωκα — give
  - aor. inf. δοῦναι
δίδωμι δίκην — pay the penalty
διηγέομαι — describe in full
*δίκη - ης ἡ — justice
*δοκεῖ - aor. ἔδοξε — it seems (+ dat.)
δοκιμάζω — hold in high regard
*δόξα - ης ἡ — opinion, reputation

δόρυ - ατος τό — spear
δορυφόρος - ου ὁ — spear-carrier, bodyguard
δουλεία - ας ἡ — slavery
*δοῦλος - ου ὁ — slave
δραχμή - ῆς ἡ — drachma
*δράω - aor. pass. — do
  ἐδράσθην
*δύναμαι — be able
*δύναμις - εως ἡ — power
*δυνατός - ή - όν — able
δυστυχία - ας ἡ — misfortune
δώδεκα — twelve

*ἐάω — allow
Ἐγεσταῖοι - ων οἱ — people of Egesta
ἐγκαλέω — accuse (+ dative)
ἐγχειρίδιον - ου τό — dagger
*ἐγώ — I
*εἰ — if
εἰκάζω - aor. pass. — compare
  ἠκάσθην
εἰκοστός - ή - όν — twentieth
εἰκότως — reasonably
*εἰμί - fut. ἔσομαι — to be
εἴπερ — if
εἴργω — exclude, prevent
εἷς - μία - ἕν — one
εἰσέρχομαι - impf. — come upon
  εἰσῄα
εἴσκειμαι — to be put on board
  ship
*εἴωθα — be accustomed
*ἐκ — from (+ gen.)
*ἕκαστος - η - ον — each
ἑκατόν — 100
*ἐκεῖ — there
*ἐκεῖθεν — from there
*ἐκεῖνος - η - ο — that
ἐκεχειρία - ας ἡ — truce
ἐκκρίνω - aor. pass. — choose
  ἐξεκρίθην
ἐκλέγω — choose
ἐκπλέω — sail out
ἐκπλήσσω - perf. pass. — strike with fear
  ἐκπέπληγμαι
ἔκπλους - ου — sailing out, expedition
ἐκπονέω - aor. pass. — work at, finish off
  ἐξεπονήθην
ἔκπωμα - ατος τό — cup
ἐκφοβέω — scare
ἐλάσσων - ον — less
ἐλάχιστα — least
*ἐλευθερία - ας ἡ — freedom
Ἑλληνικός - ή - όν — Greek
Ἑλληνίς - ιδος — Greek

*ἐλπίζω — hope
ἐλπίς - ίδος ἡ — hope
ἐμαυτοῦ - ἐμαυτῆς — of myself
ἔμμισθος - ον — paid
ἐμποδών — in the way, under their feet
ἔμπορος - ου ὁ — merchant
ἐν τούτῳ — meanwhile
*ἐναντίος - α - ον — opposite
ἔνειμι — be in
*ἐνθένδε — from there
ἐνθυμέομαι — ponder
ἐνιαύσιος - α - ον — annual
ἐνίημι — send in
ἐξαιρέω - aor. pass. ἐξῃρέθην — remove, deter
ἐξαρτύω - aor. pass. ἐξήρτυθην — equip, kit out
ἐξελαύνω - aor. ἐξήλασα — drive out
ἑξήκοντα — sixty
ἐξουσία - ας ἡ — wealth, resources
*ἔξω — outside
*ἑορτή - ῆς ἡ — festival
ἐπαγγέλλω - aor. ἐπήγγειλα — announce
ἐπαιτιάομαι — bring a charge against
ἐπαίτιος - ον — responsible
ἐπακτός - όν — imported
ἐπαναχωρέω — retreat
ἐπαχθής - ές — burdensome
ἐπέρχομαι - pres. inf. ἐπιέναι — come against
*ἐπί — against (+ acc.), for (+ dat.)
ἐπιβάτης - ου ὁ — marine
ἐπιβουλεύω — plot against (+ dat.)
ἐπιβουλή - ῆς ἡ — plot
ἐπίγραμμα - ατος τό — epigram
Ἐπίδαυρος - ου ὁ — Epidaurus
ἐπιδείκνυμι - aor. ἐπέδειξα — show
ἐπίδειξις - εως ἡ — show, display
ἐπιδίδωμι - impf. ἐπεδίδουν — give
ἐπιθυμία - ας ἡ — desire
ἐπικηρυκεύομαι — announce
ἐπιλέγω — collect
ἐπιμαρτύρομαι — bear witness
ἐπιμέλομαι — care about (+ gen.)
ἐπιμεταπέμπω — send after
ἐπίπλους - ου ὁ — attack, expedition
*ἐπίσταμαι — know
ἐπιτάσσω - aor. ἐπέταξα — order

*ἐπιτήδειος - α - ον — necessary
ἐπιτήδευμα - ατος τό — practice, behaviour, activity
ἐπιτηδεύω — practise
ἐπιφορά - ᾶς ἡ — addition, bonus
*ἐπιχειρέω - aor. pass. ἐπεχειρήθην — attempt
ἐπιχώριον - ου τό — custom of the place
ἐπιχώριος - ου ὁ — native
ἑπτά — seven
ἐραστὴς - οῦ ὁ — lover
*ἐργάζομαι - perf. εἴργασμαι — be busy, work
ἐργασία - ας ἡ — workmanship
*ἔργον - ου τό — work, task
*ἔρημος - ον — isolated, in absentia
Ἑρμῆς - οῦ ὁ — herm
Ἑρμοκράτης - ου ὁ — Hermocrates
Ἕρμων - ωνος ὁ — Hermon
*ἔρχομαι - fut. εἶμι pres./fut. inf. ἰέναι — go
ἐρωτικός - ή - όν — concerning love
ἐσκομίζω — bring in
ἐσφέρω — bring in
*ἕτερος - α -ον — other
*ἔτι — still, yet
ἑτοιμάζω - aor. mid. ἡτοιμασάμην — make ready, prepare
*ἕτοιμος - η - ον — ready
*ἔτος - ἔτους τό — year
εὔελπις - ιδος — of good hope
εὐεργέτης - ου ὁ — benefactor
*εὐθύς — immediately
εὔνους - ουν — sympathetic, supportive
εὐπρέπεια - ας ἡ — display, splendour
εὐπρεπής - ές — splendid
εὐπρόσοδος - ον — approachable
*εὑρίσκω - aor. ηὗρον — find
εὐτυχέω — be lucky
*ἔφην — said
ἐφόδιον - ου τό — living allowance, pay for food
ἐφορμέομαι — anchor, moor
ἐφόρμησις - εως ἡ — mooring, place to anchor
*ἐχθρός - οῦ ὁ — enemy
*ἔχω - fut. σχήσω - aor. ἔσχον — have

*ζητέω — seek
ζήτησις - εως ἡ — search

*ἤ — than
*ἡγέομαι — lead
*ἥκιστα — least
*ἥκω - fut. inf. ἥξειν — have come

ἡλικία - ας ἡ	youth, age, young men	*κατά	according to, on account of, for the sake of (+ acc.)
*ἡμέρα - ας ἡ	day		
*ἡμέτερος - α - ον	our		
*ἤν	if	καταβαίνω - aor.	go down
ἡσυχία - ας ἡ	silence, quiet	κατέβην	
		καταγιγνώσκω - aor.	condemn
θάμβος - ους τό	wonder, amazement	κατέγνων	
*θάνατος - ου ὁ	death	καταγορεύω	accuse
θέα - ας ἡ	sight-seeing	καταδαρθάνω - aor.	fall asleep
*θεός - οῦ ὁ	god	κατέδαρθον	
*θεραπεύω	take care of, protect	καταδέω	imprison
Θεσσαλός - οῦ ὁ	Thessalian	καταιτιάομαι - aor.	bring an accusation against
Θησεῖον - ου τό	shrine of Theseus	pass. part.	
θορυβέω	make a noise, cause trouble	καταιτιαθείς	
		κατακρατέω	overcome
Θουρία - ων τά	Thurii, a city in southern Italy	+ gen.	
		καταλαμβάνω	seize
θρανίτης - ου ὁ	rower on the top bench of a trireme	καταλείπω - aor.	leave, abandon
		κατέλιπον	
*θυγάτηρ - θυγατέρος ἡ	daughter	κατάλογος - ου ὁ	service list
		κατάλυσις - εως ἡ	destruction
*θύω	sacrifice	καταλύω - aor. pass.	destroy
		κατελύθην	
Ἰαπυγίος - α - ον	Iapygian	Κατάνη - ης ἡ	Catana, a city in Sicily
*ἴδιος - α - ον	personal, private	κατασκοπέω	oversee, keep watch over
ἰδιώτης - ου ὁ	private citizen	κατασκευή - ῆς ἡ	ornament, tackle
*ἱερόν - οῦ τό	holy place, shrine, temple	καταστρέφομαι - fut.	subdue
		καταστρέψομαι	
*ἱκανός - ή - όν	sufficient	καταφρονέω	despise (+ gen.)
ἱκετεύω	beg, act as a suppliant	κατέχω - aor.	check, prevent, (intrans.) reach land
*ἵνα	in order that	κατέσχον	
Ἵππαρχός - οῦ ὁ	Hipparchus	*κατηγορέω	accuse (+ gen.)
*ἱππεύς - έως ὁ	cavalryman	κατοικίζω - fut.	settle
ἱππικόν - οῦ τό	cavalry	κατοικιῶ	
*ἵππος - ου ὁ	horse	*κεῖμαι	lie
Ἰσθμός - οῦ ὁ	Isthmus (of Corinth)	*κελεύω	order
*ἵστημι - aor. pass.	set up	*κενός - ή - όν	empty
ἐστάθην		Κεραμεικός - οῦ ὁ	Keramaikos, an area of Athens
ἰσχυρίζομαι	assert strongly		
		κεράννυμι - aor.	mix
καθέζομαι	sit down, take up a position, besiege	ἐκέρασα	
		κεύθω - perf. κέκευθα	hide
καθέλκω - aor.	drag down	*κῆρυξ - υκος ὁ	herald
καθείλκυσα		*κηρύσσω - aor.	announce
*καθίστημι - pres. mid. καθίσταμαι - aor. Mid. κατεστησάμην	place, set up	ἐκήρυξα	
		*κινδυνεύω	take a risk
		*κίνδυνος - ου ὁ	danger
*καίρος - ου ὁ	moment	κομιδή - ῆς	food, provisions
κακόνους - ουν	of ill will	κόνις - εως ἡ	dust
*καλέω	call	*κόρη - ης ἡ	young girl
*καλῶς	beautifully	*κρατέω	overcome (+ gen.)
κανοῦς - κανοῦ ὁ	basket	κρατήρ - ῆρος ὁ	mixing bowl
κατ' ἀμφότερα	for both purposes (on land and sea)	κράτιστος - η - ον	strongest, best
		Κρήτη - ης ἡ	Crete
		κριθή - ῆς ἡ	barley

*κρίνω	judge	μήν	indeed, very
κρίσις - εως ἡ	judgement		(strengthening particle)
*κτάομαι - fut.	obtain, get	*μήν - μηνός ὁ	month
κτήσομαι - aor.		μήνυμα - ατος τό	denunciation
ἐκτησάμην - perf.		μηνυτής - οῦ ὁ	informer
κέκτημαι		μήνυτρον - ου τό	reward for information
		μηνύω	reveal, pass information
*Λακεδαιμόνιοι -	Spartans	μιμνήσκομαι	remember
ὧν οἱ		*μισθός - οῦ ὁ	payment
Λάμαχος - ου ὁ	Lamachus, an Athenian	μισθοφορά - ᾶς ἡ	wages, pay
	general	μνῆμα - ατος τό	memorial
*λαμβάνω - aor.	take	*μόλις	with difficulty
ἔλαβον - aor. pass.		*μόνον	only
ἐλήφθην		μύλων - ωνος ὁ	mill
λαμπρός - ά - όν	shining, famous	μυστήρια - ων τά	(Eleusinian) mysteries
λαμπρότης - ητος ἡ	splendour	μυστικός - ή - όν	connected with the
*λέγω - aor. εἶπον -	say		Mysteries
aor. pass. ἐλέχθην			
perf. pass. εἴρημαι		Νάξος - ου ὁ	Naxos, a city in Sicily
Λεοντίνοι - ων οἱ	Leontini	*ναῦς - νεώς ἡ	ship
Λεωκόρειον - ου τό	Leocoreion, a shrine in	ναύσταθμον - ου τό	mooring place
	Athens	*ναύτης - ου ὁ	sailor
*λιμήν - λιμένος ὁ	harbour	ναυτικός - ή - όν	naval
λογίζομαι	calculate	νεώτερος - α - ον	younger, newer, (hence)
*λόγος - ου ὁ	word, speech		revolutionary
*λυπέω	cause to grieve	*νῆσος - ου ἡ	island
λύπη - ης ἡ	pain, grief	*νομίζω	think
		*νόμος - ου ὁ	law
*μακρότατος - η - ον	greatest	*νοῦς - νοῦ ὁ	mind, intention
μαλακίζομαι	go soft on	*νύξ - νυκτός ἡ	night
*μάλιστα	most		
*μᾶλλον	more	*ξένος - ου ὁ	foreigner, non-citizen
μάχιμος - η - ον	fit for battle	ξυγγένεια - ας ἡ	relationship by blood
μεγαλύνω	make a fuss, make a	ξυγγενής - ές	related
	noise	ξυγκαταβαίνω - aor.	go down together
*μέγας - μεγάλη -	great, big	ξυγκατέβην	
μέγα		ξυλλαμβάνω - aor.	seize
μέγιστος - η - ον	greatest	act. ξυνέλαβον - aor.	
μεθίστημι - aor. trans.	change	pass. ξυνελήφθην	
μετέστησα		ξυλλέγω	collect
μειζόνως	very seriously	ξυμβαίνει - aor.	it happens
*μέλλω	intend	ξυνέβη	
*μέν	on the one hand	ξύμβασις - εως ἡ	agreement
*μέρος - ους τό	part	ξυμμαχέω	be an ally
*μέσος - η - ον	middle of	*ξύμμαχος - ου ὁ	ally
μεσόω	be in the middle	ξυμπᾶς - πᾶσα - πᾶν	all
Μεσσηνίοι - ὧν οἱ	Messanians	ξυμπλέω	sail together
*μετά	after (+ acc.)	ξυμπληρόω aor.	fill
μεταβολή - ῆς ἡ	change	ξυνεπλήρωσα	
μεταπεμπτέος - ον	must be sent for	ξυστρατεύω	
μετάπεμπτος - ον	sent for	ξυμφέρει - aor.	it happens
μετάστασις - εως ἡ	change	ξυνήνεγκε	
*μέτοικος - ου ὁ	resident alien	*ξυμφορά - άς ἡ	event, luck, chance
*μέχρι	until (+ gen.)	ξυνάρχων - οντος ὁ	fellow commander
μῆκος - ους τό	size	ξυνδεσμώτης - ου ὁ	fellow prisoner

ξυνδιαβάλλω - perf. pass. ξυνδιαβέβλημαι	join in abusing	*ὁπλίτης - ου ὁ	hoplite
		ὁπλιτικός - ή - όν	relating to hoplites
ξυνελευθερόω	set free	ὁποσοιοῦν	somehow
ξυνεπαμύνω	ward off together	*ὁπότερος - α - ον	which of two
ξυνεπεύχομαι	join in prayer	*ὅπως	how
ξυνεπιτίθημι - fut. mid. ξυνεπιτίθησομαι	join in attacking	*ὁράω - fut. ὄψομαι - aor. εἶδον	see
ξυνέπομαι - impf. ξυνειπόμην	follow (+ dat.)	*ὀργίζομαι	become angry
		ὅρκιον - ου τό	oath
*ξύνεσις - εως ἡ	understanding, intelligence	*ὁρμάομαι - aor. ὡρμήθην - perf. ὥρμημαι	set out
ξυνεχῶς	continually	*ὅς - ἥ - ὅ	who (relative)
ξυνήθης - ες	shared	ὅσοσπερ - ὅσηπερ - ὅσοσπερ	as great as
ξυνίστημι - aor. ξυνέστησα	set up together	*ὅτε	when
		*ὅτι	that
ξυνόμνυμι - perf. ξυνομώμοκα	swear together, form a conspiracy	*οὐ/οὐκ	not
		*οὐδέ	not even
ξυντρέχω - aor. ξυνέδραμον	run together	*οὔτε	neither/nor
		*οὗτος - αὕτη - τοῦτο	this
ξυντυχία - ας ἡ	chance	*οὕτως	so
ξυνωμοσία - ας ἡ	conspiracy	ὄχλος - ου ὁ	crowd, mob
ξυνωμότης - ου ὁ	conspirator	ὀχλώδης - ες	like a mob, riotous
ξυσστρατεύω	join in the expedition		
		παιανίζω - aor. ἐπαιάνισα	sing the paean
*ὁδός - οῦ ἡ	road	παιδιά - ᾶς ἡ	playfulness
*ὅθεν	from where	*παῖς - παιδός ὁ	child
*οἶδα - inf. εἰδέναι - fut. εἴσομαι - impf. ᾔδη	know	πανταχόθεν	from everywhere
		πάντως	totally
		*πάνυ	completely
οἰκεῖος - α - ον	domestic	πάππος - ου ὁ	grandfather
οἰκείω	in a friendly way	*παραδίδωμι - aor. παρέδωκα	hand over
*οἰκία - ας ἡ	house		
οἰκίζω - fut. οἰκιῶ	settle	παρακαλέω - aor. παρεκάλεσα	summon, call upon
*οἶνος - ου ὁ	wine		
*οἶος τ'εἰμί - fut. ἐσόμαι	to be able	παραμένω - aor. παρέμεινα	remain, await
οἰωνός - οῦ ὁ	(bird of) ill omen	παρανομία - ας ἡ	lawlessness
ὀλιγαρχικός - ή - όν	oligarchic	παραπλέω - aor. παρέπλευσα	sail by
ὁλκας - άδος ἡ	cargo ship		
ὀλοφυρμός - οῦ ὁ	lamentation	*παρασκευάζω	prepare
ὅμηρος - ου ὁ	hostage	παρασκευή - ῆς ἡ	preparation
ὁμιλέω - perf. ὡμιλήκα	accompany	παραχρῆμα	immediately
		*πάρειμι	be present
ὅμιλος - ου ὁ	crowd	παρέρχομαι - aor. παρῆλθον	come forwards
*ὅμοιος - α - ον	like, similar		
ὁμοιότροπως	similarly	παρέχω - aor. παρέσχον	provide
*ὁμολογέω	agree		
*ὅμως	nevertheless	παρίημι	give up
*ὄνομα - ατος τό	name	παροξύνω	sharpen, intensify
ὀνομάζω - aor. pass. ὠνομάσθην	call	*πᾶς - πᾶσα -πᾶν	all
		*πάσχω - fut. πείσομαι	suffer
ὁπλιταγωγός - όν	troop carrying	*πατήρ - πατρός ὁ	father

παῦλα - ης ἡ	delay	πολλαχόθεν	from everywhere
*παύω - aor. pass. ἐπαύθην	stop, check	*πολύς - πολλή - πολύ	much, many
*πεζός - οῦ ὁ	infantry	πολυτελής - ές	expensive
*πείθω - aor. act. ἔπεισα - aor. pass. ἐπείσθην	persuade	πομπεύς - έως ὁ	escort, attendant
		πομπή - ῆς ἡ	procession
		πονηρία - ας ἡ	wickedness
*πειράομαι	try	πονηρός - ά - όν	wicked
πείρασις - εως ἡ	attempt	πορίζω - perf. pass. πεπόρισμαι	provide
Πεισίστρατος - ου ὁ	Peisistratos		
Πελοπόννησος - ου ἡ	Peloponnese	πόρος - ὁ	crossing
*πέμπω	send	*ποταμός - οῦ ὁ	river
πεντακισχίλιοι - ων	5,000	Ποτείδαια - ας ἡ	Potidaea
πεντήκοντα	fifty	*πρᾶγμα - ατος τό	matter
περαιόω - aor. pass. ἐπεραιώθην	make to cross	πρασσω perf. pass. πέπραγμαι	do
*περί	about (+ gen.)	πρέπει	it is fitting
περιαλγέω	be much troubled	πρεσβεύω	carry out an embassy
περιβόητος - ον	much talked about	*πρέσβυς - πρεσβύτερος - πρεσβύτατος	old, older, oldest
περιγίγνομαι	survive		
περιδεής - ές	very frightened		
περίειμι	survive	*προδίδωμι - aor. pass. προεδόθην	betray
περιίστημι - aor. intrans. περιέστην, perf. περιεστήκα	stand around, happen	προέχω - fut. προέξω	be superior
		*προθυμία - ας ἡ	eagerness, enthusiasm
Περικλῆς - οῦς ὁ	Pericles	πρόθυρον - ου τό	porch
περικοπή - ῆς ἡ	mutilation	προίστημι - perf. inf. προεστάναι	be in control, in power
περικόπτω - aor. pass. περιεκόπην	mutilate, deface		
		πρόοιδα - pres. part. προειδώς	know before
περιμένω	await		
περισκοπέω	look around, inspect	προπέμπω	send off
περιτυγχάνω - aor. περιέτυχον	meet	προπηλακίζω - fut. προπηλακιῶ	abuse, insult
περιφανῶς	clearly	*πρός	towards (+ acc.)
*πιστεύω	trust	προσάγω - aor. προσήγαγον	lead towards
πίστις - εως ἡ	trust		
πλασσω - aor. mid. ἐπλασάμην	mould, form	προσβολή - ῆς ἡ	attack
		προσδεῖ - impf. προσέδει	need in addition
*πλεῖστος - η - ον	most		
πλευστέον	one must sail	προσδέχομαι - aor. προσεδεξάμην	accept
*πλέω - aor. ἔπλευσα	sail		
πλέων - πλέον	more	προσδοκία - ας ἡ	expectation
*πλῆθος - ους τό	crowd	πρόσειμι - fut. προσέσομαι	be on side
*πλήν	except (+ gen.)		
πλήρης - ες	full	προσέτι	still, yet, furthermore
*πληρόω - fut. πληρώσω	fill	προσκτάομαι - fut. προσκτήσομαι	gain in addition
*πλοῖον - ου τό	ship	προσοικοδομέω	build
*πλοῦς - οῦ ὁ	voyage	προσπίπτω - aor. προσέπεσον	fall upon
*ποιέω	make, do		
*πολεμέω	wage war	προστάσσω - aor. pass. προσετάχθην	assign
πολεμητέον	one must go to war		
*πολέμιος - α - ον	hostile	προστίθημι - aor. mid. προσεθέμην	give, hand over
*πόλις - εως ἡ	city		
*πολίτης - ου ὁ	citizen	*πρόσωπον - ου τό	face

προτελέω - perf. προτετέλεκα — spend beforehand

*πρότερον — before

προτιμωρέω - aor. mid. προετιμωρησάμην — take vengeance on

προφασίζομαι — make excuses

*πρῶτος - η - ον — first

Πύθιος - α - ον — Pythian

πυρός - οῦ ὁ — wheat

*ῥάδιος - α - ον comp. ῥάων — easy - easier

ῥητός - ή - όν — fixed, specified

*ῥήτωρ - ορος ὁ — speaker

*ῥώμη - ης ἡ — strength, power

Σαλαμινία - ας ἡ — Salaminia, Athens' state trireme

σάλπιγξ - ιγγος ἡ — trumpet

*σαφής - ές — clear

σαφῶς — clearly

Σελινοῦς - οῦντος ὁ — Selinus

*σημαίνω - fut. σημανῶ — show

σημεῖον - ου τό — standard, figurehead

σιτοποιός - οῦ ἡ — baker

*σῖτος - ου ὁ — food

σιωπή - ῆς ἡ — silence

σκεύη - ῶν τά — tackle, baggage

σπένδω — pour libations

*σπονδή - ῆς ἡ — libation

σπουδή - ῆς ἡ — urgency, energy

*στόλος - ου ὁ — expedition

*στράτευμα - ατος τό — army, expedition

*στρατεύομαι — make an expedition

*στρατιά - ᾶς ἡ — army

Συράκουσαι - ῶν αἱ — Syracuse

Συρακούσιοι - ων οἱ — Syracusans

σφάλλω - aor. pass. ἐσφάλην — trip up

*σφεῖς - σφῶν — them(selves)

σφενδονήτης - ου ὁ — slinger

*σφέτερος - α - ον — their own

*σῶμα - ατος τό — body

*σωτηρία - ας ἡ — safety

*σώφρων - σῶφρον - comp. σωφρονέστερος — sensible, reasonable

τάλαντον - ου τό — a talent, 6,000 drachmas

*τάχ' ἄν — perhaps

ταχυναυτέω — to be fast at sailing

*ταχύς - εῖα - ύ — fast

τεκμήριον - ου τό — evidence

τελειόω - aor. ἐτελείωσα — fulfil, complete

*τελευτάω — end, die

*τέλος — in the end

τέμενος - ους τό — sacred enclosure

τεσσαράκοντα — forty

τέσσαρες - άρων — four

τέταρτος - η - ον — fourth

τετράγωνος - ον — four-sided

τετράκισχίλιοι — four thousand

τῇδε — here

*τίθημι - aor. ἔθακα — place

τιμωρέω - perf. pass. τετιμώρημαι — take revenge

*τις - τι — someone/something

τοιόσδε - τοιάδε - τοιόνδε — of such a kind

*τοιοῦτος - αὕτη - οὗτο — of this kind

*τόλμα - ης ἡ — courage

*τολμάω — dare

τόλημα - ατος τό — deed of daring

*τοξότης - ου ὁ — archer

*τοσοῦτος - τοσαύτη - τοσοῦτο — so great

τρία - τρίων — three

τριακόσιοι - ων — three hundred

τριηράρχος - ου ὁ — captain of a trireme, the person who funded the trireme

*τριήρης - ους ἡ — trireme

*τρόπος - ου ὁ — way

τροφή - ῆς ἡ — provisions

*τυγχάνω - aor. ἔτυχον — happen

*τύπτω — hit

τυραννεύω — act as a tyrant

τυραννίς - ίδος ἡ — tyranny

*τύραννος - ου ὁ — tyrant

*τύχη - ης ἡ — chance

*ὑβρίζω - perf. pass. ὕβρισμαι — abuse, insult

ὕβρις - εως ἡ — act of arrogance, insulting behaviour

*υἱός - οῦ ὁ (plural υἱεῖς) — son

*ὑμεῖς - ὑμῶν — you

ὑπάρχω - fut. ὑπάρξω — to be, exist

ὑπερβάλλω — outdo, excel

ὑπερβολή - ῆς ἡ — excess

ὑπήκοος - ον — subject

ὑπηρεσία - ας ἡ — ship's crew

*ὑπό — by (+ gen.)

ὑποδέχομαι - aor. ὑπεδεξάμην — accept, receive

ὑπολαμβάνω - aor. ὑπέλαβον — take

ὑπομιμνήσκω	remember	φράζω - aor. ἔφρασα	say, tell
ὑποπτεύω - aor. pass. ὑπωπτεύθην	suspect	φρύγω aor. pass. πέφρυγμαι	roast, toast
ὑπόπτης - ου	suspicious	*φυγάς - φυγάδος ὁ	fugitive
ὕποπτος - ον	suspected		
ὑπόπτως	suspiciously	χειμερινός - ή - όν	of winter
ὑποσημαίνω - aor. pass. ὑπεσημάνθην	to give a signal	*χράομαι	use (+ dat.)
		*χρή - inf. χρῆναι	it is necessary
ὑπόσπονδος - ον	under truce	*χρῆμα - ατος τό	thing
ὑποψία - ας ἡ	suspicion	*χρήσιμος - η - ον	useful
*ὑστεραία	on the next day	χρηστός - ή - όν	useful
*ὕστερον	later	χρονίζω	delay
		χρόνιος - α - ον	for a long time
*φαίνω - aor. pass. ἐφάνην	show	*χρόνος - ου ὁ	time
		*χρύσεος - η - ον	golden
φαῦλος - ον	poor	*χώρα - ας ἡ	country
*φερω - fut. οἴσω - aor. ἤνεγκον	carry, bear, bring	*χωρέω	come
		*χωρίον - ου τό	place
*φημί - aor. ἔφην	say	*χωρὶς	apart from (+ gen.)
*φθάνω - aor. ἔφθασα	anticipate, do something first		
*φιλία - ας ἡ	friendship	*ὥρα - ας ἡ	time, season
*φίλος - η - ον	dear	*ὡς	that
*φοβέομαι - aor. ἐφοβήθην	fear	*ὡς τάχιστα	as quickly as possible
		*ὥστε	and so
φοβερός - ά - όν	fearful	*ὠφελέω - aor. ὠφελῆσα	help

Plato, *Symposium*

Introduction, Commentary Notes and
Vocabulary by Simon Allcock

AS: 189c2–194e2

A Level: 201d–206b

Introduction

Plato's *Symposium* has been consistently one of the most popular of Plato's dialogues, and is one of the most influential treatments of love in Western literature. But it is characteristic of Platonic humour that it all starts with a giant hangover – the characters turn to speech-making because they can't face any more drinking. Any student of Plato's dialogues needs to appreciate Plato the philosopher and Plato the literary artist, including how these two roles complement and enrich each other. This is especially true of the reader of the *Symposium*, which is one of Plato's most literary and dramatic creations.

Part of the reason for the popularity of the *Symposium* is that Plato the philosopher takes as his subject Love. Love is curiously a universal human concept – everyone is happy to talk about it as if we understand what it is, and most people would claim to experience it – and yet it is also very hard to define. In the *Symposium*, Plato takes up the challenge to say what love is and what it does. The dialogue captures the power of sexual desire and the experience of being 'in love', but Plato suggests that love is much broader and deeper, that it is actually a desire for the permanent possession of happiness found through the knowledge of goodness and beauty. For the reader, this raises important questions about what the goal of human life is, and how we can gain knowledge and happiness. It has particularly been an inspiration for many religious and mystic writings with its description of an ascent from the physical world to the attainment of true knowledge and beauty. Every subsequent attempt to understand love, whether Aristotle, St. John, Nietzsche or Freud, has been a continuation of the conversation started by Plato.

But in the *Symposium* (a symposium was a formal drinking party), we also see the brilliance of Plato the literary artist and dramatist. We see his imagination in creating the fifth-century Athenian equivalent of Celebrity Big Brother, with a wonderful variety of A-list celebrities of the time, leading figures from the worlds of politics, the arts, philosophy and high society. We see his humanity as he creates a group of friends who banter and tease with real affection. We see his humour as he puns on names, mocks the foibles of human nature and creates absurd fantasies. We see his literary skill as he writes different speeches for different characters with unique rhetorical styles, often recognizable parodies of particular rhetorical schools or individuals. And there is drama as we are drawn into a complex web of relationships, involving current lovers in a scandalous relationship, ex-lovers, triangles of flirtation and jealousy, and awkward clashes of personality.

However, this is not a case of a beautiful painting being given a beautiful frame. The philosophy and the art each shine a light on the other. No detail of the drama is merely for entertainment, but each one also sharpens our understanding of the ideas. For example, Aristophanes' hiccups, while obviously adding to the humour, also serve to delay his speech so that it can answer the speech of Eryximachus and be juxtaposed with the speech of Agathon. Similarly, we see the philosophical ideas illustrated in the lives and interactions of the characters. Not least Diotima's description of the true lover as philosopher is seen in the life of Socrates as described in the *Symposium*, both in the narrative and by Alcibiades.

The dramatic form of the dialogue also serves a philosophical purpose – it showcases the process of philosophy in action. For Plato, Philosophy is not a body of knowledge, but a process, that of critically examining ideas among friends, known as dialectic, that leads towards greater understanding. Love, as a personal and experiential phenomenon, makes a particularly fertile subject matter for the application of dialectic. Many criticisms have been levelled at the views of love in the *Symposium*: that no reason is given for humans to want to pursue the good; that loving someone seems to be reduced to loving that person's qualities, not the person themselves; that love seems to be egocentric, always looking for what the lover can 'get'; that the ideal of ascending towards knowledge seems to deny aspects important to our humanity. But whatever one's views, the dialogue form invites us to join the conversation.

Plato

Life

Plato (*c.* 428–347 BCE) can easily be seen as the father of the Western philosophical tradition. His range of interests included metaphysics (the study of what is), epistemology (the study of what it is to know), ethics, political theory, language, art, love, maths, science and religion, and thus he established the big issues which are still discussed today. He was the first to unite these in a coherent system of thought, and the first to give written philosophy a distinctive intellectual method, and happily a large amount of his work has survived.

Surprisingly little is known about the life of Plato. Plato grew up as a wealthy aristocrat in Athens, and it is clear from several of his works (*Apology, Phaedo*) that he was part of the circle around Socrates. The dialogues are set in this world: young men of ambition and connections, interested in intellectual pursuits, visiting the gymnasium, and enjoying dinner parties and symposia with their peers.

Plato doesn't seem to have started writing before the 390s BCE, and by then some big events had overturned this world in which he grew up. Athens had lost the Peloponnesian War in 404 BCE, and this was closely followed by a short-lived but brutal period of oligarchy ('The Thirty') before democracy was restored in 403 BCE. Then in 399 BCE, Socrates, who had clearly been a mentor and huge inspiration in the life of Plato, was put to death on the twin charges of denying the city's gods and corrupting the youth.

In the 380s BCE Plato visited Sicily for the first time as the guest of Dion at the court of Dionysius I, tyrant of Syracuse. It is likely that the increasing interest in politics that we see in the later dialogues is partly a result of his involvement in Syracusan politics, but this period was also important for exposing Plato to the Pythagorean philosophers in southern Italy, and it is possible to see an increasing interest in maths and the afterlife in his later dialogues. It is likely that soon after his return to Athens he founded 'The Academy', which has come to be regarded as something akin to the world's first university, in a gymnasium in Athens. In fact, it was probably more of a place where intellectuals would gather to discuss philosophy, perhaps with communal meals at Plato's nearby home.

Works

We are unable to date many of the dialogues with certainty, but over time a consensus has developed among scholars to group them into three periods: early, middle and late. Beside the occasional historical reference which helps fix particular works (e.g. *Symposium* 193a2 seems to refer to the Spartans breaking up Arcadian Mantinea in 385 BCE), the two main ways of fixing on an order have been to look for a progression of thought or for patterns and progression in the style of Greek.

The early period includes *Apology* (an account of Socrates' speeches at his trial), *Euthyphro* and *Crito*, classic examples of the Socratic technique of *elenchus* (question-and-answer) applied to an individual who has supposed expertise. The middle period includes the *Symposium* and the *Republic*, perhaps Plato's most famous works. There is a much greater interest in metaphysics and the soul, and where the earlier dialogues can leave a reader with a sense of frustration (*aporia*) that the dismantling of an expert hasn't led to a positive conclusion, these works contain much more of a coherent and positive philosophy. The late period includes the *Timaeus*, *Sophist* and *Laws*.

How 'Socratic' is Plato's philosophy?

Socrates (like Jesus Christ) is unusual in having a profound influence without ever writing anything down (he explains his reasons for this in *Phaedrus* 274f – an argument written down cannot speak to defend itself when misunderstood). The young Plato was clearly a devoted follower and he chose to make Socrates the prime interlocutor in almost all his dialogues. This leaves us with the problem of being unsure what ideas to attribute to Socrates the speaker, and what views to attribute to Plato, the author. The general consensus (partly because it is suggested by Aristotle, *Metaphysics* 1.6) is that the early dialogues, which show a much greater interest in ethical questions and particularly the search for definitions of terms used in ethical contexts, such as 'courage', 'piety', or 'self-control', and in how to live well, reflect the historical Socrates. Plato inherited from Socrates the idea that we need to search for the single uniting factor behind the application of a term to a diverse set of examples (e.g. what unites all examples of courage) and the method of seeking truth through discussion. But Socrates repeatedly stressed that he didn't have wisdom, and so as the middle dialogues move on to more abstract and metaphysical thinking and put forward positive ideas, it is thought that this is much more the philosophy of Plato. He presumably kept Socrates as his primary interlocutor as a mark of honour to his former teacher, and the distinction, over which much ink has been shed, is largely unimportant.

Why dialogues?

The dialogue form, a literary account of a supposed conversation, is initially surprising to a modern reader who is used to philosophy in the form of treatises and lectures, but it was a happy marriage of philosophical and literary advantage. The philosophical impetus came from a desire to reflect the conversations of his teacher Socrates. For Socrates, and Plato, philosophy was an inquiry rather than a body of knowledge, and the dialogue form could model the process of philosophy as well as putting forward ideas. The reader has to think about what each speaker says to the others, what needs further defence, what hints we get from the characterization and structure – in other words, Plato forces his readers to engage in just the same Socratic dialectic that we see in the dialogues. The form also allows a natural way of airing readers' challenges through the challenges of the interlocutors, and shows the process of rational argument convincing a 'normal' or initially sceptical interlocutor. It also had literary advantages. Plato began to write philosophy when this discipline had no established literary form: many pre-Socratics followed Homer in writing verse. But the idea of airing arguments in competing speeches was already accepted in the *agons* of tragedy and in the set-piece debates of Herodotus and Thucydides. The dialogue form offered the advantage of being more entertaining: like comedy, the unlikely hero often deflates the pretentious, famous and arrogant. And the dramatic setting offered the possibility of characters exemplifying the ideas in action.

Plato's intellectual influences

Aristotle (*Metaphysics* 987a32f) tells us that Plato was influenced by Cratylus (a follower of Heraclitus) and then Socrates. Heraclitus was one of a number of Greek natural philosophers now known as the pre-Socratics, including Pythagoras, Anaxagoras, Zeno, Parmenides, Empedocles and Democritus. These thinkers were part of a rational movement which tried to move from the μύθοι of Homer, in which capricious and arbitrary gods interfere in the world, to a rational understanding of a world governed by laws in nature. Early questions on nature (matter, cosmology, etc.) moved on to questions of what can be known, and how, and then on to questions of morality and politics. Heraclitus held the view that all matter is in a state of flux (i.e. the river I jump into is not the same one as the one you jump into seconds later) and therefore nothing can be known (because whatever one knows instantly changes). The challenge to knowledge that this presented is taken up by Socrates in Plato's dialogues. He frequently grapples with the issue of 'what makes all examples of X to be X' (e.g. what makes all beautiful things beautiful) in an attempt to know what 'beauty' is. This led to what is now known as Plato's 'Theory of Forms' – for us to know anything (and we feel we do!), there must be something constant and unchanging behind the examples found in the world which we can know. Plato calls these eternal unchanging forms of things an εἶδος or ἰδέα, a thing that can only be apprehended through νοῦς, the mind, for sense-organs can only see physical things. But in referring to these forms, he usually uses the locution 'the X itself', e.g. αὐτὸ τὸ καλὸν ('the Beautiful itself') (211e1), and then reiterated: αὐτὸ τὸ θεῖον καλὸν . . . μονοειδὲς ('the Beautiful itself, simple and divine') (211e3).

Historical setting

The *Symposium* is a story within a story: a party in 416 BCE is described in a conversation many years later. The conversation is between Apollodorus, a close friend of Socrates, and an unnamed friend of his. By the time of this conversation, Agathon, the tragedian and host of the party, is described as having left Athens several years earlier (172c) (which happened *c.* 407 BCE) but there is no mention of Agathon having died (*c.* 399 BCE) and Socrates is clearly alive (172c) (he died 399 BCE). This points to a dramatic date for this conversation around 406–400 BCE. The friend asks Apollodorus for an account of the symposium. Apollodorus explains that he had been too young to be there, but has heard an account of the party from Aristodemus, and checked some of the particulars with Socrates himself. The main bulk of the dialogue, therefore, is Apollodorus' narrative of what Aristodemus had told him about the party.

Like the opening conversation, the account of the drinking party is fictitious – there is no need to suppose that such a party took place on that or any other occasion. But the fictional party is set in a very specific historical context. Agathon, an up-and-coming tragic poet, had just won first prize for his tragedy in the Lenaea of 416 BCE, a dramatic festival held in honour of Dionysus in Athens in January. This symposium, hosted by Agathon at his own house (173a), is imagined as being held the evening after the official victory party, which was probably a lavish affair funded by the choregos (the wealthy sponsor). The context explains why the guests are complaining of hangovers (176a), a plausible narrative excuse for why this party will take the form of speeches on love rather than having a focus on drinking.

The year 416 BCE is a high point in Athenian history, and the culture, wealth and confidence are obvious in this account. Athens had been fighting the Peloponnesian War against Sparta and her allies since 431 BCE. She had now come through the difficult years of a terrible plague, and while not every element of the struggle had gone her way, the victory at Pylos and the capture of 292 Spartan hoplites had helped her secure peace in 421 BCE (the 'peace of Nicias') on good terms. By 416 BCE Athenian confidence was high, and this can be seen by the decision to send a great expedition to Sicily, a means of expanding Athenian interest and harming Spartan influence without technically breaking the terms of the peace. Alcibiades' star was burning particularly brightly, both in Athens as a politician and general (and indeed he was the prime-mover of the Sicilian expedition) and across the Greek world as Olympic victor and bon viveur.

The city was also flourishing culturally, with Sophocles, Euripides and Aristophanes all producing plays regularly, and great works of art and architecture being created. The characters in the *Symposium* can quote from Homer and Hesiod, from tragedy and the pre-Socratics, and expect the others to understand the context. The characters are also familiar with the sophists, mentioning Prodicus (177b) and Gorgias (198c) as if they were all familiar with their ideas and the way they spoke.

But for Plato's readers, this party must have looked like those enjoying the *Titanic* as it headed towards the iceberg. Alcibiades, so confident and glamorous in 416 BCE, was accused of sacrilege within a year, and Phaedrus and possibly Eryximachus, were caught up in that scandal too. The charge was that at a similar symposium, they had parodied the Eleusinian mysteries (a mystery cult in honour of Demeter of great religious significance to Athens) and had mutilated the statues of Hermes found outside most Athenian houses by knocking off the erect phalluses. Whether Alcibiades did it or not, he was convicted as he left the city on the Sicilian expedition and had to jump ship for Sparta where he found refuge in exile. The Sicilian expedition, which had set out looking so powerful and with such high hopes, turned out to be a disaster so huge that Athens never fully recovered. Athens was now short of manpower and money to pay for its fleet and riven by civil strife. There was a revolution and brief period of oligarchic rule in 411 BCE (the rule of 'the 400', then 'the 4000'), and another after the Peloponnesian War was lost in 404 BCE (the rule of 'the 30'). The characters in this dialogue may well have been involved in or sympathetic to these mainly aristocratic oligarchies, and may have suffered in the subsequent reprisals.

Worst of all, in 399 BCE, Socrates was dead, executed by the city on the charges of not believing in the city's gods, and corrupting just the sort of youths we see at this party. Given what follows, it is hard not to see Plato setting this dialogue in this particular moment to make various points in defence of Socrates. Some of the elements of Alcibiades' speech in praise of Socrates, about his courageous service as an Athenian hoplite at Potidaea (219d) and Delium (221a), repeat ideas from Plato's *Apology*, a probably fictional account of Socrates' own defence speech. Scholars have also seen the speech of Alcibiades as absolving Socrates from any responsibility for Alcibiades' failures and treacheries. Alcibiades, who was well-known for having consorted with Socrates as a youth, and then turned out so disastrously for the city, was perhaps used as a prime example by Socrates' accusers of a youth he had corrupted, but in the *Symposium*, Plato shows that Alcibiades had rejected the higher ideals of Socrates for sensual pleasures.

Characters

The *Symposium* is a fictitious party, but the party is set in a particular historical moment and the characters are real historical figures.

One can assume that the individual characters bear some relation to the real people (we would need more historical evidence to know to what extent they are distorted or caricatured) and also that this is a plausible group for such a symposium in 416 BCE: these characters are all members of the same social circle – wealthy, aristocratic and intellectual. They seem to be men of means, with the leisure that comes from not having to work for a living. This section is a quick biography of them as historical figures (taken in order of mention); consideration of their characters and speeches in the dialogue will come elsewhere.

All the speakers, with the exception of Aristophanes, are also mentioned in Plato's *Protagoras* as among those who flocked to Callias' house to attend the sophists gathered there. As he enters Callias' house, Socrates spots Phaedrus and Eryximachus around Hippias, and Agathon and Pausanias hanging on the words of Prodicus. Alcibiades joins the company shortly afterwards.

Apollodorus

A close friend of Socrates. In the *Apology* he is one of Socrates' young friends present at the trial and willing to put up money for a fine. In *Phaedo*, he is present at Socrates' death, and his tears cause the others to break down, earning a rebuke from Socrates.

Agathon *c.* 445–399 BCE

The most celebrated tragic poet after the three great masters, Aeschylus, Sophocles and Euripides: when Dionysus is hunting for a tragic poet in *Frogs*, Agathon is the next one considered. His first victory came in 416 BCE in the Lenaea (the occasion of the *Symposium* is a victory party at his house). He is portrayed as a boy in *Protagoras* who keeps the company of the sophist Prodicus, and he appears to have been influenced by the sophist Gorgias. He was famous as a modernizer (e.g. plots which didn't come from myth; choral odes unconnected to the plot) and for his flowery poetry, but no plays are extant. He is said to have been strikingly beautiful, and is ridiculed for effeminacy and passive homosexuality in Aristophanes' *Thesmophoriazusae* in 411 BCE. In about 407 BCE he left Athens for the court of Archelaus of Macedon, a great patron of the arts. In this dialogue, he is a strikingly hospitable and graceful host, and has A-list figures from the aristocracy and intellectual elite to his dinner, but is perhaps also a flatterer; there are strong hints that at the age of thirty he remains beautiful, youthful and attracted to older men.

Socrates *c.* 470–399 BCE

Socrates must have been a well-known figure in Athens at the time. In some ways he was like many other Athenian males of the intellectual and leisured circle in which he mixed: at different times of life he was on campaign as a hoplite in the army and he was involved as a citizen in Athenian politics. But he was also a very distinctive figure: he was famous for his unkept appearance, for hanging around the public spaces of Athens engaging in philosophical conversation, and for his friendships with many young aristocrats (he was famous enough to have been parodied by Aristophanes in *Clouds*). From his portrayal in the *Symposium* and other dialogues, he is a fully human character – he makes puns, he enjoys drinking, and he engages in flirtations and perhaps love affairs with those in his circle. But he is also superhuman – in his tolerance of drink, in his endurance of cold and sleeplessness, and in his long, concentrated contemplations. He was tried for impiety and corrupting the youth in 399 BCE and executed by being forced to drink hemlock.

Alcibiades 451–404 BCE

Alcibiades was from a noble family, and, after his father's death, was brought up by Pericles. He showed great promise as a politician and military strategist, and he had great wealth and huge personal charisma. The *Symposium* catches him at the height of his brilliance in Athens.

In 415 BCE he persuaded the Athenians to send a great expedition to Sicily with him in charge, a project which turned out disastrously for Athens. Even as the expedition departed, he was tried and exiled for alleged sacrilege (an alleged parody of the Eleusinian mysteries and mutilation of the Herms) and he jumped ship for Sparta. After helping the Spartans for a few years, he fled to the Persian satrap Tissaphernes in 411 BCE, before rejoining the Athenian fleet at Samos. In 407 BCE he was restored to Athens and given an extraordinary naval command in the Aegean. But after a subordinate was defeated at Notium in 406 BCE he retired to Thrace, and then to Persia where he was murdered.

Glaucon

A common name and it is unclear who this is. It is possible it is Plato's brother Glaucon who is an interlocutor in *Republic*.

Aristodemus

We know no more than we are told here – he was a short, shoeless, humble friend of Socrates.

Eryximachus

We don't know anything from outside this dialogue. He is a doctor who comes across as pompous and humourless. He too may have been exiled in 415 BCE.

Pausanias

Notoriously devoted to Agathon, probably aristocratic, and otherwise largely unknown.

Aristophanes *c.* 450–385 BCE

The greatest playwright of Old Comedy. He combined fantasy, slapstick, toilet-humour, parody, social and political satire. All aspects and people in contemporary Athens were fair game, and he made attacks on Socrates in *Clouds* and Agathon in *Thesmophoriazusae*.

Phaedrus

A recurrent minor figure in the Platonic dialogues, and with one dialogue named after him (*Phaedrus*, in which the topic, once again, is love). In 415 BCE he was exiled as part of the 'mutilation of the Herms' scandal. He may have returned to Athens under the general amnesty of 403 BCE.

Eros

Eros (ὁ Ἔρως) is the subject of the dialogue as those at the party all agree to speak in praise of so great a god. Eros was understood both as the god and as the human experience, and so as translator, one is constantly unsure whether to refer to 'Eros' or 'Love' (and 'him' or 'it').

Eros, as a human emotion, was understood as a strong desire aroused by something καλός. This was usually a sexual desire (contrast it with φιλία/ἀγάπη, more general words applicable to relationships within families and between friends), and so Eros was closely related to Aphrodite, but could metaphorically be extended to other strong desires. We need to put aside Judaeo-Christian notions of the unconditional love of God, and modern conceptions of 'Platonic love' (usually now understood to be a love of one soul for another soul, free of sensual desire). Eros was desire for something, usually sex with someone found attractive, but Diotima describes a rational transference of this desire away from people found beautiful to the Beautiful itself.

Eros was also understood as a winged deity, and as such has been a favourite subject for artists through the ages (see the *Eros Farnese*, by Praxiteles). However, there was no agreed story of his origin, as comes out in the speeches of Phaedrus and Pausanias. In contrast, Eryximachus suggests that it is a universal force, while Socrates argues that he is really a *daimon*, an intermediary between gods and men.

Greek sexuality

While Love is a universal human experience, the reader of the *Symposium* will immediately notice that it is set in a world of very different expectations regarding human sexuality. I will attempt to outline these expectations in as far as they are relevant to the understanding of the text, and in what follows, I am heavily indebted to Kenneth Dover: *Greek Homosexuality*.

It also needs saying that care must be taken with the *Symposium* as a source on this topic. The characters in this dialogue are literary constructions of Plato, so the views expressed in their speeches cannot be taken as representative of the views of these historical figures or of Plato himself. Furthermore, the characters, and Plato himself, were part of an Athenian social, political and intellectual elite, and so it is also dangerous to assume that their practices and values are representative of Athenian males in general (and Pausanias makes it clear that different Greek city states had different practices). Nevertheless, the views expressed in this dialogue must have been plausible for such people at that time.

An Athenian male had three main accepted contexts within which sexual relationships might occur. The first was within marriage, which at this time had to be with a free-born Athenian woman. At least among the wealthy and powerful, a marriage was usually arranged for mutual benefits of wealth, social standing and connections. The other purpose of the union was the producing of children. Wives remained largely segregated in the home, partly to ensure the legitimacy of children, and also because for any other male to have sex with her would be seen as an act of *hubris* against the husband. Pausanias makes it clear that it was a social norm for an Athenian male to marry irrespective of desire, but one imagines there must have been a full spectrum of degrees of love between husbands and wives.

The second option was sex with a slave or prostitute of either gender. It is clear from the sources that slaves could be used for this purpose, and Old Comedy suggests that brothels were commonplace. This option was about the satisfying of sexual desires, and emotion was not expected to play a part. A greyer area was *hetairai*: a *hetaira* differed from a prostitute in the sense that payment might take the form of being a kept mistress, and we know of some *hetairai* who were educated and artistically talented, and formed long-term relationships with male lovers (most famously Aspasia with Pericles); nevertheless, this was in origin a transactionary relationship.

The third option was a particular type of homosexual relationship, which was not a pairing of equals. Dover (*Greek Homosexuality* p. 84) describes how 'homosexual relationships in Greek society are regarded as the product not of the reciprocated sentiment of equals but of the pursuit of those of lower status by those of higher status.' The relationship was pederastic, between an *erastes* and an *eromenos*. The *erastes* was an adult male; the *eromenos* was typically a youth – the most attractive age was thought to be after the onset of puberty but before full beard growth. The speech of Pausanias (180c–185c) and other sources make clear that there were expectations about how such relationships should be conducted. The *erastes* was expected to pursue the boy, and excessive behaviour in the pursuit of a beloved could indulgently be forgiven. He should mentor the young man into adult life, helping him to grow intellectually and morally and understand how an Athenian should behave. The *eromenos* was expected to be coy and resist, and might be dissuaded or protected by his father, tutor or friends. The *eromenos* was not to seek or expect sensual pleasure from the relationship and should begrudge contact until the *erastes* proved himself worthy. He could reasonably give-in out of admiration, or the desire to learn from the more experienced man, or out of pity for his lover's passion. There is reticence about what sexual favours the *eromenos* might grant, although he should not 'play the woman' by accepting a subordinate position of contact. While the *erastes* could respectably be in love with his beloved and might find satisfaction of his sexual desires, the *eromenos* was not expected to love (ἐϱᾶν) but might return affection (φιλεῖν), as the names suggest (*erastes* = the one who loves; *eromenos* = the one who is loved).

An Athenian male, particularly of the leisured classes, might engage in all three of these relationships during his life, and indeed potentially at the same stage of his life. It was assumed that virtually everyone responded at some time to both homosexual and heterosexual stimuli. And an Athenian could be both an *erastes* and an *eromenos* at the same stage of life, but importantly not with the same person. For at the heart of every sexual relationship, the Athenians saw a power imbalance: on the one side the active ('male', pursuing, dominant, loving) and on the other the passive ('female', pursued, yielding, loved).

But following this outline of the sexual world of the Athenian male, it still needs explaining why the third option, *erastes–eromenos* relationships, is assumed for much of this dialogue. A partial explanation is that Pausanias and Agathon were in just such a long-term relationship (albeit unusually prolonged), as expressed both by the characters in this dialogue (177d, 193bc) and by other historical sources. This dynamic also clearly underlies the relationship between Socrates and Alcibiades, and is perhaps in the background of other relationships among those at the party. But it is also the case that the subject for their speeches is *Eros* and there was an assumption that such a strong emotion could only be found in these *erastes–eromenos* relationships which combined physical beauty, sexual desire and an admiration of character and cultured qualities in the beloved. Sexual relations with women might satisfy lust, but women, particularly wives who rarely left the home, were not thought to have any of the higher qualities (intelligence, culture, courage, etc.) which might satisfy a man's highest and noblest aspirations.

The question of whether Socrates was ever in such a relationship is probably not a fruitful one. It is clear that he lived in the world of such relationships: he regularly frequented the gymnasium, surely a homoerotically charged environment and a common place to pursue boys. He also surrounded himself with the wealthy young men of Athens and in other dialogues he discusses their difficulties in such relationships. In the *Symposium*, he makes it clear that he recognizes and is attracted by male beauty. But Alcibiades' story suggests that Socrates practised self-restraint, and may have never become fully involved in such a relationship. In later dialogues (e.g. *Republic*, *Laws*) he seems to suggest banning them, as an example of being enslaved by our base appetites and as a distraction from the philosopher's true love – the Good.

Symposia

The symposium is a distinctive feature of the life of wealthy men in classical Athens, full of ritual and religion, but its core act of men getting drunk together makes it timeless.

A symposium would frequently follow a dinner. Guests would be welcomed by a slave, their hands and feet would be washed and perfumed, and they would be shown into a reception room in the men's quarters. Here they would recline, typically two to a couch, leaning on their left elbows and propped on cushions while eating and drinking with their right hands. Guests would be garlanded, and begin by offering prayers and libations to gods and heroes, particularly Zeus, and in this case to Dionysus (both as god of wine, and because they are celebrating the Lenaea, a festival in his honour).

In the centre of the room would be a κρατήρ, a large mixing bowl. The pure wine would be kept in a vase that acted as a 'cooler' before being mixed with water in the κρατήρ at a ratio of about 3:1, giving the actual drink a strength of about 5 per cent abv. The wine would be served in goblets by slave boys. Often someone would be appointed or elected to be in charge of the drinking (the symposiarch) and he would get to control the dilution of the wine and the quantity and frequency of the drinking. Hosts would often put on a variety of entertainments which might include music (often in the form of a pipe player), dancers, or games (kottabos, a game that involved flicking wine-dregs, was a favourite). Sex was also in the background or foreground – there was a strong homoerotic element to such gatherings, but hosts might also arrange for the presence of *hetairai* and prostitutes, and pipe-girls and slaves were assumed to be available. But as a gathering of wealthy men, it might also serve the purpose of business networking or political scheming.

The party, if it didn't end in unconsciousness, might descend into a *komos*, a revel, through the streets, as we see with the arrival of Alcibiades from another party (212d) and the final interruption (223b).

Encomia

The guests at this symposium agree to hymn (ὑμνέω), praise (ἐπαινέω) and deliver an encomium *(ἐγκώμιον)* of *Eros*. Such encomia were common in honour of victors (e.g. Olympic victors), in politics and as rhetorical practice exercises. The expectations of the genre, later codified, were that the speaker should praise: i) the blessings that the subject possessed (e.g. family, riches); ii) the virtues of the subject (usually σοφία, δικαιοσύνη, ἀνδρεία); iii) the subject's forebears; and iv) his achievements. These expectations can be seen in all of the speeches, most obviously in the speech of Agathon.

Summary

172a–174a Prologue: Apollodorus talks to a companion

The dialogue opens with Apollodorus talking to an unnamed companion (or companions), a wealthy businessman – a fictional conversation set *c.* 407–400 BCE. He is clearly responding to a request to give an account of a symposium at the house of Agathon, at which Socrates and Alcibiades were among the guests. He says that he is in a good position to give such an account as just a few days previously he had met another friend, Glaucon, on the road, who had also asked him for such an account. In describing his conversation with Glaucon, we learn that the symposium had taken place in 416 BCE after Agathon had won his first victory with a tragedy in the Lenaea. Apollodorus had heard an account of the party from Aristodemus who had been there, and had checked the accuracy of it with Socrates himself. Apollodorus then begins his account of Aristodemus' account.

In Plato's dialogues, Socrates is normally the narrator, and so this account is surprising. We are told that this is an account (Apollodorus') of an account (Aristodemus') of what was said at the party, leaving us doubly distanced from the occasion itself – while the dialogue has a very specific historical setting, we are to understand that this is a literary fiction. It is also points to the central importance of the speech of Alcibiades in praise of Socrates, which would be awkward in the mouth of Socrates.

174a–175e Aristodemus' prologue: arrival at the party

Aristodemus meets Socrates in the street and is surprised to see him smartly dressed for a party. Socrates explains that he is dining at Agathon's and invites Aristodemus to join the party. Aristodemus arrives and is generously welcomed in, but Socrates has been delayed, standing in a trance on a neighbour's porch while he thinks, and he doesn't enter until dinner is well advanced. Agathon welcomes him, seats him beside himself on the end couch, and expresses a hope that they will hear what Socrates has been thinking.

There is clearly meant to be humour in this situation. Aristodemus, a man we have been told is a little fellow who never wears shoes, is persuaded to turn up to a party with the most fashionable members of Athenian society – so fashionable that even Socrates has for once dressed up. Aristodemus only agrees on condition they say that Socrates invited him, so it must be particularly embarrassing for him to turn up at the door to find that Socrates has disappeared.

The party is a literary construct and so nothing happens without a purpose and none of the events are merely incidental: Socrates' late arrival means that he shares a couch with Agathon, thus putting him last in the order of speeches.

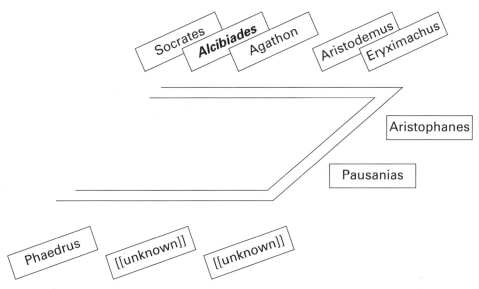

FIGURE 1 *Diagram showing the seating plan. Diners recline, leaning on their left elbows and facing inwards, either one or two to a couch (until Alcibiades arrives at the end of the meal and squeezes between Agathon and Socrates).*

176a–177e Agreement to make speeches in praise of Eros

Following dinner, libations and hymns, it is the time to drink, but Pausanias admits to being hungover and struggling from the victory party the night before, and Aristophanes and Agathon share that feeling. Eryximachus makes a suggestion (attributing the idea to Phaedrus): they should make beautiful speeches in praise of the god Eros, for such a great god has been neglected by poets and sophists. All agree.

We see that narrative amusement (the image of them all nursing hangovers) also has literary/philosophical motivation (it explains why these speeches will be given). Again we see Plato's humour in the characterization of the pompous and pedantic doctor Eryximachus who wants to lecture them all on health. And we see the agonistic culture of Athens in Socrates' (ironic?) concern that those going last will have a hard job to compete. Socrates' surprising comment that he knows nothing except the things of love (τα ἐρωτικά) foreshadows his account of his education from Diotima.

178a–180b Speech 1: Phaedrus

Thesis – Eros is an ancient god, who benefits society.

Phaedrus starts with the origins of Eros – a primordial god without parents. Then he describes the benefits for both *erastes* and *eromenos*: love is the means of imparting the virtue necessary for the good life (being καλός not αἰσχρός). Someone would feel shame at being caught acting disgracefully especially if caught by lover/beloved and would feel pride if seen acting well. Examples:

- the bravest soldiers – a lover would never run from battle leaving his beloved.
- the most self-sacrificial people, e.g. Alcestis and Achilles. The gods rewarded their love.

This speech is in one sense very conventional for an encomium: Hesiod, Homer and the poets are accepted as authoritative sources and mythological exempla are given as evidence. There is little originality and some inconsistency in the speech, and also evidence of sophistic influence.

180c–185c Speech 2: Pausanias

Thesis – common Eros, the indulgence of physical lust, gives Love a bad name, but heavenly Eros, with honourable intentions, is a noble thing.

Pausanias 'corrects' Phaedrus – since there are two Aphrodites (the ancient one called 'heavenly' and the younger called 'common'), there must be two forms of Eros. Actions are neither good nor bad; it depends how they are done.

- Common Eros – for women and boys; of body, not minds; aiming for sexual satisfaction; leading to irrational actions.
- Heavenly Eros – for boys post-puberty pre-beard; for their mind and character; acceptable for an *eromenos* to gratify an *erastes*.

Pausanias then gives a defence of this last statement: common people don't accept it because they only see common love leading to immorality; Elis and Boeotia accept it because they are too lazy to argue it; Persians don't accept it because these relationships create powerful bonds which bring down tyranny. Athenian habits are more sophisticated: an *erastes* is accepted and encouraged by society in his attempts, however humiliating; an *eromenos* is discouraged from accepting the lover by his family, friends and tutor – this is to test the motives of the *erastes*, to see that he is a lover of mind not body, and in it for the long-term benefit of the *eromenos* and not for short-term gratification. In this case, submission is acceptable. It is morally good if done for the sake of gaining virtue, and such a relationship benefits the state and the individual.

It is unsurprising that someone in a long-term relationship with Agathon attacks sexual relations with women and immature boys. He appears at times to be morally relativist, and one wonders if he is finding worthy arguments to justify his own sexual behaviour. The 'lawyer-like' speech and emphasis on νόμος *and outcome show the marks of sophistic training.*

185c-e Aristophanes' hiccups

Aristophanes, who was next to speak, asks Eryximachus to take his place while he overcomes his hiccups.

No element of the story is accidental: the device of hiccups allows the amusing speech of Aristophanes to come after the self-important speech of Eryximachus, is eminently suitable for a comic playwright who has such fun with scatological humour, and is a pun on the name of Eryximachus ('fighter of belches').

185e–188e Speech 3: Eryximachus

Thesis – love is much broader: there is good and bad eros in everything, and things flourish when the good eros in them is cultivated.

The health of any organism is a harmony: having the right loves and not the wrong ones. Medicine is the science of encouraging good loves and removing bad. He then shows the same principle in musicians, the climate, astrologers and seers. The love which leads us to a virtuous harmonious life is most powerful and important.

Eryximachus follows Pausanias in describing two types of eros, but extends the sense of love from romantic/sexual relationship to universal principle (which will become important in the speech of Diotima). Some see him as an expert scientific witness; others see him characterized as a pompous pedant; most see a monotonous unornamented style suitable for a scientist with little literary taste.

189a-c Aristophanes' hiccups cured

189c–193e Speech 4: Aristophanes

[189c2–194e2: Group 1 set text]

Thesis – love is a very powerful god, for he brings human happiness.

Aristophanes begins with a myth: humans were originally round wholes, with eight limbs/two heads, etc., in three genders (male, female and mixed). In their strength and arrogance, they challenged the gods, and so Zeus decided to chop them in half to weaken them, with Apollo turning round their heads and sewing up their front at the navel. But humans so missed their other halves that they grew apathetic and starved. So Zeus moved their genitals round to the front and gave them a way to 'reunite' through sex – this brought procreation in male–female pairs and satisfaction in male–male and female–female. Love is our desire to be made whole again, returned to our original form, and this explains different tendencies (heterosexual, homosexual). But the strongest love is if we find our original other half – this brings a lifelong relationship of love and sense of fulfilment as being closest to our original wholeness. If we suitably revere Love and the gods, they will help us to find love and true satisfaction.

Aristophanes is the first to engage with what love actually is and feels like. While the pseudo-myth is absurd, the idea of 'finding the one', 'the one who makes me whole', 'the other half' chimes with modern readers and expresses a great romantic ideal of love as far more than just sex. This is also a rare recognition of lesbianism in classical literature, although it is ignored as soon as it is introduced. There is little agreement whether Aristophanes is serious in claiming that those with homosexual inclinations (like Pausanias and Agathon) are the most masculine, as derived from original all-male wholes; more likely this is sarcastic (given that he mocks them in his comedies for effeminacy). It is not to be taken too literally – it only makes sense for one generation of humans who were originally wholes; homosexuality would die out in one generation, etc.) but it does bring Eros back to a single natural force.

Aristophanes had recently satirized Socrates in his comedy the Clouds *(423* BCE*), and this portrayal was so forceful that Socrates (in the form of his defence speech handed down to us in Plato's* Apology*) laid some of the blame for his conviction on it. Nonetheless, the Symposium shows him belonging to that same wealthy intellectual world, and gives him a speech of humour, of poetic style, and deep insight into the human condition.*

193e–194e Interlude: Socrates and Agathon

Socrates tries to drag Agathon into an argument, but the others call them back to speeches.

Here we get a glimpse of the Socratic technique of elenchus, the question-and-answer pattern we see throughout the Platonic dialogues.

This is also the moment (according to the seating order) when Aristodemus should speak, but he either chooses not to recall his speech, or he was overlooked at the party.

194e–197e Speech 5: Agathon

Thesis – Love is the most beautiful and virtuous of the gods, and he causes these things in other people.

Agathon says that unlike the other speakers, he will describe Love himself. In regard to beauty, Love is young, sensitive, supple and lovely. In regard to his virtue, he is fair, self-disciplined, courageous, wise. Therefore, he creates these same traits in those he inspires: poetic creation, physical procreation, all the gods' skills come from love of beauty.

This speech is full of beauty as we'd expect from a prize-winning tragedian of famous personal beauty (the fact that it is largely a description of himself must have been meant to be humorous), but full of weak sophistic arguments (e.g. the argument that love is particularly self-disciplined, which flies in the face of experience). Opinions differ about the style – it is almost certainly a parody of Gorgias, and some find the figures of speech forced to the point of absurdity. It is enthusiastically received by the other guests, but Socrates immediately criticizes it for a lack of truthfulness. It does set up well for Socrates' speech by distinguishing between love itself and what it causes (but then it lapses into confusion by giving Love itself the characteristics of a person who is in love), and by the important idea that love is always of the beautiful.

198a–212c Speech 6: Socrates

198a–199c defining an encomium

Socrates suggests that all the previous encomia have been wonderful in their language and the qualities they have ascribed to Eros, but untrue. He will speak the truth, even if unstylishly.

This seems a rather jarring note at a party of friends, but this helps to give Socrates' speech authority. It echoes the portrayal of Socrates in the Apology *where he says that he will rely on truth rather than rhetoric (a common topos at the start of a speech).*

199c–201c elenchus of Agathon

Socrates will start like Agathon asking 'what is love?'. He establishes love is 'love of X', love is 'desiring to have possession of X'. One cannot desire to have something that one already has (e.g. one can't desire health if one is healthy, although one might desire its continuance). Love is 'love of beauty', therefore love must lack beauty and cannot be beautiful. Then good is equated with beauty, so love is shown not to be good.

As with so much Socratic elenchus, it leads to ἀπορία, *but it is important that the popular image (the beautiful charming god) is shot down early on.*

201d–212c Diotima

[201d–206b10: Group 2 set text]

Diotima is introduced, a Mantinean woman expert in love and many other matters relating to the gods. Socrates' account builds from where he left off with Agathon.

1. If Love isn't beautiful/good, is it bad? No. It can be neither (like true belief is between knowledge and ignorance).

2. Every god is fortunate and beautiful. Love isn't beautiful, so therefore can't be a god. Love is a *daimon*, between god and human.

3. Love is the child of Poverty (explains its neediness) and Plenty (explains its ingenuity, energy and skills).

4. Wisdom is beautiful and Love is of beauty, so Love desires wisdom.

So Love is a lover, not the object of love (204c2-3), and the true philosopher (204b4).

5   Eros (and the lover) loves beautiful/good things because they bring happiness.

6.   Eros is the desire for anything good (but common usage just applies it to romantic relationships).

People love goodness, to get it for themselves, for ever (206a11).

7   Love's purpose is procreation (body and soul) in beauty, e.g. human procreation by sex – this needs a beautiful medium!

8   If the aim is permanent possession, this is really the desire for possession and immortality. Procreation is the closest we can get to immortality. Therefore, the aim of love must be goodness and immortality.

9   The closest that we mortals get to immortality is that we constantly renew ourselves, physically (e.g. hair, blood, etc.) and intellectually (e.g. revision, practice), but we also love immortality and aim for it:

• Some are pregnant with respect to bodies: physical procreation (i.e. children) in a beautiful medium (attractive woman) brings an element of physical immortality.

• Some are pregnant with respect to soul: e.g. creative procreation (e.g. art) in a beautiful medium to produce great art; e.g. virtue procreation (e.g. justice) in a beautiful medium (other just characters) to create good laws. Such a relationship of beautiful souls is the most powerful and lasting since they are united by the most beautiful offspring.

Diotima then suggests that the ways of love are like a mystery cult, and that there is a higher level still. She describes the proper way for someone to go about this ascent to knowledge, later likening each step to the rungs on a ladder.

The Ladder of Love (209e5–211d1)
(In the medium of beauty) the Beautiful itself (i.e. the Form of Beauty). Eternal. Unchanging.

↑

beautiful knowledge → love of that knowledge → love of all knowledge + begets knowledge.

↑

a beautiful soul → love of that soul → love of all virtue (individual and physical fade) + begets practical virtue

↑

A beautiful body (boy) → love of that body → love of all physical beauty (individual fades) + begets children

There is complete satisfaction/happiness to gaze upon the Good. This union begets wisdom and virtue.

Why is Diotima introduced so that this account is second hand? It certainly softens the criticism of Agathon and the others by showing that Socrates had been in the same position. It also avoids Socrates giving an account of the true lover of wisdom which looks very like himself.

The language is that of initiation into a mystery cult. Socrates talks about the need for divination and instruction, and Diotima first purifies him by the cross-examination. She then takes him through the steps of the initiation, until 210a1 marks a particular moment of revelation of the higher mysteries (some have read this as a hint that this is where the historical Socrates stopped – with his interest in the practical virtues of the good life – and the following section is truly Platonic, but this is speculation!). The climax is described metaphorically as a sight, but needing the appropriate faculty, a mystical union which gives birth to true virtue.

It is clear that different humans will get to different stages on the ladder. Many will physically procreate in a 'physically beautiful medium' but perhaps never begin to see beauty separate from that instance. Diotima assumes that the ones who begin to ascend will start from the beauty of a boy (although not necessary), and for the second stage of beauty in a soul, it is assumed this could only be found in another man, and physical attraction is seen as a helpful medium. But while this pursuit might start in the context of Greek pederasty, it is clear that the one who rises higher in his understanding will lose interest in the physical, and then in the individual as he sees greater things. Diotima is clear on how the philosopher moves from the specific to the general, but not how the philosopher moves between the rungs of the ladder. Perhaps we need a teacher to harness the power of our desire and to lead us up the ladder through rational argument.

212b-c Socrates' conclusion

Eros should be honoured above all, as the desire that drives us towards the forms themselves.

Eros has turned out to be the desire for the good (το ἀγαθόν) for it brings happiness (εὐδαιμονία), and the highest form of the good is wisdom (σοφία), so Eros is the philosophic impulse. Eros will help lead the philosopher from the sensual, through the intellectual, to the eternal, all in the medium of beauty.

212c–215a Alcibiades arrives

Alcibiades arrives, very drunk, with friends, to crown Agathon and hoping to join the party. He squeezes in between Agathon and Socrates, and then notices Socrates. Alcibiades suggests that Socrates was sitting beside Agathon because of Agathon's beauty. Socrates suggests that Alcibiades gets jealous if his lovers talk to anyone else.

Alcibiades decides some serious drinking is needed and starts them off, followed by Socrates. Eryximachus tells Alcibiades that he has entered during a series of speeches and that it is his turn to speak in praise of Love. Alcibiades, using the excuse of drunkenness and Socrates' jealousy, says that he won't praise Love but agrees to praise Socrates.

This interlude is important for the characterization of Alcibiades (charismatic, unrestrained, loved by all) and of Socrates (said to be a 'lover' of Alcibiades and Agathon, and a great drinker who never gets drunk). It provides an important comic relaxation after the philosophical climax of Diotima and the form of the Beautiful.

215a–222b Speech 7: Alcibiades

Alcibiades declares that Socrates is like Silenus or Marsyas (both wise satyrs) – outrageous on the outside, divine on the inside; in appearance; in possessing people through his words. But Alcibiades says that he has blocked his ears and fled, for he knows the good life that Socrates calls him to, but he prefers the honours of the multitude and is ashamed.

Socrates is erotically disposed towards handsome people, yet temperate within and despises worldly benefits. Alcibiades illustrates this with his own story. He had thought that Socrates wanted to become his *erastes* because of his beauty, charisma and success, and was minded to accept for the benefits of wisdom and education it would bring. Socrates continued to converse with him philosophically and never made a move, even as Alcibiades offered himself more and more overtly, culminating in an explicit offer which was rejected as they spent a night together on a couch after dinner. This left Alcibiades wounded at the rejection and yet even more drawn to Socrates for his extraordinary restraint.

Following this, Alcibiades served in the army with Socrates at Potidaea, where Socrates showed greater endurance than all others of cold, great perseverance when standing contemplating, and great courage in saving Alcibiades' life. Similarly, Socrates showed courage and confidence in the retreat at Delium, helping to save his comrades' lives.

Alcibiades also suggests Socrates' arguments are like Silenus: they look ridiculous on the outside but deep-down they have divine wisdom leading to a noble life.

This speech on one level provides relief from the previous heavy and abstract speeches. It is a love story: while it starts with Socrates as the erastes and Alcibiades as the eromenos, it becomes clear that Alcibiades is in love, the erastes, and he takes the role of the rejected lover, telling the story at his own expense.

But while this speech seems light and trivial, this is just as philosophically important as the others. The story starts as if it is going to be a living example of the sort of relationship that Pausanias had outlined in his speech – an eromenos (Alcibiades) giving in to an erastes (Socrates) for the sake of educational benefits, and offering sexual gratification. However, the story doesn't lead that way, but instead we see in the actions of Socrates a lived-out example of the ascent to knowledge that Diotima had described. Socrates had started from the physical beauty of one individual (and presumably moved on to contemplate all physical beauty) and in that individual was an extraordinary character (and this had led to fruitful conversations that could have produced virtue). But for Socrates, his ascent had gone higher, until having fallen in love with the Good itself, through the medium of the beautiful, he had little interest left for the physical beauty of Alcibiades. The examples of Socrates' virtuous and courageous behaviour are proof that knowledge of the Good itself leads to all human virtue. Socrates turns out to be the true philosopher, the true lover, the one whom love has led to the point of grasping the Good itself.

And therefore Alcibiades represents everyman. He became a lover of the beauty in the soul of Socrates and as such was started on the ascent of the ladder of love/ knowledge. Alcibiades, as Beauty incarnate, should have been just the sort of beautiful medium in which Socrates, the true philosopher, could have given birth to true virtue. And yet Alcibiades rejected this path, as he himself admits (216a-b) in favour of a life of physical beauty, pleasures and honour-seeking. The disastrous events which follow soon after this dialogue mean that this dialogue acts as a sort of parable illustrating the dangers of rejecting philosophy and the pursuit of the Good. It leaves us the reader with the question – will we be a lover of the Alcibiades or Socrates type?

222c–223d The party ends

Alcibiades provokes laughter with his speech and Socrates wins a (good-natured?) argument to have Agathon move to recline next to him. The party is interrupted by a group of revellers and collapses into heavy drinking. Eryximachus and Phaedrus leave, some pass out, and Aristodemus awakes near dawn to find Socrates still talking to Aristophanes and Agathon, arguing that anyone who can write tragedy could also write comedy. Aristophanes and Agathon fall asleep, at which point Socrates potters off for a bath and a normal day in the Lycaeum.

Agathon said at the beginning (175e) that Dionysus would judge whether he or Socrates was the wiser. Alcibiades, in a sense the embodiment of Dionysus, has voted for Socrates, and now Socrates overcomes Dionysus while Agathon is overcome. The argument about poets follows a description of Aristophanes, who, although comic, was profound, and Agathon, who although beautiful, was ridiculous; it is Plato, the creator of this tragi-comic drama, in his portrayal of Socrates, a ridiculous yet wise figure, who shows that both are possible.

Structural analysis

This account of the party is a literary construct and a work of philosophy, so no event just happens. A first observation is that speeches and dramatic interludes alternate, the interludes often giving illustrations of the characters or ideas as well as light relief (the exception is the back-to-back speeches of Phaedrus and Pausanias – perhaps we are to take the latter speech as an extension of the former).

Some divide the dialogue into three main acts: the first five speeches, the speech of Socrates, and the scene with Alcibiades. The speeches of Socrates and Alcibiades seem to contain the important Platonic ideas, so this leads to much discussion about the purpose of the first five speeches (Plato must have written them for a reason) and how they relate to the rest.

Others see the six speeches of the original guests, and then the intervention of Alcibiades. Various patterns have been seen in these six speeches: two groups of three (two vs one type of love); or a ring composition (Eros a powerful god → a universal force → a powerful god); three about the experience of love and then three about what it is; or three pairs (perhaps antagonistic), based on various criteria.

The early speeches all contain some elements that Socrates accepts and builds on. Phaedrus gives us the power of love, Pausanias the educational potential, Eryximachus the idea of love as a universal principle, Aristophanes love as our drive for fulfilment which goes deeper than sex, Agathon love's role as procreator.

They also contain some elements of popular (mis)conception which Socrates reacts against: those who treated love as a god are corrected – it is a *daimon*; Aristophanes is explicitly corrected (205e) that love is not for physical or emotional wholeness but for the Good; Agathon is shown to have confused love itself with its objects.

Further Reading

Translations

Plato. *The Symposium*. Tr. Christopher Gill. Penguin 1999.
Plato. *Symposium*. Tr. A. Nehamas and P. Woodruff. In *Plato: Complete Works*. Ed. John M. Cooper. Indianapolis: Hackett Publishing Company 1997.
Plato. Symposium. Tr. Robin Waterfield. Oxford: OUP 1994.
Plato. *The Symposium*. Tr. W. Hamilton. Penguin 1951.

Commentaries

Plato Symposium. K. Dover. Cambridge 1980.
The Symposium of Plato. R. G. Bury. Cambridge 1909.
The Symposium. R. E. Allen. Yale 1991.
Plato: Symposium. C. J. Rowe. A&P 1998.

Plato is often the best commentary on Plato. The *Phaedrus* and *Apology* are most useful starting points.

Clay, D. 'The Tragic and Comic poet of the Symposium'. In *Essays in Ancient Greek Philosophy vol 2*. Ed. J. P. Anton and A. Preus, 186–202. Albany 1983.
Cornford, F. M. 'The doctrine of Eros in Plato's Symposium'. In *The unwritten philosophy and other essays*, 68–80. Cambridge 1950.
Dover, K. *Greek Homosexuality*. Duckworth 1978.
Dover, K. 'Aristophanes' speech in Plato's Symposium'. *JHS* 1966, 41–50.
Eisner, Robert. 'A case of poetic justice: Aristophanes' speech in Plato's Symposium'. *CW* 1979, 417–419.
Hunter, Richard. *Plato's Symposium*. OUP 2004.
Kraut, Richard (ed.). *Cambridge Companion to Plato*. CUP 2012.
Levy, Donald. 'The definition of Love in Plato's Symposium'. *Journal of History of Ideas*, 1979.
Schofield, Malcolm. 'Plato in his time and space'. In *The Oxford Handbook of Plato*. Ed. Fine, 36–62. OUP 2008.

Scott, Dominic. 'Socrates and Alcibiades in the Symposium'. *Hermathena* 168, 25–37.
Von Blanckenhagen. Peter H. 'Stage and Actors in Plato's Symposium'. *Greek, Roman and Byzantine Studies* 33, 1992, 51–68.

Acknowledgements

The text is based on the Oxford text of John Burnet, OUP 1903, with some changes of punctuation, particularly the addition of speech marks. I am heavily indebted to the commentaries of Dover and Bury in particular, and my several reviewers who made many valuable corrections and suggestions.

Text

‘καὶ μήν, ὦ Ἐρυξίμαχε,’ εἰπεῖν τὸν Ἀριστοφάνη, ‘ἄλλη   189c2
γέ πῃ ἐν νῷ ἔχω λέγειν ἢ ᾗ σύ τε καὶ Παυσανίας εἰπέτην.
ἐμοὶ γὰρ δοκοῦσιν ἄνθρωποι παντάπασι τὴν τοῦ ἔρωτος
δύναμιν οὐκ ᾐσθῆσθαι, ἐπεὶ αἰσθανόμενοί γε μέγιστ᾿ ἂν   5
αὐτοῦ ἱερὰ κατασκευάσαι καὶ βωμούς, καὶ θυσίας ἂν ποιεῖν
μεγίστας, οὐχ ὥσπερ νῦν τούτων οὐδὲν γίγνεται περὶ αὐτόν,
δέον πάντων μάλιστα γίγνεσθαι. ἔστι γὰρ θεῶν φιλαν-
θρωπότατος, ἐπίκουρός τε ὢν τῶν ἀνθρώπων καὶ ἰατρὸς   d
τούτων ὧν ἰαθέντων μεγίστη εὐδαιμονία ἂν τῷ ἀνθρωπείῳ
γένει εἴη. ἐγὼ οὖν πειράσομαι ὑμῖν εἰσηγήσασθαι τὴν
δύναμιν αὐτοῦ, ὑμεῖς δὲ τῶν ἄλλων διδάσκαλοι ἔσεσθε.
δεῖ δὲ πρῶτον ὑμᾶς μαθεῖν τὴν ἀνθρωπίνην φύσιν καὶ τὰ   5
παθήματα αὐτῆς. ἡ γὰρ πάλαι ἡμῶν φύσις οὐχ αὐτὴ ἦν
ἥπερ νῦν, ἀλλ᾿ ἀλλοία. πρῶτον μὲν γὰρ τρία ἦν τὰ γένη
τὰ τῶν ἀνθρώπων, οὐχ ὥσπερ νῦν δύο, ἄρρεν καὶ θῆλυ,
ἀλλὰ καὶ τρίτον προσῆν κοινὸν ὂν ἀμφοτέρων τούτων, οὗ   e
νῦν ὄνομα λοιπόν, αὐτὸ δὲ ἠφάνισται· ἀνδρόγυνον γὰρ ἓν
τότε μὲν ἦν καὶ εἶδος καὶ ὄνομα ἐξ ἀμφοτέρων κοινὸν τοῦ
τε ἄρρενος καὶ θήλεος, νῦν δὲ οὐκ ἔστιν ἀλλ᾿ ἢ ἐν ὀνείδει
ὄνομα κείμενον. ἔπειτα ὅλον ἦν ἑκάστου τοῦ ἀνθρώπου τὸ   5
εἶδος στρογγύλον, νῶτον καὶ πλευρὰς κύκλῳ ἔχον· χεῖρας
δ τέτταρας εἶχε, καὶ σκέλη τὰ ἴσα ταῖς χερσίν, καὶ πρόσωπα
δύ᾿ ἐπ᾿ αὐχένι κυκλοτερεῖ, ὅμοια πάντῃ· κεφαλὴν δ᾿ ἐπ᾿   190a
ἀμφοτέροις τοῖς προσώποις ἐναντίοις κειμένοις μίαν, καὶ
ὦτα τέτταρα, καὶ αἰδοῖα δύο, καὶ τἆλλα πάντα ὡς ἀπὸ
τούτων ἄν τις εἰκάσειεν. ἐπορεύετο δὲ καὶ ὀρθὸν ὥσπερ
νῦν, ὁποτέρωσε βουληθείη· καὶ ὁπότε ταχὺ ὁρμήσειεν θεῖν,   5
ὥσπερ οἱ κυβιστῶντες καὶ εἰς ὀρθὸν τὰ σκέλη περιφερό-
μενοι κυβιστῶσι κύκλῳ, ὀκτὼ τότε οὖσι τοῖς μέλεσιν
ἀπερειδόμενοι ταχὺ ἐφέροντο κύκλῳ. ἦν δὲ διὰ ταῦτα τρία

τὰ γένη καὶ τοιαῦτα, ὅτι τὸ μὲν ἄρρεν ἦν τοῦ ἡλίου τὴν   b
ἀρχὴν ἔκγονον, τὸ δὲ θῆλυ τῆς γῆς, τὸ δὲ ἀμφοτέρων μετέχον
τῆς σελήνης, ὅτι καὶ ἡ σελήνη ἀμφοτέρων μετέχει· περιφερῆ
δὲ δὴ ἦν καὶ αὐτὰ καὶ ἡ πορεία αὐτῶν διὰ τὸ τοῖς γονεῦσιν
ὅμοια εἶναι. ἦν οὖν τὴν ἰσχὺν δεινὰ καὶ τὴν ῥώμην, καὶ   5
τὰ φρονήματα μεγάλα εἶχον, ἐπεχείρησαν δὲ τοῖς θεοῖς,
καὶ ὃ λέγει Ὅμηρος περὶ Ἐφιάλτου τε καὶ Ὤτου, περὶ
ἐκείνων λέγεται, τὸ εἰς τὸν οὐρανὸν ἀνάβασιν ἐπιχειρεῖν
ποιεῖν, ὡς ἐπιθησομένων τοῖς θεοῖς. ὁ οὖν Ζεὺς καὶ οἱ   c
ἄλλοι θεοὶ ἐβουλεύοντο, ὅ τι χρὴ αὐτοὺς ποιῆσαι, καὶ ἠπό-
ρουν· οὔτε γὰρ ὅπως ἀποκτείναιεν εἶχον καὶ ὥσπερ τοὺς
γίγαντας κεραυνώσαντες τὸ γένος ἀφανίσαιεν – αἱ τιμαὶ
γὰρ αὐτοῖς καὶ ἱερὰ τὰ παρὰ τῶν ἀνθρώπων ἠφανίζετο –   5
οὔθ᾽ ὅπως ἐῷεν ἀσελγαίνειν. μόγις δὴ ὁ Ζεὺς ἐννοήσας
λέγει ὅτι "δοκῶ μοι," ἔφη, "ἔχειν μηχανήν, ὡς ἂν εἶέν
τε ἄνθρωποι καὶ παύσαιντο τῆς ἀκολασίας ἀσθενέστεροι
γενόμενοι. νῦν μὲν γὰρ αὐτούς," ἔφη, "διατεμῶ δίχα ἕκαστον,   d
καὶ ἅμα μὲν ἀσθενέστεροι ἔσονται, ἅμα δὲ χρησιμώτεροι
ἡμῖν διὰ τὸ πλείους τὸν ἀριθμὸν γεγονέναι· καὶ βαδιοῦνται
ὀρθοὶ ἐπὶ δυοῖν σκελοῖν· ἐὰν δ᾽ ἔτι δοκῶσιν ἀσελγαίνειν
καὶ μὴ ἐθέλωσιν ἡσυχίαν ἄγειν, πάλιν αὖ," ἔφη, "τεμῶ δίχα,   5
ὥστ᾽ ἐφ᾽ ἑνὸς πορεύσονται σκέλους ἀσκωλιάζοντες." ταῦτα
εἰπὼν ἔτεμνε τοὺς ἀνθρώπους δίχα, ὥσπερ οἱ τὰ ὠὰ τέμ-
νοντες καὶ μέλλοντες ταριχεύειν, ἢ ὥσπερ οἱ τὰ ὠὰ ταῖς   e
θριξίν· ὅντινα δὲ τέμοι, τὸν Ἀπόλλω ἐκέλευε τό τε
πρόσωπον μεταστρέφειν καὶ τὸ τοῦ αὐχένος ἥμισυ πρὸς
τὴν τομήν, ἵνα θεώμενος τὴν αὑτοῦ τμῆσιν κοσμιώτερος
εἴη ὁ ἄνθρωπος· καὶ τἆλλα ἰᾶσθαι ἐκέλευεν. ὁ δὲ τό τε   5
πρόσωπον μετέστρεφε, καὶ συνέλκων πανταχόθεν τὸ δέρμα
ἐπὶ τὴν γαστέρα νῦν καλουμένην, ὥσπερ τὰ σύσπαστα
βαλάντια, ἓν στόμα ποιῶν ἀπέδει κατὰ μέσην τὴν γαστέρα,
ὃ δὴ τὸν ὀμφαλὸν καλοῦσι. καὶ τὰς μὲν ἄλλας ῥυτίδας
τὰς πολλὰς ἐξελέαινε καὶ τὰ στήθη διήρθρου, ἔχων τι   191a
τοιοῦτον ὄργανον οἷον οἱ σκυτοτόμοι περὶ τὸν καλάποδα
λεαίνοντες τὰς τῶν σκυτῶν ῥυτίδας· ὀλίγας δὲ κατέλιπε,
τὰς περὶ αὐτὴν τὴν γαστέρα καὶ τὸν ὀμφαλόν, μνημεῖον
εἶναι τοῦ παλαιοῦ πάθους. ἐπειδὴ οὖν ἡ φύσις δίχα   5
ἐτμήθη, ποθοῦν ἕκαστον τὸ ἥμισυ τὸ αὑτοῦ συνῄει, καὶ
περιβάλλοντες τὰς χεῖρας καὶ συμπλεκόμενοι ἀλλήλοις,
ἐπιθυμοῦντες συμφῦναι, ἀπέθνῃσκον ὑπὸ λιμοῦ καὶ τῆς

ἄλλης ἀργίας διὰ τὸ μηδὲν ἐθέλειν χωρὶς ἀλλήλων ποιεῖν.　　　b
καὶ ὁπότε τι ἀποθάνοι τῶν ἡμίσεων, τὸ δὲ λειφθείη, τὸ
λειφθὲν ἄλλο ἐζήτει καὶ συνεπλέκετο, εἴτε γυναικὸς τῆς
ὅλης ἐντύχοι ἡμίσει, ὃ δὴ νῦν γυναῖκα καλοῦμεν, εἴτε
ἀνδρός· καὶ οὕτως ἀπώλλυντο. ἐλεήσας δὲ ὁ Ζεὺς ἄλλην　　5
μηχανὴν πορίζεται, καὶ μετατίθησιν αὐτῶν τὰ αἰδοῖα εἰς
τὸ πρόσθεν· τέως γὰρ καὶ ταῦτα ἐκτὸς εἶχον, καὶ ἐγέννων
καὶ ἔτικτον οὐκ εἰς ἀλλήλους ἀλλ᾽ εἰς γῆν, ὥσπερ οἱ τέτ-　　c
τιγες. μετέθηκέ τε οὖν οὕτω αὐτῶν εἰς τὸ πρόσθεν καὶ
διὰ τούτων τὴν γένεσιν ἐν ἀλλήλοις ἐποίησε, διὰ τοῦ
ἄρρενος ἐν τῷ θήλει, τῶνδε ἕνεκα, ἵνα ἐν τῇ συμπλοκῇ
ἅμα μὲν εἰ ἀνὴρ γυναικὶ ἐντύχοι, γεννῷεν καὶ γίγνοιτο τὸ　　5
γένος, ἅμα δ᾽ εἰ καὶ ἄρρην ἄρρενι, πλησμονὴ γοῦν γίγνοιτο
τῆς συνουσίας καὶ διαπαύοιντο καὶ ἐπὶ τὰ ἔργα τρέποιντο
καὶ τοῦ ἄλλου βίου ἐπιμελοῖντο. ἔστι δὴ οὖν ἐκ τόσου
ὁ ἔρως ἔμφυτος ἀλλήλων τοῖς ἀνθρώποις καὶ τῆς ἀρχαίας　　d
φύσεως συναγωγεὺς καὶ ἐπιχειρῶν ποιῆσαι ἓν ἐκ δυοῖν καὶ
ἰάσασθαι τὴν φύσιν τὴν ἀνθρωπίνην. ἕκαστος οὖν ἡμῶν
ἐστιν ἀνθρώπου σύμβολον, ἅτε τετμημένος ὥσπερ αἱ ψῆτται,
ἐξ ἑνὸς δύο. ζητεῖ δὴ ἀεὶ τὸ αὑτοῦ ἕκαστος σύμβολον.　　5
ὅσοι μὲν οὖν τῶν ἀνδρῶν τοῦ κοινοῦ τμῆμά εἰσιν, ὃ δὴ
τότε ἀνδρόγυνον ἐκαλεῖτο, φιλογύναικές τέ εἰσι καὶ οἱ
πολλοὶ τῶν μοιχῶν ἐκ τούτου τοῦ γένους γεγόνασιν, καὶ
ὅσαι αὖ γυναῖκες φίλανδροί τε καὶ μοιχεύτριαι, ἐκ τούτου　　e
τοῦ γένους γίγνονται. ὅσαι δὲ τῶν γυναικῶν γυναικὸς
τμῆμά εἰσιν, οὐ πάνυ αὗται τοῖς ἀνδράσι τὸν νοῦν προσ-
έχουσιν, ἀλλὰ μᾶλλον πρὸς τὰς γυναῖκας τετραμμέναι
εἰσί, καὶ αἱ ἑταιρίστριαι ἐκ τούτου τοῦ γένους γίγνονται.　　5
ὅσοι δὲ ἄρρενος τμῆμά εἰσι, τὰ ἄρρενα διώκουσι, καὶ τέως
μὲν ἂν παῖδες ὦσιν, ἅτε τεμάχια ὄντα τοῦ ἄρρενος, φιλοῦσι
τοὺς ἄνδρας καὶ χαίρουσι συγκατακείμενοι καὶ· συμπεπλεγμένοι τοῖς ἀνδράσι, καὶ εἰσιν οὗτοι βέλτιστοι τῶν παίδων　　192a
καὶ μειρακίων, ἅτε ἀνδρειότατοι ὄντες φύσει. φασὶ δὲ δή
τινες αὐτοὺς ἀναισχύντους εἶναι, ψευδόμενοι· οὐ γὰρ ὑπ᾽
ἀναισχυντίας τοῦτο δρῶσιν ἀλλ᾽ ὑπὸ θάρρους καὶ ἀνδρείας
καὶ ἀρρενωπίας, τὸ ὅμοιον αὑτοῖς ἀσπαζόμενοι. μέγα δὲ　　5
τεκμήριον· καὶ γὰρ τελεωθέντες μόνοι ἀποβαίνουσιν εἰς
τὰ πολιτικὰ ἄνδρες οἱ τοιοῦτοι. ἐπειδὰν δὲ ἀνδρωθῶσι,
παιδεραστοῦσι καὶ πρὸς γάμους καὶ παιδοποιίας οὐ προσ-　　b
έχουσι τὸν νοῦν φύσει, ἀλλ᾽ ὑπὸ τοῦ νόμου ἀναγκάζονται·

ἀλλ᾽ ἐξαρκεῖ αὐτοῖς μετ᾽ ἀλλήλων καταζῆν ἀγάμοις. πάντως
μὲν οὖν ὁ τοιοῦτος παιδεραστής τε καὶ φιλεραστὴς γίγνεται,
ἀεὶ τὸ συγγενὲς ἀσπαζόμενος. ὅταν μὲν οὖν καὶ αὐτῷ   5
ἐκείνῳ ἐντύχῃ τῷ αὑτοῦ ἡμίσει καὶ ὁ παιδεραστὴς καὶ
ἄλλος πᾶς, τότε καὶ θαυμαστὰ ἐκπλήττονται φιλίᾳ τε καὶ
οἰκειότητι καὶ ἔρωτι, οὐκ ἐθέλοντες, ὡς ἔπος εἰπεῖν χωρί-   c
ζεσθαι ἀλλήλων οὐδὲ σμικρὸν χρόνον. καὶ οἱ διατελοῦντες
μετ᾽ ἀλλήλων διὰ βίου οὗτοί εἰσιν, οἳ οὐδ᾽ ἂν ἔχοιεν εἰπεῖν
ὅ τι βούλονται σφίσι παρ᾽ ἀλλήλων γίγνεσθαι. οὐδενὶ γὰρ
ἂν δόξειεν τοῦτ᾽ εἶναι ἡ τῶν ἀφροδισίων συνουσία, ὡς   5
ἄρα τούτου ἕνεκα ἕτερος ἑτέρῳ χαίρει συνὼν οὕτως ἐπὶ
μεγάλης σπουδῆς· ἀλλ᾽ ἄλλο τι βουλομένη ἑκατέρου ἡ ψυχὴ
δήλη ἐστίν, ὃ οὐ δύναται εἰπεῖν, ἀλλὰ μαντεύεται ὃ βού-   d
λεται, καὶ αἰνίττεται. καὶ εἰ αὐτοῖς ἐν τῷ αὐτῷ κατακειμένοις ἐπιστὰς ὁ Ἥφαιστος, ἔχων τὰ ὄργανα, ἔροιτο "τί
ἔσθ᾽ ὃ βούλεσθε, ὦ ἄνθρωποι, ὑμῖν παρ᾽ ἀλλήλων γενέσθαι;" καὶ εἰ ἀποροῦντας αὐτοὺς πάλιν ἔροιτο "ἆρά γε   5
τοῦδε ἐπιθυμεῖτε, ἐν τῷ αὐτῷ γενέσθαι ὅτι μάλιστα ἀλλήλοις, ὥστε καὶ νύκτα καὶ ἡμέραν μὴ ἀπολείπεσθαι ἀλλήλων; εἰ γὰρ τούτου ἐπιθυμεῖτε, ἐθέλω ὑμᾶς συντῆξαι καὶ
συμφυσῆσαι εἰς τὸ αὐτό, ὥστε δύ᾽ ὄντας ἕνα γεγονέναι   e
καὶ ἕως τ᾽ ἂν ζῆτε, ὡς ἕνα ὄντα, κοινῇ ἀμφοτέρους ζῆν,
καὶ ἐπειδὰν ἀποθάνητε, ἐκεῖ αὖ ἐν Ἅιδου ἀντὶ δυοῖν ἕνα
εἶναι κοινῇ τεθνεῶτε· ἀλλ᾽ ὁρᾶτε εἰ τούτου ἐρᾶτε καὶ
ἐξαρκεῖ ὑμῖν ἂν τούτου τύχητε·" ταῦτ᾽ ἀκούσας ἴσμεν ὅτι   5
οὐδ᾽ ἂν εἷς ἐξαρνηθείη οὐδ᾽ ἄλλο τι ἂν φανείη βουλόμενος,
ἀλλ᾽ ἀτεχνῶς οἴοιτ᾽ ἂν ἀκηκοέναι τοῦτο ὃ πάλαι ἄρα ἐπε-
θύμει, συνελθὼν καὶ συντακεὶς τῷ ἐρωμένῳ ἐκ δυοῖν εἷς
γενέσθαι. τοῦτο γάρ ἐστι τὸ αἴτιον, ὅτι ἡ ἀρχαία φύσις
ἡμῶν ἦν αὕτη καὶ ἦμεν ὅλοι· τοῦ ὅλου οὖν τῇ ἐπιθυμίᾳ   10
καὶ διώξει ἔρως ὄνομα. καὶ πρὸ τοῦ, ὥσπερ λέγω, ἓν   193a
ἦμεν, νυνὶ δὲ διὰ τὴν ἀδικίαν διῳκίσθημεν ὑπὸ τοῦ θεοῦ,
καθάπερ Ἀρκάδες ὑπὸ Λακεδαιμονίων· φόβος οὖν ἔστιν,
ἐὰν μὴ κόσμιοι ὦμεν πρὸς τοὺς θεούς, ὅπως μὴ καὶ αὖθις
διασχισθησόμεθα, καὶ περίιμεν ἔχοντες ὥσπερ οἱ ἐν ταῖς   5
στήλαις καταγραφὴν ἐκτετυπωμένοι, διαπεπρισμένοι κατὰ
τὰς ῥῖνας, γεγονότες ὥσπερ λίσπαι. ἀλλὰ τούτων ἕνεκα
πάντ᾽ ἄνδρα χρὴ ἅπαντα παρακελεύεσθαι εὐσεβεῖν περὶ
θεούς, ἵνα τὰ μὲν ἐκφύγωμεν, τῶν δὲ τύχωμεν, ὡς ὁ Ἔρως
ἡμῖν ἡγεμὼν καὶ στρατηγός. ᾧ μηδεὶς ἐναντία πραττέτω   b

– πράττει δ' ἐναντία ὅστις θεοῖς ἀπεχθάνεται – φίλοι γὰρ
γενόμενοι καὶ διαλλαγέντες τῷ θεῷ ἐξευρήσομέν τε καὶ
ἐντευξόμεθα τοῖς παιδικοῖς τοῖς ἡμετέροις αὐτῶν, ὃ τῶν νῦν   5
ὀλίγοι ποιοῦσι. καὶ μή μοι ὑπολάβῃ Ἐρυξίμαχος, κωμῳδῶν
τὸν λόγον, ὡς Παυσανίαν καὶ Ἀγάθωνα λέγω – ἴσως μὲν
γὰρ καὶ οὗτοι τούτων τυγχάνουσιν ὄντες καὶ εἰσιν ἀμφότεροι   c
τὴν φύσιν ἄρρενες – λέγω δὲ οὖν ἔγωγε καθ' ἁπάντων καὶ
ἀνδρῶν καὶ γυναικῶν, ὅτι οὕτως ἂν ἡμῶν τὸ γένος εὔδαιμον
γένοιτο, εἰ ἐκτελέσαιμεν τὸν ἔρωτα καὶ τῶν παιδικῶν τῶν
αὑτοῦ ἕκαστος τύχοι εἰς τὴν ἀρχαίαν ἀπελθὼν φύσιν· εἰ   5
δὲ τοῦτο ἄριστον, ἀναγκαῖον καὶ τῶν νῦν παρόντων τὸ
τούτου ἐγγυτάτω ἄριστον εἶναι· τοῦτο δ' ἐστὶ παιδικῶν τυχεῖν
κατὰ νοῦν αὐτῷ πεφυκότων· οὗ δὴ τὸν αἴτιον θεὸν ὑμνοῦντες
δικαίως ἂν ὑμνοῖμεν Ἔρωτα, ὃς ἔν τε τῷ παρόντι ἡμᾶς   d
πλεῖστα ὀνίνησιν εἰς τὸ οἰκεῖον ἄγων, καὶ εἰς τὸ ἔπειτα
ἐλπίδας μεγίστας παρέχεται, ἡμῶν παρεχομένων πρὸς θεοὺς
εὐσέβειαν, καταστήσας ἡμᾶς εἰς τὴν ἀρχαίαν φύσιν καὶ
ἰασάμενος μακαρίους καὶ εὐδαίμονας ποιῆσαι.   5
οὗτος,' ἔφη, 'ὦ Ἐρυξίμαχε, ὁ ἐμὸς λόγος ἐστὶ περὶ
Ἔρωτος, ἀλλοῖος ἢ ὁ σός. ὥσπερ οὖν ἐδεήθην σου, μὴ
κωμῳδήσῃς αὐτόν, ἵνα καὶ τῶν λοιπῶν ἀκούσωμεν τί ἕκαστος
ἐρεῖ, μᾶλλον δὲ τί ἑκάτερος· Ἀγάθων γὰρ καὶ Σωκράτης   e
λοιποί.'
'ἀλλὰ πείσομαί σοι,' ἔφη φάναι τὸν Ἐρυξίμαχον· 'καὶ
γάρ μοι ὁ λόγος ἡδέως ἐρρήθη. καὶ εἰ μὴ συνῄδειν Σω-
κράτει τε καὶ Ἀγάθωνι δεινοῖς οὖσι περὶ τὰ ἐρωτικά, πάνυ   5
ἂν ἐφοβούμην μὴ ἀπορήσωσι λόγων διὰ τὸ πολλὰ καὶ
παντοδαπὰ εἰρῆσθαι· νῦν δὲ ὅμως θαρρῶ.'
τὸν οὖν Σωκράτη εἰπεῖν 'καλῶς γὰρ αὐτὸς ἠγώνισαι,   194a
ὦ Ἐρυξίμαχε· εἰ δὲ γένοιο οὗ νῦν ἐγώ εἰμι, μᾶλλον δὲ
ἴσως οὗ ἔσομαι ἐπειδὰν καὶ Ἀγάθων εἴπῃ εὖ, καὶ μάλ' ἂν
φοβοῖο καὶ ἐν παντὶ εἴης ὥσπερ ἐγὼ νῦν.'
'φαρμάττειν βούλει με, ὦ Σώκρατες,' εἰπεῖν τὸν Ἀγάθωνα,   5
'ἵνα θορυβηθῶ διὰ τὸ οἴεσθαι τὸ θέατρον προσδοκίαν μεγάλην
ἔχειν ὡς εὖ ἐροῦντος ἐμοῦ.'
'ἐπιλήσμων μεντἂν εἴην, ὦ Ἀγάθων,' εἰπεῖν τὸν Σω-
κράτη, 'εἰ ἰδὼν τὴν σὴν ἀνδρείαν καὶ μεγαλοφροσύνην   b
ἀναβαίνοντος ἐπὶ τὸν ὀκρίβαντα μετὰ τῶν ὑποκριτῶν, καὶ
βλέψαντος ἐναντία τοσούτῳ θεάτρῳ, μέλλοντος ἐπιδείξεσθαι
σαυτοῦ λόγους, καὶ οὐδ' ὁπωστιοῦν ἐκπλαγέντος, νῦν

οἰηθείην σε θορυβήσεσθαι ἕνεκα ἡμῶν ὀλίγων ἀνθρώπων.'   5
'τί δέ, ὦ Σώκρατες;' τὸν Ἀγάθωνα φάναι, 'οὐ δήπου με
οὕτω θεάτρου μεστὸν ἡγῇ, ὥστε καὶ ἀγνοεῖν ὅτι νοῦν ἔχοντι
ὀλίγοι ἔμφρονες πολλῶν ἀφρόνων φοβερώτεροι.'
'οὐ μεντἂν καλῶς ποιοίην,' φάναι, 'ὦ Ἀγάθων, περὶ σοῦ   c
τι ἐγὼ ἄγροικον δοξάζων· ἀλλ᾿ εὖ οἶδα ὅτι εἴ τισιν ἐντύχοις
οὓς ἡγοῖο σοφούς, μᾶλλον ἂν αὐτῶν φροντίζοις ἢ τῶν
πολλῶν· ἀλλὰ μὴ οὐχ οὗτοι ἡμεῖς ὦμεν· ἡμεῖς μὲν γὰρ
καὶ ἐκεῖ παρῆμεν καὶ ἦμεν τῶν πολλῶν· εἰ δὲ ἄλλοις   5
ἐντύχοις σοφοῖς, τάχ᾿ ἂν αἰσχύνοιο αὐτούς, εἴ τι ἴσως
οἴοιο αἰσχρὸν ὂν ποιεῖν· ἢ πῶς λέγεις;'
'ἀληθῆ λέγεις,' φάναι.
'τοὺς δὲ πολλοὺς οὐκ ἂν αἰσχύνοιο εἴ τι οἴοιο αἰσχρὸν
ποιεῖν;'   10
καὶ τὸν Φαῖδρον ἔφη ὑπολαβόντα εἰπεῖν ' ὦ φίλε   d
Ἀγάθων, ἐὰν ἀποκρίνῃ Σωκράτει, οὐδὲν ἔτι διοίσει αὐτῷ
ὁπῃοῦν τῶν ἐνθάδε ὁτιοῦν γίγνεσθαι, ἐὰν μόνον ἔχῃ ὅτῳ
διαλέγηται, ἄλλως τε καὶ καλῷ. ἐγὼ δὲ ἡδέως μὲν ἀκούω
Σωκράτους διαλεγομένου, ἀναγκαῖον δέ μοι ἐπιμεληθῆναι   5
τοῦ ἐγκωμίου τῷ Ἔρωτι καὶ ἀποδέξασθαι παρ᾿ ἑνὸς ἑκάστου
ὑμῶν τὸν λόγον· ἀποδοὺς οὖν ἑκάτερος τῷ θεῷ οὕτως ἤδη
διαλεγέσθω.'
'ἀλλὰ καλῶς λέγεις, ὦ Φαῖδρε,' φάναι τὸν Ἀγάθωνα,   e
'καὶ οὐδέν με κωλύει λέγειν· Σωκράτει γὰρ καὶ αὖθις ἔσται
πολλάκις διαλέγεσθαι.'

Agathon speaks, describing Love (Eros) himself. Socrates follows, first defining an encomium and then refuting Agathon's speech.

'καὶ σὲ μέν γε ἤδη ἐάσω· τὸν δὲ λόγον τὸν περὶ τοῦ   201d
Ἔρωτος, ὅν ποτ᾽ ἤκουσα γυναικὸς Μαντινικῆς Διοτίμας, ἣ
ταῦτά τε σοφὴ ἦν καὶ ἄλλα πολλά – καὶ Ἀθηναίοις ποτὲ
θυσαμένοις πρὸ τοῦ λοιμοῦ δέκα ἔτη ἀναβολὴν ἐποίησε τῆς
νόσου, ἣ δὴ καὶ ἐμὲ τὰ ἐρωτικὰ ἐδίδαξεν— ὃν οὖν ἐκείνη   5
ἔλεγε λόγον, πειράσομαι ὑμῖν διελθεῖν ἐκ τῶν ὡμολογημένων ἐμοὶ καὶ Ἀγάθωνι, αὐτὸς ἀπ᾽ ἐμαυτοῦ, ὅπως ἂν
δύνωμαι. δεῖ δή, ὦ Ἀγάθων, ὥσπερ σὺ διηγήσω, διελθεῖν
αὐτὸν πρῶτον, τίς ἐστιν ὁ Ἔρως καὶ ποῖός τις, ἔπειτα τὰ   e
ἔργα αὐτοῦ. δοκεῖ οὖν μοι ῥᾷστον εἶναι οὕτω διελθεῖν, ὡς
ποτέ με ἡ ξένη ἀνακρίνουσα διῄει. σχεδὸν γάρ τι καὶ ἐγὼ
πρὸς αὐτὴν ἕτερα τοιαῦτα ἔλεγον οἷάπερ νῦν πρὸς ἐμὲ
Ἀγάθων, ὡς εἴη ὁ Ἔρως μέγας θεός, εἴη δὲ τῶν καλῶν·   5
ἤλεγχε δή με τούτοις τοῖς λόγοις οἷσπερ ἐγὼ τοῦτον, ὡς
οὔτε καλὸς εἴη κατὰ τὸν ἐμὸν λόγον οὔτε ἀγαθός.
καὶ ἐγώ, "πῶς λέγεις," ἔφην, "ὦ Διοτίμα; αἰσχρὸς ἄρα ὁ
Ἔρως ἐστὶ καὶ κακός;"
καὶ ἥ, "οὐκ εὐφημήσεις;" ἔφη· "ἢ οἴει, ὅτι ἂν μὴ καλὸν   10
ᾖ, ἀναγκαῖον αὐτὸ εἶναι αἰσχρόν;"
"μάλιστά γε."   202a
"ἢ καὶ ἂν μὴ σοφόν, ἀμαθές; ἢ οὐκ ᾔσθησαι ὅτι ἔστιν
τι μεταξὺ σοφίας καὶ ἀμαθίας;"
"τί τοῦτο;"
"τὸ ὀρθὰ δοξάζειν καὶ ἄνευ τοῦ ἔχειν λόγον δοῦναι οὐκ   5
οἶσθ᾽," ἔφη, "ὅτι οὔτε ἐπίστασθαί ἐστιν (ἄλογον γὰρ
πρᾶγμα πῶς ἂν εἴη ἐπιστήμη;) οὔτε ἀμαθία (τὸ γὰρ τοῦ
ὄντος τυγχάνον πῶς ἂν εἴη ἀμαθία;) ἔστι δὲ δή που
τοιοῦτον ἡ ὀρθὴ δόξα, μεταξὺ φρονήσεως καὶ ἀμαθίας."
"ἀληθῆ," ἦν δ᾽ ἐγώ, "λέγεις."   10
"μὴ τοίνυν ἀνάγκαζε ὃ μὴ καλόν ἐστιν αἰσχρὸν εἶναι,   b
μηδὲ ὃ μὴ ἀγαθόν, κακόν. οὕτω δὲ καὶ τὸν Ἔρωτα ἐπειδὴ
αὐτὸς ὁμολογεῖς μὴ εἶναι ἀγαθὸν μηδὲ καλόν, μηδέν τι
μᾶλλον οἴου δεῖν αὐτὸν αἰσχρὸν καὶ κακὸν εἶναι, ἀλλά τι
μεταξύ," ἔφη, "τούτοιν."   5
"καὶ μήν," ἦν δ᾽ ἐγώ, "ὁμολογεῖταί γε παρὰ πάντων μέγας
θεὸς εἶναι;"
"τῶν μὴ εἰδότων," ἔφη, "πάντων λέγεις, ἢ καὶ τῶν εἰδότων;"

"συμπάντων μὲν οὖν."

καὶ ἡ γελάσασα· "καὶ πῶς ἄν," ἔφη, "ὦ Σώκρατες,   10

ὁμολογοῖτο μέγας θεὸς εἶναι παρὰ τούτων, οἵ φασιν αὐτὸν   c

οὐδὲ θεὸν εἶναι;"

"τίνες οὗτοι;" ἦν δ᾽ ἐγώ.

"εἷς μέν," ἔφη, "σύ, μία δ᾽ ἐγώ."

κἀγὼ εἶπον, "πῶς τοῦτο," ἔφην, "λέγεις;"   5

καὶ ἥ, "ῥᾳδίως," ἔφη. "λέγε γάρ μοι, οὐ πάντας θεοὺς

φὴς εὐδαίμονας εἶναι καὶ καλούς; ἢ τολμήσαις ἄν τινα μὴ

φάναι καλόν τε καὶ εὐδαίμονα θεῶν εἶναι;"

"μὰ Δί᾽ οὐκ ἔγωγ᾽," ἔφην.

"εὐδαίμονας δὲ δὴ λέγεις οὐ τοὺς τἀγαθὰ καὶ τὰ καλὰ   10

κεκτημένους;"

"πάνυ γε."

"ἀλλὰ μὴν Ἔρωτά γε ὡμολόγηκας δι᾽ ἔνδειαν τῶν   d

ἀγαθῶν καὶ καλῶν ἐπιθυμεῖν αὐτῶν τούτων ὧν ἐνδεής

ἐστιν."

"ὡμολόγηκα γάρ."

"πῶς ἂν οὖν θεὸς εἴη ὅ γε τῶν καλῶν καὶ ἀγαθῶν ἄμοιρος;"   5

"οὐδαμῶς, ὥς γ᾽ ἔοικεν."

"ὁρᾷς οὖν," ἔφη, "ὅτι καὶ σὺ ἔρωτα οὐ θεὸν νομίζεις;"

"τί οὖν ἄν," ἔφην, "εἴη ὁ Ἔρως; θνητός;"

"ἥκιστά γε."

"ἀλλὰ τί μήν;"   10

"ὥσπερ τὰ πρότερα," ἔφη, "μεταξὺ θνητοῦ καὶ ἀθανάτου."

"τί οὖν, ὦ Διοτίμα;"

"δαίμων μέγας, ὦ Σώκρατες· καὶ γὰρ πᾶν τὸ δαιμόνιον

μεταξύ ἐστι θεοῦ τε καὶ θνητοῦ."   e

"τίνα," ἦν δ᾽ ἐγώ, "δύναμιν ἔχον;"

"ἑρμηνεῦον καὶ διαπορθμεῦον θεοῖς τὰ παρ᾽ ἀνθρώπων

καὶ ἀνθρώποις τὰ παρὰ θεῶν, τῶν μὲν τὰς δεήσεις καὶ

θυσίας, τῶν δὲ τὰς ἐπιτάξεις τε καὶ ἀμοιβὰς τῶν θυσιῶν,   5

ἐν μέσῳ δὲ ὂν ἀμφοτέρων συμπληροῖ, ὥστε τὸ πᾶν αὐτὸ

αὑτῷ συνδεδέσθαι. διὰ τούτου καὶ ἡ μαντικὴ πᾶσα χωρεῖ

καὶ ἡ τῶν ἱερέων τέχνη τῶν τε περὶ τὰς θυσίας καὶ τελετὰς

καὶ τὰς ἐπῳδὰς καὶ τὴν μαντείαν πᾶσαν καὶ γοητείαν. θεὸς   203a

δὲ ἀνθρώπῳ οὐ μίγνυται, ἀλλὰ διὰ τούτου πᾶσά ἐστιν ἡ

ὁμιλία καὶ ἡ διάλεκτος θεοῖς πρὸς ἀνθρώπους, καὶ ἐγρη-

γορόσι καὶ καθεύδουσι· καὶ ὁ μὲν περὶ τὰ τοιαῦτα σοφὸς

δαιμόνιος ἀνήρ, ὁ δὲ ἄλλο τι σοφὸς ὢν ἢ περὶ τέχνας ἢ   5

χειρουργίας τινὰς βάναυσος. οὗτοι δὴ οἱ δαίμονες πολλοὶ
καὶ παντοδαποί εἰσιν, εἷς δὲ τούτων ἐστὶ καὶ ὁ Ἔρως."
"πατρὸς δέ," ἦν δ᾽ ἐγώ, "τίνος ἐστὶ καὶ μητρός;"
"μακρότερον μέν," ἔφη, "διηγήσασθαι· ὅμως δέ σοι ἐρῶ.   b
ὅτε γὰρ ἐγένετο ἡ Ἀφροδίτη, ἡστιῶντο οἱ θεοὶ οἵ τε ἄλλοι
καὶ ὁ τῆς Μήτιδος ὑὸς Πόρος. ἐπειδὴ δὲ ἐδείπνησαν,
προσαιτήσουσα οἷον δὴ εὐωχίας οὔσης ἀφίκετο ἡ Πενία, καὶ
ἦν περὶ τὰς θύρας. ὁ οὖν Πόρος μεθυσθεὶς τοῦ νέκταρος   5
– οἶνος γὰρ οὔπω ἦν – εἰς τὸν τοῦ Διὸς κῆπον εἰσελθὼν
βεβαρημένος ηὗδεν. ἡ οὖν Πενία ἐπιβουλεύουσα διὰ τὴν
αὑτῆς ἀπορίαν παιδίον ποιήσασθαι ἐκ τοῦ Πόρου, κατακλίνεταί τε παρ᾽ αὐτῷ καὶ ἐκύησε τὸν ἔρωτα. διὸ δὴ καὶ   c
τῆς Ἀφροδίτης ἀκόλουθος καὶ θεράπων γέγονεν ὁ Ἔρως,
γεννηθεὶς ἐν τοῖς ἐκείνης γενεθλίοις, καὶ ἅμα φύσει ἐραστὴς ὢν περὶ τὸ καλὸν καὶ τῆς Ἀφροδίτης καλῆς οὔσης.
ἅτε οὖν Πόρου καὶ Πενίας ὑὸς ὢν ὁ Ἔρως ἐν τοιαύτῃ τύχῃ   5
καθέστηκεν. πρῶτον μὲν πένης ἀεί ἐστι, καὶ πολλοῦ δεῖ
ἁπαλός τε καὶ καλός, οἷον οἱ πολλοὶ οἴονται, ἀλλὰ σκληρὸς
καὶ αὐχμηρὸς καὶ ἀνυπόδητος καὶ ἄοικος, χαμαιπετὴς ἀεὶ   d
ὢν καὶ ἄστρωτος, ἐπὶ θύραις καὶ ἐν ὁδοῖς ὑπαίθριος κοιμώμενος, τὴν τῆς μητρὸς φύσιν ἔχων, ἀεὶ ἐνδείᾳ σύνοικος.
κατὰ δὲ αὖ τὸν πατέρα ἐπίβουλός ἐστι τοῖς καλοῖς καὶ τοῖς
ἀγαθοῖς, ἀνδρεῖος ὢν καὶ ἴτης καὶ σύντονος, θηρευτὴς   5
δεινός, ἀεί τινας πλέκων μηχανάς, καὶ φρονήσεως ἐπιθυμητὴς καὶ πόριμος, φιλοσοφῶν διὰ παντὸς τοῦ βίου,
δεινὸς γόης καὶ φαρμακεὺς καὶ σοφιστής· καὶ οὔτε ὡς
ἀθάνατος πέφυκεν οὔτε ὡς θνητός, ἀλλὰ τοτὲ μὲν τῆς αὐτῆς e
ἡμέρας θάλλει τε καὶ ζῇ, ὅταν εὐπορήσῃ, τοτὲ δὲ ἀποθνή-
σκει, πάλιν δὲ ἀναβιώσκεται διὰ τὴν τοῦ πατρὸς φύσιν, τὸ
δὲ ποριζόμενον ἀεὶ ὑπεκρεῖ· ὥστε οὔτε ἀπορεῖ Ἔρως ποτὲ
οὔτε πλουτεῖ, σοφίας τε αὖ καὶ ἀμαθίας ἐν μέσῳ ἐστίν.   5
ἔχει γὰρ ὧδε. θεῶν οὐδεὶς φιλοσοφεῖ οὐδ᾽ ἐπιθυμεῖ σοφὸς   204a
γενέσθαι· ἔστι γάρ· οὐδ᾽ εἴ τις ἄλλος σοφός, οὐ φιλοσοφεῖ.
οὐδ᾽ αὖ οἱ ἀμαθεῖς φιλοσοφοῦσιν οὐδ᾽ ἐπιθυμοῦσι σοφοὶ
γενέσθαι· αὐτὸ γὰρ τοῦτό ἐστι χαλεπὸν ἀμαθία, τὸ μὴ
ὄντα καλὸν κἀγαθὸν μηδὲ φρόνιμον δοκεῖν αὑτῷ εἶναι   5
ἱκανόν· οὔκουν ἐπιθυμεῖ ὁ μὴ οἰόμενος ἐνδεὴς εἶναι οὗ ἂν
μὴ οἴηται ἐπιδεῖσθαι."
"τίνες οὖν," ἔφην ἐγώ, "ὦ Διοτίμα, οἱ φιλοσοφοῦντες,
εἰ μήτε οἱ σοφοὶ μήτε οἱ ἀμαθεῖς;"

A
Level

"δῆλον δή," ἔφη, "τοῦτό γε ἤδη καὶ παιδί, ὅτι οἱ μεταξὺ   b
τούτων ἀμφοτέρων, ὧν ἂν εἴη καὶ ὁ Ἔρως. ἔστι γὰρ δὴ τῶν
καλλίστων ἡ σοφία, Ἔρως δ᾽ ἐστὶν ἔρως περὶ τὸ καλόν,
ὥστε ἀναγκαῖον Ἔρωτα φιλόσοφον εἶναι, φιλόσοφον δὲ
ὄντα μεταξὺ εἶναι σοφοῦ καὶ ἀμαθοῦς. αἰτία δὲ αὐτῷ καὶ   5
τούτων ἡ γένεσις· πατρὸς μὲν γὰρ σοφοῦ ἐστί καὶ εὐπόρου,
μητρὸς δὲ οὐ σοφῆς καὶ ἀπόρου· ἡ μὲν οὖν φύσις τοῦ
δαίμονος, ὦ φίλε Σώκρατες, αὕτη· ὃν δὲ σὺ ᾠήθης Ἔρωτα
εἶναι, θαυμαστὸν οὐδὲν ἔπαθες. ᾠήθης δέ, ὡς ἐμοὶ δοκεῖ   c
τεκμαιρομένη ἐξ ὧν σὺ λέγεις, τὸ ἐρώμενον Ἔρωτα εἶναι,
οὐ τὸ ἐρῶν· διὰ ταῦτά σοι οἶμαι πάγκαλος ἐφαίνετο ὁ
Ἔρως. καὶ γὰρ ἔστι τὸ ἐραστὸν τὸ τῷ ὄντι καλὸν καὶ
ἁβρὸν καὶ τέλεον καὶ μακαριστόν· τὸ δέ γε ἐρῶν ἄλλην   5
ἰδέαν τοιαύτην ἔχον, οἵαν ἐγὼ διῆλθον."
καὶ ἐγὼ εἶπον· "εἶεν δή, ὦ ξένη· καλῶς γὰρ λέγεις·
τοιοῦτος ὢν ὁ Ἔρως τίνα χρείαν ἔχει τοῖς ἀνθρώποις;"
"τοῦτο δὴ μετὰ ταῦτ᾽," ἔφη, "ὦ Σώκρατες, πειράσομαί σε   d
διδάξαι. ἔστι μὲν γὰρ δὴ τοιοῦτος καὶ οὕτω γεγονὼς ὁ
Ἔρως, ἔστι δὲ τῶν καλῶν, ὡς σὺ φῄς. εἰ δέ τις ἡμᾶς
ἔροιτο· τί τῶν καλῶν ἐστιν ὁ Ἔρως, ὦ Σώκρατές τε
καὶ Διοτίμα; ὧδε δὲ σαφέστερον. ἐρᾷ ὁ ἐρῶν τῶν καλῶν·   5
τί ἐρᾷ;"
καὶ ἐγὼ εἶπον ὅτι "γενέσθαι αὑτῷ."
"ἀλλ᾽ ἔτι ποθεῖ," ἔφη, "ἡ ἀπόκρισις ἐρώτησιν τοιάνδε· τί
ἔσται ἐκείνῳ ᾧ ἂν γένηται τὰ καλά;"
οὐ πάνυ ἔφην ἔτι ἔχειν ἐγὼ πρὸς ταύτην τὴν ἐρώτησιν   10
προχείρως ἀποκρίνασθαι.
"ἀλλ᾽," ἔφη, "ὥσπερ ἂν εἴ τις μεταβαλὼν ἀντὶ τοῦ καλοῦ   e
τῷ ἀγαθῷ χρώμενος πυνθάνοιτο 'φέρε, ὦ Σώκρατες, ἐρᾷ ὁ
ἐρῶν τῶν ἀγαθῶν· τί ἐρᾷ;'
"γενέσθαι," ἦν δ᾽ ἐγώ, "αὑτῷ."
"καὶ τί ἔσται ἐκείνῳ ᾧ ἂν γένηται τἀγαθά;"   5
"τοῦτ᾽ εὐπορώτερον," ἦν δ᾽ ἐγώ, "ἔχω ἀποκρίνασθαι, ὅτι
εὐδαίμων ἔσται."
"κτήσει γάρ," ἔφη, "ἀγαθῶν οἱ εὐδαίμονες εὐδαίμονες, καὶ   205a
οὐκέτι προσδεῖ ἐρέσθαι ἵνα τί δὲ βούλεται εὐδαίμων εἶναι
ὁ βουλόμενος, ἀλλὰ τέλος δοκεῖ ἔχειν ἡ ἀπόκρισις."
"ἀληθῆ λέγεις," εἶπον ἐγώ.
"ταύτην δὴ τὴν βούλησιν καὶ τὸν ἔρωτα τοῦτον πότερα   5
κοινὸν οἴει εἶναι πάντων ἀνθρώπων, καὶ πάντας τἀγαθὰ

A
Level

βούλεσθαι αὐτοῖς εἶναι ἀεί, ἢ πῶς λέγεις;"

"οὕτως," ἦν δ᾽ ἐγώ, "κοινὸν εἶναι πάντων."

"τί δὴ οὖν," ἔφη, "ὦ Σώκρατες, οὐ πάντας ἐρᾶν φαμέν,

εἴπερ γε πάντες τῶν αὐτῶν ἐρῶσι καὶ ἀεί, ἀλλά τινάς φαμεν   b

ἐρᾶν, τοὺς δ᾽ οὔ;"

"θαυμάζω," ἦν δ᾽ ἐγώ, "καὶ αὐτός."

"ἀλλὰ μὴ θαύμαζ᾽," ἔφη, "ἀφελόντες γὰρ ἄρα τοῦ ἔρωτός

τι εἶδος ὀνομάζομεν, τὸ τοῦ ὅλου ἐπιτιθέντες ὄνομα, ἔρωτα,   5

τὰ δὲ ἄλλα ἄλλοις καταχρώμεθα ὀνόμασιν."

"ὥσπερ τί;" ἦν δ᾽ ἐγώ.

"ὥσπερ τόδε, οἶσθ᾽ ὅτι ποίησίς ἐστί τι πολύ· ἡ γὰρ

τοι ἐκ τοῦ μὴ ὄντος εἰς τὸ ὂν ἰόντι ὁτῳοῦν αἰτία πᾶσά ἐστι

ποίησις, ὥστε καὶ αἱ ὑπὸ πάσαις ταῖς τέχναις ἐργασίαι   c

ποιήσεις εἰσὶ καὶ οἱ τούτων δημιουργοὶ πάντες ποιηταί."

"ἀληθῆ λέγεις."

"ἀλλ᾽ ὅμως," ἦ δ᾽ ἥ, "οἶσθ᾽ ὅτι οὐ καλοῦνται ποιηταὶ ἀλλὰ

ἄλλα ἔχουσιν ὀνόματα, ἀπὸ δὲ πάσης τῆς ποιήσεως ἓν   5

μόριον ἀφορισθὲν τὸ περὶ τὴν μουσικὴν καὶ τὰ μέτρα τῷ

τοῦ ὅλου ὀνόματι προσαγορεύεται. ποίησις γὰρ τοῦτο

μόνον καλεῖται, καὶ οἱ ἔχοντες τοῦτο τὸ μόριον τῆς ποιήσεως

ποιηταί."

"ἀληθῆ λέγεις," ἔφην.   10

"οὕτω τοίνυν καὶ περὶ τὸν ἔρωτα· τὸ μὲν κεφάλαιόν ἐστι   d

πᾶσα ἡ τῶν ἀγαθῶν ἐπιθυμία καὶ τοῦ εὐδαιμονεῖν, ὁ μέ-

γιστός τε καὶ δολερὸς ἔρως παντί· ἀλλ᾽ οἱ μὲν ἄλλῃ

τρεπόμενοι πολλαχῇ ἐπ᾽ αὐτόν, ἢ κατὰ χρηματισμὸν ἢ κατὰ

φιλογυμναστίαν ἢ κατὰ φιλοσοφίαν, οὔτε ἐρᾶν καλοῦνται   5

οὔτ᾽ ἐρασταί, οἱ δὲ κατὰ ἕν τι εἶδος ἰόντες τε καὶ ἐσπου-

δακότες τὸ τοῦ ὅλου ὄνομα ἴσχουσιν, ἔρωτά τε καὶ ἐρᾶν καὶ

ἐρασταί."

"κινδυνεύεις ἀληθῆ," ἔφην ἐγώ, "λέγειν."

"καὶ λέγεται μέν γέ τις," ἔφη, "λόγος, ὡς οἳ ἂν τὸ ἥμισυ   10

ἑαυτῶν ζητῶσιν, οὗτοι ἐρῶσιν· ὁ δ᾽ ἐμὸς λόγος οὔτε ἡμίσεός   e

φησιν εἶναι τὸν ἔρωτα οὔτε ὅλου, ἐὰν μὴ τυγχάνῃ γέ που,

ὦ ἑταῖρε, ἀγαθὸν ὄν· ἐπεὶ αὑτῶν γε καὶ πόδας καὶ χεῖρας

ἐθέλουσιν ἀποτέμνεσθαι οἱ ἄνθρωποι, ἐὰν αὐτοῖς δοκῇ τὰ

ἑαυτῶν πονηρὰ εἶναι. οὐ γὰρ τὸ ἑαυτῶν οἶμαι ἕκαστοι   5

ἀσπάζονται, εἰ μὴ εἴ τις τὸ μὲν ἀγαθὸν οἰκεῖον καλεῖ καὶ

ἑαυτοῦ, τὸ δὲ κακὸν ἀλλότριον· ὡς οὐδέν γε ἄλλο ἐστὶν οὗ

ἐρῶσιν ἄνθρωποι ἢ τοῦ ἀγαθοῦ. ἢ σοὶ δοκοῦσιν;"   206a

A
Level

"μὰ Δί᾽ οὐκ ἔμοιγε," ἦν δ᾽ ἐγώ.
"ἆρ᾽ οὖν," ἦ δ᾽ ἥ, "οὕτως ἁπλοῦν ἐστι λέγειν ὅτι οἱ
ἄνθρωποι τἀγαθοῦ ἐρῶσιν;"
"ναί," ἔφην.   5
"τί δέ; οὐ προσθετέον," ἔφη, "ὅτι καὶ εἶναι τὸ ἀγαθὸν
αὑτοῖς ἐρῶσιν;"
"προσθετέον."
"ἆρ᾽ οὖν," ἔφη, "καὶ οὐ μόνον εἶναι, ἀλλὰ καὶ ἀεὶ
εἶναι;"
"καὶ τοῦτο προσθετέον."   10
"ἔστιν ἄρα συλλήβδην," ἔφη, "ὁ ἔρως τοῦ τὸ ἀγαθὸν αὑτῷ
εἶναι ἀεί."
"ἀληθέστατα," ἔφην ἐγώ, "λέγεις."
"ὅτε δὴ τοῦτο ὁ ἔρως ἐστὶν ἀεί," ἦ δ᾽ ἥ, "τῶν τίνα τρόπον   b
διωκόντων αὐτὸ καὶ ἐν τίνι πράξει ἡ σπουδὴ καὶ ἡ σύντασις
ἔρως ἂν καλοῖτο; τί τοῦτο τυγχάνει ὂν τὸ ἔργον; ἔχεις
εἰπεῖν;"
"οὐ μεντἂν σέ," ἔφην ἐγώ, "ὦ Διοτίμα, ἐθαύμαζον ἐπὶ   5
σοφίᾳ καὶ ἐφοίτων παρὰ σὲ αὐτὰ ταῦτα μαθησόμενος."
"ἀλλ᾽ ἐγώ σοι," ἔφη, "ἐρῶ. ἔστι γὰρ τοῦτο τόκος ἐν
καλῷ καὶ κατὰ τὸ σῶμα καὶ κατὰ τὴν ψυχήν."
"μαντείας," ἦν δ᾽ ἐγώ, "δεῖται ὅτι ποτε λέγεις, καὶ οὐ
μανθάνω."   10

Commentary Notes

189c2–193e2: Aristophanes' speech

Aristophanes' speech is the fourth speech reported in this work, after Phaedrus, Pausanias and Eryximachus. He promises at the beginning of his speech (189c2) that he is going to approach the praise of Eros in a different way to the previous speeches: he doesn't pick up on the genealogies of Eros, or the distinction of a heavenly/earthly Eros, or the idea of Eros as a universal force which moderates or unbalances all the processes of the world. Instead he says that he is going to reveal how powerful Eros is, and he gives a story about human development, a (pseudo?) aetiology of human physical characteristics, sexuality and love.

One of the issues for the reader is to decide how serious Aristophanes is. He prefaces his speech (189b6) saying that to be amusing (γελοῖα) would be an advantage, but he is afraid of being laughed at (καταγέλαστα), and at 193b6 he tells Eryximachus not to treat what he is saying as funny. The reader will have to decide whether to accept this at face value, or treat it as mock-solemnity designed to make a satire funnier. His references to Eros as healer, the way that his dual humans appear to caricature some of the 'scientific' thinking of the time, and the contrived hiccups which forced him to speak after Eryximachus, may suggest that this speech is partly an extended mockery of Eryximachus. More broadly, the fantastical nature of the aetiology, and occasional jokes about individuals and politicians certainly seem consistent with the comedy we know from his plays.

But this speech does tackle some serious ideas. It recognizes different forms of sexual attraction and that societal norms and individual desires aren't necessarily aligned. Above all, Aristophanes suggests that Eros is a desire for wholeness: that sometimes one can meet another person who seems a perfect complement to you. In those circumstances, we seek 'oneness' with that person as far as we can – and that Love is not to be valued as a benefit to society, but as an end in itself which brings the truest human happiness (compare these ideas to modern expressions like 'my other half' and, from the Christian marriage service, 'the two become one flesh'). To the modern reader, this is perhaps simultaneously the most absurd speech, and the one that most closely mirrors how we talk about love.

189c2-d4 Introduction

Aristophanes begins from the idea that people underestimate the power of Eros, for as the god who cures mankind's greatest ills and brings us happiness, he should be worshipped with great temples and altars.

189c

καὶ μήν ... ἄλλη γέ πη: 'well, yes indeed ... in some other way'; picking up Eryximachus in 188e 'you may be planning a quite different kind of eulogy of the god'. Aristophanes will be different in style, content and entertainment, and his speech will mock the pompous manner and pretentious content of Eryximachus in particular.

εἰπεῖν τὸν Ἀριστοφάνη: 'Aristophanes said'. Indirect statement (accusative + infinitive) – the whole story of the party is an account given by Apollodorus to an unnamed companion (direct speech). But his account is what Aristodemus had told him so the events are in indirect speech. The speeches are in direct speech, i.e. the full version of this: (Apollodorus speaking) 'Aristodemus told me that Aristophanes said'. Also at 193e3; 194a1; 194a5; 194a9; 194b6; 194c1; 194c8.

ἢ ἧ: 'than (the way) in which'.

εἰπέτην: 3rd person dual ending, aorist indicative active, in place of the more logical 2nd person dual (εἴπετον) that one would expect.

ἐμοὶ γὰρ δοκοῦσιν ἄνθρωποι: literally 'for men seem to me' – 'I think that men'. The promotion of ἐμοὶ seems to emphasize that this is his own opinion, one that he doesn't see widely shared. ἄνθρωποι is a crasis of οἱ ἄνθρωποι.

ᾐσθῆσθαι: perfect middle infinitive – 'to have appreciated'.

αἰσθανόμενοί γε: 'if they *did* appreciate it' – present participle acting as protasis in present/past counterfactual condition.

ἂν ... κατασκευάσαι: infinitive following δοκοῦσιν; apodosis of past counterfactual condition – '(I think that) they would have built'.

αὐτου: here, and frequently in the next few sentences, referring to Love.

ἂν ποιεῖν: 2nd (parallel) apodosis following δοκοῦσιν, now with present infinitive – 'they would now make'.

οὐχ ὥσπερ νῦν: literally 'not in the way in which now' – 'whereas now'.

περὶ αὐτόν: περὶ + accusative – 'in the case of him'.

δέον: present participle in accusative absolute (like a genitive absolute, but for impersonal verbs), with concessive force – 'although it should happen most of all'.

189d

ὤν: present participle ('being') giving an explanation – 'for he is'.

ἰατρὸς τούτων: it is hard to hear ἰατρός without thinking of Eryximachus, the doctor, with whom Aristophanes has had some playful banter. The claim that Eros's acts of healing actually contribute to human happiness may be a dig at Eryximachus.

ὧν ἰαθέντων: genitive absolute (aorist passive participle) with relative pronoun (antecedent τούτων), acting as the protasis of a future remote condition – '(of those things) which if they were cured'.

AS

ἂν ... εἴη: apodosis of the future remote condition – 'there would be'. However, while technically a future remote condition, Aristophanes is arguing that Eros should be recognized for the great benefits he *does* already bring to humans, so it must be translated more like 'he is the healer of those things, the healing of which brings the greatest happiness to the human race'.

189d5–191d1 The story of humans

Humans originally had three genders, and were whole people, with double the number of faces and limbs as now. Being very powerful, they threatened the gods, and so Zeus split them in half to weaken them and had them sown-up at the navel where they had been cut. But these new 'halves' pined so much for their other halves that they did nothing and began to die out. Therefore Zeus had their genitalia moved to their new fronts to make sexual union possible, providing a means of satisfaction as well as procreation.

This aetiology has a number of elements typical of this type of story: it starts 'in the beginning', it contains ridiculous explanations (descent from sun, earth and moon explains three genders), it describes uninspiring gods (motivated to act out of fear and desire for more honours) and claims even trivial things as supporting evidence (e.g. wrinkles on stomachs).

ἐγὼ οὖν πειράσομαι: picking up (and possibly parodying) the language of Phaedrus (180d) and Eryximachus (186a).

ὑμεῖς δὲ: here with the sense of 'you in turn'.

τῶν ἄλλων: just 'others' (rather than 'the others').

τὰ παθήματα αὐτῆς: literally 'the sufferings of it' – 'what has happened to it'.

αὐτή: a crasis of ἡ αὐτὴ 'the same', picked up by ἥπερ 'as', and contrasted with ἀλλοία 'different'.

τὰ γένη: 'types'; it soon becomes clear that this means 'sexes/genders'.

ἄρρεν καὶ θῆλυ: both neuter accusative, in apposition to τὰ γένη and more specifically explaining the δύο.

189e

καί: as often, used here adverbially ('also') to emphasize the next word.

τρίτον: understand γένος.

κοινὸν ὄν: literally 'being shared in by' + genitive – 'which had elements in common with both of these'.

οὗ: the antecedent is the τρίτον (γένος).

ὄνομα λοιπόν: supply ἐστί.

ἠφάνισται: perfect passive – 'has disappeared' – the perfect tense emphasizing that this is also the present state. This is set against λοιπόν (ἐστί) just as οὐ ... ὄνομα is set against αὐτὸ δὲ – 'the name of which ..., but it itself'.

τότε μὲν ... νῦν δὲ: the contrast is between the original times when the 'androgynous' was a distinct sex and the time of the party when it is nothing but a name and one used only for abuse, denoting an effeminate man. One can't hear this without thinking of the effeminate host of the party, Agathon.

ἓν: 'one sex/type' – understand γένος. This 'one' is the third sex/type mentioned at 189e1.

καὶ εἶδος καὶ ὄνομα: take these as accusatives of respect – '(androgynous) both in its form and its name'.

ἐξ ἀμφοτέρων κοινὸν τοῦ τε ἄρρενος καὶ θήλεος: 'a combination of both the male and the female'. κοινὸν agrees with ἕν.

ἀλλ᾽ ἤ: 'other than' or 'except' (after negatives).

ἐν ὀνείδει . . . κείμενον: 'used as an insult'.

ἔπειτα: 'secondly' picks up from πρῶτον μὲν in 189d7. It seems as though the being described here (contrary to many re-imaginings) had two backs on the outside, and no visible chest or belly. Its limbs (four arms, four legs) came out of the sides, there was one head on top with two faces, each face looking outwards above a back, and genitals on the outside (where the buttocks are now).

ὅλον ἦν ἑκάστου τοῦ ἀνθρώπου τὸ εἶδος στρογγύλον: ὅλον and στρογγύλον are adjectives describing the original form of humans – 'the form of each human was both whole and round'.

τὰ ἴσα: 'the same number as' + dative.

νῶτον καὶ πλευρὰς . . . χεῖρας . . . σκέλη . . . πρόσωπα . . . κεφαλὴν . . . ὦτα . . . αἰδοῖα: notice how the body part comes first in the clause each time: Aristophanes takes us to the part and then tells us how it was set up in this original being. From χεῖρας, these are all objects of εἶχε.

190a

ἐπ᾽ αὐχένι κυκλοτερεῖ: 'on a cylindrical neck'.

ὅμοια πάντῃ: 'alike in every way'. This helps to emphasize the 'oneness' of this original human, but it is not clear if it means that the two faces actually look identical. This would seem to present a problem in the later idea of searching for one's original other half, for there are no two people (excepting twins) who look exactly alike and we are not attracted necessarily to those who look identical to us.

ἐπ᾽ ἀμφοτέροις τοῖς προσώποις ἐναντίοις κειμένοις: 'for the two faces facing in different directions'.

ὡς ἀπὸ τούτων ἄν τις εἰκάσειεν: 'as someone would imagine/infer from these things'. εἰκάσειεν (aorist optative active) + ἄν – a potential optative.

ὀρθὸν: 'upright'. The subject is still the 'one androgynous sex/form'.

ὁποτέρωσε βουληθείη: literally 'in whichever direction (of two directions faced) it wished' – aorist optative for an indefinite (-ever) clause (historic sequence).

ὁρμήσειεν: aorist optative for indefinite. ὁρμάω + infinitive – 'start eagerly to'.

ὥσπερ οἱ κυβιστῶντες . . . κύκλῳ: literally 'just as those tumbling and bringing their limbs around (sticking) straight out, actually tumble in a circle'. Translate as 'just as acrobats perform tumbles, bringing their limbs round in a circle'. Think of the linked somersaults and cartwheels (tumbles) that modern gymnasts perform in a floor routine.

ὀκτὼ τότε οὖσι τοῖς μέλεσιν: 'on their eight limbs which they had then' (οὖσι is dative plural present participle, literally 'being').

ἀπερειδόμενοι: present middle participle – 'supporting themselves on' + dative.

ἐφέροντο: 'they used to go'.

διὰ ταῦτα: 'for these reasons'. Looks ahead to ὅτι ('because').

AS

190b

τρία and **τοιαῦτα** both agree with **τὰ γένη**. The explanation will cover both why three genders exist and why they are as they are.

The sun was seen as a male deity; earth as a female deity; the idea of the moon (while a feminine noun) being bisexual also occurs in other later works.

τὴν ἀρχὴν: adverbial accusative – 'at first', 'originally'.

τὸ μὲν ἄρρεν: understand γένος.

τὸ δὲ θῆλυ: understand γένος ἦν ἔκγονον.

τὸ δὲ ἀμφοτέρων μετέχον: again understand γένος ἦν ἔκγονον – 'the gender sharing both (male and female) was the offspring'.

ὅτι: 'because'.

περιφερῆ δὲ δὴ ἦν καὶ αὐτὰ καὶ ἡ πορεία αὐτῶν: the subject is **τὰ γένη** – 'both they themselves and their movement really were circular'. **δὴ** emphasizes the adjective before it.

διὰ τὸ . . . εἶναι: 'on account of (them) being' (articular infinitive).

τὴν ἰσχὺν . . . τὴν ῥώμην: accusatives of respect, the first being purely physical, and the second carrying the idea of confidence in strength.

τὰ φρονήματα μεγάλα: the implication is not just 'great ambition' but 'excessive'.

καὶ ὁ . . . τοῖς θεοῖς: 'the attempt to make an ascent into heaven, to make an attack on the gods, which Homer says about Ephialtes and Otus, is actually talking about those creatures (the whole/double humans)'.

καὶ ὃ λέγει Ὅμηρος περὶ Ἐφιάλτου τε καὶ Ὤτου: Iliad 5.385ff; Odyssey 11.307ff. These two, the tallest men on earth, had once imprisoned Ares for 13 months in a bronze jar, and had planned to make an attempt on the gods in Olympus by piling mountains on top of each other.

τὸ . . . ἐπιχειρεῖν: this noun phrase (articular infinitive) is (in a sense) the antecedent to the relative clause (ὃ λέγει) and the subject of **λέγεται**. Plato is 'interpreting the Homeric passage as a covert or confused allusion to the double humans' (Dover). It is interesting that many accounts of humanity have in common the idea of humans wanting to be gods or replace the gods.

190c

ὡς ἐπιθησομένων τοῖς θεοῖς: ὡς + future participle (of ἐπιτίθημι) for purpose or intention. Genitive case could agree back to **ἐκείνων**, or be a switch to genitive absolute (Dover).

ὅ τι . . . αὐτοὺς ποιῆσαι: 'what (it was necessary) to do with them'. ποιέω + accusative + accusative – 'to do X to Y', or 'to do X with Y'.

οὔτε . . . εἶχον: 'they could not see'. This isn't the physical possibility, but a question of will: they were not willing to do this given the cost.

ὅπως ἀποκτείναιεν . . . ἀφανίσαιεν: indirect question, the optative because historic sequence, the aorist by aspect. The original question was probably a deliberative question in the present subjunctive: 'how might we kill them'.

ὥσπερ τοὺς γίγαντας κεραυνώσαντες: referring to the so-called 'gigantomachy' in Greek mythology, when Zeus and the Olympian gods fought against the giants. A popular theme in Greek art (e.g. east metopes of the Parthenon). The thunderbolt is Zeus' weapon, appropriate for a sky god.

AS

ἠφανίζετο: imperfect indicative for a present counterfactual conditional, ἂν omitted – 'honours etc. would be gone (sc. if the gods did this)'.

ἐῷεν: present optative of ἐάω. This clause is a second indirect question after εἶχον. Understand 'them' as object.

ἀσελγαίνειν: 'to keep behaving outrageously'. The infinitive is present by aspect, giving the sense of repeated action.

μόγις δὴ: is there an element of comedy here over how hard Zeus has to think?

δοκῶ μοι ἔχειν μηχανήν: δοκέω μοι + nominative (omitted) + infinitive – 'I think that I have a scheme/way'.

ὡς ἂν εἶέν τε ἄνθρωποι: a clause after a verb of 'striving'. The ἂν is potential, and Plato uses the optative because the sequence is historic (λέγει is historic present) – 'how mankind might exist'.

190d

γενόμενοι: (instrumental sense of the participle) 'by becoming (weaker)'.

διατεμῶ: epsilon contract future.

ἕκαστον: in apposition to αὐτούς – 'each of them'.

ἅμα μὲν ἀσθενέστεροι ... ἅμα δὲ χρησιμώτεροι: the anaphora and the balancing comparatives show that Zeus believes he has solved his 'catch-22'. The gods look (comically?) greedy. Such a view of the gods is typical of Aristophanic comedy (e.g. Dionysus in Frogs).

διὰ τὸ πλείους τὸν ἀριθμὸν γεγονέναι: τὸ γεγονέναι (perfect active infinitive) makes an accusative noun phrase after δια; πλείους is accusative plural of πλείων, the comparative of πολύς; τὸν ἀριθμὸν is accusative of respect – 'because there will be more of them'.

βαδιοῦνται: epsilon contract future.

ἐπὶ δυοῖν σκελοῖν: dual genitive – 'on two legs'.

ἐὰν ... δοκῶσιν: future open condition – the protasis is two present subjunctives, apodosis is future indicative.

ἀσκωλιάζοντες: 'hopping', with a possible reference to a game involving hopping on greased wineskins and trying to stay upright.

ἔτεμνε τοὺς ἀνθρώπους δίχα: note the triple repeat of this key idea of cutting in two.

τὰ ὄα: small red-brown sorb apples that used to be cut in half and pickled.

190e

ὥσπερ οἱ τὰ ᾠὰ ταῖς θριξίν: understand τεμόντες. This is possible if the egg is hard-boiled and shelled, and was proverbial for doing something with ease. Aristophanic comedy is full of such everyday life.

ὅντινα δὲ τέμοι: indefinite clause in historic sequence – 'whomever he cut (in two)'.

ἵνα θεώμενος ... εἴη ὁ ἄνθρωπος: purpose clause in historic sequence. The participle is causal – 'so that the man would be better behaved because he could see his own bisection'.

τἆλλα ἰᾶσθαι: Apollo has clearly been given the task as the 'healer'. τἆλλα a crasis of τὰ ἄλλα – a catch-all for the other wounds needing fixing, most obviously all the way up the body.

AS

ὁ δὲ: i.e. Apollo. As usual, the δὲ marks the change of subject to someone just mentioned.

τε ... καὶ: echoes the two parts of the instruction.

ἐπὶ τὴν γαστέρα νῦν καλουμένην: 'on to the stomach, as it is now called'.

τὰ σύσπαστα βαλλάντια: 'draw-string purses'.

ἀπέδει: 'he tied it up/off'. This and the following imperfects perhaps reflect the many humans on which Apollo had to operate!

τὸν ὀμφαλὸν: i.e. the belly button.

191a

διήρθρου: 3rd person imperfect indicative active – 'he moulded'. It is not stated here, but it must be understood that Apollo fashioned the chests of the male and female forms differently.

ἔχων: this participle often best translates as 'with'.

οἷον: picks up τοιουτον – 'with some tool like'.

οἱ σκυτοτόμοι: anyone who cuts leather, but here specifically a shoemaker.

περὶ τὸν καλάποδα λεαίνοντες: 'smoothing (the wrinkles) around the cobbler's last'. A cobbler's 'last' is a wooden or metal foot-shaped block around which a cobbler fashions shoes.

ὀλίγας δὲ κατέλιπε: this δὲ contrasts the μὲν (190e9) of the many other wrinkles which Apollo smoothed out.

τὰς περὶ αὐτὴν τὴν γαστέρα καὶ τὸν ὀμφαλόν: this is a sort of comic aetiology for why people have a few (or more!) 'wrinkles', i.e. folds of skin/fat on their stomachs!

μνημεῖον εἶναι: the infinitive carries the sense of purpose after κατέλιπε.

ἐπειδὴ οὖν ἡ φύσις δίχα ἐτμήθη: this marks the end of the description of the 'operation' to cut humans in two. φύσις refers to our original/natural state.

ποθοῦν ἕκαστον τὸ ἥμισυ τὸ αὑτοῦ συνῄει: ποθοῦν is nominative singular neuter of the present participle agreeing with ἕκαστον τὸ ἥμισυ, i.e. literally 'each half, desiring, tried to join with'. But translate as 'each half longed to join with its own other half'. συνέρχομαι also carries a sexual sense, a double entendre appropriate to the context.

ἐπιθυμοῦντες συμφῦναι: note all the συμ- prefixes expressing the desire for togetherness.

191b

ὑπὸ λιμοῦ καὶ τῆς ἄλλης ἀργίας: 'from hunger and general inactivity' (Bury); being unwilling to separate even for a moment, these beings could not grow, find or eat food, or look after any of their other needs. ὑπὸ + genitive is unusual for an abstract cause.

διὰ τὸ ... ἐθέλειν: 'because they were (not) willing'. διὰ + accusative (articular infinitive).

μηδὲν ... ποιεῖν: μηδὲν is the object of ποιεῖν.

καὶ ὁπότε τι ἀποθάνοι τῶν ἡμίσεων, τὸ δὲ λειφθείη: 'whenever one of the halves died and the other was left behind'. An indefinite temporal clause in historic sequence (ὁπότε + optative). τι ... τῶν ἡμίσεων is subject.

τὸ λειφθὲν: article + aorist passive participle – 'the one left behind'.

ἄλλο: must mean 'another', rather than 'the other half' (which was now dead).

εἴτε γυναικὸς τῆς ὅλης ἐντύχοι ἡμίσει ... εἴτε ἀνδρός: 'whether it met with the half of a female whole ... or a male whole'. εἰ + optative for the protasis of a past open (general) condition. ἐντυγχάνω + dative – 'to meet with'. Aristophanes seems to be ignoring the third gender, the 'androgynous whole', perhaps because once it is cut in half, it offers the same two (man/woman) options, just from a different origin.

ὃ δὴ νῦν γυναῖκα καλοῦμεν: the antecedent of the relative is ἡμίσει.

καὶ οὕτως ἀπώλλυντο: imperfect middle – 'they were (in the process of) dying out'. οὕτως describes the state of these beings – they were only interested in embracing the other half, and dying out because they showed no interest in the basics of survival.

ἐλεήσας δὲ ὁ Ζεὺς ἄλλην μηχανὴν πορίζεται: this account of the nature/ creation of man makes humans the result of a series of reactions to circumstances rather than a designed whole. One moment Zeus is afraid of humans, the next he pities them when his 'solution' has gone too far.

καὶ μετατίθησιν: μετα- as a prefix again speaking of change – 'he moved'.

τέως γὰρ καὶ ταῦτα ἐκτὸς εἶχον: 'for up to this point they had these too on the outside'. i.e. until they were cut in two, these were on the outside of the old wholes, along with their faces, etc.

191c

καὶ ἐγέννων καὶ ἔτικτον οὐκ εἰς ἀλλήλους ἀλλ᾽ εἰς γῆν: 'they used to plant seed and procreate not into each other but into the ground'. These two verbs are virtually synonymous here.

ὥσπερ οἱ τέττιγες: Dover tells us that 'cicadas' in fact mate in the normal way, but Plato may have confused them with grasshoppers: the females of some species lay eggs directly into the ground with a hard ovipositor which may have been mistaken for a penis.

μετέθηκέ τε οὖν οὕτω αὐτῶν εἰς τὸ πρόσθεν: Aristophanes repeats the idea of μετατίθησιν after his digression. Understand τα αἰδοῖα with αὐτῶν as before.

καὶ διὰ τούτων τὴν γένεσιν ἐν ἀλλήλοις ἐποίησεν: ἐν ἀλλήλοις is contrasting with the former state of begetting εἰς γῆν.

διὰ τοῦ ἄρρενος ἐν τῷ θήλει: the Greek understanding of reproduction was of the male providing all the (genetic) material and the female merely the 'incubation'.

τῶνδε ἕνεκα: τῶνδε as usual looks forward, to the two reasons given in the purpose clauses. It may be omitted in translation.

ἵνα ... γεννῷεν καὶ γίγνοιτο, ... γίγνοιτο ... διαπαύοιντο ... τρέποιντο ... ἐπιμελοῖντο: a purpose clause in historic sequence with six optatives, all present by aspect (the first involves an alpha contraction), to reflect the general truth of this.

ἐν τῇ συμπλοκῇ: 'in the embrace' – Aristophanes describes one embrace whatever the two constituent members.

ἅμα μὲν εἰ ἀνὴρ γυναικὶ ἐντύχοι ... ἅμα δ᾽ εἰ καὶ ἄρρην ἄρρενι: the two possibilities imagined are a male half (a man) meeting/joining with a female half

AS

(a woman), or a male half (a man) with a male half (a man). Clearly female + female is possible, but this omission perhaps reflects a Greek male's lack of interest in female sexuality!

ἅμα δ᾽ εἰ καὶ: 'and even if'.

πλησμονὴ γοῦν γίγνοιτο τῆς συνουσίας καὶ διαπαύοιντο καὶ ἐπὶ τὰ ἔργα τρέποιντο καὶ τοῦ ἄλλου βίου ἐπιμελοῖντο: 'satisfaction at least would happen from the intercourse, and they might rest (from their unending desire for their other half) and might turn to the works and take care of the rest of life'. Solving the problem of 191a8-b1. It is presumably deliberate that γίγνοιτο echoes the polyptoton of γεννῷεν/ γίγνοιτο/ τό γένος.

191c8–193e1 The application of this story

The preceding myth is said to explain different sexual orientations (hetero- and homosexual) as the desire for original halves to find other halves of the type they had once been united to (e.g. half of an original all-man will desire men). True love of the sort that lasts a lifetime is the experience of meeting the actual original other-half. In these cases, the two desire the greatest union they can achieve. Like many such aetiologies, it comes with a moral lesson: revere the gods so that they don't cut us in half again; and revere Eros particularly who can help find our other half and bring us happiness.

In some parts, this application aligns very closely with how many people now might see the world. Aristophanes seems to capture the human longing for love and the hope that it will provide wholeness and satisfaction. But he also seems to capture the sense of incompleteness and separation that we experience in life, and how we want an even greater union than sex can provide (consider the frequency of pain/ despair/death themes in romantic poetry). The whole explanation ignores the obvious issue that this only makes sense for one generation – any offspring would never have experienced the state of being a whole (double) human, although perhaps it might be claimed that such a longing was in our nature (even if not in our experience). However, such a confusion between individual and species is typical of this kind of myth (consider 'how the elephant got his trunk' in the 'Just So' stories).

191d
οὖν: this is the conclusion of the preceding story.

ἐκ τόσου: 'from so long ago', i.e. from the time original whole people were divided into man or woman halves by Zeus.

ἔστι . . . ὁ ἔρως has three different subject complements: ἔμφυτος ('innate' or 'in-born'. I.e. nature, not nurture); συναγωγεὺς (it is the force driving us to bring back together our ancient nature); ἐπιχειρῶν ('and one who tries').

ἓν ἐκ δυοῖν: 'one from two'.

σύμβολον: a 'tally', i.e. a unique half. Earlier societies broke objects (e.g. knuckle-bones, raggedly torn paper, etc.) in half, giving the halves to the two sides in a contract. This way, the parties could prove their identity by supplying the two unique (and hence fitting) halves of the tally.

ἅτε τετμημένος: ἅτε + participle – 'seeing that'.

ζητεῖ δὴ ἀεὶ τὸ αὑτοῦ ἕκαστος σύμβολον: τὸ αὑτοῦ ... σύμβολον το αὑτου
– 'his own tally'/'his own other-half'. Perhaps this is the origin of our phrase 'my
other half'? This would suggest there really is 'the one' out there!

ὅσοι μὲν οὖν τῶν ἀνδρῶν τοῦ κοινοῦ τμῆμά εἰσιν: τῶν ἀνδρῶν is partitive
after ὅσοι – 'and so all men who are an off-cut from the common sex'.

ὃ δὴ τότε ἀνδρόγυνον ἐκαλεῖτο: as explained at 189e2-4.

φιλογύναικές τέ εἰσι: 'are lovers of women', i.e. heterosexual males.

καὶ οἱ πολλοὶ τῶν μοιχῶν ἐκ τούτου τοῦ γένους γεγόνασιν: 'most adulterers
are born from this (i.e. the androgynous) race'. As Dover points out, marriage was
a matter of compliance with social convention, in no way reflecting sexual
inclination. Adultery here stands for any other heterosexual relationship in which
desire is the driving force.

191e

ὅσαι αὖ γυναῖκες φίλανδροί τε καὶ μοιχεύτριαι: 'and so too all women who
are lovers of men and adulteresses'. αὖ signposts a second parallel point.

ὅσαι δὲ τῶν γυναικῶν γυναικὸς τμῆμά εἰσιν: 'all the women who are an off-
cut from the female sex'. The δὲ picks up ὅσοι μὲν 191d6.

οὐ πάνυ: 'not much'.

ἀλλὰ μᾶλλον πρὸς τὰς γυναῖκας τετραμμέναι εἰσί: 'but they are more inclined
towards women'. τετραμμέναι is the perfect passive participle of τρέπω –
'turned' – just as we now use the language of 'sexual orientation'.

καὶ αἱ ἑταιρίστριαι: i.e. female homosexuals. The modern term 'lesbian' derives
from the way the female poet Sappho, from the island of Lesbos, wrote Love
Poetry about girls, but this association comes later than Plato.

ὅσοι δὲ ἄρρενος τμῆμά εἰσι: the next possibility – 'all men who are an off-cut of
a (original) male (whole)'.

διώκουσι: the men are described with a more active aggressive verb (contrast
τετραμμέναι εἰσί) reflecting the gender stereotypes of the time.

καὶ τέως μὲν ἂν παῖδες ὦσιν: here τέως (= ἕως) + ἂν + subjunctive for an
indefinite temporal clause in primary sequence.

ἅτε τεμάχια ὄντα τοῦ ἄρρενος: again ἅτε + participle – 'seeing that'. τεμάχια
– 'slices'. i.e. each one is a slice (or a sliced-off half) of an original male whole.

φιλοῦσι τοὺς ἄνδρας: it is probably significant that this is the first group to have
the word φιλέω applied to it, rather than words denoting sexual orientation or
pursuit, as this makes the male–male pattern sound nobler.

192a

καὶ χαίρουσι συγκατακείμενοι καὶ συμπεπλεγμένοι τοῖς ἀνδράσι: 'they
love to lie down next to and be embraced by men'. The vague euphemisms perhaps
reflect the variety of patterns in these physical relationships, the passive second
participle reflecting the passive role of the boy, as well as the repeated prefix συν-
emphasizing togetherness.

τῶν παίδων καὶ μειρακίων: if there is a difference between these, the latter refers
to older youths, perhaps up to twenty-one.

ἅτε ἀνδρειότατοι ὄντες φύσει: a play on the root of ἀνδρεῖος – they are most
brave by nature because they are 'all-male' by origin. This statement recognizes

AS

that not all of Greek (and probably not all of Athenian) society shared the sexual mores that seem accepted among the group at this symposium, particularly concerning pederasty.

αὐτοὺς ἀναισχύντους εἶναι: 'that they are shameless'. Accusative + infinitive after φημί. αὐτοὺς is talking about these boys who are attracted to men, because they are halves of original male wholes.

ψευδόμενοι: a blunt statement. ψεύδομαι here just means 'are wrong' rather than implying that they are deliberately misleading people.

οὐ γὰρ ὑπ' ἀναισχυντίας τοῦτο δρῶσιν ἀλλ' ὑπὸ θάρρους καὶ ἀνδρείας καὶ ἀρρενωπίας: a good example of the literary device of 'negative-positive restatement'. Here, after the negative is rejected, the positive is emphasized by a list of three with polysyndeton – 'courage and manliness and masculinity'.

τὸ ὅμοιον: 'the same [character]'.

ἀσπαζόμενοι: 'recognizing with joy', 'valuing' or 'welcoming'. The thought is that these boys love men because of their own hyper-manliness, leading them to be attracted to the same characteristic in others.

μέγα δὲ τεκμήριον: understand ἐστί – 'there is a clear proof [of this]'.

καὶ γὰρ τελεωθέντες μόνοι ἀποβαίνουσιν εἰς τὰ πολιτικὰ ἄνδρες οἱ τοιοῦτοι: 'for in fact (καὶ) these sort of men alone, when grown up, prove fit for politics'. At face value, Aristophanes offers as proof of their courage/manliness/masculinity that men of this sort turn out to be the best politicians (and it is no surprise that Aristophanes and the others should consider those who share similar values to them to be those most fit for political roles). But Aristophanes in his comedies frequently suggests the opposite: homosexuality, particularly sexual passive submission, is equated with effeminacy (not manliness), and politicians are often assumed to be the worst sort of people. We can either read this speech as sincere, expressing the real opinions of Aristophanes (and in this view his comedies are playing on prejudices he knows the masses have), or we don't take Aristophanes seriously here, and think that he is pushing the logic of his story to absurdity.

192b

ἐπειδὰν δὲ ἀνδρωθῶσι: = ἐπεί + ἄν + (aorist passive) subjunctive – indefinite clause – 'when they become men'.

παιδεραστοῦσι: 'they love boys', carrying none of the negative connotations of the modern 'pederasty'.

καὶ πρὸς γάμους καὶ παιδοποιίας οὐ προσέχουσι τὸν νοῦν φύσει, ἀλλ' ὑπὸ τοῦ νόμου ἀναγκάζονται: then, as now, there was much intellectual debate about what is caused by nature (φύσις) and what by nurture (here νόμος – all the influences on a person from law, society, family, upbringing, etc). In a conservative society, these pressures are here described as 'forcing' one into a conventional lifestyle whatever one's inclinations.

ἀλλ' ἐξαρκεῖ αὐτοῖς: impersonal verb – 'they would be quite satisfied'.

καταζῆν: the prefix gives the sense 'to live out their life'.

πάντως μὲν οὖν: this marks the summing up of the position of the argument – 'and so in summary'.

παιδεραστής τε καὶ φιλεραστής: these are the two sides of this sort of relationship – the man who loves a boy and the boy who loves a (man) lover. The repeated ἐραστής might suggest the reciprocal nature of this relationship, but the imbalance of the two descriptions (why is the latter not 'boys who love men'?) might suggest that in practice some of the boys didn't love their lovers back.

ἀεὶ τὸ συγγενὲς ἀσπαζόμενος: this phrase echoes 192a5. τὸ συγγενές is that which is of the same kind.

ὅταν ... ἐντύχῃ: ὅτε + ἄν + (aorist by aspect) subjunctive for an indefinite temporal clause.

αὐτῷ ἐκείνῳ τῷ αὑτοῦ ἡμίσει: dative after ἐντυγχάνω. αὐτῷ is emphatic; ἐκείνῳ is definite – '(whenever X meets) with that very other-half of himself'.

καὶ ὁ παιδεραστὴς καὶ ἄλλος πᾶς: i.e. the lover of boys, and every other lover of any sort (as previously outlined).

θαυμαστὰ: neuter plural adjective as adverb – 'wonderfully'.

ἐκπλήττονται: ἐκπλήττω is used of being struck by any sudden passion or emotion.

192c

φιλίᾳ τε καὶ οἰκειότητι καὶ ἔρωτι: the first is a general love; the second the sort of love one has for family; the third is sexual desire. The effect is emphasized by the list of three.

ὡς ἔπος εἰπεῖν: 'so to speak a word' – this is commonly used to excuse emphatic statements which are not meant to be taken too literally.

οὐκ ἐθέλοντες .... χωρίζεσθαι ἀλλήλων οὐδὲ σμικρὸν χρόνον: the compound negative after the single negative strengthens (rather than cancels) – 'not being willing to be apart from each other, not even for a second'. σμικρὸν χρόνον is accusative for time how long.

οἱ διατελοῦντες μετ᾽ ἀλλήλων διὰ βίου: διατελέω here means to live. Aristophanes is describing two partners who stay together for life.

οὗτοί εἰσιν: i.e. two halves of an original whole who have found each other.

οἵ: the relative pronoun. The antecedent is οἱ διατελοῦντες.

ἂν ἔχοιεν εἰπεῖν: 'who could not say'. ἔχω has the sense of 'to be able'. ἄν + present (by aspect) optative is for a potential clause (or consider it as a future remote conditional, with the implied protasis 'if they were to try').

ὅ τι βούλονται σφίσι παρ᾽ ἀλλήλων γίγνεσθαι: indirect question, indicative mood by sequence (from εἰσίν) – 'what they want to happen to themselves from each other'.

οὐδενὶ γὰρ ἂν δόξειεν τοῦτ᾽ εἶναι: τοῦτο (subject) must refer back to 'the thing that these two want for themselves from each other'. The optative (aorist by aspect) is potential (see note 190a, here understanding 'if someone were to think about it'). Literally 'for this would seem to no one to be' – 'no one would think that this is'.

ἡ τῶν ἀφροδισίων συνουσία: a periphrastic phrase for sexual intercourse, both hetero- and homosexual.

ὡς ἄρα: this introduces a restatement of the idea in the first half of the sentence, dependent on οὐδενὶ δόξειεν – 'that'.

τούτου ἕνεκα: τούτου refers to ἡ τῶν ἀφροδισίων συνουσία.

ἕτερος ἑτέρῳ χαίρει συνὼν: ἕτερος repeated in a different case (like 'alius' in Latin) can have the sense of 'one Xs one, another another'. So here 'one person rejoices to be with one person, another with another'.

AS

οὕτως ἐπὶ μεγάλης σπουδῆς: treat like an adverbial phrase – 'with such great enthusiasm'/'so passionately'.

ἄλλο τι: i.e. something other/more than sexual intercourse. The word order of the sentence emphasizes this. This idea becomes much more important in the speech of Diotima, who claims that Eros should lead on to a longing for higher things.

192d

βουλομένη ἑκατέρου ἡ ψυχὴ δήλη ἐστίν: δῆλος ἐστί + participle – 'X clearly . . ./ it is clear that X'.

ὃ οὐ δύναται εἰπεῖν: the antecedent of ὃ is ἄλλο τι. The thought picks up from 192 c2-3.

ἀλλὰ μαντεύεται ὃ βούλεται, καὶ αἰνίττεται: μαντεύομαι is 'to prophesy'; αἰνίττομαι is literally 'to speak of something in riddles'. Here the thought of the former is that the person has some sense (of what he wishes), but not as clearly as knowledge; and the latter that the person can make some attempt at explaining it, but unclearly.

καὶ εἰ . . . ὁ Ἥφαιστος . . . ἔροιτο: 'suppose Hephaestus were to ask'. εἰ + optative for the protasis of a future remote conditional. The apodosis comes at 192e5 ἴσμεν. Hephaestus is introduced as the god of crafts and creative devices. Many have seen here a reference to the myth (sung by Demodocus in *Odyssey* 8) about Hephaestus catching his wife Aphrodite and her lover Ares in a net while making love, and exposing them to the mockery of the other gods. While the net had the potential to hold them together permanently, this story is a curious counterpart in binding two people against their wishes until they are set free. Does this undermine Aristophanes' claim that this would bring happiness?

αὐτοῖς κατακειμένοις ἐπιστάς: ἐφίστημι + dative – 'to stand over'. Strong aorist active participle with present sense.

ἐν τῷ αὐτῷ: 'together'.

ὅτι μάλιστα: 'as much as possible'.

ἔχων τὰ ὄργανα: Hephaestus was a blacksmith, and the tools of his trade would have included the anvil, hammer, bellows and tongs.

'τί ἔσθ᾽ ὃ βούλεσθε, ὦ ἄνθρωποι, ὑμῖν παρ᾽ ἀλλήλων γενέσθαι;': this closely imitates the wording of 192c3-4. Aristophanes, having rejected sexual intercourse as the desired end of the relationship, comes back to the question. The question is directed towards ἄνθρωποι as befits a god speaking to humans, and would apply to a homo- or heterosexual pair. ἔσθ᾽ is ἐστί, with the iota elided before a vowel, and the tau aspirated before a rough breathing.

καὶ εἰ ἀποροῦντας αὐτοὺς πάλιν ἔροιτο: εἰ + optative – grammatically a restatement of the protasis, but the question has been rephrased to provide a suggested answer. ἀπορία, the state of being at a loss what to say or think next, is a stage reached by many of Socrates' interlocutors in Plato's dialogues, a stage when they realize that they don't know what they thought they knew, usually an important step on the road towards knowledge.

ἀρά γε τοῦδε ἐπιθυμεῖτε: γε – 'in fact' (i.e. as opposed to sex). τοῦδε looks forward to the following infinitive phrase, and as such does not need to be translated.

AS

ἐν τῷ αὐτῷ γενέσθαι ὅτι μάλιστα ἀλλήλοις: 'to be together with each other as much as possible' (ὅτι + superlative like the more familiar ὡς + superlative).

ὥστε καὶ νύκτα καὶ ἡμέραν μὴ ἀπολείπεσθαι ἀλλήλων: a result clause with infinitive (present by aspect) giving a potential (rather than realized) result. Understand a 'you' as subject of the infinitive.

εἰ γὰρ τούτου ἐπιθυμεῖτε: the protasis is repeated, with τούτου looking back.

192e

θέλω ὑμᾶς συντῆξαι καὶ συμφυσῆσαι εἰς τὸ αὐτό: συντήκω is aorist active infinitive from τήκω 'I weld, melt'; συμφυσάω is aorist active infinitive from φυσάω 'I blow' (the idea of the bellows); but here they are virtually synonymous, the repeated prefix συν- being the key idea – 'I am willing to melt down and weld you together into one and the same thing'.

ὥστε δύ' ὄντας ἕνα γεγονέναι: again a result clause with infinitive (here perfect active stressing the finished nature of this event) for a potential result. Again 'you' is to be understood as a subject of the infinitive, with δύ' ὄντας agreeing. See 191a8 for the idea earlier. Notice the parallel structures of the rest of the result clause.

καὶ ἕως τ' ἂν ζῆτε: indefinite temporal clause – ἂν + subjunctive in primary sequence – 'as long as you live'.

ὡς ἕνα ὄντα: ὡς points to the participle being causal – 'since you are now one'. ὄντα is adapted to the singular of its predicate, although describing ἀμφοτέρους.

κοινῇ ἀμφοτέρους ζῆν: a second infinitive in the result clause – 'you will both live a common/shared life'.

καὶ ἐπειδὰν ἀποθάνητε: another indefinite clause, grammatically the same as and parallel to ἕως τ' ἂν ζῆτε.

ἐκεῖ αὖ ἐν Ἅιδου: 'there in Hades too'.

ἀντὶ δυοῖν ἕνα εἶναι κοινῇ τεθνεῶτε: '(you), being one instead of two, will share a common death'. A third infinitive in this result clause. δυοῖν is the genitive case, dual. τεθνεῶτε is the perfect active participle, dual accusative masculine ending (agreeing with ὑμᾶς which has been understood as the subject throughout this result clause).

ἀλλ' ὁρᾶτε: present imperative, metaphorically meaning 'consider' rather than literally 'see'.

εἰ τούτου ἐρᾶτε καὶ ἐξαρκεῖ ὑμῖν: 'whether you desire this and it is enough for you'. Indirect question – present indicative verbs in primary sequence. The second part of the question is key – sexual intercourse had already been established as something desired, but as not enough.

ἂν τούτου τύχητε: ἂν = ἐάν. grammatically a protasis of a future open condition – 'if you obtain this'.

ταῦτ' ἀκούσας: aorist participle with conditional sense, agreeing with 'no one'.

ἴσμεν ὅτι οὐδ' ἂν εἷς ἐξαρνηθείη οὐδ' ἄλλο τι ἂν φανείη βουλόμενος: 'we know that no one would refuse and would clearly not want anything else'. After Hephaestus' words, the original conditional (192d3, rephrased 192d8) is picked up. It is a future remote condition, hence here ἂν + optatives (aorist by aspect). οὐδ' ἂν εἷς is the equivalent of καί + οὐδείς + ἄν, but more forceful. φαίνομαι + participle = I am clearly X-ing/it is clear that I'.

AS

ἀτεχνῶς: 'simply'.

οἴοιτ᾽ ἄν: another ἄν + optative (present by aspect) as this is still the apodosis of this condition.

ἀκηκοέναι τοῦτο: an indirect statement – the subject (being the same as the subject of οἴοιτο has been omitted) + perfect infinitive + object. τοῦτο is the antecedent to the relative clause, commonly included in Greek but best not translated in English – 'he would simply think that he had heard what'.

πάλαι ἄρα: 'in fact for a long time already'.

συντακεὶς τῷ ἐρωμένῳ: aorist passive participle of συντήκω + dative – 'welded to the one he loves'.

ἐκ δυοῖν εἷς γενέσθαι: a slight variation on the phrase at 192e3.

τοῦτο γάρ ἐστι τὸ αἴτιον: this clearly marks the completion of the (mock?) aetiology of love, started at 189e.

ὅτι ἡ ἀρχαία φύσις ἡμῶν ἦν αὕτη: ἀρχαία refers to the time before the split performed by Zeus. αὕτη – 'this', i.e. as outlined in the previous chapters.

καὶ ἦμεν ὅλοι: the number of modern self-help books offering 'wholeness' suggests Aristophanes has put his finger on a deep and permanent longing.

193a

τοῦ ὅλου οὖν τῇ ἐπιθυμίᾳ καὶ διώξει ἔρως ὄνομα: understand ἐστί. This conclusion had first been reached at 191d1 and is now repeated. Note the word order, with τοῦ ὅλου first so that it repeats ὅλοι and the subject last to give weight to the conclusion. Consider S. T. Coleridge *Notebooks* 3.70 'Love is a desire of the whole being to be united to some thing, or some being, felt necessary to its completeness'.

καὶ πρὸ τοῦ = προ τουτου.

ἕν: neuter singular – 'a single entity'.

διῳκίσθημεν: aorist passive – 'we have been broken up and separated'. This is a story with many parallels to 'the Fall' in Christian theology.

καθάπερ: introduces a comparison.

Ἀρκάδες ὑπὸ Λακεδαιμονίων: Mantinea, in Arcadia (in the centre of the Peloponnese) was besieged and captured by the Spartans in 385 BCE. After its capture, the city wall was pulled down and Mantinea was separated into four villages. This is clearly an anachronism in a speech set in 416 BCE, but perhaps reflects a recent event for Plato and points towards a date of composition soon after 385 BCE. Such anachronistic references to contemporary events were typical of Aristophanic comedy.

φόβος οὖν ἔστιν, ... ὅπως μὴ καὶ αὖθις διασχισθησόμεθα: 'and so there is a fear that ... we will be split again'. A fear clause: ὅπως μὴ + future indicative, equivalent to the usual μη + subjunctive/optative. Zeus recognized this option of a further splitting at 190d5.

ἐὰν μὴ κόσμιοι ὦμεν πρὸς τοὺς θεούς: a future open conditional, subjunctive present by aspect. κόσμιος is 'orderly/well-behaved'.

ἔχοντες: 'being'.

ὥσπερ οἱ ἐν ταῖς στήλαις καταγραφὴν ἐκτετυπωμένοι: perfect passive participle of ἐκτυπόω – 'just like those (figures) moulded in profile on stelae'. A stele is an upright stone slab, used for, among other things, grave stones.

AS

διαπεπρισμένοι κατὰ τὰς ῥῖνας: continuing the simile. Perfect passive participle of διαπρίζω – 'sawn through'.

γεγονότες ὥσπερ λίσπαι: perfect active participle followed by second simile – 'having become like half-dice'. Like the tallies of 191d4-5, the matching two halves of a dice might be kept by friends.

193b

ἀλλὰ τούτων ἕνεκα πάντ᾽ ἄνδρα χρὴ ἅπαντα παρακελεύεσθαι εὐσεβεῖν περὶ θεούς: πάντ᾽ ἄνδρα is an accusative going with χρὴ; ἅπαντα is a neuter plural accusative of respect after εὐσεβεῖν – 'but on account of these things it is necessary for every man to exhort (others) to be pious in all respects'.

ἵνα τὰ μὲν ἐκφύγωμεν, τῶν δὲ τύχωμεν: ἵνα + subjunctive (aorist by aspect) for purpose clause in primary sequence. τὰ μὲν must refer to being further cut in two; τῶν δὲ must be becoming one with the person you love, given the verbal echo of τυγχάνω from 192e5.

ὡς ὁ Ἔρως ἡμῖν ἡγεμὼν καὶ στρατηγός: the sense of ὡς is difficult here, but perhaps (as LSJ: relative I.3) 'in as far as'. Understand ἐστί. A striking military metaphor.

ᾧ μηδεὶς ἐναντία πραττέτω: the verb is 3rd person singular present imperative. The antecedent of ᾧ could be the thought 'this principle', but is more likely to be the person 'Eros/Love' – 'let no one act in opposition to Eros'.

πράττει δ᾽ ἐναντία ὅστις θεοῖς ἀπεχθάνεται: 'whoever is hated by the gods is acting in opposition (to Eros)'.

φίλοι γὰρ γενόμενοι καὶ διαλλαγέντες τῷ θεῷ: aorist passive participle of διαλλάσσω; the participles have conditional sense – 'if we become his friends and are reconciled to the god'.

ἐξευρήσομέν τε καὶ ἐντευξόμεθα: the latter is future of ἐντυγχάνω – 'we will meet with'.

τοῖς παιδικοῖς τοῖς ἡμετέροις αὐτῶν: 'a genitive plural following ὁ ἡμέτερος refers to the "we" implicit in the possessive adjective' (Dover) – 'our very own beloved'.

ὃ τῶν νῦν ὀλίγοι ποιοῦσι: 'a thing which few people today achieve'.

καὶ μή μοι ὑπολάβῃ Ἐρυξίμαχος: 'and let Eryximachus not reply to me, . . . , supposing that (I'm talking about . . .)'. μή + subjunctive (aorist by aspect) for a prohibition. ὑπολαμβάνω has a sense of 'reply (to me)' and 'interpreting/ supposing'. At 189b1 Eryximachus warned Aristophanes not to make jokes and said that he would be on the look-out for them. In denying to Eryximachus that his speech is a comedy aimed at Agathon and Pausanias, Aristophanes gets to make the joke anyway, but pins the blame on the hapless Eryximachus.

κωμῳδῶν τὸν λόγον: κωμῳδέω can be to mock, but here must mean 'treat as comedy'. But perhaps this assertion is only included to make a joke at the expense of Pausanias and Agathon. Such a relationship between the aristocratic thirty-something Pausanias, and the effeminate beardless almost-thirty Agathon must have been at the least unusual, and perhaps scandalous to some.

ὡς Παυσανίαν καὶ Ἀγάθωνα λέγω: indirect statement. See Introduction for these two.

193c

ἴσως μὲν γὰρ καὶ: 'for it may well be that'.

τούτων: i.e. two of these sort he has been talking about – those from original male wholes who love males.

τυγχάνουσιν ὄντες: τυγχάνω + participle – 'I happen to be'.

τὴν φύσιν ἄρρενες: 'male as to their nature' (accusative of respect). It is unclear whether we are also to assume that they are two halves of the same original male whole. The idea of Agathon as particularly masculine is clearly meant to be funny. In the opening scene of Aristophanes *Thesmophoriazusae*, Euripides and Mnesilochus visit Agathon to persuade him to dress as a woman and spy on the festival of the Thesmophoria. The jokes in the scene make it clear that Agathon was so far from being strong, bearded or manly in any way that this idea was laughable.

λέγω δὲ οὖν ἔγωγε: adversative – 'but I am saying'.

καθ' ἁπάντων καὶ ἀνδρῶν καὶ γυναικῶν: κατά + genitive – 'about'.

ὅτι οὕτως ἂν ἡμῶν τὸ γένος εὔδαιμον γένοιτο, εἰ ἐκτελέσαιμεν τὸν ἔρωτα καὶ τῶν παιδικῶν τῶν αὑτοῦ ἕκαστος τύχοι: optative + ἄν, εἰ + optative (aorists by aspect), for a future remote condition (here in indirect statement). The subject is **ἡμῶν τὸ γένος** (our race, i.e. the human race). ἐκτελέω is 'to accomplish/achieve'. τυγχάνω + genitive is 'I get together with'. **αὑτοῦ** – note the rough breathing (= ἑαυτοῦ) – 'his very own'. The second half of the apodosis explains what it means to achieve love. This might be to someone of the same or opposite sex depending on the nature of the original whole.

εἰς τὴν ἀρχαίαν ἀπελθὼν φύσιν. ἀπέρχομαι – 'I return, am restored'.

εἰ δὲ τοῦτο ἄριστον: understand ἐστί. The condition is present open. **τοῦτο** refers to our original whole condition.

ἀναγκαῖον: understand ἐστί.

καὶ τῶν νῦν παρόντων: καί – 'also'. The genitive is 'time during which' – 'in our present situation'.

τὸ τούτου ἐγγυτάτω ἄριστον εἶναι: ἐγγυτάτω is the irregular superlative ending of ἐγγύς + genitive is 'near', here with **τὸ** forming a noun phrase, acting as the accusative subject of the accusative + infinitive – (it is necessary that) 'the nearest (condition) to this is best'.

τοῦτο δ' ἐστί: **τοῦτο** picks up the whole idea of 'the nearest condition to this'.

κατὰ νοῦν αὑτῷ πεφυκότων: the participle, agreeing with **παιδικῶν**, is the perfect active participle of φύω. This is intransitive in the perfect tense, meaning 'I am born', and therefore 'I am by nature' – 'the one by nature in line with his own mind'.

οὗ δὴ τὸν αἴτιον θεὸν ὑμνοῦντες: 'and if we were to praise the god (who is) responsible for this'. This participle phrase is in place of the protasis of a future remote condition (εἰ + optative). **οὗ** is a connecting relative, the antecedent being the idea of finding our own true beloved.

193d

δικαίως ἂν ὑμνοῖμεν ἔρωτα: the apodosis of the future remote condition (present by aspect) – 'we would be right to praise Love'.

ἡμᾶς πλεῖστα ὀνίνησιν: 3rd person singular present indicative active of ὀνίνημι, with a superlative adverb.

εἰς τὸ οἰκεῖον ἄγων: instrumental sense of participle. οἰκείος means 'one's own' or 'suitable'.

εἰς τὸ ἔπειτα: prepositional phrase acting adverbially – 'for the future'.

ἡμῶν παρεχομένων πρὸς θεοὺς εὐσέβειαν: genitive absolute, with (future) conditional sense. Normally the genitive elements would 'sandwich' the phrase, but here εὐσέβειαν is given emphasis by its position – 'if we show due reverence to the gods'.

καταστήσας ἡμᾶς εἰς τὴν ἀρχαίαν φύσιν καὶ ἰασάμενος: the weak aorist active of καθίστημι is transitive, meaning 'to put someone in a certain state'. These two participles are also part of the 'great hopes' that Eros gives us. They are grammatically subordinate both because they have to happen before we may become happy, and in order that the climactic vision of human happiness has more weight.

μακαρίους καὶ εὐδαίμονας ποιῆσαι: infinitives following verbs of 'hoping' (here ἐλπίδας μεγίστας παρέχεται – 'he gives us great confidence that') can take a future infinitive or present/aorist by aspect when with future sense – 'he will make us blessed and happy'.

Notice how this provides fitting closure to the speech by echoing the language at the beginning (189d1-2).

ἀλλοῖος ἢ ὁ σός: 'different to yours'; as he had promised at 189c2-3.

ὥσπερ οὖν ἐδεήθην σου: aorist passive of the deponent verb δέομαι – 'just as I asked you'.

μὴ κωμῳδήσῃς αὐτόν: μή + aorist subjunctive = prohibition. αὐτόν refers to the speech.

ἵνα καὶ τῶν λοιπῶν ἀκούσωμεν: subjunctive in a purpose clause in primary sequence (aorist by aspect). ἀκούω takes a genitive when hearing a person.

193e

τί ἕκαστος ἐρεῖ: indirect question in primary sequence, retaining the tense of the original question (future).

μᾶλλον δὲ τί ἑκάτερος: the correction to ἑκάτερος implies 'two' (Agathon and Socrates). Aristodemus should have come next, but his literary role is as narrator rather than speaker, and he is conveniently forgotten.

193e2–194e2 Socrates and Agathon

Socrates and Agathon both claim to be worried about whether they can live up to the high standard of speeches. Socrates uses Agathon's claim to try to draw him into a philosophical discussion, but Phaedrus interrupts to get the speeches back on track.

This interlude is important (like all the others) both to break up the speeches, and also for the characterization: the modesty of Socrates and Agathon (real or feigned?); Socrates' concern for logical argument and true reasons; Agathon's conceit. It continues the theme of the contest between Socrates and Agathon in wisdom (begun 175e; settled when Alcibiades crowns Socrates 213e).

καὶ γάρ μοι ὁ λόγος ἡδέως ἐρρήθη: 'for I have enjoyed your speech'. **ἐρρήθη** is the aorist passive of λέγω. Take **μοι** closely with **ἡδέως** – literally 'gladly to me'.

καὶ εἰ μὴ συνῄδη: the verb is 1st person singular imperfect indicative active of σύνοιδα; σύνοιδα + dative – 'to know a thing about X'. The condition is present counterfactual: εἰ + indicative, indicative + ἄν – 'if I did not know about'.

Σωκράτει τε καὶ Ἀγάθωνι δεινοῖς οὖσι περὶ τὰ ἐρωτικά: indirect statement with participle after a verb of knowing.

πάνυ ἂν ἐφοβούμην: the apodosis of the condition – 'I would be very afraid'.

μὴ ἀπορήσωσι λόγων: **μή** + subjunctive = fear clause in (virtual) primary sequence (aorist by aspect).

διὰ τὸ πολλὰ καὶ παντοδαπὰ εἰρῆσθαι: το ... εἰρῆσθαι (perfect passive infinitive of λέγω) making a noun phrase after **διά** (+ accusative). Literally 'because of the having been spoken many and of all sorts things' – 'because of the number and variety of things said'.

194a

καλῶς γὰρ αὐτὸς ἠγώνισαι: perfect passive (but with active sense) of ἀγωνίζομαι – 'for you yourself have competed well'. Classical Athens was an 'agonistic' (competition-based) culture – sport and warfare are obviously competitive, but they also competed in competitions for poetry, song, theatre and rhetoric.

εἰ δὲ γένοιο ... ἂν φοβοῖο: future remote conditional εἰ + optative (aorist by aspect), optative (present by aspect) + **ἄν** – 'if you were to be ..., you would be afraid'.

οὗ: relative adverb – here 'in the position in which'.

μᾶλλον δὲ ἴσως οὗ ἔσομαι: Socrates corrects himself – 'or rather I'm sure where I will be' – for the sake of flattering Agathon.

ἐπειδὰν καὶ Ἀγάθων εἴπῃ εὖ: **ἄν** + subjunctive (aorist by aspect) = indefinite clause in (virtual) primary sequence. Here, the indefinite clause is not 'whenever', but a temporal clause in the future.

ἐν παντί: idiomatic for '(to be) at your wit's end'.

φαρμάττειν βούλει: 'you wish to put a hex on' (LSJ) – excessive praise was thought to risk nemesis from envious gods, or just to pile paralysing pressure on a speaker by raising expectations.

ἵνα θορυβηθῶ: aorist passive subjunctive in purpose clause, primary sequence (aorist by aspect) – 'so that I am thrown into confusion'.

διὰ τὸ οἴεσθαι τὸ θέατρον προσδοκίαν μεγάλην ἔχειν: indirect statement (accusative and infinitive) after **οἴεσθαι** – 'because of the thought that my audience has great expectations'. Agathon thinks of the other guests as 'his audience', appropriately for a playwright who is still high from winning.

ὡς εὖ ἐροῦντος ἐμοῦ: the genitive **ἐμοῦ** follows **προσδοκίαν**, the participle phrase agreeing.

ἐπιλήσμων: Socrates commonly claims forgetfulness as a means of drawing out answers, but here he claims the opposite.

μεντἄν = μέντοι ἄν – 'oh, but'.

ἂν εἴην ... εἰ ... οἰηθείην: a future remote condition (tenses of optative by aspect) – 'I would be ..., if I were to think'.

194b

ἰδών: Socrates is talking about the 'proagon', an event which took place just before the dramatic festival, in the Odeion, a large hall next to the theatre of Dionysus in Athens. In front of a large audience, the choregos (wealthy producer) and the poet-playwright would introduce their play(s) and actors.

μεγαλοφροσύνην: 'self-confidence' (Dover).

ἀναβαίνοντος . . . βλέψαντος . . . μέλλοντος . . . ἐκπλαγέντος: understand σου (Agathon) with all these participles – 'of you going up . . . when you had looked out at . . . and when you were about to . . ., frightened'.

ἐπὶ τὸν ὀκρίβαντα: onto the stage/platform.

βλέψαντος ἐναντία τοσούτῳ θεάτρῳ: 'having looked straight out at such a big audience'. The experience of being on stage, with everything 'facing' and the seating area looking 'so big'.

ἐπιδείξεσθαι σαυτοῦ λόγους: σαυτοῦ is the reflexive possessive pronoun 'of your own'. An actor only exposes his performance (not himself) to public criticism, while a playwright (or author) exposes his own words.

οὐδ' ὁπωστιοῦν: 'not in any way'.

σε θορυβήσεσθαι: accusative + (future) infinitive after οἴομαι.

τί δέ: 'really?'.

οὐ δήπου . . . ἡγῇ: 'surely you don't consider'.

οὕτω θεάτρου μεστὸν: i.e. 'so full of myself because of my success in the theatre'. An example of Plato's humour – most readers do find him very full of himself!

ὥστε καὶ ἀγνοεῖν: result clause, with infinitive for potential result. Subject 'I' omitted.

ὅτι: indirect statement. Understand εἰσί.

νοῦν ἔχοντι: 'to anyone with a mind'. This phrase coming first carries the emphasis.

ἔμφρονες . . . ἀφρόνων: these are antonyms – 'wise/silly', the latter being genitive of comparison. Such contempt for his audience seems to fit the intellectual and artistic snobbery of Agathon.

οὐ μεντἂν = οὐ μέντοι ἄν – 'no', affirming the statement of 194b6.

194c

οὐ . . . ἂν καλῶς ποιοίην: 'I would not be doing right'. A potential optative (consider it as the apodosis of a future remote condition; understand 'if I were to do such a thing').

τι . . . ἄγροικον δοξάζων: 'entertaining any uncultured opinion . . .' ἄγροικον literally means 'of the countryside' i.e., an opinion of Agathon as uncultured. Notice the dichotomy between city and countryside, the city representing what is intelligent and cultured and the countryside the opposite.

ἀλλ' εὖ οἶδα ὅτι: introduces an indirect statement containing a conditional.

εἴ τισιν ἐντύχοις . . . μᾶλλον ἂν αὐτῶν φροντίζοις ἢ τῶν πολλῶν: an original future remote condition – 'if you were to meet with some people . . . you would care more about them than the many'.

οὓς ἡγοῖο σοφούς: the relative clause naturally keeps the optative mood because it is still expressing the condition (future remote).

AS

μὴ οὐχ οὗτοι ἡμεῖς ὦμεν: μή οὐ + subjunctive may express a cautious negation or suspicion that something may not be true – 'but I rather think that we here are not (wise)'.

ἡμεῖς μὲν ... δὲ ἄλλοις: Socrates contrasts those at the table with hypothetical others.

ἐκεῖ παρῆμεν: i.e. in the theatre.

εἰ ... ἐντύχοις ... ἂν αἰσχύνοιο, εἴ ... οἴοιο: 'if you did meet ... you would be ashamed ... if you thought'. The type of condition is future remote, with two protases.

εἴ τι ἴσως οἴοιο αἰσχρὸν ὂν ποιεῖν: indirect statement after οἴομαι of the sort – nominative omitted (σύ) + infinitive. **ὂν** (present participle of εἰμί) agrees with **τι** – 'if perhaps you thought that you were doing something shameful'.

ἢ πῶς λέγεις: typical Socratic way of seeking agreement.

τοὺς δὲ πολλοὺς: this contrasts with **αὐτούς** 194c6.

οὐκ ἂν αἰσχύνοιο εἴ τι οἴοιο αἰσχρὸν ποιεῖν: the same form of future remote condition, but this time the **οὐκ** shows Socrates pushing for the obvious answer.

Socrates has shown the incoherence in Agathon's position. Agathon claimed to have not been nervous on stage because a sensible person only gets nervous in front of wise people (194b8). Socrates showed that: a) the same wise people were in the theatre audience (194c4); b) it was not the wisdom or number of the audience but the feeling that one was doing something shameful which would make Agathon ashamed (194c6, 9). Agathon should probably have said that he had felt confident on stage because he thought he had a good play to show, but either his modesty or desire to flatter this group led him to an untenable statement.

194d

καὶ τὸν Φαῖδρον ἔφη ὑπολαβόντα εἰπεῖν: again, we are reminded that this is a story told by Aristodemus (subject of **ἔφη**). **τὸν Φαῖδρον ὑπολαβόντα εἰπεῖν** is accusative + infinitive – 'and he said that Phaedrus spoke up, interrupting'.

ἐὰν ἀποκρίνῃ Σωκράτει, οὐδὲν ἔτι διοίσει αὐτῷ: a future open conditional: **ἐὰν** + subjunctive (aorist by aspect), future indicative (of διαφέρω) – 'if you answer Socrates, it will no longer make any difference to him'.

ὁπηοῦν τῶν ἐνθάδε ὁτιοῦν γίγνεσθαι: accusative + infinitive – 'that any of the things here (i.e. their planned speeches) happen in any way'.

ἐὰν μόνον ἔχῃ ὅτῳ διαλέγηται: a second protasis of the future open type, followed by an indirect question (an original deliberative subjunctive question) – 'if only he has someone to converse with'.

ἄλλως τε καὶ καλῷ: καλῷ agrees with ὅτῳ – 'especially someone handsome'.

ἐγὼ δὲ ἡδέως μὲν ἀκούω Σωκράτους διαλεγομένου: present indicative for a statement of general truth. **ἀκούω** + genitive of persons.

ἀναγκαῖον δέ μοι: understand ἐστί.

ἀποδέξασθαι παρ᾽ ἑνὸς ἑκάστου ὑμῶν τὸν λόγον: 'to exact a speech from each one of you'. The verb carries the sense of what one has a moral duty to supply.

ἀποδοὺς οὖν ἑκάτερος τῷ θεῷ οὕτως ἤδη διαλεγέσθω: 'and so let each (of the two of you) converse then, only after having paid his dues to the god'. **διαλεγέσθω**

is a 3rd person imperative; this verb refers to the conversation Socrates wants to have rather than the speech which is demanded by Phaedrus (and the others).

194e

καὶ οὐδέν με κωλύει λέγειν: there is a hint here that Agathon is rather glad to be rescued from his self-contradictory position (see note on 194c10).

Σωκράτει γὰρ καὶ αὖθις ἔσται: 'it will be possible for Socrates again later'.

AS

198a-201c: Socrates began by criticizing the previous encomia as being speeches which made Eros as attractive as possible, but were not true (198d). He continued by setting out how he intended to speak (199b): his speech would tell the truth about Eros, and would not worry about rhetorical artistry.

He then questioned Agathon, saying that he wished to establish a couple of principles before speaking. These turn out to be: i) that Love is of love of something, and that something must be something that Love lacks (200e); ii) Love is love of beautiful things, therefore Eros himself lacks beauty and is not beautiful (201a) (the second is later disputed by Diotima, who says that Love is of the good, and beauty is the medium in which this is best obtained).

The speech of Diotima (201d–212b)

Socrates moves from questioning Agathon to what is known as the speech of Diotima. The character of Diotima allows the 'wrong opinions' of Agathon, Aristophanes and the general public to be corrected, without making Socrates less likeable. It also means that, although required to give a speech about Love, Socrates manages to include the dialectic process (*elenchus*) which he saw as essential to the pursuit of philosophy.

Diotima introduced 201d1–201e2

Diotima is otherwise unknown and may or may not be based on a real person. Armand D'Angour has recently argued that this name is Plato's disguise for a real woman, Aspasia of Miletus (who later became the long-term partner of Pericles), and that Aspasia was the key influence on the philosophical development of the young Socrates. Plato's views on the intellectual and philosophical potential of women are hard to make out clearly. There are moments in the *Republic* where he seems to suggest that women, given access to the same education as men, could equally become philosopher kings. But in other parts of the Platonic corpus, women are claimed to be inferior in almost every way. The introduction of a female character as the authoritative voice on Love (and it turns out, philosophy) is surprising given that girls at the time would rarely have received a good education, although women with religious roles and expertise are seen in Greek literature. Besides Diotima, the dialogue assumes that intellectual development occurs in male environments, particularly pederastic relationships.

201d

καὶ σὲ μέν γε ἤδη ἐάσω: the future tense of ἐάω. This phrase marks the end of the questioning of Agathon, begun at 199c3 – 'anyway, now indeed I'll leave you alone'.

τὸν δὲ λόγον: grammatically this is the object of **πειράσομαι ὑμῖν διελθεῖν** (201d6) but try to keep it first in translating. Speaking a λόγος in praise of love was the original requirement of 177d2.

ὅν ποτ᾽ ἤκουσα: Plato's device of introducing Diotima allows Socrates to remain on a level with the others. He can claim that he too was ignorant about love until enlightened by Diotima.

γυναικὸς Μαντινικῆς Διοτίμας: all of these details make Diotima sound real, and yet there is no reason for her to be so, and the lack of definite article shows that she isn't known to the others. The fact that Plato chooses a woman may be to avoid the appearance of the *Symposium* being an extended self-interested defence of homosexuality. Mantinea was a real place on the Peloponnese, but the place name was presumably chosen for its associations with words for prophecy. Similarly, the name 'Diotima' (meaning 'honouring' or 'honoured by Zeus') is presumably significant.

ἢ ταῦτά τε σοφὴ ἦν καὶ ἄλλα πολλά: relative clause, the antecedent being Διοτίμας. ταῦτά … ἄλλα πολλά are accusatives of respect – 'who was wise regarding these things and many others'.

καὶ Ἀθηναίοις ποτὲ θυσαμένοις πρὸ τοῦ λοιμοῦ δέκα ἔτη ἀναβολὴν ἐποίησε τῆς νόσου: 'when the Athenians once sacrificed … she caused', i.e. her religious expertise prescribed the right sacrifices which were believed to have appeased the gods and bought ten years. Plague had famously struck Athens 430–428 BCE (see *Thuc.* 2.47), so this may refer to a real moment *c.* 440 BCE when plague first threatened. Natural disasters were commonly believed to be brought on a city by an angry god (e.g. *Oedipus Tyrannus*).

ἣ δὴ καὶ ἐμὲ τὰ ἐρωτικὰ ἐδίδαξεν: another relative clause, antecedent Διοτίμας – 'the very one who'. There is an obvious double entendre, typical of Greek comedy.

ὃν οὖν ἐκείνη ἔλεγε λόγον: this relative clause picks up τον λόγον from the beginning of the sentence in case it has been forgotten in the introduction of Diotima – 'so the account which that woman spoke, I'.

ἐκ τῶν ὡμολογημένων ἐμοὶ καὶ Ἀγάθωνι: 'building on the things agreed between me and Agathon'. The participle is perfect passive.

αὐτὸς ἐπ᾽ ἐμαυτοῦ: 'by myself', as opposed to in dialogue with Agathon.

ὅπως ἂν δύνωμαι: 'as far as I can'. Indefinite adverb + ἄν + subjunctive (present by aspect) for an indefinite clause in primary sequence.

ὥσπερ σὺ διηγήσω: 2nd singular aorist middle indicative. Bury suggests the choice of verb suggests 'veiled contempt'; or is this an attempt to build bridges after he spectacularly took apart Agathon's speech?

201e

αὐτὸν πρῶτον, τίς ἐστιν: an indirect question in the typically Greek form: '(describe) him who he is', where we say '(describe) who he is'. τίς ἐστιν is a significant addition from the two aims of Agathon at 195a. Socrates is interested in definitions and what something really is.

ῥᾷστον εἶναι: 'to be easiest'.

οὕτω διελθεῖν, ὥς: ὥς picks up οὕτω – 'to go through it (in this way) as'.

με … ἀνακρίνουσα διῄει: the main verb is 3rd person singular, imperfect indicative active of διέρχομαι, used intransitively. με is object of ἀνακρίνουσα. This must mean more than just that Diotima was answering his question; she used a question-and-answer technique.

A
Level

The character of Love 201e3–202b5

Love is not beautiful nor ugly but in-between (just as right opinion is in-between knowledge and ignorance (an idea treated at length in *Meno*). This is a restatement of the principles agreed between Socrates and Agathon.

Notice how many layers of narration we now have: this is now Apollodorus describing what Aristodemus said that Socrates said that Diotima said.

σχεδὸν ... τι ... ἕτερα τοιαῦτα: '(for I said to her) nearly the same sort of things (which)'. τι goes closely with σχεδὸν, and doesn't need translating.

οἷάπερ νῦν πρὸς ἐμὲ Ἀγάθων: the relative οἷά follows the antecedent ἕτερα. Understand ἐλέγεν.

ὡς εἴη ὁ Ἔρως μέγας θεός, εἴη: indirect statements, with optative in historic sequence. These are the two key errors of Agathon's position which Socrates is going to correct.

τῶν καλῶν: the genitive is for the objects of Eros, as agreed at 200e8.

ἤλεγχε δή με: 'indeed she corrected me'. Socrates' characteristic humility can be preserved by the introduction of Diotima even as he corrects Agathon.

οἷσπερ ἐγὼ τοῦτον: relative clause, the antecedent of οἷς is τούτοις τοῖς λόγοις. Understand ἤλεγχον. Socrates' refutation of Agathon is the section 199c–201d.

ὡς οὔτε καλὸς εἴη ... οὔτε ἀγαθός: again, indirect statements with optative in historic sequence.

κατὰ τὸν ἐμὸν λόγον: this reflects the Socratic technique – interlocutors are led to a position where they are contradicting themselves.

πῶς λέγεις: 'what do you mean', expressing both shock and a genuine question.

αἰσχρὸς ἄρα ὁ Ἔρως ἐστὶ καὶ κακός: αἰσχρὸς (the contradictory notion of καλος) put first for emphasis. Bury says that Socrates ironically pretends not to recognize the rules of logic: what is not καλός is οὐ-καλός, not αἰσχρός.

καὶ ἥ ... ἔφη: the relative pronoun meaning 'she' survived in some fixed expressions, especially with φημί (Dover).

οὐκ εὐφημήσεις: εὐφημέω was to speak words of good omen, but also to avoid unlucky words or keep an appropriate silence (e.g. during a sacrifice) – 'you can't say that'.

ἢ οἴει ... ἀναγκαῖον αὐτὸ εἶναι αἰσχρόν: an indirect statement (accusative and infinitive) following οἴομαι (2nd person singular, present). There is another εἶναι implied with ἀναγκαῖον. αὐτὸ picks up the indefinite clause and can be omitted in English.

ὅτι ἂν μὴ καλὸν ᾖ: indefinite clause – ὅστις + ἄν + subjunctive – 'whatever isn't beautiful'.

202a

μάλιστά γε: strong positive agreement – 'yes'.

ἦ καὶ ἂν μὴ σοφόν, ἀμαθές: each ἦ adds another case to consider. Lots of words are left out, assumed from 201e10-11 – 'or also (do you think that whatever) is not wise (is) foolish'. 'Diotima is drawing the logical distinction between contraries (good/bad) and contradictories (good/not good)' (Rose).

ἢ οὐκ ᾔσθησαι: 2nd person singular, perfect indicative active of αἰσθάνομαι.

**A
Level**

ὅτι ἔστιν τι μεταξὺ σοφίας καὶ ἀμαθίας: μεταξύ as a preposition takes the genitive – 'that there is something between wisdom and foolishness'.

τί τοῦτο; understand ἐστίν.

οὐκ οἶσθ'. . . ὅτι: take this first in the sentence – 'do you not think that'.

τὸ ὀρθὰ δοξάζειν καὶ ἄνευ τοῦ ἔχειν λόγον δοῦναι: the articles with the two infinitives (δοξάζειν . . . ἔχειν; δοῦναι is dependent on ἔχειν which has the sense of 'be able') make a noun phrase which is grammatically the subject of the ὅτι clause: 'thinking rightly even without being able to give a reason (for that thought)'. The difference between knowledge and right opinion is of great interest to Plato and the subject of the dialogue *Meno*, where it is agreed that right opinion needs to be allied with a rational explanation for it to be knowledge.

οὔτε ἐπίστασθαί ἐστιν: the infinitive here virtually makes an abstract noun – 'is neither knowledge'.

ἄλογον γὰρ πρᾶγμα πῶς ἂν εἴη ἐπιστήμη: πῶς ἂν + optative – 'how could an unexplained thing be knowledge'.

οὔτε ἀμαθία: understand ἐστίν.

τὸ γὰρ τοῦ ὄντος τυγχάνον: τυγχάνω + genitive – 'what meets with the truth'. εἰμί here has its strong sense of 'that which really is', i.e. what is true in reality.

ἔστι δὲ δήπου τοιοῦτον: 'there is clearly some such thing as'.

φρονήσεως: φρόνησις seems to be used interchangeably with σοφία and ἐπιστήμη.

ἀληθῆ: neuter plural adjective but translate as abstract noun – '(you speak) the truth'.

ἦν: variant on ἔφην, usually combined with δέ and a pronoun – 'I said'.

202b

μὴ τοίνυν ἀνάγκαζε: ἀναγκάζω + accusative + infinitive – 'to contend that a thing is necessarily so' (LSJ).

ὃ μὴ καλόν ἐστιν αἰσχρὸν εἶναι: the relative clause acts as the accusative.

οὕτω δὲ καὶ τὸν ἔρωτα: take these words separately, applying to the whole sentence – 'so too regarding Eros'.

ἐπειδὴ αὐτὸς ὁμολογεῖς μὴ εἶναι ἀγαθὸν μηδὲ καλόν: Eros is the understood accusative in this indirect statement – 'since you yourself agree that it is not good nor beautiful'. μὴ may be used in indirect speech after a verb of agreeing.

μηδέν τι μᾶλλον οἴου: οἴου is 2nd singular present middle imperative – 'do not think any the more for that' (Dover).

δεῖν αὐτὸν αἰσχρὸν καὶ κακὸν εἶναι: δεῖν + accusative + infinitive. αὐτὸν refers to Eros.

ἀλλά τι μεταξύ, ἔφη, τούτοιν: τούτοιν is genitive plural dual – 'but (consider him to be) something between these things, she said'.

The status of Love 202b6–203a7

Love is not a god nor a mortal, but in-between – a δαίμων. For gods are beautiful and good, and it has been agreed that Love is not. This is a major departure from traditional Greek mythology and from all that has been assumed so far.

A
Level

καὶ μήν: used to introduce a further point, often in disagreement or counter-argument – 'But'.

ὁμολογεῖταί γε παρὰ πάντων μέγας θεὸς εἶναι: this is a very unusual story of the young Socrates holding the same wrong opinions as everyone else and appealing to popular agreement for backing. Eros is the subject of the main verb, and therefore followed by nominative + infinitive.

τῶν μὴ εἰδότων, ἔφη, πάντων λέγεις, ἢ καὶ τῶν εἰδότων: the genitives follow naturally on from πάντων after παρά. μή is for a generic participle phrase – 'do you mean by all those who don't know, or also by those who know'.

συμπάντων μὲν οὖν: μὲν οὖν makes the response more emphatic.

καὶ πῶς ἄν: see 202a8 – 'how could'.

202c

ὁμολογοῖτο μέγας θεὸς εἶναι: Eros is the subject of the verb.

παρὰ τούτων, οἵ φασιν αὐτὸν οὐδὲ θεὸν εἶναι: 'by people who deny that he is even a god'.

εἷς μέν . . . σύ, μία δ᾽ ἐγώ: understand the appropriate form of εἰμί each time.

κἀγὼ εἶπον "πῶς τοῦτο" ἔφην, "λέγεις;": there is an apparent tautology of εἶπον and ἔφην (one needs to be ignored when translating). Some have suggested taking εἶπον as aorist imperative, inside the direct speech. κἀγὼ is a crasis of καί and ἐγώ.

καὶ ἥ: see note on 201e10.

οὐ πάντας θεοὺς φῂς εὐδαίμονας εἶναι καὶ καλούς: the emphasis of the question is on πάντας, and οὐ goes closely with it. Clearly in traditional myth, not all the gods are beautiful (e.g. Hephaestus), but this more intellectual belief (that they are all happy and beautiful) has been put forward by Agathon 195a.

ἢ τολμήσαις ἄν: the aorist optative is potential – 'would you dare to'.

τινα μὴ φάναι καλόν τε καὶ εὐδαίμονα θεῶν εἶναι: 'say that any of the gods is not beautiful and fortunate'. Note the chiastic reordering of the adjectives in this restatement.

μὰ Δί᾽ οὐκ ἔγωγ᾽: μα + accusative for an oath with a god's name.

εὐδαίμονας δὲ δὴ λέγεις οὐ τοὺς τἀγαθὰ καὶ τὰ καλὰ κεκτημένους: εὐδαίμονας has been promoted for emphasis but should be translated last in the indirect statement – 'do you not in fact call those who have acquired good and beautiful things fortunate'.

πάνυ γε: a way of giving a clear affirmative.

202d

ἀλλὰ μὴν Ἔρωτά γε: 'yet truly about Love'. Like 202b1, take this first, signposting the move from talking about the gods to talking about Love.

ὡμολόγηκας δι᾽ ἔνδειαν τῶν ἀγαθῶν καὶ καλῶν ἐπιθυμεῖν αὐτῶν τούτων: this was agreed at 201e6. The word order is emphatic – 'you have agreed that it is because of lack of good and beautiful things it (Love) desires these very things'.

ὧν ἐνδεής ἐστιν: the antecedent of the relative is τούτων; the relative is in the genitive after ἐνδεής.

ὡμολόγηκα γάρ: γάρ gives the sense of 'yes, for' or 'no, for'. Here 'yes, for I did agree (that)'.

A Level

πῶς ἂν οὖν θεὸς εἴη: for the form of the question, see 202a8n.

ὅ γε τῶν καλῶν καὶ ἀγαθῶν ἄμοιρος: 'someone who is bereft of beautiful and good things'. ὅ is the definite article.

The logic of the argument has been

1 All gods are happy
2 Happiness is having good and beautiful things
3 Eros doesn't have what is good and beautiful
4 So Eros isn't happy, so Eros isn't a god.

Accepting point 1 as a definition, this argument seems open to attack at points 2 and 3 about whether happiness is having ALL good and beautiful things, and whether Eros lacks ALL that is good and beautiful.

καὶ σὺ: καί is emphatically placed – 'you too'.

τί οὖν ἄν, ἔφην, εἴη: ἄν + optative is potential – 'what then could (Love) be'.

ἥκιστά γε: an emphatic negative – 'not at all'.

ἀλλὰ τί μήν: 'but what, then'. μήν gives the sense of there being no other options.

ὥσπερ τὰ πρότερα: at 202a5.

δαίμων μέγας: 'a great Spirit'. In Homer, this word could be applied to the great gods, but only masculine and singular, and stood more for their divine power. After Homer, it could be applied to the ghosts of heroes or kings, and sometimes meant virtually 'fate'. Plato gives it this new sense, which stuck. Socrates, in his speech at his trial (see Plato's *Apology*) says that a δαίμων speaks to him and turns him away from things like politics. Any translation/understanding needs to get away from the negative connotations of demon/demonic, but since we have no category of intermediate being between gods and mortals, there is no ideal word.

καὶ γὰρ πᾶν τὸ δαιμόνιον: the article + adjective is used to form a vague abstract concept – 'the whole spiritual world'.

202e

τίνα ... δύναμιν ἔχον: the participle (neuter singular nominative) agrees back to το δαιμόνιον.

ἑρμηνεῦον καὶ διαπορθμεῦον: again, the participles (neuter singular nominative) agree with το δαιμόνιον.

θεοῖς τὰ παρ᾽ ἀνθρώπων καὶ ἀνθρώποις τὰ παρὰ θεῶν: arranged in two grammatically similar halves (and yet also chiastic!) to reflect the balance of the relationship – each gives and expects what is appropriate.

τῶν μὲν τὰς δεήσεις καὶ θυσίας – 'the requests and sacrifices of men'.

τῶν δὲ τὰς ἐπιτάξεις τε καὶ ἀμοιβὰς τῶν θυσιῶν – 'the instructions and the responses to sacrifices of the gods'. Note again the parallel structures (and μέν ... δέ) suggesting the balanced reciprocal relationship.

ἐν μέσῳ δὲ ὂν ἀμφοτέρων: again, the participle (neuter singular nominative) agrees with το δαιμόνιον – 'both' i.e. mortal and immortal.

συμπληροῖ: the verb is 3rd person singular, present indicative active (omicron contract). The subject is πᾶν τὸ δαιμόνιον – 'it fills in the gap'.

A Level

ὥστε τὸ πᾶν αὐτὸ αὑτῷ συνδεδέσθαι: τὸ πᾶν αὐτὸ is the accusative subject of the result clause; αὑτῷ is reflexive; συνδεδέσθαι perfect passive infinitive – 'with the result that universe is connected together with itself'.

διὰ τούτου καὶ ἡ μαντικὴ πᾶσα χωρεῖ: τούτου refers to δαιμόνιον, the spiritual system that fills the space between gods and mortals. Prophecy is seen as the art of extracting messages from that system. καὶ – 'too/also'. χωρέω here has the sense 'passes' and therefore 'works'.

203a

καὶ ἡ τῶν ἱερέων τέχνη τῶν τε περὶ τὰς θυσίας καὶ τελετὰς καὶ τὰς ἐπῳδὰς καὶ τὴν μαντείαν πᾶσαν καὶ γοητείαν: following μαντικὴ, this covers all religious skills performed by priests, which might include a prophetic role. Understand χωρεῖ with this second subject too – 'and the art of priests, the ones concerned with sacrifices and rites and spells and all prophecy and magic'. The polysyndeton emphasizes the wide range of forms of communication with the divine through the 'spiritual'.

θεὸς δὲ ἀνθρώπῳ οὐ μείγνυται: as before, this assumes a more sophisticated view of god/gods. Gods understood in Homeric terms clearly did interact directly with humans.

ἀλλὰ διὰ τούτου: repeating the idea of 202e7; again understand 'spiritual medium'.

πᾶσά ἐστιν ἡ ὁμιλία καὶ ἡ διάλεκτος θεοῖς πρὸς ἀνθρώπους: a catch-all expression – 'is all interaction and conversation for the gods with humans'.

καὶ ἐγρηγορόσι καὶ καθεύδουσι: these participles (dative masculine plural of perfect and present respectively) grammatically agree with θεοῖς but in sense need to be taken with ἀνθρώπους (this problem has had various suggested solutions including text emendation).

καὶ ὁ μὲν περὶ τὰ τοιαῦτα σοφὸς δαιμόνιος ἀνήρ: understand ἐστί after σοφός.

ὁ δὲ ἄλλο τι σοφὸς ὢν ἢ περὶ τέχνας ἢ χειρουργίας τινὰς βάναυσος: notice the variation in these parallel phrases: ὁ . . . σοφός has become ὁ . . . σοφὸς ὤν, and περὶ τὰ τοιαῦτα has become ἄλλο τι (accusative of respect). βάναυσος is set up in contrast to δαιμόνιος – the contrast must be something like a 'man concerned with the spiritual world' vs a 'man concerned with the material world' (generally pejorative).

παντοδαποί: 'of every kind'.

The nature of Eros 203a8–204c6

Diotima describes how Eros was born as a result of a liaison between Poros (Resource) and Penia (Want) and as a result has conflicting characteristics reflecting both parents. This includes being between knowledge and ignorance and therefore loving wisdom. Diotima explains that the heart of Socrates'/Agathon's mistake was to describe Eros like the objects of love, rather than describing Eros as the lover of those objects. While Diotima/Socrates/Plato wants to draw important conclusions from this story, one can't help being surprised and amused at the story of Eros being

A Level

conceived from a drunken liaison between two wholly unsuitable gods, and the frequent word play helps to create the humour. This story is meant to balance the theogonies of the earlier speeches and the pseudo-myth of Aristophanes – Socrates can match them in his creativity. The narrative also brings light relief to the frequent question-and-answer.

πατρὸς δέ ... τίνος ἐστὶ καὶ μητρός: literally 'he is of which father and mother' (genitive of source). Phaedrus (178a) has claimed that Eros is primordial and has no parents; Agathon (195b) has claimed that Eros is one of the youngest gods but without giving parentage.

203b

μακρότερον ... διηγήσασθαι: understand ἐστί. μακρότερον here carries the sense of 'rather long'. This is perhaps a typical way of introducing a change of pace from argument to myth. This seems to be a Platonic invention, but such aetiological myths were common in Greek writing.

ἐρῶ: future of λέγω.

ὅτε γὰρ ἐγένετο ἡ Ἀφροδίτη: γίγνομαι with the strong sense of 'be born'. Phaedrus had described two versions of the birth of Aphrodite (180d); Diotima seems to be accepting the version where she is daughter of Zeus and Dione.

ἡστιῶντο οἱ θεοὶ οἵ τε ἄλλοι καὶ ὁ τῆς Μήτιδος υὸς Πόρος: Greek typically says 'the gods were feasting, the other ones and Poros' to set the scene generally (gods feasting) and then zoom in on a specific character of interest. Πόρος describes any 'means/resource', e.g. a route for a journey, money for a purchase, a scheme to achieve something. Μῆτις (wisdom/skill/craft) in Hesiod's tradition is the first wife of Zeus and mother of Athena (which is used to explain Athena's wisdom).

προσαιτήσουσα: future participle for sense of purpose, promoted for emphasis.

οἷον δὴ εὐωχίας οὔσης: οἷον + genitive absolute – 'just as (happens) when there is a party'.

ἡ Πενία: Poverty had been personified by Aristophanes in *Wealth* (388 BCE). It has just been agreed that the gods are 'happy/blessed' and have 'good and fine things' (202c) and so it seems that Penia is not a goddess. She appears to be the opposite of Poros, and the combination of the two creates a *daimon*, between god and mortal, so Bury concludes that Penia is a personification of mortal nature in all our impoverishment (relative to the gods).

ὁ οὖν Πόρος μεθυσθεὶς τοῦ νέκταρος: Greek gods traditionally enjoyed ambrosia and nectar (both with immortality-bringing properties). It is an anthropomorphic stretch to imagine a god drunk on nectar.

οἶνος γὰρ οὔπω ἦν: in Greek mythology, Dionysus, the son of Zeus and the Theban princess Semele, discovered wine on Mt. Nysa, and bestowed the gift on mankind, becoming the god of wine. According to Homer (*Iliad* 5.341f), the gods continued to drink ambrosia not wine.

βεβαρημένος ηὗδεν: perfect passive participle of βαρέω – 'overcome, he slept'.

ἡ οὖν Πενία ἐπιβουλεύουσα διὰ τὴν αὑτῆς ἀπορίαν παιδίον ποιήσασθαι ἐκ τοῦ Πόρου: notice the play on words – the solution to ἀπορία comes from Πόρος.

**A
Level**

203c

κατακλίνεταί τε παρ᾽ αὐτῷ καὶ ἐκύησε τὸν ἔρωτα: κυέω is a variant of κύω – 'she fell pregnant with'.

διὸ: crasis of διά ὅ – 'on account of which'.

ἀκόλουθος καὶ θεράπων: the former particularly implies following, and the latter ministering.

γεννηθεὶς ἐν τοῖς ἐκείνης γενεθλίοις: aorist passive participle with causal sense – 'because he was conceived on the birthday of that (goddess Aphrodite)'. The polyptoton makes the logic clear, the key assumption being a Greek belief that the circumstances of a conception affect the character of the child.

καὶ ἅμα φύσει ἐραστὴς ὢν περὶ τὸ καλὸν καὶ τῆς Ἀφροδίτης καλῆς οὔσης: ἅμα links γεννηθεὶς and ὢν, both causal participles, followed by a causal genitive absolute. Eros is a lover of the beautiful in general, and therefore of Aphrodite who is beautiful, and these are further reasons he is an attendant on Aphrodite.

ἅτε οὖν Πόρου καὶ Πενίας υὸς ὤν: ἅτε makes the causal sense of the participle clear – 'and so, seeing that he is the son of Poros and Penia'.

ὁ Ἔρως ἐν τοιαύτῃ τύχῃ καθέστηκεν: the verb is intransitive perfect – 'Eros turned out in the following way'. We now begin a description of what Eros is like, based on the characteristics of his parents. This description will counter Agathon's description of 195b–197c.

πρῶτον μὲν πένης ἀεί ἐστι: the lover as a poor man is a trope in comedy and poetry, playing on the idea either that he has spent all his money in the pursuit of his beloved, or that in his devotion to his beloved he has forgotten/lost interest in his work. Here it is Eros so described, and πένης deliberately plays on his mother's name Πενία.

καὶ πολλοῦ δεῖ: 'he is far from'; literally 'he is lacking of much from'.

ἁπαλός: delicate, usually in a positive sense. Agathon used this word repeatedly from 195c7 about Eros.

οἷον οἱ πολλοὶ οἴονται: 'as most people think'. Socrates puts Agathon among οἱ πολλοί, perhaps pointedly since Agathon contrasted himself with them 194b.

203d

ἀλλὰ σκληρὸς: 'rough' or 'harsh' to the touch, sight, smell. This adjective was specifically rejected by Agathon 196a4. The trope of the lover looking rough, because of nights lying at his beloved door or a neglect for his own care, is another literary commonplace. Note the strong polysyndeton.

καὶ αὐχμηρὸς: 'squalid' of hair, or 'dry' of skin.

καὶ ἀνυπόδητος καὶ ἄοικος: 'and shoeless and homeless'. This list (note the polysyndeton) is reminiscent of Aristophanic comedy.

χαμαιπετής: a range of suitable meanings: 'falling to the ground' – the trope of the awkward lover; 'grovelling on the ground' – the trope of the lover trying to win over a beloved; 'lying on the ground' – again, the lover who sleeps outside the beloved's house. The next adjective may point towards the last meaning.

ἐπὶ θύραις καὶ ἐν ὁδοῖς: this is one idea (hendiadys) – 'at house doors by the roadside'. Penia was described as being at the door of the gods' party.

A Level

ὑπαίθριος κοιμώμενος: 'sleeping in the open air'.

τὴν τῆς μητρὸς φύσιν ἔχων: 'having the nature of his mother', i.e. Πενία. These are all characteristics which a lover shares with a beggar!

ἀεὶ ἐνδείᾳ σύνοικος: 'always tied to poverty'.

It is noticeable that this description fits Socrates very well – poor, rough-looking, shoeless (cf. 174a), often bedless, often hanging out in the streets and public places. This will make sense as Socrates is gradually revealed as the ideal lover – the lover of wisdom.

κατὰ δὲ αὖ τὸν πατέρα: 'and then again in conformity with his father'. αὖ carries the sense of 'next' or 'in turn'.

ἐπίβουλός: 'plotting'. Curiously the verb was used about Πενία at 202b7.

τοῖς καλοῖς καὶ τοῖς ἀγαθοῖς: the dative case follows naturally from the ἐπι-compound, showing the direction or target of the plotting. These are probably neuter for a generalization, although masculine would fit the description of Eros.

ἴτης: a variant of ἰταμός – 'eager' or 'vigorous'. Again, note the polysyndeton giving a parallel list of attributes inherited from his father.

ἀεί τινας πλέκων μηχανάς: πλέκω is originally to weave, but came to mean 'devise'.

φρονήσεως ἐπιθυμητὴς: 'a desirer of understanding'.

πόριμος: 'resourceful'. Note the play on words with Πόρος.

φιλοσοφῶν διὰ παντὸς τοῦ βίου: 'a lover of wisdom through his whole life'. This is at this stage a surprising description but anticipates where the argument is going.

δεινὸς γόης καὶ φαρμακεὺς καὶ σοφιστής: could be as mystical as 'a clever wizard, sorcerer and sophist' or as pejorative as 'a clever cheat and poisoner and sophist'. When reading this triplet, one thinks of the psychological tricks, alcohol and 'chat' that lovers have used in their 'seductions' over the years.

203e

καὶ οὔτε ὡς ἀθάνατος πέφυκεν οὔτε ὡς θνητός: 'by nature he is neither like an immortal nor a mortal'. φύω in the perfect active is intransitive – 'to be born' and therefore 'to be X by nature'.

τοτὲ μὲν . . . τοτὲ δὲ: 'at one moment . . . at another'.

τῆς αὐτῆς ἡμέρας: 'in the same day', genitive of time during which/within which.

ὅταν εὐπορήσῃ: 'whenever he has resources'. ὅταν is a crasis of ὅτε + ἄν, introducing an indefinite clauses (subjunctive in primary sequence, aorist tense by aspect). Another play on the name Πόρος.

πάλιν δὲ ἀναβιώσκεται διὰ τὴν τοῦ πατρὸς φύσιν: i.e. his life lurches between the energy and success of his father, and the poverty and failure of his mother. This description perhaps reflects the inconstant emotions of love, or the divine discontent that the true lover of beauty will feel until he apprehends Beauty itself.

τὸ δὲ ποριζόμενον: 'his income' (Dover), literally 'that which is provided', the neuter article + participle making a noun phrase.

ἀεὶ ὑπεκρεῖ: 'always wastes away gradually'. The verb is a compound: ὑπό + ἐκ + ῥέω (I flow out from under).

ὥστε οὔτε ἀπορεῖ Ἔρως ποτὲ οὔτε πλουτεῖ: 'with the result that Eros is never either in want nor rich'. ὥστε + indicative for actual result.

**A
Level**

σοφίας τε αὖ καὶ ἀμαθίας ἐν μέσῳ ἐστίν: this seems to be an important new
   direction to the description (αὖ marking a new point) even if it is tacked on to the
   end of the sentence. Perhaps translate in a new sentence.

204a

ἔχει γὰρ ὧδε: 'for it's like this'. ἔχω (used impersonally) + adverb has the sense of
   'to be'.
ἔστι γάρ: 'for he (already) is (wise)'. The singular subject follows οὐδείς.
οὐδ᾽ εἴ τις ἄλλος σοφός, οὐ φιλοσοφεῖ: 'nor does any other wise person pursue
   wisdom'. εἴ τις can be treated like an indefinite adjective, but reflects the fact that
   this is hypothetical (no human is actually wise, and therefore all should be
   philosophers). The second οὐ reinforces the negative connective οὐδέ.
οὐδ᾽ αὖ οἱ ἀμαθεῖς φιλοσοφοῦσιν οὐδ᾽ ἐπιθυμοῦσι σοφοὶ γενέσθαι: this
   αὖ points us to the other side of a balance (see note on 203d4). The language
   deliberately imitates the opening sentence of this section about the gods
   (204a1).
αὐτὸ γὰρ τοῦτό: 'for with respect to this very thing', accusative of respect.
ἐστι χαλεπὸν ἀμαθία: 'ignorance is damaging'.
τὸ μὴ ὄντα καλὸν κἀγαθὸν μηδὲ φρόνιμον δοκεῖν αὑτῷ εἶναι ἱκανόν: 'in
   that while not being beautiful and good nor wise, it seems to itself to be sufficient'.
   The whole phrase τὸ . . . ἱκανόν stands in apposition to, and explains, τοῦτό. It
   seems true that often the most ignorant are most happy being ignorant.
οὔκουν ἐπιθυμεῖ ὁ μὴ οἰόμενος ἐνδεὴς εἶναι οὗ ἂν μὴ οἴηται ἐπιδεῖσθαι:
   'therefore a person thinking that he doesn't lack anything doesn't desire whatever
   he doesn't think he lacks'. ὁ μὴ οἰόμενος ἐνδεὴς εἶναι acts as subject. μή is
   used with the generic participle, and the subject of the indirect statement (being
   the same as the subject of οἰόμενος) is left out. οὗ ἂν μὴ οἴηται ἐπιδεῖσθαι –
   the relative clause is indefinite (hence ἂν + μή + subjunctive in primary sequence),
   and οὗ is genitive as object of ἐπιδεῖσθαι. The antecedent of οὗ (τούτου –
   genitive after ἐπιθυμέω) has been omitted.
τίνες . . . οἱ φιλοσοφοῦντες: εἰσίν understood.

204b

δῆλον δή . . . τοῦτό γε ἤδη καὶ παιδί: note the piling-up of emphasis:
   δή/γε/ἤδη/καί. This is quite a pointed put-down by Diotima. In *Meno*, Socrates
   uses a child to explore the difference between right opinion and knowledge,
   assuming the child can make these basic logical steps.
ὅτι οἱ μεταξὺ τούτων ἀμφοτέρων: οἱ is οἱ φιλοσοφοῦντες, τούτων are the
   wise and ignorant.
ὧν ἂν εἴη καὶ ὁ Ἔρως: a relative clause – the antecedent is οἱ, the genitive is
   partitive. ἂν + optative must be potential, although some editions have indicative
   – 'of whom Eros would be one'.
ἔστιν γὰρ δὴ τῶν καλλίστων ἡ σοφία: 'wisdom is (one) of the finest things'.
   καλός is much broader than physical beauty.
Ἔρως δ᾽ ἐστὶν ἔρως περὶ τὸ καλόν: 'Eros is love of the beautiful'.
ὥστε ἀναγκαῖον: understand ἐστί, an indicative for actual result.
ἔρωτα φιλόσοφον εἶναι: accusative and infinitive (after 'it is necessary').

A
Level

φιλόσοφον δὲ ὄντα μεταξὺ εἶναι σοφοῦ καὶ ἀμαθοῦς: ἔρωτα is the (accusative) subject of the infinitive, with φιλόσοφον δὲ ὄντα agreeing.

αἰτία δὲ αὐτῷ καὶ τούτων ἡ γένεσις: 'his birth is the cause of these things too'. αὐτῷ is dative of advantage, and understand ἐστί.

πατρὸς μὲν γὰρ σοφοῦ ἐστι καὶ εὐπόρου, μητρὸς δὲ οὐ σοφῆς καὶ ἀπόρου. The genitives are genitives of source, like 203a9. Notice the balancing halves.

ἡ μὲν οὖν φύσις τοῦ δαίμονος ... αὕτη: this completes Socrates description of the nature of Eros, started at 203c5. αὕτη (οὗτος), as often, looks backward.

204c

ὃν δὲ σὺ ᾠήθης ἔρωτα εἶναι, θαυμαστὸν οὐδὲν ἔπαθες: literally 'with respect to who you thought Eros to be, you suffered nothing surprising'. But it is perhaps more clearly put – 'it is not at all surprising that you thought as you did who Eros was'. οἴομαι has aorist ᾠήθην.

ὡς ἐμοὶ δοκεῖ τεκμαιρομένη: τεκμαίρομαι is to judge from evidence.

ἐξ ὧν σὺ λέγεις: a compressed form of ἐξ τούτων ἅ. The relative has been 'attracted' into the case of its antecedent, which has been left out.

τὸ ἐρώμενον ἔρωτα εἶναι, οὐ τὸ ἐρῶν: accusative and infinitives (x2) after ᾠήθης. Socrates had thought (and this was the view of Agathon in his speech) that Eros was the thing beloved (τὸ ἐρώμενον, i.e. the beautiful), not the thing doing the loving (τὸ ἐρῶν).

διὰ ταῦτά σοι οἶμαι πάγκαλος ἐφαίνετο ὁ Ἔρως: notice the word order. The promotion of σοι gives it an edge of criticism, ostensibly of Socrates, although it is clear that it applies to Agathon and the others who liked that speech more than Socrates; πάγκαλος, the critical wrong idea, is also put ahead of Eros.

καὶ γὰρ ἔστι τὸ ἐραστὸν τὸ τῷ ὄντι καλὸν καὶ ἁβρὸν καὶ τέλεον καὶ μακαριστόν: literally 'for it is the thing loved which is the actually beautiful and charming and perfect and blessed thing'. τὸ ἐραστὸν – 'the thing loved'. τῷ ὄντι is the article + participle, but used adverbially to mean 'actually'.

τὸ δέ γε ἐρῶν ἄλλην ἰδέαν τοιαύτην ἔχον: understand ἐστί. ἔχον ἐστί is virtually the same as ἔχει – 'but the thing actually doing the loving has another form'.

οἵαν ἐγὼ διῆλθον: as done at 201e–204b. The relative picks up τοιαύτην.

The purpose of Love 204c7–206b1

Crucial to the next section are the agreements: i) at 201a5 it was agreed that Love (ἔρως) is love of beauty; and ii) at 201c7 that ἀγαθά (good things) are also καλά (beautiful) (from now on, these qualities will be treated as synonymous). Love is now defined as the desire to have good things forever, because this brings happiness. This raises interesting questions about whether people can love someone even when we know that they are not good or are destructive to our own happiness. Diotima deals with the popular use of the term 'love' for romantic/sexual feelings and explains that this is just one example of what Love really is. This section is the key moment when Plato lifts Eros above the issue of sexual attraction and turns it into the driving force for humans in seeking the good, which ultimately brings happiness.

A
Level

εἶεν δή: 'very well, then'. The particle is used to pass on to the next point.

καλῶς γὰρ λέγεις: this is a way of stating agreement with what has been said (not approval of how it was said).

τοιοῦτος ὤν: 'since (Eros) is like this', the participle is causal.

ὁ Ἔρως τίνα χρείαν ἔχει τοῖς ἀνθρώποις: 'what use does Eros have for humans'.

204d

τοῦτο δὴ μετὰ ταῦτ': τοῦτο refers back to what Socrates has just requested; ταῦτα to those things that have just been discussed.

ἔστι μὲν γὰρ δὴ τοιοῦτος καὶ οὕτω γεγονὼς ὁ Ἔρως, ἔστι δὲ τῶν καλῶν, ὡς σὺ φής: a quick recap! τοιοῦτος refers to Eros' character; γεγονὼς (perfect active participle of γίγνομαι) refers to his birth (which helps explain his character); the third element, the basis for the following argument, Socrates stated at 201e5, and something close again at 204b3.

εἰ δέ τις ἡμᾶς ἔροιτο: 'if someone were to ask us'. This takes the form of the protasis of a future remote condition: εἰ + optative.

τί τῶν καλῶν ἐστιν ὁ Ἔρως: 'in what respect is Eros of fine things'. τί is accusative of respect; τῶν καλῶν is objective genitive.

ὧδε δὲ σαφέστερον: understand 'it is' or 'I will say it'.

ἐρᾷ ὁ ἐρῶν τῶν καλῶν· τί ἐρᾷ: 'the lover loves fine things: why does he love (them)'.

καὶ ἐγὼ εἶπον ὅτι "γενέσθαι αὑτῷ": 'and I said "that beautiful things become his"'. ὅτι can be used even with direct speech, and isn't translated here (this is not indirect statement). The verb ἐράω can take accusative and infinitive to mean 'desire that', which explains the infinitive γενέσθαι. The reflexive αὑτῷ (= ἑαυτῷ) refers back to the understood subject Eros.

ἀλλ' ἔτι ποθεῖ . . . ἡ ἀπόκρισις ἐρώτησιν τοιάνδε: 'but your answer still requires a question like this'. Diotima calls Socrates out for not answering the question. Notice the striking juxtaposition.

τί ἔσται ἐκείνῳ: 'what (benefit/use/gain) will there be'.

ᾧ ἂν γένηται τὰ καλά: 'for the one who gets beautiful things' (literally 'for whom the beautiful things become'). ἂν + subjunctive for an indefinite clause in primary sequence (aorist by aspect). The dative ᾧ is possessive.

οὐ πάνυ ἔφην ἔτι ἔχειν ἐγώ: 'I said that I was still not at all able'. The construction is indirect statement with nominative and infinitive. ἔχω, as often with the infinitive, has the sense of 'to be able'.

προχείρως: the root of this word is for something to be 'at hand'.

204e

ὥσπερ ἂν εἰ τις μεταβαλὼν ἀντὶ τοῦ καλοῦ τῷ ἀγαθῷ χρώμενος πυνθάνοιτο: treat this as a future remote condition – 'just as (you would answer) if someone, making a change and using 'good' instead of 'beautiful' were to ask (it)'. The apodosis is omitted.

ἐρᾷ ὁ ἐρῶν τῶν ἀγαθῶν· τί ἐρᾷ: the question of 204d5, with 'good' substituted for 'beautiful'.

γενέσθαι, ἦν δ' ἐγώ, αὑτῷ: the same reply as 204d7 (see note). This is the conclusion to step 1 of this argument: love (ἔρως) for καλά/ἀγαθά (beautiful/ good things) is desire to have them.

A Level

καὶ τί ἔσται ἐκείνῳ ᾧ ἂν γένηται τἀγαθά: the same question as 204d8 (see note), with 'good' substituted. The next step is to establish why one wants to have καλά/ἀγαθά.

τοῦτ᾽ εὐπορώτερον ... ἔχω ἀποκρίνασθαι: ἔχω again with the sense of 'be able'. εὐπορώτερον – 'more easily'. Again probably a pun on Πόρος.

ὅτι εὐδαίμων ἔσται: indirect statement after ἀποκρίνασθαι – 'that he will be happy'.

205a

κτήσει ... ἀγαθῶν οἱ εὐδαίμονες εὐδαίμονες: 'it is the possession of good things that makes the happy happy'. Literally 'the happy are happy by the possession of good things'. Understand εἰσίν. This is the conclusion to step 2: a person desires to have καλά/ἀγαθά because this brings happiness.

καὶ οὐκέτι προσδεῖ ἐρέσθαι: 'it is not necessary to ask any further'. The verb is impersonal. Both οὐκέτι and the προσ- prefix give the idea of 'further' or 'in addition'.

ἵνα τί: understand γένηται – literally 'in order for what to happen'. i.e. 'why'.

βούλεται εὐδαίμων εἶναι ὁ βουλόμενος: εὐδαίμων εἶναι goes with both the participle and the finite verb.

ἀλλὰ τέλος δοκεῖ ἔχειν ἡ ἀπόκρισις: 'the answer seems to have a conclusion'. Every argument at some stage has to fall back on something that is just accepted as true without argument (an axiom), and for Plato, the wish to be εὐδαίμων is axiomatic (we don't need to ask 'why does he wish to be happy' – it is just obviously true). This perhaps makes more sense when one understands that the Greek verb εὐδαιμονέω (and related εὐδαιμονία, εὐδαίμων) describes an objective state, where all is well with a man (unlike the English 'happiness' which has more of a sense of subjective feelings). The idea that 'well-being' is the ultimate good or the obvious object of all human longing fits with a lot of modern thinking, but is not necessarily the case.

ἀληθῆ λέγεις: ἀληθῆ is neuter plural of the adjective, but a standard way of expressing the abstract notion 'the truth'. This phrase is little more than 'I agree'.

ταύτην δὴ τὴν βούλησιν καὶ τὸν ἔρωτα τοῦτον: this sentence begins with the accusative (of the indirect statement) 'this desire and this love', referring back to the desire of good things for the sake of being happy.

πότερα κοινὸν οἴει εἶναι πάντων ἀνθρώπων: 'do you think that (this desire and this love) are common to all people'. The construction is indirect statement (accusative and infinitive) after οἴομαι. πότερα introduces questions with an alternative – here in the phrase ἢ πῶς λέγεις (and doesn't need translating). κοινὸν takes the genitive.

καὶ πάντας τἀγαθὰ βούλεσθαι αὑτοῖς εἶναι ἀεί: this continues the indirect statement – πάντας is the accusative and βούλεσθαι the infinitive. αὑτοῖς is reflexive (= ἑαυτοῖς). This is an addition to step 2 – now ALL people desire to have καλά/ἀγαθά ALWAYS because this brings happiness. ἀεί has been added to this formulation and will become vitally important, although it is not clear whether it is going with βούλεσθαι or εἶναι.

ἢ πῶς λέγεις: a standard way of checking agreement.

οὕτως: a natural reply to πῶς – 'yes, as you say'.

A Level

κοινὸν εἶναι πάντων: indirect statement, after the λέγω implied by the question.

τί δὴ οὖν ... οὐ ... φαμεν: 'so why then do we not say', + accusative + infinitive. The main argument now gets paused to consider why most people don't use the term 'love' in this way. It will be picked up again at 205d1.

205b

εἴπερ γε: the suffix -περ and γε add emphasis – 'if indeed'.

πάντες τῶν αὐτῶν ἐρῶσι καὶ ἀεί: 'all men desire the same things always' (i.e. the good, that it should be theirs always).

ἀλλά τινάς φαμεν ἐρᾶν, τοὺς δ᾽ οὔ: the 'but' contrasts to the 'why' question. Diotima is pointing out the apparent contradiction between their conclusion (all men all the time love the good, wanting it in order to be happy) and the common use of the verb love, which we apply to some people in a particular time of romantic attachment.

θαυμάζω ... καὶ αὐτός: καὶ carries the sense of '(I) too'. It is an unusual (and humorous?) reversal from the other dialogues for Socrates to be the one who is slow in understanding and not seeing where the argument is going, but is an important example of intellectual humility.

ἀφελόντες γὰρ ἄρα τοῦ ἔρωτός τι εἶδος: 'for in fact, having separated out one type of love'. ἀφελόντες is aorist active participle agreeing with the subject 'we'.

ὀνομάζομεν, τὸ τοῦ ὅλου ἐπιτιθέντες ὄνομα, ἔρωτα: 'we call it 'love', applying the name of the whole concept'. τοῦ ἔρωτός τι εἶδος (one type of love, i.e. 'romantic love') is also the object of the main verb.

τὰ δὲ ἄλλα ἄλλοις καταχρώμεθα ὀνόμασιν: 'with respect to other things too, we thoughtlessly apply other names'. This has been understood in two different ways: (i) with τὰ δὲ ἄλλα referring to other types of love, for which we use other names; (ii) this refers to other things (i.e. other examples), where we give the name of the whole to a specific sub-type. Either way τὰ ... ἄλλα is best taken as accusative of respect. The κατα- prefix suggests 'misuse/misapplication'.

ὥσπερ τί: 'like what', but perhaps less blunt in Greek!

ὥσπερ τόδε: as usual, ὅδε looks forward.

τι πολύ: 'something of many forms'.

ἡ γάρ τοι ἐκ τοῦ μὴ ὄντος εἰς τὸ ὂν ἰόντι ὁτῳοῦν αἰτία πᾶσά ἐστι ποίησις: 'for surely every cause for anything whatever going from a state of not being into a state of being is "creation"'. τό (μή) ὄν is the way of describing the abstract notion of existing (not existing). ὁστισοῦν is a more emphatic version of ὅστις – 'anything whatsoever' – the ὅστις element declining normally, and ἰόντι agreeing. This section relies on the fact that the Greek word for a poet (ποιητής) has its root in the verb ποιέω, and therefore a ποιητής could logically be anyone who creates anything. This ambiguity doesn't exist in English, making this section very difficult to translate. The point is that we have words which could apply to a broad range of contexts, but are normally used for one specific example of such a context.

205c

ὥστε: expressing logical consequence.

καὶ αἱ ὑπὸ πάσαις ταῖς τέχναις ἐργασίαι: ἐργασία is something laboured at or manufactured (usually with the hands). LSJ says that ὑπό + dative here describes the subordination of things under a class. i.e. 'even things manufactured by what we would call all technical skills', e.g. out of wood, metal, clay, etc.

ποιήσεις: 'creations'.

οἱ τούτων δημιουργοὶ πάντες ποιηταί: 'skilled workmen of such things are all "creators"'. ποιηταί usually refers to poets, but 'poet' makes no sense here: a skilled workman/artisan is certainly 'creating' or 'making' something.

ἦ δ᾽ ἥ: see note 202a10.

οἶσθ᾽ ὅτι οὐ καλοῦνται ποιηταὶ ἀλλὰ ἄλλα ἔχουσιν ὀνόματα: 'do you know that they are not called "poets/creators" but have other names'. The subject is still δημιουργοί. Note the emphasis on ἄλλα through its promotion.

ἀπὸ δὲ πάσης τῆς ποιήσεως: 'but from all (forms of) creation'.

ἓν μόριον ἀφορισθὲν τὸ περὶ τὴν μουσικὴν καὶ τὰ μέτρα τῷ τοῦ ὅλου ὀνόματι προσαγορεύεται: 'one part, separated off, the part concerning music and metre, is called by the name of the whole'. ἀφορισθὲν is aorist passive participle (neuter nominative) agreeing with the subject ἓν μόριον, which also has the article phrase (τὸ . . . μέτρα) in apposition.

ποίησις γὰρ τοῦτο μόνον καλεῖται: start with τοῦτο μόνον.

καὶ οἱ ἔχοντες τοῦτο τὸ μόριον τῆς ποιήσεως ποιηταί: understand εἰσίν.

205d

οὕτω τοίνυν καὶ περὶ τὸν ἔρωτα: 'in the same way accordingly also about Eros'.

τὸ μὲν κεφάλαιόν: κεφάλαιος means 'of the head', but like our words to do with 'capital' can metaphorically mean the chief point or sum; here it is probably accusative of respect and can be treated as virtually an adverb – 'in summary'.

ἐστι πᾶσα ἡ τῶν ἀγαθῶν ἐπιθυμία καὶ τοῦ εὐδαιμονεῖν: '(love) is every desire for good things and to be happy'. There is much disagreement about how to understand this summary. The most popular construal is to understand ὁ Ἔρως as an understood subject and the rest as predicate.

ὁ μέγιστός τε καὶ δολερὸς ἔρως παντί: 'Eros, very great and deceitful to all' – to be taken in apposition to the understood subject. δολερός doesn't fit the context and is not a common word in Attic prose leading most people to think this is a quotation from poetry; μέγιστός is the relevant element, and quoting poetry for confirmation has been a frequent feature in these speeches. The polyptoton of πᾶς adds universality and emphasis to the summary.

ἀλλ᾽ οἱ μὲν: contrasted with οἱ δέ shortly. The contrast is between those seeing good/happiness in various ways, with those seeking it through romantic love.

ἄλλη τρεπόμενοι πολλαχῇ: the participle is middle or passive with the sense of 'turning themselves in many other ways'.

ἐπ᾽ αὐτόν: referring to the desire of good things and to be happy.

ἢ κατὰ χρηματισμὸν ἢ κατὰ φιλογυμναστίαν ἢ κατὰ φιλοσοφίαν: this list is three possible examples of the 'many other ways'. χρηματισμόν can be money-making or administration.

οὔτε ἐρᾶν καλοῦνται οὔτε ἐρασταί: 'are neither said "to love" nor to be "lovers"'.

οἱ δὲ κατὰ ἕν τι εἶδος ἰόντες τε καὶ ἐσπουδακότες: these participles balance τρεπόμενοι. ἐσπουδακότες is perfect active participle. The two should be seen as a sort of hendiadys – 'those eagerly going after just one type'.

ἴσχουσιν: a variant of ἔχω, particularly having the sense of 'hold on to'.

A
Level

ἔρωτά τε καὶ ἐρᾶν καὶ ἐρασταί: ἔρωτα fits grammatically in apposition to τὸ
  ὄνομα, while we understand καλοῦνται from the first half of the sentence with
  ἐρᾶν and ἐρασταί – 'love, and are said "to love" and are called "lovers"'.
κινδυνεύεις ἀληθῆ . . . λέγειν: κινδυνεύω + infinitive expresses what is probable
  or likely – 'you are probably right'.
καὶ λέγεται μέν γέ τις . . . λόγος: as articulated by Aristophanes 191d–193d.
ὡς . . . οὗτοι ἐρῶσιν: indirect statement after λέγεται.
οἳ ἂν τὸ ἥμισυ ἑαυτῶν ζητῶσιν: 'whoever seeks their own other half'. ἄν +
  subjunctive (present by aspect) for an indefinite clause. The article + adjective τὸ
  ἥμισυ acts as an abstract noun.

205e

ὁ δ᾽ ἐμὸς λόγος φησιν: introduces an indirect statement.
οὔτε ἡμίσεός εἶναι τὸν ἔρωτα οὔτε ὅλου: 'that love is neither of a half nor of a
  whole'. τὸν ἔρωτα is accusative in an accusative and infinitive. The two genitives
  are objective.
ἐὰν μὴ τυγχάνῃ γέ που . . . ἀγαθὸν ὄν: 'unless (the half or whole) happens to be
  good of course'. τυγχάνω + participle – 'to happen to be X'. που – 'as may be the
  case in given circumstances' (Dover). For Socrates/Diotima, it is the good that is
  the object of love; for Aristophanes, it is the fact of once having been whole that
  makes another half the object of love (goodness doesn't come into it.)
αὑτῶν = ἑαυτων – 'their own'.
ἐθέλουσιν ἀποτέμνεσθαι: 'are willing to cut off'.
ἐὰν αὐτοῖς δοκῇ τὰ ἑαυτῶν πονηρὰ εἶναι: 'if these things of theirs seem to them
  to be bad'. The construction is a generalized present open conditional (ἐάν +
  subjunctive). τὰ ἑαυτῶν is the subject, referring generally to the person's hands/
  feet/any other part, and the neuter plural subject takes a singular verb ending. The
  point seems to be that wholeness of body is not something we love per se, but only
  when that wholeness is good.
τὸ ἑαυτῶν: best translated periphrastically – 'what is his own'.
οἶμαι: take as if a side statement, not grammatically part of the sentence.
εἰ μὴ εἴ τις: 'unless someone', present open conditional.
τὸ μὲν ἀγαθὸν οἰκεῖον καλεῖ καὶ ἑαυτοῦ, τὸ δὲ κακὸν ἀλλότριον: 'calls what
  is related to him and his own "good", and what is not his own "bad"'. The point
  is that something belonging to a person is not what makes it welcome/desirable to
  that person, but rather the goodness of that thing. e.g. a foot with gangrene is
  'one's own', and yet is not desirable and we would amputate it to save our life.

206a

ὡς: causal.
οὗ ἐρῶσιν ἄνθρωποι: 'which men love'. The relative pronoun is in the genitive
  following ἐράω; the antecedent is οὐδέν ἄλλο.
ἢ τοῦ ἀγαθοῦ: this is logically the opposite of οὐδέν ἄλλο but has been attracted
  into the genitive of οὗ, the object of ἐρῶσιν.
ἢ σοὶ δοκοῦσιν: 'or do you think (they love something else)'. The subject is 'men'.
μὰ Δί᾽ οὐκ ἔμοιγε: an emphatic negative. δοκοῦσιν is understood with ἔμοι from
  the question, i.e. he does agree that men love the good.

ἆρ᾽ οὖν . . . οὕτως ἁπλοῦν ἐστι λέγειν: 'therefore can we say without qualification that', literally 'therefore is it thus simple to say that'.

τἀγαθοῦ: crasis of τοῦ ἀγαθοῦ.

τί δέ: literally 'what', but perhaps no stronger than 'but'.

οὐ προσθετέον: understand ἐστί. This is the verbal noun, with a sense of obligation – 'shouldn't it be added'.

ὅτι καὶ εἶναι τὸ ἀγαθὸν αὑτοῖς ἐρῶσιν: take in this order: ὅτι καὶ ἐρῶσιν τὸ ἀγαθὸν εἶναι αὑτοῖς – 'that they also desire the good to be theirs'. This had been agreed at 204e4.

προσθετέον: understand ἐστί – 'it should be added'.

ἆρ᾽ οὖν . . . καὶ οὐ μόνον εἶναι, ἀλλὰ καὶ ἀεὶ εἶναι: the first καί introduces this new addition. ἀεί is the key addition.

καὶ τοῦτο προσθετέον: again understand ἐστί – 'this too must be added'.

συλλήβδην: 'in summary'. This updates the summary of 206a3.

ἔστιν ἄρα ὁ ἔρως τοῦ τὸ ἀγαθὸν αὑτῷ εἶναι ἀεί: 'love is therefore of the good being one's own always'. This restates the conclusion of 205a5, but now τὸ ἀγαθὸν has replaced ἀγαθά, giving a 'more metaphysical turn' to the discussion (Dover).

The activity of Love 206b1–209e5

This text just begins this section of the speech. Diotima will argue that the activity of Eros is procreation in the context of the beautiful. See the Introduction for where this argument leads.

206b

ὅτε δὴ τοῦτο ὁ ἔρως ἐστὶν ἀεί: ὅτε has a causal sense and δή is emphatic – 'seeing that this is love always'.

τῶν τίνα τρόπον διωκόντων αὐτὸ καὶ ἐν τίνι πράξει ἡ σπουδὴ καὶ ἡ σύντασις ἔρως ἂν καλοῖτο: 'how and by what activity must men pursue it if their eagerness and effort is to be called "Eros"'. Literally 'the eagerness and effort of those pursuing it in what way and in what activity might be called Eros'. i.e. having established the object of the pursuit of love (to acquire the good for oneself forever), how might one go after that in such a way that one's effort and enthusiasm might be called Eros. ἂν + optative represents a virtual future remote conditional, with the participle phrase taking the part of the protasis. In Greek, there is no problem having multiple questions in one sentence, or that the questions are grammatically subordinate (here dependent on the participle).

τί τοῦτο τυγχάνει ὂν τὸ ἔργον: again τυγχάνω + participle – 'to happen to be'.

ἔχεις εἰπεῖν: again ἔχω + infinitive with the sense of 'to be able'.

οὐ μεντἂν: crasis of μέντοι + ἄν. μέντοι – 'no, of course not'.

οὐ μεντἂν σέ . . . ἐθαύμαζον ἐπὶ σοφίᾳ καὶ ἐφοίτων παρὰ σέ: the construction is the apodosis of a present counterfactual conditional (ἂν + imperfect indicative x2) – 'I would not admire you for your wisdom or come to you'. The implied protasis is 'if I could say that'. φοιτάω is the normal Greek word for going to someone for instruction, but Plato must have been aware that it could refer to sexual intercourse (following the double entendre of Diotima as his teacher in τὰ ἐρωτικά).

αὐτὰ ταῦτα μαθησόμενος: future participle for purpose – 'in order to learn these very things'.

ἐρῶ: future of λέγω.

ἔστι γὰρ τοῦτο: understand ἔργον from 206b3 – 'the work (of Eros) is this'.

τόκος ἐν καλῷ: 'the production of offspring in beauty'. The sense of ἐν as 'in the medium/conditions of' becomes clearer in the ensuing discussion.

καὶ κατὰ τὸ σῶμα καὶ κατὰ τὴν ψυχήν: 'both in terms of the body and the soul'. These qualify **τόκος** – it is not just talking about the physical procreation of offspring.

Μαντείας . . . δεῖται ὅτι ποτε λέγεις: the relative clause acts as subject of δεῖται – 'whatever you are saying needs divination (for me to understand it)'.

καὶ οὐ μανθάνω: our text ends with Socrates admitting he doesn't understand – in line with his presentation here of himself as just as ignorant as those at the party until Diotima educated him.

Vocabulary

An asterisk * denotes a word in OCR's Defined Vocabulary List for AS.

ἁβρός -ά -όν — graceful, splendid
*ἀγαθός -ή -όν — good, virtuous
Ἀγάθων -ωνος, ὁ — Agathon
ἀγάμος -ον — unmarried
*ἀγνοέω — I do not know
ἄγροικος -ον — uncultured, boorish, of the countryside

*ἄγω, ἤγαγον — I lead, keep, stay
ἀγωνίζομαι, (perf. pass. with active sense) ἠγώνισμαι — I contend, compete with

*ἀδικία -ας, ἡ — injustice, wrongdoing
*ἀεί — always, at every moment
ἀθάνατος -ον — immortal
*Ἀθηναῖος -α -ον — Athenian
Ἅιδης -ου, ὁ — Hades
αἰδοῖον -ου, τό — male or female genitalia, private parts

αἰνίττομαι — I allude to
*αἰσθάνομαι, ἠσθόμην, (perf.) ἤσθημαι — I notice, perceive (+ acc. or gen.)

*αἰσχρός -ή -όν — shameful
*αἰσχύνομαι — I feel ashamed in front of X (acc.)

*αἴτια -ας, ἡ — cause
*αἴτιος -η -ον — responsible
ἀκολασία -ας, ἡ — intemperance, lack of self-control

ἀκόλουθος -ον — follower
*ἀκούω, (perf.) ἀκήκοα — I hear, listen to (acc. of person, gen. of thing)

*ἀληθής -ές — true
*ἀλλά — but
*ἀλλήλους -ας -α (no nom.) — each other

ἀλλοῖος -α -ον — different
*ἄλλος -η -ο — other
ἀλλότριος -α -ον — belonging to another, foreign

ἄλλως — otherwise
ἄλλως τε καί — especially
ἄλογος -ον — irrational, without an account

*ἅμα — at once, at the same time
ἀμαθής -ές — ignorant, foolish
ἀμαθία -ας, ἡ — ignorance, folly
ἀμοιβή -ῆς, ἡ — reply, recompense
ἄμοιρος -ον — without a share of
*ἀμφότερος -α -ον — both (of two)
*ἄν — hypothetical or indefinite particle; a contraction of ἐάν

ἀνάβαινω, ἀνέβην — I go up, appear before the court

ἀνάβασις -εως, ἡ — ascension, journey up
ἀναβιώσκομαι — I come back to life
ἀναβολή -ῆς, ἡ — postponement, delay
*ἀναγκάζω — I compel
ἀναγκαῖος -α -ον — necessary
ἀναίσχυντος -ον — I am shameless, behave impudently

ἀναισχυντία -ας, ἡ — shamelessness
ἀνακρίνω — I examine, ask questions
*ἀνδρεία -ας, ἡ — bravery, manliness
*ἀνδρεῖος -α -ον — brave, manly
ἀνδρόγυνος -ον — androgynous, common to men and women

ἀνδρόω, (aor. pass.) ἠνδρώθην — I become a man, reach manhood

*ἄνευ (+ gen.) — without
*ἀνήρ ἀνδρός, ὁ — man
ἀνθρωπεῖος -α -ον — human

ἀνθρώπινος -η -ον — human, of man, attainable by man

*ἄνθρωπος -ου, ὁ — human, man

ἀντί (+ gen.) — instead of

ἀνυπόδητος -ον — unshod

ἄοικος -ον — homeless

ἀπαλός -ή -όν — soft, delicate

*ἄπας, ἄπασα, ἄπαν (ἀπαντ-) — all, the whole, every

ἀπερείδομαι — I support myself

ἀπέρχομαι — I return, am restored

ἀπεχθάνομαι, ἀπηχθόμην — I am hated

ἁπλοῦς -ῆ -οῦν — single, simple

*ἀπό (+ gen.) — from, away from

ἀποβαίνω, ἀποβήσομαι — I turn out, result, prove fit for

ἀποδέχομαι — I recover, I exact (a legal/ moral duty)

ἀποδέω — I fasten off

ἀποδίδωμι — I give back, pay what is due

*ἀποθνήσκω, ἀποθανοῦμαι, ἀπέθανον, (perf.) τέθνηκα — I die

*ἀποκρίνομαι — I reply

ἀπόκρισις -εως, ἡ — answer, reply

*ἀποκτείνω, (perf.) ἀπέκτονα — I kill

ἀπολείπω, ἀπέλιπον — I leave behind, abandon

ἀπολείπομαι (pass.) — I am absent from, separated from (+ gen.)

*ἀπόλλυμι — I destroy, kill; (intransitive mid.) die

Ἀπόλλων -ωνος, ὁ — Apollo

*ἀπορέω — I am at a loss for (+ gen.)

*ἀπορία -ας, ἡ — difficulty, lack

ἄπορος -ον — resourceless

ἀποτέμνω — I cut off

*ἄρα — (introduces a yes/no question)

ἀργία -ας, ἡ — inactivity, idleness

*ἀριθμός -οῦ, ὁ — number

*ἄριστος -η -ον — best, very good (sup. of ἀγαθός)

Ἀριστοφάνης -ους, ὁ — Aristophanes

Ἀρκάδες -ων, οἱ — The Arcadians

ἀρρενωπία -ας, ἡ — manliness, manly look

ἄρρην -εν — male, masculine

ἀρχαῖος -α -ον — old, original

*ἀρχή -ῆς, ἡ — beginning; authority, magistracy, office

ἀσελγαίνω — I act outrageously

*ἀσθενής -ές — weak

ἀσκωλιάζω — I hop on one leg

ἀσπάζομαι — I welcome kindly, greet

ἄστρωτος -ον — without bedding

*ἅτε (+ participle) — since, because

ἀτεχνῶς — simply, absolutely

*αὖ — again; moreover; in turn

αὖθις — again, hereafter

*αὐτός -ή -ό — -self (emphatic adjective); him, her, it, them (pronoun in oblique cases)

αὐχήν -ένος, ὁ — neck

αὐχμηρός -ά -όν — hard

ἀφαιρέω, ἀφεῖλον — I isolate, separate

ἀφανίζω, ἠφάνισα, (perf. pass.) ἠφάνισμαι — I make to disappear, hide, destroy; (pass.) I disappear

*ἀφικνέομαι, ἀφικόμην — I come, arrive

ἀφορίζω, (aor. pass.) ἀφωρίσθην — I mark off with boundaries

*ἀφροδίσια -ων, τά — sexual pleasures

Ἀφροδίτη -ης, ἡ — Aphrodite

ἄφρων -ον — foolish, senseless

*βαδίζω, βαδιοῦμαι — I go, walk

βαλλάντιον -ου, τό — money-bag, purse

βάναυσος -ον — artisan, mechanic

βαρέω, (perf. pass.) βεβάρημαι — I weigh down, make heavy

*βέλτιστος -η -ον (sup. of ἀγαθός) — best

*βίος -ου, ὁ — life

*βλέπω — I look

*βουλεύομαι — I take counsel, deliberate

βούλησις -εως, ἡ — desire, willingness

*βούλομαι, ἐβουλήθην — I wish, want

*βωμός -οῦ, ὁ — altar

γάμος -ου, ὁ — marriage, wedding

*γάρ — for, that is to say

γαστήρ -έρος, τό — stomach

*γε — indeed (emphasises preceding word); at least, at any rate

*γελάω — I laugh

γενέθλιος -ον — of a birthday, birthday party

*γένος -ους, τό — race

γένεσις -εως, ἡ — coming into being, origin, becoming

γεννάω, (aor. pass.) ἐγεννήθην — I beget, create

*γῆ -ῆς, ἡ — earth, ground

γίγας -αντος, ὁ — giant

*γίγνομαι, ἐγενόμην, (perf.) γέγονα — I happen, become, turn out, result, am born; (perf.) have arisen, am

γόης -ητος, ὁ — sorcerer, wizard, cheat

γοητεία -ας, ἡ — witchcraft, magic

γονεύς -έως, ὁ — father

*γοῦν — at all events, at any rate

*γυνή -αικός, ἡ — woman, female

δαιμονίον -ου, τό — divinity

δαιμόνιος -α -ον — spiritual, in touch with the gods

δαίμων -ονος, ὁ — spirit, divinity

*δέ — but, and

δέησις -εως, ἡ — prayer, entreaty

*δεῖ — it is necessary (+ acc. + inf.)

*δεινός -ή -όν — fearful, dangerous; skilful, clever

δειπνέω — I dine

δέκα — ten

*δέομαι, ἐδεήθην — I ask for X (acc.) from Y (gen.); need (+ gen.)

δέρμα -ατος, τό — skin

δέω, ἔδησα (+ gen.) — I lack, need

*δή — (emphatic particle) indeed, in truth, then, so, accordingly

*δῆλος -η -ον — clear

δημιουργός -οῦ, ὁ — craftsman, workman

*δήπου — of course, indeed, presumably, I suppose

*διά (+ acc.) — on account of

*διά (+ gen.) — through

*διαλέγομαι, διελέχθην, (perf.) διείλεγμαι — I converse with, talk to (+ dat.)

διάλεκτος -ου, ὁ — conversation

διαλλάσσω, (aor. pass.) διηλλάγην — I reconcile

διαπαύομαι — I find an end, find rest

διαπορθμεύω — I communicate

διαπρίζω, (perf. pass.) διαπέπρισμαι — I saw in half

διαρθρόω — I divide by joints

διασχίζω, (fut. pass.) διασχισθήσομαι — I cut in two

διατελέω — I live through to the end

διατέμνω, διατεμῶ — I cut in two

διαφέρω — I will make a difference

διδάσκαλος ου, ὁ — teacher

*διδάσκω — I teach X (acc.) to Y (acc.), inform

*δίδωμι, ἔδωκα — I give

διέρχομαι, διῆλθον — I explain, go through

*διηγέομαι — I explain, describe

*δικαίως — justly

*διό — for which reason (= δι' ὅ)

διοικίζω, (aor. pass.) διῳκίσθην — I scatter, cause to live apart

Διοτίμα -ας, ἡ — Diotima

δίχα — in two, apart

*διώκω — I pursue

*δοκέω, ἐδόξα — I think, have an opinion; intend; seem

δολερός -ά -όν — deceitful, treacherous

*δόξα -ας, ης — opinion, judgement; glory

δοξάζω — I think, suppose

*δράω — I do

*δύναμαι — I am able to

*δύναμις -εως, ἡ — power

*δύο, (gen. / dat.) δυοῖν — two

*ἐάν — if (future open conditional)

*ἑαυτόν -ήν -ό — himself, herself, itself (reflexive)

*ἐάω — I allow

*ἐγγύς (+ gen.) — near

ἐγείρω, (intransitive perf.) ἐγρήγορα — I rouse, wake up

ἐγχώμιον -ου, τό — eulogy, speech in praise of

*ἐγώ — I

*ἐθέλω — I want

*εἰ — if

εἶδος -ους, τό — appearance, form, shape

εἶεν — well then

εἰκάζω, εἴκασα — I infer, guess

*εἰμί, ἔσομαι, (impf.) ἦν — I am, exist

*εἰρῆσθαι — perf. pass. inf. of λέγω

*εἰς (+ acc.) — into, onto

*εἷς, μία, ἕν — one

εἰσέρχομαι — I come/go into

εἰσηγέομαι — I bring in, introduce X (acc) to Y (dat), instruct

*εἴτε — either, or

*ἐκ — from, out of

*ἕκαστος -η -ον — each

*ἑκάτερος -α -ον — each (of two)

ἔκγονος -ον — born of, sprung from

*ἐκεῖ — there

*ἐκεῖνος -η -ο	that
ἐκλεαίνω	I smooth out
ἐκπλήττω, (aor. pass.) ἐξεπλάγην	I shock, amaze, astound
ἐκτελέω, ἐξετέλεσα	I accomplish, fulfil
ἐκτός	outside
ἐκτυπόω, (perf. pass.) ἐκτετύπωμαι	I work in relief
*ἐκφεύγω	I escape
ἐλέγχω	I refute, test, question, cross-examine
ἐλεέω, ἠλέησα	I pity, show mercy
ἐλπίς -ίδος, ἡ	hope, expectation, reason to believe
ἐμαυτόν -ήν	myself
*ἐμός -ή -όν	my, of me
ἔμφρων -ον	sensible, rational
ἔμφυτος -ον	inborn, natural
*ἐν (+ dat.)	in, at, over
*ἐναντίος -α -ον	opposite
ἐνδεής -ές (+ gen.)	lacking, in need of
ἔνδεια -ας, ἡ	lack, absence
*ἕνεκα (+ gen.)	on account of, for the sake of
*ἐνθάδε	here
*ἐννοέω	I have in mind, think about, consider
*ἐντυγχάνω, ἐντεύξομαι, ἐνέτυχον	I meet with (+ dat.)
ἐξαρκέι	it is sufficient
ἐξαρνέομαι, ἐξηρνήθην	I deny, refuse
ἐξευρίσκω	I find out
ἔοικα	I seem, seem likely; resemble (+ dat.)
*ἐπεί	since; for; although
*ἐπειδάν	whenever (= ἐπειδή + ἄν)
*ἐπειδή	since; when
*ἔπειτα	then; besides
*ἐπί (+ acc.)	to, towards, onto, for the sake of
*ἐπί (+ dat.)	on, at ,for, for the sake of
*ἐπί (+ gen.)	upon
ἐπιβουλεύω	I plot against
ἐπίβουλος -ον	plotting against, treacherous
ἐπιδείκνυμι, ἐπέδειξα	I tell, relate, show
ἐπιδέομαι	I am in want of (+ gen.)
ἐπιθυμέω	I desire, be eager (+ gen.)
ἐπιθυμητής -οῦ, ὁ	one who desires
ἐπιθυμία -ας, ἡ	desire
ἐπίκουρος -ου, ὁ	helper, ally
ἐπιλήσμων -ον	forgetful
ἐπιμελέομαι	I have a concern for (+ gen.)
*ἐπίσταμαι	I know, understand; (+ inf.) know how to
ἐπιστήμη -ης, ἡ	knowledge, wisdom
ἐπίταξις -εως, ἡ	command
ἐπιτίθεμαι, ἐπιθήσομαι	I make an attack/attempt (+ dat.)
ἐπιχειρέω	I try, attempt, challenge
*ἔπος -ους, τό	word
ἐπῳδή -ῆς, ἡ	spell
ἐραστής -οῦ, ὁ	lover
ἐράω	I love (+ gen.)
ἐργασία -ας, ἡ	manufacture, work
*ἔργον -ου, τό	deed, work, task
ἑρμηνεύω	I interpret, translate
*ἐρρήθην	see λέγω
Ἐρυξίμαχος -ου, ὁ	Eryximachus
*ἐρῶ	see λέγω
ἔρως -ωτος, ὁ	Eros (the god), love, desire
*ἐρωτάω, ἠρόμην	I ask
ἐρώτησις -εως, ἡ	question
ἐρωτικός -η -ον	concerned with love
ἑστιάομαι	I entertain
ἑταιρίστρια -ας, ἡ	lesbian
*ἑταῖρος -ου, ὁ	friend, companion
*ἕτερος -α -ον	one, the other (of two)
*ἔτι	still, besides, moreover
*ἔτος -ους, τό	year
*εὖ	well
εὐδαιμονέω	I am happy, prosperous
εὐδαιμονία -ας, ἡ	happiness
*εὐδαίμων -ον	happy, prosperous, fortunate
εὕδω	I sleep
εὐπορέω	I find a means
εὐπόρος -ον	resourceful
εὐσέβεια -ας, ἡ	piety, reverence
εὐσεβέω	I live or act piously/ reverently
εὐφημέω	I speak a word of good omen
εὐωχία -ας, ἡ	feasting
Ἐφιάλτης -ου, ὁ	Ephialtes
ἐφίσταμαι (mid. of ἐφίστημι)	I stand over
*ἔχω, (impf.) εἶχον, ἔσχον, (perf.) ἔσχηκα	I have, possess; (aor. and perf.) obtain, get; am able
*ζάω, (inf.) ζῆν	I live
*Ζεύς, Διός, ὁ (acc. Δία)	Zeus
*ζητέω	I seek, investigate

*ἤ	indeed (emphatic particle)
*ἤ	or
*ἤ. . . ἤ	either. . .or
*ἤ	or (sometimes introducing a question)
*ἤ	than, from (in a comparison)
*ἡγέομαι	I consider
*ἡγεμών -όνος, ὁ	leader, guide
*ἦν δ᾽ ἐγώ	I said
*ἡδέως	gladly, pleasingly
*ἤδη	already, now, furthermore
*ἥκιστα	least, very little
*ἥλιος -ου, ὁ	sun
*ἡμεῖς	we
*ἡμέρα -ας, ἡ	day
*ἡμέτερος -α -ον	our
ἥμισυς -εια -υ	half
ἤσθημαι	see αἰσθάνομαι
ἡσυχία -ας, ἡ	peace, quiet
Ἥφαιστος -ου, ὁ	Hephaistus
θάλλω	I thrive, prosper
*θαρρέω	I take courage
θάρρος -ους, τό	courage
*θαυμάζω	I am amazed at
θαυμαστός -ή -όν	wonderful, marvelous
*θεάομαι	I see
θέατρον -ου, τό	audience, theatre
*θέλω = ἐθέλω	
*θεός -οῦ, ὁ	god
*θεράπων -οντος, ὁ	minister
θέω	I run
θῆλυς -εια -υ	female, feminine
θηρευτής -οῦ, ὁ	hunter
θνητός -ή -όν	mortal
θορυβέω	I confuse by noise
θρίξ, τριχός, ἡ	hair
*θύρα -ας, ἡ	door
θυσία -ας, ἡ	sacrifice
*θύω	I sacrifice
ἰάομαι, (aor. pass.) ἰάθην	I heal, cure
*ἰατρός -οῦ, ὁ	doctor, healer
ἰδέα -ας, ἡ	form, shape
*ἱερεύς -έως, ὁ	priest
*ἱερόν -οῦ, τό	temple; (pl.) sacrificial offerings
*ἱκανός -ή -όν	sufficient
*ἵνα (+ subj. / opt.)	in order that, so that
*ἴσος -η -ον	equal, balanced
ἰσχύς -ύος, ἡ	strength
ἴσχω	I retain

*ἴσως	perhaps, probably
ἴτης = ἰταμός -ή -όν	reckless
καθάπερ	according, just as
*καθεύδω	I sleep
*καθίστημι	I establish, restore
*καί	and; and yet; even; also
*κακός -ή -όν	bad, evil
καλάπους -οδος, ὁ	shoe-maker's last
*καλέω	I call
*καλλίστος -η -ον	finest, best
*καλός -ή -όν	fine, good, beautiful
*καλῶς	well
*κατά (+ acc.)	according to, in accordance with, along, down
καταγραφή -ης, ἡ	a figure in profile, in 'bas-relief'
καταζῶ	I live my life
κατάκειμαι	I lie together
κατακλίνω	I lie down
καταλείπω	I leave behind
κατασκευάζω	I build
καταχράομαι	I use/apply thoughtlessly
*κεῖμαι	(of names) I am given, used
*κελεύω	I order
κεραυνόω	I strike with a thunderbolt
κεφάλαιος -α -ον	principal, main
*κεφαλή -ης, ἡ	head
κῆπος -ου, ὁ	garden
*κινδυνεύω	I run the risk of; am likely to (+ inf.)
κοιμάομαι	I go to bed
*κοινός -ή -όν	common, shared, mutual
κόσμιος -α -ον	well-behaved, moderate
*κτάομαι	I obtain
κτῆσις -εως, ἡ	possession, having
κυβιστάω	I tumble, somersault head first
κύκλος -ου, ὁ	circle
κυκλοτερής -ές	round, circular, made round
κύω	I conceive
*κωλύω	I stop, prevent
κωμῳδέω	I satirise, treat as funny
*Λακεδαιμόνιοι -ων, οἱ	Spartans
λεαίνω	I smooth
*λέγω, ἐρῶ, εἶπον, (aor. pass.) ἐρρήθην	I say, speak, mention, tell, speak about (+ acc.)
*λείπω, (aor. pass.) ἐλείφθην	I leave

λιμός -οῦ, ὁ	hunger	*μηχανή -ῆς, ἡ	contrivance, device; way, means
λίσπαι -ων, αἱ	dice cut in half		
λοιμός -οῦ, ὁ	plague	μίγνυμι / μείγνυμι	I mix
*λοιπός -ή -όν	remaining, rest of	μνημεῖον -ου, τό	reminder
		μόγις	with difficulty, with reluctance
μά (+ acc.)	by X!		
μακάριος -α -ον	happy, blessed	μοιχεύτρια -ας, ἡ	adulteress
*μακρός -ά -όν	long	μοιχός -ου, ὁ	adulterer
*μάλιστα (sup. of μάλα)	especially	*μόνος -η -ον, adv. μόνον	only, alone
*μᾶλλον (comp. of μάλα)	more, rather	μόριον -ου, τό	piece
		μουσική -ης, ἡ	music
*μανθάνω	I learn		
μαντεία -ας, ἡ	prophecy	*ναί	yes
μαντεύομαι	I prophesy, consult the oracle	νέκταρ -αρος, τό	nectar
		*νομίζω	I think, consider, believe
μαντική -ῆς, ἡ	prophetic art	*νόμος -ου, ὁ	law, custom
Μαντινικος -η -ον	of/from Mantinea	*νόος -ου, ὁ	mind, attention
μεγαλοφροσύνη -ης, ἡ	self-confidence	*νόσος -ου, ἡ	disease
		*νοῦς -οῦ, ὁ	mind
*μέγας, μεγάλη, μέγα, (adv.) μέγα	big, great	*νῦν	now
		*νυνί = νῦν	now
		*νύξ, νυκτός, ἡ	night
*μέγιστος -η -ον (sup. of μέγας)	biggest, greatest	νῶτον -ου, τό	back
μεθύσκω, (aor. pass.) ἐμεθύσθην	I make drunk on/with X (gen.)	*ξένος -ου, ὁ	stranger, foreigner, friend
		ξύλον -ου, τό	(piece of) wood
μείζων -ον (comp. of μέγας)	bigger, greater	*ὁ, ἡ, τό	the (definite article)
μειράκιον -ου, τό	young lad, teenager	*ὅδε, ἥδε, τόδε	this, this here, the following
*μέλλω	I am likely to, intend to; (+ fut. inf.) going to	*ὁδός -οῦ, ἡ	street, road
		*οἶδα	know
μέλος -εος, τό	limb	οἰκείος, α, ον	belonging to one's family, one's own
*μέν ... δέ	on the one hand ... on the other (articulates a contrast)	οἰκειότης -ητος, ἡ	kinship
		*οἶνος -ου, ὁ	wine
*μεντἄν	crasis of μέντοι ἄν	οἴομαι / οἶμαι, ᾠήθην	I think, consider
*μέντοι	however		
*μέσος -η -ον	middle	*οἷον	such as
μεστός -ή -όν	full of	*οἷος -α -ον	of what sort, such as, as
μεταβάλλω	I change, exchange	ὀκρίβας -αντος, ὁ	the platform/stage in the Odeion
μεταξύ (+ gen.)	between		
μεταστρέφω	I turn around	*ὀκτώ	eight
μετατίθημι	I place differently	*ὀλίγος -η -ον	few, little
μετέχω	I have a share in, partake of	ὅλος -η -ον	whole, complete
		Ὅμηρος -ου, ὁ	Homer
μέτρον -ου, τό	rhythm	ὁμιλία -ας, ἡ	intercourse, interaction
*μή	not	*ὅμοιος -α -ον	similar
*μηδέ	and ... not, but not, not even, nor	*ὁμολογέω	I agree
		ὀμφαλός -ου, ὁ	navel, belly-button
*μηδείς -εμία -έν	no one, nothing	*ὅμως	yet, nevertheless
μήν	truly, indeed	ὀνείδος -εος, τό	reproach, abuse
*μήτε	neither, nor	ὀνίνημι	I delight, bring benefit
*μήτηρ μητρός, ἡ	mother	*ὄνομα, -ατος, τό	name, reputation
Μῆτις -ιδος, ἡ	Metis, 'Wisdom'	ὀνομάζω	I call, name

ὄον -ου, το	sorb-apple
ὄπηοῦν	how, in whatever way
ὁπότε	when
ὁποτέρωσε	in whichever of two directions
*ὅπως	how, that, in order that, to
ὁπωστιοῦν	in any way
*ὁράω, (impf.) ἑώρων, εἶδον	I see
ὄργανον -ου, τό	tool
*ὀρθός -ή -όν	upright, straight; correct
*ὁρμάω, ὥρμησα	I start, stir up, rush into, be eager
*ὅς, ἥ, ὅ	who, which (relative pronoun)
*ὅσος -η -ον	as much as; (plur.) all who, as many as
ὅσπερ, ἥπερ, ὅπερ	the very one who, the very thing which
*ὅστις, ἥτις, ὅτι	who/what (indirect pronoun), whoever/ whatever (indefinite)
ὁστισοῦν, ὁτιοῦν	anyone whosoever, anything whatsoever
*ὅταν	whenever
*ὅτε	when
*ὅτι	because; the fact that, that
*ὅτι (= ὅ τι)	neuter singular of ὅστις
*οὐ, οὐκ, οὐχ	not
*οὐδαμῶς	not at all
*οὐδέ	and . . . not, but not, not even, nor
*οὐδείς -εμία -έν	no, nobody, nothing
*οὐκέτι	no longer
*οὐκοῦν	surely?; therefore
*οὖν	therefore, and so; actually, in fact
οὔπω	not yet
*οὐρανός -ου, ὁ	sky, heaven, home of the gods
οὖς, ὠτός, τό	ear
*οὔτε	neither, nor
*οὗτος, αὕτη, τοῦτο	this; he, she, it
*οὕτω(ς)	thus, in this way; so
πάγκαλος -η -ον	very beautiful, fine
πάθημα -ματος, τό	suffering, misfortune
πάθος -ους, τό	experience, suffering, emotion
παιδεραστέω	I am a lover of boys
παιδεραστής -οῦ, ὁ	lover of boys
παιδικά -ῶν, τά	beloved (pl. for sg.)
παιδίον -ου, τό	diminutive of παῖς
παιδοποιία -ας, ἡ	procreation of children

*παῖς, παιδός, ὁ/ἡ	child, boy, girl
*πάλαι	long ago, some time ago, a while ago
*παλαιός -ά -όν	old, of old
*πάλιν	back, again
παντάπασι	all in all, wholly
πανταχόθεν	from all quarters, from everywhere
πάντη	in every way
παντοδαπός -ή -όν	of every kind
πάντως	at any rate
πάνυ	very, great, altogether, at all
*παρά (+ acc.)	to
*παρά (+ gen.)	from
παρακελεύομαι	I exhort
*πάρειμι	I am present
*παρέχω	I provide, supply, furnish
*πᾶς, πᾶσα, πᾶν (παντ-)	all, every; the whole
*πάσχω, ἔπαθον, (perf.) πέπονθα	I suffer, experience
*πατήρ, πατρός, ὁ	father
Παυσανίας -ου, ὁ	Pausanias
*παύω	I stop; (mid.) cease (+ gen.)
*πείθομαι, πείσομαι	I obey; believe, trust
*πειράομαι	I try, attempt
πένης -ητος	poor
πενία -ας, ἡ	poverty
*περί (+ acc. / gen.)	about, concerning, at
περιβάλλω	I throw around
περίειμι	I go around
περιφερής -ές	curved, circular
περιφέρω	I carry around
πη	in some way, somehow
*πλεῖστος -η -ον (sup. of πολύς)	greatest, most
*πλείων -ον or πλέων -ον (comp. of πολύς)	more
πλέκω	I weave, contrive
πλευρά -ᾶς, ἡ	rib, side
πλησμονή -ῆς, ἡ	fullness, satisfaction
πλουτέω	I am rich
πόθεω	I desire
*ποιέω	I make, do, compose; (mid.) value, produce
ποίησις -εως, ἡ	any act of creation, often specifically poetry
ποιητής -οῦ, ὁ	poet, someone who creates
*ποῖος -α -ον	what sort of?
πολιτικός -ή -όν	political, relating to public life, befitting a citizen

*πολλάκις	often, many times	*σαφής -ές	clear
πολλαχῇ	in many places, in many ways	*σαυτοῦ = σεαυτοῦ	your own (reflexive)
		σελήνη -ης, ἡ	moon
πολλοῦ δεῖ	he is far from	σκέλος -εος, τό	leg
*πολύς, πολλή, πολύ	much, great; (pl.) many, a lot of	σκληρός -ά -όν	rough
		σκῦτος -ους, τό	leather
πονηρός -ά, -όν	wicked, bad	σκυτοτόμος -ου, ὁ	shoe-maker
πορεία -ας, ἡ	movement	σμικρός -ά -όν	small, little
*πορεύομαι	I make a journey, move around	*σός -ή -όν	your
		*σοφία -ας, ἡ	wisdom, expertise
πορίζω	I provide	σοφιστής -οῦ, ὁ	sophist
πόριμος -ον	resourceful, inventive	*σοφός -ή -όν	wise, skilled, expert
Πόρος -ου, ὁ	Poros, 'Means'	σπουδάζω, (perf. act.) ἐσπούδακα	I am serious, dedicated
*ποτε	once, ever		
*πότερα . . . ἤ	whether . . . or? (introduces a question with two options)	σπουδή -ης, ἡ	enthusiasm, eagerness
		στῆθος -ους, τό	chest
		στήλη -ης, ἡ	a stone slab, e.g. a gravestone, monument
*πότερος -α -ον	which (of two)?	στόμα -ατος, τό	mouth, opening
*που	anywhere, somewhere, I suppose	*στρᾰτηγός -ου, ὁ	general
		στρογγύλος -η -ον,	round, spherical
*πούς, πόδος, ὁ	foot	*σύ	you (sg.)
*πρᾶγμα -ατος, τό	business, occupation, thing; (pl.) affairs, troubles	συγγενής -ές	of the same kin, of like kind
		συγκατάκειμαι	I lie with, sleep with
πρᾶξις -εως, ἡ	affair, matter	συλλήβδην	taken together (adv.), in sum
*πράττω, ἔπραξα	I do, perform; (mid.) obtain for oneself	σύμβολον -ου, τό	a unique other-half, a tally
*πρό (+ gen.)	before, in front of, in the face of	σύμπας, σύμπασα, σύμπαν (συμπαντ-)	all together
*πρός (+ acc.)	against, to, regarding, with respect to, with, in comparison with		
		συμπλέκω, (perf. pass.) συμπέπλεγμαι	I join together, become intimate with
προσαγορεύομαι	I call by name		
προσαιτέω	I beg	συμπληρόω	I fill completely
προσδέω	I need in addition	συμπλοκή -ῆς, ἡ	entwining, embrace
προσδοκία -ας, ἡ	expectation	συμφυσάω	I fuse together
πρόσειμι, (impf.) προσῆν	I am in addition	συμφύω, συνέφυσα	I unite, grow together
		συναγωγεύς -έως, ὁ	the bringer-back-together
προσέχω	I pay (attention), apply (one's mind)		
		συνδέω	I bind together
*πρόσθεν	before, in front	σύνειμι	I associate with, have sex with (+ dat.)
προστίθημι	I add		
πρόσωπον -ου, τό	face	συνέλκω	I draw together
προχείρως	readily	συνέρχομαι,	I come together with
*πρῶτον	first (adv.)	σύνειμι, συνῆλθον	(+ dat.)
*πυνθάνομαι	I inquire, find out	σύνοιδα	I join in acknowledging (+ dat.)
*πως	in some way, somehow		
*πῶς	how?	σύνοικος -ου, ὁ	someone who lives with, a companion
*ῥάδιος -α -ον, (comp.) ῥᾴων, -ον	easy, light	συνουσία -ας, ἡ	association, sex
		σύντασις -εως, ἡ	effort, exertion
*ῥᾳδίως	easily	συντήκω, συνέτηξα, (aor. pass.) συνετάκην	I weld together
ῥίς, -νός, ἡ	nose		
ῥυτίς -ίδος, ἡ	wrinkle		
ῥώμη -ης, ἡ	strength		

σύντονος -ον	intense	*τρίτος -η -ον	third
σύσπαστος -ον	capable of being closed by drawing together	*τρόπος -ου, ὁ	way
*σφεῖς	they (reflexive)	*τυγχάνω, ἔτυχον	I happen to (+ participle), obtain (+ gen.)
*σχεδόν	nearly, almost	*τύχη -ης, ἡ	fortune, fate
Σωκράτης -ους, ὁ (acc. Σωκράτη)	Socrates	*ὑμεῖς	you (pl.)
		ὑμνέω	I praise, sing of
*σῶμα -ατος, τό	body	*ὑός -οῦ or -έος, ὁ (= υἱός)	son
ταριχεύω	I preserve by drying	ὑπαίθριος -ον	under the sky
*τάχ᾽ ἄν	perhaps	ὑπεκρέω	I flow out from under
*ταχύ	quickly	*ὑπό (+ gen.)	under, by, at the hands of, because of
*τε	and, both		
τεκμαίρομαι	I form a judgment from evidence	ὑποκρίτης -ου, ὁ	actor
		ὑπολαμβάνω	I suppose, take up, reply
τεκμήριον -ου, τό	evidence		
τέλεος -α -ον	perfect, entire	Φαῖδρος, -ου, ὁ	Phaedrus
τελετή -ῆς, ἡ	priest, official	*φαίνω, (aor. pass.) ἐφάνην	I show; (pass.) appear
τελειόω, (aor. pass.) ἐτελεώθην	I complete, fulfil, accomplish		
		φαρμακεύς -έως, ὁ	druggist, apothecary
*τέλος	finally	φαρμάττω	I bewitch, drug
τεμάχιον -ου, τό	slice, piece	*φέρε	come!
*τέμνω, τεμῶ, (perf. pass.) τέτμημαι, (aor. pass.) ἐτμήθην	I cut	*φέρω, οἴσω, ἤνεγκα	I bear, carry
		*φημί, φήσω, (impf.) ἔφην	I say, assert, affirm, declare
*τέτταρες -α	four	φίλανδρος, ον	loving men
τέττιξ -ιγος, ὁ	cicada	φιλανθρωπότατος -η -ον	philanthropic, kind to humans
*τέχνη -ης, ἡ	craft, skill		
τέως = ἕως	until	φιλεραστής -οῦ, ὁ	a lover of having lovers
τίκτω	I bring forth, bear	*φιλέω	I love
*τιμή -ῆς, ἡ	honour	*φιλία -ας, ἡ	affection
*τις, τι	a (certain), one, someone, something, some, a sort of	φιλογυμναστία -ας, ἡ	love of gym/sport
		φιλογύναικες -ων, οἱ	lovers of women (no singular occurs)
"τίς, τί	who? which? what?	*φίλος -η -ον	dear, pleasing
τμῆμα -ατος, τό	part cut off	*φίλος -ου, ὁ	friend
τμῆσις -εως, ἡ	cutting, cut	φιλοσοφέω	I am a philosopher, love wisdom
*τοι	look now		
τοίνυν	well then	φιλοσοφία -ας, ἡ	philosophy
τοιόσδε -άδε -όνδε	such as this	φιλόσοφος -ου, ὁ	philosopher, lover of wisdom
τοιοῦτος, τοιαύτη, τοιοῦτο	of such a kind, such, like that, this sort of, as follows		
		*φοβέομαι	I fear
τόκος -ου, ὁ	begetting, offspring	φοβερός -ά -όν	frightening
*τολμάω	I dare	*φόβος -ου, ὁ	fear
τομή -ῆς, ἡ	cut	φοιτάω	I come, I have sexual relations
τόσος -η -ον	so much, such early times		
		φρόνημα -ματος, τό	thought, spirit, pride
*τοσοῦτος, τοσαύτη, τοσοῦτο	so much, so great, such great; (pl.) so many	φρόνησις -εως, ἡ	wisdom, thought, knowledge
*τότε	then	φρονίμος -ον	in one's right mind, sensible, wise
*τρεῖς, τρία	three		
*τρέπω, ἔτρεπον, (perf. pass.) τέτραμμαι	I turn	φροντίζω	I consider, care, be thoughtful, worry about (+ gen.)

φύσις -εως, ἡ	nature, character; origin, birth
φύω, (perf. act.) πέφυκα	I am born, grow
*χαίρω	I rejoice, enjoy; greet; say goodbye
*χαλεπός -ή -όν	difficult, harsh, painful
χαμαιπετής -ές	lying on the ground
*χείρ, χειρός, ἡ	hand
χειρουργία -ας, ἡ	handicraft, work done by hand
*χράομαι	I use, experience (+ dat.)
χρεία -ας, ἡ	function, utility, use
*χρή	it is necessary for X (acc.) to Y (inf.)
χρηματισμός -οῦ, ὁ	making money
*χρησίμος -η -ον	useful
*χρόνος -ου, ὁ	time
*χωρέω	I work

χωρίζω	I separate, divide
χωρίς (+ gen.)	apart from, without
*ψεύδομαι, (aor. pass.) ἐψεύσθην	I cheat, lie, deceive; (pass.) I am mistaken in something (+ gen.)
ψῆττα -ης, ἡ	flat fish
ψυχή -ης, ἡ	life, soul, spirit, mind
*ὧδε	thus, in the following way
ᾠήθην	aorist passive of οἴομαι
ᾠόν -οῦ, τό	egg
*ὡς	as, how, that, since
*ὡς (+ fut. participle)	in order to
*ὡς (+ sup.)	as . . . as possible
*ὥσπερ	as, like, as if, as it were
*ὥστε	with the result that, that, as to, to
Ὦτος, -ου, ὁ	Otus

Plutarch, *Alcibiades*

Introduction, Commentary Notes
and Vocabulary by Carl Hope

A Level: 10.1.1–16.5

Introduction

Plutarch: Life

Plutarch of Chaeronea was born around CE 45 and lived until around CE 120. The town of Chaeronea lay in central Greece in the region of Boeotia, east of Delphi and west of Thebes. The town had been the site of the famous Battle of Chaeronea in 338 BCE when Philip II of Macedon, the father of Alexander the Great, defeated a coalition of Greek states led by Athens and Thebes, gaining hegemony over most of southern Greece. Plutarch studied philosophy and became a Platonist, lecturing at Rome and travelling around Italy and even to Egypt, while in his last thirty or so years he held various offices in his home town and was awarded a permanent priesthood at the shrine to Apollo at Delphi. His first language was Greek, learning Latin later in his life but never mastering it. He appears to have had influence among the powerful, aiming to combine the power of Rome with the learning and history of Greece. He wrote in the period known as the Second Sophistic, a time of renaissance, encouraged by philhellenic emperors such as Trajan and Hadrian, for Greek education and rhetoric (literary style) in the Roman Empire. Intellect and learning were modelled on the teachings and oratory of fifth-century BCE Greece. Plutarch, although writing in this context, is not considered an exponent of this literary movement since his works are not preoccupied with rhetoric in the same way.

Plutarch was prolific, with over 225 works attributed to him in an ancient catalogue (the Catalogue of Lamprias). Nearly 100 of these are lost; among his extant works are 50 *Lives* and 78 compositions collected under the title *Moralia*. In these Plutarch treats various topics including politics, ethics and morals, history, religion, education and philosophy – including critiques of other philosophical schools including Stoicism and Epicureanism. His *On the Malice of Herodotus* is a famous treatise in which he accuses Herodotus of favouritism in his account of the Graeco-Persian wars and cites a number of errors in his works. Overall, he was a man with many interests who was religious, reflective and had strong convictions. His influence has been great, with translations of his works in the Renaissance providing rich source material to many writers and poets, most notably Shakespeare, whose *Julius Caesar, Antony and Cleopatra* and *Coriolanus* in particular are indebted to the relevant *Lives* of Plutarch.

Plutarch: *Lives*

Plutarch's *Lives* were likely written in the last twenty or so years of his life. Forty-six of his 50 surviving works are paired as parallel lives, nineteen including an accompanying comparison. Each pair contains the biographies of one famous Greek and one famous Roman, including legendary figures such as Theseus and Romulus, historical leaders such as Alexander the Great and Julius Caesar and orators such as Demosthenes and Cicero.

Plutarch chose his subjects carefully, writing about men whose deeds and character were worthy of mentioning – both to imitate and to avoid. He also wished to find pairs, for comparison and contrast. Alcibiades was an ideal subject since he was an Athenian general who had many successes, was charismatic and popular and was directly involved in many events during a very important part of Greek history, the Peloponnesian War of 431–404 BCE. He was also exiled by the Athenians twice, sided with two of Athens' enemies and had numerous character flaws, including being extravagant, a playboy and rather unscrupulous. This enigmatic character was a good foil for the subject of the paired biography, a strict, conservative Roman general called Coriolanus, who, like Alcibiades, also fought against his own people. As the *Life of Alcibiades* proves, there was much rich material for Plutarch to mine in this biography and historians still remain fascinated by Alcibiades today.

In a few of his biographies Plutarch gives us some indications of the aims of his project and what he himself is getting from them. In his *Life of Aemilius Paulus* – the Roman general who defeated the Macedonians at Pydna in 168 BCE – he states that he started writing his *Lives* for others but now continues it for his own sake, enjoying trying to guide his life by the virtues he discovers in his subjects. He says that he selects the most important and most noble from his subjects' deeds – τὰ κυριώτατα καὶ κάλλιστα πρὸς γνῶσιν ἀπὸ τῶν πράξεων (1.1). This, he says, is very helpful for correcting one's character or morals – πρὸς ἐπανόρθωσιν ἠθῶν (1.2).

He makes it clear in the *Life of Nicias*, a contemporary and rival of Alcibiades, that he uses historical sources and draws upon them to avoid making errors, and that he also tries to find some more obscure facts about his subject. His professed purpose, however, was not just to amass useless information (τὴν ἄχρηστον ἱστορίαν) but to hand down material providing a means of observing a subject's character and way of life – ἀλλὰ τὴν πρὸς κατανόησιν ἤθους καὶ τρόπου παραδιδούς (1.5).

Plutarch focuses on the character of his individuals, exemplified by their actions; much of his *Lives* is straightforward narrative. He explores moral and ethical judgements of his protagonists through anecdotes, in line with his own intentions. His *Life of Alexander* (1.2) starts:

οὔτε γὰρ ἱστορίας γράφομεν, ἀλλὰ βίους, οὔτε ταῖς ἐπιφανεστάταις πράξεσι πάντως ἔνεστι δήλωσις ἀρετῆς ἢ κακίας, ἀλλὰ πρᾶγμα βραχὺ πολλάκις καὶ ῥῆμα καὶ παιδιά τις ἔμφασιν ἤθους ἐποίησε μᾶλλον ἢ μάχαι μυριόνεκροι καὶ παρατάξεις αἱ μέγισται καὶ πολιορκίαι πόλεων

For I am not writing Histories, but Lives – in the most distinguished deeds there is not always evidence of virtue or vice, but a trivial matter, some phrase or joke, often reflects character more than battles with thousands dead, huge conflicts and sieges of cities

Plutarch nonetheless did choose as the subjects of his biographies mostly men who were involved in politics and led armies, engaging in battles and sieges. He uses his narration of events to show character and judge the way some great men lived their lives, contextualizing the aspect of character which the events illuminate. His *Life of Alcibiades* is no exception, starting with various anecdotes drawn from his whole life showing his character and followed by the events of his political career chronologically, with comments on his way of life or morals woven into the narration. Several character traits referred to in the early part of this *Life* appear throughout the biography as Alcibiades' boyhood actions are represented as precursors of his activities in adulthood. The *Life of Alcibiades* creates the image of an individual who is hard to pin down and whose actions cannot always be explained easily; Plutarch's assessment of him reflects this, which means we too are left to make up our own minds.

Timeline

c. 450 BCE	Alcibiades is born in Athens.
447 BCE	Alcibiades' father Cleinias is killed fighting for the Delian League, led by Athens, at the Battle of Coronea.
	Pericles becomes Alcibiades' guardian (**Section 1**)
432–429 BCE	Alcibiades fights for the Athenians in their victory at Potidaea in northern Greece, defeating the Corinthians who supported the Potidaeans' revolt against Athens. Socrates, one of his teachers, reportedly saved Alcibiades' life during this campaign (**Section 7**).
431–421 BCE	The 'Archidamian War', the first phase of the Peloponnesian War fought between Athens and Sparta and their allies.
429 BCE	Pericles dies from the plague at Athens (430–426 BCE).
425 BCE	An Athenian force defeats the Spartans in a naval battle at Pylos. Part of the Peloponnesian army, including Spartan hoplites, were isolated on the island of Sphacteria and subsequently defeated in battle. Nearly three hundred were captured and taken back to Athens as hostages (**Section 14.1, Section 14.5**).
424 BCE	Alcibiades fights for the Athenians against Boeotia in central Greece at Delium, where he is said to have saved Socrates (**Section 7**).
421 BCE	The Peace of Nicias, a fifty-year truce between Athens and Sparta, is agreed, though it is officially abandoned seven years later.
420–419 BCE	Alcibiades is elected general, having been active in speaking against the Peace of Nicias and hindering negotiations between Athens and

Sparta. He is instrumental in brokering an alliance with Argos, an important city in the Peloponnese (**Section 14–15**).

418 BCE   The Athenian force, in an alliance with Argos, Mantinea and Elis which Alcibiades helped engineer, is defeated by a Spartan-led army at the Battle of Mantinea (**Section 15**).

417–416 BCE   Alcibiades is elected general again but is involved in a vote in the Assembly to have him and Nicias exiled – an ostracism – proposed by a politician named Hyperbolus. Alcibiades and Nicias combine their influence to turn the tables and have Hyperbolus himself exiled (**Section 13**).

416 BCE   Alcibiades enters seven chariots in the Olympic Games and gains first prize (**Section 11**).

415 BCE   Alcibiades is again elected general and, against Nicias, supports the Sicilian Expedition, in which Athens would send troops to become involved in what was essentially a local dispute with a view to gaining riches and influence over Syracuse, the main power in Sicily (**Sections 17–18**).

                 The 'Mutilation of the Herms', an incident which occurs as the force is about to depart for Sicily, during which many statues of the god of travel, Hermes – *hermai* – are vandalized (**Section 18**). Alcibiades and his companions are accused of carrying out this sacrilegious act, while they are further accused of profaning the Eleusian Mysteries, an ancient, secretive cult to the goddesses Demeter and Persephone (**Section 19**).

                 Alcibiades is recalled from the expedition but he escapes from his pursuers, hiding at Thurii in the southern, Greek part of Italy called Magna Graecia; at Athens he is condemned to death in his absence (**Sections 20–22**).

413–404 BCE   The 'Ionian War', the second phase of the Peloponnesian War.

413 BCE   The Sicilian Expedition ends in defeat and disaster for Athens.

412 BCE   Alcibiades helps the Spartans encourage Athenian allies on the west coast of modern-day Turkey – the Ionian coast – to revolt from Athens.

                 Alcibiades becomes unwelcome in Sparta, so defects to the Persian satrap Tissaphernes, who had been aiding Sparta in the Peloponnesian War financially.

411 BCE   The Four Hundred, a radical form of oligarchic government, stage a coup in Athens as the city struggles with the strain of the Peloponnesian War. Internal divisions between extremists and moderates lead to their replacement by the Five Thousand.

                 Alcibiades is recalled by the Athenian fleet at Samos, partly on the promise that he would bring Persian support, through Tissaphernes, over to the Athenian side.

Alcibiades plays a decisive role for Athens in the Battle of Abydus, a naval engagement against the Spartan fleet contested near the Hellespont.

410 BCE   Alcibiades is arrested by Tissaphernes as the Persians remain on the Spartan side. Alcibiades escapes and resumes command, leading Athenian naval forces to victory at the Battle of Cyzicus, also near the Hellespont, giving Athens control of the region.

As a result of this defeat, Sparta offers Athens peace terms but these are refused. Athens restores democracy, ousting the oligarchic Five Thousand.

407 BCE   Alcibiades returns to Athens after winning some cities to the Athenian cause; there he protects a procession of followers of the Eleusinian Mysteries whose route takes them past a Spartan stronghold. He starts on a new expedition against islands in the Ionian Sea.

406 BCE   While Alcibiades is away raising funds to pay his troops he leaves the fleet in the hands of a deputy, Antiochus, with instructions not to engage the enemy. Such orders are ignored and the Athenians are defeated by Lysander and his Spartan fleet at Notium. Alcibiades is blamed – he flees to Thrace.

405 BCE   Athenians defeated at sea again by the Spartans at Aegospotami after Alcibiades had tried to warn the Athenian generals that they had to change their tactics.

404 BCE   Alcibiades is killed in Persian territory; Athens' democracy is overthrown and the oligarchic Thirty take control of the city.

c. CE 45   Plutarch is born in Chaeronea in Boeotia.

c. CE 119–125   Plutarch's death.

Alcibiades

The fascination with Alcibiades, which started with his contemporaries and ancient authors, continues today. In part this is due to our incomplete evidence for his exciting life and actions, which were central to the fate of Athens in the late fifth century BCE. Our inability to fully explain some of the decisions made either by him or about him adds to the enigma, while our sources' information on his personality serves only to increase our wish to understand him. He attracts attention as a major player in the Peloponnesian War who appears to have been persuasive, strategically insightful, arrogant, extravagant, frequently successful, popular and willing to do harm to his own city, all in equal measure.

Alcibiades' role in events surrounding the end of the Peloponnesian War ensured he appeared in many histories detailing the period, not all of which survive today. Plutarch was familiar with the *Histories* of Ephorus, for example, while the Roman biographer Cornelius Nepos says that the historians Theopompus and Timaeus agreed with Thucydides in their praise of Alcibiades' character. Plutarch's *Life* is the last ancient source to treat Alcibiades on any significant scale. A number of anecdotes about Alcibiades do appear in literature after Plutarch, such as Athenaeus' *Deipnosophistae* from second/third century CE. Athenaeus seems to include incidents relating to Alcibiades' passionate and scandalous nature in particular.

The most complete account of the end of the fifth century BCE comes from Thucydides in his *History of the Peloponnesian War*. Alcibiades is a key figure throughout his narrative, but the historian is not always complimentary towards him. As noted below, Thucydides was definitely a source for Plutarch and provides much comparable material, especially for the Spartan embassy affair (Section 14) and from the Sicilian Expedition narrative onwards in the second part of the biography (Sections 17 and following). Alcibiades also appears in the works of other historians. In Xenophon's *Hellenica* his military ability is the primary focus and in Diodorus Siculus' *Bibliotheca Historica* he is credited as having a major effect on Athenian policy, success and failure. Both authors present Alcibiades in a more positive light than Thucydides.

Aspects of his character and career are presented in three different legal orations. Isocrates' sixteenth speech, *On the Team of Horses*, is part of a speech for Alcibiades the Younger (the son of our Alcibiades about whom Plutarch writes his biography) when he was taken to court over the accusation that his father had entered another's chariot in the Olympic Games as his own. The speech praises Alcibiades throughout and defends various aspects of his career and character, in particular how loyal he was to Athens' democracy. The fourteenth and fifteenth speeches attributed to the logographer Lysias, called *Against Alcibiades 1* and *2*, concern a charge against Alcibiades the Younger of serving in the cavalry illegally during a conflict in central Greece. The prosecutor, in focusing on the charges of desertion and refusal of military service, devotes part of his argument to showing that Alcibiades' career was not as stellar as often thought, that he harmed Athens more than helped her and was not particularly democratic at all. A similarly negative portrayal of Alcibiades is found in the fourth speech attributed to Andocides (from here on called pseudo-Andocides 4). *Against Alcibiades* is presented as a speech in the ostracism vote determining the fate of Alcibiades, Nicias and one other (the speaker himself), the same vote to which our selection refers (Section 13). Tyrannical aspects of Alcibiades' character are referenced throughout, with a number of anecdotes illuminating his lack of respect for the law and for others; some of these same anecdotes are also recorded in Plutarch's *Life*.

Alcibiades' close connections with the philosopher Socrates, which Plutarch discusses in this *Life* in some of the sections in the prescribed English selection (Sections 1, 4, 6 and 7), result in him being discussed or making an appearance in four works by students of Socrates. In his *Memorabilia* Xenophon says that Alcibiades primarily associated with Socrates in order to improve his chances in politics while in Plato's *Symposium* Alcibiades turns up at a dinner party drunk with a flute-girl on his arm, insists on making the other guests drunk and decides that he will make a speech praising Socrates, not Eros as requested. The Alcibiades of this dialogue chose Athenian politics and demagoguery over the teachings of Socrates. Two dialogues attributed to Plato, *Alcibiades 1* and *2* relate conversations between Alcibiades and Socrates – their first in the case of *Alcibiades 1*. Alcibiades is seen as wanting political power and Socrates fears that the Athenian people will ultimately ruin him if he gives in to wanting to win them over.

Cornelius Nepos, the Roman biographer of the first century BCE, included a life of Alcibiades in his text 'On the Lives of Eminent Generals'. In an examination which is favourable overall, Nepos depicts him as a most patriotic individual, although he does seem to recognize Alcibiades' complexity of character, remarking at the outset (1.1):

constat enim inter omnes, qui de eo memoriae prodiderunt, nihil illo fuisse excellentius vel in vitiis vel in virtutibus

for it is agreed among all who have written about him that nothing was more remarkable than his capacity for vices or virtues

and, after contrasting his qualities – which included his beauty, military ability, eloquence, wealth, energy, generous and adaptable – with his negative characteristics, namely his extravagance, self-indulgence, lustfulness and lack of self-control, he states that (1.4):

omnes admirarentur in uno homine tantam esse dissimilitudinem tamque diversam naturam

all wondered how there was such disparity and diversity in the character of one man

Nepos' portrait of Alcibiades, however, is not especially nuanced and concentrates almost exclusively on his positive qualities.

Indeed our sources probably each contain elements of the real Alcibiades, and most likely the truth about his personality, his role in the political events of the time and his motivations lies somewhere in between all these narratives.

Stuttard (pg. 3) sums up neatly the problems with trying to find the real Alcibiades:

Throughout his life, the rumour mill of his native Athens and the wider world ground out tales of his duplicity and decadence that mired him in controversy and threatened to destroy him. Meanwhile Alcibiades himself, adept at self-promotion, countered them with testimonies of his patriotic probity, until it was impossible for anyone to know with any certainty where the truth really lay. For later generations the problem was compounded by the bias of what evidence survived, so that the sources that we have today must be approached with caution.

Plutarch: *Life of Alcibiades*

The true character of Alcibiades remains as elusive to us as it was to his contemporaries and ancient writers. Plutarch knew the traditions concerning Alcibiades and drew on many sources in composing his biography. We can never know why he made the choices he did but it is fair to assume he kept his aims at the forefront of his decisions. The result is a biography which presents a puzzling individual in an ambiguous manner, leaving many questions about him unanswered.

In twenty of Plutarch's *Lives* the Greek life is first in the pair, but of the three which break this pattern, the *Life of Alcibiades* is one, with the *Life of Coriolanus* coming before it; a comparison, or *syncrisis*, of the two comes at the end (see below). The first *Life* in a pair can often introduce themes which are then developed in the second biography. In the case of *Coriolanus*, aspects of his character which are highlighted include his arrogant and inflexible attitude to the common people of Rome, whom he refused to win over, the simplicity and straightforwardness of his life and his strict stance against bribery. These traits are starkly contrasted in the Greek *Life* as Alcibiades, constantly winning over the people through his speeches and charisma, is depicted as a complex character whose life was anything but straightforward and whose attitude towards money was one of extravagance. The two men appear to be opposites in character for the most part, but they are paired also because they both were generals who were exiled by their homelands and then caused their own cities great harm by aiding the enemy against them. As such they both are challenging figures to portray and judge.

Plutarch's *Life of Alcibiades* is a work which is effectively divided into two parts. Sections 1–16 deal with Alcibiades' ancestry and boyhood, with various anecdotes referring to aspects of his character such as ambition, outrageous behaviour, extravagance and passionate nature; chronology is not always respected here. His first entry into politics is set out and events of his early political career are detailed, including avoiding being exiled through a vote in the Assembly, arranging an alliance with rival Greek states, ruffling the feathers of the leading politician of his day, Nicias, and agitating for war during the so-called Peace of Nicias between Athens and Sparta by humiliating an embassy from Sparta and Nicias too in the process. After relating how he aided some allies against the Spartans, the final section of this part collects several anecdotes which show Alcibiades as extravagant and arrogant yet irrepressible.

The second part of the biography which takes up the rest of the *Life*, Sections 17–39, follows the narrative of Alcibiades' political life starting with the Sicilian Expedition launched in 415 BCE. Alcibiades is presented as the main proponent of the campaign, arguing against Nicias' resistance to what he believed was too dangerous an undertaking. The night before the fleet was to set sail, very many pillars with the heads of Hermes on them, called herms, were vandalized. Some accused Alcibiades and his friends of doing this after some drunken revelry. There soon followed a charge that he desecrated the Eleusinian Mysteries (a cult to Demeter and Persephone) by acting out their rites at a party. Alcibiades wanted to defend himself at once, having the support of the troops and allies he had won over on his side, but his enemies had the trial delayed until he should return. Barely after setting out he was recalled, as the fleet reached Sicily to conduct the expedition according to his plan. In the meantime a man accused of taking part in the Mutilation of the Herms, as the incident came to be known, informed on others in exchange for immunity from prosecution. This did not keep the people happy but rather seemed to increase their anger towards Alcibiades and demanded that he return to Athens to prove his innocence. Soon after boarding the ship to Athens Alcibiades, who knew things would not go well for him in Athens, escaped and went into hiding. He was found guilty by the Athenians *in absentia*, for desecrating the Eleusinian Mysteries.

This is where the selection to be read ends, at Section 22. The rest of the biography narrates Alcibiades' subsequent actions, detailed in the 'Timeline' above: his defection to Sparta, then to Persia; his return to favour, leading the Athenian fleet on the Ionian coast to some victories against the Spartans; his flight after Antiochus, his lieutenant, is defeated by Lysander at Notium; his attempt to help Athenian commanders at Aegospotami; his death in Persian territory.

Most of the second part of the *Life* records Alcibiades' actions within the context of the events of 415 BCE down to 404 BCE. These actions are to be understood in light of the Alcibiades' character, as set out in the first part of the biography. As such the focus is on the historical and on Alcibiades' behaviour. Nonetheless some anecdotes are scattered throughout these sections too. We learn from Section 23, for instance, that he could live as thriftly and frown as well as any Spartan, drink and ride horses as hard as any Thracian and live as luxuriously as any Persian; in Section 24 Plutarch notes that the Persian satrap Tissaphernes named his most beautiful garden 'Alcibiades', so taken in was he by the Athenian's flattery; and in Section 38 it is recorded that Alcibiades, just before he ended up being killed, had a dream: either he saw himself dressed in his mistress' clothes with her holding his head in her arms while she put make-up on his face, or he saw his own head being cut off by Bagaeus, the brother of Pharnabazus, and an image of his own body being burned.

The comparison (*syncrisis*) of Alcibiades and Coriolanus

Following Plutarch's biographical pairs is a syncrisis, which compares the characters of his two subjects and decides which of the Greek or Roman was a better man overall. As the *Life of Alcibiades* was placed second in the pair, the syncrisis follows, comparing Alcibiades with the Roman general Coriolanus. Plutarch starts by stating that, while both men were great generals, Alcibiades edges out Marcius Coriolanus since he did not lose a battle on land or at sea. He then notes that both won many successes for their homelands but also did significant harm to them by switching sides and joining the enemy. Alcibiades won over the common people of Athens but was hated by the noble class and was unscrupulous in his public acts – Plutarch cites his treatment of the Spartan embassy seeking peace as evidence, but then says that the ends justified the means, since his alliance with Argos and allies made Athens strong. Alcibiades' ambition and efforts to succeed amid political rivalry are mentioned, as is his anger, which did harm to the Athenians. But he is praised for rising above such feelings when necessary, for instance when he offered advice to the Athenian generals at Aegospotami even though they had replaced him and he had been exiled by the Athenians for a second time. Alcibiades' later defection from Sparta, after he had fled from Athens, is considered to have been necessary, to an extent, since the Spartans were plotting to take his life after misusing him.

Next Plutarch details how Alcibiades gained much of his money corruptly and then spent it extravagantly before discussing his adaptability and charm, which explain why, despite harming Athens, he was appointed general numerous times and indeed benefitted Athens as a solider and as a commander – Athens' disasters usually occurred when he was absent. Alcibiades enjoyed winning honours, did not want to be overlooked for important positions and would behave in whatever way was required to win people over.

In conclusion, however, Plutarch decides that Coriolanus – whose traits included arrogance and pride and who had only won significant victories when fighting against his homeland Rome, not for it – was brilliant in all other traits and that, due to his self-control, financial restraint and resistance to bribery, he deserved to be compared with the best and most honourable Greeks, not Alcibiades. These harsh, last words on Alcibiades come as a surprise, considering that throughout the syncrisis he seems to be equal to or better than Coriolanus in most respects; nevertheless Plutarch concludes that he was:

τῷ θρασυτάτῳ ... καὶ ὀλιγωροτάτῳ τοῦ καλοῦ

[regarding self-control and rising above wealth] most rash and most careless towards honour

In both his *Life* and in the syncrisis, Plutarch ends with information which does not present Alcibiades in the best light, even though the preceding material has been largely positive. His overall view of his protagonist appears to be impossible to determine and deliberately ambiguous: his assessment of Alcibiades seems to change like a chameleon, just as he described Alcibiades' own nature.

Method and aims

Plutarch's use of sources and his manipulation of the sequence of events provide an insight into his method and aims. He stays focused on his subject and selects material accordingly, arranging it in the way which best suits his purpose.

Sources

Plutarch most likely read extensively and did a lot of research; as such, the anecdotes he includes in his *Alcibiades* are consciously selected to elucidate certain aspects of his character pertinent to the actions he later carried out during his life. They are also chosen to contribute to the portrait being drawn of Alcibiades in contrast to Coriolanus.

Plutarch sometimes directly quotes his sources and sometimes paraphrases their content, often naming them. He uses his sources for a variety of purposes, but broadly speaking there seem to be three main aims:

(i)   to lend credibility to statements he makes – e.g. Eupolis' quotation on Phaeax (Section 13)

(ii)   to provide a contrasting view to a detail or engage in an existing debate – e.g. Thucydides on Alcibiades' victories (Section 11)

(iii) to offer additional or alternative information to his account – e.g. Theophrastus on Alcibiades' speaking ability (Section 10) or Plato the comic poet's view of Hyperbolus (Section 13).

Plutarch also on occasion refers to his own works, such as at the end of the ostracism event early in Alcibiades' career (Section 13), where he states that he has written about this incident at greater length in his *Life of Nicias*, Section 11. Similarities abound between the two narrations, with the identical, direct quotation of the comic poet Plato's three lines on Hyperbolus appearing in both passages. But the focus changes: in *Alcibiades* the protagonist is more proactive in siding with Nicias. Hyperbolus' character is examined in detail, to show him to be the type of demagogue the people used and exploited rather than one who influenced them. As such he is set up as a counterpoint to Alcibiades, who had genuine influence among the people, as the ostracism vote and history bears out.

The *Lives*, considered to be composed later than the *Moralia*, clearly drew on the same notes and source material as them, if not on them directly. Some anecdotes from the *Alcibiades* show this, for instance when Alcibiades carries a quail into the Athenian Assembly (Section 10). In his *Praecepta gerendae reipublicae* ('Political Precepts') 799d Plutarch writes that the Carthaginians would never have joined in hunting down a politician's quail in the manner the Athenians joined Alcibiades. Similarly, the reference to Alcibiades' manner of public speaking (also Section 10) is also reported at *Praecepta gerendae reipublicae* 804d, where some wording is the same and the information is attributed to Theophrastus.

It is clear that other sources referring to Alcibiades (discussed above, see 'Alcibiades') also influenced Plutarch's *Life*. It is interesting, for instance, that the three anecdotes related in Section 16.4 regarding Alcibiades' lawless spirit (Agatharcus, Taureas and the Melian woman) are all related in the same order as examples of his use of violence in the speech *Against Alcibiades* attributed to the orator Andocides (pseudo-Andocides 4. 17–23).

There are also many similarities between Plutarch's narration of Alcibiades' life and the last two-thirds of Thucydides 5. But there are also variations: Plutarch streamlines events, rearranges his material and is selective in details, all in order to retain focus on the character of his protagonist.

Chronology of events

From our selection of the *Life of Alcibiades* it is clear that Plutarch was not concerned with precise chronology, since it is not his purpose to give a year-by-year account of Alcibiades' life. The first part of the biography (Section 1–16) is presented with an overall chronological structure in that it takes us from his family and early childhood down to the Sicilian Expedition of 415 BCE. Sections 1–9 are concerned with the events of his boyhood before he entered politics and the public spotlight but the anecdotes related cannot be assigned a date from Plutarch's text itself and the order of their presentation cannot be assumed to be chronological. Some incidents are known from other sources, for instance the events related in Section 7 concerning Potidaea and Delium, which can be dated securely; in fact the inclusion of Delium at this point is noted by Plutarch as being out of sequence.

Sections 10–16 deal with the first few years of Alcibiades' involvement in politics, but again Plutarch is interested not in the order of events but in the presentation of his material and how it pertains to Alcibiades. Thus in Section 10 the mention of

Antiochus catching the quail leads Plutarch to note that this resulted in him becoming dear to Alcibiades; Plutarch's readers likely knew the role he was to play in Alcibiades' fate over fifteen years or so later. The references to Alcibiades' Olympic victories in Section 11 date from a number of years after the events of Section 13, which detail the ostracism vote against Alcibiades brought by Hyperbolus. This in turn is placed before Alcibiades' dealings with the Spartan assembly (Section 14) and his brokering of an alliance with Argos, Mantinea and Elis (Section 15), although the ostracism in fact took place later.

Plutarch clearly has his reasons for such chronological displacement, and it is interesting to consider the build-up of Alcibiades' character which the sequence, as presented, creates. After entering politics and winning over the people (Section 10) he is shown to be famous and a winner (Section 11). While noting the rivalry which cities indulged in to give Alcibiades the best gift, reflecting his own love of competition, Plutarch introduces a negative side of Alcibiades with the anecdote relating to Diomedes' chariot (Section 12). He is seen to be potentially duplicitous at this early stage and not an entirely straightforward character (as opposed to Marcus Coriolanus, with whom he is being compared). Alcibiades' ability to work out which way the political winds were blowing and his willingness to play a role for political gain is seen in the ostracism incident (Section 13) which introduces the rivalry with Nicias, picked up in Section 14. Here the deceitful side of Alcibiades is in evidence again with his interactions with the Spartan embassy, to the detriment of Nicias' standing, before Alcibiades' appointment as general, and his political acumen is recorded when he gains valuable allies for Athens and works for her interest in his dealings with a couple of city states (Section 15). The complexity of his character and some of the traits which will contribute to the troubles which plague his career are described in Section 16, which concludes the first part of the biography and sets up the characterization of Alcibiades neatly before what was perhaps the main event of his political life, the Sicilian Expedition. The rest of his career and his actions during it should be read in the context of the characteristics of Alcibiades which Sections 1–16 highlight, even if this is a subtly different Alcibiades to the one with which his audience was already familiar.

Overall, Plutarch should be viewed as a keen researcher with his own methodology towards the genre of writing biography. His use of his source material, his selection of anecdotes and the arrangement of the incidents contained within a *Life* are all honed to best suit his methods and aims. Only a few examples pertaining to Plutarch's methodology are noted here for the sake of brevity and where relevant some mention is made throughout the Commentary but these too are by no means exhaustive. Suggestions for where students wishing to learn more should start are made below (see Further Reading).

Themes

In our selection, many themes are packed in to a fairly short text. Since the work is biographical, a greater variety of topics and a larger number of anecdotes are encountered than when reading a historical narrative or a philosophical dialogue for the most part, since the thematic focus in those is narrower. What follows below is not a complete list, but gives an idea of a number of themes which Plutarch explores with regard to Alcibiades' character and the presentation of his life. Examples here are drawn from the selection to be read in Greek but the English selection provides further material.

A good starting point is Section 16.1: Alcibiades' positive qualities are listed, countered by negative traits. Section 10 also introduces elements of Alcibiades' character which will play a part in his life, with a focus on his charisma and wish for popular support. Many characteristics are exemplified through anecdotes or actions which Plutarch records.

These themes help provide structure to the *Life* also, since they are referred back to by Plutarch or help explain or foreshadow events involving Alcibiades.

Themes connected with Alcibiades' character and qualities include:

(i)   his wish to influence the common people and his success at this (e.g. 10.2, 13.4, 16.3)

(ii)   his cleverness at speaking (e.g. 10.2, 14.8, 16.5)

(iii)   his love of competition and honour (e.g. 11.1, 12.2, 13.1, 14.1, 16.3-4)

(iv)   his love of display (e.g. 10.1, 14.6, 16.2, 16.5)

(v)   his willingness to use others' property as his own (e.g. 12.2, 13.2)

(vi)   his two-sided character (e.g. 14.8-9, 16.5)

(vii)   his relationship with oaths (e.g. 14.8 (oath-breaker), 15.4 (supporting an oath)).

Other themes occurring within the selection which should be noted include:

(i)   how Alcibiades is given prominence in events (e.g. throughout 14, 15.2)

(ii)   Alcibiades' connection to drama and the theatricality of his life (e.g. 10.1, 11–12, 14, 16.5)

(iii)   ambiguity associated with Alcibiades' actions and life (e.g. 11.1, 12.3, 13.4).

That ambiguity be connected to Alcibiades comes as no surprise: in his presentation of his subject, Plutarch appears to wish to reflect the difficulty of evaluating him. Anecdotes are often vague and there are a number of comments on the differing views of sources, such as which places Alcibiades' chariots secured at the Olympics (11.1). Plutarch does not seek to address these ambiguities and leaves them open deliberately, for his readers to decide. He also employs the words of others, particularly comic poets, to characterize Alcibiades (11.2, 13.2, 13.5 and 16.2).

Language and style

Reading Plutarch can be challenging. He uses a lot of vocabulary which is not particularly common and which those who have primarily studied the likes of Herodotus, Plato and Xenophon will not have encountered much.

The notes in the Commentary point out a number of matters of style, but are not comprehensive. Certain sections seem more rhetorical and stylized than others, reflecting the content, such as Sections 10, 14 and 16.1-5. The following aspects of Plutarch's writing are worth bearing in mind when reading the selection:

- *Word order.* Ancient Greek is rarely as systematic as Latin in its use of subject, object, verb, but often it does follow a structure with some logic to it. Plutarch's sentences can work like this, but often a whole clause or sentence needs to be examined in detail before translation. The object of the sentence often comes first in the sentence, highlighting the focus of the sentence. The subject can sometimes be found at the very end of a clause, delayed so that the end comes as a twist or underscores the point being made. Adjectives and nouns are commonly separated from another, usually by just a word or two; often the verb they are dependent on comes between them.

- *Expression.* Plutarch sometimes uses an abstract noun where we might expect an adjective (e.g. 13.3: ἀναισχυντίαν καὶ ἀπόνοιαν and εὐτολμίαν καὶ ἀνδρείαν). Due to the irregular word order, reading Plutarch is a good test of grammar as very close attention must be paid to the form of words to work out their function in the sentence. He is also fond of using rare words (e.g. 14.4: ἐξετράχυνε, 14.7: ἀγνωμονήσει, 15.1: κραδᾶναι).

- *Sentence structure.* Plutarch writes fairly simply, without long sentences in subordination (hypotaxis), but rather with many clauses working side by side (parataxis). Relative clauses are very common. To achieve this paratactic style, participles abound, as does the genitive absolute. The accusative + infinitive construction occurs frequently after verbs of speaking, perception, etc. (sometimes where a Classical author uses accusative + participle) and multiple such clauses can depend on a single verb (see Section 10).

- *Lists.* Lists – of examples, of anecdotes, of character traits – are typical in this *Life*, and can often be identified by the use of καί or τε to indicate each item.

- *Balance.* Plutarch aims for balance throughout, with the frequent use of μέν and δέ to contrast clauses, sometimes even within a larger μέν and δέ clause. This rhetorical aim for balance results in the doubling of words, sometimes with one idea expressed by two words (hendiadys) but more commonly with two similar words adding flavour to the point (pleonasm). In the text there are numerous such couplets, of nouns, adjectives, verbs and even phrases.

- *Variety.* To break up his narrative, Plutarch presents his information in different ways. Some anecdotes are introduced vaguely, starting with λέγεται 'it is said' or a similar expression like 'some say', others are attributed to a named author. There are a number of direct quotations from other literature, often the comic poets, used to describe attitude or character. Alcibiades himself is quoted in a couple of places (14.7, 15.3). Interestingly, much of the speech to the Spartan embassy is from Thucydides but in indirect speech. Plutarch reports Alcibiades' words in direct speech, imagining how such a speech might have sounded. Breaking up the narrative, the speech is also appropriate in light of Alcibiades' ability to persuade, a thematic characteristic which Plutarch refers to repeatedly.

A close reading of the text will reveal many other idiosyncrasies of the author. It should be borne in mind that Plutarch aimed to be readable. There are rhetorical devices throughout and some sections of narrative are artfully constructed, but the *Life* is structured in such a way as to be easy to follow and to build up a picture of the biography's subject. The frequent quotation of others is usually seamless, and Plutarch does not get bogged down with citing his sources excessively or with detailed historical exposition. He selects material for his purpose and relates it in a largely straightforward manner. Certainly in the *Life of Alcibiades*, the subject matter is often lively enough and the character of Alcibiades sufficiently complex that it is enough to let them take centre stage.

Glossary

Most named individuals are discussed at the appropriate point in the Commentary but three worthy of particular mention are:

Eupolis   a comic poet of fifth century BCE who was a contemporary of Aristophanes. Only fragments survive of his works though he is thought to have won first prize seven times and nineteen plays are attributed to him. Typically of Old Comedy a number of his plays appear to attack politicians, with Hyperbolus, Phaeax and Alcibiades all targets. Among the traditions concerning his death, one tells that Eupolis had to serve under Alcibiades, having previously ridiculed him in one of his plays, on the Sicilian Expedition; on route to Sicily, Alcibiades reportedly had the poet drowned!

Hyperbolus   a politician of the popular faction in Athens who rose to prominence after Cleon, a most notorious demagogue of fifth century BCE. Plutarch's characterization of him is unrelentingly negative. Much of the material referring to him in the *Alcibiades* is included in Plutarch's *Nicias* 11, where Hyperbolus is introduced in the same way and spoken of in similarly unflattering terms.

Nicias   born c. 470 BCE, the leading Athenian politician and general at the time of Alcibiades' entry into politics. He was moderate in his views and clashed with the popular demagogues of the time. He wanted peace with Sparta in the ongoing Peloponnesian War. His role in negotiations with them led to his name being given to the pact of 421 BCE, the so-called 'Peace of Nicias'. Strongly opposing the Sicilian Expedition, he was voted to be one of the three generals and died on campaign there in 413 BCE.

Further Reading

Plutarch has been a much-studied author, especially in the last fifty years or so, while the fascination with Alcibiades has remained since ancient times. Several very recent works, including the Blackwell companion edited by Beck, serve as a good starting point for research into Plutarch, his aims, methods and his literary context. The amount of biographies of Alcibiades reflects to an extent the difficulty to characterize him with certainty, but the new book by Stuttard is a very readable account which synthesizes the various traditions existing around him. The commentary on Plutarch's *Alcibiades* by Verdegem is particularly focused on moralism and how the text is structured, but is a thoroughly-researched edition which has informed much of what is contained in this volume.

The translation by Waterfield in the Oxford World's Classics series, faithful to the Greek text but in a contemporary fashion, is an enjoyable read. Stadter's introduction serves as an excellent overview of the author for those new to him and the notes on the text give much context and explanation for the reader.

Plutarch and ancient biography

Beck, M. (ed.). *A Companion to Plutarch*. Oxford 2014.

de Blois, L. et al. (eds). *The statesman in Plutarch's works: proceedings of the sixth international conference of the International Plutarch Society*. Leiden 2004–2005; 2 volumes – especially Volume 2.

Duff, T. *Plutarch's Lives. Exploring Virtue and Vice*. Oxford 1999.

Jacobs, S. *Plutarch's Pragmatic Biographies: Lessons for Statesmen and Generals in the Parallel Lives*. Leiden 2017.

Mossman, J. (ed.). *Plutarch and his intellectual world: essays on Plutarch*. London 1997.

Mossman, J. and McGing, B. (eds.). *The limits of ancient biography*. Swansea 2006.

Pelling, C.B.R. 'Plutarch's Adaptation of his Source-Material' *JHS* 100 (1980), 127–140 (reprinted in Pelling 2002, 91–115 and in Scardigli 1995, 125–154).

Pelling, C.B.R. 'Aspects of Plutarch's Characterisation' *ICS* 13.2 (1988) 257–274 (reprinted in Pelling 2002, 283–300)

Pelling, C.B.R. *Plutarch and history: eighteen studies*. Swansea 2002.

Scardigli, B. *Essays on Plutarch's Lives*. Oxford 1995.

Stadter, P.A. (ed.) *Plutarch and the historical tradition*. London 1992.

Stadter, P.A. *Plutarch and his Roman readers*. Oxford 2015.

Plutarch's *Alcibiades*

Duff, T. 'Plutarch on the Childhood of Alcibiades (*Alk.* 20–3)' *PCPS* 49 (2003), 89–117.

Russell, D.A. 'Alcibiades 1–16', *PCPS* 12 (1966), 37–47 (reprinted in Scardigli 1995, 191–207.

Verdegem, S. *Plutarch's Life of Alcibiades: Story, Text and Moralism*. Leiden 2010.

Waterfield, R. *Greek lives: a selection of nine Greek lives*. Oxford 1998.

Alcibiades

Ellis, W.M. *Alcibiades*. London 1989.

Gribble, D. *Alcibiades and Athens: a study in literary presentation*. Oxford 1999.

Rhodes, P.J. *Alcibiades. Athenian Playboy, General and Traitor*. Barnsley 2011.

Stuttard, D. *Nemesis: Alcibiades and the fall of Athens*. Cambridge, MA 2018.

Vickers, M. J. *Aristophanes and Alcibiades: echoes of contemporary history in Athenian comedy*. Berlin 2015.

Wohl, V. 'The Eros of Alcibiades', *CA* 18.2. (1999), 349–385.

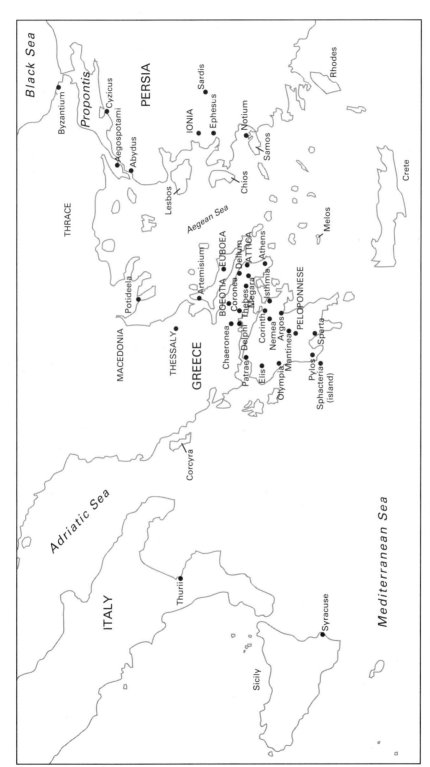

FIGURE 3 *Greece and Magna Graecia in the fifth century* BCE.

Text

10

[1] πρώτην δ᾽ αὐτῷ πάροδον εἰς τὸ δημόσιον γενέσθαι λέγουσι μετὰ χρημάτων ἐπιδόσεως, οὐκ ἐκ παρασκευῆς, ἀλλὰ παριόντα θορυβούντων Ἀθηναίων ἐρέσθαι τὴν αἰτίαν τοῦ θορύβου, πυθόμενον δὲ χρημάτων ἐπίδοσιν γίνεσθαι παρελθεῖν καὶ ἐπιδοῦναι· τοῦ δὲ δήμου κροτοῦντος καὶ βοῶντος ὑφ᾽ ἡδονῆς, ἐπιλαθέσθαι τοῦ ὄρτυγος ὃν ἐτύγχανεν ἔχων ἐν τῷ ἱματίῳ· πτοηθέντος οὖν καὶ διαφυγόντος ἔτι μᾶλλον ἐκβοῆσαι τοὺς Ἀθηναίους, πολλοὺς δὲ συνθηρᾶν ἀναστάντας, λαβεῖν δ᾽ αὐτὸν Ἀντίοχον τὸν κυβερνήτην καὶ ἀποδοῦναι· διὸ προσφιλέστατον τῷ Ἀλκιβιάδῃ γενέσθαι.

[2] μεγάλας δ᾽ αὐτῷ κλεισιάδας ἐπὶ τὴν πολιτείαν ἀνοίγοντος τοῦ τε γένους καὶ τοῦ πλούτου τῆς τε περὶ τὰς μάχας ἀνδραγαθίας, φίλων τε πολλῶν καὶ οἰκείων ὑπαρχόντων, ἀπ᾽ οὐδενὸς ἠξίου μᾶλλον ἢ τῆς τοῦ λόγου χάριτος ἰσχύειν ἐν τοῖς πολλοῖς. καὶ ὅτι μὲν δυνατὸς ἦν εἰπεῖν, οἵ τε κωμικοὶ μαρτυροῦσι καὶ τῶν ῥητόρων ὁ δυνατώτατος ἐν τῷ κατὰ Μειδίου, λέγων τὸν Ἀλκιβιάδην καὶ δεινότατον εἰπεῖν γενέσθαι πρὸς τοῖς ἄλλοις.

[3] εἰ δὲ Θεοφράστῳ πιστεύομεν, ἀνδρὶ φιληκόῳ καὶ ἱστορικῷ παρ᾽ ὁντινοῦν τῶν φιλοσόφων, εὑρεῖν μὲν ἦν τὰ δέοντα καὶ νοῆσαι πάντων ἱκανώτατος ὁ Ἀλκιβιάδης, ζητῶν δὲ μὴ μόνον ἃ δεῖ λέγειν, ἀλλὰ καὶ ὡς δεῖ τοῖς ὀνόμασι καὶ τοῖς ῥήμασιν, οὐκ εὐπορῶν δέ, πολλάκις ἐσφάλλετο καὶ μεταξὺ λέγων ἀπεσιώπα καὶ διέλειπε, λέξεως διαφυγούσης αὐτόν, ἀναλαμβάνων καὶ διασκοπούμενος.

11

[1] αἱ δ᾽ ἱπποτροφίαι περιβόητοι μὲν ἐγένοντο καὶ τῷ πλήθει τῶν ἁρμάτων· ἑπτὰ γὰρ ἄλλος οὐδεὶς καθῆκεν Ὀλυμπίασιν ἰδιώτης οὐδὲ βασιλεύς, μόνος δὲ ἐκεῖνος. καὶ τὸ νικῆσαι δὲ καὶ δεύτερον γενέσθαι καὶ τέταρτον, ὡς Θουκυδίδης φησίν, ὁ δ᾽ Εὐριπίδης τρίτον, ὑπερβάλλει λαμπρότητι καὶ δόξῃ πᾶσαν τὴν ἐν τούτοις φιλοτιμίαν.

λέγει δ᾽ ὁ Εὐριπίδης ἐν τῷ ᾄσματι ταῦτα: [2]

σὲ δ᾽ ἀείσομαι, ὦ Κλεινίου παῖ.
καλὸν ἁ νίκα: κάλλιστον δ᾽, ὃ μηδεὶς ἄλλος Ἑλλάνων,
ἅρματι πρῶτα δραμεῖν καὶ δεύτερα καὶ τρίτα,
βῆναί τ᾽ ἀπονητί, Διὸς στεφθέντα τ᾽ ἐλαίᾳ
κάρυκι βοᾶν παραδοῦναι:

12

τοῦτο μέντοι τὸ λαμπρὸν ἐπιφανέστερον ἐποίησεν ἡ τῶν πόλεων φιλοτιμία. [1]
σκηνὴν μὲν γὰρ αὐτῷ κεκοσμημένην διαπρεπῶς ἔστησαν Ἐφέσιοι, τροφὰς δὲ
ἵπποις καὶ πλῆθος ἱερείων παρεῖχεν ἡ Χίων πόλις, οἶνον δὲ Λέσβιοι καὶ τὴν
ἄλλην ὑποδοχὴν ἀφειδῶς ἑστιῶντι πολλούς. οὐ μὴν ἀλλὰ καὶ διαβολή τις ἢ
κακοήθεια γενομένη περὶ τὴν φιλοτιμίαν ἐκείνην πλείονα λόγον παρέσχε.

λέγεται γὰρ ὡς ἦν Ἀθήνησι Διομήδης, ἀνὴρ οὐ πονηρός, Ἀλκιβιάδου φίλος, [2]
ἐπιθυμῶν δὲ νίκην Ὀλυμπικὴν αὐτῷ γενέσθαι: καὶ πυνθανόμενος ἅρμα
δημόσιον Ἀργείοις εἶναι, τὸν Ἀλκιβιάδην εἰδὼς ἐν Ἄργει μέγα δυνάμενον καὶ
φίλους ἔχοντα πολλούς, ἔπεισεν αὐτῷ πρίασθαι τὸ ἅρμα.

πριάμενος δὲ ὁ Ἀλκιβιάδης ἴδιον ἀπεγράψατο, τὸν δὲ Διομήδη χαίρειν [3]
εἴασε χαλεπῶς φέροντα καὶ μαρτυρόμενον θεοὺς καὶ ἀνθρώπους. φαίνεται δὲ
καὶ δίκη συστᾶσα περὶ τούτου, καὶ λόγος Ἰσοκράτει γέγραπται περὶ τοῦ

ζεύγους ὑπὲρ τοῦ Ἀλκιβιάδου παιδός, ἐν ᾧ Τισίας ἐστίν, οὐ Διομήδης, ὁ
δικασάμενος.

13

ἐπεὶ δ᾽ ἀφῆκεν αὐτὸν εἰς τὴν πολιτείαν ἔτι μειράκιον ὤν, τοὺς μὲν ἄλλους [1]
εὐθὺς ἐταπείνωσε δημαγωγούς, ἀγῶνα δ᾽ εἶχε πρός τε Φαίακα τὸν
Ἐρασιστράτου καὶ Νικίαν τὸν Νικηράτου, τὸν μὲν ἤδη καθ᾽ ἡλικίαν προήκοντα
καὶ στρατηγὸν ἄριστον εἶναι δοκοῦντα, Φαίακα δ᾽ ἀρχόμενον, ὥσπερ αὐτός,
αὐξάνεσθαι τότε καὶ γνωρίμων ὄντα πατέρων, ἐλαττούμενον δὲ τοῖς τε ἄλλοις
καὶ περὶ τὸν λόγον.

ἐντευκτικὸς γὰρ ἰδίᾳ καὶ πιθανὸς ἐδόκει μᾶλλον ἢ φέρειν ἀγῶνας ἐν δήμῳ [2]
δυνατός. ἦν γάρ, ὡς Εὔπολίς φησι,

λαλεῖν ἄριστος, ἀδυνατώτατος λέγειν.

φέρεται δὲ καὶ λόγος τις κατ᾽ Ἀλκιβιάδου ὑπὸ Φαίακος γεγραμμένος, ἐν ᾧ
μετὰ τῶν ἄλλων γέγραπται καὶ ὅτι τῆς πόλεως πολλὰ πομπεῖα χρυσᾶ καὶ

ἀργυρᾶ κεκτημένης Ἀλκιβιάδης ἐχρῆτο πᾶσιν αὐτοῖς ὥσπερ ἰδίοις πρὸς τὴν καθ᾽ ἡμέραν δίαιταν.

[3] ἦν δέ τις Ὑπέρβολος Περιθοίδης, οὗ μέμνηται μὲν ὡς ἀνθρώπου πονηροῦ καὶ Θουκυδίδης, τοῖς δὲ κωμικοῖς ὁμοῦ τι πᾶσι διατριβὴν ἀεὶ σκωπτόμενος ἐν τοῖς θεάτροις παρεῖχεν. ἄτρεπτος δὲ πρὸς τὸ κακῶς ἀκούειν καὶ ἀπαθὴς ὢν ὀλιγωρίᾳ δόξης, ἣν ἀναισχυντίαν καὶ ἀπόνοιαν οὖσαν εὐτολμίαν ἔνιοι καὶ ἀνδρείαν καλοῦσιν, οὐδενὶ μὲν ἤρεσκεν, ἐχρῆτο δ᾽ αὐτῷ πολλάκις ὁ δῆμος ἐπιθυμῶν προπηλακίζειν τοὺς ἐν ἀξιώματι καὶ συκοφαντεῖν.

[4] ἀναπεισθεὶς οὖν ὑπ᾽ αὐτοῦ τότε τὸ ὄστρακον ἐπιφέρειν ἔμελλεν, ᾧ κολούοντες ἀεὶ τὸν προὔχοντα δόξῃ καὶ δυνάμει τῶν πολιτῶν ἐλαύνουσι, παραμυθούμενοι τὸν φθόνον μᾶλλον ἢ τὸν φόβον. ἐπεὶ δὲ δῆλον ἦν ὅτι ἑνὶ τῶν τριῶν τὸ ὄστρακον ἐποίσουσι, συνήγαγε τὰς στάσεις εἰς ταὐτὸν ὁ Ἀλκιβιάδης, καὶ διαλεχθεὶς πρὸς τὸν Νικίαν κατὰ τοῦ Ὑπερβόλου τὴν ὀστρακοφορίαν ἔτρεψεν.

ὡς δ᾽ ἔνιοί φασιν, οὐ πρὸς Νικίαν, ἀλλὰ πρὸς Φαίακα διαλεχθεὶς καὶ τὴν ἐκείνου προσλαβὼν ἑταιρίαν ἐξήλασε τὸν Ὑπέρβολον οὐδ᾽ ἂν προσδοκήσαντα.

[5] φαῦλος γὰρ οὐδεὶς ἐνέπιπτεν εἰς τοῦτον τὸν κολασμὸν οὐδ᾽ ἄδοξος, ὥς που καὶ Πλάτων ὁ κωμικὸς εἴρηκε τοῦ Ὑπερβόλου μνησθείς,

καίτοι πέπραχε τῶν προτέρων μὲν ἄξια,
αὑτοῦ δὲ καὶ τῶν στιγμάτων ἀνάξια.
οὐ γὰρ τοιούτων εἵνεκ᾽ ὄστραχ᾽ εὑρέθη.

περὶ μὲν οὖν τούτων ἐν ἑτέροις μᾶλλον εἴρηται τὰ ἱστορούμενα.

14

[1] τὸν δ᾽ Ἀλκιβιάδην ὁ Νικίας οὐχ ἧττον ἠνία θαυμαζόμενος ὑπὸ τῶν πολεμίων ἢ τιμώμενος ὑπὸ τῶν πολιτῶν. πρόξενος μὲν γὰρ ἦν ὁ Ἀλκιβιάδης τῶν Λακεδαιμονίων, καὶ τοὺς ἁλόντας αὐτῶν περὶ Πύλον ἄνδρας ἐθεράπευσεν·

[2] ἐπεὶ δ᾽ ἐκεῖνοί τε διὰ Νικίου μάλιστα τῆς εἰρήνης τυχόντες καὶ τοὺς ἄνδρας ἀπολαβόντες ὑπερηγάπων αὐτόν, ἔν τε τοῖς Ἕλλησι λόγος ἦν ὡς Περικλέους μὲν συνάψαντος αὐτοῖς, Νικίου δὲ λύσαντος τὸν πόλεμον, οἵ τε πλεῖστοι τὴν εἰρήνην Νικίειον ὠνόμαζον, οὐ μετρίως ἀνιώμενος ὁ Ἀλκιβιάδης καὶ φθονῶν ἐβούλευε σύγχυσιν ὁρκίων.

[3] καὶ πρῶτον μὲν Ἀργείους αἰσθανόμενος μίσει καὶ φόβῳ τῶν Σπαρτιατῶν ζητοῦντας ἀποστροφήν, ἐλπίδας αὐτοῖς ἐνεδίδου κρύφα τῆς Ἀθηναίων

συμμαχίας, καὶ παρεθάρρυνε πέμπων καὶ διαλεγόμενος τοῖς προεστῶσι τοῦ δήμου μὴ δεδιέναι μηδ᾽ ὑπείκειν Λακεδαιμονίοις, ἀλλὰ πρὸς Ἀθηναίους τρέπεσθαι καὶ περιμένειν ὅσον οὐδέπω μεταμελομένους καὶ τὴν εἰρήνην ἀφιέντας.

ἐπεὶ δὲ Λακεδαιμόνιοι πρός τε τοὺς Βοιωτοὺς ἐποιήσαντο συμμαχίαν καὶ [4] Πάνακτον οὐχ ἑστός, ὥσπερ ἔδει, τοῖς Ἀθηναίοις παρέδωκαν, ἀλλὰ καταλύσαντες, ὀργιζομένους λαβὼν τοὺς Ἀθηναίους ἔτι μᾶλλον ἐξετράχυνε, καὶ τὸν Νικίαν ἐθορύβει καὶ διέβαλλεν εἰκότα κατηγορῶν,

ὅτι τοὺς ἐν Σφακτηρίᾳ τῶν πολεμίων ἀποληφθέντας αὐτὸς μὲν ἐξελεῖν οὐκ [5] ἠθέλησεν στρατηγῶν, ἑτέρων δ᾽ ἐξελόντων ἀφῆκε καὶ ἀπέδωκε χαριζόμενος Λακεδαιμονίοις· εἶτ᾽ ἐκείνους μὲν οὐκ ἔπεισε φίλος ὢν Βοιωτοῖς μὴ συνόμνυσθαι μηδὲ Κορινθίοις, Ἀθηναίοις δὲ κωλύει τὸν βουλόμενον τῶν Ἑλλήνων φίλον εἶναι καὶ σύμμαχον, εἰ μὴ δόξειε Λακεδαιμονίοις.

ἐκ δὲ τούτου κακῶς φερομένῳ τῷ Νικίᾳ παρῆσαν ὥσπερ κατὰ τύχην [6] πρέσβεις ἀπὸ τῆς Λακεδαίμονος, αὐτόθεν τε λόγους ἐπιεικεῖς ἔχοντες καὶ πρὸς πᾶν τὸ συμβιβαστικὸν καὶ δίκαιον αὐτοκράτορες ἥκειν φάσκοντες. ἀποδεξαμένης δὲ τῆς βουλῆς, τοῦ δὲ δήμου τῇ ὑστεραίᾳ μέλλοντος ἐκκλησιάζειν, δείσας ὁ Ἀλκιβιάδης διεπράξατο τοὺς πρέσβεις ἐν λόγοις γενέσθαι πρὸς αὐτόν.

ὡς δὲ συνῆλθον ἔλεγε· ῾τί πεπόνθατε, ἄνδρες Σπαρτιᾶται; πῶς ἔλαθεν ὑμᾶς [7] ὅτι τὰ τῆς βουλῆς ἀεὶ μέτρια καὶ φιλάνθρωπα πρὸς τοὺς ἐντυγχάνοντάς ἐστιν, ὁ δὲ δῆμος μέγα φρονεῖ καὶ μεγάλων ὀρέγεται; κἂν φάσκητε κύριοι πάντων ἀφῖχθαι, προστάττων καὶ βιαζόμενος ἀγνωμονήσει. φέρε δή, τὴν εὐήθειαν ταύτην ἀφέντες, εἰ βούλεσθε χρήσασθαι μετρίοις Ἀθηναίοις καὶ μηδὲν ἐκβιασθῆναι παρὰ γνώμην, οὕτω διαλέγεσθε περὶ τῶν δικαίων ὡς οὐκ ὄντες αὐτοκράτορες. συμπράξομεν δ᾽ ἡμεῖς Λακεδαιμονίοις χαριζόμενοι.᾽

ταῦτα δ᾽ εἰπὼν ὅρκους ἔδωκεν αὐτοῖς καὶ μετέστησεν ἀπὸ τοῦ Νικίου, [8] παντάπασι πιστεύοντας αὐτῷ καὶ θαυμάζοντας ἅμα τὴν δεινότητα καὶ σύνεσιν, ὡς οὐ τοῦ τυχόντος ἀνδρὸς οὖσαν.

τῇ δ᾽ ὑστεραίᾳ συνήχθη μὲν ὁ δῆμος, εἰσῆλθον δ᾽ οἱ πρέσβεις. ἐρωτώμενοι δ᾽ ὑπὸ τοῦ Ἀλκιβιάδου πάνυ φιλανθρώπως ἐφ᾽ οἷς ἀφιγμένοι τυγχάνουσιν, οὐκ ἔφασαν ἥκειν αὐτοκράτορες.

εὐθὺς οὖν ὁ Ἀλκιβιάδης ἐνέκειτο μετὰ κραυγῆς καὶ ὀργῆς, ὥσπερ οὐκ ἀδικῶν, [9] ἀλλ᾽ ἀδικούμενος, ἀπίστους καὶ παλιμβόλους ἀποκαλῶν καὶ μηδὲν ὑγιὲς μήτε πρᾶξαι μήτ᾽ εἰπεῖν ἥκοντας, ἐπηγανάκτει δ᾽ ἡ βουλή, καὶ ὁ δῆμος ἐχαλέπαινε, τὸν δὲ Νικίαν ἔκπληξις εἶχε καὶ κατήφεια τῶν ἀνδρῶν τῆς μεταβολῆς, ἀγνοοῦντα τὴν ἀπάτην καὶ τὸν δόλον.

15

[1] οὕτω δὲ τῶν Λακεδαιμονίων ἐκπεσόντων, στρατηγὸς ἀποδειχθεὶς ὁ Ἀλκιβιάδης εὐθὺς Ἀργείους καὶ Μαντινεῖς καὶ Ἠλείους συμμάχους ἐποίησε τοῖς Ἀθηναίοις. καὶ τὸν μὲν τρόπον οὐδεὶς τῆς πράξεως ἐπήνει, μέγα δ᾽ ἦν τὸ πεπραγμένον ὑπ᾽ αὐτοῦ, διαστῆσαι καὶ κραδᾶναι Πελοπόννησον ὀλίγου δεῖν ἅπασαν, καὶ τοσαύτας ἀσπίδας ἐν ἡμέρᾳ μιᾷ περὶ Μαντίνειαν ἀντιτάξαι Λακεδαιμονίοις, καὶ πορρωτάτω τῶν Ἀθηνῶν ἀγῶνα κατασκευάσαι καὶ κίνδυνον αὐτοῖς, ἐν ᾧ μέγα μὲν οὐδὲν ἡ νίκη προσέθηκε κρατήσασιν, εἰ δ᾽ ἐσφάλησαν, ἔργον ἦν τὴν Λακεδαίμονα περιγενέσθαι.

[2] μετὰ δὲ τὴν μάχην εὐθὺς ἐπέθεντο καταλύειν ἐν Ἄργει τὸν δῆμον οἱ χίλιοι καὶ τὴν πόλιν ὑπήκοον ποιεῖν· Λακεδαιμόνιοι δὲ παραγενόμενοι κατέλυσαν τὴν δημοκρατίαν. αὖθις δὲ τῶν πολλῶν ἐξενεγκαμένων τὰ ὅπλα καὶ κρατησάντων, ἐπελθὼν ὁ Ἀλκιβιάδης τήν τε νίκην ἐβεβαίωσε τῷ δήμῳ, καὶ τὰ μακρὰ τείχη συνέπεισε καθεῖναι καὶ προσμίξαντας τῇ θαλάσσῃ τὴν πόλιν ἐξάψαι παντάπασι τῆς Ἀθηναίων δυνάμεως.

[3] καὶ τέκτονας καὶ λιθουργοὺς ἐκ τῶν Ἀθηνῶν ἐκόμισε καὶ πᾶσαν ἐνεδείκνυτο προθυμίαν, οὐχ ἧττον ἑαυτῷ κτώμενος ἢ τῇ πόλει χάριν καὶ ἰσχύν. ἔπεισε δὲ καὶ Πατρεῖς ὁμοίως τείχεσι μακροῖς συνάψαι τῇ θαλάσσῃ τὴν πόλιν. εἰπόντος δέ τινος τοῖς Πατρεῦσιν ὅτι ‘καταπιοῦνται ὑμᾶς Ἀθηναῖοι·’ ‘ἴσως,’ εἶπεν ὁ Ἀλκιβιάδης, ‘κατὰ μικρὸν καὶ κατὰ τοὺς πόδας, Λακεδαιμόνιοι δὲ κατὰ τὴν κεφαλὴν καὶ ἀθρόως.’

[4] οὐ μὴν ἀλλὰ καὶ τῆς γῆς συνεβούλευεν ἀντέχεσθαι τοῖς Ἀθηναίοις, καὶ τὸν ἐν Ἀγραύλου προβαλλόμενον ἀεὶ τοῖς ἐφήβοις ὅρκον ἔργῳ βεβαιοῦν. ὀμνύουσι γὰρ ὅροις χρήσασθαι τῆς Ἀττικῆς πυροῖς, κριθαῖς, ἀμπέλοις, ἐλαίαις, οἰκείαν ποιεῖσθαι διδασκόμενοι τὴν ἥμερον καὶ καρποφόρον.

16

[1] ἐν δὲ τοιούτοις πολιτεύμασι καὶ λόγοις καὶ φρονήματι καὶ δεινότητι πολλὴν αὖ πάλιν τὴν τρυφὴν τῆς διαίτης καὶ περὶ πότους καὶ ἔρωτας ὑβρίσματα, καὶ θηλύτητας ἐσθήτων ἁλουργῶν ἑλκομένων δι᾽ ἀγορᾶς, καὶ πολυτέλειαν ὑπερήφανον, ἐκτομάς τε καταστρωμάτων ἐν ταῖς τριήρεσιν, ὅπως μαλακώτερον ἐγκαθεύδοι, κειρίαις, ἀλλὰ μὴ σανίσι, τῶν στρωμάτων ἐπιβαλλομένων, ἀσπίδος τε διαχρύσου ποίησιν οὐδὲν ἐπίσημον τῶν πατρίων ἔχουσαν, ἀλλ᾽ Ἔρωτα κεραυνοφόρον.

ἅπερ ὁρῶντες οἱ μὲν ἔνδοξοι μετὰ τοῦ βδελύττεσθαι καὶ δυσχεραίνειν [2]
ἐφοβοῦντο τὴν ὀλιγωρίαν αὐτοῦ καὶ παρανομίαν, ὡς τυραννικὰ καὶ ἀλλόκοτα,
τοῦ δὲ δήμου τὸ πάθος τὸ πρὸς αὐτὸν οὐ κακῶς ἐξηγούμενος ὁ Ἀριστοφάνης
ταῦτ᾿ εἴρηκε·

ποθεῖ μέν, ἐχθαίρει δέ, βούλεται δ᾿ ἔχειν,

ἔτι δὲ μᾶλλον τῇ ὑπονοίᾳ πιέζων·

μάλιστα μὲν λέοντα μὴ ᾿ν πόλει τρέφειν·
ἢν δ᾿ ἐκτρέφῃ τις, τοῖς τρόποις ὑπηρετεῖν.

ἐπιδόσεις γὰρ καὶ χορηγίαι καὶ φιλοτιμήματα πρὸς τὴν πόλιν ὑπερβολὴν μὴ [3]
ἀπολείποντα καὶ δόξα προγόνων καὶ λόγου δύναμις καὶ σώματος εὐπρέπεια
καὶ ῥώμη μετ᾿ ἐμπειρίας τῶν πολεμικῶν καὶ ἀλκῆς πάντα τἆλλα συγχωρεῖν
ἐποίει καὶ φέρειν μετρίως τοὺς Ἀθηναίους, ἀεὶ τὰ πρᾳότατα τῶν ὀνομάτων
τοῖς ἁμαρτήμασι τιθεμένους, παιδιὰς καὶ φιλοτιμίας.

οἷον ἦν καὶ τὸ Ἀγάθαρχον εἶρξαι τὸν ζωγράφον, εἶτα γράψαντα τὴν οἰκίαν [4]
ἀφεῖναι δωρησάμενον· καὶ Ταυρέαν ἀντιχορηγοῦντα ῥαπίσαι φιλοτιμούμενον
ὑπὲρ τῆς νίκης· καὶ τὸ Μηλίαν γυναῖκα ἐκ τῶν αἰχμαλώτων ἐξελόμενον καὶ
συνόντα θρέψαι παιδάριον ἐξ αὐτῆς.

καὶ γὰρ τοῦτο φιλάνθρωπον ἐκάλουν· πλὴν ὅτι τοὺς Μηλίους ἡβηδὸν [5]
ἀποσφαγῆναι τὴν πλείστην αἰτίαν ἔσχε, τῷ ψηφίσματι συνειπών.

Ἀριστοφῶντος δὲ Νεμέαν γράψαντος ἐν ταῖς ἀγκάλαις αὐτῆς καθήμενον
Ἀλκιβιάδην ἔχουσαν, ἐθεῶντο καὶ συνέτρεχον χαίροντες. οἱ δὲ πρεσβύτεροι
καὶ τούτοις ἐδυσχέραινον ὡς τυραννικοῖς καὶ παρανόμοις. ἐδόκει δὲ καὶ
Ἀρχέστρατος οὐκ ἀπὸ τρόπου λέγειν ὡς ἡ Ἑλλὰς οὐκ ἂν ἤνεγκε δύο Ἀλκιβιάδας.

Commentary Notes

Section 10

10.1

πρώτην δ’ αὐτῷ πάροδον . . . γενέσθαι λέγουσι: the whole section is in indirect statement after λέγουσι – 'men say'. Note that Plutarch reports this anecdote in rather vague terms, with no named sources, and it is unclear how much weight we are supposed to give it: this is perhaps typical of the ambiguous nature of Alcibiades’ portrait throughout the work. πάροδον was the word used to describe the first entry of the chorus in a Greek tragedy – a suitable term for Alcibiades’ theatrical arrival on the political scene of Athens.

μετὰ χρημάτων ἐπιδόσεως: this first entry of Alcibiades into public life is fitting since this act of giving money to the state is precisely one of the qualities listed by Plutarch which caused the Athenians to tolerate his behaviour (see 16.3). The term ἐπίδοσις refers to donations which residents of Athens were requested to make to help fund-raising initiatives for specific causes, such as financing a campaign; they were subscriptions, in a sense, as making them was the civic duty of a resident Athenian, home-born or foreign. ἐπιδόσεως here is followed within this section by ἐπίδοσιν and the verb ἐπιδοῦναι, highlighting the importance of this aspect of Alcibiades’ life from the very beginning of his political career.

οὐκ ἐκ παρασκευῆς: Plutarch presents Alcibiades as an opportunist who cannot help both being curious when hearing the Athenian Assembly applauding and wanting some of that approval to be shown to himself. It is hard to imagine that Alcibiades, who had had Pericles as one of his guardians (noted by Plutarch at 1.1) and enjoyed many advantages which helped him politically (see 10.2), happened to stumble upon this situation by accident; it has been speculated that this anecdote is drawn from material from a comic poet (Russell (1972) 120) and the use of λέγουσι suggests unreliability.

παριόντα: present participle of πάρειμι, παριέναι – 'pass by'. It refers now to Alcibiades, the unexpressed subject of this and the following two indirect statements – supply αὐτόν for sense.

θορυβούντων Ἀθηναίων: from the context this clearly refers to an Athenian assembly, where contributions were being made to the state, situating this anecdote on the Pnyx, the hill in Athens where assemblies took place. The carved stone steps of its speaker’s platform are still intact today.

παρελθεῖν καὶ ἐπιδοῦναι: Alcibiades' reaction to hearing that the Athenian applause was in response to an ἐπίδοσιν was to make one himself; the verb παρελθεῖν usually refers to those coming forward to the *bema*, or speaker's platform, to address the citizens.

τοῦ δὲ δήμου κροτοῦντος καὶ βοῶντος ὑφ' ἡδονῆς: at 6.2–6.3 Plutarch has stated that Alcibiades was easily seduced by pleasures and also had a love of fame (φιλοδοξία), so here Plutarch notes the reaction of the Athenian people to Alcibiades' contribution with a couplet of verbs to emphasize how positively they felt, which was just what Alcibiades was aiming for. The frequent use of forms of the word ἡδονή, 'pleasure', throughout the *Life* reminds us of one of Alcibiades' vices.

τοῦ ὄρτυγος: 'the quail'. Birds such as quails, geese and cocks, as well as hares, hunting dogs, horses and even small panthers and leopards were standard gifts exchanged between men in a sexual relationship, as a passage from Aristophanes' *Birds* and various Attic vase paintings attest. The older male lover (the ἐραστής, or 'lover') would hunt an animal which he would present to his younger lover (the ἐρώμενος, or 'beloved'), as a symbol of his manliness and ability to fight for him. This anecdote therefore suggests that Alcibiades, whose beauty was well-known (1.3) and who had many lovers, including Socrates (6.1), was returning from a meeting with one such older male companion.

πτοηθέντος οὖν καὶ διαφυγόντος: since the whole passage is in indirect speech, Plutarch uses genitive absolutes throughout to give background information, often in couplets, as here.

πολλοὺς δὲ συνθηρᾶν ἀναστάντας: 'many stood up to join in the hunt'. He can be seen here to become one of the people, taken in by them immediately, and his entrance to public life is complete. The theatrical nature of this episode is clear, while the hunt for the quail perhaps reflects the hunt element of it being caught by a male lover in the first place – is Alcibiades taking on the role of the older lover in a relationship with Athens, with the Athenians' readiness to join him in this hunt showing their complicity in such a relationship?

λαβεῖν δ' αὐτὸν Ἀντίοχον τὸν κυβερνήτην καὶ ἀποδοῦναι: διὸ προσφιλέστατον τῷ Ἀλκιβιάδῃ γενέσθαι: the helmsman, here winning his friendship by capturing the quail, will be responsible for Alcibiades' downfall when he fails to follow instructions and is defeated by the Spartan general Lysander at the Battle of Notium in 406 BCE. In the latter years of the Peloponnesian War between Athens and Sparta, the Athenians had enjoyed some successful naval encounters off the western coast of Asia Minor. Leaving the majority of the fleet with Antiochus, Alcibiades was north, busy adding some nearby cities to the Athenian empire. His one instruction was for Antiochus to avoid engaging the Spartan fleet and await his return. Antiochus, however, sailed too close to the Spartans and was killed in the ensuing conflict, while as much as a quarter of the entire Athenian fleet was destroyed. Blamed for this disaster, Alcibiades was to be stripped of command, though he fled to Thrace in anticipation of the news.

10.2

Μεγάλας ... κλεισιάδας ἐπὶ τὴν πολιτείαν: Plutarch uses the metaphor of opening doors to opportunity as we still do today; the reference to τὴν πολιτείαν ('public service') picks up the theme of political life and Alcibiades' involvement in it introduced by τὸ δημόσιον and ἐπιδόσεως in the previous section.

ἀνοίγοντος τοῦ τε γένους καὶ τοῦ πλούτου τῆς τε περὶ τὰς μάχας ἀνδραγαθίας: genitive absolute with concessive ('although') force. A tricolon of the attributes which enabled Alcibiades to succeed in politics: his birth, his wealth and bravery in battles.

φίλων τε πολλῶν καὶ οἰκείων ὑπαρχόντων: immediately after the previous clause in genitive absolute, a further couplet in the same grammatical construction adds detail to the main clause; both genitive absolutes serve to contrast with the main sentence, which expresses Alcibiades' viewpoint.

ἠξίου ... ἰσχύειν ἐν τοῖς πολλοῖς: οἱ πολλοί is used, as often, to mean 'the many', 'the common people', as opposed to the rich elites. The verb ἰσχύειν contains the idea of defeating an opponent, of prevailing over them, but can be used more generally to mean 'have strength' or 'have influence', as here.

ἀπ᾽ οὐδενὸς ... μᾶλλον ἢ τῆς τοῦ λόγου χάριτος: χάρις here refers to the eloquence and elegance of his speech, the outward beauty of it.

δυνατὸς ἦν εἰπεῖν: Alcibiades' ability (literally 'power') in speaking is here first referred to in general terms, picked up again by δεινότατον εἰπεῖν below.

οἵ τε κωμικοὶ: refers to Greek comic poets, two of whom – Plato (not the philosopher) and Aristophanes (the only surviving example of Greek Old Comedy from fifth-century BCE Athens when Alcibiades was active) – are quoted by Plutarch in our prescribed sections.

καὶ τῶν ῥητόρων ὁ δυνατώτατος ἐν τῷ κατὰ Μειδίου: the superlative refers to Demosthenes, an Athenian politician and orator who lived through the fourth century BCE. He was a patriot who warned Athens against the increasing threat from Macedon, which was ruled by King Philip II, the father of Alexander the Great. In his speech *Against Meidias* (Speech 21.145), he says of Alcibiades that καὶ στρατηγὸς ἄριστος, καὶ λέγειν ἐδόκει πάντων, ὥς φασιν, εἶναι δεινότατος ('as people say, he was thought to be an excellent general and the most skilful of all in speaking'). Plutarch quotes the superlative δεινότατος below.

10.3

εἰ δὲ Θεοφράστῳ πιστεύομεν: the δὲ picks up the μὲν from the previous statement, contrasting the general ability of Alcibiades in speaking with the more precise ability which Theophrastus attributes to him, referred to here. Theophrastus was the successor of the philosopher Aristotle, living through much of the fourth century BCE and into the third century BCE. He was interested in all knowledge but in natural history in particular, writing nearly three hundred works with topics including botany, metaphysics, weather phenomena and general history.

ἀνδρὶ φιληκόῳ καὶ ἱστορικῷ παρ᾽ ὀντινοῦν τῶν φιλοσόφων: this description of Theophrastus is an alternative to using a superlative – literally 'a man who loved discourse and was precise compared with any philosopher'; παρά + accusative can have the meaning, as here, of 'in comparison with' but implying the subject's superiority. Like Demosthenes, Theophrastus is referred to in very flattering terms, since Plutarch wishes to emphasize the credibility of his sources.

εὑρεῖν μὲν ἦν τὰ δέοντα καὶ νοῆσαι πάντων ἱκανώτατος ὁ Ἀλκιβιάδης: 'while Alcibiades was the most capable of all at finding and understanding what was required in a situation'. The μέν will shortly be picked up by evidence of flaws in Alcibiades' delivery of speeches. Theophrastus' view of Alcibiades is not that he was generally an able speaker, but rather that he was perceptive and knew what to say in any given circumstances, highlighted by the superlative ἱκανώτατος. Note the couplet of εὑρεῖν . . . καὶ νοῆσαι to reinforce this.

ζητῶν δὲ μὴ μόνον ἃ δεῖ λέγειν, ἀλλὰ καὶ ὡς δεῖ τοῖς ὀνόμασι καὶ τοῖς ῥήμασιν, οὐκ εὐπορῶν δέ: unlike most writers' opinion of Alcibiades – that he was a very good speaker – Plutarch states that Theophrastus flagged this as his problem. The participle εὐπορῶν suggests a lack of resources, here suggesting a lack of vocabulary or the lack of a natural gift to extemporize. Note the balanced structure of this description, with the use of δέ twice, between which come μὴ μόνον and ἀλλὰ καί, the repetition of δεῖ and the couplet of τοῖς ὀνόμασι καὶ τοῖς ῥήμασιν, perhaps reflecting the charm of speech which Alcibiades strove for.

ἐσφάλλετο: in the passive the verb means 'be tripped up' or can refer to a drunkard, 'to stagger'. Here the meaning is 'he stumbled over his words'.

ἀπεσιώπα καὶ διέλειπε: couplet of main verbs. διαλείπω means 'I leave an interval'.

λέξεως διαφυγούσης αὐτόν: a genitive absolute, explaining his sudden silence. Note the same use of 'escape' or 'elude' as we use still today, e.g. 'the phrase escapes me'.

ἀναλαμβάνων καὶ διασκοπούμενος: another couplet, this time of participles. The translation of διασκοπούμενος is often given as 'proceeding with caution' but the compound δια- can mean 'in different directions' while the basic meaning of σκοπέω in the middle voice is 'look into, examine'; hence here 'expressing it in a different way'.

Section 11

11.1

αἱ δ' ἱπποτροφίαι περιβόητοι μὲν ἐγένοντο: 'while his horse-breeding was famous'. περιβόητος literally means 'shouted about'. The breeding of horses was a preserve of the rich.

καὶ τῷ πλήθει τῶν ἁρμάτων: the use of καί here defines why his horse-breeding was famous – 'especially for'.

ἑπτὰ γὰρ ἄλλος οὐδεὶς καθῆκεν Ὀλυμπίασιν ἰδιώτης οὐδὲ βασιλεύς, μόνος δὲ ἐκεῖνος: the unprecedented number of chariots Alcibiades entered (καθῆκεν) in the Olympic Games of 416 BCE – seven – is put first in the sentence to highlight the scale on which he operated. The contrast is brought out by referring to him μόνος after ἄλλος οὐδείς ('no-one else') and the couplet ἰδιώτης οὐδὲ βασιλεύς ('private citizen nor even king'). The Olympic Games, the forerunners to our own modern version started in 1896, were held every four years from 776 BCE, and the Greeks used them as a dating tool, referring to the four-year periods between Games as 'Olympiads'. Events included running, wrestling and chariot-racing among others and the festival was held at the sanctuary of Zeus in Olympia. The winners, who in the chariot-racing would be the owners of the horses rather than the actual drivers, were often celebrated in victory odes, an example of which Plutarch quotes below.

καὶ τὸ νικῆσαι δὲ καὶ δεύτερον γενέσθαι καὶ τέταρτον: the δὲ picks up the μὲν from the start of the section: while his horse-breeding was famous, it was his victories at the Olympic Games which really showed off him and his wealth. The polysyndeton referring to where three of his chariots finished, 'first and second and fourth', reflects his achievement. **τὸ νικῆσαι**: the articular infinitive in Greek is a verbal noun (the gerund in Latin) and so here means 'his winning'. Note that Euripides, in the victory ode quoted below, states that Alcibiades' chariots finished first, second and third, a discrepancy not easily explained.

ὑπερβάλλει λαμπρότητι καὶ δόξῃ πᾶσαν τὴν ἐν τούτοις φιλοτιμίαν: δόξα often refers to the opinion others have of you, your 'reputation'. Alcibiades is constantly presented as a man of extremes, often with superlatives used to describe him. Here the ὑπερ- in ὑπερβάλλει with the sense of 'beyond' ('to pass' or 'to run past' in racing contexts) and the use of πᾶσαν, 'all (ambition)', highlight how he acted – and achieved – above the expected and ordinary in all he undertook: compare Section 16.1.

11.2

ὁ Εὐριπίδης ἐν τῷ ᾄσματι: Euripides included victory songs (or 'epinician odes', from the Greek ἐπινίκιος, 'for/of a victory') within his tragedies but this one for Alcibiades is the only example attributed to him. Alcibiades would have paid the poet a large sum for such a song. It is fitting that Euripides, a tragedian of risk-taking mould who played with dramatic convention, should be commissioned by a character such as Alcibiades. Interestingly, Plutarch elsewhere (*Life of Demosthenes* 1.1) states that most reports attribute this to Euripides but notes that someone else could have been the writer (ὁ μὲν γράψας τὸ ἐπὶ τῇ νίκῃ τῆς Ὀλυμπίασιν ἱπποδρομίας εἰς Ἀλκιβιάδην ἐγκώμιον, εἴτ᾽ Εὐριπίδης, ὡς ὁ πολὺς κρατεῖ λόγος, εἴθ᾽ ἕτερός τις ἦν).

Note that such epinician poems were written in Doric, a dialect which differs to the Greek, Attic dialect used by Plutarch, particularly regarding vowels; equivalent Attic forms are noted as appropriate.

ὦ Κλεινίου παῖ: Alcibiades' father Cleinias had fought in the Persian Wars at the Battle of Artemisium (480 BCE), in a trireme he himself had fitted out (Section 1.1), and was therefore worthy of mention in a victory ode.

καλὸν ἁ νίκα: 'victory is a fine thing'; the Attic form is ἡ νίκη.

Διὸς στεφθέντα τ᾽ ἐλαίᾳ: στεφθέντα is the aorist passive participle from στέφω, 'garlanded'. ἐλαία has the Attic form ἐλάα. Winners at the Olympic Games were awarded an olive crown, made from the twigs of the sacred olive tree which grew near the Temple of Zeus at Olympia. Reportedly Heracles, to honour his father Zeus, awarded the olive crown to the winner of the running race between himself and his brothers.

κάρυκι: the Attic form is ὁ κῆρυξ, κήρυκος.

Section 12

12.1

τοῦτο μέντοι τὸ λαμπρὸν: his achievement, which seemed unsurpassable, was improved upon nonetheless. 'This splendour' refers to his success at Olympia in chariot-racing.

ἡ τῶν πόλεων φιλοτιμία: the subject of the verb ἐποίησεν ('made') comes at the end of the sentence and as such serves to leave the brilliance of Alcibiades' achievement at the start; it is thus closer to the explanation of who was involved in 'the competitive rivalry of cities' which follows. Alcibiades was a 'lover of competition' (φιλόνεικος) according to Section 2.1.

σκηνὴν μὲν γὰρ αὐτῷ κεκοσμημένην διαπρεπῶς ἔστησαν Ἐφέσιοι: to explain the previous statement, Plutarch lists three examples of cities making lavish gifts to Alcibiades to win his favour. Ephesus was a Greek city state on the Ionian coast, the west coast of modern-day Turkey. The Ionian city states were part of the Delian League, the collection of allies which Athens led through most of the fifth century BCE. Here Plutarch states that they 'set up for him a tent which was decorated magnificently'; at first glance this may seem a simple statement showing how highly Alcibiades was regarded, but there is a less flattering undertone: a magnificently decorated tent was more fitting, in the minds of the Greeks, for a ruler of Persia than for a Greek statesman like Alcibiades.

τροφὰς δὲ ἵπποις καὶ πλῆθος ἱερείων … οἶνον δὲ Λέσβιοι: the gifts provided by the Chians, whose island Chios lies just off the Ionian coast, supplied Alcibiades with the means to celebrate his Olympic victory in style. Lesbos, an island north of Chios, was known for its wines. Note how in this list of gifts the main provisions from the cities – the tent, fodder, sacrificial animals and wine – are all early accusatives.

ἀφειδῶς: 'unsparingly'. The adverb here should be considered alongside the use of διαπρεπῶς above, both of which add to the scale of the occasion. Take with ἑστιῶντι.

ἑστιῶντι πολλούς: the participle agrees with the αὐτῷ earlier in the sentence, referring to Alcibiades. He needed the provisions from cities since he was 'entertaining many'. The practice of hosting a few private guests after a victory is taken to the extreme by Alcibiades who, according to Athenaeus, entertained the whole crowd.

διαβολή τις ἢ κακοήθεια: Plutarch offers two interpretations of the incident he is about to relate from the start: either Alcibiades was the subject of a false accusation (διαβολή) or he was guilty of deliberate deceit and malpractice (κακοήθεια). Plutarch presents this couplet but does not hint at which he thinks is true, rather leaving it to the reader to decide; this is one of Alcibiades' many actions which are double-edged and impossible to interpret with confidence.

περὶ τὴν φιλοτιμίαν ἐκείνην: note the repeated use of φιλοτιμία (see 11.1).

12.2

λέγεται: Plutarch frequently introduces anecdotes or rumours in such a vague manner. This incident occurs in Diodorus Siculus 13.74.3, pseudo-Andocides 4.26

and is the subject of a lawsuit brought against Alcibiades the Younger, for whom Isocrates' speech *On the Team of Horses* (Isocrates 16) was written. Plutarch refers to this speech below in 12.3, noting the discrepancy of the names relating to the injured party.

Διομήδης, ἀνὴϱ οὐ πονηϱός, Ἀλκιβιάδου φίλος: Diomedes is presented in a way to earn readers' sympathy, if the story is to be believed. The space which Plutarch devotes to the incident seems to suggest that he wishes to report it in order to use it as evidence of the difficulty of addressing Alcibiades' life and character, since even a success story as that of the Olympic victory is tarnished by accusations and possible bad behaviour. 'Diomedes' may be a nickname for Teisias, referring to the mythical king of Thrace whose wild, man-eating horses Hercules captured and took away as one of his Labours.

Πυνθανόμενος . . . εἰδώς: two participles explain Diomedes' reasoning.

πϱίασθαι τὸ ἅϱμα: infinitive dependent on ἔπεισεν. The same verb is repeated almost immediately (πϱιάμενος, 12.3). τὸ ἅϱμα refers to and repeats the ἅϱμα at the start of the sentence; the agreement and transaction between Diomedes and Alcibiades is the focus, making Alcibiades something of a double-dealer.

12.3

ἴδιον ἀπεγϱάψατο: understand τὸ ἅϱμα as the object with which ἴδιον agrees. The middle form of ἀπογϱάφω has the sense of 'register for oneself'. This verb is also used in legal texts for the act of indicting or informing against someone, appropriate considering the next part of the incident.

χαίϱειν εἴασε: ἐᾶν χαίϱειν is a somewhat rude phrase meaning 'to dismiss from one's mind'.

χαλεπῶς φέϱοντα: 'reacting angrily' (literally – 'bearing it with difficulty'). This and the participle μαϱτυϱόμενον agree with Diomedes, best translated as a relative clause.

φαίνεται: as with λέγεται above (12.2) the use of the vague 'it seems' here adds to the idea that Plutarch is not committing to the incident but is remaining, as so often throughout the *Life*, quite ambiguous in his attitude towards it.

συστᾶσα: aorist participle (dependent on φαίνεται) from συνίστημι, 'bring about, cause', agreeing with δίκη.

λόγος Ἰσοκϱάτει γέγϱαπται ... πεϱὶ τοῦ ζεύγους: the speech written by Isocrates refers to Isocrates 16, *On the Team of Horses*, given its title from the first words of the speech: πεϱὶ μὲν οὖν τοῦ ζεύγους τῶν ἵππων.

ὑπὲϱ τοῦ Ἀλκιβιάδου παιδός: ὑπὲϱ + genitive has the meaning of 'on behalf of' as well as 'in defence of' in legal speeches, the equivalent of *pro* + ablative in Latin (Cicero's *Pro Milone*), while 'against' was κατὰ + genitive (see Section 13.2 below), the equivalent to *in* + accusative (Cicero's *In Catilinam* or *In Verrem*).

τοῦ Ἀλκιβιάδου παιδός: Not very much is known about Alcibiades the Younger. He is the only boy out of the two children Alcibiades and Hipparete are known to have had and is known from lawsuits in the fourth century BCE: Isocrates 16, *On the Team of Horses* and Lysias 14 and 15. From these sources details about the life of Alcibiades the Younger are scarce but include that he was only four when his father defected to Sparta, that he was charged of wrongdoing in connection with military service and that he was accused of incest with his sister – accusations of scandalous behaviour appear to follow the family around.

Τισίας ... οὐ Διομήδης: these were possibly the same person – see note on **Διομήδης** (12.2).

ὁ δικασάμενος: the middle form of δικάζω, 'I judge', is used for 'take to court': here it means 'the plaintiff' or 'complainant'.

Section 13

13.1

ἀφῆκεν αὑτὸν εἰς τὴν πολιτείαν: 'he threw himself into politics'. ἀφῆκεν is aorist from ἀφίημι. Notice the rough breathing on **αὑτὸν**, which stands for ἑαυτόν. The expression suits Alcibiades' passionate nature.

ἔτι μειράκιον ὤν: 'while still a young adult'. **μειράκιον** usually means 'lad', referring to someone who has just entered adulthood or is in their early twenties. Alcibiades' precocious talent and willingness to challenge Nicias, who was mid-fifties, is being highlighted. At the time of the ostracism, around 417/416 BCE, Alcibiades was probably thirty-three years old.

τοὺς μὲν ἄλλους ... δημαγωγούς: Plutarch frequently splits nouns and their dependent adjectives, often with the verb inserted between them. The μὲν, picked up by ἀγῶνα δ᾽ εἶχε, contrasts how easily Alcibiades brushed aside other popular politicians with the struggle he entered upon with Phaeax and Nicias. The reference to **δημαγωγούς** – the word used for politicians who focused on winning popular support, opposing the more conservative, aristocratic politicians – shows that Alcibiades' focus was on winning over the people.

εὐθὺς ἐταπείνωσε: the verb echoes how Socrates made Alcibiades humble (ταπεινὸν ἐποίει) in Section 6.2 but is a reminder that Alcibiades is no longer a student of Socrates and reined in as he once was.

ἀγῶνα δ᾽ εἶχε: 'he had a struggle'. Since ἀγών often refers to athletic contests, a man like Alcibiades who loves competition (see note on φιλοτιμία at 12.2 above) and becomes an Olympic victor experiences politics as he does any other competition. Plutarch's reference to Alcibiades' rivalry with Nicias here sets up the events related in Section 14 where Alcibiades takes on Nicias. The ostracism is dated to later: Plutarch is engineering the rivalry to build up to Alcibiades' clashes with Nicias over the Spartan embassy (Section 14) and subsequently the Sicilian Expedition (Sections 17–18).

Φαίακα τὸν Ἐρασιστράτου: not very much is known about Phaeax beyond what Plutarch tells us here and in a couple of related *Lives* and his brief appearance in Thucydides Book 5.

γνωρίμων ὄντα πατέρων, ἐλαττούμενον δὲ: the first participle is concessive, 'though he was from distinguished parents', contrasted with 'yet he was inferior'. The adjective and noun are split again by the verb.

τοῖς τε ἄλλοις καὶ περὶ τὸν λόγον: 'in other ways too but especially in respect to public speech'. The combination of τε ... καὶ is used to single out the main quality in which Phaeax is inferior, explored further in Section 13.2.

13.2

ἐντευκτικὸς γὰρ ἰδίᾳ καὶ πιθανός: a couplet, as so often with Plutarch, is used to describe Phaeax's ability 'in private conversation' as 'affable and persuasive'. πιθανός derives from πείθω.

ἐδόκει: perhaps best rendered here as 'he had the reputation of being'.

φέρειν ἀγῶνας: 'to win contests', with ἀγῶνας picking up the instance in Section 13.1.

ἐν δήμῳ: contrasted with his aptitude ἰδίᾳ. Since Plutarch is examining the public side of Alcibiades and in Section 10.2 referred to his 'ability in speaking' (δυνατὸς εἰπεῖν), he is backing up his statement in 13.1 that Phaeax was no match for Alcibiades in a public debate.

λαλεῖν ἄριστος, ἀδυνατώτατος λέγειν: the quotation from Eupolis' *Demes* is arranged as a chiasmus which contrasts the ability to talk and chatter (λαλεῖν) with the ability to speak publicly (λέγειν). The superlative ἀδυνατώτατος links to Plutarch's description of Alcibiades in Section 10.2 as power-hungry (and see note on ἐν δήμῳ above).

φέρεται: similar to the impersonal use of λέγεται in Section 12.2; 'there exists'. The present tense suggests the work is still in circulation in Plutarch's lifetime.

λόγος τις κατ᾿ Ἀλκιβιάδου ὑπὸ Φαίακος γεγραμμένος: the speech is usually identified with pseudo-Andocides IV in which the speaker makes a case not to be ostracized and attacks Alcibiades behaviour and record. It has been ascribed to Phaeax but the speech is thought to be a rhetorical exercise rather than an actual speech by the politician. Note the use of κατά + genitive for 'against' (see note on ὑπὲρ at 12.3).

πομπεῖα: here 'reserved for ceremonial use', i.e. items connected to and used in processions and ceremonies.

Ἀλκιβιάδης ἐχρῆτο πᾶσιν αὐτοῖς: the grammatical separation of a genitive absolute clause from the main sentence is not always observed by Plutarch. Here αὐτοῖς refers to the πολλὰ πομπεῖα, the objects of the genitive absolute.

πρὸς τὴν καθ᾿ ἡμέραν δίαιταν: 'in his day-to-day life'. δίαιτα can also have the meaning of 'banquet' or 'table', so 'at his daily table' is a possible translation. The emphasis is on Alcibiades' regular use of ceremonial vessels which were not even his own; this must mean on a day-to-day basis during his Olympic victories in 416 BCE only (in accordance with the source, pseudo-Andocides 4, which goes on to comment that later, when the vessels were used at the actual ceremonies of those Games, some people thought that Alcibiades had lent his own possessions to Athens for the ceremony).

13.3

οὐ μέμνηται μὲν ὡς ἀνθρώπου πονηροῦ καὶ Θουκυδίδης: Plutarch balances two views of Hyperbolus, Thucydides' and the comic poets', both of which show him in a bad light. Grammatically the subject of the μὲν clause is Thucydides while Hyperbolus himself is the subject of the δὲ clause. Plutarch appears to misquote Thucydides here, since the latter calls Hyperbolus a μοχθηρὸν ἄνθρωπον, not a πονηρόν one (8.73.3).

τοῖς δὲ κωμικοῖς ὁμοῦ τι πᾶσι: Plutarch makes much use of comic poets in these sections.

διατριβὴν: 'material for jokes', connecting to how he is 'always being mocked in the theatres' (ἀεὶ σκωπτόμενος ἐν τοῖς θεάτροις).

πρὸς τὸ κακῶς ἀκούειν: literally 'to being spoken badly about'.

ὀλιγωρίᾳ δόξης: 'due to his contempt for public opinion'. This quality makes him the opposite of Alcibiades and would remind a reader of Plutarch's description of Coriolanus, whose *Life* precedes that of Alcibiades and whose pride and disgust for the common people are a theme throughout.

ἦν ἀναισχυντίαν καὶ ἀπόνοιαν οὖσαν: ἦν refers to the 'contempt' politicians show the people. Another couplet here expresses Plutarch's strong personal views on the behaviour of politicians who refuse even to consider the views of the common people. Note how this behaviour is described through two pairs of abstract nouns.

εὐτολμίαν ἔνιοι καὶ ἀνδρείαν καλοῦσιν: Plutarch wants to make his view clear that he disagrees with what 'some' think: the use of the vague ἔνιοι is a common method employed by Plutarch to express a general viewpoint with which he frequently disagrees (see Section 13.4).

οὐδενὶ μὲν ἤρεσκεν, ἐχρῆτο δ᾽ αὐτῷ ... ὁ δῆμος: the chiasmus contrasts how Hyperbolus, though disliked, was exploited by the people. Both verbs take the dative case. The verb χράομαι reminds us Alcibiades' use of Athens' ceremonial vessels as his own with no sense of propriety (Section 13.1-2); so too the people have scant regard for Hyperbolus and his attitude.

τοὺς ἐν ἀξιώματι: 'those in high official positions'.

Προπηλακίζειν ... καὶ συκοφαντεῖν: both words have obscure, though interesting, origins. προπηλακίζειν is most likely connected to πηλός meaning 'mud', so the verb has the idea of 'mud-slinging', a term we still use today. The verb is used in pseudo-Andocides 4.21 referring to Alcibiades himself, insulting a rival chorus sponsor Taureas (see below, Section 16.4). The word συκοφαντεῖν is thought to be linked to σῦκον, 'fig', but its exact connection is unknown. Possibly it relates to someone who was a 'fig-revealer' (the second half of the word being associated with φαίνειν), explained as those who denounced people illegally exporting figs from Athens. The meaning of the English word 'sycophant' (flatterer) is derived from this idea of giving up information for personal gain.

13.4

ἀναπεισθείς: 'persuaded', but with the prefix ἀνα- can mean 'mislead' or 'seduce'. The subject is 'the people', continued from the previous sentence.

ὑπ᾽ αὐτοῦ: Plutarch in his *Lives* writes about this ostracism on two other occasions, in his *Life of Nicias* Section 12 and his *Life of Aristides* Section 7. Only this account specifically states that Hyperbolus initiated the vote, allowing Alcibiades to be the one who combined his and another's votes to overturn the vote, thus defeating Hyperbolus by having greater influence over the people. Hyperbolus' contempt for popular favour is parallel to that of the Roman general Coriolanus; Plutarch in his Comparison (syncrisis) explicitly states that Alcibiades was superior to Coriolanus in winning popular favour, as he is here to Hyperbolus.

τὸ ὄστρακον: the ὄστρακον was both an earthenware pot and the shard of one. It is used here by Plutarch to represent the actual vote of an ostracism. The process involved the Athenians gathering in the Athenian Agora and voting in their tribes' enclosure by putting their potsherd, inscribed with the name of the man they were voting to exile, in a large urn. This had been preceded by weeks of speeches and campaigns by factions with an interest in the vote. The purpose of an ostracism is explained below as well as in both *Nicias*, *Themistocles* and *Aristides*, while the latter also includes an explanation of the process (*Life of Aristides* Section 7.4-5), noting that a quorum of 6,000 votes was required. Plutarch clearly felt that this institution might be unfamiliar to his audience and that an understanding of it would enhance their appreciation of the context of the Athenian political climate in the fifth century BCE.

ἐπιφέρειν ἔμελλεν: μέλλω is often followed by a future infinitive but can, as here, take a present infinitive and still mean 'was about to'.

ᾧ: dative of instrument.

Κολούοντες . . . ἐλαύνουσι: the main verb is in the present tense, coupled with the temporal adverb ἀεί, to show repeated action. The people remain the subject but have moved from singular (ὁ δῆμος) to plural.

τὸν προὔχοντα δόξῃ καὶ δυνάμει τῶν πολιτῶν: 'any one of the citizens who was excelling in popularity and power'. Note the alliterative couplet of δόξῃ καὶ δυνάμει.

παραμυθούμενοι τὸν φθόνον μᾶλλον ἢ τὸν φόβον: Plutarch's portrayal of the people is usually unflattering, here attributing their votes to personal emotions and suggesting that those voted out were not a threat, simply too influential. The fact that for the most part it was the people who made politicians so powerful in the first place does not appear to prevent their voting against such men.

ἑνὶ τῶν τριῶν: ἑνὶ is the dative of disadvantage. In the other two accounts of this matter, Plutarch makes the vote between just Alcibiades and Nicias, though mentioning that it could have been between Alcibiades and Phaeax (in his *Life of Nicias* Section 12, stating this as Theophrastus' view). Here Plutarch continues the theme of the ἀγών between Alcibiades, Phaeax and Nicias from Section 13.1. Alcibiades' rivalry with Nicias, the focus of Sections 14–15 and 17f., contrasts with his apparent willingness to work with him here. As noted at 13.1 (see ἀγῶνα) the ostracism in fact came after the events of Section 14 but this sequence of events creates a more dramatic context for them.

ἐποίσουσι: future tense, 3rd person plural of ἐπιφέρω, 'carry out', 'impose upon'.

συνήγαγε τὰς στάσεις εἰς ταὐτὸν ὁ Ἀλκιβιάδης: 'Alcibiades brought together the political factions into one'. ταὐτὸν works as τὸ αὐτό, literally 'the same'. Alcibiades as the initiator of uniting politicians' supporters against Hyperbolus is a detail found only here. The delay of his name refocuses the narrative on the protagonist, who has not been mentioned since the end of Section 13.2.

διαλεχθείς: aorist participle of διαλέγομαι, 'I discuss with someone (πρός + accusative of person)'. The exact same form of this verb is repeated in the next sentence.

τὴν ὀστρακοφορίαν: 'the casting of votes'. Alcibiades' ability to turn the people's votes against Hyperbolus, the proposer of the ostracism vote himself, is highlighted here as an indicator of Alcibiades' influence with the people and aptitude for negotiating the shifting winds of politics, both of which are important elements of this *Life*.

ὡς δ᾽ ἔνιοί φασιν: the unidentified authors of an alternate version are here noted but Plutarch makes no judgement on their view. Alcibiades' willingness to look beyond rivalry and unite with Phaeax for political gain provides more evidence of his pragmatism.

τὴν ἐκείνου προσλαβὼν ἑταιρίαν: 'gaining that man's supporters in addition to his own', the idea of 'in addition' created by the prefix προσ-. ἑταιρία refers to a political club or party, the root of the word connected to 'companion'. The separation of the noun from its article by a participle (and here also the possessive ἐκείνου) is common in Plutarch.

ἐξήλασε: the use of the active voice makes Hyperbolus' banishment seem Alcibiades' personal achievement.

τὸν Ὑπέρβολον οὐδ᾽ ἂν προσδοκήσαντα: the use of οὐδ᾽ ἂν here with the aorist participle stands for the use of the aorist optative, to express something that could never have happened. Translate 'Hyperbolus, who could never have expected it'.

13.5

φαῦλος γὰρ οὐδεὶς ... οὐδ᾽ ἄδοξος: the γὰρ explains why Hyperbolus would have been so shocked at losing the ostracism vote, since it was unprecedented for a political nobody to suffer banishment through this way.

ὥς που καὶ Πλάτων ὁ κωμικὸς εἴρηκε: the use of the vague που highlights Plutarch's focus on his aims and focus – he is not preoccupied with informing his audience of precisely where every quotation he uses comes from; the content of Plato's words are the important element.

μνησθείς: the aorist passive form has the meaning 'make mention of'; followed by the genitive case.

καίτοι πέπραχε ... εὑρέθη: 'and yet he suffered what his ancestors were worthy of suffering but what he and his tattoos were unworthy of. For the vote of ostracism was not invented for such men.' This is an unknown fragment from the poet of Old Comedy, Plato, quoted identically in Plutarch's *Life of Nicias* Section 11.

περὶ ... τούτων ἐν ἑτέροις μᾶλλον εἴρηται τὰ ἱστορούμενα: 'my research about this affair has been recorded in more detail in other works', presumably referring to his *Lives* of Nicias, Themistocles and Aristides, as noted above, primarily *Life of Nicias* Section 11, where the same Plato fragment is quoted. Note the promotion of περὶ τούτων, separated by μὲν οὖν indicating a shift towards new subject matter.

Section 14

This long section narrates the actions of Alcibiades to harm Nicias, focusing primarily on his dealings with the Spartan embassy through a speech. These events date to 420 BCE and as such took place before the ostracism vote recorded in Section 13. Much of the same material as here is covered in Plutarch's *Life of Nicias* 9–11 as well as Thucydides 5.42-45, who is used here as a consistent source for the first time. The three versions contain similar content but are told in their own way without similarities of expression. Plutarch emphasizes Alcibiades' role and even words throughout, building to the humiliation of Nicias. Plutarch attributes motive to

Alcibiades in places where Thucydides does not, as the biographer examines Alcibiades' character most of all.

14.1

τὸν δ᾽ Ἀλκιβιάδην: though Nicias is the subject of this sentence, Plutarch starts with his protagonist. Section 13 has set up the rivalry between Alcibiades and Nicias, although chronologically these events came before the ostracism vote.

ὁ Νικίας ἥνία: Plutarch here makes Nicias personally responsible for Alcibiades' resentment even though it is caused by how others feel about him.

οὐχ ἧττον … θαυμαζόμενος ὑπὸ τῶν πολεμίων ἢ τιμώμενος ὑπὸ τῶν πολιτῶν: Plutarch neatly balances the contrasting views of the enemy and of Athenian citizens, with the similar sounds of πολεμίων and πολιτῶν.

πρόξενος μὲν: Alcibiades' family held hereditarily the position as the Spartan 'representative' in Athens. Holding this position, Alcibiades felt that he should be their favourite, not Nicias. The μὲν is picked up by the ἐπεὶ δ᾽ ἐκεῖνοί in Section 14.2, with the reasons why Alcibiades should be respected contained here contrasted with the reality of how the Spartans actually felt.

καὶ τοὺς ἁλόντας αὐτῶν περὶ Πύλον ἄνδρας ἐθεράπευσεν: ἁλόντας is the aorist participle passive from ἁλίσκομαι. The island Pylos and its neighbouring island Sphacteria off the west coast of Greece were the sites of battles in 425 BCE during the Peloponnesian War. The Athenians trapped a large number of Spartan hoplites and took them prisoner; when negotiations with Sparta for their release broke down, they were taken to Athens and held there; these are the men Alcibiades is said here to have 'looked after'. A Spartan surrender was unheard of and punctured their air of invincibility; over the next few years Athens became more confident and launched more expansive attacks. Only after a few defeats in these engagements was Athens willing to negotiate again with Sparta, the result of which was the so-called Peace of Nicias in 421 BCE.

14.2

ἐπεὶ δ᾽ ἐκεῖνοί τε: refers to the Spartans. ἐπεὶ introduces three subordinative causal clauses, each indicated by their own τε, which explain the motivations behind Alcibiades feelings which make up the main clause of this sentence.

διὰ Νικίου μάλιστα τῆς εἰρήνης τυχόντες … ἀπολαβόντες: the participles are best translated as causal clauses.

ὑπερηγάπων: that the Spartans 'greatly loved' Nicias would of course annoy Alcibiades, which Plutarch highlights further with ὑπερ – which often indicates excess, Alcibiades' speciality.

Περικλέους μὲν συνάψαντος αὐτοῖς, Νικίου δὲ λύσαντος τὸν πόλεμον: a balanced phrase linking the two great statesmen of Athens, Pericles and Nicias, whom Alcibiades wanted to supersede; here Nicias is seen to be bettering his predecessor. Pericles had been Alcibiades' guardian (Section 1). The genitive absolutes represent what the Greeks are saying in place of finite verbs.

οἵ τε πλεῖστοι τὴν εἰρήνην Νικίειον ὠνόμαζον: the third reason for Alcibiades' distress, again starting with τε. The treaty with Sparta was not called 'the Peace of Nicias' by Thucydides, nor does the historian say that people said Nicias had ended the war. Both statements were clearly current in Plutarch's time, and the biographer possibly thought that these views stemmed from Nicias' time. As with ἐν τοῖς Ἕλλησι above, the views of οἱ πλεῖστοι were important to Alcibiades.

οὐ μετρίως ἀνιώμενος ὁ Ἀλκιβιάδης: his passionate nature is a theme of the *Life* so the fact that 'Alcibiades was immoderately distressed' by all the plaudits Nicias was receiving comes as no surprise. ἀνιώμενος verbally links Alcibiades' reaction to the start of Section 14 where Nicias caused him distress (ἠνία).

φθονῶν ἐβούλευε σύγχυσιν ὁρκίων: Alcibiades' relationship with oaths, ὁρκία, is a theme revisited later in this section.

14.3

καὶ πρῶτον μὲν Ἀργείους: Plutarch records the two methods Alcibiades employed to break the treaty with the Spartans and undermine Nicias, starting them with the names of the enemies whom Alcibiades looked to make use of in different ways. μὲν Ἀργείους is picked up by δὲ Λακεδαιμόνιοι at the start of Section 14.4.

μίσει καὶ φόβῳ τῶν Σπαρτιατῶν: 'due to hatred and fear of the Spartans'. Both are causal datives.

ζητοῦντας ἀποστροφήν: the 'escape' the Argives were looking for was to defect from Sparta.

ἐλπίδας ... ἐνεδίδου κρύφα τῆς Ἀθηναίων συμμαχίας: these hopes are realized in the pact narrated in Section 15.1 and points to the relationship Alcibiades builds with the Argives, whom he advises on defensive planning in Section 15.2. He is portrayed as a cunning politician who acts in secret, taking advantage of opportunities he notices.

παρεθάρρυνε: introducing an accusative and infinitive (the accusative is not expressed here, and is to be taken from the Ἀργείους at the start of the section). At this juncture he can do no more than talk in secret; in the next section his talk can directly harm Nicias, by constantly levelling accusations against him.

πέμπων καὶ διαλεγόμενος: a couplet of participles denoting how Alcibiades emboldened the Argives. In Thucydides' narrative he only contacted the Argives to suggest they send an embassy to Athens to discuss the possibility of an alliance. Plutarch's account makes Alcibiades act as more of a mastermind, working in the shadows to stir up trouble for his arch-rival Nicias.

τοῖς προεστῶσι τοῦ δήμου: τοῖς προεστῶσι is dative dependent on διαλεγόμενος.

μὴ δεδιέναι μηδ' ὑπείκειν Λακεδαιμονίοις: the μὴ + infinitive indirect command construction is after παρεθάρρυνε.

ὅσον οὐδέπω μεταμελομένους καὶ τὴν εἰρήνην ἀφιέντας: ὅσον οὐδέπω + two present participles meaning 'all but'. The Athenians, Alcibiades claimed, 'were changing their minds and giving up on peace', referring to the so-called Peace of Nicias.

14.4

πρός τε τοὺς Βοιωτοὺς ἐποιήσαντο συμμαχίαν: under the terms of the so-called Peace of Nicias, there were restrictions on whom Athens and Sparta could sign treaties with. Sparta was trying to get back the hoplites who had been captured in the battles at Pylos and Sphacteria (Section 14.1) while Athens wished to get back control of Panactum, a strategic fortress in central Greece which had fallen to the Boeotians. The Spartans asked Boeotia to deliver up Panactum to Athens so she would return their hoplites. The Boeotians agreed, but only if Sparta signed a separate treaty with them, affording them some protection from Athens. In 420 BCE Sparta signed this treaty, even though it was in contravention of the peace terms agreed between Athens and Sparta a year before.

καὶ Πάνακτον οὐχ ἑστός, ὥσπερ ἔδει, τοῖς Ἀθηναίοις παρέδωκαν, ἀλλὰ καταλύσαντες: Sparta is here blamed for what was likely carried out by the Boeotians themselves, providing Alcibiades with a focus for his accusations against Nicias who was considered too pro-Spartan. ἑστός is the perfect participle active, accusative neuter singular form from ἵστημι.

ὀργιζομένους λαβὼν τοὺς Ἀθηναίους ἔτι μᾶλλον ἐξετράχυνε: Alcibiades is the unexpressed subject of this main clause; the rare verb ἐκτραχύνω literally means 'I make rough' but here is used metaphorically for 'make angry' as a variation on ὀργίζομαι. Ever the opportunist, he uses popular passions to his advantage.

ἐθορύβει καὶ διέβαλλεν: imperfect tenses suggesting repeated action.

εἰκότα κατηγορῶν: Alcibiades' ability to speak, persuade and know what to say were referred to in Section 10.2-3.

14.5

ὅτι: introducing Alcibiades' accusations against Nicias which follow for the rest of the section.

τοὺς ἐν Σφακτηρίᾳ τῶν πολεμίων ἀποληφθέντας: ἀποληφθέντας is aorist passive participle passive of ἀπολαμβάνω, here with the sense of 'take apart/away'. On Sphacteria, see note on Pylos, Section 14.1.

αὐτὸς μὲν ἐξελεῖν ... ἑτέρων δ' ἐξελόντων ἀφῆκε: note the balance of expression and the repeated use of the aorist of ἐξαιρέω in different forms. Alcibiades accuses Nicias of refusing to capture the Spartan hoplites when he was a general only to then release them when others had captured them.

χαριζόμενος Λακεδαιμονίοις: Alcibiades attacks Nicias for what he labels his pro-Spartan acts, just at the time of heightened Athenian distrust of Sparta.

εἶτ᾽ ἐκείνους μὲν οὐκ ἔπεισε: the first two accusations levelled against Nicias were balanced by μὲν and δὲ and so are these next two.

φίλος ὤν: 'since he was their friend', part of Alcibiades' frequent case against Nicias.

Βοιωτοῖς μὴ συνόμνυσθαι μηδὲ Κορινθίοις: the middle form of συνόμνυμι is used with the dative case to mean 'form an alliance with', literally meaning 'swear together' regarding the oaths they would take in forming a pact.

Ἀθηναίοις δὲ κωλύει: 'but in the case of the Athenians, he prevented'. The text is uncertain here but the sense is clear.

εἰ μὴ δόξειε Λακεδαιμονίοις: these accusations are unique to Plutarch and are an attempt to capture how Alcibiades might have targeted his opponent, riding on a wave of popular anti-Spartan sentiment. Though reported in indirect speech, the balance of the accusations perhaps replicates in small-scale the rhetoric which Alcibiades would have employed in casting his aspersions.

14.6

ἐκ δὲ τούτου κακῶς φερομένῳ τῷ Νικίᾳ παρῆσαν ὥσπερ κατὰ τύχην πρέσβεις ἀπὸ τῆς Λακεδαίμονος: τῷ Νικίᾳ is a dative of interest. Negotiations for peace may help restore Nicias' reputation. Plutarch's reference to Nicias' τύχη here is to indicate that he is not anticipating an embassy at all nor the deception which will humiliate him further at the end of this section. Sections 14.6-9 form a unit concerning the Spartan embassy and Alcibiades' tricking it. This follows the measures he has already taken to disrupt Nicias' influence and trumps them.

The Spartans' embassy likely came to Athens in response to their hearing the news that Argos was considering an alliance with Athens. These negotiations were supposedly being carried out by Alcibiades in secret (see Section 14.3), which was clearly working since Nicias is presented here as being completely unaware of such events.

αὐτόθεν τε λόγους ἐπιεικεῖς ἔχοντες: as so often, Plutarch cites the embassy's mandates in a pair, structured by the use of τε and καὶ. The use of ἐπιεικεῖς here and δίκαιον below serve to emphasize the equitable aims of the embassy, which Alcibiades plays upon when giving it advice, making his deception and misuse of it particularly reprehensible.

πρὸς πᾶν τὸ συμβιβαστικὸν: 'to [negotiate] any measure which would lead to reconciliation', a fairly compressed expression.

αὐτοκράτορες: here specifically 'in receipt of full powers to negotiate a solution', a more restricted meaning than that of our modern word 'autocrat', which is synonymous with 'dictator'.

ἀποδεξαμένης δὲ τῆς βουλῆς: the first of two genitive absolutes providing the context of Alcibiades' fear, with causal force. The Athenian Boule was an advisory council of 500 citizens who had been official magistrates (archons).

τοῦ δὲ δήμου τῇ ὑστεραίᾳ μέλλοντος ἐκκλησιάζειν: the Athenian Assembly was where questions such as declaring war or peace were debated and decided upon, so Alcibiades is pressed into taking matters into his own hands before the embassy presented themselves there. This time pressure is not noted in Thucydides or Plutarch's *Life of Nicias*; here Plutarch wants to create dramatic tension for the events to follow, which play out vividly like a theatrical scene. Like with the quail episode in Section 10.1, incidents involving Alcibiades are often portrayed theatrically, mirroring his own love of display.

ὁ Ἀλκιβιάδης διεπράξατο: Alcibiades has already been shown to be willing to orchestrate political business personally (see Section 14.3 in connection with his secret dealings with Argos) and here brings it about that the embassy will speak with him before attending the Assembly, though there was no political or legal reason for the embassy to do so. Alcibiades' position as Spartan *proxenos*, however, as well as his reputation and his influence, may have given the embassy enough reason.

14.7

ὡς δὲ συνῆλθον ἔλεγε: the direct speech which follows is the longest of its kind in this *Life* and is a rendering of much of what Thucydides reports in his account, albeit in indirect speech. Plutarch here aimed to make the episode more vivid and dramatic, attempting to capture the Alcibiades' rhetoric, with repetition of words and balancing of phrasing.

τί πεπόνθατε: 'what has happened to you . . .?' Alcibiades starts boldly, and follows it with another, longer question. Both are aimed at making the Spartan embassy question itself and be willing to listen to him.

πῶς ἔλαθεν ὑμᾶς ὅτι: ἔλαθεν used impersonally.

τὰ τῆς βουλῆς ἀεὶ μέτρια καὶ φιλάνθρωπα ... ἐστιν: 'the attitude (literally 'things') of the Boule is always moderate and courteous'. μέτρια recalls Alcibiades' inability to handle his jealousy towards Nicias moderately (μετρίως, Section 14.2).

πρὸς τοὺς ἐντυγχάνοντάς: 'towards those who obtain an audience'.

ὁ δὲ δῆμος: Alcibiades contrasts the Boule with the common people, whom Alcibiades knows well. The embassy would have known of his influence with the people of Athens and so would likely have listened to this advice; recall how Alcibiades was good at finding the right thing to say (Section 10.3).

μέγα φρονεῖ καὶ μεγάλων ὀρέγεται: this description of the common people would fit Alcibiades well. The repetition of μεγ- might be to reinforce the idea, since it could seem strange that the Boule (whose number was drawn only from ex-archons) would be moderate but the democratic Assembly proud and ambitious.

κἂν φάσκητε κύριοι πάντων ἀφῖχθαι: κἂν is crasis for καὶ ἄν, 'and if', introducing a conditional clause after φάσκητε. κύριοι πάντων is an alternate way of expressing αὐτοκράτορες, 'in receipt of full powers to negotiate a solution'.

προστάττων καὶ βιαζόμενος ἀγνωμονήσει: the unexpressed subject of this apodosis is the Athenian people and Assembly, who are again depicted in terms which apply to Alcibiades himself. The unusual verb ἀγνωμονέω literally means 'I act unfeelingly'.

φέρε δή: Alcibiades now adopts the tone of an advisor and suggests how they can avoid unfair treatment at the hands of the people, having painted an unsavoury picture of them so far.

τὴν εὐήθειαν ταύτην ἀφέντες: though a participle, it is best to render this as an imperative, 'set aside this naivety'.

εἰ βούλεσθε χρήσασθαι μετρίοις Ἀθηναίοις: Alcibiades said that only the Boule were moderate in their attitude, so he is claiming to show the ambassadors how they can make the Assembly more like the Boule and so receive them warmly. χρήσασθαι here means 'to have dealings with'.

καὶ μηδὲν ἐκβιασθῆναι παρὰ γνώμην: Alcibiades continues the theme of the danger of the embassy being pressured (compare βιαζόμενος above) and adds παρὰ γνώμην here, 'contrary to your wish' to reaffirm his point.

συμπράξομεν δ' ἡμεῖς: the 'we' here refers to Alcibiades alone, and is a fitting rhetorical touch on which to end the speech. It also makes Alcibiades' subsequent volte-face more forceful.

Λακεδαιμονίοις χαριζόμενοι: 'as a favour to the Spartans', an act made more shameless by the repetition of the phrase which Alcibiades himself used in condemning Nicias' pro-Spartan sentiments in Section 14.5.

14.8

ὅρκους ἔδωκεν: Thucydides only says he gave his pledge. Making Alcibiades an oath-breaker in this episode is a particularly negative depiction, painting him as sacrilegious, effectively the charge for which he will be exiled when he is found guilty of desecrating the Eleusinian Mysteries (see Section 22).

μετέστησεν ἀπὸ τοῦ Νικίου: 'he won them away from Nicias'. **μετέστησεν** is the aorist indicative active from μεθίστημι, 'I make move', but here in the sense of moving their loyalty.

παντάπασι πιστεύοντας: the resultant switching of sides by the embassy, shown to be effected 'completely' (**παντάπασι**), evidencing Alcibiades' ability to persuade.

ἅμα τὴν δεινότητα καὶ σύνεσιν: recall how Demosthenes described Alcibiades as being very clever when it came to speaking (Section 10.2).

ὡς οὐ τοῦ τυχόντος ἀνδρὸς οὖσαν: the article with the aorist participle of τυγχάνω means 'the everyday', 'the usual'.

τῇ δ' ὑστεραίᾳ: Plutarch appears to be compressing the timeline of events to get to the heart of the incident more quickly and concentrate on the role of Alcibiades. In Thucydides' account and in Plutarch's *Life of Nicias* events are not so compressed: an earthquake took place once the Spartan embassy was discovered to have been exaggerating their powers of negotiation and Alcibiades had stirred up resentment towards them. The people wanted to make an alliance with Argos at once, supposedly, but the earthquake prevented this. The Assembly then met the following day, before dismissing the Spartans.

συνήχθη μὲν ὁ δῆμος, εἰσῆλθον δ' οἱ πρέσβεις: Plutarch sets the common people and the ambassadors apart, their entries both noted. Like the 'contest' which is playing out between Alcibiades and Nicias – Alcibiades is said to always enjoy a contest – here the embassy is to take on the Athenian people, a prospect which Alcibiades has just made daunting for the Spartans in his speech to them in Section 14.7. The use of the passive in 'the people were led in' perhaps suggests that they are the ones without power here, compared to the ambassadors who are actively in charge of their own entry.

ἐρωτώμενοι δ' ὑπὸ τοῦ Ἀλκιβιάδου: Alcibiades is given the main role in the action by Plutarch, as the ambassadors are questioned by him regarding their powers. To them, this is part of the pact made with Alcibiades on the previous night.

πάνυ φιλανθρώπως: 'perfectly courteously'.

ἐφ' οἷς ἀφιγμένοι τυγχάνουσιν: 'on what conditions they had just come'. τυγχάνω + participle of a verb can be used to express coincidence and can have the sense of 'at that moment' like here. ἐπί + dative often means 'on the condition'.

αὐτοκράτορες: one of a number of words from Alcibiades' own speech which reappear here, as the Spartans repeat his instructions on cue.

14.9

εὐθὺς οὖν ὁ Ἀλκιβιάδης ἐνέκειτο μετὰ κραυγῆς καὶ ὀργῆς: the dramatic denouement of the incident, as Alcibiades wastes no time at all (**εὐθύς**) in verbally attacking them, angrily shouting at them. **ἐνέκειτο** is the imperfect indicative active form from ἔγκειμαι, here meaning 'to press upon' or 'act violently towards'. This type of behaviour is exactly what Alcibiades had warned the embassy about regarding the Assembly – he just had omitted to mention that he would be the one stirring it up.

ἀπίστους καὶ παλιμβόλους: the first of three couplets contained in these last few lines referring to the Spartan embassy incident, which is wrapped up rhetorically, as is appropriate to the situation and to Alcibiades' nature. The irony in Alcibiades' description of these men is clear.

μηδὲν ὑγιὲς μήτε πρᾶξαι μήτ᾽ εἰπεῖν ἥκοντας: ἀποκαλῶν introduces indirect statement. Note the three negatives and the contrast of action and speaking, a typical Greek trope. ὑγιὲς here means 'sound' or even 'solid'.

ἐπηγανάκτει δ᾽ ἡ βουλή, καὶ ὁ δῆμος ἐχαλέπαινε: the chiasmus underlines the strength of feeling captured in the verbs. By showing how both sets of people reacted, the extent of Nicias' humiliation and Alcibiades' deceit is increased.

τὸν δὲ Νικίαν ἔκπληξις εἶχε καὶ κατήφεια: Nicias is at the mercy of emotions just as he is at the mercy of Alcibiades' machinations, gripped by 'confusion and dejection'. The second couplet in these final stages of the embassy.

ἀγνοοῦντα τὴν ἀπάτην καὶ τὸν δόλον: the reversal of the politicians' influence is summed up, with Nicias' ignorance and Alcibiades' accomplishment highlighted. Alcibiades' role as the primary mover in Athenian affairs is confirmed immediately at the start of Section 15, where he orchestrates the alliance with the Argives.

Section 15

15.1

οὕτω δὲ τῶν Λακεδαιμονίων ἐκπεσόντων: the use of οὕτω in conjunction with the genitive absolute makes the appointment of Alcibiades as general follow the rejection of the Spartan embassy both in time and causation, suggesting that his actions won him approval.

Ἀργείους καὶ Μαντινεῖς καὶ Ἠλείους: this alliance was formed in 420/419 BCE. These three city states, all in the Peloponnese, feared the power of nearby Sparta and sided with Athens for protection of their own interests and land.

καὶ τὸν μὲν τρόπον: Plutarch clearly did not approve of the deceitful methods Alcibiades had employed to engineer the alliance with the Argives. The μὲν . . . δ᾽ contrasts the means with the end, however, as Plutarch notes that Alcibiades' achievements were vital.

οὐδεὶς . . . ἐπήνει: such universal distaste for Alcibiades' tricks is likely exaggerated but Plutarch wants to condemn such underhand political machinations. The account of the Spartan embassy episode in Section 14 was set up in such a way as to make Alcibiades' achievement look impressive while still showing Plutarch's disapproval of Alcibiades' tactics throughout.

τὸ πεπραγμένον ὑπ᾽ αὐτοῦ: Alcibiades had a leading role in the forging of the alliance with the Argives but Plutarch presents it as though he achieved it single-handedly.

διαστῆσαι καὶ κραδᾶναι Πελοπόννησον: a couplet of aorist active infinitives, the latter from the rare verb κραδαίνω. These and the two infinitives which follow explain Alcibiades' achievement. The strategy was for Athens to be in alliance with key sites around the Peloponnese which would destabilize Sparta's dominance there.

ὀλίγου δεῖν ἅπασαν: 'almost all'. The infinitive here stands in for the participle of δέω + genitive, which means 'I lack'. Literally 'all, lacking a little'.

πορρωτάτω τῶν Ἀθηνῶν: the superlative of the adverb πόρρω + genitive, 'far from'. Mantinea, the site of the battle in 418 BCE, is in the Arcadian region of the Peloponnese, in Spartan territory. For a full account, see Thucydides 5.

ἀγῶνα κατασκευάσαι καὶ κίνδυνον αὐτοῖς: an instance of zeugma, where a verb works with two objects and has a slightly different meaning with each. Alcibiades 'arranged the battle [very far from Athens] and put the danger on them (the Spartans)'. Note the use of ἀγῶνα again.

ἐν ᾧ: refers back to ἀγῶνα.

προσέθηκε κρατήσασιν: προσέθηκε is the aorist indicative active from προστίθημι, 'I hand over' or 'I add', so here '[victory] conferred [no great benefit] to them (the Spartans) if they won'. Here the participle should be translated as a condition, 'if'.

εἰ δ' ἐσφάλησαν: the protasis, εἰ + aorist indicative, is followed by an apodosis with corresponding aorist indicative verb (ἦν) but without the expected ἄν, perhaps to emphasize the seriousness of such an occurrence: had Sparta lost at Mantinea, her very existence really was in the balance. Plutarch makes very little of the fact that Athens and her alliance did lose the battle as this would not align with the focus of the section: the benefits Alcibiades brought to Athens through his 'policy'.

ἔργον ἦν τὴν Λακεδαίμονα περιγενέσθαι: 'it would have been a matter of survival for Sparta'. The phrase ἔργον ἐστί can be followed by an infinitive.

15.2

μετὰ δὲ τὴν μάχην: the installation of the oligarchic faction in Argos took place in the winter months of 418/417 BCE. Thucydides Book 5 and Diodorus Siculus Book 12.80 offer accounts of the battle.

ἐπέθεντο: aorist indicative middle from ἐπιτίθημι, meaning here 'they set about' + infinitive.

οἱ χίλιοι: 'the Thousand', the name given by Plutarch (and Diodorus Siculus) to the Spartan-backed oligarchic regime which was installed in Argos. This may not be accurate – Thucydides says a thousand Spartans combined with a thousand Argives were involved – but it chimes with how oligarchic coups were referred to: the 411 BCE coup in Athens installed 'the Four Hundred' and that of 404 BCE installed 'the Thirty'.

ὑπήκοον: an adjective with only two terminations, agreeing here with τὴν πόλιν. Literally it means 'listening to', derived from ἀκούω.

κατέλυσαν τὴν δημοκρατίαν: Plutarch repeats the verb for 'abolish' but here refers to the Argive 'democracy'. By doing so he has created a tricolon, variously referring to the government of Argos as first δῆμον then πόλιν and finally now δημοκρατίαν.

τῶν πολλῶν: in contrast to the oligarchic 'Thousand'.

ἐξενεγκαμένων τὰ ὅπλα καὶ κρατησάντων: the genitive absolute refers to events which took place a few months after the initial coup.

ἐπελθὼν ὁ Ἀλκιβιάδης τήν τε νίκην ἐβεβαίωσε τῷ δήμῳ: the participle and aorist main verb relating to Alcibiades' role in the events of 417 BCE after the oligarchic coup is overthrown make it seem immediate and personal, linking to the advice he gives the Argives in the next sentence, introduced by καὶ, which picks up the τε here.

καὶ τὰ μακρὰ τείχη συνέπεισε καθεῖναι: the sense of the verb is to 'carry down' the walls to the sea (as Thucydides expresses regarding Alcibiades' advice to Patrae to do the same (see below), Book 5.52: Πατρέας τε τείχη καθεῖναι ἔπεισεν ἐς θάλασσαν, 'he persuaded the people of Patrae to carry down their walls to the sea') but here Plutarch for clarity adds the expression καὶ προσμίξαντας τῇ θαλάσσῃ τὴν πόλιν. The 'long walls' of Argos would make Plutarch's audience also think of Athens' Long Walls, built in the mid-fifth century BCE to connect Athens to her harbours at Piraeus and Phalerum and so enable the city to withstand a siege by being able to rely on maintaining supply chains due to their maritime dominance. Alcibiades' relationship with Argos has been introduced already (Section 14.3), when he secretly sent messages to the democratic element of the city.

According to Thucydides, Alcibiades helped the democracy at Argos rebuild their walls at a later point, in 416 BCE, after the Spartans had torn the original wall down. Plutarch has compressed the timeline, making Alcibiades directly involved in this event and showcasing his persuasive nature and strategic planning, as well as creating a link with the anecdote about the walls of Patrae which follows.

ἐξάψαι παντάπασι τῆς Ἀθηναίων δυνάμεως: 'to fasten [their city] wholly to the power of the Athenians'. ἐξάπτω + accusative (supplied) + genitive, here used metaphorically. The expression is used in a similar context by Plutarch in his *Life of Themistocles* (19.3) where the protagonist, in directing the building of Athens' Long Walls, τὴν πόλιν ἐξῆψε τοῦ Πειραιῶς καὶ τὴν γῆν τῆς θαλάττης ('fastened the city to the Piraeus and the land to the sea').

15.3

καὶ τέκτονας καὶ λιθουργοὺς ἐκ τῶν Ἀθηνῶν ἐκόμισε: Plutarch again stresses Alcibiades' personal involvement in the process of (re-)building the walls at Argos, another detail not evident in Thucydides' account.

καὶ πᾶσαν ἐνεδείκνυτο προθυμίαν: again the verb splits the adjective and noun.

οὐχ ἧττον ἑαυτῷ κτώμενος ἢ τῇ πόλει: that Alcibiades works for the good of both himself and the city of Athens is perfectly in line with the characterization of him so far.

χάριν καὶ ἰσχύν: a couplet of what Alcibiades gained, which will help his ambitions.

ἔπεισε δὲ καὶ Πατρεῖς ὁμοίως τείχεσι μακροῖς συνάψαι τῇ θαλάσσῃ τὴν πόλιν: note the similarity of expression here with the description of the walls at Argos, with minor variations such as the prefix συν- instead of ἐξ- attached to the verb and the compression of the building of walls into the use of the dative of instrument, τείχεσι μακροῖς. The connection of this anecdote is both thematic as well as grammatical, with καὶ, 'too' and ὁμοίως, 'similarly' reinforcing this. This event is usually dated to 419 BCE, in other words before any of the developments at Argos. Its inclusion here works on a number of levels: it links to the theme of Alcibiades giving advice, specifically about building walls, and so increasing Athenian influence; it creates the sense of Alcibiades planning a network of allies relying on Athens' naval power; by coming after the reference to the

Argive walls, it allows the account of Alcibiades' involvement with Argos to follow straight from the narrative detailing the alliance he forged with the Argives and the Battle of Mantinea, where it has the most impact; and it introduces another anecdote which gives insight into Alcibiades' character, the first for a while after much narration of historical events through Sections 14 and 15.

εἰπόντος δέ τινος τοῖς Πατρεῦσιν: it is not specified at whom Alcibiades' reply is directed, this individual or the people of Patrae. The anecdote is kept vague and is peculiar to Plutarch; its inclusion serves to suggest that Alcibiades was an instrument in an Athenian style of expansion which he was not afraid to speak of and was not ashamed of, being a man fond of winning. It also provides evidence of Alcibiades' ability to cut to the heart of an issue in a pithy manner, as Theophrastus had said (see Section 10.3).

'καταπιοῦνται ὑμᾶς Ἀθηναῖοι': the choice of tense and the inverted word order highlight the inevitability of Athens' swallowing up of Patrae in the speaker's view.

'κατὰ μικρὸν καὶ κατὰ τοὺς πόδας, Λακεδαιμόνιοι δὲ κατὰ τὴν κεφαλὴν καὶ ἀθρόως.': Alcibiades' response is neatly balanced, making use of the verb from the speaker's words for his own. The first half of the reply does not include a denial that Athens' aim over the long-term was one of expansion; he sees the region of Greece as the playground of the two major powers, Athens and Sparta; Alcibiades only notes that with Athens it will be 'little by little and feet first' as opposed to Sparta's swallowing up of Patrae, which Alcibiades suggests she will achieve 'head first and completely'. The repetition of κατὰ + accusative builds up the image. Plutarch adds καὶ ἀθρόως to add to the negative depiction of Spartan expansion. The chiastic arrangement of this reply fits with the contrasting Λακεδαιμόνιοι δὲ to give Alcibiades' retort additional force.

15.4

οὐ μὴν ἀλλά: introducing a strong contrast, with the idea here of 'not only that but . . .' as Plutarch is to add that Alcibiades was not content with advising two allies to become dependent on Athenian naval power by building city walls, for he also advised the Athenians themselves to plan strategically and pay more attention to a ground force.

καὶ τῆς γῆς . . . ἀντέχεσθαι: genitive singular after the verb ἀντέχεσθαι which here means 'to attach oneself'. καὶ, 'even', at the start of the sentence stress Alcibiades' point that traditionally Athens was a sea power and not a land one.

καὶ τὸν ἐν Ἀγραύλου προβαλλόμενον ἀεὶ τοῖς ἐφήβοις ὅρκον ἔργῳ βεβαιοῦν: explanatory (exegetic) καὶ, 'that is'. τὸν . . . ὅρκον is the object of βεβαιοῦν with everything sandwiched between being dependent on the noun. ἐν Ἀγραύλου is elliptical (an element is missing) and a word such as τό ἱερόν or τό τέμενος, 'precinct' or 'sanctuary' (in the dative after ἐν), must be supplied with the possessive genitive Ἀγραύλου. Agraulus was the daughter of Cecrops, a mythical founder of Athens; her sanctuary was in central Athens near the Acropolis and she was the first goddess called on to witness the oath. It is thought that the oath dates back to the archaic period, predating this version provided by Plutarch and the version found in an inscription from the fourth century BC which is referred to below.

τοῖς ἐφήβοις: dative of agent. Plutarch often uses this where authors from the Classical period might prefer ὑπό + genitive. Ephebes were Athenians usually aged 18 who, on enrolling for the training to become soldiers, swore an oath of commitment to Athens' protection and betterment. Completion of this training was required for Athenian citizenship.

ἔργῳ: the contrast between λόγος and ἔργον, 'word and deed', is a common theme in ancient literature. Compare Alcibiades' accusations against the Spartan embassy in Section 14.9.

ὀμνύουσι γὰρ ὅροις χρήσασθαι τῆς Ἀττικῆς πυροῖς, κριθαῖς, ἀμπέλοις, ἐλαίαις: χράομαι here 'I treat' or 'I regard'. The areas where these plants grew represented most of the known world at this time. This interpretation of the oath by Plutarch may not be correct, since an inscription from the fourth century BCE of the oath suggests that 'boundaries' may in fact be something else they are to have consideration for, alongside the various crops and trees named, and are not in apposition to them. Plutarch's view, whether correct or not, explains Alcibiades' reminding the Athenians of the importance of the land and urging them to act upon this oath.

οἰκείαν ποιεῖσθαι διδασκόμενοι τὴν ἥμερον καὶ καρποφόρον: 'being taught to regard [land] which is arable and fruit-producing their own'. οἰκείαν agrees with the couplet τὴν ἥμερον καὶ καρποφόρον, all of which is dependent on understanding τὴν γῆν; Alcibiades is indicating that Athens should only let topography restrict them, not ambition. Alcibiades' own ambition is remarked on a number of times throughout the *Life*.

Section 16

16.1

ἐν δὲ τοιούτοις πολιτεύμασι . . . τοῖς τρόποις ὑπηρετεῖν: the first two sections denote a number of Alcibiades' traits, culminating in the opinions of him held by the notable citizens and common people alike.

πολιτεύμασι καὶ λόγοις καὶ φρονήματι καὶ δεινότητι: two couplets referring to Alcibiades' positive political qualities: the first couplet, with both nouns in the plural to make their connection explicit, refers to his statesmanship and oratorical skill while the second couplet, composed of abstract nouns in the singular, refers to his determination and cleverness in politics.

πολλὴν αὖ πάλιν τὴν τρυφὴν τῆς διαίτης: this object, the first of a list of Alcibiades' negative qualities, and the rest of the nouns in the accusative throughout 16.1, are objects of the participle ὁρῶντες in 16.2, showing how the notable men felt towards Alcibiades based on their observing his behaviour and actions listed here. Alcibiades' love of luxury has been noted before with an anecdote detailing Alcibiades cutting off the tail of his very expensive dog (9.1).

καὶ περὶ πότους καὶ ἔρωτας ὑβρίσματα: this has also been cited previously: an anecdote in Section 4.5 refers to both vices, when Alcibiades plays a drunken trick on his lover Anytus; his sexual appetite led to his wife Hipparete wishing to leave him (Section 8.3). περὶ + accusative here means 'in the case of'.

θηλύτητας ἐσθήτων ἁλουργῶν ἑλκομένων δι᾽ ἀγορᾶς: Alcibiades' habit of dragging his cloak, highlighting its length, has been referred to in Section 1.4 but here two further details are added: the 'effeminacy' (θηλύτης) of his clothing and its colour, 'purple', making it expensive and serving to further the depiction of Alcibiades as extravagant and a show-off. The adjective ἁλουργός literally means 'worked from the sea', referring to the extraction of purple dye from sea snails.

καὶ πολυτέλειαν ὑπερήφανον: this is particularly negative; though ὑπερήφανος can occasionally be used positively, it usually means 'arrogant' or 'excessive', reinforced by the prefix ὑπερ-, which often has connotations of being over and above what is normal or required.

ἐκτομάς τε καταστρωμάτων ... ἐγκαθεύδοι: this refers to Alcibiades having a hole cut in the ships' decks and his bedding then spread over this, tied up on cords, effectively creating a hammock. The comparative adverb μαλακώτερον clearly links back to Alcibiades' effeminacy of clothing noted above.

κειρίαις, ἀλλὰ μὴ σανίσι, τῶν στρωμάτων ἐπιβαλλομένων: a difficult phrase reliant on the genitive absolute: 'with the bedding lying upon cords, and not the planks of the ships', since the hard boards of a trireme deck would not lead to a soft sleep. The contrast between this novel arrangement and the expected circumstance is highlighted by ἀλλὰ μὴ.

ἀσπίδος τε διαχρύσου ποίησιν οὐδὲν ἐπίσημον τῶν πατρίων ἔχουσαν, ἀλλ᾽ Ἔρωτα κεραυνοφόρον: this 'production of a golden shield' is another instance of Alcibiades' extravagance in itself but the detail goes further: the shield 'bears no ancestral badge' (like a coat of arms), yet has on it 'a picture of Eros wielding a thunderbolt'. This ties to Alcibiades' connection to love (ἔρωτας) but shows him going too far – it is Zeus, the king of the gods, who should carry the thunderbolt, not the god of sexual love. Only a few important families had their own coat of arms but Alcibiades has to be different again, adding his own twist.

16.2

ἅπερ ὁρῶντες: the text is not secure at this point but the meaning seems to be clear: 'witnessing these things'.

οἱ μὲν ἔνδοξοι: the view of the 'notables' is contrasted here with that of the common people. Plutarch varies the presentation of these opposing opinions: the notable Athenians are the subjects expressing their views whereas the views of the common people, who are in the genitive, are given through two quotations from a play by Aristophanes.

μετὰ τοῦ βδελύττεσθαι καὶ δυσχεραίνειν: two articular infinitives in the genitive after μετὰ, meaning 'along with'. This allows three feelings of the notable Athenians to be presented in total, their fear and their 'loathing and disgust', emphasized here through the use of two unusual, forceful verbs.

ἐφοβοῦντο τὴν ὀλιγωρίαν αὐτοῦ καὶ παρανομίαν: two aspects of Alcibiades' character pinpointed as what the notable citizens feared.

οὐ κακῶς ἐξηγούμενος ὁ Ἀριστοφάνης ταῦτ᾽ εἴρηκε: 'interpreting it spot on, Aristophanes said this'. οὐ κακῶς is an example of litotes, so here 'not badly' to mean 'very well'. Aristophanes' plays are the only surviving complete examples of fifth-century Old Comedy. He satirized politicians in his plays and targeted those becoming too powerful, especially demagogues. Alcibiades features in a number of his plays through the 420s–410s, almost exclusively negatively.

ποθεῖ μέν, ἐχθαίρει δέ, βούλεται δ᾽ ἔχειν: '[the common people] love him, hate him, but want to have him'. This quotation is from line 1425 of Aristophanes' *Frogs*, which won first prize in 405 BCE as Athens, a year after Alcibiades was sent into exile. This quotation comes from a scene where Aeschylus and Euripides compete to escape the Underworld by giving the best advice to Athens, who is losing in the war against Sparta. This line is what the judge Dionysus says Athens thinks of Alcibiades.

ἔτι δὲ μᾶλλον τῇ ὑπονοίᾳ πιέζων: 'and adding more weight to his view with the metaphor'. ὑπόνοια can mean 'guess' or 'insinuation', where the meaning of what is being said is hidden or not immediately clear.

μάλιστα μὲν λέοντα … ὑπηρετεῖν: 'it is best not to rear a lion in a city, but if one does, it is best to humour its ways', *Frogs* lines 1431–1432, Aeschylus' view on Alcibiades. The reference to Alcibiades as a lion picks up on the anecdote included early in the *Life* (Section 2.1) where Alcibiades said he bit like a lion. Euripides' reply, which just precedes Aeschylus', says that he hates a man who slowly helps his city but quickly harms her and seeks personal gain over communal gain.

16.3

ἐπιδόσεις γὰρ καὶ χορηγίαι καὶ φιλοτιμήματα πρὸς τὴν πόλιν: a list of three of Alcibiades' financial contributions to the city of Athens. An Athenian resident had to perform certain civic duties, including helping finance undertakings such as building projects and military campaigns, paying for the chorus for plays competing in the dramatic festivals and hosting public dinners. On ἐπιδόσεις see the note on μετὰ χρημάτων ἐπιδόσεως in Section 10.1 – Alcibiades' entry into public life had been on hearing such an occasion of contributions taking place.

ὑπερβολὴν μὴ ἀπολείποντα: the word ὑπερβολή contains the idea of 'throwing beyond', something that is over and above, hence 'extravagance'. 'Overreach' and 'overshoot' express this original meaning.

καὶ δόξα προγόνων καὶ λόγου δύναμις καὶ σώματος εὐπρέπεια καὶ ῥώμη μετ᾽ ἐμπειρίας τῶν πολεμικῶν καὶ ἀλκῆς: this list of positive qualities is presented with variation of expression, referring to qualities previously noted or which will be factors in the events to follow.

πάντα τἀλλα: the object of συγχωρεῖν and φέρειν; τἀλλα is crasis for τὰ ἄλλα.

συγχωρεῖν ἐποίει καὶ φέρειν μετρίως τοὺς Ἀθηναίους: '[these attributes] made the Athenians allow and tolerably endure'. The Athenians are left to the very end of this clause so Alcibiades' qualities are the focus, reflecting his influence over them; this must refer to the common people, not all Athenians. A couplet of verbs in the infinitive dependent on ἐποίει, the subject of which is the long list of attributes. Each one is treated separately, so the verb remains in the singular.

τὰ πρᾳότατα τῶν ὀνομάτων τοῖς ἁμαρτήμασι τιθεμένους: Plutarch has previously indicated his own dislike for people not calling a spade a spade when discussing the view of some men towards Hyperbolus' attitude in Section 13.3 and as such is perhaps levelling criticism at Athens here. The present participle τιθεμένους is best translated as a relative clause, 'who assigned . . . to', agreeing with τοὺς Ἀθηναίους. Three examples of his faults follow in Section 16.4.

παιδιὰς καὶ φιλοτιμίας: a couplet of the attributes of Alcibiades which the common people of Athens used as excuses for his behaviour, 'childishness and ambition'. Both nouns are in the genitive depending on the unexpressed τὰ ὀνόματα. His youthfulness was highlighted in Section 13.1 while his ambition is a constant theme.

16.4

This section is clear in meaning but its grammar is elliptical. The three anecdotes are each introduced by a καὶ and all are after τὸ. The challenge comes in working out the uses of the participles, since there are several in the masculine accusative singular form; some agree with Alcibiades, the subject of each anecdote, and some with the object of the anecdote, be it Agatharcus or Taureas.

οἷον ἦν: 'there was for instance', an adverbial use of οἷος.

καὶ: the first of three uses of καὶ to introduce each instance of a fault of Alcibiades' which the Athenian people found excuses for. These three anecdotes are all recorded, in the same order, in pseudo-Andocides 4.17-23, with some variations in detail, and the first two are mentioned in reverse order in Demosthenes 21.147 (*Against Meidias*).

τὸ: 'the fact that'; for the rest of Section 16.4, Alcibiades is the (unexpressed) subject of the infinitive verbs – supply αὐτόν (in the accusative case after τὸ).

Ἀγάθαρχον εἷρξαι: 'he imprisoned Agatharcus'. εἷρξαι is the aorist infinitive active from ἔργω, introduced by the τὸ which governs this and the following two infinitives. Alcibiades apparently held Agatharcus hostage in his house until he finished painting it, sometime in the early 420s. Agatharcus was a noted painter from Samos and Alcibiades wanted his house decorated impressively.

τὸν ζωγράφον: literally 'someone who paints from life'.

εἶτα . . . ἀφεῖναι: 'then . . . he released'. Another infinitive with Alcibiades as its subject.

δωρησάμενον: the aorist middle participle of δωρέω, in the accusative masculine singular agreeing with Alcibiades, the unexpressed accusative, who let Agatharcus go 'after he had given him a gift'. With Alcibiades' love of extravagance, it is to be assumed that it was probably a large gift. The account in pseudo-Andocides does not mention any gift, while Demosthenes adds that Alcibiades had found him trespassing in his house; Plutarch's version recalls Alcibiades doing wrong then trying to make amends when he hit his future father-in-law Hipponicus for fun only to offer himself for punishment (Section 8) and is an example of the behaviour which gave the Athenians a pretext for excusing his misdemeanours.

καὶ Ταυρέαν ἀντιχορηγοῦντα ῥαπίσαι φιλοτιμούμενον ὑπὲρ τῆς νίκης: the καὶ introduces the second anecdote. ἀντιχορηγοῦντα agrees with Taureas, but φιλοτιμούμενον agrees with Alcibiades. The last participle, as with δωρησάμενον above, ends the anecdote with a positive spin after an act of violence and lawlessness. The notable Athenians were disgusted at such behaviour (Section 16.2: τὴν ὀλιγωρίαν αὐτοῦ καὶ παρανομίαν), but are excused by the common people.

Taureas had questioned the right of a member of the chorus Alcibiades was sponsoring to compete, arguing that the boy was not registered. In trying to settle the dispute before the judges, Alcibiades ends up hitting Taureas and does not get in trouble for it. The anecdote likely dates to the 420s, before Alcibiades becomes a major political figure. From pseudo-Andocides IV we are given additional details, such as the fact that the judges sided with Alcibiades in the dispute because they recognized he was a powerful figure and they did not wish to get on the wrong side of him; they even awarded him the prize at the end. It is not clear how serious the physical attack was: the verb ῥαπίζω means 'I strike' but can represent striking with a club, thrashing or even just slapping someone's face.

καὶ τὸ Μηλίαν γυναῖκα ἐκ τῶν αἰχμαλώτων ἐξελόμενον καὶ συνόντα: for the third example of Alcibiades' conduct, Plutarch starts with καὶ again and reintroduces τὸ, making its form parallel to the first anecdote. The two participles agree with the unexpressed Alcibiades. ἐξελόμενον is the aorist infinitive middle from ἐξαιρέω, here 'I choose for myself'. σύνειμι has both the meaning of 'I live with' and 'I have sexual intercourse with', the latter of which, in light of the following statement, may be what is meant here.

θρέψαι παιδάριον ἐξ αὐτῆς: 'he brought up a child she had with him'. This is the last infinitive in the list of anecdotes, introduced by its own τὸ. Θρέψαι is the aorist infinitive active from τρέφω. Alcibiades is accused of being the main advocate for the enslavement of the women and children (pseudo-Andocides 4.22); that he should gain personally from such a measure is not surprising in the case of Alcibiades.

In all three anecdotes the objects of Alcibiades' wrongdoing – Agatharcus, Taureas and the Melian woman – each come at the very start of their anecdote, but this anecdote diverges from the pattern at the end by not ending with a participle lessening the negativity of Alcibiades' action. This incident is related positively, only to be undercut subsequently by Plutarch referring to the context, which makes Alcibiades seem anything but philanthropic. The presentation of these anecdotes is devised to show how difficult it was (and is) to formulate an opinion of the man.

16.5

καὶ γὰρ τοῦτο φιλάνθρωπον ἐκάλουν: 'for they even called this act philanthropic'. The subject is 'the Athenians', referring back to the common people who excused his behaviour at the end, last mentioned at the end of Section 16.3. Alcibiades acting in a kind way to others is considered unlikely by Plutarch, who stated in Section 5 that he did help one man once, highlighting the rarity of the event, especially by also noting that even then Alcibiades had a personal grudge with the tax-collectors against whom he helped this man. This sentence starts the shift away from the positivity of the anecdote.

πλὴν ὅτι: 'except that', introducing a strong contrast to what has just been stated.

τοὺς Μηλίους: accusative in the accusative + infinitive construction which follows τὴν πλείστην αἰτίαν ἔσχε below. The Melians, on an island in the Aegean Sea south of Athens and remaining neutral in the Peloponnesian War, had refused to surrender to the Athenians when invaded in 416 BCE. The famous Melian Dialogue

(Thucydides 5. 84–116) has the Athenians urge the Melians to be practical and submit in the face of a larger enemy and foe. The refusal led to a siege and Melos fell some months later. The adult males were put to death while the women and children were sold into slavery.

ἡβηδὸν ἀποσφαγῆναι: 'were slaughtered from the youth upwards'. ἡβηδὸν is an adverb from ἥβη, 'youth'. ἀποσφαγῆναι is the aorist infinitive passive from ἀποσφάζω, part of the accusative + infinitive construction after τὴν πλείστην αἰτίαν ἔσχε.

τὴν πλείστην αἰτίαν ἔσχε: Alcibiades here is singled out as particularly blameworthy for the fate of the Melian men, the superlative of πολύς an exaggeration finishing off the anecdote on an extreme note. The details of who decided on this course of action are unknown, with Thucydides' account merely stating that all the captured grown men were put to death.

τῷ ψηφίσματι συνειπών: 'after speaking in support of the decree'. συνειπών is the aorist participle active from συναγορεύω, 'I advocate', the future and aorist of the verb supplied by forms of συνερερῶ. In pseudo-Andocides 4.22 Alcibiades is accused of being the main advocate for the enslavement of the women and children, as noted above, but Plutarch is clearly pinpointing the decree which led to the death of the males. Plutarch does not agree with the common people's tendency to play down the significance of Alcibiades' wrongdoings, a theme continued in the three anecdotes which follow. These serve as a transitional prelude to the narrative detailing his first setback, the Sicilian Expedition.

Ἀριστοφῶντος δὲ Νεμέαν γράψαντος ἐν ταῖς ἀγκάλαις αὑτῆς καθήμενον Ἀλκιβιάδην ἔχουσαν: read in the order of Ἀριστοφῶντος γράψαντος δὲ Νεμέαν καθήμενον, ἔχουσαν Ἀλκιβιάδην ἐν ταῖς ἀγκάλαις αὑτῆς. This next anecdote, introduced by a genitive absolute, again starts with the name of the person other than Alcibiades involved in the incident. On this occasion, however, Alcibiades is not the subject, but rather the Athenians, who had been the subject of ἐκάλουν in Section 16.4, as Plutarch returns to his theme of how others perceived him and his actions.

Nemea was the location of one of the four meetings making up the Panhellenic (all-Greece) Games, the others being Olympia, Isthmia and Delphi (which hosted the Pythian Games). Alcibiades' victory in the Olympic Games had already been recorded by Plutarch (Section 12). The anecdote here is also referenced in Athenaeus' *Deipnosophistae*. The commissioning of this painting by Aristophon (or Aglaophon, according to Athenaeus), depicting a personified Nemea sat down and cradling Alcibiades in her arms, certainly seems a rather arrogant act. Athenaeus adds that Alcibiades had another painting of himself, in which personifications of the Olympian and Pythian festivals were crowning him. Plutarch omits this detail, though it would make Alcibiades appear even more disrespectful. We cannot know why, but his inclusion of the Nemean painting perhaps connects Nemea, Alcibiades and lions – Hercules killed the Nemean lion for his first Labour and Alcibiades' association with lions has been established already in the *Life* (Sections 2 and 16.1).

ἐθεῶντο καὶ συνέτρεχον χαίροντες: the Athenian common people are the subject here, continuing their take on Alcibiades with regard to the three anecdotes related in Section 16.4.

οἱ δὲ πρεσβύτεροι: on this occasion Plutarch refers to the opinion of the 'older citizens', concerned with Alcibiades' reckless and lawless attitude. Broadly speaking we are probably meant to identify this group of citizens with the οἱ ἔνδοξοι from Section 16.2; here their views contrast with the common people, but on this occasion the two views are presented in relation to the same incident, Aristophon's painting.

καὶ τούτοις ἐδυσχέραινον: 'were disgusted at this too'. The same verb was used when Plutarch first gave the notable Athenians' opinion on Alcibiades' behaviour in Section 16.1 and the καὶ here reminds the audience of those anecdotes, pointing out that this was just one more in a series of incidents which made Alcibiades seem too self-important.

ὡς τυραννικοῖς καὶ παρανόμοις: the couplet neatly sums up the fears about Alcibiades, that he acted like a tyrant and with no regard for the law. Both these exact aspects of his character were said to have stirred up hatred for Alcibiades among the notable Athenians in Section 16.2 (παρανομίαν ... τυραννικὰ).

ἐδόκει: after dividing up the views of either the common people or the notable people for the other anecdotes, here Plutarch keeps the reaction to the saying entirely vague.

καὶ Ἀρχέστρατος οὐκ ἀπὸ τρόπου λέγειν ὡς: 'also that Archestratus did not speak absurdly when he said that'. Take ἀπὸ τρόπου λέγειν as a phrase. Elsewhere (*Life of Lysander* 19) Plutarch says that Theophrastus recorded this saying from Archestratus.

ἡ Ἑλλὰς οὐκ ἂν ἤνεγκε δύο Ἀλκιβιάδας: this comment, neatly summing up the enigmatic nature of Alcibiades, points both to the fact that he was unique in character and that, perhaps fortunately, there was only one of him.

Vocabulary

While there is no Defined Vocabulary List for A Level, words in the OCR Defined Vocabulary List for AS are marked with * so that students can quickly see the vocabulary with which they should be particularly familiar.

Ἀγάθαρχος, -ου, ὁ — Agatharcus (painter)
*ἀγαθός, -ή, -όν — good
ἀγκάλη, -ης, ἡ — arm
*ἀγνοέω — be unaware
ἀγνωμονέω — act without feeling
*ἀγορά, -ᾶς, ἡ — market-place
Ἀγραύλου — of Agraulus
*ἀγών, -ῶνος, ὁ — struggle, contest, trial
*ἀδικέω — wrong, injure (someone)
ἄδοξος, -ον — disreputable
ἀδύνατος, -ον — incapable
*ἀεί — always
ἀείδω, fut. ἀείσομαι — sing
*Ἀθῆναι, -ῶν, αἱ — Athens
*Ἀθηναῖοι, -ων, οἱ — Athenians
ἀθρόος, -α, -ον — all at once
*αἰσθάνομαι — perceive, notice
αἰτία, -ας, ἡ — cause, charge, blame
αἰχμάλωτος, -ον — prisoner of war, captive
*ἀκούω — hear, listen, be spoken of/ about
ἁλίσκομαι — be captured
Ἀλκιβιάδης, -ου, ὁ — Alcibiades (Greek statesman)
ἀλκή, -ῆς, ἡ — might, strength
*ἀλλά — but
ἀλλόκοτος, -ον — monstrous, of unusual form
*ἄλλος, -η, -ο — other, another
ἁλουργής, -ές — purple-dyed
*ἅμα — at the same time, together with
ἁμάρτημα, -ατος, τό — fault, failure
ἄμπελος, -ου, ὁ — vine
*ἄν — would, (indefinite) could
ἀναισχυντία, -ας, ἡ — shamelessness

ἀναλαμβάνω — take up again, resume, collect oneself
ἀνάξιος, -α, -ον — unworthy, undeserving
ἀναπείθω — persuade, induce, lead on
ἀνδραγαθία, -ας, ἡ — bravery
*ἀνδρεία, -ας, ἡ — courage, manliness
*ἀνήρ, ἀνδρός, ὁ — man, husband
*ἄνθρωπος, -ου, ὁ — man
ἀνιάω — feel distress, grieve
ἀνίστημι — stand up
ἀνοίγνυμι — open
ἀντέχομαι + gen. — hold on
Ἀντίοχος, -ου, ὁ — Antiochus (quail-catcher, later Alcibiades' deputy)
ἀντιτάσσω — set up for battle against
ἀντιχορηγέω — be a rival choregos
*ἄξιος, -ία, -ιον — worthy, deserving
*ἀξιόω — I think fit, demand
ἀξίωμα, -ατος, τό — positions of rank, honour
ἀπαθής, -ές — unaffected
*ἅπᾶς, ἅπᾶσα, ἅπᾶν — all, every
ἀπάτη, -ης, ἡ — deceit
ἄπιστος, -ον — untrustworthy, faithless
*ἀπό + gen. — from
ἀπογράφω — register
ἀποδέχομαι — receive favourably, approve
ἀποδίδωμι — give up, hand over
ἀποκαλέω — label, address
ἀπολαμβάνω, aor. pass. ἀπελήφθην — capture, take away
ἀπολείπω — leave out, omit
ἀπονητί — without fatigue
ἀπόνοια, -ας, ἡ — foolishness

ἀποσιωπάω — stop speaking and fall silent

ἀποστροφή, -ῆς, ἡ — escape

ἀποσφάζω, aor. pass. -εσφάγην — slaughter, cut the throat

Ἀργεῖοι, -ων, οἱ — Argives

Ἄργος, -εος, ὁ — Argos

*ἀργυροῦς, -ᾶ, -οῦν — made of silver

ἀρέσκω + dat. — please

*ἄριστος, -η, -ον — superlative of ἀγαθός

Ἀριστοφάνης, Ἀριστοφάνεος, ὁ — Aristophanes (Greek tragic poet)

Ἀριστοφῶν, Ἀριστοφῶντος, ὁ — Aristophon (painter)

*ἅρμα, -ατος, τό — chariot

*ἄρχομαι — begin

ᾆσμα, -ατος, τό — song

*ἀσπίς, -ίδος, ἡ — shield

ἄτρεπτος, -ον — unmoved

Ἀττική, Ἀττικῆς, ἡ — Attica (region of mainland Greece encompassing Athens)

*αὖ — in turn

*αὖθις — again

*αὐξάνω — increase

αὐτόθεν — at once

αὐτοκράτωρ, -ορος, ὁ — possessing full powers

*αὐτός, -ή, -ό — (emphatic adjective) -self; (pronoun in oblique cases) him, her, it

αὐτοῦ, αὐτῆς, αὐτοῦ — his/her/its, of one's own

ἀφειδής, -ές — unsparing, lavish

ἀφίημι, perf. ἀφῆκα, aor. part. ἀφείς — throw, give up on, release

*ἀφικνέομαι, perf. ἀφῖγμαι, perf. inf. ἀφῖχθαι — come, arrive

*βαίνω, aor. ἔβην — go

*βασιλεύς, -έως, ὁ — king

βδελύσσομαι — feel loathing

βεβαιόω — make secure

βιάζομαι — force, press hard

*βοάω — shout

*βοή, -ᾶς, ἡ — shout

βοιωτοί, -ῶν, οἱ — Boeotians

*βουλεύω — plan, consider

*βουλή, -ῆς, ἡ — Boule, Athenian council

*βούλομαι — want

*γάρ — for

*γένος, -εος/-ους, τό — race, family, birth, type

*γῆ, γῆς, ἡ — land

*γίγνομαι — become, happen, come to be

*γνώμη, -ης, ἡ — judgement, wish

γνώριμος, -ον — distinguished, well-known

*γράφω, perf. pass. γέγραμμαι — write, paint (16.4; 5)

*γυνή, γυναικός, ἡ — woman

*δέ — but, and

*δεῖ + acc. — it is necessary

δείδω, perf. inf. δεδιέναι — fear

*δεινός, -ή, -όν — skilled, clever, fearful, terrible, strange

δεινότης, -ητος, ἡ — cleverness

*δεύτερος, -α, -ον, — second

δέω — lack

δῆλος — clear, certain

δημαγωγός, -οῦ, ὁ — popular leader, demagogue

δημοκρατία, -ας, ἡ — democracy

*δῆμος, -ου, ὁ — people, community

δημόσιος, -η, -ον — public

*διά + gen. — through

διαβάλλω — slander

διαβολή, -ῆς, ἡ — false accusation, slander

δίαιτα, -ας, ἡ — way of life, diet

διαλέγομαι — discuss, have a conversation

διαλείπω — leave an interval

διαπράσσω — bring about, accomplish

διαπρεπής, -ές — magnificient

διασκοπέω — express in a different way, proceed with caution

διατριβή, -ῆς, ἡ — material for jokes, amusement

διαφεύγω — escape

διάχρυσος, -ον — golden

*διδάσκω — teach, train

*δίδωμι, aor. ἔδωκα — give

διίστημι — divide, set at variance

δικάζομαι — be a plaintiff, take to court

*δίκαιος, -α, -ον — just, fair

*δίκη, -ης, ἡ — trial, lawsuit

διό — for which reason

Διομήδης, -ου, ὁ — Diomedes (cheated out of a chariot)

*δοκέω — be reputed, seem (+ dat – seem good to)

*δόλος, -ου, ὁ — trickery
*δόξα, -ης, ἡ — reputation
*δύναμαι — be able
*δύναμις, -εως, ἡ — power
*δυνατός, -ή, -όν — powerful, able, capable
*δύο — two
δυσχεραίνω — feel disgust
δωρέω — give a present

*ἐάν / ἤν — if
*ἑαυτόν, -ήν, -ό — oneself
ἐάω χαίρειν — dismiss from one's mind
ἐγκαθεύδω — sleep
ἔγκειμαι — press upon, act violently towards
*ἐθέλω — be willing
*εἰ — if
εἰκώς, εἰκυῖα, εἰκός — reasonable
*εἰμί — be
εἵνεκα + gen. (=ἕνεκα) — for, for the sake of
*εἰρήνη, -ης, ἡ — peace
*εἰς + acc. — into
*εἷς, μία, ἕν — one
εἰσέρχομαι — enter
εἶτα — then
*ἐκ + gen — out of, from
ἐκβιάζω — force out
ἐκβοάω — shout out
*ἐκεῖνος, ἐκείνη, ἐκεῖνο — that, he, she, it, they
ἐκκλησιάζω — hold an assembly
ἐκπίπτω — fail
ἔκπληξις, -εως, ἡ — confusion, dismay
ἐκτομάζω — cut out
ἐκτραχύνω — make angry, embitter
ἐκτρέφω — rear, raise
ἐκφέρω, aor. mid. ἐξηνεγκάμην — bring out
ἐλαία, -ας, ἡ — olive-tree
ἐλαττόω — (passive) be inferior
*ἐλαύνω — drive out, banish
*ἕλκω — drag, (middle) trail behind
*Ἑλλάς, -άδος, ἡ — Greece
*Ἕλληνες, Ἑλλήνων, οἱ — the Greeks
ἐλπίς, -ίδος, ἡ — hope
ἐμπειρία, -ας, ἡ — experience
ἐμπίπτω — fall in
*ἐν + dat — in, on, among
ἐνδείκνυμι — display, exhibit
ἐνδίδωμι — cause, excite

ἔνδοξος, -ον — held in high regard
*ἔνιοι, -αι, -α — some
ἐντευκτικός, -ή, -όν — affable
ἐντυγχάνω — obtain an audience, appeal
ἐξαιρέω, aor. ἐξεῖλον — capture, pick out
ἐξάπτω — fasten
ἐξελαύνω — drive out, exile
ἐξηγέομαι — interpret
ἐπαγανακτέω — be aggrieved, be upset, be indignant
ἐπαινέω — praise
*ἐπεί — when, since
ἐπέρχομαι — come up
*ἐπί + acc — to, onto, at
*ἐπί + dat — on condition of
ἐπιβάλλω — throw upon
ἐπιδίδωμι — make a contribution
ἐπίδοσις, -εως, ἡ — contribution to the state
ἐπιεικής, -ές — suitable, fitting, reasonable
ἐπιθυμέω — desire, wish
*ἐπιλανθάνομαι + gen — forget
ἐπίσημον, -ου, τό — distinguishing badge
ἐπιτίθημι, aor. mid. ἐπεθέμην — (middle) set about, apply oneself to
ἐπιφανής, -ές — manifest, evident, conspicuous
ἐπιφέρω — carry out, bring on
*ἑπτά — seven
Ἐρασίστρατος, -ου, ὁ — Erasistratus (father of Phaeax)
*ἔργον, -ου, τό — deed, matter
ἔργω, aor. inf. εἶρξαι — shut in
ἔρομαι, aor. inf. ἐρέσθαι — ask
ἔρως, -ωτος, ὁ — sexual passion
Ἔρως-ωτος, ὁ — Eros (son of Venus, goddess of love)
*ἐρωτάω — ask (a question)
ἐσθής, -ῆτος, ἡ — clothing
ἑστιάω — entertain, feast
ἑταιρία, -ας, ἡ — political support, friendship
*ἕτερος, -α, -ον — other
*ἔτι — still, yet
εὐήθεια, -είας, ἡ — naivety, simplicity
*εὐθύς — at once, immediately
Εὔπολις, Εὐπόλιδος, ὁ — Eupolis (Greek comic poet)
εὐπορέω — find means, be able
εὐπρέπεια, -ας, ἡ — attractiveness, comeliness

Εὐριπίδης, -ου, ὁ — Euripides (Greek tragic poet)

*εὑρίσκω, aor. εὗρον — find, invent

εὐτολμία, -ας, ἡ — courage, boldness

Ἐφέσιοι, -ων, οἱ — Ephesians

ἔφηβος, -ου, ὁ — ephebe (18-year old soldier recruit)

ἐχθαίρω — hate

*ἔχω — have, hold

ζεῦγος, -εος, τό — team of horses, chariot

Ζεύς, Διός, ὁ — Zeus

*ζητέω — I seek

ζωγράφος, -ου, ὁ — painter

*ἤ — than, or

ἡβηδόν — from the youth upwards

*ἤδη — already, (by) now

ἡδονή, -ῆς, ἡ — pleasure

*ἥκω — have come

Ἠλεῖοι, -ων, οἱ — people of Elis

*ἡμεῖς, ἡμῶν — we

*ἡμέρα, -ας, ἡ — day

ἥμερος, -ον — cultivated, arable

ἥττων, ἧττον — less

*θάλασσα, -ης, ἡ — sea

*θαυμάζω — admire

*θεάομαι — look at

θέατρον, -ου, τό — theatre

*θεός, -οῦ, ὁ — god

Θεοφράστος, -ου, ὁ — Theophrastus (philosopher after Aristotle)

θεραπεύω — take care of

θηλύτης, -ητος, ἡ — effeminacy

θορυβέω — make a loud noise, cause an uproar

θόρυβος, -ου, ὁ — loud noise, din

Θουκυδίδης, -ου, ὁ — Thucydides (Greek historian)

ἴδιος, -α, -ον — one's own

ἰδιώτης, -ου, ὁ — private citizen, individual

ἱερεῖον, -ου, τό — sacrificial animal

*ἱκανός, -ή, -όν — capable, sufficient

ἱμάτιον, -ου, τό — cloak

*ἵππος, -ου, ὁ — horse

ἱπποτροφία, -ας, ἡ — breeding of horses

Ἰσοκρατής, Ἰσοκράτους, ὁ — Isocrates (Greek orator)

*ἵστημι, aor. ἔστησα, perf. part. ἑστώς — set up, make to stand, stand

ἱστορέω — research, record, inquire into

ἱστορικός, -ή, -όν — precise, exact, scientific

ἰσχύς, -ύος, ἡ — power, might

ἰσχύω — have strength, have influence

*ἴσως — perhaps

καθ᾽ ἡλικίαν — to one's prime of life, to maturity

καθ᾽ ἡμέραν — daily, day-to-day

*καθίζω — sit down

καθίημι, aor. καθῆκα, aor. inf. καθεῖναι — enter for racing (11.1), run down (15.2)

*καί — and, even, also, actually

*καίτοι — and yet

κακοήθεια, -ας, ἡ — malpractice, bad manners

*κακός, -ή, -όν — bad, evil

*καλέω — call

*καλός, -ή, -όν — beautiful, fine, noble

καρπόφορος, -ον — fruit-producing

*κατά + acc. — down, according to, by, against

κατά + gen. — against

καταλύω — destroy, break up

καταπίνω, fut. -πιοῖμαι — swallow up

κατασκευάζω — arrange, establish

κατάστρωμα, -ατος, τό — deck

*κατηγορέω — accuse

κατήφεια, -ας, ἡ — dejection, shame

κειρία, -ας, ἡ — cord

κεραυνοφόρος, -ον — wielding the thunderbolt

*κεφαλή, -ῆς, ἡ — head

*κῆρυξ, -υκος, ὁ — herald

*κίνδυνος, -ου, ὁ — danger

Κλεινίας, Κλεινίου, ὁ — Cleinias (father of Alcibiades)

κλεισιάδες, -ων, αἱ — doors

κολασμός, -οῦ, ὁ — punishment

κολούω — discredit, curtail

*κομίζω — bring

κοσμέω — adorn, embellish, equip

κραδαίνω — agitate

*κρατέω — prevail, get the upper hand

κρατήσασις, -εως, ἡ — advantage, benefit

κραυγή, -ῆς, ἡ — shouting

κριθή, -ῆς, ἡ — barley

κροτέω — applaud

κρύφα — secretly

*κτάομαι, perf. κέκτημαι — obtain, get

κυβερνήτης, -ου, ὁ — helmsman

κύριος, -α, -ον — have power, have authority

*κωλύω — I prevent (someone from doing), hinder

κωμικός, -ή, -όν — comic

*Λακεδαιμόνιοι, -μονίων, οἱ — Spartans

Λακεδαίμων, -ονος, ἡ — Sparta

λαλέω — chatter, prattle on

*λαμβάνω — I take, capture

λαμπρός, -ά, -όν — splendid, brilliant

λαμπρότης, -ητος, ἡ — brilliance

*λανθάνω — escape the notice of

*λέγω, aor. εἶπον, perf. εἴρηκα — say, tell, speak, mention

λέξις, -εως, ἡ — word, phrase

Λέσβιοι, -ων, οἱ — people of Lesbos

λέων, -οντος, ὁ — lion

λιθουργός, -οῦ, ὁ — stone-mason

*λόγος — speech, argument, story, word

*λύω — release, set free

*μακρός, -ά, -όν — long

μαλακός -ή, -όν — soft

*μάλιστα — especially, very much

*μᾶλλον — more

Μαντίνεια, -ας, ἡ — Mantinea

Μαντινεῖς, -έων, οἱ — Mantineans

μαρτυρέω — bear witness, give evidence

*μάχη, -ης, ἡ — fight, battle

μέγα φρονέω — be high-minded, be arrogant

*μέγας, μεγάλη, μέγα — great, big

μεθίστημι — make move

Μειδίας, Μειδίου, ὁ — Meidias

μειράκιον, -ου, τό — young adult, lad

*μέλλω + infinitive — be about to

*... μέν ... δέ — on the one hand ... on the other ... [marks a contrast]

*μέντοι — however, certainly

*μετά + acc — after

*μετά + gen — with

μεταβολή, -ῆς, ἡ — reversal, change of heart

μεταμέλομαι — repent, regret, change one's mind

μεταξύ — in the midst; (here: + part) in the middle of

μετρίος, -α, -ον — moderate

*μή (and compounds) — not (see under οὐ)

Μήλιος, -α, -ον — from Melos (an island in the Aegean sea)

μήν — indeed, truly

*μικρός, -ά, -όν — little, small

μιμνήσκω, perf. mid/pass μέμνημαι — (+ gen) make mention of

μῖσος, -εος, τό — hatred

*μόνον — only

*μόνος, -η, -ον — alone, only

Νεμέα, -ας, ἡ — Nemea (one site of Panhellenic Games)

*νικάω — conquer, win

*νίκη, -ης, ἡ — victory

Νικηράτος, -ου, ὁ — Niceratus (father of Nicias)

Νικίας, -ου, ὁ — Nicias (Greek general, rival to Alcibiades)

Νικίειος — of Nicias

νοέω — think, understand, apprehend

*οἶδα, perf. part. εἰδώς — know

οἰκείος, -α, -ον — related, kin, one's own

*οἰκία, -ας, ἡ — house

*οἶνος, -ου, ὁ — wine

*οἷος, οἵα, οἷον — such

*ὀλίγος, -η, -ον — small, few, little

ὀλιγωρία, -ας, ἡ — contempt

Ὀλυμπιάδες, -ων, αἱ — the Olympic Games

Ὀλυμπικός, -ή, -όν — Olympic

*ὄμνυμι — swear (an oath)

*ὅμοιος, -α, -ον — similar

ὁμοῦ τι — absolutely, in all

*ὄνομα, -ατος, τό — name, term

ὀνομάζω — name, call

*ὅπλα, -ων, τά — weapons, arms

ὅπως — so that

ὁράω — see

*ὀργή, -ῆς, ἡ — anger

*ὀργίζομαι — grow angry

ὀρέγω + gen — aim at, grasp for

ὅρκια, ὁρκίων, τά — treaty, oaths

*ὅρκος, -ου, ὁ — oath, pledge

ὅρος, -ου, ὁ — boundary

ὄρτυξ, -υγος, ὁ — quail

*ὅς, ἥ, ὅ — who, which (relative pronoun)

*ὅσος, -η, -ον	as much, as big, plural 'as many as'	*περί + acc	around, regarding, concerning
ὅστις, ἥτις, ὅ τι	whoever, whatever, anybody, anything	*περί + gen	about
ὄστρακον, -ου, τό	vote of ostracism, potsherd used for voting	περιβόητος, -ον	famous
		περιγίγνομαι	survive
		Περιθοίδης	from the deme Perithoedae (a region in Athens)
ὀστρακοφορία, -ας, ἡ	casting of votes in an ostracism	Περικλεῆς, Περικλέους, ὁ	Pericles (Athenian politician and general)
*ὅτι	that, because		
*οὐ / οὐκ / οὐχ	not	περιμένω	await, wait for
*οὐδέ	and not, nor, not even	πιέζω	add weight, weigh down on
*οὐδείς, οὐδεμία, οὐδέν	no one, nothing		
		πιθανός, -ή, -όν	persuasive
οὐδέπω	not yet	*πιστεύω + dat	believe, trust
*οὖν	and so, therefore	Πλάτων, -ωνος, ὁ	Plato (Greek comic poet)
*οὔτε ... οὔτε	neither ... nor	*πλεῖστος, -η, -ον	superlative of πολύς
*οὗτος, αὕτη, τοῦτο	this	*πλείων, πλεῖον	comparative of πολύς
*οὕτω	in this way		
		*πλῆθος, -εος, τό	large number, crowd
παιδάριον, -ου, τό	child, little boy	*πλήν	except
παιδιή, -ῆς, ἡ	childishness	πλοῦτος, -ου, ὁ	wealth, riches
*παῖς, παιδός, ὁ	son, child	ποθέω	yearn for, desire
παλίμβολος, -ον	untrustworthy, unstable	*ποιέω	make, do, (middle) consider
*πάλιν	back, again		
Πάνακτον, -ου, τό	Panactum (fortress in Boeotia)	ποίησις, -εως, ἡ	creation, production
		πολεμικός, -ή, -όν	of war, for war
παντάπασι	completely	*πολέμιος, -α, -ον	enemy
πάνυ	altogether, very	*πόλεμος, -ου, ὁ	war
*παρά + acc	in comparison with, contrary to, along	*πόλις, -εως, ἡ	city-state, city
		πολιτεία, -ας, ἡ	state
παραγίγνομαι	arrive, come to support	πολίτευμα, -ατος, τό	statesmanship, governing a city
*παραδίδωμι	provide, offer, hand over		
		*πολίτης, -ου, ὁ	citizen
παραθαρρύνω	encourage, embolden	*πολλάκις	often, many times
παραμυθέομαι	alleviate, mitigate	*πολύς, πολλή, πολύ	much, many
παρανομία, -ας, ἡ	lawlessness	πολυτέλεια, -ας, ἡ	extravagance
παράνομος, -ον	lawless	πομπεῖον, -ου, ὁ	vessel used for ceremonial purposes
παρασκευή, -ῆς, ἡ	preparation		
*πάρειμι	be present	πονηρός, -ά, -όν	worthless
παρέρχομαι, fut. πάρειμι	pass by, go along	*πόρρω	far from
		πότος, -ου, ὁ	drinking-bouts
*παρέχω	provide, cause, produce	πού	somewhere
πάροδος, -ου, ἡ	entry	*πούς, ποδός, ὁ	foot
*πᾶς, πᾶσα, πᾶν	all, every	πρᾶξις, -εως, ἡ	deed, achievement
*πάσχω, perf. πέπονθα	suffer	πρᾶος, -ον	mild
		*πράσσω, perf. πέπραχα	experience, do, manage
*πατήρ, πατρός/ πατέρος, ὁ	father		
		*πρέσβεις, -εων, οἱ	ambassadors
Πατρεῖς, -έων, οἱ	people of Patrae	*πρέσβυς, -εως/-εος, ὁ	old man (comparative 16.5 – elders)
πάτριος, -α, -ον	ancestral		
*πείθω	persuade	πρίαμαι	buy
Πελοπόννησος, -ου, ἡ	the Peloponnese	προβάλλω	set before, lay upon
		*πρόγονοι, -ων, οἱ	ancestors
*πέμπω	send	προεστῶτες, -ων, οἱ	leaders

προέχω — excel, be first

προήκω — have advanced

*προθυμία, -ας, ἡ — eagerness, zeal

πρόξενος, -ου, ὁ — representative

προπηλακίζω — spatter with mud, smear

*πρός + acc — against, towards, for

*πρός + dat — in addition to

προσδοκάω — expect

προσλαμβάνω — gain in addition, take hold of

προσμείγνυμι, aor. -έμειξα — make sth. (acc.) reach sth. (dat.)

προστάττω — give orders, instruct

προστίθημι, aor. προσέθηκα — add, give also

προσφιλής, -ές — beloved, dear

πρότερος, -α, -ον — preceding, previous, earlier

*πρῶτος, -η, -ον — first

πτοέω — terrify, scare

Πύλος, -ου, ὁ — Pylos (on west coast of the Peloponnese, Greece)

*πυνθάνομαι — ascertain, learn, ask

πυρός, -οῦ, ὁ — wheat

*πῶς; — how?

ῥαπίζω — strike

ῥῆμα , -ατος, τό — phrase, saying

*ῥήτωρ, -ορος, ὁ — orator, speaker, politican

ῥώμη, -ης, ἡ — bodily strength

σανίς, -ίδος, ἡ — plank

*σκηνή, -ῆς, ἡ — tent

σκώπτω — mock

Σπαρτιάτης, -ου, ὁ — Spartan

στάσις, -εως, ἡ — (here) faction, political party

στέφω — crown, encircle

στίγμα, -ατος, τό — tattoo-mark

*στρατηγέω — be general

*στρατηγός, -οῦ, ὁ — general, commander

στρῶμα, -ατος, τό — bedding

σύγχυσις, -εως, ἡ — violation

*συγχωρέω — allow

συκοφαντέω — denounce, criticize

συμβιβαστικός, -ή, -όν — leading to reconciliation

*συμβουλεύω + dat — advise

*συμμαχία, -ας, ἡ — alliance

*σύμμαχος, -ου, ὁ — ally

συμπείθω — persuade

συμπράττω — cooperate, join in, help

συνάγω, aor. pass. συνήχθην — bring together, lead together

συνάπτω — join together

σύνειμι — live with, have sexual intercourse with

συνεῖπον + dat — spoke in support of

συνέρχομαι — assemble

σύνεσις, -εως, ἡ — intelligence, wisdom, judgement

συνθηράω — hunt together, join a hunt

συνίστημι — bring about, cause, put together

συνόμνυμι — sweat together, (middle) form an alliance

συντρέχω — run together

Σφακτηρία, -ας, ἡ — Sphacteria (island off the coast of Pylos)

σφάλλω — stumble, trip, fail

*σῶμα, -ατος, τό — body

ταπεινόω — humble

Ταυρέας, Ταυρέου, ὁ — Taureas (a rival choregos whom Alcibiades hits)

*τε — and

*τε ... καί / τε ... τε — both ... and

*τεῖχος, -εος, τό — wall

τέκτων, -ονος, ὁ — carpenter

*τέταρτος, -η, -ον — fourth

*τίθημι — place

*τιμάω — honour

*τις, τι — a

*τίς; τί; — who? what?

Τισίας, Τισίου, ὁ — Teisias (possibly the name of Diomedes)

*τοιοῦτος, -αύτη, -οῦτο — such (a kind)

*τοσοῦτος, -αύτη, -οῦτο — so great, so many

*τότε — at that time, then

*τρεῖς, τριῶν — three

*τρέπω — turn

τρέφω, aor. inf. θρέψαι — rear, raise

*τρέχω, aor. ἔδραμον — run

τριήρης, τριήρεος, ὁ — trireme

*τρίτος, -η, -ον — third

*τρόπος, -ου, ὁ — manner, way

τροφή, -ῆς, ἡ — food

τρυφή, -ῆς, ἡ — luxuriousness

*τυγχάνω + gen — obtain, (+ participle) happen to

τυραννικός, -ή, -όν	despotic, fitting for a tyrant	*φθόνος, -ου, ό	envy, jealousy
*τύχη, -ης, ή	fortune (good or bad), chance	φιλάνθρωπος, -ον	kind, courteous
		φιλήκοος, -ον	fond of (hearing) discussion
ὕβρισμα, -ατος, τό	outrageous act	*φίλος, -ου, ό	friend
ὑγιής, -ές	sound, solid	φιλόσοφος, -ου, ό	philosopher
*ὑμεῖς, ὑμῶν	you (pl)	φιλοτιμέομαι	be ambitious
ὑπάρχω	already exist, be	φιλοτίμημα, -ατος, τό	act of ambition
ὑπείκω	yield, give in		
*ὑπέρ + gen.	on behalf of, in defence of	φιλοτιμία, -ας, ή	ambition, love of honour
ὑπεραγαπάω	excessively love	φοβέομαι	fear
ὑπερβάλλω	surpass, excel	*φόβος, -ου, ό	fear
ὑπερβολή, -ῆς, ή	excess	φρονήματα, -ατων, τά	high purposes, proud design
Ὑπέρβολος, Ὑπερβόλου, ό	Hyperbolus (populist politician, rival to Alcibiades)		
		*χαίρω	rejoice
		χαλεπαίνω	be angry, be outraged
ὑπερήφανος, -ον	arrogant, excessive	*χαλεπός, -ή, -όν	difficult, harsh
ὑπήκοος, -ον	subject, obedient	χαρίζομαι	gratify, indulge, give as a favour
ὑπηρετέω	(here) humour		
*ὑπό + gen	by, from, at the hands of	χάρις, χάριτος, ή	charm, grace, favour
		χίλιοι, -ων, οί	thousand
ὑποδοχή, -ῆς, ή	means for entertaining	Χίος, -ου, ό	Chios
ὑπόνοια, -ας, ή	suspicion, guess, (here) metaphor	χορηγία, -ας, ή	financial support towards public choruses
*ὑστεραία, -ας, ή	next day	*χράομαι + dat	use, treat
		*χρήματα, -άτων, τά	money
Φαίαξ, Φαίακος, ό	Phaeax (Greek politican, rival to Alcibiades)	*χρυσοῦς, -ῆ, -οῦν	made of gold
		ψήφισμα, -ατος, τό	vote, decree
*φαίνομαι	seem, appear		
φάσκω	say, assert	ὠ	(used when addressing someone)
φαῦλος, -η, -ον	worthless		
*φέρω, aor. ἤνεγκα	bear, endure, carry	*ὡς	as, when, that, because, how
*φημί	say		
*φθονέω	feel envy	*ὥσπερ	just as, as if

Homer, *Odyssey*

Introduction and Vocabulary by
Sarah Harden and Alastair Harden

Commentary Notes to Book 1 by
Sarah Harden

Commentary Notes to Book 6 by
Alastair Harden

AS: Book 1: 213–444

A Level: Book 6: 85–331

Introduction

Who was Homer?

Homer is the name traditionally given to the author or composer of both the *Iliad* and the *Odyssey,* but in fact we know very little about the authorship of these poems, and even less about the identity of Homer himself. We have no reliable evidence for the life of Homer, his dates of birth and death, or any evidence that there was such a man or that he composed either of the poems we now know as the *Iliad* and the *Odyssey*. The ancient Greeks likewise knew little about Homer – many cities including Chios, Smyrna and Cyme claimed to be linked with him, but there is no evidence for the truth of this.

It is clear that a single poet composed and crafted each of the extant poems attributed to Homer, but many scholars believe that the *Iliad* and the *Odyssey* were composed by two different poets for a wide range of reasons including linguistic differences between the epics as well as seeming theological and stylistic differences. The differences between these two epics were noted already in antiquity: the scholar Longinus hypothesized that the *Iliad,* with its heroic theme of war, was a product of the master poet's youth while the *Odyssey*, a poem about a middle-aged man returning home from war, was a work from his old age. What we do now know is that the *Odyssey* (and the *Iliad*) are the product of a tradition of oral poetry in Greece (see below for more details on oral poetry), and even if we cannot be sure who composed the final versions which were eventually written down and survive today, the poems are both masterpieces of poetic skill which can be appreciated today even if we do not know who composed them.

The *Odyssey* in context

The date of the *Odyssey*

The dates of the Homeric poems are not entirely secure, but most scholars agree on a date between 725 and 650 BCE, using a mixture of linguistic, historical and religious evidence from the poems themselves. The references to temples, narrative art and the wide expanse of places mentioned by the poet imply a date after 800–750 BCE when the Greek world began to expand after a 'dark age' following the collapse of the Mycenean palace culture, while Homer begins to be mentioned in other poetic texts around 650 BCE, showing that the poems were very well known across the Greek world by that date.

The epic 'genre'

The *Odyssey* (along with the *Iliad*) is an example of epic poetry, a wide-ranging generic classification which will need some explanation in its own right. The word 'epic' derives ultimately from the Greek word *epos*, 'word', and Greek epic poetry has some clear defining characteristics which would have been recognized at once by any ancient Greek audience. The primary feature is that epic poetry is composed in dactylic hexameter, a poetic metre with a set pattern of long and short syllables and six 'feet' or metrical units in each line (see below for detailed discussion of Homeric hexameter). All poems in this metre in early Greece were seen as 'epic', even when the themes of the poems were quite different from each other. In addition to the use of hexameter metre, epic poems tend to be long narratives (the *Iliad* and *Odyssey* are each many thousands of lines long) and their subject matter revolves around the actions of gods and mythical heroes such as Achilles and Odysseus. The *Iliad* tells the story of a short time during the Trojan War, but uses flashbacks and flash-forward techniques to encompass a much wider timescale. The *Odyssey* tells the story of the homecoming from Troy of Odysseus, one of the Greek heroes.

The Greeks would also have seen the works of Hesiod, another early Greek poet from *c.* eighth century BCE, as epic: his extant works are a *Theogony*, or story of how all the gods were born and got their particular responsibilities, and *The Works and Days*, a didactic poem on how to live a morally upright life, farm the land and observe religious customs. Other epic poems, now very fragmentary, exist from what is known as the 'Epic Cycle'; the subject matter of these poems ranges from the Trojan War to the Theban myth of Oedipus and the adventures of the heroes Heracles and Theseus. Ancient critics deemed the Homeric epics to be superior to these now fragmentary poems, but so little of them remains that it is difficult for modern critics to make a firm judgement on this. The fragments we do have serve to show the richness of oral epic tradition in which Homer was composing his work.

Oral poetry

Although we know little of the master poet (whom we shall call Homer) who composed the *Iliad* and *Odyssey* in their final form, we do know that he was part of an ancient tradition of oral poetry in Greece, stretching back hundreds of years. The work of Milman Parry and Albert Lord was the turning point in Homeric studies when scholars began to realize that the Homeric poems were different from modern literature. Parry and Lord used comparative studies of oral poets in Yugoslavia to identify the way oral poems differ from written verse.

That the Homeric epics are in fact orally-derived is clear from the fabric of the poems themselves, which contain all sorts of clues of oral composition: primarily the obvious use (also seen in the Yugoslavian oral tradition) of formulaic (repeated) language to aid the poet in oral composition and performance.

The modern reader of the *Odyssey* is instantly struck by various repetitions in the story: these can be very small, for instance the use of the same adjective, over and over, to describe the same character. So in *Odyssey* book 1, Telemachus is repeatedly called Τηλέμαχος πεπνυμένος 'wise Telemachus' and Athena referred to as Παλλὰς Ἀθήνη 'Pallas Athena' or γλαυκῶπις Ἀθήνη 'flashing-eyed Athena'. These noun + adjective pairings are the smallest example of the 'Homeric formula', a unit of oral poetry which makes it easier for the poet to compose long stretches of poetry at a time, since he has these building blocks ready to slot into a line of verse.

Characters in Homer tend to have a set of two or three familiar 'epithets' or adjectives, which are always used with their name and which usually fall in the same place in the line (due to the need for the syllable lengths to fit with the hexameter metre). Thus the poet, composing on the spot, has a toolkit of phrases to draw upon.

A larger unit again exists, of a whole line which may be repeated at will. These are often lines opening or closing a character's direct speech (see below for direct speech in Homer) or phrases indicating the passage of time. The phrase τὴν δ᾽ αὖ Τηλέμαχος πεπνυμένος ἀντίον ηὔδα 'and so wise Telemachus answered her' is repeated several times in *Odyssey* book 1, and similarly the usual Homeric phrases for the fall of night ('and the sun went down and all the ways grew dark') or the break of dawn ('and dawn came early with her rosy fingers') are repeated so often in both epics that they have become famous in later English and American literature. Such lines allow the poet to structure his composition, remind the listening audience who has been speaking in the poem, and buy the poet a little time to think of what he is going to sing next.

There is a larger unit again, of a whole short scene or series of actions, which may be repeated at the poet's leisure. These scenes tend to be routine actions conducted by the characters such as arming scenes, bathing scenes, the preparation of food or going to bed. This large-scale repetition may seem odd to a modern, reading audience, but in an oral context it forms a vital range of flexible, adaptable units of poetry ready for the oral poet to incorporate into his work.

It is important to note that the repetition of fixed formulae, or units of verse, does not rob Homer of the power to craft original, meaningful and highly effective poetry. Homer was working in an oral tradition where the conditions of learning the craft (memorizing hundreds of lines of traditional verse) and of performance (singing these poems in front of a largely illiterate audience) meant that repetition of this kind was essential for both poet and audience, but it did not stop the skilled poet from re-shaping this traditional material in exciting and creative ways. That Homer did this successfully is clear from the unity of the poems, their subtle treatment of recurring themes, their development of character and plot and the many cross-references between the *Odyssey* and the *Iliad* which show that the poet of the *Odyssey* was aware of the *Iliad* and interested in interacting with it.

From song to text: when and how was the *Odyssey* written down?

The poems as we have them now were finalized and written down at some point in their history. Frustratingly, we do not know exactly when or how this happened.

Many scholars believe that Homer himself may have been a sort of hybrid – an oral poet who became literate and who was able to write down the poems he composed. If we accept the rough dates of 725–650 BCE for the composition of the *Odyssey*, and we also want to argue that Homer himself wrote his poems down, we would be proposing that Homer was one of the very earliest adopters of the new technology of writing. Writing came to Greece from Phoenicia around 800 BCE and we start to see archaeological evidence for writing from about 750 BCE. Some scholars have argued from comparative studies of modern oral poets that oral poets never write, or that writing somehow prevents oral poets from having the capacity for memory needed to successfully memorize and perform long oral poems. However, we must at least allow the possibility that an oral poet, trained in the tradition, who later learnt to write, may well have used the new format to record his work.

Others have proposed that Homer had a scribe who wrote down his poems as he sang, or that a wealthy patron arranged for this to be done for him. The idea of someone else writing down the Homeric poems is not a modern one. Ancient sources ascribe the recording of the Homeric poems to Peisistratus, an Athenian tyrant of the sixth century BCE, who is said to have made a project of writing down these precious poems for posterity. William Allan dismisses this theory on the grounds that it would be impractical for a poet to perform such long pieces at the appropriate pace for a scribe to keep up, and that it fundamentally misunderstands the concept of oral poetry, which is designed to allow the poet to reshape and improve his poems over multiple performances.

It is also possible that the poems were composed by a master poet or poets and handed down orally for some time before being written down. This model raises its own questions, as the language of the epics seems reasonably fixed as pre-650 BCE, which means that poets were memorizing very accurately (and not updating Homer's language to their own dialects), and although we have some ancient sources for a guild of rhapsodes (singers) called the 'Homeridae' who may have been responsible for memorizing and preserving the Homeric poems, we don't know enough about them or how they may have worked to make a conclusion possible.

We may never have a firm answer to the question of when or how the Homeric epics were finally written down, but we know that they were, and that the texts were considered of canonical importance in ancient Greece, forming the backbone of education as well as informing Greek attitudes to the gods, ethics and morality.

What was the performance context of the *Odyssey*?

What would be the occasion, then, for a poem like the *Odyssey* to be performed? We aren't entirely sure of the performance context for poems such as the *Iliad* and *Odyssey*, but we have lots of clues which help to build a picture of how these epics would have been received in their original performance context.

Homer includes within his poem several examples of bards (*aoidoi*) who perform epic poetry. This is helpful at least as an indication of how Homer *wants us* to see his own poetry being performed, even if it is an idealized version of reality. So in book 1 of the *Odyssey* we see Phemius, the bard at Odysseus' house, performing at a banquet of the suitors. Phemius' subject matter is very close to that of the *Odyssey* itself, for he sings of the 'painful homecoming' *lugron noston* of the Greeks from Troy. Its heroic subject matter identifies his song as epic, like the *Odyssey*, and we see his song has a powerful effect on its audience: the rowdy suitors are silenced, and Penelope, Odysseus' long-bereaved wife, is deeply moved. Later in the *Odyssey* we see another court bard, Demodocus, who also sings at the banquets and feasts of his king. Demodocus too has a powerful effect on his audience and is held in high esteem in the court.

Some bards would very likely have been permanently attached to aristocratic families and performed precisely the function that we see Phemius and Demodocus filling in the *Odyssey*. Homer, however, is more likely to have been itinerant, travelling to different courts or communities and performing at public festivals or funeral games, perhaps also at funerals and weddings. Often such occasions would involve poetic contests which were held in much the same way as athletic contests, with prizes for the best poet. Homer's work is silent on its own performance context (i.e. he does not say in the poem where or when it is performed) and its appeal is 'Panhellenic', i.e. it is not coloured by bias for or mention of one aristocratic clan or one city state. It seems from this that Homer was aiming for wider appeal, and perhaps deliberately composed his poem in this way to ensure it would appeal to any Greek audience who heard it.

The *Odyssey* is over ten thousand lines long, and would take days to recite at a festival; it is no coincidence that the poem naturally falls into discrete chunks or stories which could be told separately. Thus *Odyssey* Books 1–4 (often called the 'Telemachy') tell the story of Telemachus' journey to mainland Greece in search of his father, set up the terrible situation with the suitors in Ithaca and establish Penelope's loyalty to her husband. Books 9–12 are another famous self-contained unit: Odysseus' own narrative of all his adventures with monsters, witches and giants on his long voyage home. In this way the poet could offer a focus on different themes by choosing sections of the longer poem to fit with the particular audience or context in which he found himself.

Homer and history

The world depicted in Homer is one of wealthy, aristocratic heroes who rule their local area in a sort of fiefdom from a palace. It is for this reason that many scholars have identified the society depicted in the Homeric poems with the era of the Bronze Age Mycenean palaces in Greece, a society which left behind large palace structures and evidence of aristocratic lifestyles which seem (at least superficially) similar to those depicted in Homer. The Mycenean palaces collapsed in the twelfth century BCE, for reasons which are still unclear, and Greece entered a 'dark age' which lasted until the ninth century BCE; we would thus be hypothesizing that the Homeric poems were composed in a tradition which was preserved through this 'dark age' into the eighth century when the poems took their current form.

What historical facts, if any, is it possible to recover from Homer? The only evidence we have for the Mycenean age is material evidence from archaeological sources, and it is notoriously difficult to match such evidence up with the poetry of Homer as we have it. The famous archaeologist Heinrich Schliemann dug a site in Turkey at a place called Hissarlik which he was convinced was the site of ancient Troy, as well as digging the sites of ancient Mycenae (home of the hero Agamemnon) and Pylos (home of the Iliadic hero Nestor). The Greek sites probably are geographically the same areas Homer refers to as Mycenae and Pylos, as the sites show evidence of continuous occupation from the twelfth century BCE onwards, but whether the heroes Agamemnon and Nestor ever lived there, or existed at all, is a matter of much less certainty.

Hissarlik, the site Schliemann identified as Troy, is even more problematic. It is in roughly the right area of Asia Minor to be a contender for Homer's Troy as described in the poems, but more modern archaeological explorations of the site have not thrown up any firm evidence of a Greek conquest and sacking of the area, so there is no firm archaeological evidence for the Trojan War as described by Homer.

Similarly, the site of Ithaca and its geography have caused problems for scholars for many years. There seems to be no evidence for a palace there, and the poet's description of the island in book 9 does not match the island's real physical location and features. It may therefore be that we are dealing with a fictionalized Ithaca, based loosely on a real Greek place, and certainly not a description from which we can safely draw any detailed historical inferences. This is ultimately unsurprising: the Homeric epics are works of poetic fiction and it is always extremely dangerous to seek historical facts in fictional texts. It is also important to note that, although the Homeric poems may have elements which stretch back to the Mycenean palace age, they are also likely to contain elements of Greek culture and society from the intervening period down to 750 BCE. This is exemplified in some of the objects mentioned in the poems: for instance the armour and weapons of the heroes is made of bronze, implying a Mycenean date, but in book 9 of the *Odyssey* there is mention made of tempering iron, a much later technique unknown to Mycenean Greeks. This microcosmic example makes clear the likelihood that the poems as we have them contain a rich mixture of elements drawn from several hundred years of Greek culture and history, plus probably a good deal of completely fictional elements, and are not simply a reflection of any one age or time.

Homeric language (for linguistic forms used in Homer see below) is a similarly mixed bag. It is an artificial form of Greek, in which words from different eras and dialects are combined into a patois never spoken by a particular Greek community. There are some elements of Mycenean Greek preserved in the Homeric language, as well as a large smattering of Ionic Greek and some Aeolian Greek used to make constructing hexameter verse easier. Although the Greek used in Homer does not reflect one period or geographical area, it would have been understood by its audiences across Greece and is, in this way, Panhellenic.

Xenia and Homeric society

Xenia (ξενία) in the world of Homer is the reciprocal culture of guest/host friendship, and in origin it may represent a culture which was united primarily by ties of language, culture (particularly the practices revolving around washing and eating) and religion. It is the mechanism by which a traveller can, under the protection of Zeus Xenios, be guaranteed a safe reception at the home of another Greek, and violation of xenia provides the *Odyssey* and, ultimately, the *Iliad* with their narrative premises: the entire Trojan War was waged as a result of Paris violating *xenia* in abducting Helen. More specifically, the entire *Odyssey* can be seen as a one-man portrait of the rights and wrongs of xenia. Odysseus' return from Troy is beset with horrifying disaster as he encounters monstrous disrespecters of *xenia* on his voyage home, and in book 6 he finally alights on a place where xenia is upheld; from here, back in civilized society, he begins his narration of those spectacular events which fill books 9–12 of the poem. On the back of Phaeacian xenia, provided with a ship and crew for the purpose, Odysseus then sets sail to his own palace where the conventions of xenia are being trounced by the suitors who neither abide by its conventions as guests in Odysseus' home nor uphold the conventions as surrogate masters there. The culmination of the poem is the wholesale slaughter of the suitors and the reunion of the ruling family with Odysseus' reinstallation.

The practice of xenia is mutually understood by those individuals and peoples who uphold it. It features prominently in book 1, where Telemachus' receiving the disguised Athena (from line 119) establishes the theme within the poem and serves as an exemplary model. Athena, disguised as Mentes, approaches the palace but is not admitted by the suitors, quickly establishing their lack of heed for xenia. Telemachus is angered that a stranger should be left waiting outside, so (unaware that he is addressing a goddess) he takes her hand, relieves her of her spear, and admits the guest with these words:

χαῖρε, ξεῖνε, παρ᾽ ἄμμι φιλήσεαι: αὐτὰρ ἔπειτα
δείπνου πασσάμενος μυθήσεαι ὅττεό σε χρή.

(1.123–124)

'Greetings, stranger: you will be welcomed in our house.
But when you have taken a meal, you will tell us what you need.'

Note the words of welcome that are given to the xenos (addressed here in the vocative, ξεῖνε): he is assured hospitality and invited to dine, and assured also that his needs will be met. This all takes place before 'Mentes' has said anything at all: Telemachus does not even ask his name, but basic hospitality is the standard moral response to a stranger at your door and Telemachus is embarrassed and enraged that the practice of xenia is not upheld under the suitors' occupation of his father's palace.

The standard formula for the treatment of a guest has been studied closely by scholars as there are several instances of xenia in the *Odyssey* and they differ slightly according to context, but the following points are common to most instances and can be considered some basic elements of Homeric xenia:

- A declaration of xenia in the form of a hospitable greeting and welcoming invitation.
- Washing, providing with a seat and eating.
- Participating in some ritual act such as a libation or a prayer.
- When the meal is finished, asking the xenos (in the following order) their name, their father's name, where they came from and what they are doing.
- Exchanging gifts.

Instances of xenia may not always contain all of these elements, but they establish the moral parameters for how a guest should be treated and stretching the flexibility of xenia or inverting its provisions altogether provide a cultural backdrop for some of the defining episodic moments of the *Odyssey*: the episodes of Circe, the Laestrygonians and the Cyclopes can all be analysed in terms of xenia, and as noted above it gives the poem its primary narrative arc, i.e. the homecoming of Odysseus and his vengeance on those who have exploited his household.

Given the centrality of xenia to the *Odyssey*, and particularly to books 1 and 6, it might first be wondered where this pre-eminent practice originated from. Scholars see it as belonging to a pre-literate and pre-monetary Greek world, where exchange of manufactured goods was important among the aristocratic elite as a means of building trust and forging connections, and where letters of introduction (which have been central to the movement of people throughout history and gave rise to the modern passport) did not exist: Odysseus himself is able to partake of xenia as a guest under a false identity with no trouble, so trust is assumed when xenia is employed. Archaeological evidence gives some corroboration to the real practice of xenia: a royal tomb dating from the tenth century BCE excavated at Lefkandi on Euboea contains items from across the Mediterranean including an already-antique piece of Babylonian jewellery, which provide evidence that xenia might have operated within aristocratic echelons at a time when some elements of the Homeric epics were starting to take shape. It seems likely that this cultural practice, like several aspects of Homeric language which were already centuries-old at the time of the poem's composition, reflects a Greece that was already in the distant past during the lifetime of the poet.

The practice of xenia in the *Odyssey* gives some insight into the parameters of Homeric society. It has just been described as an aristocratic practice, which Telemachus as the son of Odysseus is able to use as he travels around elite circles in search of news of his father, but in the character of Eumaeus the swineherd in book 14 the poet seems to use xenia as a clear means to establish good and bad character traits, to build sympathy for the lowly servant and to prepare the audience for the slaughter of the suitors. Eumaeus provides the meat which the suitors so unrestrainedly eat (thus both exploiting xenia and, as we have seen, denying it to others) but when the disguised Odysseus comes to his door he follows the textbook practice of xenia by making a seat for him, offering him food from his herd, and only later asking his identity. It is as a proud member of Odysseus' household that he so diligently welcomes the guest, and his vocal longing for his master's return also reinforces the notion of Odysseus as the ultimate embodiment and enforcer of the correct treatment of strangers, in contrast to the suitors on whom Odysseus will soon take vengeance.

The most notable inversion of xenia is to be found in book 9, in the episode of the Cyclops Polyphemus, which helps explain Odysseus' present gratitude and comfort at the hands of the Phaeacian king Alcinous. His reception by Polyphemus contains several elements which map directly onto the proprieties of xenia and characterize the Cyclopes as an ungodly and monstrous people. (It is interesting to note that the Phaeacians, who embody a selfless xenia and the best aspects of human society, are described at the beginning of book 6 as having once been neighbours of the Cyclopes who left for Scheria after being attacked by them too often.) The first words from

Polyphemus to Odysseus and his men are 'Strangers (ξεῖνοι), who are you?' (9.252), and Odysseus (narrating the episode) tells his Phaeacian listeners that 'my heart broke', instantly recognizing as he did that the rules of xenia would not apply here, that consequently he and his men would not be under the protection of Zeus Xenios, and that they might therefore be in enormous danger. Nevertheless he pushes on: he reminds the Cyclops of the gods' protection for guests, and at lines 267, 268 and 271 he uses different versions of the Greek word ξένια in his explicitly requesting hospitality from the Cyclops. But things go from bad to worse: far from offering his guests a place to sit and a meal, Polyphemus explicitly dismisses the very notion of reverence to the gods, then seizes two of Odysseus' men, smashes their heads against the wall of his cave, and eats them.

In the chronology of the poem's events, Phaeacia represents Odysseus' much longed-for return to the conventions of xenia after having suffered various perversions of it at the hands of the Cyclops, the Laestrygonians, Circe and Calypso. Odysseus' caution in book 6 on landing in Phaeacia (see note to book 6 lines 118 and 119) is born out of his terrible experiences of xenia gone wrong, as he will subsequently tell his hosts, but the moment of his welcome from Nausicaa heralds the beginning of his return to his palace and the bloody triumph of xenia which he will bring to Ithaca.

Characters

Odysseus

The eponymous hero of the poem is announced in its opening lines ('Tell me, Muse, of that many-sided man who wandered for so long after he sacked the sacred town of Troy'), and named in line 21 ('[Poseidon] continued to rage unceasingly against godlike Odysseus'). He is discussed by Athena at line 44, and is never far from the lips of his son Telemachus, but does not make an appearance until the beginning of book 5 where we find him sitting disconsolate on the shore of Ogygia. In the *Iliad* he is a persuasive speaker and commanding presence among the turbulent Greek leaders. He is one of the heroes sent to try to persuade Achilles to return to the battlefield, and is himself a warrior of considerable prestige and ability.

In the *Odyssey*, his characterization is more complex. He relies more on his wits than his strength, and presents some contradictions and flaws. He yearns for his home and family, but stays with Calypso for seven years in a state of quasi-marriage; he deplores the godless hubris of the Cyclopes but his triumph on escaping from Polyphemus leads indirectly to the wholesale destruction of his crew as he boasts to the blind Cyclops that it was Odysseus who blinded him, thereby allowing Polyphemus to invoke the wrath of his father Poseidon. He fails to keep his crew from making disastrous decisions, such as opening the bag of winds given by Aeolus, and slaughtering the cattle of Helios the sun-god. Book 6 sees him as suspicious, battered figuratively by cumulative occurrence and physically by the elements after a bumpy journey from Ogygia, modest, eloquent and cautious. Perhaps the most complex aspects of his character are brought out in Ithaca on his return, where his lengthy and savage revenge on the suitors and on those of his household who served them is described in gruesome detail.

Telemachus

Telemachus, as Odysseus' only son and the heir of his household, is a central figure in the *Odyssey*. His importance is made clear by the fact that the first four books of the poem focus on Telemachus – we do not even meet Odysseus until book 5. Of course, Odysseus' importance is emphasized by his absence from books 1–4, and especially by the state of affairs in Ithaca, the pathos of his family's plight without him, and the impressive stories Telemachus hears about him during these books of the poem. When we meet Telemachus in book 1, he is still basically a child, but he is starting to grow up into manhood and he deeply resents the bad behaviour of the suitors. At this point, however, we are told that he is 'imagining how his noble father might come from somewhere and throw the suitors from the palace': so he is not quite yet at the stage of manhood where he feels confident to try and restore justice himself. In book 1, Athena's visit (in the disguise of Mentes) gives Telemachus the confidence to leave home in search of his father.

Although he may lack confidence and to some extent maturity, Telemachus has all the right instincts for a Greek hero, as is clear from his polite reception of Mentes: unlike the suitors, who are so busy enjoying themselves that they fail to welcome the guest, Telemachus greets Athena at once and makes the correct offer of food and rest before he questions her about her origins and aims.

Telemachus, as one might expect for a young man whose home is overrun by rapacious suitors seeking to marry his mother, has something of a pessimistic streak in book 1. When Athena asks him if Odysseus is his father, he replies that he does not know, commenting that 'no man can be certain of who his father is', and he is convinced that the suitors will consume his wealth and murder him. He begins to show more confidence after just a short conversation with Athena/Mentes: he is commanding in his tone to Penelope when she asks for the bard Phemius to change his song, claiming the authority in the house directly. He is then brave enough to criticize the suitors' behaviour openly and to threaten them with eventual retribution for their actions.

Telemachus learns a lot about his father in books 2–4, and shows himself to be a polite and respectful guest who understands the rules of *xenia*. On his return to Ithaca, he narrowly escapes a murder plot from the suitors and soon meets the disguised Odysseus, whom he eagerly helps to overthrow the suitors.

Penelope

Penelope makes just one appearance in book 1, but her character here is consistent with her behaviour elsewhere in the poem. In book 1, she is drawn downstairs from her chamber by the song of Phemius, Odysseus' court bard. Phemius is singing of the Greeks and their difficult return home from Troy, a subject which is obviously painful for a woman still waiting for her husband to return from this very war. Penelope is careful to maintain a distance from the suitors – she stops at the entrance to the hall and she is accompanied by two slave women. She also covers her face modestly with a veil before speaking. Throughout the poem, Penelope refuses to mix with the suitors or encourage them. For instance, we are told elsewhere that she devised a clever strategy for putting them off, by asking them to wait while she wove a shroud for her father-in-law Laertes. The suitors agree to this, but Penelope gets up every night and unpicks her work so that she does not make any progress on the shroud. This trick works for three years, until a faithless slave-girl betrays her mistress to the suitors.

In this scene in book 1 we see Penelope's genuine grief and love for Odysseus: she asks Phemius to change his song, stating that she cannot bear it and commenting that she bears a greater sadness than any other woman. When Telemachus dismisses her, she goes to her room and weeps for her husband. Penelope throughout the poem is characterized by her loyalty to Odysseus and her respectable behaviour: she acts as a Greek wife should by staying in the women's' quarters, overseeing housework and awaiting her husband's return.

Athena

Athena is a central character in the *Odyssey*: she influences the plot and the characters constantly throughout the poem. Odysseus is her favourite and she is determined to get him home safely: this is made clear in book 1, when we see her at a council of the gods defending Odysseus and reminding Zeus that he had promised Odysseus could return home. She visits Ithaca (in disguise as a human – this is often the case when she interacts with mortals) to encourage Telemachus to travel and to stand up to the suitors more – this is to prepare him for the heroic deeds he will need to perform at his father's side to get rid of the suitors at the end of the poem. Similarly, in book 1 it is Athena who takes Penelope's grief away and sends sleep to her, offering the suffering wife some relief in her pain. It is Athena who inspires Nausicaa to go to the shore in book 6, thus ensuring that Odysseus will be met by a sympathetic host in Phaeacia, and she then appears to Odysseus in the guise of a local girl with further advice on his way to Alcinous' palace. Similarly, when Odysseus finally reaches the shores of Ithaca, it is Athena who meets him first, with both praise and advice for the next step of his revenge against the suitors.

It is thus impossible to imagine the plot without Athene's direction and involvement, but it is important to recognize that her guidance does not, for a Greek audience, in any way diminish Odysseus' achievements as a hero. Rather, the very fact of her support and interest would raise Odysseus' standing, as only the best of mortals receive such attention from the gods. This is linked to the Greek idea of 'double determination' by which a mortal's actions (or his fate) could be divinely controlled and yet seen to be his own responsibility. A simple example of this is the scene in *Iliad* 1, where Hera restrains the angry Achilles from stabbing Agamemnon, his comrade, with a sword. We are not supposed to see Achilles as a mere puppet of the gods, but rather, Hera's involvement shows how important he is to the gods and the importance of this interaction between two of the top Greek heroes. It is also possible to read the inspiration of Hera allegorically as a metaphor for Achilles' own sudden sense of restraint in a moment of anger. A Greek would see Achilles, or any Greek hero, as ultimately responsible for his own behaviour, for better or for worse. Thus Athena's constant involvement in the plot does not diminish, but rather increases, Odysseus' heroism.

Nausicaa

The daughter of the Phaeacian king and queen, Alcinous and Arete, Nausicaa is given plenty of space in book 6 as the narrative pace slows and tension builds in anticipation of Odysseus rejoining civilized society. She is tall and beautiful, and likened to the gods in her appearance: she is unmarried but of marriageable age, and Athena lures her to the beach to wash her clothes partly by scolding her for risking her reputation among the menfolk through not being well turned-out. Nausicaa asks her father if she can borrow the waggon to take her laundry to the shore, and the narrator tells us that she was embarrassed to mention the subject of her own marriage but that her father read between the lines and was happy to let her go on this basis. Readiness for marriage, ready wit and reputation are her defining characteristics.

On the shore, she is likened by the narrator to Artemis in her stature and demeanour among her maidservants, and she keeps her cool when the salt-encrusted naked Odysseus emerges and asks for a rag to wrap around himself. She displays an exemplary knowledge of how to treat a stranger (see above on *xenia*), but her modesty makes her concerned for her reputation so she advises Odysseus on exactly how to walk beside the waggon on their return to town so as not to be seen in her company. She also advises Odysseus on exactly how to approach her royal parents so that he can get what he wants (i.e. bypass her father and go straight for Queen Arete). Overall, despite the artificial frisson of potential marriage to the mysterious stranger on her shores she nevertheless serves as a reminder of the wife and family that await Odysseus in Ithaca.

The language of epic

The epic hexameter

Because of its origin as oral poetry composed for performance, the sound of Homeric Greek contributes more to the meaning of the poem than the more sophisticated verse forms of later Classical and modern writers for whom the written word is paramount. In addition to the usual assonances, alliterations, aural contrasts and other poetic 'sound effects', the reader of Homeric epics should also be keenly aware of the impact of rhythm and pace driving the narrative forwards at varying speeds for various effects particularly as the entire poem is composed in only one type of metre. While the poet of the *Odyssey* does employ a vast array of descriptive language, the words in each line are hung on the frame of the verse structure: language and versification have each received the careful attention of Homeric scholars throughout the centuries, and both elements need to be considered when reading and appreciating the text.

The hexameter line: metre, feet and breaks

Unlike English poetry, where metre comprises an arrangement of stressed and unstressed syllables ('Tiger, tiger, burning bright . . .'), the rhythm of Greek verse can be understood as an arrangement of long and short syllables (so-called 'quantitative verse'). When analysing metre, long syllables are marked with a macron (–) and short syllables with a breve (∪) though what precisely makes a syllable long or short will be considered below. Each line of verse can be divided into a number of 'feet', and there are many types of metrical foot combining various permutations of long and short syllables, but the only true feet we will encounter are dactyls (– ∪ ∪) and spondees (– –). Dactyls take their name from the Greek word for 'finger' (coming from the relative lengths of bone along a finger, i.e. long-short-short); spondees (– –) are named after the Greek word for 'libation', which refers to the ritual pouring of wine as an offering to the gods. Broadly speaking, a line that is largely dactylic is faster-paced than a mostly-spondaic line, which will feel slower and more stately, but the effect of varying dactyls and spondees is particular to each clause, line or episode, and the reader should in general make their own decisions about their literary effect after analysing particular lines for their metrical quantity.

The Homeric epics are composed in a metre called 'dactylic hexameter', i.e. six dactyls (although the sixth foot is only two syllables, either – ∪ or – –). In practice, the feet of an epic hexameter line can be a mixture of dactyls and spondees, and in reality there are further permissible variations within the epic hexameter, but the basic format is as follows:

– ∪∪ | – ∪∪ | – ∪∪ | – ∪∪ | – ∪∪ | – ∪

The possible variations of dactyl and spondee are neatly caught in the mnemonic English line:

'Down in a | deep dark | dell sat an | old cow | munching a | beanstalk.'

which, when scanned, runs thus:

– ∪∪ | – – | – ∪∪ | – – | – ∪∪ | – –

But the *Odyssey* is far more than simply 12,000 lines each practically the same shape at the others: each hexameter line is in fact a variation on this theme, and it is the nature of these variations which gives Homeric verse its richness and life. While it is true that the feet of a line are what give it its overall shape and rhythm, which can be easily calculated for each line once some basic rules are learnt (on which see below), nevertheless the arrangement of words and clauses on the line is far more subtle and may ultimately be more important to the creation of the hexameter line than the starting point provided by a simple arrangement of 'six dactylic feet'.

Verses and breaks: caesurae, diaereses, enjambment

One of the ways that Homeric hexameter lines vary is by having one or more points on each line where there is a break in sense: these can be noted either as a 'caesura' (when 'cutting' a foot, i.e. placed in the middle of a foot) or as a 'diaeresis' (when 'dividing' two feet) and both are marked in texts with the symbol ‖. These phenomena have been studied, named and categorized by scholars since antiquity, with a vast array of technical descriptions depending on whether they fall (for example) after the second syllable of the third foot (which is a 'weak penthemimeral caesura', the most common break in the Homeric epics) or between the fourth and fifth foot (a 'bucolic diaeresis'), and detailed analysis has contributed a vast amount to the deeper understanding of the history of the language and the verse form, but for the student and general reader the key skill is to notice how the poet uses breaks within the line to create mood, vary pace, or emphasize words and phrases within a metre that in itself actually offers little flexibility and is not especially suited to the vocabulary of the Greek language (as discussed below). For the effect of sense-breaks which caesurae and diaereses bring to versification, consider an extreme example: the indignant tone of the imagined Phaeacian man who Nausicaa fears will question her motives in bringing the stranger Odysseus to her parents' palace:

'τίς δ ὅδε Ναυσικάᾳ ἕπεται ‖ καλός τε μέγας τε
ξεῖνος; ‖ ποῦ δέ μιν εὗρε; ‖ πόσις νύ οἱ ἔσσεται αὐτῇ.
ἤ τινά που πλαγχθέντα κομίσσατο ‖ ἧς ἀπὸ νηὸς
ἀνδρῶν τηλεδαπῶν, ‖ ἐπεὶ οὔ τινες ἐγγύθεν εἰσίν . . .'

(6.276–279)

'Who's this man following Nausicaa – a fine chap, and strapping –
A foreigner? Where did she pick him up? Well, he'll make a fine husband for her.
Perhaps it's some traveller she's taking care of – someone fresh off the boat,
From some overseas race – since no-one here's good enough for her!'

This loose and prosey English version is slightly paraphrased to help convey the scornful and abrasive tone which a literal translation might struggle to convey but which the breaks make very evident in the Greek. Note in particular the 'run-on' position, where a word expressed the beginning of a line (e.g. ξεῖνος above) grammatically belongs with the clause above but is spotlit in enjambment. The placement of clauses along the line also contributes much to the flow of the text: choppy, skewed verse can suggest informality, uncertainty or urgency, whereas whole-line clauses or couplets can give the impression of good-ordered eloquence, although the precise effect of the versification will depend on narrative context and characterization.

It is these 'between the lines' enhancements of what is actually said which make the use of diaereses, caesurae and enjambment so important alongside word-order, juxtaposition, pace, sound effects and all the other devices in the poet's toolkit beyond the mere selection of lexical terms. Even a cursory glance at a few lines of Homeric verse in books 1 and 6 can show the richness that these breaks add to the verse form: they can highlight a prepositional phrase, a relative clause, or an appositional afterthought, and modern editors' punctuation in particular can make them very easy to spot. The breaks make very clear the fact that in a gigantic epic poem (unlike, for example, the mannered and neatly-structured English sonnet) the metre itself is not an end but a means to accommodate expressive units of language. Students interested in learning more about the effect of metre should consult the commentaries listed in the 'Further Reading' below.

Long and short syllables

As noted above, each foot of a line is to be understood not in terms of stressed and unstressed syllables, but of 'quantity', i.e. whether the syllables in each foot are long or short. For the purposes of analysing quantity, Greek has an advantage over other languages in that it distinguishes certain vowels as long or short by using different letter-forms for them, i.e. ε and η, o and ω, but even then the quantity of α, ι and υ can only be known from entries in larger or specialist dictionaries where long vowels can be marked ᾱ ῑ ῡ and shorts marked ᾰ ῐ ῠ.

In its most basic form, the difference between long and short syllables is as follows:

- A syllable is usually short if it contains a short vowel not followed by anything which might lengthen it;
- A syllable is usually long if it contains a long vowel or diphthong, or a short vowel that is lengthened by the anything which follows it.

To scan a line, therefore, the student should start by noting (though not yet marking) the long vowels η and ω, and any long α, ι or υ which they deduce to be long. The position of short vowels can often make them long 'by position', generally when followed by certain pairs of consonants. It is worth understanding the following table to get a sense of how these groups of letters behave:

	labial	palatal	dental
voiced	β	Γ	δ
plosive	π	K	τ
aspirated	φ	χ	θ
liquids: λ, μ, ν, ϱ			

Before proceeding to scan a line, therefore, note the following points, in rough order of how much impact they have on scansion:

- At the ends of words, short vowels α ε o, common endings such as verb terminations -μαι, -σθαι etc., and dative endings -ι and -οι, can all be 'elided' or struck out when the next word begins with a vowel (so at 6.209 δότ' stands for δότε).
- In general, two consonants or double-consonants lengthen short vowels (so e.g. ἕσπετο should be scanned – ∪∪ even though it begins with a short ε).
- In a two-consonant pair, when the first is plosive (π, κ, τ) or aspirated (φ, χ, θ) and the second is liquid (λ, μ, ν, ϱ), i.e. in pairs such as τϱ, πλ etc., this need not lengthen a short vowel (so e.g. in ἀποπλύνεσκε, the first short ε is lengthened by σκ, whereas the short o is not lengthened by the πλ).

- Liquids λ, μ, ν, and also σ, can lengthen short vowels.
- A short syllable can become long when the next word begins with a ϱ.
- A long vowel or diphthong can be shortened if followed by a short one ('correption').
- Two distinct vowels can be scanned together as one ('synizesis').

An additional complication is that by the time the Homeric epics attained written form the Greek alphabet had long ceased to record the letter digamma (ϝ, roughly equivalent to the English W), which was known to the poet of the *Odyssey* but had already fallen out of use. As a result of its disappearance, a 'lost' digamma can play havoc on the rules of scansion: its ghost can be detected in words such as δείδω, which had as its root δϝι (= dwi) rather than just δει. The weak aorist of δείδω is ἔδεισα: this looks as if it should be scanned ∪ – ∪, but in fact is scanned – – ∪ as the lost digamma makes the δ act as a double-consonant δϝ, i.e. *edweisa* rather than *edeisa*, thereby lengthening the augment ε. The digamma can also prevent elision by acting as an imaginary barrier between adjacent vowels in neighbouring words: ἄναξ and ἄνασσα were originally ϝάναξ and ϝάνασσα, so e.g. at 6.175, ἀλλά ἄνασσα, we see ἀλλά retain its final alpha before ἄνασσα.

There are further variations which complicate scansion. While it is generally assumed that (for example) iambic verse is very suited to English, the same cannot be said for the dactylic hexameter and the Greek language, containing as it does many words which do not fit the metre, because of their containing either – ∪ – or ∪∪∪. For this reason, there are many more tweaks which the poet is free to use if the metre doesn't fit (such as the so-called 'headless line' which begins ∪∪∪) and in many cases there are several competing theories for why a particular syllable might have been lengthened/shortened which are discussed in scholarly articles and commentaries. As noted above, modern scholarship has revealed that Homeric Greek is a patchwork of different dialects drawn from different ages of the Greek language and this may account for some of the complexities of pinning down the Homeric hexameter. For the A-level student, the starting point should be to be able to tell if a line is largely dactylic or spondaic, and to spot and comment on the caesurae and diaereses and the effects they have on the text, and to consult a specialist commentary for more specific detail on scansion if needed.

Homeric Greek

As we have just noted, the Homeric language is an amalgam of different dialects of Greek and also of words used at different times in Greek history. Thus it can look very different at first glance from the type of Greek normally taught in schools (Attic Greek), as some of the noun and verb endings are spelled differently from how you are used to.

The following is a list of some of the most common deviations from Attic Greek, more exhaustive lists can be found in the commentaries referred to under 'Further Reading' at the end of this Introduction.

Some general principles to be aware of:

- Homer often does not contract vowels where Attic Greek would (e.g. in contract verbs).
- Words usually spelled with a double consonant may appear with a single consonant (ʼΟδυσσεα/ʼΟδυσηος).
- Words with a single consonant may have it doubled (so e.g. ὅτι becomes ὅττι).
- Vowels may be lengthened – so ξενος ('stranger') becomes ξεινος. Frequent substitutions of this sort are ει for ε, η for α and ου for ο.
- Verbs with prepositions as prefixes (e.g. ἀποβαινω) are sometimes written as two separate words with the preposition usually occurring before the verb in the line. This is called tmesis, and is referred to in the Commentary Notes where appropriate.

Accidence

First declension nouns

- The nominative singular of feminine nouns ends in -η, rather than -ᾱ, even after ϱ, ε, and ι.
- The genitive singular of masculine nouns ends in -ᾱο or -εω, (-ου in Attic).
- The genitive plural of often ends in -ᾱων or -εων (a leftover from Mycenean Greek).
- The dative plural ends in -ῃσι or -ῃς (-αις in Attic).

Second declension nouns

- The genitive singular ends in -οιο (Attic – ου) e.g. Od.1.441 θαλαμοιο 'of his bedroom'.
- The dative plural ends in -οισι (Attic -οις) e.g. Od. 1.313 ξεινοισι 'to the guests'.

Third declension nouns

- The dative plural: ends in -εσσι(ν) (Attic -σι) e.g. Od.1.430 κτεατεσσιν 'with his own possessions'.

Verbs

- The augment can be (and is very often) omitted from indicative past tenses.
- Imperfect verbs can take the ending -εσκε/-εσκον.

- The present infinitive ending is often -μεναι (-ειν in Attic).
- Subjunctives do not always take lengthened endings, and in some instances are even augmented.
- Consonants may be doubled e.g. ἐκαλεσα becomes ἐκαλεσσα, ἐλαβε becomes ἐλλαβε.

Pronouns

- μιν is used for αὐτον/ αὐτην (him/her).
- σφεις is used for 'they' (acc. σφας, dat. σφιν or σφισι).
- οἱ is used for αὐτῳ (to/for him).
- the article ὁ, ἡ, το is used as a demonstrative pronoun.
- ὁς, ἡ, το is used as a possessive adjective.

Further Reading

Translations

Fitzgerald, R. *Homer, Odyssey*. New York 2007.
Rieu, E. V. *Homer, Odyssey*, revised translation of D. C. H. Rieu. London 2003.
Wilson, E. *Homer, Odyssey*. New York 2018.

Companions, introductions and general studies

Camps, W. A. *An introduction to Homer*. Oxford 1980.
de Jong, I. *A narratological commentary on the Odyssey*. Cambridge 2001.
Doherty, L. *Oxford readings in Homer's Odyssey*. Oxford 2009.
Finlay, M. I. *The world of Odysseus*, revised edition. New York 2002.
Griffin, J. *Homer*. Bristol 2001.
Jones, P. *Homer's Odyssey: a companion to the English translation of Richmond Lattimore*. Bristol 1991.
Morris, I. and B. Powell (eds.). *A new companion to Homer*. Leiden 1997.

Commentaries to Books 1 and 6

Garvie, A. F. *Homer: Odyssey, books VI-VIII*. Cambridge 1994.
Hainsworth, S. et al. (ed.). *A commentary on Homer's Odyssey, volume 1: introduction and books I-VIII*. Oxford 1990.
Jones, P. V. *Homer: Odyssey 1 & 2*. Warminster 1991.
Pulleyn, S. *Odyssey Book 1*. Oxford 2018.
Stanford, W. B. *The Odyssey of Homer, vol.1, Books I-XII*, second edition. Basingstoke 1959.
Watson, J. *Homer, Odyssey VI and VII*. Bristol 2002.

Acknowledgements

We would each like to express our deep and profound thanks to Stephen Anderson for his limitless and patient help with every aspect of compiling these notes.

Alastair Harden thanks Sarah for the opportunity to contribute to this edition, and extends his warmest gratitude to Chloe Hamill and to Peter, Ellie and Balthazar Thackrey, without whose generous hospitality his contribution would not have been possible.

Sarah Harden would like to thank Alastair for his patience and kindness as a co-author, without which this commentary would not have been written.

Text

Odyssey 1

1–213: At a meeting of the gods, Athena convinces Zeus to take pity on the marooned Odysseus and allow him to return home. She adopts a mortal disguise and enters the palace of Odysseus at Ithaca, which has been overrun with the suitors of his wife Penelope. Posing as Odysseus' friend Mentes she tells Telemachus that his father is definitely alive, and asks him more about his parentage.

τὴν δ' αὖ Τηλέμαχος πεπνυμένος ἀντίον ηὔδα:
"τοιγὰρ ἐγώ τοι, ξεῖνε, μάλ' ἀτρεκέως ἀγορεύσω.
μήτηρ μέν τέ μέ φησι τοῦ ἔμμεναι, αὐτὰρ ἐγώ γε   215
οὐκ οἶδ': οὐ γάρ πώ τις ἑὸν γόνον αὐτὸς ἀνέγνω.
ὡς δὴ ἐγώ γ' ὄφελον μάκαρός νύ τευ ἔμμεναι υἱὸς
ἀνέρος, ὃν κτεάτεσσιν ἑοῖς ἔπι γῆρας ἔτετμε.
νῦν δ' ὃς ἀποτμότατος γένετο θνητῶν ἀνθρώπων,
τοῦ μ' ἔκ φασι γενέσθαι, ἐπεὶ σύ με τοῦτ' ἐρεείνεις."   220

τὸν δ' αὖτε προσέειπε θεά, γλαυκῶπις Ἀθήνη:
"οὐ μέν τοι γενεήν γε θεοὶ νώνυμνον ὀπίσσω
θῆκαν, ἐπεὶ σέ γε τοῖον ἐγείνατο Πηνελόπεια.
ἀλλ' ἄγε μοι τόδε εἰπὲ καὶ ἀτρεκέως κατάλεξον:
τίς δαίς, τίς δὲ ὅμιλος ὅδ' ἔπλετο; τίπτε δέ σε χρεώ;   225
εἰλαπίνη ἠὲ γάμος; ἐπεὶ οὐκ ἔρανος τάδε γ' ἐστίν:
ὥς τέ μοι ὑβρίζοντες ὑπερφιάλως δοκέουσι
δαίνυσθαι κατὰ δῶμα. νεμεσσήσαιτό κεν ἀνὴρ
αἴσχεα πόλλ' ὁρόων, ὅς τις πινυτός γε μετέλθοι."

τὴν δ' αὖ Τηλέμαχος πεπνυμένος ἀντίον ηὔδα: 230
"ξεῖν', ἐπεὶ ἂρ δὴ ταῦτά μ' ἀνείρεαι ἠδὲ μεταλλᾷς,
μέλλεν μέν ποτε οἶκος ὅδ' ἀφνειὸς καὶ ἀμύμων
ἔμμεναι, ὄφρ' ἔτι κεῖνος ἀνὴρ ἐπιδήμιος ἦεν:
νῦν δ' ἑτέρως ἐβόλοντο θεοὶ κακὰ μητιόωντες,
οἳ κεῖνον μὲν ἄιστον ἐποίησαν περὶ πάντων   235
ἀνθρώπων, ἐπεὶ οὔ κε θανόντι περ ὧδ' ἀκαχοίμην,

εἰ μετὰ οἷς ἑτάροισι δάμη Τρώων ἐνὶ δήμῳ,
ἠὲ φίλων ἐν χερσίν, ἐπεὶ πόλεμον τολύπευσεν.
τῷ κέν οἱ τύμβον μὲν ἐποίησαν Παναχαιοί,
ἠδέ κε καὶ ᾧ παιδὶ μέγα κλέος ἦρατ' ὀπίσσω.   240
νῦν δέ μιν ἀκλειῶς ἅρπυιαι ἀνηρείψαντο·
οἴχετ' ἄιστος ἄπυστος, ἐμοὶ δ' ὀδύνας τε γόους τε
κάλλιπεν. οὐδέ τι κεῖνον ὀδυρόμενος στεναχίζω
οἶον, ἐπεί νύ μοι ἄλλα θεοὶ κακὰ κήδε' ἔτευξαν.
ὅσσοι γὰρ νήσοισιν ἐπικρατέουσιν ἄριστοι,   245
Δουλιχίῳ τε Σάμῃ τε καὶ ὑλήεντι Ζακύνθῳ,
ἠδ' ὅσσοι κραναὴν Ἰθάκην κάτα κοιρανέουσιν,
τόσσοι μητέρ' ἐμὴν μνῶνται, τρύχουσι δὲ οἶκον.
ἡ δ' οὔτ' ἀρνεῖται στυγερὸν γάμον οὔτε τελευτὴν
ποιῆσαι δύναται· τοὶ δὲ φθινύθουσιν ἔδοντες   250
οἶκον ἐμόν· τάχα δή με διαρραίσουσι καὶ αὐτόν."

τὸν δ' ἐπαλαστήσασα προσηύδα Παλλὰς Ἀθήνη·
"ὢ πόποι, ἦ δὴ πολλὸν ἀποιχομένου Ὀδυσῆος
δεύῃ, ὅ κε μνηστῆρσιν ἀναιδέσι χεῖρας ἐφείη.
εἰ γὰρ νῦν ἐλθὼν δόμου ἐν πρώτῃσι θύρῃσι   255
σταίη, ἔχων πήληκα καὶ ἀσπίδα καὶ δύο δοῦρε,
τοῖος ἐὼν οἷόν μιν ἐγὼ τὰ πρῶτ' ἐνόησα
οἴκῳ ἐν ἡμετέρῳ πίνοντά τε τερπόμενόν τε,
ἐξ Ἐφύρης ἀνιόντα παρ' Ἴλου Μερμερίδαο—
ᾤχετο γὰρ καὶ κεῖσε θοῆς ἐπὶ νηὸς Ὀδυσσεὺς   260
φάρμακον ἀνδροφόνον διζήμενος, ὄφρα οἱ εἴη
ἰοὺς χρίεσθαι χαλκήρεας· ἀλλ' ὁ μὲν οὔ οἱ
δῶκεν, ἐπεί ῥα θεοὺς νεμεσίζετο αἰὲν ἐόντας,
ἀλλὰ πατήρ οἱ δῶκεν ἐμός· φιλέεσκε γὰρ αἰνῶς—
τοῖος ἐὼν μνηστῆρσιν ὁμιλήσειεν Ὀδυσσεύς·   265
πάντες κ' ὠκύμοροί τε γενοίατο πικρόγαμοί τε.
ἀλλ' ἦ τοι μὲν ταῦτα θεῶν ἐν γούνασι κεῖται,
ἤ κεν νοστήσας ἀποτίσεται, ἦε καὶ οὐκί,
οἷσιν ἐνὶ μεγάροισι· σὲ δὲ φράζεσθαι ἄνωγα,
ὅππως κε μνηστῆρας ἀπώσεαι ἐκ μεγάροιο.   270
εἰ δ' ἄγε νῦν ξυνίει καὶ ἐμῶν ἐμπάζεο μύθων·
αὔριον εἰς ἀγορὴν καλέσας ἥρωας Ἀχαιοὺς
μῦθον πέφραδε πᾶσι, θεοὶ δ' ἐπὶ μάρτυροι ἔστων.
μνηστῆρας μὲν ἐπὶ σφέτερα σκίδνασθαι ἄνωχθι,
μητέρα δ', εἰ οἱ θυμὸς ἐφορμᾶται γαμέεσθαι,   275
ἂψ ἴτω ἐς μέγαρον πατρὸς μέγα δυναμένοιο·
οἱ δὲ γάμον τεύξουσι καὶ ἀρτυνέουσιν ἔεδνα
πολλὰ μάλ', ὅσσα ἔοικε φίλης ἐπὶ παιδὸς ἕπεσθαι.
σοὶ δ' αὐτῷ πυκινῶς ὑποθήσομαι, αἴ κε πίθηαι·
νῆ' ἄρσας ἐρέτῃσιν ἐείκοσιν, ἥ τις ἀρίστη,   280
ἔρχεο πευσόμενος πατρὸς δὴν οἰχομένοιο,

AS

ἤν τίς τοι εἴπῃσι βροτῶν, ἢ ὄσσαν ἀκούσῃς
ἐκ Διός, ἥ τε μάλιστα φέρει κλέος ἀνθρώποισι.
πρῶτα μὲν ἐς Πύλον ἐλθὲ καὶ εἴρεο Νέστορα δῖον,
κεῖθεν δὲ Σπάρτηνδε παρὰ ξανθὸν Μενέλαον·   285
ὃς γὰρ δεύτατος ἦλθεν Ἀχαιῶν χαλκοχιτώνων.
εἰ μέν κεν πατρὸς βίοτον καὶ νόστον ἀκούσῃς,
ἦ τ' ἂν τρυχόμενός περ ἔτι τλαίης ἐνιαυτόν·
εἰ δέ κε τεθνηῶτος ἀκούσῃς μηδ' ἔτ' ἐόντος,
νοστήσας δὴ ἔπειτα φίλην ἐς πατρίδα γαῖαν   290
σῆμά τέ οἱ χεῦαι καὶ ἐπὶ κτέρεα κτερεΐξαι
πολλὰ μάλ', ὅσσα ἔοικε, καὶ ἀνέρι μητέρα δοῦναι.
αὐτὰρ ἐπὴν δὴ ταῦτα τελευτήσῃς τε καὶ ἔρξῃς,
φράζεσθαι δὴ ἔπειτα κατὰ φρένα καὶ κατὰ θυμὸν
ὅππως κε μνηστῆρας ἐνὶ μεγάροισι τεοῖσι   295
κτείνῃς ἠὲ δόλῳ ἢ ἀμφαδόν· οὐδέ τί σε χρὴ
νηπιάας ὀχέειν, ἐπεὶ οὐκέτι τηλίκος ἐσσι.
ἦ οὐκ ἀίεις οἷον κλέος ἔλλαβε δῖος Ὀρέστης
πάντας ἐπ' ἀνθρώπους, ἐπεὶ ἔκτανε πατροφονῆα,
Αἴγισθον δολόμητιν, ὅ οἱ πατέρα κλυτὸν ἔκτα;   300
καὶ σύ, φίλος, μάλα γάρ σ' ὁρόω καλόν τε μέγαν τε,
ἄλκιμος ἔσσ', ἵνα τίς σε καὶ ὀψιγόνων ἐὺ εἴπῃ.
αὐτὰρ ἐγὼν ἐπὶ νῆα θοὴν κατελεύσομαι ἤδη
ἠδ' ἑτάρους, οἵ πού με μάλ' ἀσχαλόωσι μένοντες·
σοὶ δ' αὐτῷ μελέτω, καὶ ἐμῶν ἐμπάζεο μύθων."   305

τὴν δ' αὖ Τηλέμαχος πεπνυμένος ἀντίον ηὔδα·
"ξεῖν', ἦ τοι μὲν ταῦτα φίλα φρονέων ἀγορεύεις,
ὥς τε πατὴρ ᾧ παιδί, καὶ οὔ ποτε λήσομαι αὐτῶν.
ἀλλ' ἄγε νῦν ἐπίμεινον, ἐπειγόμενός περ ὁδοῖο,
ὄφρα λοεσσάμενός τε τεταρπόμενός τε φίλον κῆρ,   310
δῶρον ἔχων ἐπὶ νῆα κίῃς, χαίρων ἐνὶ θυμῷ,
τιμῆεν, μάλα καλόν, ὅ τοι κειμήλιον ἔσται
ἐξ ἐμεῦ, οἷα φίλοι ξεῖνοι ξείνοισι διδοῦσι."

τὸν δ' ἠμείβετ' ἔπειτα θεά, γλαυκῶπις Ἀθήνη·
"μή μ' ἔτι νῦν κατέρυκε, λιλαιόμενόν περ ὁδοῖο.   315
δῶρον δ' ὅττι κέ μοι δοῦναι φίλον ἦτορ ἀνώγῃ,
αὖτις ἀνερχομένῳ δόμεναι οἶκόνδε φέρεσθαι,
καὶ μάλα καλὸν ἑλών· σοὶ δ' ἄξιον ἔσται ἀμοιβῆς."

ἡ μὲν ἄρ' ὣς εἰποῦσ' ἀπέβη γλαυκῶπις Ἀθήνη,
ὄρνις δ' ὣς ἀνοπαῖα διέπτατο· τῷ δ' ἐνὶ θυμῷ   320
θῆκε μένος καὶ θάρσος, ὑπέμνησέν τέ ἑ πατρὸς
μᾶλλον ἔτ' ἢ τὸ πάροιθεν. ὁ δὲ φρεσὶν ᾗσι νοήσας
θάμβησεν κατὰ θυμόν· ὀίσατο γὰρ θεὸν εἶναι.
αὐτίκα δὲ μνηστῆρας ἐπῴχετο ἰσόθεος φώς.

τοῖσι δ' ἀοιδὸς ἄειδε περικλυτός, οἱ δὲ σιωπῇ   325
ἥατ' ἀκούοντες: ὁ δ' Ἀχαιῶν νόστον ἄειδε
λυγρόν, ὃν ἐκ Τροίης ἐπετείλατο Παλλὰς Ἀθήνη.
τοῦ δ' ὑπερωιόθεν φρεσὶ σύνθετο θέσπιν ἀοιδὴν
κούρη Ἰκαρίοιο, περίφρων Πηνελόπεια:
κλίμακα δ' ὑψηλὴν κατεβήσετο οἷο δόμοιο,   330
οὐκ οἴη, ἅμα τῇ γε καὶ ἀμφίπολοι δύ' ἕποντο.
ἡ δ' ὅτε δὴ μνηστῆρας ἀφίκετο δῖα γυναικῶν,
στῆ ῥα παρὰ σταθμὸν τέγεος πύκα ποιητοῖο,
ἄντα παρειάων σχομένη λιπαρὰ κρήδεμνα:
ἀμφίπολος δ' ἄρα οἱ κεδνὴ ἑκάτερθε παρέστη.   335
δακρύσασα δ' ἔπειτα προσηύδα θεῖον ἀοιδόν:

"Φήμιε, πολλὰ γὰρ ἄλλα βροτῶν θελκτήρια οἶδας,
ἔργ' ἀνδρῶν τε θεῶν τε, τά τε κλείουσιν ἀοιδοί:
τῶν ἕν γέ σφιν ἄειδε παρήμενος, οἱ δὲ σιωπῇ
οἶνον πινόντων: ταύτης δ' ἀποπαύε' ἀοιδῆς   340
λυγρῆς, ἥ τέ μοι αἰεὶ ἐνὶ στήθεσσι φίλον κῆρ
τείρει, ἐπεί με μάλιστα καθίκετο πένθος ἄλαστον.
τοίην γὰρ κεφαλὴν ποθέω μεμνημένη αἰεί,
ἀνδρός, τοῦ κλέος εὐρὺ καθ' Ἑλλάδα καὶ μέσον Ἄργος."

τὴν δ' αὖ Τηλέμαχος πεπνυμένος ἀντίον ηὔδα: 345
"μῆτερ ἐμή, τί τ' ἄρα φθονέεις ἐρίηρον ἀοιδὸν
τέρπειν ὅππη οἱ νόος ὄρνυται; οὐ νύ τ' ἀοιδοὶ
αἴτιοι, ἀλλά ποθι Ζεὺς αἴτιος, ὅς τε δίδωσιν
ἀνδράσιν ἀλφηστῇσιν, ὅπως ἐθέλησιν, ἑκάστῳ.
τούτῳ δ' οὐ νέμεσις Δαναῶν κακὸν οἶτον ἀείδειν: 350
τὴν γὰρ ἀοιδὴν μᾶλλον ἐπικλείουσ' ἄνθρωποι,
ἥ τις ἀκουόντεσσι νεωτάτη ἀμφιπέληται.
σοί δ' ἐπιτολμάτω κραδίη καὶ θυμὸς ἀκούειν:
οὐ γὰρ Ὀδυσσεὺς οἶος ἀπώλεσε νόστιμον ἦμαρ
ἐν Τροίῃ, πολλοὶ δὲ καὶ ἄλλοι φῶτες ὄλοντο.   355
ἀλλ' εἰς οἶκον ἰοῦσα τὰ σ' αὐτῆς ἔργα κόμιζε,
ἱστόν τ' ἠλακάτην τε, καὶ ἀμφιπόλοισι κέλευε
ἔργον ἐποίχεσθαι: μῦθος δ' ἄνδρεσσι μελήσει
πᾶσι, μάλιστα δ' ἐμοί: τοῦ γὰρ κράτος ἔστ' ἐνὶ οἴκῳ."

ἡ μὲν θαμβήσασα πάλιν οἰκόνδε βεβήκει: 360
παιδὸς γὰρ μῦθον πεπνυμένον ἔνθετο θυμῷ.
ἐς δ' ὑπερῷ' ἀναβᾶσα σὺν ἀμφιπόλοισι γυναιξὶ
κλαῖεν ἔπειτ' Ὀδυσῆα φίλον πόσιν, ὄφρα οἱ ὕπνον
ἡδὺν ἐπὶ βλεφάροισι βάλε γλαυκῶπις Ἀθήνη.

μνηστῆρες δ' ὁμάδησαν ἀνὰ μέγαρα σκιόεντα,   365
πάντες δ' ἠρήσαντο παραὶ λεχέεσσι κλιθῆναι.
τοῖσι δὲ Τηλέμαχος πεπνυμένος ἤρχετο μύθων:

"μητρὸς ἐμῆς μνηστῆρες ὑπέρβιον ὕβριν ἔχοντες,
νῦν μὲν δαινύμενοι τερπώμεθα, μηδὲ βοητὺς
ἔστω, ἐπεὶ τό γε καλὸν ἀκουέμεν ἐστὶν ἀοιδοῦ   370
τοιοῦδ' οἷος ὅδ' ἐστί, θεοῖς ἐναλίγκιος αὐδήν.
ἠῶθεν δ' ἀγορήνδε καθεζώμεσθα κιόντες
πάντες, ἵν' ὕμιν μῦθον ἀπηλεγέως ἀποείπω,
ἐξιέναι μεγάρων: ἄλλας δ' ἀλεγύνετε δαῖτας,
ὑμὰ κτήματ' ἔδοντες, ἀμειβόμενοι κατὰ οἴκους.   375
εἰ δ' ὕμιν δοκέει τόδε λωίτερον καὶ ἄμεινον
ἔμμεναι, ἀνδρὸς ἑνὸς βίοτον νήποινον ὀλέσθαι,
κείρετ': ἐγὼ δὲ θεοὺς ἐπιβώσομαι αἰὲν ἐόντας,
αἴ κέ ποθι Ζεὺς δῷσι παλίντιτα ἔργα γενέσθαι:
νήποινοί κεν ἔπειτα δόμων ἔντοσθεν ὄλοισθε."   380

ὣς ἔφαθ', οἱ δ' ἄρα πάντες ὀδὰξ ἐν χείλεσι φύντες
Τηλέμαχον θαύμαζον, ὃ θαρσαλέως ἀγόρευεν.

τὸν δ' αὖτ' Ἀντίνοος προσέφη, Εὐπείθεος υἱός:
"Τηλέμαχ', ἦ μάλα δή σε διδάσκουσιν θεοὶ αὐτοὶ
ὑψαγόρην τ' ἔμεναι καὶ θαρσαλέως ἀγορεύειν: 385
μὴ σέ γ' ἐν ἀμφιάλῳ Ἰθάκῃ βασιλῆα Κρονίων
ποιήσειεν, ὅ τοι γενεῇ πατρώιόν ἐστιν."

τὸν δ' αὖ Τηλέμαχος πεπνυμένος ἀντίον ηὔδα:
"Ἀντίνο', ἦ καί μοι νεμεσήσεαι ὅττι κεν εἴπω;
καὶ κεν τοῦτ' ἐθέλοιμι Διός γε διδόντος ἀρέσθαι.   390
ἦ φὴς τοῦτο κάκιστον ἐν ἀνθρώποισι τετύχθαι;
οὐ μὲν γάρ τι κακὸν βασιλευέμεν: αἶψά τέ οἱ δῶ
ἀφνειὸν πέλεται καὶ τιμήεστερος αὐτός.
ἀλλ' ἦ τοι βασιλῆες Ἀχαιῶν εἰσὶ καὶ ἄλλοι
πολλοὶ ἐν ἀμφιάλῳ Ἰθάκῃ, νέοι ἠδὲ παλαιοί,   395
τῶν κέν τις τόδ' ἔχῃσιν, ἐπεὶ θάνε δῖος Ὀδυσσεύς:
αὐτὰρ ἐγὼν οἴκοιο ἄναξ ἔσομ' ἡμετέροιο
καὶ δμώων, οὕς μοι ληίσσατο δῖος Ὀδυσσεύς."

τὸν δ' αὖτ' Εὐρύμαχος Πολύβου πάϊς ἀντίον ηὔδα:
"Τηλέμαχ', ἦ τοι ταῦτα θεῶν ἐν γούνασι κεῖται,   400
ὅς τις ἐν ἀμφιάλῳ Ἰθάκῃ βασιλεύσει Ἀχαιῶν:
κτήματα δ' αὐτὸς ἔχοις καὶ δώμασι σοῖσιν ἀνάσσοις.
μὴ γὰρ ὅ γ' ἔλθοι ἀνὴρ ὅς τίς σ' ἀέκοντα βίηφιν
κτήματ' ἀπορραίσει, Ἰθάκης ἔτι ναιεταούσης.
ἀλλ' ἐθέλω σε, φέριστε, περὶ ξείνοιο ἐρέσθαι,   405
ὁππόθεν οὗτος ἀνήρ, ποίης δ' ἐξ εὔχεται εἶναι
γαίης, ποῦ δέ νύ οἱ γενεὴ καὶ πατρὶς ἄρουρα.
ἠέ τιν' ἀγγελίην πατρὸς φέρει ἐρχομένοιο,
ἦ ἑὸν αὐτοῦ χρεῖος ἐελδόμενος τόδ' ἱκάνει;
οἷον ἀναΐξας ἄφαρ οἴχεται, οὐδ' ὑπέμεινε   410
γνώμεναι: οὐ μὲν γάρ τι κακῷ εἰς ὦπα ἐῴκει."

τὸν δ' αὖ Τηλέμαχος πεπνυμένος ἀντίον ηὔδα:
"Εὐρύμαχ', ἦ τοι νόστος ἀπώλετο πατρὸς ἐμοῖο:
οὔτ' οὖν ἀγγελίῃ ἔτι πείθομαι, εἴ ποθεν ἔλθοι,
οὔτε θεοπροπίης ἐμπάζομαι, ἥν τινα μήτηρ   415
ἐς μέγαρον καλέσασα θεοπρόπον ἐξερέηται.
ξεῖνος δ' οὗτος ἐμὸς πατρώιος ἐκ Τάφου ἐστίν,
Μέντης δ' Ἀγχιάλοιο δαΐφρονος εὔχεται εἶναι
υἱός, ἀτὰρ Ταφίοισι φιληρέτμοισιν ἀνάσσει."
ὣς φάτο Τηλέμαχος, φρεσὶ δ' ἀθανάτην θεὸν ἔγνω.   420

οἱ δ' εἰς ὀρχηστύν τε καὶ ἱμερόεσσαν ἀοιδὴν
τρεψάμενοι τέρποντο, μένον δ' ἐπὶ ἕσπερον ἐλθεῖν.
τοῖσι δὲ τερπομένοισι μέλας ἐπὶ ἕσπερος ἦλθε:
δὴ τότε κακκείοντες ἔβαν οἰκόνδε ἕκαστος.
Τηλέμαχος δ', ὅθι οἱ θάλαμος περικαλλέος αὐλῆς   425
ὑψηλὸς δέδμητο περισκέπτῳ ἐνὶ χώρῳ,
ἔνθ' ἔβη εἰς εὐνὴν πολλὰ φρεσὶ μερμηρίζων.
τῷ δ' ἄρ' ἅμ' αἰθομένας δαΐδας φέρε κεδνὰ ἰδυῖα
Εὐρύκλει', Ὦπος θυγάτηρ Πεισηνορίδαο,
τήν ποτε Λαέρτης πρίατο κτεάτεσσιν ἑοῖσιν   430
πρωθήβην ἔτ' ἐοῦσαν, ἐεικοσάβοια δ' ἔδωκεν,
ἶσα δέ μιν κεδνῇ ἀλόχῳ τίεν ἐν μεγάροισιν,
εὐνῇ δ' οὔ ποτ' ἔμικτο, χόλον δ' ἀλέεινε γυναικός:
ἥ οἱ ἅμ' αἰθομένας δαΐδας φέρε, καί ἑ μάλιστα
δμῳάων φιλέεσκε, καὶ ἔτρεφε τυτθὸν ἐόντα.   435
ὤιξεν δὲ θύρας θαλάμου πύκα ποιητοῖο,
ἕζετο δ' ἐν λέκτρῳ, μαλακὸν δ' ἔκδυνε χιτῶνα:
καὶ τὸν μὲν γραίης πυκιμηδέος ἔμβαλε χερσίν.
ἡ μὲν τὸν πτύξασα καὶ ἀσκήσασα χιτῶνα,
πασσάλῳ ἀγκρεμάσασα παρὰ τρητοῖσι λέχεσσι   440
βῆ ῥ' ἴμεν ἐκ θαλάμοιο, θύρην δ' ἐπέρυσσε κορώνῃ
ἀργυρέῃ, ἐπὶ δὲ κληῖδ' ἐτάνυσσεν ἱμάντι.
ἔνθ' ὅ γε παννύχιος, κεκαλυμμένος οἰὸς ἀώτῳ,
βούλευε φρεσὶν ᾗσιν ὁδὸν τὴν πέφραδ' Ἀθήνη.

Commentary Notes

Odyssey 1

For all vocabulary, please refer to the Vocabulary section after *Odyssey* 6 Commentary Notes.

1–213: *The poem begins with an invocation to the Muse 'Sing, Muse of the man of many wiles, who wandered far and wide ...' introducing the protagonist of the poem, Odysseus, and the subject matter, his journey home to Ithaca after the Greek victory in the Trojan War. At the start of the poem, Odysseus has been wandering for almost ten years, his return home delayed by various adventures and misfortunes.*

The scene shifts at line 22 to heaven, where the gods have a conversation about mortals and Athena, who especially supports Odysseus, takes the opportunity to persuade Zeus that it is time for her favourite to return home after all his suffering. She reminds the gods that Odysseus is currently trapped against his will on the island of the nymph Calypso, where he has been for seven years.

Athena vows to travel to Ithaca and inspire Telemachus, Odysseus' son, to travel around Greece visiting his father's old friends, so that he can try to learn his father's whereabouts. She immediately makes this visit in the disguise of a human (Mentes, a guest-friend of the family) and witnesses the excessive feasting of the many suitors who have taken up residence in Odysseus' house during his long absence, courting his wife Penelope and eating and drinking all his food and wine. Telemachus welcomes Mentes/Athena with courtesy and offers him the hospitality due to such a friend. Telemachus discusses his frustration at the outrageous behaviour of the suitors with Mentes/Athena and asks for his advice as to how he might find news of his father and precipitate his return. Mentes/Athena reassures Telemachus that his father is still alive and prophesies his return to Ithaca. (S)he then asks Telemachus who his father is, noting that he is very like to Odysseus in appearance.

213

τὴν: 'her', i.e. Athena in her disguise as Mentes. Note the use of the definite article as a demonstrative pronoun.

πεπνυμένος: 'wise' – lit. perfect middle participle of πέπνυμαι 'I am conscious', used frequently in Homer as an epithet of Telemachus. In Homer more generally this word is used of young, inexperienced characters rather than of great heroes, but it nonetheless denotes a positive trait in Telemachus. For Homeric epithets, see Introduction p. 247.

αὖ: a particle literally meaning 'again, on the contrary' but which is often used when a speaker changes in Homer. Can be omitted in translation or rendered as 'then'.

ηὔδα: 3rd person sing. imperf. indicative active of the contract verb αὐδάω 'I speak'.

214

τοι – an emphatic particle, often difficult to translate into fluent English. 'Look you' or 'mark my words'.

215–220

Telemachus says he is unsure if he is really Odysseus' son. This reflects the young man's insecurity, caused by growing up in his father's absence.

215

ἔμμεναι: = εἶναι 'to be'.

τοῦ 'his', 'of him' refers to Odysseus. Athena/Mentes has just asked Telemachus if he is Odysseus' son.

215–216

μήτηρ μέν . . . οὐκ οἶδ: Telemachus' doubt at his parentage is emphasized by the enjambment of οὐκ οἶδ 'I don't know'.

216

ἀνέγνω – 3rd singular aor. of ἀναγιγνώσκω 'I know well, I know for sure'.

217

ὡς δὴ ἐγώ γ᾿ ὄφελον: 'would that I had . . .' + infinitive, expresses a wish for the past which has not been fulfilled.

τευ: = τινος.

218

ὃν κτεάτεσσιν ἑοῖς ἔπι γῆρας ἔτετμε: Telemachus' wish that his father had grown old at home shows the extent of his despair; he would rather have an inglorious father who had remained in Ithaca than an absent, albeit heroic one. The reference to possessions (κτεάτεσσιν) reminds us that the suitors are at present consuming large quantities of Odysseus' household, a problem Telemachus and Penelope are unable to deal with in the absence of Odysseus.

219

ἀποτμότατος: the superlative emphasizes Odysseus' misfortunes.

γένετο – unaugmented 3rd pl. aorist of γίγνομαι. The augment is often omitted in Homeric verse.

221

αὖτε: 'in turn' often denotes a transition.

γλαυκῶπις Ἀθήνη: 'grey-eyed Athena', 'flashing-eyed Athena' – a regular epithet of the goddess in Homer.

AS

222

γενεήν: 'heritage', 'family'.

ὀπίσσω: 'hereafter', 'in the future'.

223

θῆκαν: unaugmented 3rd pl. aorist of τίθημι, here '[the gods] have appointed', 'have laid out'.

σέ ... τοῖον: 'such a son as you'.

224

μοι: dative with εἰπέ 'tell me'.

κατάλεξον: weak aor. imperative 2nd sing. of καταλέγω 'I recount'.

225

ἔπλετο: 3rd person sing. aor. middle of πέλω 'I am' (an alternative to εἰμί often used in Homer).

τίπτε: 'why on earth', 'why ever'.

χρεώ: an irregular feminine noun, nominative singular 'necessity', 'need'. The verb is omitted and must be supplied: 'Why ever has [this] necessity *come to* you?'.

226

εἰλαπίνη ἠὲ γάμος; ἐπεὶ οὐκ ἔρανος τάδε γ᾽ ἐστίν: there are three types of feast mentioned here: an εἰλαπίνη (a private party), γάμος (wedding feast) and ἔρανος (a communal dinner to which the guests each contribute something).

ἠέ: = ἤ in Attic Greek, i.e. 'or'.

227

ὥς τέ μοι ὑβρίζοντες ὑπερφιάλως δοκέουσι: the ὥς here is dependent on a missing [I say this] because. It thus has the force of a γαρ and could be translated as 'For they seem to me to be behaving outrageously [ὑβρίζοντες] and arrogantly [ὑπερφιάλως]'. The audience have not yet seen the suitors misbehaving, but we are prepared for their later riotous behaviour by this statement, which is given greater authority because it is spoken by Athena.

228

δαίνυσθαι The infinitive (present middle of δαίνυμι 'I dine', 'I feast') is dependent on δοκέουσι in the line above.

κατὰ δῶμα: 'throughout [your] house'.

νεμεσσήσαιτο: 3rd person. sing. aor. optative. middle of νεμεσάω 'I feel anger' in a potential optative clause 'A man would be angry . . .'.

229

αἴσχεα: accusative plural of the neuter noun αἶσχος -εος (shame, disgrace), unusually used here to mean 'shameful deeds, shameful things' as if it were an adjective.

ὁρόων: = ὁρῶν in Attic Greek (masc. nom. sing. of the present participle of ὁράω (I see).

ὅς τις: 'any man who . . .'.

μετέλθοι: 3rd person sing. aor. optative active μετέρχομαι (I come among, mingle with) continuing the potential optative clause from the line above 'any sensible man who should come among [them]'.

230

= line 213 an example of an Homeric formula (see Introduction pp. 246–247)

231

ξεῖν': = elided masc. vocative sing. of ξεῖνος which is the Homeric spelling for the Attic Greek noun ξένος (stranger/foreigner/guest-friend). Telemachus shows that he is courteous and knows the protocol of how to treat guests and strangers by addressing Athena/Mentes in this way.

ἄρ: = a form of ἄρα used when the next word begins with a consonant. This particle indicates the natural sequence of ideas and is often difficult to translate, particularly when it is combined (as here) with δη, which means 'indeed'.

ἀνείρεαι: 2nd person present indicative middle ἀνέρομαι 'I ask', 'I question'.

232

μέλλεν: 'was likely to be' (unaugmented 3rd person singular imperfect indicative active of μέλλω).

233

ἔμμεναι: Homeric form of the present infinitive of εἰμί 'I am', i.e. 'to be'.

ὄφρα: 'so long as', 'while'.

κεῖνος: poetic spelling of the pronoun ἐκεῖνος 'he', 'that man'. Telemachus does not name his father here – this distant language reflects his lack of connection with the man he has never met.

ἦεν: Homeric spelling of Attic Greek ἦν (3rd person indicative active of εἰμί 'I am').

234

ἐβόλοντο: = ἐβούλοντο.

μητιόωντες: present participle masc. nom. pl. of μητιάω 'I plot', 'I devise', here describing the gods.

235

κεῖνον: = ἐκεῖνον, here referring to Odysseus as before.

235–236

περὶ πάντων ἀνθρώπων: 'above all other men'.

236

ἀκαχοίμην: 1st person singular aorist optative middle of ἀχεύω 'I grieve'.

κε: is the Homeric version of ἄν, used here with the optative in a future counterfactual 'I would not grieve . . .'.

πέρ: is an enclitic particle which gives emphasis to an idea. Translate as 'really', 'at least'.

237

δάμη: unaugmented 3rd person singular aorist indicative passive of δαμάζω 'I overpower'.

ἑτάροισι: = dat. pl. of ἑταῖρος (2nd decl. masc.) 'companion'.

ἐνί: = ἐν 'in' (+ dative).

238

χερσίν: dat. pl. of χείρ 'hand' (3f.).

τολύπευσεν: 3rd person singular aorist indicative active (unaugmented) of τολυπεύω 'I wind (wool)', thus 'I finish', 'I complete'. This is a metaphor from wool-working: translate 'when he wound up the war'.

239

τῷ: 'then', 'in that case'.

κέν: = ἄν, marking a past counterfactual condition 'All the Greeks *would have* made a tomb for him'.

οἱ: = αὐτῷ 'for him'.

Παναχαιοί: 'all the Greeks'.

240

ᾧ: = 'his'.

ἤρατ': 3rd person singular aorist indicative middle of αἴρω (here 'I win', literally 'I lift').

241

μιν: = αὐτόν 'him'

ἅρπυιαι: 'whirlwinds', imagined here most likely as a natural phenomenon on the sea rather than as a mythological personification such as the Harpies.

ἀνηρείψαντο 3rd person plural aorist indicative middle of ἀνερείπομαι 'I snatch up'

242

οἴχετ': present tense with perfect meaning, 'he has gone'.

243

κάλλιπεν: = 3rd person singular aorist indicative active of καταλείπω 'I leave behind'.

τι: 'at all', 'in any way'.

244

νύ: = νῦν.

ἄλλα: 'other' (in agreement with κήδε' 'troubles').

245

ὅσσοι: = epic spelling of the masc. nom. pl. of ὅσος 'as many as', 'all of'.

νήσοισιν: dative plural of νῆσος, ἡ (2f.) island.

ἐπικρατέουσιν: in Homer contract verbs regularly written in their uncontracted forms, as here with the 3rd person plural present indicative active of ἐπικρατέω (+ dative) 'I rule over'.

ἄριστοι: literally 'the best [men]', i.e. the chiefs, the leaders.

246

Δουλιχίῳ τε Σάμη τε καὶ ὑλήεντι Ζακύνθῳ: 'Dulichium and Same and wooded Zacynthus': all these islands are in the dative after ἐπικρατέω in the previous line.

247

κάτα: 'throughout'.

κοιρανέουσιν: another epsilon contract verb written in uncontracted form.

248

τόσσοι: 'all these men', 'so many men' – correlative with ὅσσοι in line 245.

μνῶνται: 3rd person present indicative middle of μνάομαι 'I woo'.

249

τοί: = οἱ (masc. nom. plural of the definite article). Refers here to the suitors: the δε immediately following indicates a change of subject.

251

με διαρραίσουσι καὶ αὐτόν: 'they will also destroy me myself'.

252

ἐπαλαστήσασα: feminine nominative singular aorist active participle of ἐπαλαστέω 'I am full of wrath at'. The aorist here implies a sudden surge of feeling (Stanford 226 n.252).

προσηύδα: 3rd person singular imperfect indicative active of προσαυδάω 'I speak to'.

253

ὢ πόποι: a common address in Homer used when the speaker is very upset or angry. Translate as 'alas!' or 'oh no!'.

ἦ: 'truly'.

πολλόν: adverbial with δεύῃ (2nd person singular present indicative middle of δεύω + gen. 'I miss, I lack'). Translate as 'you greatly miss, you greatly lack'.

ἀποιχομένου Ὀδυσῆος: genitive after δεύῃ in the next line.

254

μνηστῆρσιν: dat. pl. of μνηστήρ (3m.) 'wooer', 'suitor'.

ἐφείη: 3rd person singular aorist optative active of ἐφίημι 'I put on', 'I lay on'. The optative is used here in a future counterfactual phrase (NB the κε = ἄν earlier in the line) 'who [Odysseus] would lay his hands on the shameless suitors'.

255

εἰ γάρ: introduces a wish for the future and is used with the optative σταίη in the next line 'I wish he were standing . . .', 'would that he were standing . . .'.

ἐν πρώτῃσι θύρῃσι: 'at the outer door'.

256

ἐών: masc. nom. sing. of the present participle of εἰμί (= ὤν in Attic Greek).

AS

257

τοῖος ... οἷόν: 'such a man ... as'.

τὰ πρῶτ᾽: 'first' (adverbial).

259

ἐξ Ἐφύρης: Ephyra, either a town in Thesprotia or in Elis (there are two towns of this name and scholars disagree on which is meant here).

παρ᾽ Ἴλου Μερμερίδαο: 'from the house of Ilus, son of Mermerus. Μερμερίδαο (nom. Μερμερίδης) is the patronymic form of the noun (distinguished usually by the -ίδης in the ending). This Ilus is otherwise unknown. His father Mermerus was the son of Jason and Medea.

260

κεῖσε: = ἐκεῖσε 'to there'.

θοῆς ἐπὶ νηός: 'in a swift ship'. The adjective θοῆς 'swift' is an example of a Homeric epithet (see Introduction pp. 246–247) and is the most common epithet for a ship in Homer.

261–262

ὄφρα: = ἵνα (introducing a purpose clause); ὄφρα οἱ εἴη.

ἰοὺς χρίεσθαι χαλκήρεας: 'so that he might have it for anointing his bronze-tipped arrows'.

262

χαλκήρεας: 'bronze-tipped'.

ὁ μέν: = Ilus, Odysseus' host on this journey.

οἱ: = αὐτῷ 'to him', i.e. to Odysseus.

263

δῶκεν: = unaugmented 3rd person singular aorist indicative active of δίδωμι 'I give'.

θεοὺς αἰὲν ἐόντας: another example of a Homeric epithet or formula, the gods are frequently described using this phrase 'the gods who are/exist forever'.

νεμεσίζετο: 'he was in awe of'.

264

φιλέεσκε: = 3rd person singular imperfect indicative active of φιλέω 'I love', indicating a continuous or repeated action.

αἰνῶς: literally 'terribly', 'dreadfully' used here hyperbolically to express very strong emotion: 'excessively'.

265

τοῖος ἐών: 'in this manner', 'in such a way'.

ὁμιλήσειεν: 3rd person singular aorist optative active of ὁμιλέω, literally 'I meet with' but here used in the sense of 'I meet in battle'. The optative picks up on the wish for the future introduced in line 255; translate 'Would that Odysseus meet the suitors in battle in this manner'.

AS

266

ὠκύμοροι: 'swift-dying', 'swift to die' – an unusual adjective which draws attention to the suitors' imagined fate at Odysseus' hands.

γενοίατο: 3rd person plural aorist optative middle of γίγνομαι. Translate 'they would become', 'they would be'.

267

ταῦτα: 'these things' i.e. this situation, used with the singular verb κεῖται as is usual with neuter plural subjects.

πικρόγαμοι: another unusual adjective, used ironically here as it literally means 'attaining a bitter marriage' – the suitors, of course, will not succeed in marrying Penelope but will die at the hands of her husband.

268

ἤ . . . ἠε: 'whether . . . or . . .'.

νοστήσας: aorist active participle masc. nom. sing of νοστέω 'I go home' – this verb is of special resonance in the *Odyssey*, as the poem's main theme is the homecoming of the protagonist from Troy. The *Odyssey* fits into a wider story-group of the 'nostoi' or 'homecomings' of the Greek heroes from Troy, and indeed the poem deals in briefer terms with many of the other stories in this group, for example Telemachus finds out about the homecoming of Menelaus when he visits him in Sparta in book 4 of the poem.

ἀποτίσεται: 3rd person singular future middle of ἀποτίνω 'I take revenge on'.

οὐκί: a common epic form of οὐκ.

269

οἷσιν ἐνὶ μεγάροισι: 'in his own halls'. The megaron was a form of architecture common to Bronze Age palaces of the sort inhabited by the Homeric heroes. It consisted of an open porch and a hallway leading into a large open room with a central hearth vented through a hole in the ceiling. The ceiling of the rectangular central room was often supported by four columns.

ἄνωγα: perfect tense used as present tense, 'I command': Athena is speaking very authoritatively to Zeus, a sign of how much she cares for Odysseus.

270

ὅππως: = ὅπως 'how'.

ἀπώσεαι: 2nd person singular aorist subjunctive middle of 'ἀποθέω ' I drive out'. Translate 'you might remove'.

271

εἰ δ᾽ ἄγε νῦν: 'come on now'.

ξυνίει: 2nd person singular present imperative of συνίημι 'I send with', 'I bring with', used metaphorically here to mean 'give heed'.

ἐμπάζεο: 2nd person singular present imperative middle of ἐμπάζομαι 'I pay attention to' (+ gen.). The tautology with ξυνίει indicates the urgency with which Athena demands Telemachus' attention.

272

ἀγορήν: = accusative singular of ἀγορά 'assembly'.

AS

273

πέφραδε: 2nd person singular aorist imperative active of φράζω 'I point out'. Translate here as 'speak'.

ἔστων: 3rd person plural imperative of εἰμί 'I am': 'let the [gods] be'.

274

ἐπὶ σφέτερα: 'to their own [homes]'.

σκίδνασθαι: present middle infinitive of σκίδνημι 'I scatter', 'I disperse'.

ἄνωχθι: 2nd person singular perfect imperative of ἄνωγα, the defective perfect tense verb used as a present tense. Translate 'Order', 'Command'.

275

οἱ: = αὐτῇ.

γαμέεσθαι: present middle infinitive of γαμέω 'I marry'. If a woman is the subject of this verb, the middle must be used (only a man may be the subject of the active form of the verb).

276

ἴτω: 3rd person singular imperative of εἶμι 'I will go' used as present tense. 'Let her go'. The change from indirect command in the previous lines to a direct imperative is striking and makes Athena/Mentes' words even more forceful.

μητέρα: translate the accusative as 'as for your mother'.

ἐς: = εἰς 'to'.

δυναμένοιο: = masculine genitive singular of the present middle participle of δύναμαι 'I am able'. Here it is used as an adjective 'powerful' and agrees with πατρός.

277

οἱ δὲ: the identity of the subject here is much disputed. It seems most likely to refer to Penelope's family, present in the megaron of her father.

ἔεδνα: neuter acc. pl. of ἔδνον 'dowry'.

278

πολλὰ μάλ᾽: it is easiest to supply a noun with this (although it technically agrees with ἔεδνα in the line before) 'very many [gifts]'.

ὅσσα: = ὅσα 'as many as' (referring back to the many gifts).

ἔοικε: 3rd person singular perfect active of the defective verb ἔοικα 'I am like, I resemble'. This impersonal usage is frequently used in Homer with the meaning 'it is right', 'it is fitting'.

φίλης ἐπὶ παιδὸς: the meaning of the preposition is difficult here, but it is easiest to take it with the verb, translating it as [follow] 'after a dear daughter'.

279

ὑποθήσομαι: 1st person singular future indicative middle of ὑποτίθημι 'I advise'.

αἴ κε: = ἐαν, forming a future open conditional with the subjunctive πίθηαι.

πίθηαι: 2nd singular aorist subjunctive middle of πείθω (literally 'I persuade', used in Homer often, as here, in the sense of 'I pay heed'). Translate as 'if you will pay attention'.

AS

280

ἄρσας: masculine nominative singular aorist participle ἀραρίσκω 'I equip', 'I fit'. A twenty-oared ship is quite small (fifty-oared ships were the normal outfit at Troy): this size implies secrecy and perhaps is also a recognition that the suitors will try to prevent Telemachus having a larger outfit.

ἐρέτῃσιν: = dat. pl. of ἐρέτης 'rower'.

ἐείκοσιν: = εἴκοσι 'twenty'.

ἥ τις ἀρίστη: 'the best [ship you have]'.

281

ἔρχεο: = ἔρχου 2nd sing. pres. imperative middle.

πευσόμενος: masc. nom. sing. fut. middle participle of πυνθάνομαι (+ gen.) 'I find out about'. The future participle is used here to form a purpose clause. 'Go and find out'.

282

ἤν: = ἐάν.

εἴπῃσι: 3rd singular aorist subjunctive active of λέγω.

284

εἴρεο: 2nd sing. pres. imperative middle ἔρομαι 'I ask'.

285

παρὰ ξανθὸν Μενέλαον: 'to the house of auburn-haired Menelaus'.

287

πατρὸς βίοτον καὶ νόστον: literally: 'the life and homecoming of your father', i.e. 'that your father is alive and coming home'.

288

τρυχόμενός περ: 'although suffering'.

ἔτι: 'still', 'yet'.

τλαίης: 'you could endure' (to be taken with ἂν earlier in the line).

289

τεθνηῶτος: masc. gen. sing. perfect active participle of θνήσκω. 'If you hear that he has died . . .'.

291

χεῦαι: 2nd person singular aorist imperative middle of χέω 'I heap up'.

ἐπὶ κτέρεα κτερεΐξαι: 'and over it perform funeral rites'.

292

δοῦναι: aorist active infinitive used as imperative. Translate 'give your mother to a [new] man'.

293

ἔρξῃς: 2nd sing. aorist subjunctive active of ἔρδω 'I do, I achieve'. The subjunctive reflects the uncertainty of the timeframe.

AS

294

φράζεσθαι: 'consider' (infinitive as imperative).

295

ὅππως: = ὅπως 'how'.

296

νηπιάας ὀχέειν: 'to behave childishly'.

297

ἐσσι: = εἶ – 'you are'.

298

ἀίεις: is technically present tense but best translated here as perfect 'have you not heard?'.

ἔλλαβε: is the Homeric spelling for ἔλαβε, 3rd person singular aorist indicative active of λαμβάνω.

299

πάντας ἐπ᾽ ἀνθρώπους: 'among all mankind'.

πατροφονῆα: 'his father's killer'.

300

ὅ οἱ πατέρα κλυτὸν ἔκτα: 'who killed his famous father' ἔκτα is from κτείνω.

302

ἔσσο: imperative from εἰμί 'I am': 'be'.

ὀψιγόνων: 'of those yet to be born'.

ἵνα ... ἐὺ εἴπῃ: purpose clause '[that someone] might praise you'.

303

κατελεύσομαι: 1st person singular future indicative middle κατέρχομαι 'I go down'.

305

σοὶ δ᾽ αὐτῷ μελέτω: 'let [these things] be a concern to you yourself', i.e. 'take care of these things yourself'.

καὶ ἐμῶν ἐμπάζεο μύθων: a striking repetition of the end of line 271.

307

φίλα φρονέων: literally 'thinking kindly things', i.e. 'with kind intentions'.

308

λήσομαι: 'I will [not] forget'. NB λανθάνω takes the genitive (here αντων).

309

ἐπίμεινον: aorist imperative active 'stay!'.

ἐπειγόμενός περ ὁδοῖο: 'although eager for the road'.

AS

310

λοεσσάμενος: aorist middle participle of λούω 'I bathe', 'having washed [yourself]'.

τεταρπόμενος: aorist middle participle of τέρπω 'I enjoy, I satisfy', so 'having satisfied'.

311

κίῃς: 2nd singular present subjunctive κίω 'I go' in a purpose clause after ὄφρα.

312

τιμῆεν: 'precious' (agreeing with δῶρον in the previous line) neuter acc. sing. of τιμήεις.

313

οἷα φίλοι ξεῖνοι ξείνοισι διδοῦσι: 'of the sort that kind hosts give to guests'. Telemachus shows that, although he is young, he is well-versed in the rules of Greek hospitality. See introduction, pp. 250–253.

315

λιλαιόμενόν περ ὁδοῖο: the περ here is an intensifier 'greatly longing for the road'.

317

δόμεναι: infinitive as imperative 'and give'.

318

σοὶ δ᾽ ἄξιον ἔσται ἀμοιβῆς: 'it will bring you full value in terms of its return' – she means that Telemachus will receive an equally valuable gift if he visits her. This reciprocity is characteristic of the Greek custom of *xenia*.

320

ὄρνις δ᾽ ὣς ἀνοπαῖα διέπτατο: 'she flew up into the air [in the shape of] a bird'. Athena departs human company in the shape of a bird again later in the poem, when she visits Pylos. The word ἀνοπαῖα has caused considerable confusion and debate since antiquity, and corrections to the text have been suggested by scholars; it could also potentially mean 'unseen', or 'up the smoke-vent'.

321

ὑπέμνησεν: 'she reminded him'.

322

μᾶλλον ἔτ᾽ ἢ τὸ πάροιθεν: 'even more than before'.

φρεσὶν ᾗσι: 'in his mind'.

323

θάμβησεν: unaugmented aorist of θαμβέω 'I am amazed'.

κατὰ θυμόν: 'in his heart'.

ὀίσατο: 3rd person singular aorist middle of οἴομαι 'I think'.

324

ἐπῴχετο: 3rd person singular imperfect middle of ἐποίχομαι 'I go towards'.

326

ἥατ': 'they sat' 3rd person plural pluperfect indicative middle of ἥμαι 'I sit'.

327

ἐπετείλατο: 'she laid upon them'. Athena caused difficulties for the Greeks returning
from Troy because they had offended her when the Greek Ajax raped the Trojan
princess and priestess Cassandra after dragging her out of Athena's temple at
Troy. She does however continue to support Odysseus as her special favourite.

328

τοῦ: 'his' (Phemius').
σύνθετο: 'she heard'.
οἷο δόμοιο: 'from her chamber'.

332

δῖα γυναικῶν: 'fair lady'.

333

παρὰ σταθμὸν: 'by the doorpost'.

334

σχομένη: 'holding' (aorist middle participle of ἔχω).
λιπαρὰ κρήδεμνα: 'a shining veil' – plural for singular. Penelope shows her modesty
by coming to the hall accompanied by two maids and by covering her face with a
veil before the suitors. This makes clear that she is not encouraging their attentions.

335

παρέστη: 'stood beside'; 3rd person singular aorist indicative active of παρίστημι.

336

δακρύσασα: although this is an aorist participle, it is best translated as present:
'weeping' or perhaps 'bursting into tears'.
θεῖον ἀοιδόν: 'the divine singer': bards and poets were seen as divine because they
were inspired by the muses, goddesses of poetry.

337

πολλὰ γὰρ ἄλλα βροτῶν θελκτήρια οἶδας: 'for you know many other things
that charm mortals'. οἶδας is the epic form of 2nd person singular of οἶδα 'I
know'.

339

τῶν ἕν: 'one of these'.
σφιν: = αὐτοῖς 'for them', i.e. the suitors.
παρήμενος: 'as you sit here', perfect participle of ἥμαι 'I sit'.

340

πινόντων: 'let them drink' 3rd person present imperative of πίνω 'I drink'.

ἀποπαύε᾽: 2nd person sing. middle imperative 'cease'.

342

ἐπεί με μάλιστα καθίκετο πένθος ἄλαστον: 'since upon me especially has come unbearable grief'.

343

τοίην γὰρ κεφαλήν: literally 'such a head [of a man]' to be taken with ἀνδρός in the next line. She means she misses the person of Odysseus. This form of emotional language is often used in Homer when characters talk about dead loved ones. Translate 'so dear a man' or 'such a man'.

344

κλέος: 'glory' is one of the major preoccupations of the *Iliad* and a primary focus of any hero in Homeric culture. Penelope is proud of her husband's wide renown. A hero's glory would be spread, in part, by bards such as Phemius singing the heroic exploits of men like Odysseus at aristocratic feasts.

καθ᾽ Ἑλλάδα καὶ μέσον Ἄργος: 'across all of Greece and central Argos' – Hellas is properly only the territory of Peleus, Achilles' father, but is used here to mean all of Northern Greece, while Argos is used as a catch-all term for the rest of Greece south of the isthmus of Corinth.

346

τί τ᾽ ἄρα: 'Why indeed' – Telemachus is clearly annoyed with Penelope here. He speaks to her in a rebellious tone, rebuking her for trying to curb the poet in his work.

ἐρίηρον: 'trusty' – this epithet is only used in Homer of bards (poets) and dear companions. It has connotations of loyalty and service which reflect well on Phemius.

347

ὅππῃ: 'in whatever way'.

347–348

οὔ νύ τ᾽ ἀοιδοὶ αἴτιοι: 'for bards are not at all to blame' – the τ᾽ here is an (elided) generalising τε.

348

ποθι: 'I suppose' – this softens the starkness of Telemachus' claim that Zeus is responsible for the suffering of men. Compare to Achilles' famously pessimistic claim in *Iliad* book 24 that Zeus doles out fortunes to men from two urns: one with only suffering and bad things in it, and one with a mixture of good and bad things.

349

ἀλφηστῇσιν: – dative plural of ἀλφηστής 'wage-earning' or perhaps 'grain-eating'– an unusual word for Homer (it is not found in the *Iliad* at all). The

AS

idea seems to be that this group of men are distinguished from both gods and savages.

ὅπως ἐθέλησιν: indefinite clause 'however he wishes', 'in whatever way he wants'.

ἐθέλησιν: is the 3rd person singular present active subjunctive of ἐθέλω 'I want'.

350

τούτῳ δ᾽ οὐ νέμεσις: 'there is no [reason for] anger with this man', i.e. Phemius. *nemesis*, often translated as 'revenge' or 'retribution' is a significant motivating moral factor in the Homeric world, and indeed more widely in Greek literature and thought: heroes fear *nemesis* in the form of public shame and potentially divine punishment also if they behave wrongly.

352

ἀκουόντεσσι: = masc. dative plural of active present participle of ἀκούω. lit. 'to those hearing'. The phrase ἀκουόντεσσι νεωτάτη ἀμφιπέληται is best translated as 'the newest to meet their ears'. Telemachus argues here that people very naturally praise most those poems which are new to them. This is interesting in a poem composed in the highly formulaic oral tradition, but poets could of course use traditional language to tell a new story.

353

σοί: 'as for you', an ethic dative.

ἐπιτολμάτω: 3rd singular present imperative with κραδίη καὶ θυμὸς as its subject. 'Let your heart and spirit endure . . .'.

354

νόστιμον ἦμαρ: 'the day of his return'.

355

ὄλοντο: 3rd person plural aorist (unaugmented) from ὄλλυμι. Translate as '[they] died'.

356–359

These lines appear also at *Iliad* 6.490ff. where Hector tells his wife Andromache to go into the house and busy herself with women's work, dismissing her advice about the war. The lines have a different, less compassionate tone here. Their repetition shows the mechanism of oral poetics at work: the poet has re-used the lines in a new context where they take on a new meaning and nuance.

356

εἰς οἶκον: not 'into the house', for they are already in the house, but 'into your own room'. Telemachus here acts out the role of the male head of the household in dismissing his mother from the public gathering.

τὰ σ᾽ αὐτῆς ἔργα κόμιζε: 'busy yourself with your own work', i.e. women's work of weaving, as he goes on to clarify.

357

ἱστόν τ᾽ ἠλακάτην τε: 'the loom and the distaff': Greek women were expected to take charge of the production of clothing for the family using large, upright wooden looms. Wealthy women would of course have (as Penelope does here) the help of slaves and servants. The distaff was a spindle used to spin the wool. Even aristocratic women are depicted weaving: it is thus a universal activity for females of all classes and a sign of a good, respectable wife. Penelope is famous for her skill at the loom (see book 2.116–117) and was particularly well known for her stratagem for putting the suitors off, by which she said she would marry one of them when she had finished weaving a shroud for her father-in-law, Laertes, but spent each night unpicking the work so that it should never be finished. She was eventually discovered when one of her maids betrayed her.

ἀμφιπόλοισι: dative plural of ἀμφίπολος, a two-termination adjective here used as a feminine noun meaning 'handmaids' – a special class of female servant who accompanied their mistress in public and worked closely with her on her tasks. The dative is after the verb of ordering.

358

μῦθος δ᾽ ἄνδρεσσι μελήσει: 'speech shall be a concern for men' – Telemachus' speech here adapts the speech of Hector to Andromache in book 6 of the *Iliad*, where Hector tells his wife that war is a concern for men. Telemachus is denying his mother the right to voice her opinion in public. Most scholars have seen this as adolescent rudeness and it is hard to rehabilitate Telemachus from this accusation.

359

τοῦ γὰρ κράτος ἔστ᾽ ἐνὶ οἴκῳ: 'for the power in this house is mine'. τοῦ here = 'ἐμοῦ'. This is rather an arrogant statement (and clearly not true, as the suitors have been able to run riot over the house, eating and drinking Odysseus' food and courting his wife). Telemachus is grasping for the rights he will have as a fully grown man, a position he is on the cusp of in this poem.

360–361

ἥμεν . . . ἔνθετοθμμς Penelope obeys Telemachus without question, which throws an interesting light on his actions and how the audience would have perceived his speech to Penelope.

βεβήκει: is 3rd singular pluperfect indicative active from βαινω, used here to mark the end of the episode rather than with a true pluperfect meaning. Translate as 'she went'.

363

κλαῖεν: 3rd person singular imperfect indicative active (unaugmented). The imperfect tense neatly conveys the extended nature of Penelope's weeping. Her genuine love for Odysseus is clearly shown here.

364

βάλε: 3rd person singular aorist indicative active of βάλλω (unaugmented). Athena is very fond of Odysseus and helps him often throughout the poem. Here she takes pity on his wife and helps her sleep.

AS

365

ὁμάδησαν: another unaugmented aorist, from ὁμαδέω 'I make an uproar'. The suitors are inflamed by the sight of Penelope and, characteristically, they act boorishly and misbehave.

μέγαρα σκιόεντα: 'shadowy halls'. σκιόεντα 'shadowy, shady' is a fixed epithet of μέγαρα 'halls' but is more likely to indicate cool shade from the hot Greek sun rather than gloom.

366

παραὶ: = παρα (beside [her]).

λεχέεσσι: = dative plural of λέχος 'bed'. The plural here is just the frequent 'plural for singular' used in poetry, while the dative has a locative force 'in bed'.

κλιθῆναι: aor. pass. infinitive of κλίνω – the passive of this verb has the sense 'I lie down' in Homer.

367

τοῖσι: 'among them', i.e. the suitors.

368

ὑπέρβιον ὕβριν ἔχοντες: lit. 'having excessive insolence' i.e. 'excessive in your insolence' – Telemachus does not hold back in his criticism of the suitors. He is continuing to exercise his new sense of authority, awoken by the visit of Athena/ Mentes. The concept of *hubris*, or excessive arrogance and violence, looms large in Greek literature. It is associated with human characters who overstep the mark either in terms of religious law, social custom or by over-reaching the bounds set down for mortals. Here the rude, uncivilized behaviour of the suitors is contrasted with civilized behaviour and respect for the gods. A Greek audience will expect to eventually see the suitors punished, as *hubris* rarely goes unpunished in Greek literature.

369

νῦν μὲν δαινύμενοι τερπώμεθα: 'for now let us enjoy feasting'. τερπώμεθα is jussive subjunctive.

369–370

μηδὲ βοητὺς ἔστω: 'let there be no brawling' – the enjambement emphasizes the authority in the 3rd person imperative ἔστω.

370

τό γε καλὸν ἀκουέμεν ἐστὶν ἀοιδοῦ: translate in the order ἐστὶν καλὸν [τό γε] ἀκουέμεν ἀοιδοῦ. τό γε ἀκουέμεν is an articular infinitive (lit. 'listening to'); so translate 'it is good (or 'a good thing') to listen to'. Telemachus uses the power of Phemius' excellent song as an incentive to quieten the suitors down.

371

τοιοῦδ' οἷος ὅδ' ἐστί: 'such as this man is'.

AS

αὐδήν: accusative of respect, so translate 'with respect to his voice', 'as regards his voice'.

372–380

Telemachus attempts to take control of the situation. The suitors are abusing the Greek custom of *xenia*, under which religious and cultural rules a host could not refuse food and shelter to a guest, and in the absence of an adult man in the house, have been getting away with it. Telemachus is now telling them that their behaviour is unacceptable, which indeed is implied by Antinous himself later in the poem (16.384) where he demonstrates that he knows the correct way of wooing a woman.

372

καθεζώμεσθα: another jussive subjunctive 'let us sit down'.

373

ἀποείπω: aorist subjunctive in a purpose clause. This verb of speaking has negative connotations of refutation and rebuke, and is strengthened by the striking adverb ἀπηλεγέως 'bluntly'. Telemachus is making it very clear that he intends to call the suitors out for their behaviour in the public forum of the assembly.

374

ἐξιέναι μεγάρων: this blunt command is emphasized further by its position at the start of the line. This could be seen as indirect statement, as Telemachus is reporting what he will say in the assembly the next day, or an example of the infinitive used in place of the imperative, a common phenomenon in Homeric Greek.

ἀλεγύνετε: the imperative continues the strong tone established by Telemachus in the previous lines. 'you sort out other feasts'.

375

ὑμὰ κτήματ' ἔδοντες: 'eating your own possessions'. The possessive adjective ὑμὰ is made even more pointed by its position in the line.

ἀμειβόμενοι κατὰ οἴκους: 'swapping between houses'. Telemachus is suggesting (sarcastically of course) that the suitors, since they like feasting so much, should take it in turns to host each other at their own homes.

376

λωίτερον: 'more agreeable' – Telemachus is being deeply sarcastic.

378

κείρετ': 2nd person plural imperative of κείρω 'I waste'. 'Waste it, then!'.

ἐπιβώσομαι: future middle of ἐπιβοάω. The middle of this verb has the sense 'I call on X for help' or 'I call X as witness'. Telemachus immediately mentions the gods to reinforce the idea that the suitors are in the wrong, and to imply that they can expect divine punishment for their bad behaviour.

AS

379

αἴ κέ ποθι: 'if by chance . . .'.

δῷσι: 3rd person singular aorist subjunctive of δίδωμι. '[Zeus] may grant'.

παλίντιτα ἔργα: 'deeds of revenge'.

380

νήποινοί κεν ἔπειτα δόμων ἔντοσθεν ὄλοισθε: 'then indeed you would perish without [the opportunity for] revenge in my halls'. Telemachus cleverly repeats the adjective and verb used in line 377 of the suitors wasting Odysseus' household, turning the language onto them to strengthen the idea of their punishment being deserved, and caused directly by their own actions. His words here are bold: he is openly threatening the suitors with death.

381

ὀδὰξ ἐν χείλεσι φύντες: 'biting their lips hard with their teeth'.

382

θαύμαζον: = ἐθαύμαζον.

ὃ θαρσαλέως ἀγόρευεν: the relative pronoun here ὃ is causal 'because he spoke boldly'. ἀγόρευεν: = ἠγόρευεν (imperfect).

383

The name Antinous means 'hostile' and this 'speaking name' makes the character of this ringleader of the suitors very clear. Throughout the poem Antinous is openly hostile to Telemachus whereas (as we shall see below) the other very prominent suitor, Eurymachus, is more subtle and deceptive in his approach.

384

μάλα: 'truly'. Antinous mocks Telemachus here – it is clear that he is not alarmed by Telemachus' threats but rather finds them amusing.

385

ἔμεναι: = εἶναι.

386

ἀμφιάλῳ: a two-termination adjective, so fem. dat. sing. 'sea-girt', 'surrounded by sea'.

Κρονίων: (masc. nom. sing.) 'the son of Kronos', i.e. Zeus.

386–387

μὴ . . . ποιήσειεν: a wish for the future with the aorist optative 'may [Zeus] never make you . . .'.

387

πατρώιον: 'inheritance' (neuter singular of the adjective πατρώιος 'ancestral' used as a noun).

γενεῇ: dative singular of γενεά. Translate as 'by birth'.

389

νεμεσήσεαι: 2nd person singular future middle of νεμεσάω 'I am angry at'. This verb takes the dative.

ὅττι κεν εἴπω: 'whatever I say', indefinite construction with the Homeric κεν for the usual ἄν.

390

καὶ κεν τοῦτ᾽ ἐθέλοιμι Διός γε διδόντος ἀρέσθαι: 'Even this I would be glad to accept if Zeus gave it'.

Διός γε διδόντος: is a genitive absolute with the present participle of δίδωμι.

ἀρέσθαι: aorist infinitive middle from αἴρω 'I take'.

391

ἦ φής: 'or do you claim that . . .' the ἦ is scornful, implying that Telemachus despises Antinous' obsession with royal power. φής will introduce an accusative and infinitive of indirect statement.

τετύχθαι: perfect infinitive of τεύχω 'I prepare, furnish' here used to mean 'to happen', 'to occur'.

392

βασιλευέμεν: = βασιλεύειν (i.e. present infinitive active, 'to rule'). 'For it is no bad thing to rule as a king'. Telemachus admits, in an example of litotes or deliberate understatement, that it is a good thing to have kingly power, but he also understands that it is not everything in life. The litotes thus reflects his perspective and moderation.

οἱ: = αὐτῷ 'for him', 'his'.

δῶ: = a Homeric form for the nominative singular of the neuter noun δῶμα 'house'.

393

τιμηέστερος: 'more honoured' (nominative masc. sing. comparative of τιμήεις). Telemachus here shows knowledge of τιμή, 'honour', one of the major preoccupations of heroes in the *Iliad*. One way of obtaining τιμή in the Homeric world is through warfare, but the acquisition of wealth and royal power is also a major source of honour for these heroes.

394

ἦ τοι: 'truly'.

βασιλῆες Ἀχαιῶν εἰσὶ καὶ ἄλλοι: 'there are other kings of the Greeks . . .'. Ἀχαιῶν is used here to mean 'Greek' rather than specifically 'Achaean' (Achaea was a region in Greece). This statement raises important questions about what the word βασιλεύς (usually translated as 'king') means in Homeric culture. It clearly does not mean a monarch, but something more like 'lord' or 'chief'. It is not clear in the *Odyssey* exactly how the political system in Ithaca works, but Odysseus does seem to have been the most important of these lords and thus, in some senses, the king. Telemachus here seems to reject Antinous' words at line 387, where he said that royal power in Ithaca was Telemachus' birthright (πατρώϊον), and to suggest that another aristocrat may well end up taking the lead.

AS

396

τῶν κέν τις τόδ' ἔχῃσιν: 'let one of them have it'. ἔχῃσιν is 3rd person singular present subjunctive active of ἔχω 'I have'. The subjunctive here expresses certainty 'one of them may surely have it' rather than doubt. τόδ' is deliberately vague – Telemachus is not naïve enough to sign away any specific political rights.

ἐπεὶ θάνε δῖος Ὀδυσσεύς: Telemachus has been encouraged by Athena/Mentes to think Odysseus may have survived, but of course he will not wish to share this information with the hostile suitors.

397

ἐγών: = the usual form of ἐγώ used before a word beginning with a vowel in Homer.

ἔσομ': = ἔσομαι 'I will be'. Telemachus makes a proud statement of his right to rule in his own house. This is further emphasized by the μοι in the next line, where Telemachus states that Odysseus has captured slaves 'for me'.

398

δμώων: 'of the house-slaves'. A δμώς is technically a slave captured in war or in piracy. (Eumaeus later tells Odysseus the story of how he, originally of noble family, was captured by pirates and ended up as a slave.) The use of this word here emphasizes Odysseus' prowess as a hero, as he has captured many slaves to work in his household.

ληίσσατο: 3rd singular aorist of ληίζομαι 'I seize as booty'.

399

Εὐρύμαχος Πολύβου πάϊς: 'Eurymachus son of Polybus'. Eurymachus is, along with Antinous, one of the most prominent suitors. Although what he says here seems conciliatory, his behaviour elsewhere (and indeed, the guarded tone of Telemachus' reply to him here) indicates that his speech is insincere. His questions about Mentes indicate his worry that Telemachus is building allies to move against the suitors. Eurymachus, unlike Antinous, does not have a particularly meaningful 'speaking name'.

400

ἢ τοι ταῦτα θεῶν ἐν γούνασι κεῖται: 'surely indeed these things lie on the laps of the gods'. A commonplace of Greek philosophy: Eurymachus is taking a didactic, fatherly tone with Telemachus and also seeking to imply that he has no particular interest in ruling Ithaca, but is happy to see what destiny brings. This is clearly not the case judging from his behaviour elsewhere (e.g. the plot to kill Telemachus).

402

κτήματα δ' αὐτὸς ἔχοις καὶ δώμασι σοῖσιν ἀνάσσοις: Eurymachus uses the optative wish for the future 'may you yourself have your possessions and be lord in your own halls'.

403–404

μὴ γάρ ... ἔτι γαιεταούσης 'Never may that man come who would, against your will and by force deprive you of your possessions, [not] while Ithaca is still inhabited'.

Given that the suitors have been for years feasting and drinking at Telemachus' expense, this is a patently disingenuous statement. The participle ναιεταούσης implies the meaning 'as long as Ithaca exists' and this hyperbole in itself points to a lack of sincerity.

404

ἀπορραίσει: 3rd person singular future indicative active of ἀπορραίω 'I deprive' + accusative of person deprived and accusative of the object taken away from them.

405

φέριστε: masc. vocative singular of φέριστος (= φέρτατος) 'best', 'bravest'. Eurymachus' use of the hyperbolic superlative to address the younger man is again evidence of his lack of sincerity.
ἐρέσθαι: aorist infinitive middle of ἔρομαι 'I ask'.

406

ὁππόθεν: = ὁπόθεν 'from where'.

406–407

ποίης δ' ἐξ εὔχεται εἶναι γαίης: translate in the order ἐξ ποίης γαίης εὔχεται εἶναι, remembering that this is an indirect question. 'From what . . .'.

407

γενεή: = γενεά 'family'.
πατρὶς ἄρουρα: 'ancestral lands' (lit. 'the field(s) of his father'). The tautology inherent in Eurymachus' series of questions indicates a strong desire to know all about Mentes: the suitor is clearly worried that Mentes will prove a strong ally for Telemachus.

408

ἠέ: = ἤ 'either' and is picked up by the ἤ 'or' at the start of the next line.
ἐρχομένοιο: = masculine genitive singular of the present participle, in agreement with πατρός.

409

ἑὸν αὐτοῦ χρεῖος: 'his own business', to be taken as the object of ἐελδόμενος (NB the epic double epsilon at the start of this word, the present participle from ἔλδομαι 'I desire').
τόδ' ἱκάνει: 'does he come this way', a frequent use of τόδε in epic.

410

οἷον ἀναΐξας ἄφαρ οἴχεται: 'how he darted up and went straightaway'. οἷον introduces an exclamation of surprise here. Eurymachus has not failed to notice Athena/Mentes' swift departure. The aorist participle ἀναΐξας 'having darted' is more natural rendered as a main verb in English here.

410–411

οὐδ' ὑπέμεινε γνώμεναι: 'nor did he stay [for us] to know [him]'. γνώμεναι = γνῶναι (root aorist infinitive of γιγνώσκω 'I get to know'). Eurymachus reveals

AS

his surprise and annoyance that the visitor did not think it worth introducing himself to the suitors and spoke only to the teenage son of Odysseus. This arrogance is characteristic of the suitors throughout the poem.

411

ἐῴκει: is the 3rd person singular pluperfect of the defective verb ἔοικα 'I seem' (a perfect tense verb which is used as the present tense). Translate 'he seemed', 'did he seem'. It takes the dative of a person, hence it is used here with κακῷ.

εἰς ὦπα literally 'to the eye', i.e. 'to look at', 'to look upon'. Eurymachus reveals his shallow nature, seen later par excellence when Odysseus returns home, disguised as a poor beggar, and is treated cruelly by the suitors. They do not show respect for anyone unless there is something in it for them. Their lack of respect for Odysseus and his household is clear by their excessive feasting and mistreatment of his wife, son and slaves.

413

ἦ τοι νόστος ἀπώλετο πατρὸς ἐμοῖο: 'surely my father's homecoming is lost'. Telemachus wisely does not reveal to Eurymachus that he has reason to believe his father may be returning home after all.

414

εἴ ποθεν ἔλθοι: 'no matter where it comes from'. Telemachus pretends to be cynical about any reports of Odysseus' homecoming, and indeed Eumaeus, Odysseus' most faithful servant and a lynchpin of his successful revenge against the suitors, does mention later in the poem that many people have given false accounts of Odysseus to try and gain rewards from his family.

415

ἐμπάζομαι: + genitive 'I care about', 'I take heed of'. Usually used with the negative in Homer. A θεοπροπία is an oracle or prophecy, so it may at first glance seem like a risky claim for Telemachus to make (that he does not trust oracles regarding Odysseus' return), as oracles and prophecies come from the gods. However, the Greeks were aware of false prophets and seers who pretended to deliver prophecies for monetary gain, and it is probably this sort of practice which Telemachus refers to here. In any case, Telemachus is using this reference to oracles to strengthen the (false) impression that he no longer believes his father to be alive.

ἥν τινα: 'any prophecy which my mother asks for' (take this accusative relative with the subjunctive verb ἐξερέηται in the next line, as part of an indefinite relative clause).

416

θεοπρόπον: 'prophet'.

417

πατρώιος: 'ancestral friend', 'hereditary guest-friend'.

ἐκ Τάφου: 'from Taphos'. Taphos is a small island in the sea between Ithaca and mainland Greece, very close to Ithaca itself.

418–419

Μέντης δ᾽ Ἀγχιάλοιο δαΐφρονος εὔχεται εἶναι υἱός: 'he claims he is Mentes the son of warlike Anchialus'. In Greek hospitality it was customary to feed and water your guest before asking them where they were from and what family they were from. Mentes' reply, quoted here by Telemachus is thus a standard formula in a guest-host exchange.

420

φρεσὶ δ᾽ ἀθανάτην θεὸν ἔγνω: 'but in his heart he knew the immortal goddess'. It is a mark of Telemachus' intelligence and sensitivity that he recognizes the intervention of the goddess where other mortals have failed to see the signs.

421

οἱ δ᾽: 'the suitors'. The suitors here turn to the leisurely pursuits of dance and song.
ἱμερόεσσαν: 'lovely' in agreement with ἀοιδὴν.

422

μένον: = ἔμενον.
ἐπὶ ἕσπερον ἐλθεῖν: an example of tmesis, where the preposition in a compound verb is written separately. Translate 'for evening to come'. Note the mirroring construction in the following line, μέλας ἐπὶ ἕσπερος ἦλθε 'black evening came upon [them . . .]; the repetition reflects the passing of time. The repetition of the verb τέρπομαι: 'I enjoy myself' in lines 422 and 423 emphasizes the suitors' hedonistic lifestyle, all of course at Odysseus' expense.

424

κακκείοντες: present participle of κατακείω/κακκείω, acting as a future of κατάκειμαι, the future participle is used in the sense here of 'desiring to lie down', 'with the intention of lying down'. This line shows that the suitors do not sleep at Odysseus' house, but go home each night. It raises a logistical problem (to which we are not given the answer) about what happens to those suitors who live too far away from Odysseus' house for this to be practical.
ἔβαν: 3rd person plural aorist active of βαίνω.

425

ὅθι οἱ θάλαμος περικαλλέος αὐλῆς: 'to where his bedchamber [was built] in the very beautiful courtyard'. περικαλλέος αὐλῆς is an example of a 'locative' genitive (the genitive case used to mean 'in' or 'at'). Scholars have argued that this detailed description of Telemachus going to bed is intended to emphasize his youth.

426

ὑψηλός: in agreement with θάλαμος in the previous line.
ἐδμητο: 'was built' (pluperfect of defective verb δέμω).

428

τῷ δ᾽ ἄρ᾽ ἅμ᾽: 'and with him'.

AS

φέρε: = ἔφερε '[she] carried'.

κεδνὰ ἰδυῖα: 'true-hearted'.

429

Εὐρύκλει᾽, Ὦπος θυγάτηρ Πεισηνορίδαο: 'Eurycleia, daughter of Ops, son of Peisenor'. Eurycleia is given a lineage much like a Homeric hero, to mark her out as superior to the other slaves. Her name, similarly, is a speaking name meaning 'widely-famed'. Eurycleia is of key importance later in the poem, where she helps Telemachus sneak away on his journey to try and find his father and also helps Odysseus achieve his successful revenge against the suitors.

430

πρίατο: = ἐπρίατο, 3rd sing. of ἐπριάμην (from *πρίαμαι), used as aorist of ὠνέομαι.

κτεάτεσσιν ἑοῖσιν: 'with his wealth'.

431

ἐοῦσαν: = οὖσαν (acc. sing. fem. participle of εἰμί 'I am'). This participle describes Eurycleia, who is the object of πρίατο in the previous line.

ἐεικοσάβοια: 'twenty oxen'. This is a high price for a female slave as is made clear at *Iliad* 23, during the funeral games for Patroclus, where a skilled female slave is said to be worth four oxen. A male prisoner is worth a hundred oxen and a metal tripod, twelve oxen.

432

ἴσα: adverbial 'equally', used with the dative of comparison κεδνῇ ἀλόχῳ 'to his trusty wife'.

μιν: = αὐτήν 'her', i.e. Eurycleia.

τίεν: = unaugmented imperfect tense of τίω 'I honour'.

433

ἔμικτο: aorist pass. 3rd sing. of μίγνυμι (literally 'I mix', but frequently used metaphorically of sexual intercourse. Translate 'I never slept with her in bed'.

ἀλέεινε 3rd person singular imperfect indicative active of ἀλεείνω 'I avoid'.

434

ἑ: = αὐτόν (i.e. Telemachus).

435

δμῳάων: 'of the female slaves' = gen. plural. (epic spelling) of δμωή.

φιλέεσκε: = 3rd person singular imperfect indicative active of φιλέω 'I love'. Eurycleia's affection for Telemachus is emphasized both by the imperfect tense (indicating that her love was ongoing) and by the superlative adverb μάλιστα 'most' in the previous line.

ἔτρεφε τυτθὸν ἐόντα: 'she had nursed him when he was a child'. We later discover that Eurycleia has also nursed Odysseus as a child and she is thus entirely loyal to the master of the house and his son.

436

ὤιξεν: = 3rd person singular aorist indicative active of οἴγω 'I open'.

437

μαλακὸν δ' ἔκδυνε χιτῶνα: 'he took off his soft tunic'. A short tunic is implied as Telemachus is able to remove it while sitting down.

438

τόν: 'it', i.e. the tunic.

γραίης πυκιμηδέος: 'of the wise old woman'.

439

πτύξασα: aorist participle of πτύσσω, best translated here as a main verb 'she folded'.

ἀσκήσασα: the aorist participle from ἀσκέω. Translate 'and she smoothed [the tunic]' (literally 'she took care of').

440

ἀγκρεμάσασα: 'and she hung [it] . . .'.

441

ἐπέρυσσε: 'she pulled' (aorist of ἐπερύω).

442

ἐπὶ δὲ κληῖδ' ἐτάνυσσεν ἱμάντι: 'she fastened the bolt with the leather strap'. The bolt is imagined as being on the inside of the door, but a leather thong passing through a hole in the door enables it to be opened from the outside as well as from the inside.

443–444

Telemachus does not sleep, but stays awake all night thinking of the advice Athena has given him. He is thus shown to be leaving childhood behind and taking on adult responsibilities.

443

κεκαλυμμένος οἰὸς ἀώτῳ: 'wrapped up in the fleece of a sheep'. Telemachus is well-wrapped in woollen blankets.

444

βούλευε: = ἐβούλευε 'he pondered'.

φρεσὶν ᾗσιν: 'in his mind'.

πέφραδ': = 3rd person singular aorist indicative active of φράζω 'I show'.

Text

Odyssey 6

–84 The Phaeacian princess Nausicaa leads a party of young women to wash clothes by the seashore. Unbeknownst to them, Odysseus sleeps in a shelter nearby.

αἱ δ᾽ ὅτε δὴ ποταμοῖο ῥόον περικαλλέ᾽ ἵκοντο,   85
ἔνθ᾽ ἦ τοι πλυνοὶ ἦσαν ἐπηετανοί, πολὺ δ᾽ ὕδωρ
καλὸν ὑπεκπρόρεεν μάλα περ ῥυπόωντα καθῆραι,
ἔνθ᾽ αἵ γ᾽ ἡμιόνους μὲν ὑπεκπροέλυσαν ἀπήνης.
καὶ τὰς μὲν σεῦαν ποταμὸν πάρα δινήεντα
τρώγειν ἄγρωστιν μελιηδέα: ταὶ δ᾽ ἀπ᾽ ἀπήνης   90
εἵματα χερσὶν ἕλοντο καὶ ἐσφόρεον μέλαν ὕδωρ,
στεῖβον δ᾽ ἐν βόθροισι θοῶς ἔριδα προφέρουσαι.
αὐτὰρ ἐπεὶ πλῦνάν τε κάθηράν τε ῥύπα πάντα,
ἑξείης πέτασαν παρὰ θῖν᾽ ἁλός, ἧχι μάλιστα
λάιγγας ποτὶ χέρσον ἀποπλύνεσκε θάλασσα.   95
αἱ δὲ λοεσσάμεναι καὶ χρισάμεναι λίπ᾽ ἐλαίῳ
δεῖπνον ἔπειθ᾽ εἵλοντο παρ᾽ ὄχθῃσιν ποταμοῖο,
εἵματα δ᾽ ἠελίοιο μένον τερσήμεναι αὐγῇ.
αὐτὰρ ἐπεὶ σίτου τάρφθεν δμῳαί τε καὶ αὐτή,
σφαίρῃ ταὶ δ᾽ ἄρ᾽ ἔπαιζον, ἀπὸ κρήδεμνα βαλοῦσαι: 100
τῇσι δὲ Ναυσικάα λευκώλενος ἤρχετο μολπῆς.
οἵη δ᾽ Ἄρτεμις εἶσι κατ᾽ οὔρεα ἰοχέαιρα,
ἢ κατὰ Τηΰγετον περιμήκετον ἢ Ἐρύμανθον,
τερπομένη κάπροισι καὶ ὠκείῃς ἐλάφοισι:
τῇ δέ θ᾽ ἅμα νύμφαι, κοῦραι Διὸς αἰγιόχοιο,   105
ἀγρονόμοι παίζουσι, γέγηθε δέ τε φρένα Λητώ:
πασάων δ᾽ ὑπὲρ ἥ γε κάρη ἔχει ἠδὲ μέτωπα,
ῥεῖά τ᾽ ἀριγνώτη πέλεται, καλαὶ δέ τε πᾶσαι:
ὣς ἥ γ᾽ ἀμφιπόλοισι μετέπρεπε παρθένος ἀδμής.
ἀλλ᾽ ὅτε δὴ ἄρ᾽ ἔμελλε πάλιν οἶκόνδε νέεσθαι   110
ζεύξασ᾽ ἡμιόνους πτύξασά τε εἵματα καλά,
ἔνθ᾽ αὖτ᾽ ἀλλ᾽ ἐνόησε θεά, γλαυκῶπις Ἀθήνη,
ὡς Ὀδυσεὺς ἔγροιτο, ἴδοι τ᾽ ἐυώπιδα κούρην,

ἥ οἱ Φαιήκων ἀνδρῶν πόλιν ἡγήσαιτο.
σφαῖραν ἔπειτ᾽ ἔρριψε μετ᾽ ἀμφίπολον βασίλεια: 115
ἀμφιπόλου μὲν ἅμαρτε, βαθείῃ δ᾽ ἔμβαλε δίνῃ:
αἱ δ᾽ ἐπὶ μακρὸν ἄυσαν: ὁ δ᾽ ἔγρετο δῖος Ὀδυσσεύς,
ἑζόμενος δ᾽ ὥρμαινε κατὰ φρένα καὶ κατὰ θυμόν:

"ὤ μοι ἐγώ, τέων αὖτε βροτῶν ἐς γαῖαν ἱκάνω;
ἦ ῥ᾽ οἵ γ᾽ ὑβρισταί τε καὶ ἄγριοι οὐδὲ δίκαιοι,   120
ἦε φιλόξεινοι καί σφιν νόος ἐστὶ θεουδής;
ὥς τέ με κουράων ἀμφήλυθε θῆλυς ἀυτή:
νυμφάων, αἲ ἔχουσ᾽ ὀρέων αἰπεινὰ κάρηνα
καὶ πηγὰς ποταμῶν καὶ πίσεα ποιήεντα.
ἦ νύ που ἀνθρώπων εἰμὶ σχεδὸν αὐδηέντων;   125
ἀλλ᾽ ἄγ᾽ ἐγὼν αὐτὸς πειρήσομαι ἠδὲ ἴδωμαι.'

ὣς εἰπὼν θάμνων ὑπεδύσετο δῖος Ὀδυσσεύς,
ἐκ πυκινῆς δ᾽ ὕλης πτόρθον κλάσε χειρὶ παχείῃ
φύλλων, ὡς ῥύσαιτο περὶ χροῖ μήδεα φωτός.
βῆ δ᾽ ἴμεν ὥς τε λέων ὀρεσίτροφος ἀλκὶ πεποιθώς,   130
ὅς τ᾽ εἶσ᾽ ὑόμενος καὶ ἀήμενος, ἐν δέ οἱ ὄσσε
δαίεται: αὐτὰρ ὁ βουσὶ μετέρχεται ἢ ὀίεσσιν
ἠὲ μετ᾽ ἀγροτέρας ἐλάφους: κέλεται δέ ἑ γαστὴρ
μήλων πειρήσοντα καὶ ἐς πυκινὸν δόμον ἐλθεῖν:
ὣς Ὀδυσεὺς κούρῃσιν ἐυπλοκάμοισιν ἔμελλε   135
μίξεσθαι, γυμνός περ ἐών: χρειὼ γὰρ ἵκανε.
σμερδαλέος δ᾽ αὐτῇσι φάνη κεκακωμένος ἅλμῃ,
τρέσσαν δ᾽ ἄλλυδις ἄλλη ἐπ᾽ ἠιόνας προὐχούσας:
οἴη δ᾽ Ἀλκινόου θυγάτηρ μένε: τῇ γὰρ Ἀθήνη
θάρσος ἐνὶ φρεσὶ θῆκε καὶ ἐκ δέος εἵλετο γυίων.   140
στῆ δ᾽ ἄντα σχομένη: ὁ δὲ μερμήριξεν Ὀδυσσεύς,
ἢ γούνων λίσσοιτο λαβὼν ἐυώπιδα κούρην,
ἢ αὔτως ἐπέεσσιν ἀποσταδὰ μειλιχίοισι
λίσσοιτ᾽, εἰ δείξειε πόλιν καὶ εἵματα δοίη.
ὣς ἄρα οἱ φρονέοντι δοάσσατο κέρδιον εἶναι,   145
λίσσεσθαι ἐπέεσσιν ἀποσταδὰ μειλιχίοισι,
μή οἱ γοῦνα λαβόντι χολώσαιτο φρένα κούρη.
αὐτίκα μειλίχιον καὶ κερδαλέον φάτο μῦθον.

'γουνοῦμαί σε, ἄνασσα: θεός νύ τις, ἦ βροτός ἐσσι;
εἰ μέν τις θεός ἐσσι, τοὶ οὐρανὸν εὐρὺν ἔχουσιν,   150
Ἀρτέμιδί σε ἐγώ γε, Διὸς κούρῃ μεγάλοιο,
εἶδός τε μέγεθός τε φυήν τ᾽ ἄγχιστα ἐίσκω:
εἰ δέ τίς ἐσσι βροτῶν, τοὶ ἐπὶ χθονὶ ναιετάουσιν,
τρὶς μάκαρες μὲν σοί γε πατὴρ καὶ πότνια μήτηρ,
τρὶς μάκαρες δὲ κασίγνητοι: μάλα πού σφισι θυμὸς   155
αἰὲν ἐυφροσύνῃσιν ἰαίνεται εἵνεκα σεῖο,
λευσσόντων τοιόνδε θάλος χορὸν εἰσοιχνεῦσαν.

A
Level

κεῖνος δ᾽ αὖ περὶ κῆρι μακάρτατος ἔξοχον ἄλλων,
ὅς κέ σ᾽ ἐέδνοισι βρίσας οἶκόνδ᾽ ἀγάγηται.
οὐ γάρ πω τοιοῦτον ἴδον βροτὸν ὀφθαλμοῖσιν,   160
οὔτ᾽ ἄνδρ᾽ οὔτε γυναῖκα: σέβας μ᾽ ἔχει εἰσορόωντα.
Δήλῳ δή ποτε τοῖον Ἀπόλλωνος παρὰ βωμῷ
φοίνικος νέον ἔρνος ἀνερχόμενον ἐνόησα:
ἦλθον γὰρ καὶ κεῖσε, πολὺς δέ μοι ἕσπετο λαός,
τὴν ὁδὸν ᾗ δὴ μέλλεν ἐμοὶ κακὰ κήδε᾽ ἔσεσθαι.   165
ὣς δ᾽ αὕτως καὶ κεῖνο ἰδὼν ἐτεθήπεα θυμῷ
δήν, ἐπεὶ οὔ πω τοῖον ἀνήλυθεν ἐκ δόρυ γαίης,
ὡς σέ, γύναι, ἄγαμαί τε τέθηπά τε, δείδια δ᾽ αἰνῶς
γούνων ἅψασθαι: χαλεπὸν δέ με πένθος ἱκάνει.
χθιζὸς ἐεικοστῷ φύγον ἤματι οἴνοπα πόντον: 170
τόφρα δέ μ᾽ αἰεὶ κῦμ᾽ ἐφόρει κραιπναί τε θύελλαι
νήσου ἀπ᾽ Ὠγυγίης. νῦν δ᾽ ἐνθάδε κάββαλε δαίμων,
ὄφρ᾽ ἔτι που καὶ τῇδε πάθω κακόν: οὐ γὰρ ὀίω
παύσεσθ᾽, ἀλλ᾽ ἔτι πολλὰ θεοὶ τελέουσι πάροιθεν.
ἀλλά, ἄνασσ᾽, ἐλέαιρε: σὲ γὰρ κακὰ πολλὰ μογήσας   175
ἐς πρώτην ἱκόμην, τῶν δ᾽ ἄλλων οὔ τινα οἶδα
ἀνθρώπων, οἳ τήνδε πόλιν καὶ γαῖαν ἔχουσιν.
ἄστυ δέ μοι δεῖξον, δὸς δὲ ῥάκος ἀμφιβαλέσθαι,
εἴ τί που εἴλυμα σπείρων ἔχες ἐνθάδ᾽ ἰοῦσα.
σοὶ δὲ θεοὶ τόσα δοῖεν ὅσα φρεσὶ σῇσι μενοινᾷς,   180
ἄνδρα τε καὶ οἶκον, καὶ ὁμοφροσύνην ὀπάσειαν
ἐσθλήν: οὐ μὲν γὰρ τοῦ γε κρεῖσσον καὶ ἄρειον,
ἢ ὅθ᾽ ὁμοφρονέοντε νοήμασιν οἶκον ἔχητον
ἀνὴρ ἠδὲ γυνή: πόλλ᾽ ἄλγεα δυσμενέεσσι,
χάρματα δ᾽ εὐμενέτῃσι, μάλιστα δέ τ᾽ ἔκλυον αὐτοί.᾽   185

τὸν δ᾽ αὖ Ναυσικάα λευκώλενος ἀντίον ηὔδα:
"ξεῖν᾽, ἐπεὶ οὔτε κακῷ οὔτ᾽ ἄφρονι φωτὶ ἔοικας:
Ζεὺς δ᾽ αὐτὸς νέμει ὄλβον Ὀλύμπιος ἀνθρώποισιν,
ἐσθλοῖς ἠδὲ κακοῖσιν, ὅπως ἐθέλῃσιν, ἑκάστῳ:
καί που σοὶ τάδ᾽ ἔδωκε, σὲ δὲ χρὴ τετλάμεν ἔμπης.   190
νῦν δ᾽, ἐπεὶ ἡμετέρην τε πόλιν καὶ γαῖαν ἱκάνεις,
οὔτ᾽ οὖν ἐσθῆτος δευήσεαι οὔτε τευ ἄλλου,
ὧν ἐπέοιχ᾽ ἱκέτην ταλαπείριον ἀντιάσαντα.
ἄστυ δέ τοι δείξω, ἐρέω δέ τοι οὔνομα λαῶν.
Φαίηκες μὲν τήνδε πόλιν καὶ γαῖαν ἔχουσιν,   195
εἰμὶ δ᾽ ἐγὼ θυγάτηρ μεγαλήτορος Ἀλκινόοιο,
τοῦ δ᾽ ἐκ Φαιήκων ἔχεται κάρτος τε βίη τε.᾽

ἦ ῥα καὶ ἀμφιπόλοισιν ἐυπλοκάμοισι κέλευσε:
‘στῆτέ μοι, ἀμφίπολοι: πόσε φεύγετε φῶτα ἰδοῦσαι;
ἦ μή πού τινα δυσμενέων φάσθ᾽ ἔμμεναι ἀνδρῶν;   200
οὐκ ἔσθ᾽ οὗτος ἀνὴρ διερὸς βροτὸς οὐδὲ γένηται,
ὅς κεν Φαιήκων ἀνδρῶν ἐς γαῖαν ἵκηται

δηιοτῆτα φέρων: μάλα γὰρ φίλοι ἀθανάτοισιν.
οἰκέομεν δ᾽ ἀπάνευθε πολυκλύστῳ ἐνὶ πόντῳ,
ἔσχατοι, οὐδέ τις ἄμμι βροτῶν ἐπιμίσγεται ἄλλος.   205
ἀλλ᾽ ὅδε τις δύστηνος ἀλώμενος ἐνθάδ᾽ ἱκάνει,
τὸν νῦν χρὴ κομέειν: πρὸς γὰρ Διός εἰσιν ἅπαντες
ξεῖνοί τε πτωχοί τε, δόσις δ᾽ ὀλίγη τε φίλη τε.
ἀλλὰ δότ᾽, ἀμφίπολοι, ξείνῳ βρῶσίν τε πόσιν τε,
λούσατέ τ᾽ ἐν ποταμῷ, ὅθ᾽ ἐπὶ σκέπας ἔστ᾽ ἀνέμοιο.'   210

ὣς ἔφαθ᾽, αἱ δ᾽ ἔσταν τε καὶ ἀλλήλησι κέλευσαν,
κὰδ δ᾽ ἄρ᾽ Ὀδυσσῆ᾽ εἷσαν ἐπὶ σκέπας, ὡς ἐκέλευσεν
Ναυσικάα θυγάτηρ μεγαλήτορος Ἀλκινόοιο:
πὰρ δ᾽ ἄρα οἱ φᾶρός τε χιτῶνά τε εἵματ᾽ ἔθηκαν,
δῶκαν δὲ χρυσέῃ ἐν ληκύθῳ ὑγρὸν ἔλαιον,   215
ἤνωγον δ᾽ ἄρα μιν λοῦσθαι ποταμοῖο ῥοῇσιν.
δή ῥα τότ᾽ ἀμφιπόλοισι μετηύδα δῖος Ὀδυσσεύς:

"ἀμφίπολοι, στῆθ᾽ οὕτω ἀπόπροθεν, ὄφρ᾽ ἐγὼ αὐτὸς
ἅλμην ὤμοιιν ἀπολούσομαι, ἀμφὶ δ᾽ ἐλαίῳ
χρίσομαι: ἦ γὰρ δηρὸν ἀπὸ χροός ἐστιν ἀλοιφή.   220
ἄντην δ᾽ οὐκ ἂν ἐγώ γε λοέσσομαι: αἰδέομαι γὰρ
γυμνοῦσθαι κούρῃσιν ἐυπλοκάμοισι μετελθών.'
ὣς ἔφαθ᾽, αἱ δ᾽ ἀπάνευθεν ἴσαν, εἶπον δ᾽ ἄρα κούρῃ.
αὐτὰρ ὁ ἐκ ποταμοῦ χρόα νίζετο δῖος Ὀδυσσεὺς
ἅλμην, ἥ οἱ νῶτα καὶ εὐρέας ἄμπεχεν ὤμους,   225
ἐκ κεφαλῆς δ᾽ ἔσμηχεν ἁλὸς χνόον ἀτρυγέτοιο.
αὐτὰρ ἐπεὶ δὴ πάντα λοέσσατο καὶ λίπ᾽ ἄλειψεν,
ἀμφὶ δὲ εἵματα ἕσσαθ᾽ ἅ οἱ πόρε παρθένος ἀδμής,
τὸν μὲν Ἀθηναίη θῆκεν Διὸς ἐκγεγαυῖα
μείζονά τ᾽ εἰσιδέειν καὶ πάσσονα, κὰδ δὲ κάρητος   230
οὔλας ἧκε κόμας, ὑακινθίνῳ ἄνθει ὁμοίας.
ὡς δ᾽ ὅτε τις χρυσὸν περιχεύεται ἀργύρῳ ἀνὴρ
ἴδρις, ὃν Ἥφαιστος δέδαεν καὶ Παλλὰς Ἀθήνη
τέχνην παντοίην, χαρίεντα δὲ ἔργα τελείει,
ὣς ἄρα τῷ κατέχευε χάριν κεφαλῇ τε καὶ ὤμοις.   235
ἕζετ᾽ ἔπειτ᾽ ἀπάνευθε κιὼν ἐπὶ θῖνα θαλάσσης,
κάλλεϊ καὶ χάρισι στίλβων: θηεῖτο δὲ κούρη.

δή ῥα τότ᾽ ἀμφιπόλοισιν ἐυπλοκάμοισι μετηύδα:
"κλῦτέ μευ, ἀμφίπολοι λευκώλενοι, ὄφρα τι εἴπω.
οὐ πάντων ἀέκητι θεῶν, οἳ Ὄλυμπον ἔχουσιν,   240
Φαιήκεσσ᾽ ὅδ᾽ ἀνὴρ ἐπιμίσγεται ἀντιθέοισι:
πρόσθεν μὲν γὰρ δή μοι ἀεικέλιος δέατ᾽ εἶναι,
νῦν δὲ θεοῖσιν ἔοικε, τοὶ οὐρανὸν εὐρὺν ἔχουσιν.
αἲ γὰρ ἐμοὶ τοιόσδε πόσις κεκλημένος εἴη
ἐνθάδε ναιετάων, καὶ οἱ ἅδοι αὐτόθι μίμνειν.   245
ἀλλὰ δότ᾽, ἀμφίπολοι, ξείνῳ βρῶσίν τε πόσιν τε.'

A
Level

ὣς ἔφαθ᾽, αἱ δ᾽ ἄρα τῆς μάλα μὲν κλύον ἠδ᾽ ἐπίθοντο,
πὰρ δ᾽ ἄρ᾽ Ὀδυσσῆι ἔθεσαν βρῶσίν τε πόσιν τε.
ἦ τοι ὁ πῖνε καὶ ἦσθε πολύτλας δῖος Ὀδυσσεὺς
ἁρπαλέως: δηρὸν γὰρ ἐδητύος ἦεν ἄπαστος.   250
αὐτὰρ Ναυσικάα λευκώλενος ἄλλ᾽ ἐνόησεν:
εἵματ᾽ ἄρα πτύξασα τίθει καλῆς ἐπ᾽ ἀπήνης,
ζεῦξεν δ᾽ ἡμιόνους κρατερώνυχας, ἂν δ᾽ ἔβη αὐτή,
ὤτρυνεν δ᾽ Ὀδυσῆα, ἔπος τ᾽ ἔφατ᾽ ἔκ τ᾽ ὀνόμαζεν:

"ὄρσεο δὴ νῦν, ξεῖνε, πόλινδ᾽ ἴμεν ὄφρα σε πέμψω   255
πατρὸς ἐμοῦ πρὸς δῶμα δαΐφρονος, ἔνθα σέ φημι
πάντων Φαιήκων εἰδησέμεν ὅσσοι ἄριστοι.
ἀλλὰ μάλ᾽ ὧδ᾽ ἔρδειν, δοκέεις δέ μοι οὐκ ἀπινύσσειν:
ὄφρ᾽ ἂν μέν κ᾽ ἀγροὺς ἴομεν καὶ ἔργ᾽ ἀνθρώπων,
τόφρα σὺν ἀμφιπόλοισι μεθ᾽ ἡμιόνους καὶ ἄμαξαν   260
καρπαλίμως ἔρχεσθαι: ἐγὼ δ᾽ ὁδὸν ἡγεμονεύσω.
αὐτὰρ ἐπὴν πόλιος ἐπιβήομεν, ἣν πέρι πύργος
ὑψηλός, καλὸς δὲ λιμὴν ἑκάτερθε πόληος,
λεπτὴ δ᾽ εἰσίθμη: νῆες δ᾽ ὁδὸν ἀμφιέλισσαι
εἰρύαται: πᾶσιν γὰρ ἐπίστιόν ἐστιν ἑκάστῳ.   265
ἔνθα δέ τέ σφ᾽ ἀγορὴ καλὸν Ποσιδήιον ἀμφίς,
ῥυτοῖσιν λάεσσι κατωρυχέεσσ᾽ ἀραρυῖα.
ἔνθα δὲ νηῶν ὅπλα μελαινάων ἀλέγουσι,
πείσματα καὶ σπεῖρα, καὶ ἀποξύνουσιν ἐρετμά.
οὐ γὰρ Φαιήκεσσι μέλει βιὸς οὐδὲ φαρέτρη,   270
ἀλλ᾽ ἱστοὶ καὶ ἐρετμὰ νεῶν καὶ νῆες ἐῖσαι,
ᾗσιν ἀγαλλόμενοι πολιὴν περόωσι θάλασσαν.
τῶν ἀλεείνω φῆμιν ἀδευκέα, μή τις ὀπίσσω
μωμεύῃ: μάλα δ᾽ εἰσὶν ὑπερφίαλοι κατὰ δῆμον:
καί νύ τις ὧδ᾽ εἴπῃσι κακώτερος ἀντιβολήσας: 275
'τίς δ᾽ ὅδε Ναυσικάᾳ ἕπεται καλός τε μέγας τε
ξεῖνος; ποῦ δέ μιν εὗρε; πόσις νύ οἱ ἔσσεται αὐτῇ.
ἦ τινά που πλαγχθέντα κομίσσατο ἧς ἀπὸ νηὸς
ἀνδρῶν τηλεδαπῶν, ἐπεὶ οὔ τινες ἐγγύθεν εἰσίν:
ἦ τίς οἱ εὐξαμένῃ πολυάρητος θεὸς ἦλθεν   280
οὐρανόθεν καταβάς, ἕξει δέ μιν ἤματα πάντα.
βέλτερον, εἰ καὐτή περ ἐποιχομένη πόσιν εὗρεν
ἄλλοθεν: ἦ γὰρ τούσδε γ᾽ ἀτιμάζει κατὰ δῆμον
Φαίηκας, τοί μιν μνῶνται πολέες τε καὶ ἐσθλοί.'

ὣς ἐρέουσιν, ἐμοὶ δέ κ᾽ ὀνείδεα ταῦτα γένοιτο.   285
καὶ δ᾽ ἄλλῃ νεμεσῶ, ἥ τις τοιαῦτά γε ῥέζοι,
ἥ τ᾽ ἀέκητι φίλων πατρὸς καὶ μητρὸς ἐόντων,
ἀνδράσι μίσγηται, πρίν γ᾽ ἀμφάδιον γάμον ἐλθεῖν.
ξεῖνε, σὺ δ᾽ ὦκ᾽ ἐμέθεν ξυνίει ἔπος, ὄφρα τάχιστα
πομπῆς καὶ νόστοιο τύχῃς παρὰ πατρὸς ἐμοῖο.   290
δήεις ἀγλαὸν ἄλσος Ἀθήνης ἄγχι κελεύθου

αἰγείρων: ἐν δὲ κρήνη νάει, ἀμφὶ δὲ λειμών:
ἔνθα δὲ πατρὸς ἐμοῦ τέμενος τεθαλυῖά τ᾽ ἀλωή,
τόσσον ἀπὸ πτόλιος, ὅσσον τε γέγωνε βοήσας.
ἔνθα καθεζόμενος μεῖναι χρόνον, εἰς ὅ κεν ἡμεῖς   295
ἄστυδε ἔλθωμεν καὶ ἱκώμεθα δώματα πατρός.
αὐτὰρ ἐπὴν ἡμέας ἔλπη ποτὶ δώματ᾽ ἀφῖχθαι,
καὶ τότε Φαιήκων ἴμεν ἐς πόλιν ἠδ᾽ ἐρέεσθαι
δώματα πατρὸς ἐμοῦ μεγαλήτορος Ἀλκινόοιο.
ῥεῖα δ᾽ ἀρίγνωτ᾽ ἐστί, καὶ ἂν πάϊς ἡγήσαιτο   300
νήπιος: οὐ μὲν γάρ τι ἐοικότα τοῖσι τέτυκται
δώματα Φαιήκων, οἷος δόμος Ἀλκινόοιο
ἥρωος. ἀλλ᾽ ὁπότ᾽ ἄν σε δόμοι κεκύθωσι καὶ αὐλή,
ὦκα μάλα μεγάροιο διελθέμεν, ὄφρ᾽ ἂν ἵκηαι
μητέρ᾽ ἐμήν: ἡ δ᾽ ἧσται ἐπ᾽ ἐσχάρη ἐν πυρὸς αὐγῇ,   305
ἠλάκατα στρωφῶσ᾽ ἁλιπόρφυρα, θαῦμα ἰδέσθαι,
κίονι κεκλιμένη: δμωαὶ δέ οἱ εἵατ᾽ ὄπισθεν.
ἔνθα δὲ πατρὸς ἐμοῖο θρόνος ποτικέκλιται αὐτῇ,
τῷ ὅ γε οἰνοποτάζει ἐφήμενος ἀθάνατος ὥς.
τὸν παραμειψάμενος μητρὸς περὶ γούνασι χεῖρας   310
βάλλειν ἡμετέρης, ἵνα νόστιμον ἦμαρ ἴδηαι
χαίρων καρπαλίμως, εἰ καὶ μάλα τηλόθεν ἐσσί.
εἴ κέν τοι κείνη γε φίλα φρονέησ᾽ ἐνὶ θυμῷ,
ἐλπωρή τοι ἔπειτα φίλους τ᾽ ἰδέειν καὶ ἱκέσθαι
οἶκον ἐυκτίμενον καὶ σὴν ἐς πατρίδα γαῖαν."   315

ὣς ἄρα φωνήσασ᾽ ἵμασεν μάστιγι φαεινῇ
ἡμιόνους: αἱ δ᾽ ὦκα λίπον ποταμοῖο ῥέεθρα.
αἱ δ᾽ ἐὺ μὲν τρώχων, ἐὺ δὲ πλίσσοντο πόδεσσιν:
ἡ δὲ μάλ᾽ ἡνιόχευεν, ὅπως ἅμ᾽ ἐποίατο πεζοὶ
ἀμφίπολοί τ᾽ Ὀδυσεύς τε, νόῳ δ᾽ ἐπέβαλλεν ἱμάσθλην.   320
δύσετό τ᾽ ἠέλιος καὶ τοὶ κλυτὸν ἄλσος ἵκοντο
ἱρὸν Ἀθηναίης, ἵν᾽ ἄρ᾽ ἕζετο δῖος Ὀδυσσεύς.
αὐτίκ᾽ ἔπειτ᾽ ἠρᾶτο Διὸς κούρῃ μεγάλοιο:
"κλῦθί μευ, αἰγιόχοιο Διὸς τέκος, Ἀτρυτώνη:
νῦν δή πέρ μευ ἄκουσον, ἐπεὶ πάρος οὔ ποτ᾽ ἄκουσας   325
ῥαιομένου, ὅτε μ᾽ ἔρραιε κλυτὸς ἐννοσίγαιος.
δός μ᾽ ἐς Φαίηκας φίλον ἐλθεῖν ἠδ᾽ ἐλεεινόν."
ὣς ἔφατ᾽ εὐχόμενος, τοῦ δ᾽ ἔκλυε Παλλὰς Ἀθήνη.
αὐτῷ δ᾽ οὔ πω φαίνετ᾽ ἐναντίη: αἴδετο γάρ ῥα
πατροκασίγνητον: ὁ δ᾽ ἐπιζαφελῶς μενέαινεν   330
ἀντιθέῳ Ὀδυσῆι πάρος ἣν γαῖαν ἱκέσθαι.

A
Level

Commentary Notes

Odyssey 6

1–84: At the close of book 5 Odysseus landed at the island of the Phaeacians after a storm-tossed voyage from Calypso's island Ogygia, and has walked to a wood near the water's edge. Here he bedded down anxiously in a secure shelter in a reed-bed, unaware of his location and uncertain of what awaits him. At the opening of book 6, while Odysseus sleeps, Minerva hurries to the home of the Phaeacian king Alcinous, and in disguise as a friend she convinces his daughter Nausicaa to venture to the shore to wash her clothes. Nausicaa convinces her father to allow her to borrow the mule-cart and take a party down to the beach. Within these lines the theme of marriage is firmly established: Minerva spurs Nausicaa to action by emphasizing that as she was near marriageable age she and her companions should be well turned-out ('Beauty, in these, will make the folk admire', lines 29–30, translated by Robert Fitzgerald). The subject of marriage is also hanging in the air when Nausicaa asks her father Alcinous if she can borrow the waggon for her laundry outing: she was too ashamed (literally, the word is αἴδετο) to come straight out and admit her real motives for arranging this laundry expedition, but the narrator tells us that Alcinous reads between the lines and happily assents (line 66–67). The notion that Nausicaa regards the stranger as a potential husband provides a light irony which colours the entire action of the book (see for example notes to lines 109, 154, 183 and 209).

85–109

Although we are aware of the nearby sleeping Odysseus, the narrator allows the audience to share the hero's uncertainty by suspending his meeting with Nausicaa until after a long description – eked out with careful patient irony including a long simile – of the princess and her attendants laundering clothes and playing a ball-game on a beach close to where the hero is nervously sleeping in a makeshift bed.

85

αἱ δ’ ὅτε δὴ: ‘But when indeed they . . .’; the subject of the verb ἵκοντο is Nausicaa and her attendants (ἀμφίπολοι), indicated by αἱ used as a demonstrative pronoun.

ποταμοῖο: = ποταμοῦ, the Homeric second declension genitive singular.

περικαλλέ’: = περικαλλέα, masculine accusative singular agreeing with ῥόον.

86

ἔνθ’: this word initiates a series of complex assonances and repetitions which slow the narrative and emphasize the details: ἔνθ’ (86), ἔνθ’ (88); ἀπήνης (88), ἀπ’ἀπήνης (90); ὑπεκπρόρεεν (87), ὑπεκπροέλυσαν (88) interwoven with υ and ε/η sounds and other alliterations.

ἦ τοι: the narrator addresses the audience: ‘you see . . .’.

πλυνοί . . . ἐπηετανοί: on the shore are basins presumably fed with water from a series of pipes. Describing them as ἐπηετανοί (‘plentiful’, the word is perhaps related to ἔτος and meaning ‘year on year’, or ‘all year round’) reinforces the notion of Phaeacia as a land of plenty and wholesome toil: here there is always clean water for laundry, where in other lands the streams and rivers are subject to seasonal drying.

πολὺ δ’ὕδωρ: note the unusual late caesura (see Introduction, ‘The epic hexameter’), extending the description of the basins.

87

ὑπεκπρόρεεν: a triple compound verb, literally ‘under-out-forth flowed’. The verb is an uncontracted imperfect third person singular, the subject is the ὕδωρ, which (being Phaeacian) is both πολύ and καλὸν.

μάλα περ: modifies ῥυπόωντα, ‘even very dirty [things, neuter plural; here = clothes]’.

καθῆραι: the sense is a result clause: lit. ‘the water flowed out [so as] to clean . . .’.

88

ἔνθ’: = ἔνθα. As with the ἔνθ’ in line 86 above, we are given a clear and precise description of the place where Nausicaa and her attendants have come. The anaphora serves to slow the pace of the narrative and heighten the suspense.

αἵ γ’: the γε helps reiterate the subject (αἱ, the washing-party) after two lines of digression, picking up from αἱ δ’ in line 85. The limiting quality of γε may serve to remind us that they, ‘at any rate’, are busying themselves with their laundry while the hero sleeps nearby.

μεν: Homeric Greek is less insistent on an answering δε, and the particle here may have the force of an ‘indeed’ or ‘in fact’.

ὑπεκπροέλυσαν: a superficially extraordinary re-use of the same triple-prefix as ὑπεκπρόρεεν two lines above (here ‘under-out-forth released’), perhaps with labouring precision to increase the suspense.

ἀπήνης: genitive of separation (‘from the waggon’), after an unexpressed ἀπό.

89

τάς: i.e. the mules.

**A
Level**

μέν: answered by δέ in line 90, neatly marking out the two actions of the washing-party.

σεῦαν: unaugmented weak aorist third person plural.

δινήεντα: 'eddying' or 'whirling'; the choice of words foreshadows the discovery of Odysseus by a δίνη in line 115 below.

90

τρώγειν: the infinitive expresses purpose after the verb σεῦαν above, '[they drove them . . .] to munch'.

ταί: = αί, as a demonstrative third person pronoun.

ἀπ'ἀπήνης: here alliteratively with its ἀπό, the position of ἀπήνης at the end of this line echoes line 88.

91

μέλαν ὕδωρ: accusative of motion towards. We are used to the sea described as 'wine-dark' in Homer but on the presumably-bright beach μέλας is more difficult to explain here. Garvie suggests that the word invokes the deep source of the pure clean water which fills the washing tanks.

92

θοῶς: adverb taken with προφέρουσαι: 'quickly displaying rivalry', as the girls get started on the work.

ἔριδα: it may seem odd for ἔρις ('strife') to make an appearance at this tranquil scene: the personified Eris was the cause of the Trojan War, and the word is also a battlefield term in the *Iliad*, but it here indicates a spirit of good-natured competitive rivalry and is not a straightforwardly negative term in the *Odyssey*. There are some mock-heroic flavours in this very un-Iliadic episode (see note to lines 110–117 below), and it may be that this ἔρις is the first of them.

93

τε . . . τε: a 'soft' connecting τε, the first one not requiring a 'both' in English.

94

ἐξείης: adverb, 'in a row'.

θῖν': θῖνα, accusative singular of θίς, 'shore'.

ἁλός: genitive singular of ἅλς, which when feminine means 'the sea' (not 'salt', the meaning of the masculine version).

ἧχι: = Attic ᾗ, 'where'.

95

λάιγγας: accusative, direct object of ἀποπλύνεσκε. The image is of a clean shingly beach, where you could safely dry laundry without fear of sand or seaweed.

ποτὶ χέρσον: literally 'towards the dry land', an apt choice of words for a laundering image where the wet clothes are left between the sea and the land. W. B. Stanford helpfully notes that 'they could safely leave there clothes there, as there is almost no tide in the Mediterranean', although within the narrative the image is one of harmony between humans and the natural environment in the idyllic fairyland of Phaeacia.

97

ἔπειθ': = ἔπειτα, 'then, they . . .'.

ὄχθησιν: epic plural for singular (comfortably rendered into English as 'on the river's banks'); dative after παρά.

98

μένον: this governs an accusative infinitive construction, lit. 'they awaited their clothes (εἵματα) to be dried (τερσήμεναι)' i.e. 'they waited for their clothes to dry'.

τερσήμεναι: aorist passive infinitive of τέρσομαι.

αὐγῇ: instrumental dative, with genitive ἠελίοιο. The sense is 'in the sunshine'.

99

τάρφθεν: third person plural aorist passive of τέρπω.

δμωαί τε καὶ αὐτή: at 6.16 Nausicaa had already been singled out as particularly special in stature and appearance ('a heaven of charms, divine Nausicaa', in Alexander Pope's version): the overly-wordy arrangement here of ἐπεὶ σίτου τάρφθεν δμωαί τε καὶ αὐτή ('when they had had their fill of food, both her handmaids and herself') and position of αὐτή at the end of the line lend her further emphasis.

100

σφαίρῃ ταὶ δ᾽ ἄρ᾽ ἔπαιζον: the arrangement of words is careful and unorthodox, giving particular emphasis to the ball (which is to play a vital role in the following sequence). We would expect δε second in its clause, followed by the often-untranslatable ἄρα; as the pronoun ταὶ would normally begin such a clause, we see that the normal order is shunted along to allow the σφαῖρα a prominent position on the line.

ἀπό . . . βαλοῦσαι: tmesis; the girls 'throw off' (ἀποβάλλω) their veils.

κρήδεμνα: literally 'head binding' (from κάρη and δέω), there is no clear evidence of what this looked like but tradition suggests that it was a short hair-covering very practical for a laundry excursion. Its discarding here by the washing-party has caused some comment and warrants discussion, particularly in the light of recent sexual politics. Garvie states that that 'by [removing the garment] they unconsciously render themselves vulnerable to any sexual advance.' Hainsworth goes further and sees an explicit 'erotic overtone' to the act, stating that they have 'almost courted' their fear of the revealed and naked Odysseus in line 138. The erotic aspect is entirely subjective; the act may only convey a lightly ironic gentleness among the washing-party, building up a picture of idyllic intimacy which the audience knows will be shattered by the entrance of Odysseus and adding to the suspense of his discovery – which we still keenly await.

101

τῇσι: = ταις, dative of reference.

A Level

λευκώλενος: literally 'white-elbowed' or 'white-forearmed', but traditionally rendered 'white-armed', the word is two-termination (hence here feminine) and is an epithet of Hera.

μολπῆς: genitive after ἄρχομαι. The word denotes a combination of song and dance; the Muse Melpomene, whose name is cognate, governed the chorus in particular. Its use here has provoked and contributed to much comment since antiquity regarding the precise meaning of μολπή, but in the current passage it is safe to suppose that ball-game, singing and dancing were somehow combined.

102–109

οἵη δ᾽ ... παρθένος ἀδμής: This simile is one of the longest in the *Odyssey* and one of only nine extended similes in the poem. Its main analogues are clear: Nausicaa = Artemis and attendants = nymphs, and the simile's purpose is to enhance the audience's view of Nausicaa, but other aspects are also pertinent. The remote location of Artemis' hunt reflects the sea-shore location outside the citadel, and the smiling maternal Leto hints at the strong family bond of Alcinous and Arete; Hainsworth comments that the simile emphasizes 'the purity of Nausicaa and the innocence of her sport'.

102

οἵη δ᾽ Ἄρτεμις εἶσι: οἵη introduces the simile (literally 'she was like ...', but translatable as 'just as ...'), and this would normally be picked up with the correlative τοίη but the length of the simile forces the narrator to reset the narrative flow by capping the description with ὥς ('just so was ...') at 109.

103

ἤ ... ἤ: 'whether ... or ...'.

Τηΰγετον: Taÿgetus, a very high mountain range south-west of Sparta.

Ἐρύμανθον: Erymanthus, a mountain in the northern Peloponnese later home to the Erymanthian boar, whom Heracles would deliver to Eurystheus as part of his labours though this tale is not known in the Homeric poems. The point of mentioning both mountains seems to be to evoke far-off places which (particularly if the poems were composed in Ionia) were probably known to the poet only though folk-tales of heroes.

104

κάπροισι ... ἐλάφοισι: instrumental datives after τέρπομαι: 'gladdened with ...'.

105

τῇ: 'with her ...'.

θ᾽: = τε. This 'generalizing' τε is common in similes and widens their scope, here to include the nymphs and other details beyond the primary analogues Nausicaa and Artemis; Artemis besports herself with the daughters of Zeus, where Nausicaa is in the company of her handmaids.

A
Level

106

γέγηθε: third person singular perfect indicative active of γηθέω.

φρένα: accusative of respect, difficult to render into literal English. The clause is translated by Fitzgerald as 'Leto's heart delights'.

107

πασάων: = Attic πασῶν, feminine genitive plural (of πᾶς πᾶσα πᾶν) after ὑπέρ, 'above them all'.

ὑπέρ: tallness was a valued physical attribute among the Greeks in both men and women, down to the statuesque Phye being able to garb herself as Athena and assist Peisistratus to regain the tyranny of Athens (Herodotus 1.60). As Stanford notes, 'a small person could [not be] καλός'.

γε: this adds force to the ἤ and singles out Artemis.

μέτωπα: often translated 'brow' but literally meaning 'the space between the eyes', logically a person can have only one μέτωπον so we here have poetic plural for singular. Translate as 'face'.

108

ῥεῖά τ᾽ ἀριγνώτη πέλεται: ῥεῖα is an adverb ('easily'); 'she is easily known/ recognizable'.

καλαὶ δέ τε πᾶσαι: understand εἰσί. The phrase is tacked on, almost as an afterthought, and feels concessive: 'Over all other [daughters of Zeus, i.e. her attendant nymphs] she holds her head and face / and she is easily known – **although they all are beautiful**'.

109

ὥς: the simile is rounded off: 'just so was . . .'.

ἥ γ᾽: note the same combination of article and particle as used above, line 107.

ἀμφιπόλοισι: the dative follows μετέπρεπε (the latter frequently used of heroes in the *Iliad*), she 'went among her handmaids'.

παρθένος ἀδμής: the final words of the simile remind us of Nausicaa's youth and unmarried state, which here has the effect of further aligning her with the (unmarried) goddess Artemis with whom Odysseus claims to confuse her on first sight (below at lines 149–152). It also highlights her being the complete opposite of the rough and salty warrior whom she is about to meet.

110–117

The gentle suspense which has been hanging over the audience all this time is brought to a pitch, and then relieved as the narrator steers us towards the sleeping Odysseus. The mock-heroic tone continues (see below on ἅμαρτε, line 116): the whole Nausicaa episode in fact shows several parallels with an Iliadic battle scene and, from the ironic perspective of the hero's relative safety, it takes on a light, mock-epic flavour. The battle-parallel began at the start of book 6, when Athena first assumes a disguise to spur Nausicaa into action, as she did most memorably to Hector in *Iliad* 22, and the goddess will shortly intervene

A Level

directly in the physical world although instead of diverting a spear from its target (the normal Iliadic intervention) she directs a thrown ball towards the sleeping Odysseus.

110

ἀλλ᾽ ὅτε δὴ ἄρ᾽: the tension is ramped up considerably with ἀλλα ('but') and the combination of δὴ and ἄρα ('after all', 'actually'). The sense is 'But when it actually looked like she was about to go back home . . .', instead, that is, of encountering Odysseus as per Athena's plan: thus the goddess swings into action.

ἔμελλε: De Jong points out that the imperfect indicative here indicates that an action will be postponed or will not happen, again adding to the tension: 'she was going to . . .', but didn't.

111

ζεύξασ᾽ ... πτύξασα: this pair of aorist infinitives are used temporally with νέεσθαι above: it looked as if she was about to leave, 'after having [first] yoked . . . and folded . . .'. The assonance and alliteration add to the gentle tension.

112

ἔνθ᾽: 'thereupon'; having set out the possibility, the narrator now tells us that Athena has other ideas.

αὖτ᾽: the adverb αὖτε ('on the other hand') reinforces the turnaround.

ἄλλ᾽: = ἄλλο, describing an unexpressed cognate accusative object after ἐνόησε, literally 'she intended another [intention]'.

113

ὡς: plus the following three optatives (ἔγροιτο, ἴδοι, ἡγήσαιτο) expressing purpose (i.e. Athena's intentions).

ἔγροιτο: aorist optative of ἐγείρω. This purpose will be fulfilled very shortly, with the verb's indicative ἔγρετο used in line 117.

ἐυώπιδα: εὖ and ὤψ, 'fair-eyed'.

114

ἥ: relative, with κούρην as its antecedent.

οἱ: Attic αὐτῷ, dative following ἡγέομαι.

πόλιν: accusative of motion towards.

115–116

This pair of lines is carefully structured, with Nausicaa's action described in 115 and the outcomes co-ordinated with μέν and δέ in the following line showing us the ball missing its mark, all highlighted with assonances in α, ε and ει and alliterative labial consonants β/π/φ. The goddess's intentions, stated in lines 113–114, now take physical form in the world of mortals: Nausicaa's ball is diverted off-course and lands in an eddy close to where Odysseus sleeps.

115

σφαῖραν: note again the position, for emphasis (see line 100).

A
Level

ἔρριψε: the subject of this verb, and ἅμαρτε in the following line, is βασίλεια. The verbs are arranged in chiasmus with ἀμφίπολον ... ἀμφιπόλου, perhaps invoking the criss-crossing of the thrown ball and its missing its mark.

μετ’ : = μετά, with accusative here meaning she threw the ball ‘at’ or ‘to’ a handmaid.

116

ἀμφιπόλου: genitive of separation after ἅμαρτε. Note again the position and polyptoton: ‘to a handmaid then the princess threw the ball; / the handmaid, indeed, [the princess] missed . . .’.

ἅμαρτε: third person singular strong aorist of ἁμαρτάνω, a word which recalls the missed spear-throws of the *Iliad*.

117

αἱ δ’: ‘and they’; the verb’s subject is the whole group of girls.

ἐπὶ μακρὸν ἄυσαν: another Iliadic borrowing, this formula describes the military, masculine ‘wide cry’ which follows a spear-throw: here it is re-cast as domestic, playful and feminine. ἐπί is adverbial, and μακρόν an accusative of extent describing an unexpressed cognate object (i.e. αὐδήν).

118–129

After such a disastrous journey, Odysseus’ first thoughts are understandably suspicious but his tone lightens as he hears the sounds of the laughing girls nearby.

118

ὥρμαινε: imperfect tense, possibly inceptive (‘he began to ponder’).

κατὰ φρένα καὶ κατὰ θυμόν: a common formula which appears tautological but distinguishes between the φρήν (the midriff, wherein is found the seat of the soul – roughly, the English ‘heart’) and the θυμός (a person’s driving force, their emotional ‘mind’ or ‘soul’). This overly-wordy expression (pleonasm) – where else would he ponder? – is simply a way of saying that ‘he thought to himself’.

119

ὤ μοι ἐγώ: a pessimistic opening to his speech: these words are a common plaintive lament.

τέων: Attic τίνων.

αὖτε: his tone is exasperated. (‘To what sort of mortals’ land have I come **now**?’).

120

ἦ: anticipates ἦε in the following line: ‘Are they . . . ? Or are they . . .?’, as Odysseus posits answers to his own question. Supply εἰσί in each clause.

ῥ’: = ἄρα, not easily translatable here.

A
Level

ὑβρισταί: masculine nominative plural of ὑβριστής. Hubris and its consequences are a major theme of the *Odyssey*, and Odysseus' fear of ὑβρισταί is quite natural given the events which have preceded his arrival.

121

ὥς: to Odysseus' suspicious ears, the sound is 'as though' from maidens.

σφιν: = αὐτοῖς, dative of possessor (lit. 'is there to them a mind reverent to the gods?', i.e. 'do they have . . .?').

ἀμφήλυθε: strong aorist of ἀμφέρχομαι, the subject is the θῆλυς αὐτή.

ἀϋτή: 'a cry' (note the diaeresis and the position of the breathing).

122

νυμφάων: having experienced life with demigods, the worldly Odysseus corrects himself: not maidens, perhaps, but nymphs. His choice of words recalls the simile (see line 105) which likened the Phaeacian handmaids to nymphs, and the unbiased judgement of the sounds he hears does add to the 'fantasy island' flavour of his surroundings.

αἵ: relative, 'who'.

ἔχουσ': = ἔχουσι, here 'haunt' or 'inhabit'.

124

ποιήεντα: neuter accusative plural of ποιήεις, 'grassy', describing πίσεα.

125

ἦ νύ που: 'Can it be that . . .?'. νύ is a soft 'now', not necessarily indicating time (as in 'now, how about lunch?'). The indefinite που back-pedals from the certainty of ἦ: the sense is 'am I – **somehow** – near people of human speech?'

αὐδηέντων: this word denotes particularly human utterance, and would mark out the girls as being mortals rather than gods or nymphs.

126

ἀλλ' ἄγ': 'but come, . . .'.

ἐγών: = ἐγώ.

πειρήσομαι ἠδὲ ἴδωμαι: hortatory aorist subjunctives: 'let me try and see . . .'.

127

θάμνων: genitive of separation (i.e. understand ἔκ or ἀπό).

128

χειρὶ παχείῃ: instrumental dative, 'with his stout hand'.

129

φύλλων: descriptive genitive after πτόρθον, 'a leafy branch'; the enjambment emphasizes the good use to which the dense foliage will now be put.

ῥύσαιτο ... φωτός: ῥύσαιτο is optative showing purpose, after ὡς, and the subject is the 'leafy branch'. The verb's object is Odysseus' μήδεα φωτός and the whole phrase can be translated as 'so that around his body it might cover his genitals'.

χροΐ: the χρώς is the body as pertains to its outward appearance, i.e. the skin.

130

βῆ: unaugmented root aorist of βαίνω, third person singular.

ἴμεν: = ἰέναι; in Homer, βῆ δ᾽ ἰέναι translates as 'he set out to go' (perhaps here 'started forth').

ὥς τε λέων ὀρεσίτροφος ἀλκὶ πεποιθώς: the formula is Iliadic (e.g. *Iliad* 5.299) and used of warriors blazing into the throng; its use here adds to the mock-epic tone.

ἀλκί: = ἀλκῆ, this is a rare survival of a first declension dative singular without its η. Dative after πεποιθώς.

131

ὅς τ᾽ εἶσ᾽: 'who goes'; the τε is generalizing. εἶσ᾽ = εἶσι, from εἶμι 'I shall go', which does not have its future-tense meaning here.

ἐν δέ οἱ: 'and in him his eyes blaze'.

ὄσσε: dual, here with the singular verb δαίεται.

132

αὐτάρ: the strong contrast signalled by this word is between the lion's battered and windswept state and his action in nevertheless having the strength and the need to go among the sheep and cattle; this is the crux of Odysseus' current dilemma.

133–134

The whole simile is Iliadic, but these particular lines are very similar to *Iliad* 12.300–301, when Zeus gives his son Sarpedon extra encouragement to break through the Greek fortifications. Garvie notes, however, that Sarpedon's lion was driven by his 'proud spirit' (θυμὸς ἀγήνωρ) whereas here an 'unheroic γαστήρ' drives the lion here and that difference adds further depth to the mock-epic tone.

133

ἀγροτέρας: the comparative -τερος ending shows that these deer inhabit the fields **rather than** e.g. the mountains.

ἑ: = Attic αὐτόν.

134

μήλων: genitive after πειράω, 'I make a trial *of* X'.

πειρήσοντα: future participle, masculine accusative singular (i.e. the lion, direct object of κέλεται).

καί: used adverbially: the sentence literally runs: 'his stomach drives [him], being about to make an attempt on the flock, to go **even** into the well-built sheep-fold'.

135

ἐυπλοκάμοισιν: 'fair-tressed', again a reminder of the absolute contrast between the recently-bathed handmaids and the grimy and windswept Odysseus.

**A
Level**

ἔμελλε: another 'frustrated' imperfect tense (see line 110).

136

μίξεσθαι: the ambiguity of μίγνυμι (literally 'to mix', as of liquids) adds further lightness and humour to the simile's resolution, compounded by the enjambment and the word's emphatic position (the 'run-on' position, where the enjambment spotlights a word in isolation on the following line; see φύλλων above, line 129, and various points throughout the passage). The word can be friendly or hostile, and can refer to sexual contact. Any good translation should be laden with irony and double entendre: 'enter into relations with' may convey the sense.

πεϱ: concessive in sense with the participle; 'naked though he was'.

χϱειὼ γὰϱ ἵκανε: 'for the need had come upon him'. It is unclear how much of the sexual overtone of a literal English translation was felt among a pre-classical Greek audience; the emphasis is clearly on Odysseus' uncertainty about how to approach the well-known rites of supplication – which involve physical contact (see below, line 142) – while in a state of complete undress and having only young women to supplicate. Cunning Odysseus knows that if he is in a land of mortals, he will need to come out of this situation well if he is to continue his journey home.

137

φάνη: unaugmented third person singular aorist of φαίνω.

κεκακωμένος: this cacophonous word derives from κακός: 'be*kak*ossed'. The contrasts between Odysseus and his freshly-washed (line 96) audience are now at a high point.

ἄλμη: 'with brine', from ἅλς (salt). The word initiates a neat triplet of 'αλ' alliterations with the line below.

138

ἄλλυδις ἄλλη: 'hither and thither', adverbs.

139

οἴη: 'alone', placed for emphasis.

Ἀλκινόου θυγάτηϱ: we are reminded of Nausicaa's noble status.

τῇ: personal pronoun, referring to Nausicaa: either an ethic dative or dative of reference/advantage.

140

θάϱσος … γυίων: this elegant line is deceptively straightforward and concisely expresses Athena's influence on Nausicaa: the subject of the verbs is stated above, and the line is balanced around the central καί joining the two verbal phrases (parataxis), one of placing (ἐνί … θῆκε) and one of removal (ἐκ … εἵλετο). The good order can be contrasted with the description of the fleeing attendants above.

141

στῆ: intransitive aorist of ἵστημι, 'she stood'.

σχομένη: aorist participle middle of ἔχω, 'holding herself firm'.

A Level

142

ἤ: answered by ἤ on the following line: 'whether . . . or'. Odysseus wonders whether to supplicate Nausicaa in the customary manner (see below), or to keep his distance.

γούνων: genitive plural of γόνυ, genitive 'of the part seized' (LSJ), after λαβών. The standard knee-touching part of the supplication process obviously presents Odysseus with a quandary in his current naked and unwashed state.

λίσσοιτο: 'he should entreat', optative in a deliberative question in historic sequence after μερμήριξεν above.

ἐυώπιδα κούρην: the phrase was used (in the same position on the line) of Athena's intention at line 113 that Odysseus should see Nausicaa: the second of her intentions has now been fulfilled. We are also given a reminder of Nausicaa's beautiful (εὐῶπις) appearance, and an implicit reminder of Odysseus' state.

143

αὔτως: adverb from αὐτός, 'just as he was' (with ἀποσταδά).

ἀποσταδά: adverb, 'standing away from [her]'.

ἐπέεσσιν . . . μειλιχίοισι: instrumental datives, '[entreat her] with soothing words'.

144

εἰ δείξειε . . . δοίη: the sense of εἰ + optative here is 'to see if' or 'in the hope that [she might]' (etc.).

δείξειε πόλιν καὶ εἵματα δοίη: the chiasmus (and possibly the framing alliterated δ of the verbs) neatly unites πόλιν καὶ εἵματα, two things that Odysseus is currently lacking, both within the episode (clothes) and in the wider narrative (a city).

145

ἄρα: this ἄρα draws our attention back to the main thread after the brief digression; any attempt to translate it would sound artificial although 'so' or 'anyway' would work verbally.

οἱ: dative, 'to him [as he considered]', after the Homeric δοάσσατο which equates to the Attic ἔδοξε, 'it seemed'.

κέρδιον: 'better' or 'preferable', neuter nominative singular describing the notional 'it' of δοάσσατο. This comparative adjective has no positive form.

146

λίσσεσθαι . . . μειλιχίοισι: this patterned line has an ABAB structure that carefully echoes and re-employs the vocabulary of lines 143–144.

λίσσεσθαι: infinitive after δοάσσατο.

147

μή . . . κούρη: literally, 'lest the girl should be angered in her heart at him taking her knees', a negative purpose clause.

148

αὐτίκα . . . κερδαλέον: note the alliterated κ/χ, which also draws attention to κερδαλέον (see below).

**A
Level**

μειλίχιον: to be 'soothing' is Odysseus' mission, and the narrator puts it at the front of the line straight after αὐτίκα ('straightaway').

κερδαλέον: Odysseus' cunning, well-sharpened after his wanderings, ensures that his story will be as crafty as it is soothing.

149

γουνοῦμαί: the word is related to γόνυ (see line 142) and is used more generally to mean 'I beseech' here as Odysseus has ruled out physical contact.

ἄνασσα: the feminine of ἄναξ ('lord', 'master'); the masculine form is used of gods as well as of mortals but the feminine is used of goddesses, for which the Artemis simile has prepared us.

θεός . . . ἐσσι: having just come from the island of Calypso, and encountered several divine beings on his journey, the question is not one of mere flattery although Odysseus' subsequent remarks about her parentage and family indicate that he thinks it more likely that she is mortal.

θεός . . . βροτός: θεός can be either masculine or feminine; βροτός is grammatically masculine and means 'a mortal'.

ἐσσι: = Attic εἶ, from εἰμί 'I am'.

150

τοί: = Attic οἵ, relative.

151

Ἀρτέμιδί: dative after ἐίσκω in the following line; 'I liken you . . . **to Artemis**'.

152

εἰδός τε μέγεθός τε φυήν τ': accusatives of respect.

153

εἰ δέ: this picks up εἰ μέν from line 150, and as this second member of the μέν . . . δέ pairing is longer the assumption is that having pondered whether she is a god or a mortal Odysseus has settled on the second option (as is customary in Homer when characters consider two options).

154

τρὶς μάκαρες μέν: Odysseus gives three ways in which Nausicaa makes those around her 'thrice blessed': first, her parents, then her siblings and finally the man who will eventually marry her. In Homeric texts the word μάκαρ primarily refers to gods (i.e. the 'blessed gods') and its use here is appropriate not only following the Artemis simile but also given the air of divine approval with which the narrator describes Phaeacia.

σοί: possessive dative.

πότνια: this word, 'queen' or 'master', is also used both of gods (including Artemis, as 'master of the wild beasts', *Iliad* 21.470) and mortals (e.g. Hecuba, at *Iliad* 22.239 and 341), again blurring the line between mortal and divine, although the whole phrase πατὴρ καὶ πότνια μήτηρ is a formula ('your father and **Lady** mother').

**A
Level**

156

αἰέν: Attic ἀεί.

ἰαίνεται: present passive of ἰαίνω, literally 'I warm'.

ἐυφροσύνῃσιν: 'with gladness'.

εἵνεκα: Attic ἕνεκα, here placed before its genitive rather than its customary place after.

157

λευσσόντων: 'seeing'. The subject of this participle is clearly Nausicaa's family, but it is not immediately clear why they should be genitive; it is as if σφισι above, which has the same referent, were a possessive genitive rather than a dative.

θάλος: = θαλλός, a young shoot or branch. This form of the word is only used metaphorically to refer to a son/daughter; 'offspring' fits the sense.

εἰσοιχνεῦσαν: the expected ending is -ουσαν, feminine accusative singular present active participle. Grammatically it agrees with θάλος, but it is feminine as it ultimately refers to Nausicaa ('constructio ad sensum').

158

κεῖνος: = ἐκεῖνος.

αὖ: 'again', preparing for the next and last instance of μάκαρ in the speech.

περί κῆρι: this rhyming pair is a set phrase in Homer meaning 'most heartily'.

ἔξοχον ἄλλων: ἔξοχον is used here adverbially with a genitive: 'far beyond others'.

159

κέ: = ἄν, the form is particularly common in Homer when following a relative pronoun (as here).

σ': this is the accusative object (σε) of the verb ἀγάγηται.

ἐέδνοισι βρίσας: the aorist participle is used temporally: 'having prevailed with his gift-offers'.

ἀγάγηται: aorist subjunctive after κέ (= ἄν), giving a generic or indefinite tone to the relative clause, 'he who . . . should lead you to his home' (i.e. 'whoever he may be').

160

ἴδον: = Attic εἶδον.

161

σέβας μ' ἔχει εἰσορόωντα: 'awe holds me as I look on [you]'. σέβας is a strong word denoting reverential awe and wonder.

162

Δήλῳ: dative of place; note the alliteration and assonance with the following δή.

τοῖον: this agrees with the νέον ἔρνος below, direct object of ἐνόησα. 'I noticed such a thing, once, a young shoot . . .'.

Ἀπόλλωνος παρὰ βωμῷ: 'beside the altar of Apollo'.

163

φοίνικος: descriptive genitive, a new shoot 'of a date-palm'.

A Level

164

ἦλθον . . . λαός: Odysseus gives Nausicaa a bit of his back-story (though his alleged Delos visit is not otherwise attested in the Epic Cycle) and reveals that he is more than his washed-up appearance suggests. The alliterative γ-κ-κ prefaces him revealing that he came with 'many people' (πολύς . . . λαός) who followed (ἕσπετο) him there.

καὶ: adverbial: 'For I **also** went there . . .', hinting at his wider wanderings.

165

τὴν ὁδόν: accusative of 'ground traversed' (Garvie).

ἣ δή: there is bitter emphasis in his reference the turnaround in his fortunes: 'That journey, **on which indeed** . . .'

μέλλεν . . . ἔσεσθαι: literally 'were about to be'; translate as 'were in store' or similar.

κήδε': κήδεα, neuter plural nominative, subject (with κακά) of μέλλεν. The harsh κ-sounds crash against the soft liquid sounds of μέλλεν ἐμοί.

166

ὡς: correlative with ὡς below, i.e. '**so** [at that time] was I astounded . . . **as** I am astounded [now]', a reversal of the normal order of a simile.

ἐτεθήπεα: pluperfect of the defective verb τέθηπα, here translated as an aorist (as is also the case with e.g. οἶδα).

167

ἀνήλυθεν: strong aorist of ἀνέρχομαι (compare Attic ἦλθον), the verb used of the shoot when it was first mentioned at line 163.

168

γύναι: vocative singular of γυνή.

τε . . . τε . . . δ': τε and τε co-ordinate the two verbs ἄγαμαί and τέθηπά, and δέ (here 'and') introduces a new and longer idea. Note the alliterated δ and τ sounds.

δείδια: perfect of δείδω, used with present meaning. Its combination with αἰνῶς makes this a very strongly-worded appeal: 'I am horribly afraid that . . .', more appropriate to a person fearing for their life.

169

χαλεπὸν δέ με πένθος ἱκάνει: the δε shows contrast: '**but** dreadful suffering has come to me [i.e. so I have to supplicate you, despite my fears]'.

170

χθιζός: although this is an adjective (masculine nominative singular agreeing with the subject, i.e. the speaker, literally 'yesterday-me') it is to be treated as a time adverb and translated 'yesterday'.

ἐεικοστῷ: Attic εἰκοστῷ, 'twentieth' (agreeing with ἤματι), dative of time when.

φύγον: 'I escaped', used transitively with πόντον as its object.

οἴνοπα: masculine accusative singular of οἶνοψ, agreeing with πόντον, the famous Homeric formula the 'wine-dark sea'.

171

τόφρα: 'up to that point', picked up by the correlative ὄφρα two lines below.

μ': = με, accusative object of the verb ἐφόρει,

κῦμ: = κῦμα, the verb's subject (neuter singular).

ἐφόρει: imperfect indicative of φορέω, the frequentative of φέρω meaning 'keep on carrying', an apt word for a twenty-day storm-tossed voyage. The verb is singular after κῦμα, and is used again with the plural θύελλαι.

172

κάββαλε: from καταβάλλω, the Attic would be κατέβαλε. Again, another vivid word: a spirit 'threw [him] down' on to the Phaeacian shore.

173

ὄφρ': = ὄφρα, showing purpose. Translate to που as follows: 'so that even now, no doubt . . .'.

τῇδε: i.e. in this place.

πάθω: aorist subjunctive of πάσχω.

174

ἔτι: note the repetition from the previous line.

τελέουσι: future tense (the form could also be present).

175

σε: this accusative will be resolved in the following line, running on in enjambment as ἐς [σε] πρώτην. Its unusual isolation on this line is neatly emphatic, following Odysseus' imperative and preceding the explanatory γάρ.

176

τῶν δ' ἄλλων: again, we have to wait until the following line for the noun which this adjective describes.

178

δεῖξον, δός: aorist imperatives (from δείκνυμι and δίδωμι), juxtaposed and alliterated (each also with a δέ).

δὸς δὲ ῥάκος ἀμφιβαλέσθαι: the sense is clear ('give me a rag to throw around myself'), though the syntax is more complex; μοι is re-used from the previous request, and the strong aorist middle infinitive ἀμφιβαλέσθαι conveys result. The naked man's words are clipped and direct on this matter.

179

τι: indefinite here (its accent is from the enclitic που) and describes εἴλυμα, 'some wrapping'.

σπείρων: descriptive genitive, literally 'a wrapper of cloth' (plural for singular), presumably a laundry-sling. Odysseus' request is modest, and is modestly expressed (τι, που).

A Level

180

τόσα ... ὅσα: accusative neuter plurals. These are correlatives: 'may the gods give you **such** things **as** . . .'.

δοῖεν: optative expressing a wish.

181

ἄνδρα ... οἶκον: these are accusative objects of δοῖεν, in apposition to τόσα above.

ὀπάσειαν: the subject is still θεοί.

182

ἐσθλήν: describes ὁμοφροσύνην on the line above; note the enjambment.

οὐ μέν: an emphatic denial, μέν here to be translated as μὴν, 'for truly, [nothing is] . . .'. (There is no verb, and no subject.)

τοῦ: genitive of comparison, 'than this' (neuter pronoun, the antecedent of which is the following phrase from ὅθ' to γυνή).

κρεῖσσον καὶ ἄρειον: κρεῖσσον is the Attic κρεῖττον; ἄρειον is a Homeric comparative from the same root at the superlative ἄριστος. The apparent tautology is very emphatic as Odysseus lays on his proposed blessings.

183

ἤ: this 'pivoting' ἤ which normally joins comparisons ('than') is redundant and incorrect here as we have already been given the comparative genitive above. Hainsworth notes that this basic syntactical error 'is a common slip in all authors'.

ὅθ': = ὅτε, 'whenever . . .', governing the subjunctive ἔχητον.

ὁμοφρονέοντε: a dual form (with ἔχητον), present participle active, 'being of the same mind'. The dual form is not necessary (as is seen below when it is not employed) and serves here to unite the husband and wife, raising the theme of marriage which hangs over book 6.

ἔχητον: present active subjunctive third person dual.

184

ἀνὴρ ἠδὲ γυνή: enjambment; the run-on from the previous line puts the ἀνήρ and γυνή together on the line.

δυσμενέεσσι: dative of reference/disadvantage, with an unexpressed ἐστί: 'there are many woes for their foes'. The word is a compound of δυσ- and μένος ('will' or 'spirit').

185

εὐμενέτῃσι: another compound with μένος: chosen to answer δυσμενής above, the word is extremely rare and may be an invention for this passage.

μάλιστα δέ τ' ἔκλυον αὐτοί: debate has raged for decades over the meaning of this clause and the text may be corrupt. ἔκλυον comes from κλύω which ultimately means 'I hear', and the literal meaning, 'but they themselves hear it especially', makes little sense. The aorist is gnomic (expressing a wider truth rather

A Level

than a historical event) which helps the reading. Two alternative readings are 'They themselves have the highest reputation' and 'They themselves know it most especially'. The latter has the virtue of being closer to the Greek, as with κλύω the leap from 'I hear' to 'I know' is a minor one (οἶδα, for example, originally meant 'I have seen'). The former reading takes the view that 'I hear' can mean 'I am spoken of', and by extension 'I am spoken well of', which has good parallels in Greek and is probably preferable.

186–197

Nausicaa's answering speech is crucial to her characterization: it is stately, precise, and well-structured (see e.g. lines 191–192) and comparing it with Odysseus' requests shows that she answers his questions fully and carefully (see individual notes below).

186

τὸν δ' αὖ ... ἀντίον ηὔδα: this is a common formula introducing a speech of reply; the αὖ has the effect of 'in turn', and ἀντίον ηὔδα is 'addressed in reply'.

187

ἐπεί: 'since'; this introduces a subordinate clause, but in the following lines Nausicaa digresses and no main clause arrives.

ξεῖν': vocative, ξεῖνε.

ἄφρονι: there is high irony in Nausicaa addressing the famously-cunning Odysseus as 'not unclever'; see also line 258.

188

ὄλβον Ὀλύμπιος: in these words, and elsewhere in the poem when his identity is unknown, the narrator comes close to letting Odysseus' name slip: here the alternative Ὀλυττεύς may be hanging in the air (though the point is debatable). See the essay 'Terrible, Wonderful Odysseus: The Meanings of his Epithets, His Name(s) and How We Read Him' at sententiaeantiquae.com (accessed April 2019). See also notes to lines 200 and 206.

189

ἐσθλοῖς ἠδὲ κακοῖσιν: to men 'both good and wicked'.

ἐθέλῃσιν: third person singular present active subjunctive (in epic, ἐθέλω becomes a -μι verb in the subjunctive). The subject is still Zeus.

190

που: 'I suppose': Nausicaa politely sums up the fact that Zeus allots happiness regardless of character, and lets Odysseus know that she does not necessarily feel that he deserves his present circumstances.

σὲ δὲ χρὴ τετλάμεν ἔμπης: with χρή, the young princess Nausicaa ironically advises the long-suffering hero Odysseus that he should put up with his fate: 'nevertheless, you must endure [such things, i.e. τάδε]'.

A Level

τετλάμεν: perfect infinitive, best translated as present.

191

νῦν δ': a strong statement of contrast. Nausicaa has consoled Odysseus' hardships, 'but now' she will answer his entreaties.

192

οὔτ' ... ἐσθῆτος ... οὔτε τευ ἄλλου: the genitives co-ordinated with οὔτε ... οὔτε, depend on the verb δευήσεαι, second person future indicative active (the future takes middle endings, here the Homeric -εαι) of δεύω, 'I lack/need'.

οὖν: as with νῦν δέ above, this οὖν marks the speech's logical order and good structure: 'you will not, therefore, lack ...'.

ἐσθῆτος: this answers Odysseus' request for clothing at line 178.

τευ: = Attic τινός.

193

ὧν ... ἀντιάσαντα: the antecedent of the relative ὧν is an unexpressed ἐκείνων; ἱκέτην is the subject of an unexpressed infinitive verb meaning 'not to lack' (re-using the idea of δευήσεαι in the previous line) introduced by the impersonal ἐπέοιχε, 'it is proper for', 'it befits'. Running from δευήσεαι in the previous line, the sense is as follows: '[nor will you lack (δευήσεαι) any other (τευ ἄλλου) of those things (unexpressed ἐκείνων)] which (ὧν) it befits (ἐπέοιχε) a much-suffering suppliant (ἱκέτην ταλαπείριον) who has come to meet with us (ἀντιάσαντα) not to lack (unexpressed infinitive of having or not lacking)'.

194

ἄστυ δέ τοι δείξω: this answers Odysseus' request at line 178, asking him to show her the city, and also resolves Athena's plan expressed at line 114. (ἄστυ and πόλις are effectively interchangeable in Homer.)

ἐρέω δέ τοι οὔνομα λαῶν: see line 177. ἐρέω is future of λέγω, Attic ἐρῶ.

197

τοῦ: relative pronoun, genitive after ἐκ (the antecedent is Ἀλκινόοιο).

Φαιήκων: possessive genitive, referring to the κάρτος and βίη.

ἔχεται: present middle of ἔχω. The middle ἔχομαι with ἐκ means 'I depend on', so the line runs 'on whom the power and strength of the Phaeacians depends'.

198

ἦ ῥα: 'she spoke', a very common formula for capping a speech.

199

στῆτέ: 'stand still' or 'stop'. Having herself 'stood' (line 141) when Odysseus first emerged into view, Nausicaa enjoins her handmaids to do the same: the last we had seen of them they were fleeing in disorder (line 138).

μοι: ethic dative, merely indicating that the action involves (in this case) the speaker Nausicaa, and difficult to translate.

ἰδοῦσαι: almost concessive, 'even though you've seen ...'.

A Level

200

ἦ μή που: expecting the answer 'no' (like ἄρα μή), 'surely you don't think . . .'.

δυσμενέων: another possible echo of Odysseus' name (see note to line 188), adding to the lightness of the episode.

φάσθ': = φάσθε, second person plural aorist indicative of φημί (middle ending; the form is unusual and this instance is cited in LSJ).

ἔμμεναι: = εἶναι.

201

ἔσθ': = ἔστι, the τ is aspirated into a θ by the rough breathing in οὗτος. Translate as 'exist' here.

οὗτος ἀνὴρ: i.e. someone who might be hostile to the Phaeacians.

διερὸς βροτὸς: in apposition to οὗτος ἀνὴρ, 'as a living mortal'.

οὐδὲ γένηται: the subjunctive γένηται here with οὐδέ expresses futurity: 'nor will such a person be born'.

202

κεν: = ἄν, with the subjunctive ἵκηται ('who would come').

Φαιήκων ἀνδρῶν: possessive genitives, referring to γαῖαν.

203

δηιοτῆτα φέρων: this is the key point, spotlit in enjambment at the start of the line.

μάλα . . . ἀθανάτοισιν: supply εἰσί.

205

ἄμμι: = ἡμῖν.

ἐπιμίσγεται: from ἐπιμίσγομαι, an epic/Ionic form of the Attic ἐπιμίγνυμαι.

206

ὅδε τις δύστηνος: ὅδε is now Odysseus, and it might not be a coincidence that the words ὅδε τις δύστηνος should so strongly echo the name that is still unknown to Nausicaa and will be purposely withheld from the Phaeacians for some time (until the start of Book 9).

207

τόν . . . χρὴ: understand ἡμᾶς: 'whom we now must'.

πρὸς Διός: 'under the protection of Zeus'.

208

ξεῖνοί . . . τε: note the alliterative patterning of τ/δ and ξ/χ/γ across the whole line (with λ) in the last two nouns; the sounds soften as the line progresses.

ξεῖνοί: The Phaeacians correctly observe ξενία, giving the stranger a bath and food and drink before asking his identity, and Nausicaa initiates this at the earliest possible state by ordering her attendants to provide this stranger with food and drink.

A
Level

πτωχοί: there is irony in Nausicaa's using the word 'beggar': Odysseus is not a
  beggar (though he will pretend to be one when he arrives at Ithaca).

τε ... τε: note this linking with τε happens three times in these two lines.

ὀλίγη τε φίλη: a neat statement of the advantage of showing ξενία to strangers: it
  is 'slight' to the giver but 'welcome' to the recipient.

209

δότ': = δότε, aorist imperative of δίδωμι.

210

ὅθ': relative, with ἔστ' (= ἐστί), 'where there is . . .'.

ἐπὶ: 'moreover', an adverb here.

σκέπας: nominative here, with ἔστι.

211

ἔφαθ': = ἔφατο, third person singular middle imperfect (with aorist meaning) of
  φημί. The phrase ὣς ἔφατο, 'so he spoke', is another customary way of capping
  a speech.

αἱ ... κέλευσαν: halted by Nausicaa, the handmaids stand and discuss their
  orders.

212

κάδ: = κατά.

ἄρ': probably 'then'; the particle appears three times in this description (here and in
  lines 214 and as ῥα in 217) and sets out the orderly sequence of events.

Ὀδυσσῆ': i.e. Ὀδυσσέα, direct object of εἷσαν (from ἵζω).

ἐπὶ σκέπας: here a prepositional phrase, 'to a sheltered spot'.

213

Ναυσικάα ... Ἀλκινόοιο: note the repetition from line 196 (and the entire line
  reproduces line 17 of book 6).

214

πάρ: = παρά, taking the dative οἱ (= αὐτῷ), 'beside him'.

φᾶρός ... ἔθηκαν: 'and they put a cloak (φᾶρός) and a tunic (χιτών) as clothes
  (εἵματα)'.

216

ἤνωγον ... λοῦσθαι: having been ordered to 'wash' the stranger at line 210
  (λούσατέ, active), they instead supply him with the materials (line 214) and ask
  (ἤνωγον) him to wash himself (λοῦσθαι, middle). This atmosphere of modesty is
  continued by Odysseus' request below that he bathe himself alone.

217

μετηύδα: third person singular imperfect active of μεταυδάω (with contraction
  and augment).

**A
Level**

218

στῆθ': = στῆτε, intransitive aorist imperative of ἵστημι.

οὕτω: 'thus', i.e. 'just as you are'.

ἀπόπροθεν: adverb, made from ἀπό + πρό with the 'from' suffix -θεν, 'from far away'.

219

ὤμοιιν: genitive or dative of the dual, here genitive of separation ('from my shoulders').

ἀπολούσομαι: aorist subjunctive (as χρίσομαι in the next line), expressing purpose after ὄφρα in the previous line. The Homeric subjunctive is not as simple as the Attic.

ἀμφί: this is an adverb here, '[and that I may] anoint myself **all around** with oil'.

220

ἦ: 'certainly'.

δηρὸν: adverb related to δήν, meaning 'for too long'.

ἀπὸ χροός ἐστιν ἀλοιφή: literally 'oil is away from my skin', i.e. '[for too long] has oil been away from my skin'.

221

ἄντην: adverb, 'in front of [you]'.

λοέσσομαι: from λούω, either future indicative active with middle form ('I will not . . .') or aorist subjunctive, translated by aspect ('I would not . . .').

222

γυμνοῦσθαι: middle present infinitive; Odysseus is reluctant to put down his branch in the presence of the handmaids. From αἰδέομαι to μετελθών a literal translation is 'for I am ashamed to strip myself naked after coming into the company of fair-haired maidens.'

223

αἱ δ': 'but they', i.e. the handmaids.

ἴσαν: third person plural imperfect of εἶμι (compare Attic ἴασιν).

224

αὐτάρ: usually translated 'however', this word need not have a strong adversative sense and here (as well as in 227 below) it is just a soft 'but' or even 'and'.

ἐκ ποταμοῦ: understand ὕδατι, '[with water] from the river'

νίζετο: the verb (imperfect of νίζω) takes two accusatives, χρόα (his body) and, on the next line, ἅλμην (the salt he is washing off).

225

ἥ: relative pronoun, with the antecedent ἅλμην.

νῶτα: 'back' accusative plural (for singular), direct object of ἄμπεχεν, linked by καί to the 'broad shoulders' (εὐρέας ὤμους).

ἄμπεχεν: from ἀμφί and ἔχω, the dried sea-salt forms a crust which 'clings around' Odysseus.

**A
Level**

226

ἀτρυγέτοιο: the compound adjective is two-termination and here feminine, agreeing with ἁλὸς (which hence means 'sea', see note to line 94). This interesting word could either mean 'unharvested', i.e. barren, or 'untiring'.

227

λίπ': λίπα, 'richly'. Usually this expression includes ἐλαίῳ, 'with oil'.

228

ἀμφὶ: adverbial, 'around himself'.

ἕσσαθ': = ἕσσατο, aorist of ἕννυμι.

ἅ... ἀδμής: the verb is πορε, strong aorist of (πόρω the present tense of which was back-formed from the aorist stem, see LSJ).

229–235

Athena enhances Odysseus' appearance, and the enhancement is illustrated with a simile. This crucial point in the poem marks the beginning of the end of Odysseus' troubles, as he heads to the peaceful city of Scherie and thence onward to Ithaca. The simile likens him to piece of silver which Athena gilds to make it more beautiful – a marked contrast from the wind-battered lion with which he was previously compared.

229

τόν: article for demonstrative: 'him'.

θῆκεν: aorist of τίθημι, here translatable as 'made' or 'caused [to be]', with accusative adjectives in the following lines agreeing with the object (τόν).

ἐκγεγαυῖα: perfect participle of ἐκγίγνομαι, 'born of'.

230

εἰσιδέειν: explanatory ('epexegetic') infinitive, explaining μείζονά. (The sense is like the English 'that food is good **to eat**'.)

κάδ: = κατά, taking the genitive κάρητος: 'down from his head'.

231

ὁμοίας: accusative plural (in apposition to οὔλας κόμας), governing the dative ὑακινθίνῳ ἄνθει and neatly translated with the biblical English 'like unto'.

232

ὡς δ' ὅτε: 'and just as when . . .', ὡς introduces a simile and is answered with ὥς ('so . . .') in line 235.

χρυσὸν ... ἀργύρῳ: the simile is very apt, likening Athena's embellishment of the hero Odysseus to a craftsman (ἀνὴρ ἴδρις) laying gold leaf onto an already-precious silver vessel; the simile also highlights the irony of Nausicaa thinking him a beggar.

A Level

233

δέδαεν: aorist, the reduplicated form being particular to the meaning 'teach' (i.e. 'cause to learn', rather than the usual meaning of δάω, 'learn'). Note the double accusative, 'taught [him] skill'.

235

κεφαλῇ ... ὤμοις: in apposition to τῷ, '[on him], his head and shoulders'.

237

θηεῖτο: = ἐθεᾶτο, imperfect of θεάομαι, here 'gazed in wonder'.

238

δή ῥα τότ' ... μετηύδα: 'then indeed she did speak among ...': the combination of particles δή and ῥα along with τότε is very emphatic, and indicates that the following speech is a consequence of Nausicaa's amazement.

239

κλῦτέ: aorist imperative plural of κλύω.
μευ: genitive of source after a verb of hearing (like Attic ἀκούω).
τι: direct object of εἴπω; 'so that I may say something'.

240

οὐ πάντων ἀέκητι θεῶν: these words modify the main verb ἐπιμίσγεται in the line below: 'it is not contrary to the will of all the gods ... that he approaches'.

242

δέατ': = δέατο, weak aorist, 'he seemed'.

244

αἲ γάρ: used with the optative (here εἴη), the phrase introduces a wish: 'if only such a man might be called my husband!' See summary to lines 1–84 above.
πόσιν: in this instance, this word is from πόσις meaning 'husband' but at 246 it is from the homonym meaning 'drink'.

245

καὶ οἱ ἅδοι: 'and it might please him', i.e. 'and he would decide', the verb is still optative (from ἀνδάνω) after αἲ γάρ above.

249

πῖνε καὶ ἦσθε: the verbs are both imperfect; πῖνε is unaugmented, ἦσθε is augmented.

250

ἁρπαλέως: 'greedily'. Possibly related to ἁρπάζω, 'I snatch', the enjambment highlights Odysseus' zeal for his meal.
ἦεν: imperfect of εἰμί, best translated here as 'he had been ...'.

A
Level

255

πόλινδ': = πόλινδε, the -δε suffix indicating motion towards.

ἴμεν: infinitive (see line 130) expressing purpose, following the aorist imperative ὄρσεο.

257

πάντων ... ἄριστοι: ὅσσοι is relative, its antecedent an unexpressed object of εἰδησέμεν. The formula ὅσσοι ἄριστοι with a genitive is a very common Homeric way of saying 'the bravest of the ...'.

εἰδησέμεν: future infinitive (in indirect statement after φημί in the line above) from the same root as εἶδον and οἶδα: 'I tell you that **you will get to know** ...'.

258

ἀλλὰ μάλ' ὧδ': 'but very much as follows': Nausicaa makes her instructions very clear.

ἔρδειν: infinitive as imperative (as is ἔρχεσθαι in line 261).

259

ὄφρ': = ὄφρα, here 'while', 'for as long as' correlative with τόφρα ('for that long') in the following line.

ἄν ... κ': κε and ἄν are synonyms; they introduce the indefinite subjunctive ἴομεν but their doubling-up here does not affect the translation.

ἀγροὺς ἴομεν καὶ ἔργ': 'we go through the fields and worked lands'.

260

σύν ... μεθ': Nausicaa is very precise in her instructions to Odysseus. σύν and μετά are not synonyms: σύν (with dative ἀμφιπόλοισι) here means 'together with', while μετά (with accusatives ἡμιόνους and ἄμαξαν) is 'behind' or 'after'.

261

καρπαλίμως ἔρχεσθαι: the position on the line emphasizes this important instruction.

262–288

The conjunction ἐπήν (ἐπεί + ἄν, 'when ...') in line 262 introduces an indefinite time clause which is never answered by a main clause but instead leads to a series of descriptive digressions on Phaeacia; the careful and well-ordered vignettes are linked with a series of soft δέ conjunctions and contain various verbal echoes and assonances. Nausicaa recaps her instructions at line 289.

262

ἐπιβήομεν: aorist subjunctive, following ἐπήν and governing the genitive πόλιος (Attic πόλεως), 'when we set foot on the city'.

ἥν: supply ἐστί in the relative clause, 'around which there is ...'.

A Level

263

ἑκάτεϱθε: the adverb governs the genitive πόληος (echoing the alternate form πόλιος above): 'on each side of the city'.

264

νῆες ... ἀμφιέλισσαι: metrically this phrase echoes ἐγὼ δ'ὁδὸν ἡγεμονεύσω in line 261, and δ'ὁδόν is placed in an identical position on the line. For the accusative ὁδόν here, the sense is that the boats are placed 'up along' the road.

265

πᾶσιν ... ἑκάστῳ: the well-run and orderly docks are described with alliterative σ/σт sounds and assonance of ι and ε. The tautological πᾶσιν ... ἑκάστῳ can be translated as 'for each and every one has a dockyard'.

266

σφ': = σφι, possessive dative, 'their ἀγοϱή'.

ἀγοϱή: not the familiar 'marketplace' of classical Athens, the ἀγοϱή in Homer's Greek is the people's assembly itself, or (as here) the place where the assembly is held.

ἀμφίς: this governs the accusative καλόν Ποσιδήιον: the assembly-place of the seafaring Phaeacians has in its centre a sanctuary of Poseidon.

267

ῥυτοῖσιν: this echoes the cognate εἰϱύαται in line 265 above, and is one of three ϱυ sounds in this line.

κατωϱυχέεσσ': dative plural (κατωϱυχέεσσι) agreeing with ῥυτοῖσιν and λάεσσι. Garvie notes that the area was not paved, but the 'hauled and quarried stones' were either seating for the assembly or a walled enclosure.

ἀϱαϱυῖα: feminine nominative singular, perfect active participle of ἀϱαϱίσκω: this describes the ἀγοϱή and takes the datives on this line ('fitted out with ...').

268

ἔνθα δὲ: note the repetition, picking up line 266 (as in lines 86 and 88).

ὅπλα: not the 'weapons' of Attic Greek, the word here means 'tools' or 'equipment' (or nautical 'tackle') and is qualified by the genitives νηῶν ... μελαινάων.

269

ἀποξύνουσιν: the action on the oars is uncertain: either 'they scrape off', i.e. they clean, or 'they plane/sharpen', i.e. they maintain the edges.

270

μέλει: this verb has as its subject both the pair of negatives οὐ ... βιὸς οὐδὲ φαϱέτϱη and the positive antitheses ἱστοὶ καὶ ἐϱετμὰ ... καὶ νῆες ἐῖσαι.

271

ἐῖσαι: Attic ἴσαι, 'equal', here 'well-balanced' or 'well-keeled' ('ship-shape').

A Level

272

ᾗσιν: relative pronoun, after ἀγαλλόμενοι, 'rejoicing in which'.

πεϱόωσι: present indicative active, third person singular of πεϱάω, 'I traverse', with πολιὴν θάλασσαν as its direct object.

274

μωμεύῃ: the enjambment spotlights the verb (subjunctive after μή τις on the previous line); throughout the whole book several key words are suspended into the 'run-on position' but particularly in Nausicaa's speech to Odysseus the versification lends much emphasis to key terms.

275

καί νύ ... ὧδε: 'Thus, then, ...'.

κακώτεϱος: = Attic κακίων, the adjective describes τις ('and indeed, some rather base fellow may say ...').

276

ὅδε ... τε: 'Who's this strapping fine fellow following Nausicaa ...?' The princess pays Odysseus an indirect compliment here: after having assessed his qualities earlier in the passage, it is now taken for granted that an onlooker would describe Odysseus as καλός and μέγας, although the evidently pejorative and insulting ξεῖνος qualifying τίς ('some foreigner?') is suspended to the run-on position on the following line.

277

Garvie notes the increasing length of the three units on this line and the 'coarse and offensive' tone of the question ποῦ δέ μιν εὗϱε; ('and where did she find him?').

οἱ: dative personal pronoun, here feminine and used with αὐτῇ (referring to Nausicaa).

278

ἦ: introducing a potential explanation (as line 120 above), and picked up by a second with ἦ at line 280: 'is it ...? Or maybe ...'.

ἦς ἀπὸ νηός: ἦς is possessive: 'from his ship' (following πλαγχθέντα).

279

ἀνδϱῶν τηλεδαπῶν: this expands on τινα in the previous line.

281

ἤματα πάντα: 'for all of her days', accusatives expressing duration of time.

282

βέλτεϱον: = Attic βέλτιον, understand ἐστί.

καὐτή: = καὶ αὐτή.

283

ἄλλοθεν: like ξεῖνος in line 277, the enjambment highlights the key 'runover' word.

κατὰ δῆμον: note the echo of line 274.

284

πολέες: = Attic πολλοί.

285

ἐμοί ... γένοιτο: 'these things would be a reproach to me'. κε = ἄν, with the potential optative γένοιτο.

286

ἄλλη ... ἥ τις τοιαῦτά γε: 'at any other girl who would do that sort of thing'. τις and γε highlight Nausicaa's righteous indignation at the improper behaviour of someone (τις) who would do 'that sort of thing, at least' (τοιαυτά γε) and, by extension (for the benefit of her mysterious guest), the unlikelihood of her doing it herself.

289–315

After the digression on the townspeople's imagined response to her escorting a strange man to her family home, Nausicaa gets to the point and gives Odysseus a clear set of instructions on how to get to her father's palace and what to do there. The language is precise, uncomplicated and occasionally repetitive, the verse in places carefully skewed highlighting key words in enjambment, as Nausicaa sets out her directions in detail.

289

ὦκ': = ὦκα, adverb.

ἐμέθεν: = ἐμοῦ.

ξυνίει: imperative of ξυνίημι. Note the word-play with the accompanying vocative ξεῖνε.

290

πομπῆς ... νόστοιο: genitives after τυγχάνω, which here means 'I obtain'.

291

δήεις: present tense, but with future meaning: 'you will find'.

ἄλσος: neuter accusative singular, direct object of δήεις and vividly described by αἰγείρων in the run-on position on following line: 'a grove ... of poplars'.

292

ἐν ... λειμών: 'and in [this grove] a spring wells up, and around it, a meadow': this compact line, with its several elisions, contains the precise description of the grove where Odysseus is to wait.

294

τόσσον ... βοήσας: literally 'as (τόσσον) far from the city as (ὅσσον) a man makes his voice heard having shouted'. (Understand τις as the subject of γέγωνε.)

πτόλιος: = Attic πόλεως.

A Level

295

μεῖναι: infinitive as imperative, taken with χρόνον: 'wait for some time . . .'.

εἰς ὅ: 'until'.

296

ἄστυδε: see πόλινδε, line 255.

δώματα: the first of four instances of this word in the space of seven lines. (Note that at 302 below it is a 'real' plural, 'houses', as opposed to a plural for singular.)

298

ἴμεν: infinitive as imperative.

300

ῥεῖα δ' ἀρίγνωτ' ἐστί: note the similarity to line 108, though the speaker here is Nausicaa rather than the narrator.

301

νήπιος: note the run-one position: a child could do it, '[even] a baby'. Note also the enjambment which features the increasing length of the run-on elements in the following lines up to line 307.

303

κεκύθωσι: reduplicated aorist subjunctive of κεύθω.

306

στρωφῶσ': = στρωφῶσα, nominative present participle of στρωφάω (related to στρέφω) describing Arete who is 'constantly turning' the wool as she weaves.

307

εἴατ': = εἴατο, third person plural pluperfect of ἕζομαι (the subject is δωμαί).

309

τῷ: 'on which'.

ἀθάνατος ὥς: i.e. ὡς ἀθάνατος, 'like an immortal god'.

310

παραμειψάμενος: 'passing him by . . .': note how perfunctory the description of Alcinous is, compared with the precision of Nausicaa's instructions regarding how Odysseus should approach Arete.

μητρός: with ἡμετέρης in the following line, the two genitives frame the phrase which describes how Odysseus is to make his supplication and lay extra emphasis on Arete.

311

ἴδηαι: = Attic ἴδῃ, aorist middle subjunctive after ἵνα, 'so that you may see'.

A
Level

312

εἰ καί τηλόθεν ἐσσί: lit. 'even if you are from far away'. ἐσσί is Attic εἶ.

313

κείνη: = Attic ἐκείνη, the subject of φρονέησ'.

φρονέησ': = φρονέησι, epic subjunctive taken with φίλα meaning 'to be well-disposed'.

314

ἐλπωρή τοι: understand ἐστί in the apodosis of the conditional: 'then there is hope for you'.

315

οἶκον ... γαῖαν: his οἶκος is the ultimate aim of his journey, so we are told here that Odysseus will reach his 'home and fatherland' although he will in fact reach his homeland long before he returns home. (In forecasting Odysseus' potential homecoming treats, Nausicaa neglects to mention a long-awaiting wife: see Introduction.)

316

μάστιγι φαεινῇ: the whip is described as 'gleaming' either from the gloss of tightly-wound leather or from some metal or polished wooden handle. Note the related word ἱμάσθλην framing the description at line 320 below.

318

ἐύ μέν ... ἐύ δέ: 'well did they run, and well did they trot with their feet.' Note again the labouring precision, the pleonasm in πλίσσοντο πόδεσσιν, and the plodding π alliteration starting in the latter halves of line 317–319 and culminating in ἀμφίπολοί at line 320.

320

νόῳ: Nausicaa drives the waggon 'with [her] mind', i.e. 'wisely' so that the waggon and walkers are carefully aligned.

322

ἵν: = ἵνα, lit. 'in which place'; translate as 'where' (more commonly ὅπου in Attic).

325

νῦν ... ἄκουσον: the insistent νῦν δή πέρ and repetitive μευ ἄκουσον (re-stating κλῦθί μευ from the line above) add emphasis to Odysseus' stating that his prayers have hitherto been unanswered (and it is clear in the subsequent books that he has every reason to suppose that Athena has not been at his side during his recent catastrophes).

326

ῥαιομένου ... ἔρραιε: the related words emphasize Odysseus' shipwrecked state.

A Level

329

αἴδετο γάǫ: as the more junior deity, Athena has so far been reluctant to defy Poseidon's wrath, which was born of Odysseus' disrespect for his son, the Cyclops Polyphemus and will last (as the narrator here states) until Odysseus reaches Ithaca.

330–331

ἐπιζαφελῶς ... ἱκέσθαι: Poseidon 'furiously raged against god-like Odysseus, until at last he reached his homeland'. These closing words to book 6 recall the first appearance of Odysseus' name, in book 1, lines 20–21: ὁ δ᾽ ἀσπεǫχὲς μενέαινεν / ἀντιθέῳ Ὀδυσῆι πάǫος ἦν γαῖαν ἱκέσθαι.

Vocabulary

An asterisk * denotes a word in OCR's Defined Vocabulary List for AS.

ἀγάλλομαι	to take delight in
ἄγαμαι	to admire
ἀγγελίη -ης, f.	message
ἀγλαός -ή -όν	splendid
ἀγορεύω (fut. ἀγορεύσω)	to speak, tell
*ἀγορή -ῆς, f.	place of assembly
ἄγριος -η -ον	wild
ἀγρονόμος -ον	haunting the countryside
*ἀγρός -οῦ, m.	field
ἀγρότερος -η -ον	that lives in the wild
ἄγρωστις -ιδος, f.	grass
ἄγχι/ἀγχοῦ	+ gen. near
Ἀγχίαλος -ου/-οιο, m.	Anchialus
ἄγχιστα	most closely
*ἄγω	to lead, bring (mid.) to escort, take with one
ἄγε (imper.)	come!
ἀδευκής -ές	malicious, unpleasant
ἀδμής -ῆτος	unmarried, unwed
ἀείδω	to sing
ἀεικέλιος -ον	unseemly, shameful
ἀέκητι	+ gen. against the will of
ἀέκων -ουσα -ον	unwilling
ἀήμενος -η -ον	wind-beaten
ἀθάνατος -ον	immortal
Ἀθήνη/Ἀθηναίη -ης, f.	Athene, goddess of wisdom and the arts
αἲ γάρ	would that, I wish that ...
αἴγειρος -ου, f.	poplar
αἰγίοχος -ον	aegis-bearing
Αἴγισθος -ου m.	Aegisthus, lover of Clytemnestra
*αἰδέομαι	to respect; + infin. to be ashamed to
αἰεί/αἰέν	always, ever
αἰνῶς	terribly
αἰπεινός -ή -όν	high, lofty

*αἱρέω (aor. εἷλον)	to take, seize
αἴθομαι	to burn
ἄιστος -ον	unseen
αἶσχος -εος, n.	shame
αἴτιος -α -ον	responsible, guilty
αἶψα	quickly, soon
ἀίω	to perceive
ἀκλεής -ές (adv. ἀκλειῶς)	inglorious
ἀκούω	+ gen. (of person) to listen to, hear
ἀλάομαι	to wander
ἄλαστος -ον	insufferable
ἄλγος -εος, n.	grief, pain
ἀλέγω	to attend to, care for
ἀλεγύνω	to attend to, care for
ἀλεείνω	to avoid, shun
ἀλείφω	to anoint
ἁλιπόρφυρος -ον	of sea purple
ἀλκή -ῆς, f.	strength
ἄλκιμος -ον	brave
Ἀλκίνοος -ου, m.	Alcinous, king of the Phaeacians
*ἀλλά	but
*ἀλλήλους -ας -α	each other
ἄλλοθεν	from another place
*ἄλλος -η -ο	other, another
ἄλλυδις	to another place
ἄλλυδις ἄλλη	each in different directions
ἅλμη -ης, f.	sea-water, brine
ἀλοιφή -ῆς, f.	anointing
ἄλοχος -ου, f.	wife
ἅλς, ἁλός, f.	sea
ἄλσος -εος, n.	grove
ἀλφηστής -οῦ, m.	enterprising man
ἀλωή -ῆς, f.	orchard, garden, vineyard
*ἅμα	at the same time; + dat. at the same time as

ἄμαξα -ης, f. — cart, waggon
*ἁμαρτάνω — + *gen.* to miss
ἀμείβομαι — to answer, to swap (line 375)
ἄμμι — = ἡμῖν
ἀμοιβή -ῆς, f. — gift in return
ἀμπέχω — to cover
ἀμύμων -ονος — excellent, blameless
ἀμφάδιος -η -ον — public, open
ἀμφαδόν — openly
ἀμφέρχομαι (aor. ἀμφήλυθον) — to surround
ἀμφίαλος -ον — sea-girt
ἀμφιβάλλομαι — to put on oneself
ἀμφιέλισσα -ης f. adj. — curved (at both ends)
ἀμφιπέλομαι — to meet, to reach
ἀμφίς — + *acc.* around, about
ἀμφί — *adv.* round, about, round about
ἀμφίπολος -ου, m.f. — attendant
*ἄν — (i) *conditional etc particle*; (ii) = ἀνά
*ἀνά — + *acc.* up, up along, through
ἀναβαίνω — to go up, mount
ἀναγιγνώσκω (aor. ἀνέγνων) — to know well
ἀναιδής -ές — shameless
ἀναΐσσω (aor. part. ἀναΐξας) — to dart up, spring up
ἀνακρεμάννυμι — to hang up
ἄναξ, ἄνακτος, m. — lord
ἄνασσα -ης, f. — queen
ἀνάσσω — to be lord, to rule
ἁνδάνω (aor. ἔαδον, ἅδον) — to please
ἀνδροφόνος -ον — man-killing
ἄνειμι — to go up
ἄνεμος -ου, m. — wind
ἀνερείπομαι (aor. 3 pl. ἀνηρείψαντο) — to carry off
ἀνέρομαι — to question, ask
ἀνέρχομαι — to shoot up, come up
*ἀνήρ, ἀνέρος, m. — man, husband
ἄνθος -εος, n. — flower
*ἄνθρωπος -ου, m. — man, human being
ἀγκρεμάσασα — aor. part of ἀνακρεμάννυμι
ἀνοπαῖα — unseen
ἄντα — facing, before
ἄντην — facing, before
ἀντίαω — to encounter, meet
ἀντιβολέω — to encounter, meet accidentally
ἀντίθεος -ον — godlike
ἀντίον — in reply

ἄνωγα/ἀνώγω — to order, bid
ἄξιος -α -ον — worthy
ἀοιδή -ῆς, f. — song
ἀοιδός -οῦ, m. — bard, poet
ἀπάνευθε(ν) — apart
*ἅπας, ἅπασα, ἅπαν — all, the whole
ἄπαστος -ον — + *gen.* without tasting
ἀπεῖπον — (*aor.*) spoke out
ἀπηλεγέως — bluntly
ἀπήνη -ης, f. — cart, waggon
ἀπινύσσω — to be lacking in understanding
*ἀπό — + *gen.* from, away from
Ἀπόλλων -ωνος, m. — Apollo, god of prophecy, music and archery
ἀποβάλλω — to cast aside, throw down
ἀποβαίνω (aor. ἀπέβην) — to go away
ἀπόλλυμι — to destroy, to lose
ἀπολούομαι — + *gen.* to wash off from one's . . .
ἀποίχομαι — to be away, to be gone
ἀποπαύω — to stop (*in middle* to cease)
ἀποπλύνω — to wash clean
ἀποξύνω — to sharpen off, taper
ἀπόπροθεν — at a distance, far away
ἀπορραίω — to deprive
ἀποστάδα — standing at a distance
ἀποτίνω (fut. ἀποτίσομαι) — (*in middle*) to take revenge
ἄποτμος, -ον — unlucky, ill-starred
*ἅπτομαι — + *gen.* to touch, clasp
ἄπυστος -ον — unheard of
ἀπωθέω (3 sing. aor. ἀπέωσε) — to drive out
ἀπώλεσε — 3rd person singular aorist of ἀπόλλυμι
*ἄρα/ῥα — then, so
ἀράομαι — to pray
ἄρσας (m. weak aor. part of ἀραρίσκω) — having fitted, having equipped
ἀραρυῖα (f. perf. part. of ἀραρίσκω) — fitted
Ἄργος -εος, n. — Argos (a city in central Greece)
ἀργύρεος -α/η -ον — silver
ἄργυρος -οῦ, m. — silver
ἀρείων -ον — better, stronger, more excellent
ἀρίγνωτος -ον — recognizable
ἄριστος -η -ον — best, foremost
ἀρνέομαι — to refuse, reject
ἄρουρα -ας, f. — land, earth

ἁρπαλέως — greedily
Ἅρπυιαι -ων, f. — Whirlwinds, Hurricanes (personified)
Ἄρτεμις -ιδος, f. — Artemis, goddess of hunting, sister of Apollo
ἀρτύνω — to prepare
*ἄρχω/ἄρχομαι — to begin
ἀσκέω (aor. ἤσκησα) — to smooth out
ἀσπίς -ίδος, f. — shield
*ἄστυ -εος, n. — city
ἀσχαλάω — to be distressed
ἀτιμάζω — to dishonour
ἀτρεκέως — exactly, precisely
ἀτρύγετος -ον — unharvested
Ἀτρυτώνη -ης, f. — Atrytone (an epithet of Athene)
*αὖ — again, in turn
αὐγή -ῆς, f. — radiance, light
αὐδάω — to speak
αὐδήεις -εσσα -εν — endowed with human speech
αὐλή -ῆς, f. — courtyard
αὔριον — tomorrow
αὐτάρ — but, and
αὖτε — again, this time, in turn
ἀϋτή -ῆς, f. — cry, shout
*αὐτίκα — at once, immediately
*αὐτός -ή -ό — self; him, her, it, them
αὔτως — just as one is/was, just so
αὔω — to shout
ἄφαρ — straightaway
*ἀφικνέομαι — to arrive at, reach
ἀφνειός -όν — rich
ἄφρων -ον — foolish
ἀχεύω (3 sing. aor. ἤκαχε) — to mourn
Ἀχαιός -ά -όν — Greek (Achaean)
ἄψ — back again
ἄωτον -ου, n. — wool

*βαθύς -εῖα -ύ — deep
*βαίνω (aor. ἔβην) — to go
*βάλλω — to throw, shoot
*βασίλεια -ης, f. — princess
*βασιλεύς -έως, m. — king
βασιλεύω — to rule
βέλτερος -η -ον — better
*βίη -ης, f. — strength, might
βίηφιν — by force
βιός -οῦ, m. — bow
βίοτος -ου m. — life
βλέφαρον -ου, n. — eyelid
*βοάω — to shout
βοητύς - ύος, f. — a shout
βόθρος -ου, m. — hole, trough

βόλομαι = βούλομαι — to want
βουλεύω — to consider
βοῦς, βοός, m.f. — ox, cow
βρίθω — to prevail
βροτός -οῦ, m. — mortal
βρῶσις -ιος, f. — food
βωμός -οῦ, m. — altar

γαῖα -ης, f. — land, ground
γάμος -ου, m. — marriage
*γάρ — for
γαστήρ -έρος, f. — stomach
*γε — at least, at any rate
γέγωνα (perf. w. pres. sense) — to make one's voice heard
γείνομαι (aor. ἐγεινάμην) — to give birth
γενεά -ᾶς, f. (acc. γενεήν) — family, race
γηθέω — to rejoice, be glad
γῆρας -αος, n. — old age
γλαυκῶπις -ιδος — bright-eyed
γόνος -ου, m. — child
γόνυ -ατος, n. (pl. γούνατα, γούνων) — knee
γόος -ου, m. — weeping, lamenting
γουνόομαι — to beseech by the knees, supplicate
γραίη -ης, f. — old woman
γυῖα -ων, n.pl. — limbs
γυμνόομαι — to be naked, to strip off
*γυμνός -ή -όν — naked
*γυνή -αικός, f. — woman, wife

δαίμων -ονος, m. — god, divinity
δαίνυμι — to give a banquet; (mid.) to participate in a banquet
δαίς, δαΐδος, f. — torch
δαίς, δαιτός, f. — meal, feast
δαίτη -ης, f. — meal, feast
δαΐφρων -ονος — wise
δακρύω — to weep
δαμάζω (aor. pass. ἐδάμην) — to master, conquer, subdue
Δαναοί -ων, m. — Greeks
*δέ — and, but
δέατο — = ἐδόκει
δέδαον (aor. of δάω) — taught
δέδμητο — 3 sing. plup. mid/pass. of δέμω
δείδω/δείδια — to be afraid, fear
*δείκνυμι — to show
*δεῖπνον -ου, n. — meal, dinner
δέμω — to build
δέος -ους, n. — fear

δεύομαι — + *gen.* to lack
δεύτατος -η -ον — last
*δή — indeed
δηϊότης -ητος, f. — battle, warfare
Δῆλος -ου, f. — Delos, sacred island in the Aegean
*δῆμος -ου, m. — district, land
δήν — long, for a long while
δηρόν — for a long time
δήω — to find
διαπέτομαι (aor. διεπτάμην) — to fly away
διαρραίω (fut. διαρραίσω) — to destroy
*διδάσκω — to teach
*δίδωμι (aor. ἔδωκα) — to give
διερός -ή -όν — vigorous, living
διέρχομαι — to pass through
δίζημαι — to seek
δίκαιος -η -ον — just
δινή -ῆς, f. — eddy, whirlpool
δινήεις -εσσα -εν — eddying, whirling
δῖος -α -ον — noble, illustrious, goodly
δμωαί -ῶν, f.pl. — maidservants
δοάσσατο — = ἔδοξε
*δοκέω — to seem
δολομήτης -ου, m. — wily, sneaky
δόλος -ου, m. — trick
δόμος -ου, m. — house
δόρυ, δούρατος/ δουρός, n. — spear, shaft; tree
δόσις -ιος, f. — gift
Δουλίχιον -ου, n. — Dulichium (an island near Ithaca)
δοῦρε — *dual of* δόρυ
δύναμαι — to be able
δύο — two
δύομαι — to set (of sun); to enter
δυσμενής -ές — hostile; (*pl as noun*) enemies
δύστηνος -ον — wretched, miserable, unhappy
δῶμα -ατος, n. — house, palace
δμωή -ῆς, f. — female slave
δῶρον -ου, n. — gift
ἑ (gen. ἕο, dat. οἷ) — him, her, it
ἐγγύθεν — nearby
ἐγείρω (aor. mid. ἐγρόμην) — to rouse, waken; (*mid.*) to wake up
*ἐγώ, ἐγών — I
ἐδητύς -ύος, f. — food
ἔδω — to eat
ἕεδνα -ων, n.pl. — bridal gifts
εἰκοσάβοιος -ον — worth twenty oxen

ἐείκοσιν — twenty
(ἐ)εικοστός -ή -όν — twentieth
ἐέλδομαι — + *gen.* to want
ἕζομαι — to sit down
*ἐθέλω — to wish, be willing
*εἰ — if
εἰδησέμεν — *fut. infin. of* οἶδα
εἶδος -εος, n. — appearance, beauty
εἰλαπίνη -ης, f. — feast
εἴλυμα -ατος, n. — wrapper
εἷμα -ατος, n. (also pl.) — clothes, clothing
*εἰμί — to be
*εἶμι — to go
εἵνεκα — + *gen.* on account of
εἴρομαι (inf. ἐρέεσθαι) — to ask, enquire
*εἰς, ἐς — + *acc.* into, to
εἷς, μία, ἕν (m/n. gen. ἑνός) — one
εἰσίθμη -ης, f. — entrance
ἐΐσκω — + *dat.* to liken to, compare with
εἰσοιχνέω — to enter
εἰσοράω — to look upon
ἔϊσος -η -ον — well-balanced
*ἐκ/ἐξ — + *gen.* out of, from
*ἕκαστος -η -ον — each
ἑκάτερθε(ν) — on either side
ἐκγεγαυῖα (f. perf. part. of ἐκγίγνομαι) — born of
ἐκδύνω — to strip off
ἔλαιον -ου, n. — olive oil
ἐμβάλλω — to throw in, throw on
ἔμπης — nevertheless
ἔλαφος -ου, f. — deer
ἐλεαίρω — to pity
ἐλεεινός -ή -όν — pitied
Ἑλλάς -άδος, f. — Greece
ἔλπομαι — to expect, think likely
ἐλπωρή -ῆς, f. — hope, expectation
ἐμέ/με (gen. ἐμέθεν/ μευ, dat. ἐμοί/μοι) — me
ἔμικτο — 3rd *sing. aorist passive of* μίγνυμι
*ἐμός -ή -όν — my
ἐμπάζομαι — + *gen.* to take heed (of)
*ἐν/ἐνί — + *dat.* in, on
ἐναλίγκιος -ον — + *dat.* like, resembling
*ἐναντίος -η -ον — face to face
*ἔνθα — here, there, where, then
*ἐνθάδε — here, hither
ἔνθετο — 3 *sing. aor. mid. of* ἐντίθημι
ἐνιαυτός -ου, m. — year
ἐννοσίγαιος -ου, m. — earthshaker (*an epithet of Poseidon*)

ἕννυμι — to put (clothes) on; (*mid.*) to put (clothes) on oneself

ἐντίθημι — to place in, to put in

ἔντοσθεν — from within

ἐξείης — in order

ἐξέρομαι — to enquire

ἐξονομάζω — to call by name

ἔξοχον — beyond, especially

ἔοικα (part. ἐοικώς) — to be like

ἐπαλαστέω (fem. aor. part. ἐπαλαστήσασα) — to be angry at

*ἐπεί — when, since

ἐπείγω — to press on, urge on; (*mid.*) to be eager for

*ἔπειτα — then, next

ἐπέοικε — it is fitting, right

ἐπερύω (aor. ἐπέρυσσε) — to draw closed, draw to

ἐπηετανός -όν — abundant, ever full

ἐπήν — when(ever)

*ἐπί — *adv.* thereupon, thereat, on, besides
+ *acc.* to, over, on, in
+ *dat.* upon, at, over and above

ἐπιβαίνω — to mount; set foot in/on

ἐπιβάλλω — to lay on

ἐπιβοάω (fut. ἐπιβώσομαι) — to call as witness

ἐπιδήμιος -ον — at home, among the people

ἐπιζαφελῶς — furiously

ἐπικλείω — to praise

ἐπιμάρτυρος -ου m. — witness

ἐπιμένω — to stay, wait

ἐπιμίσγομαι — to mingle with, have dealings with

ἐπίστιον -ου, n. — slipway

ἐπιτέλλω (3 sing. aor. mid. ἐπετείλατο) — to lay upon

ἐπιτολμάω — to endure

ἐποίχομαι — to go about

*ἕπομαι (aor. ἑσπόμην) — to follow

ἔπος -εος, n. — word

ἔρανος -ου, m. — shared meal, festival

*ἔργον -ου, n. — work, deed

ἔρδω — to do, act, perform

ἐρεείνω — to ask, enquire

ἐρέτης -ου m. — rower, oarsman

ἐρετμόν -οῦ, n. — oar

ἐρίηρος -ον — trusty

ἔρις -ιδος, f. — strife, rivalry

ἔρνος -εος, n. — sapling, shoot

Ἐρύμανθος -ου, m. — Erymanthus (mountain in Arcadia)

ἐρύω (3 pl. perf. pass. εἰρύαται) — to drag, draw up

ἔρχομαι (aor. ἦλθον/ἤλυθον) — to come, go

ἐς — = εἰς

ἔσσατο — 3 sing. aor. mid. of ἕννυμι (*q.v.*)

ἐσθής -ῆτος, f. — clothes, clothing

ἐσθλός -ή -όν — excellent, brave, noble

ἔσθω = *ἐσθίω — to eat

ἕσπερος -ου, m. — evening

ἐσφορέω — to carry into

ἐσχάρη -ης, f. — hearth

*ἔσχατος -η -ον — uttermost, furthest, remotest

ἔταρος = ἑταῖρος -ου, m. — companion, friend

ἑτέρως — otherwise

*ἔτι — still, yet

*ἐΰ/εὐ — well

ἐϋκτίμενος -η -ον — well-built

εὐμενέτης -ου, m. — well-wisher

εὐνή -ῆς, f. — bed

ἐϋπλόκαμος -ον — fair-tressed, with beautiful hair

*εὑρίσκω — to find

Εὐρύκλεια -ας, f. — Eurycleia

*εὐρύς -εῖα -ύ — broad

εὐφροσύνη -ης, f. — joy, happiness

*εὔχομαι — to pray

εὐῶπις -ιδος — beautiful, fair-faced

ἔφημαι — + *dat.* to be seated on

ἐφίημι (3 sing. aor. opt. ἐφείη) — to apply, to set (one's hand to . . .)

ἐφορμάω — to urge, stir up

Ἐφύρα -ης, f. — Ephyra (Corinth)

*ἔχω (aor. part. mid. σχόμενος) — to have, hold; (*mid.*) to hold one's ground

Ζάκυνθος -ου, f. — Zacynthus (an island near Ithaca)

*Ζεύς, Ζηνός/Διός, m. — Zeus, king of the gods

ζεύγνυμι — to yoke

ἦ — indeed, surely; *interrog.* can it be that; or

ἦ (from ἠμί) — he/she spoke

*ἤ — or; than

ἤ . ἤ (ἤ) — whether . . . or

ἡγεμονεύω — to show the way

*ἡγέομαι — + *dat.* lead, show the way

ἠδέ — and

ἡδύς, ἡδεῖα, ἡδύ — sweet
ἦε — = ἤ
ἠέλιος -ου, m. — sun
ἠΐων -ονος, f. — sand-spit
ἠλακάτη -ης, f. — distaff (a tool used in weaving)
ἠλάκατα -ων, n. pl. — thread, yarn
ἦμαι — to sit, be seated
ἦμαρ -ατος, n. — day
*ἡμεῖς -ῶν — we
*ἡμέτερος -α -ον — our
ἡμίονος -ου, m.f. — mule
ἡνιοχεύω — to drive
ἥρως -ωος, m. — hero
ἦτορ -ορος, n. — heart
Ἥφαιστος -ου, m. — Hephaestus, god of fire
ἦχι — where
ἦῶθεν — at morning

θάλαμος -ου, m. — bedroom
*θάλασσα -ης, f. — sea
θάλλω τεθαλυῖα (perf. part. f.) — to flourish flourishing
θάλος -εος, n. — young shoot, branch
θαμβέω (aor. ἐθάμβησα) — to be astonished at
θάμνος -ου, m. — bush
θάνε — 3 sing. unaugmented aor. of θνήσκω
θαρσαλέως — boldly
θάρσος -εος, n. — courage
θαῦμα -ατος, n. — wonder
*θεά -ᾶς, f. — goddess
θεῖος -α -ον — divine, holy
θελκτήριον -ου, n. — charm
θεοπροπία -ας, f. — prophecy
θεοπρόπος -ου, m. — prophet
*θεός -οῦ, m. — god
θεουδής -ές — god-fearing
θέσπις -ιος — divine, inspired
θηέομαι — to gaze at in wonder
θῆλυς -εια -υ — female
θίς, θινός, m. — shore, beach
θνήσκω (aor. ἔθανον) — to die
θνητός -ή -όν — mortal
θοός -ή -όν — swift
θοῶς — swiftly
θρόνος -ου, m. — chair, seat
*θυγάτηρ -έρος, f. — daughter
θύελλα -ης, f. — storm, squall
θυμός -οῦ, m. — heart, mind, soul
θύρη -ης f. — door

ἰαίνω — to warm

ἴδρις -ιος — skilful
*ἱερός -ή -όν — sacred, holy
*ἵημι (aor. ἧκα) — to let fall
Ἰθάκη -ης, f. — Ithaca
ἱκάνω — to come
Ἰκάριος -ου, m. — Icarius, father of Penelope
ἱκνέομαι (aor. ἱκόμην) — to come, arrive, reach
Ἶλος -ου, m. — Ilus, a Greek hero
ἱμάσθλη -ης, f. — whip
ἱμάς ἱμάντος, m. — leather strap
ἱμάσσω — to whip on
ἱμερόεις -εσσα -εν — lovely
*ἵνα — in order that; where
ἰός -ου m. — arrow
ἱρός -ή -όν — = ἱερός
ἰσόθεος -ον — equal to a god, god-like
ἴσος -η -ον — equal
*ἵστημι — to set, place; (mid. + intrans. tenses of active) to stand, stand still
ἱστός -οῦ, m. — mast; loom (at 1.357)

κάδ — = κατά
καθαίρω — to cleanse, clean
καθέζομαι — to sit down, be seated
*καθίζω — to make to sit down, to seat
καθικνέομαι (aor. καθικόμην) — to reach, to touch
*καί — and; also even
κακκείοντες — fut. part. of κατάκειμαι
*κακός -ή -όν — bad, harmful, evil
κακόω — to disfigure, make unsightly
*καλέω (perf. part. pass. κεκλημένος) — to call
κάλλος -εος, n. — beauty
*καλός -ή -όν — beautiful, fine, fair
κάπρος -ου, m. — boar
κάρη -ητος, n. — head
κάρηνα -ων, n.pl. — heads, peaks
καρπαλίμως — swiftly
κάρτος -εος, n. — strength
κασίγνητος -ου, m. — brother
*κατά — + acc. throughout, over, in
καταβαίνω (aor. κατέβην) — to come down
καταβάλλω — to throw down
καταλέγω (aor. imper. κατάλεξον) — to recount, tell at length
καταλείπω (3 sing. aor. κάλλιπεν) — to leave behind

καταχέω	to pour over	Κρονίων -ωνος, m.	son of Cronus
κατερύκω	to restrain	κτέαρ (dat. pl.	possession
κατέρχομαι (fut.	to go down	κτεάτεσσιν) n.	
κατελεύσομαι)		κτέρεα n. pl.	funeral gifts
κατάκειμαι	to lie down	*κτείνω	to kill
κατωρυχής -ές	dug out, quarried	κτερεΐζω	to bury with honours
κε, κεν	= ἄν	κτῆμα -ατος, n.	possession
κεδνός -ή -όν	trusty	κῦμα -ατος, n.	wave
κεῖθεν	from there		
κεῖμαι	to lie	λᾶας -ος, m.	stone
κειμήλιον -ου, n.	heirloom	Λαέρτης -ου, m.	Laertes, father of
κεῖνος -η -ο	that; he, she, it		Odysseus
κεῖσε	thither, there	λάϊγγες -ων, f.pl.	pebbles
κεκαλυμμένος	wrapped (perf. pass.	*λαμβάνω	to take
	part. of καλύπτω)	λανθάνω	I escape notice
κέλευθος -ου, f.	road, way	λαός -οῦ, m.	people
*κελεύω	to order, instruct, tell	*λέγω (aor. εἶπον)	to say
κέλομαι	to bid, order, tell	λειμών -ῶνος, m.	meadow
κερδαλέος -η -ον	cunning, artful;	λέκτρον -ου, n.	couch, bed
	advantageous	λεπτός -ή -όν	narrow, delicate
κερδίων -ον	better	λευκώλενος -ον	white-armed
κεύθω	to cover, conceal; to	λεύσσω	to see
	hold, contain,	λέχος -εος, n. (dat. pl.	bed
		λεχέεσσι)	
*κεφαλή -ῆς, f.	head		
κῆδος -εος, n.	trouble	λέων -οντος, m.	lion
κῆρ, (dat. κῆρι), n.	heart	λήκυθος -ου, m.	oil-flask
κίον (part. κιών)	they went	Λητώ -οῦς, f.	Leto, mother of Artemis
κίων -ονος, m./f.	pillar, column		and Apollo
κλάω	to break, break off	λιλαίομαι	to long for, to desire
κλαίω	to weep	*λιμήν -ένος, m.	harbour
κλείς, κλειδός, f.	latch	λίπα	richly
κλείω	to make famous	λιπαρός -ά -όν	shining
κλέος n.	glory	λίσσομαι	to beg, beseech
κλιθῆναι	aor. pass. inf. of κλίνω	λούω	to wash; (mid.) to bathe
κλῖμαξ -ακος, f.	stair(s)	(aor. mid.	
κλίνω	to lean, (pass.) to lie	part.λοεσσάμενος)	
	down	λυγρός -ά -όν	painful, sorrowful
κεκλιμένος -η -ον	leaning against	λωίων -ον	more agreeable
κλυτός -ή -όν	famous, renowned		
κλύω	to hear	μάκαρ -αρος	happy, fortunate
κοιρανέω	to be lord, to rule	*μακρός -ή -όν	long, tall
κόμαι -ων, f. pl.	hair, tresses	μακρόν	aloud
κομέω	to look after, care for	*μάλα	very, quite, just
*κομίζομαι	to take care of, rescue	μαλακός -ή -όν	soft
κομίζω	to convey, to take	*μάλιστα	most of all, above all
	care of	*μᾶλλον	more, rather
κορώνη -ης, f.	handle	μάστιξ -ιγος, f.	whip
κούρη -ης, f.	girl, daughter	μεγαλήτωρ -ορος	great-hearted
κραδίη -ης, f.	heart	μέγαρον -ου, n.	hall, house
κραιπνός -ή -όν	swift	*μέγας, μεγάλη, μέγα	great, tall, large
κραναός -ή -όν	rocky	μέγεθος -εος, n.	size
κρατερῶνυξ -υχος	stout-hoofed	μειλίχιος -η -ον	gentle, soothing
κρείσσων -ον	stronger, more powerful,	μέλας -αινα -αν	black, dark
	better	μελιηδής -ές	honey-sweet
κρήδεμνον -ου, n.	head-dress	*μέλλω	to be about to
κρήνη -ης, f.	spring, fountain	μέλω	to be a care to

μεμνημένη	fem. pf. part. middle of μιμνήσκω	νέμω	to dispense, distribute
		νέομαι	to return
μέν	*slightly emphasizes previous word; often contrasted with* δέ *or* ἀλλά.	*νέος -η -ον	young, fresh, new
		Νέστωρ -ορος, m.	Nestor (a Greek hero who served at Troy)
μενεαίνω	to rage	νήπιος -η -ον	of tender years; silly
Μενέλαος -ου, m.	Menelaus	νήποινος -ον	without compensation
μενοινάω	to desire	*νῆσος -ου, f.	island
μένος -εος, n.	might	νηῦς, νηός/νεός, f.	ship
Μέντης -ου, m.	Mentes	νίζω/νίζομαι	to wash
*μένω	to remain; wait for	νοέω	to notice, perceive, understand, think of, devise
Μερμερίδης -αο, m.	son of Mermesus		
μερμηρίζω	to deliberate, ponder	νόημα -ατος, n.	thought, mind, understanding
μέσος -η -ον	middle, central		
*μετά	+ *acc.* after	νόος -ου, m.	mind, sense
μεταλλάω	to enquire	νοστέω	to go home
μεταπρέπω	+ *dat.* to stand out among	νόστιμος -ον	of one's homecoming
		νόστος -ου, m.	return, return home
μεταυδάω	to speak among, address	νυ, νυν	then, surely, now
		νύμφη -ης, f.	nymph
μετέρχομαι	+ *dat.* to come, go among; + *acc.* to go after, pursue	*νῦν	now
		νώνυμνος -ον	nameless
		νῶτον -ου, n.	back
μέτωπον -ου, n.	forehead	ξανθός -ή -όν	blond(e)
*μή	not	*ξεῖνος -ου, m.	stranger, guest
μήδεα -ων, n.pl.	genitals	ξυνίημι	to mark, heed
μῆλον -ου, n.	sheep, goat		
*μήτηρ -έρος, f.	mother	ὁ, ἡ, τό	he, she, it; who, which; the
μητιάω	to plan, deliberate		
μίγνυμαι	to mix with, have dealings with, have sexual intercourse with	ὀδάξ	with the teeth, biting
		*ὅδε, ἥδε, τόδε	this
		ὁδός -οῦ, f.	journey, way, road
		ὀδυνη -ης, f.	pain
μιμνήσκω	to remind; (*mid.*) remember	ὀδύρομαι	to lament
		Ὀδυσ(σ)εύς -ῆος, m.	Odysseus, ruler of Ithaca
μίμνω	to remain, stay		
μιν	him, her, it	ὅθι	where
μίσγομαι	to mix with, associate with	οἱ	dative of ἑ (*q.v.*)
		οἴγω (3 sing aor. ὤιξεν)	to open
μνάομαι	to court	*οἶδα	to know
μνηστήρ -ῆρος, m.	suitor	*οἴκαδε/οἴκονδε	home, homewards
μογέω	to suffer, undergo	*οἰκέω	to live
μολπή -ῆς, f.	song and dance	οἶκος -ου, m.	house
*μῦθος -ου, m.	word, speech	οἰνοποτάζω	to quaff wine
μωμεύω	to reproach, censure	οἰνοψ -οπος	wine-dark
		οἴομαι	to think
ναιετάω	to live, be inhabited, be situated	οἶος -η -ον	alone
		οἷος -η -ον	such as
Ναυσικάα -ας, f.	Nausicaa, daughter of Alcinous	ὄϊς -ος, m.f.	sheep
		οἶτος -ου, m.	doom
νάω	to flow	οἴχομαι (impf. ᾤχετο)	to have gone, to go
νεμεσάω	+ *dat.* to be indignant with	ὀΐω	to think
		ὄλβος -ου, m.	prosperity
νεμεσίζομαι	+ *dat.* to be angry with	*ὀλίγος -η -ον	small
νέμεσις -εως, f.	wrath, anger, revenge		

ὄλλυμι	to destroy; (mid.) to perish	ὀχέω	to engage in
		ὄχθη -ης, f.	bank
ὄλοντο	3rd plural aorist middle of ὄλλυμι	ὀψίγονος -ον	yet to be born
Ὀλύμπιος -η -ον	Olympian	παίζω	to play
ὁμαδέω	to make a noise	*παῖς/παῖς, παιδός, m. f.	child
ὁμιλέω	to associate, to be in a throng	παλαιός -ά -όν	old
ὅμιλος -ου m.	crowd, throng of people	*πάλιν	back, back again
*ὁμοῖος -η -ον	like	παλίντιτος -ον	avenged
ὁμοφρονέω	to be of one mind, be in harmony	Παλλάς -άδος, f.	Pallas
		Παναχαιοί -ων, m.	all the Achaeans, all the Greeks
ὁμοφροσύνη -ης, f.	like-mindedness, harmony	παννυχιος -ον	all night long
		παντοῖος -η -ον	of every kind
ὄνειδος -εος, n.	(source of) reproach	πάρ	= παρά
ὀπάζω	to grant	*παρά	+ acc. beside, along; + dat. by, near
*ὄπισθε(ν)	behind		
ὀπίσ(σ)ω	in the future, hereafter; back	παραὶ	beside
		παραμείβομαι	to go past
*ὅπλα -ων, n.pl.	(here) ship's tackle	παρειά -ας, f.	cheek
ὅποτε	= ὅτε	παρέστη	= 3 sing. strong aor. of παρίστημι
ὅπως	how, however		
*ὁράω/ὁράομαι	to see	πάρημαι (perf. mid. part. παρήμενος)	to sit beside
ὀρεσίτροφος -ον	mountain-bred		
Ὀρέστης -ου, m.	Orestes (son of Agamemnon)	*παρθένος -ου, f.	maiden, unmarried woman
ὁρμαίνω	to deliberate, ponder	παρίσταμαι	to stand beside
*ὄρος -εος, n.	mountain	πάροιθε(ν)	before, in front
ὁρόω	= ὁράω	πάρος	before
ὄρνις, ὄρνιθος, m.f.	bird	*πᾶς, πᾶσα, πᾶν	all, every
ὄρνυμι	to stir up, arouse	πάσσαλος -ου, m.	peg
ὀρχηστύς -ύος, f.	dance	πάσσων -ον	stouter, thicker, chunkier
ὅς ἥ ὅ	who, which; his, her, its	*πάσχω (aor. ἔπαθον)	to suffer, endure
ὄσσα -ης, f.	rumour	*πατήρ -έρος, m.	father
*ὅσ(σ)ος -η -ον	as much, (pl.) as many	*πατρίς -ίδος	(fem. adj.) of one's fathers
ὄσσε, -ων, n.	eyes		
*ὅτε	when	πατροκασίγνητος -ου, m.	father's brother, uncle
ὀτρύνω	to urge, rouse		
*οὐ/οὐκ/οὐκί/οὐχί	not	πατροφονεύς -έως, m.	murderer of one's father
*οὐδέ	and not, neither	πατρώιον -ου, n.	patrimony
*οὔτε	neither, nor	*παύω	to stop; (mid.) to cease
οὖλος -η -ον	thick, woolly	παχύς -εῖα -ύ	sturdy, chunky
οὔνομα = ὄνομα -ατος, n.	name	*πεζός -ή -όν	on foot
		*πείθω	to persuade; (mid.) to obey, trust
*οὐρανός -οῦ, m.	heaven		
οὐρανόθε(ν)	from heaven	*πειράω	+ gen. to make an attempt on; (mid.) to put to the test, try to find out
οὔρεα -ων, n.pl.	mountains		
*οὕτω(ς)	in this way, thus, so		
ὀφείλω (aor. ὄφελον)	to owe, also used in wishes 'would that', 'if only'.	πεῖσμα -ατος, n.	cable
		πήληξ -ηκος, f.	helmet
		πέλω/πέλομαι	to be
*ὀφθαλμός -οῦ, m.	eye	*πέμπω	to conduct, escort, send
ὄφρα	so that, in order that; while, so long as	Πηνελόπεια -ας, f.	Penelope
ὄφρα . . . τόφρα	for as long as . . . so long	*πένθος -εος, n.	grief, sorrow, distress

πεποιθώς -ότος	(*perf. part. of* πείθω) + *dat.* trusting in	ποτί	= πρός
πεπνυμένος -η -όν	wise, sagacious	ποτικέκλιται (3 sing. perf. pass of προσκλίνω)	leans against
περ	(*with participle*) although	πότνια (fem. adj.)	august, revered
περάω	to make one's way across	πότνια μήτηρ	lady mother
*περί	+ *acc., gen., or dat.* about, around *adv.* exceedingly	*που	somewhere, anywhere; I suppose, perhaps
		*πούς, ποδός, m.	foot
περικαλλής -ές	very beautiful	πρίαμαι	to buy
περικλυτός -ή -όν	very famous	*πριν	before, until
περιμήκετος -ον	very high	προέχω	to jut, project
περίσκεπτος -ον	far-seen	*πρός	+ *gen.* on the side of, from, under the protection of
περίφρων -ονος	very thoughtful		
περιχέω	to pour round, spread over	προσαυδάω (3 sing. imperf. προσηύδα)	to address
πετάννυμι	to spread	προσεῖπον	(*aorist*) spoke to
πηγή -ῆς, f.	spring, source	πρόσθε(ν)	before
πικρόγαμος -ον	having a bitter marriage	προφέρω	to display, engage in
πινυτός -ή -όν	prudent, discreet	πρωθήβης -ου, m.	in the prime of youth
*πίνω (aor. (ἔ)πιον)	to drink	πρῶτος -η -ον	first
πίσεα -ων, n.pl.	meadows	πτόρθος -ου, m.	branch, shoot
Πεισηνορίδης -αο, m.	son of Pisenor	πτωχός -οῦ, m.	beggar
πλάζομαι (aor. part. pass.) πλαγχθείς)	to wander	πτύσσω	to fold
		πύκα	well, strongly
πλίσσομαι	to prance, trot	πυκιμηδής -ές	shrewd
πλυνός -οῦ, m.	washing trough	πυκινός/πυκνός -ή -όν	dense, compact, strongly built
πλύνω	to wash		
ποθέω	to long for, to desire	Πύλος -ου m./f.	Pylos (the city of Nestor)
ποθι	I suppose, probably		
ποιέω	to do, make	πυνθάνομαι (fut. πεύσομαι)	to learn
ποιήεις -εσσα -εν	grassy		
ποιητός -ή -όν	built	*πῦρ, πυρός, n.	fire
ποῖος -α -ον	of what sort	πύργος -ου, m.	fortification, fortified wall
*πόλεμος -ου, m.	war		
πολιός -ή -όν	grey	πω	yet, at all
*πόλις/πτόλις -ιος/-ηος, f.	city		
		ῥαίω	to break, shatter, wreck
πολυάρητος -ον	much prayed to	ῥάκος -εος, n.	rag
Πόλυβος -ου, m.	Polybus, father of Eurymachus	ῥέεθρον -ου, n.	stream
		ῥέζω	to do, act, perform
πολύκλυστος -ον	much-surging	ῥεῖα	easily
*πολύς, πολλή, πολύ (nom. pl. m.) πολέες	much, many	ῥίπτω	to throw
		ῥοή -ῆς, f.	= ῥόος
πολύτλας -αντος	much-enduring	ῥόος -ου, m.	stream
πομπή -ῆς, f.	escort, guidance	ῥύομαι	to cover, protect
πόντος -ου, m.	sea	ῥύπα -ων, n.pl.	dirt, stains
πόποι (with ὦ)	oh strange!	ῥυπόω	to be dirty
πόρον/ἔπορον (aor.)	gave	ῥυτός -ή -όν	hauled
πόσε	to where, whither		
Ποσιδήϊον -ου, n.	sanctuary of Poseidon	Σάμη -ης, f.	Same (an island near Ithaca)
πόσις -ιος, f.	drink		
πόσις -ιος, m.	husband	σέβας (no gen.), n.	astonishment, awe
*ποταμός -οῦ, m.	river	σεύω	to drive, chase
*ποτε	once, ever		

σῆμα -ατος, n. — (here) tomb, burial mound

*σῖτος -ου, m. — food

σιωπῇ — in silence

σκέπας -αος, n. — shelter

σκίδνημι — to scatter

σκιόεις -εσσα -εν — shadowy

σμερδαλέος -η -ον — terrifying

σμήχω — to wash off

*σός, σή, σόν — your

Σπάρτηνδε — to Sparta

σπεῖρα -ων, n.pl. — pieces of cloth; sails

σταθμός -ου, m. — door-post

στείβω — to tread, stamp

στεναχίζω — to groan

στῆθος -εος, n. — chest

στίλβω — to shine, gleam

στρωφάω — to twist, spin

στυγερός -ά -όν — hateful

*σύ, σεῖο — you

σφαίρη -ης, f. — ball

*σφέας -ων (dat. σφιν, σφισι) — them

σφέτερος -α -ον — their

*σχέδον — + gen. near; nearly

ταλαπείριος -ον — much-suffering

τανύω — to stretch

τάχα — quickly, soon

*ταχύς -εῖα -ύ — quick, fast

Τάφιοι -ων, m. — Taphians

Τάφος -ου, f. — Taphos

*τε — and

τέγος -εος, n. — roof

τεθαλυῖα — see θάλλω

τέθηπα — to be astonished, be amazed

τεθνηῶτος (m. gen. sing. perf. part. of θνήσκω) — dead

τείρω — to distress

τέκος -εος, n. — child

τελευτάω — to accomplish

τελευτή -ης, f. — end

τελέω/τελείω — to bring to completion, bring about, accomplish

τέμενος -εος, n. — precinct, family estate

τέρπομαι — + dat to take pleasure in; + gen.to have one's fill of (+ gen.)

(aor. pass. (ἐ) τάρφθην)

τέρσομαι — to be dry, become dry

τέτμον (also ἔτετμον) — (aorist form used as present) to overtake

τεύχω (3 sing. perf. pass. τέτυκται) — to make

*τέχνη -ης, f. — skill, art

τέων — = τίνων (from τίς)

τηλεδαπός -ή -όν — from a distant land

Τηλέμαχος -ου, m. — Telemachus, the son of Penelope and Odysseus

τηλίκος -η -ον — of such an age

τηλόθεν — from far away

Τηΰγετον -ου, n. — Taÿgetus, mountain range in Laconia

*τίθημι — to place, make

τιμήεις -εσσα -εν — precious, costly

τίπτε — why, pray?

*τίς τί — who? what?

*τις, τι — any(one), some(one); a certain

τίω — to honour

τλάω (perf. infin. τετλάμεν) — to endure, have the heart

τοι — = σοι

τοι — surely, let me tell you

τοιγάρ — therefore, accordingly

τοῖος -η -ον/τοιόσδε — such, of such a kind

*τοιοῦτος -αύτη -οῦτο — such, of such a kind

τολυπεύω (aor. τολύπευσα) — to finish

τόσ(σ)ος -η -ον — such, so great

*τότε — then

τόφρα — during that time, meanwhile

τρέπω (aor. mid. part. τρεψάμενος) — to turn

τρέφω — to raise, rear

τρέω — to flee in terror

τρητός -ή -όν — perforated

τρισμάκαρες -ων — thrice-blessed

τρύχω — I wear out, consume

τρώγω — to eat, munch

Τρῶες -ων, m. — Trojans

τρωχάω — to run

*τυγχάνω — to happen; + gen. to obtain, come upon

τύμβος -ου, m. — tomb

τυτθός -όν — little

ὑακίνθινος -η -ον — of hyacinth

ὑβρίζω — to run riot, behave violently

ὕβρις -εως, f. — arrogance, overwhelming violence

ὑβριστής -οῦ, m. — violent, overbearing person

ὑγρός -ή -όν — liquid, moist

*ὕδωρ -ατος, n. — water

υἱός -οῦ, m. — son
*ὕλη -ης, f. — wood, clump of trees
ὑλήεις -εσσα -εν — wooded
ὑόμενος -η -ον — drenched with rain
ὑπεκπρολύω — to set loose from under
ὑπεκπρορέω — to flow up and out
*ὑπέρ — + *gen.* above
ὑπέρβιος -ον — lawless
ὑπερφίαλος -ον — arrogant, overweening
ὑπερωιόθεν — from the upper chamber
ὑπερῷον -ου, n. — the upper part of the house
ὑποδύομαι — + *gen.* to emerge from under
ὑπομένω — to wait
ὑπομιμνήσκω (3 sing. aor. ὑπέμνησεν) — to call to mind
ὕπνος -ου, m. — sleep
ὑποτίθημι (fut. mid. ὑποθήσομαι) — (*in mid.*) to advise
ὑψαγόρας -ου, m. — boaster
*ὑψηλός -ή -όν — high, lofty

φαεινός -ή -όν — shining
Φαίηκες -ων, m. pl. — Phaeacians
*φαίνομαι (aor. ἐφάνην) — to appear
φαρέτρη -ης, f. — quiver
φάρμακον -ου, n. — drug
φᾶρος -εος, n. — cloak
φέριστε (voc.) — 'my good man'
*φέρω — to bring
*φεύγω — to escape, flee
*φημί — to say; to think
Φήμιος -ου, m. — Phemius, the bard at Odysseus' palace
φῆμις -ιος, f. — talk, speech
φθινύθω — to waste
φθονέω — to bear ill-will, begrudge
φιλέω — to love
φιλήρετμος -ον — oar-loving
φιλόξεινος -ον — hospitable, friendly to strangers
*φίλος -η -ον — dear
φοῖνιξ -ικος, f. — palm
φορέω — to carry
φράζομαι — to consider
φρήν -ενος, f. (also pl.) — heart, mind
φρονέω — to think, be minded, be disposed
φυή -ῆς, f. — stature
φύλλον -ου, n. — leaf

φύω — to put forth, produce, press (at line 1.381)
φωνέω — to speak
φώς, φωτός, m. — man

*χαίρω — to rejoice
*χαλεπός -ή -όν — heavy, painful, hard, difficult
χαλκήρης -ες — bronze
χαλκοχίτων -ωνος m.f. — bronze-clad
χαρίεις -εσσα -εν — graceful, pleasing, lovely
χάρις -ιτος, f. — grace, beauty, favour, gratitude
χάρμα -ατος, n. — joy, delight
χεῖλος -εος, n. — lip
*χείρ, χειρός, f. — hand
χέρσος -ου, f. — land, shore
χέω (aor. ἔχευα) — I pour
χθιζός -ή -όν — (of) yesterday
χθών -ονός, f. — earth, ground
χιτών -ωνος, f. — tunic
χνόος -ου, m. — brine
χολόομαι — to be angry
χόλος -ου, m. — anger
χορός -οῦ, m. — dance, dance floor
χρεῖος -ον — + *gen.* wanting, in need of
χρειώ -όος, f. (also χρεώ) — need, necessity
χρή — there is need, it is necessary
χρίω — to anoint; (*mid.*) to anoint oneself
χρόνος -ου, m. — time
χρύσειος = χρύσεος -η -ον — golden
*χρυσός -οῦ, m. — gold
χρώς, χροός, f. — skin, flesh, body
χῶρος -ου, m. — land, area

ὤ — oh!
Ὠγυγίη -ης, f. — Ogygia, Calypso's isle
*ὧδε — thus, so
ὦκα — swiftly; quickly
ὠκύμορος -ον — swift-dying
ὠκύς -εῖα -ύ — swift
ὦμος -ου, m. — shoulder
*ὡς — as; so that
ὥς — thus, so
ὤψ, ὠπός, f. — eye
Ὦψ, Ὦπος, m. — Ops, father of Eurycleia

Sophocles, *Ajax*

Introduction, Commentary Notes and
Vocabulary by Sam Baddeley

AS: 1–133, 284–347, 748–783

A Level: 430–582, 646–692, 815–865

Introduction

Sophocles

As is the case with many authors from antiquity, we know very little about the life of Sophocles. He lived for most of the fifth century BCE (*c.* early 490s–406) and wrote over 120 plays over the course of a 60-year career. Although we have many titles and fragments, only seven plays survive in full. Sophocles was clearly a popular playwright; he won first prize at Athens' main drama festival, the City Dionysia, much more frequently than his two famous rivals, Aeschylus and Euripides.

One biographical detail of note is that Sophocles held important political positions alongside his work as a playwright. He was one of the *hellenotamiai* (public treasurers responsible for the collection of tribute – see below) in 443/442, a *strategos* (general) alongside Pericles in 441, and a *proboulos* (advisor to the city after the Athenian defeat in Sicily) from 413. A career straddling the worlds of politics and literature is not unheard of today, but was much more common in the ancient world. Indeed, the highly political nature of dramatic competitions (see below) would perhaps encourage movement between these two spheres.

Historical context

We do not know the exact date of the *Ajax*, but most scholars think that it is one of Sophocles' earlier works. Some have been keen to date it to post 451/450, the year of the citizenship law of Pericles, in which he decreed that only those born of an Athenian mother and father could gain citizenship. This is because Agamemnon's reference to Teucer's illegitimacy (lines 1259–1261) seems to be speaking directly to that event. General opinion has settled on the 440s as the most likely decade, not least because the play resonates on both thematic and stylistic grounds with *Antigone* (which was probably also first produced in the 440s).

Military

The fifth century was a time of great political, military and cultural change in Greece in general, and in Athens in particular. After a series of protracted conflicts between the invading Persians and a united force of Greeks, the Persian threat was finally neutralized by a Greek victory at the Battle of Plataea in 479. However, it is only the benefit of hindsight that allows us to see such a defeat as decisive, and for many Greeks the menace of Persia remained a live issue for several decades. It was in this climate that Athens decided to take a lead in the next stage of defence against the great enemy. In 478, the Delian League was founded, with Athens at its helm. This was an association of city-states, whose aim was to protect Greece against a renewed Persian attack and – according to the historian Thucydides (1.96) – 'to compensate themselves for their losses by laying waste the territories of the King of Persia'. Athens started collecting tribute – money or ships – from her allies in the League, seemingly to fund its activities. However, she soon started using this money for her own purposes, such as the beautification of the city. Furthermore, her behaviour towards those city-states which wanted to leave the alliance became increasingly aggressive (at least, according to Thucydides). In the eyes of many scholars, this so-called 'League' became an exercise in imperial expansion. Tension rose between Athens and that other city-state which had played such a key part in the fight against Persia, Sparta, not least because Sparta also wanted control of the Greek city-states which were under Athens' sway. All of this was to result in the Peloponnesian War (which broke out in 431, about a decade after the *Ajax* was first performed), a hugely disastrous conflict for Athens.

Some of original audience of the *Ajax* will have remembered the Persian Wars, a great East–West conflict which was sometimes seen as a second Trojan war; moreover, the collective memory of the Athenian community will have kept this horror alive for the younger generation. In addition, some may have predicted and feared the likely outcome of the tension which was building between Athens and Sparta in the second and third quarters of the century (in particular due to the conflicts between Athens and Sparta/her allies which are often collectively termed the 'First Peloponnesian War'). So it seems likely that a play which deals with the after-effects of a long East–West war, especially on innocents (such as Tecmessa and Eurysaces), will have struck a chord with its original audience. Some may even have detected in Sophocles' presentation of Ajax, Menelaus and Agamemnon (all of whom are, at times, arrogant, aggressive and full of pride) a representation of the behaviour of their own city-state towards the rest of Greece.

Political

Athens' political landscape changed dramatically over the course of the sixth and fifth centuries BCE, not least due to the end of the rule of the tyrants and the reforms of Cleisthenes (508/507). These reforms were perhaps the most decisive step towards the creation of the democracy in the next century. The effect of such reforms was to reduce the power of the old aristocratic families and to ensure that checks and balances were in place to prevent any single individual from gaining too much power (an example of the latter would be the introduction of ostracism, with which Cleisthenes is often credited). Amongst other things, Cleisthenes revised the system of tribes, taking the four existing tribes (the members of which were loosely connected by family) and dividing them into ten new groups, each of which was named after a mythological hero, called the 'eponymous hero'. Statues of these so-called 'eponymous heroes' stood in the Athenian *agora*.

Each new tribe included citizens from the coastal, inland and city areas of Attica (Athens and its surrounding area), and therefore no tribe could be dominated by people from the same geographical area or by one or two aristocratic families. The eponymous hero of one of these tribes, the *Aiantis* tribe, was the Ajax after whom our play is named. It seems very likely that the original audience will have included members of this tribe, people who will have regularly left offerings at Ajax's shrine as part of the various hero-cult rituals which were such a widespread feature of ancient Greek religion.

The reforms of Ephialtes (462/461) marked another important stage in the reduction of aristocratic power in Athens, and the prominent and popular *strategos* Pericles consolidated these reforms in the 450s. By the time of the *Ajax*, Athenian democracy was in full flow.

Such a system of government was far removed from the honour-driven, individualistic society depicted in the (by-now canonical) Homeric epics. Indeed, some have argued that the tension between an archaic society (represented by Ajax) and a fifth-century democratic worldview (represented to a greater or lesser extent by Agamemnon, Menelaus and Odysseus) is central to a full understanding of the play, although other scholars see this contrast as too simplistic.

Public speaking and debate were at the heart of the democratic process and thus it is no surprise that Greek literature of the fifth century BCE shows a great interest in speech-making, debate and dialogue. We see this in the second half of our play, in which Teucer debates with Menelaus and Agamemnon over whether or not Ajax should be buried. The rhetorical techniques used by all three parties in their respective *agones* (or 'debates', a standard feature of tragedy) will have been familiar to the audience, especially the delivery of a long speech by each participant (*rhesis*) followed by a descent of the argument into *stichomythia*.

Athens and the theatre

The shifting military and political situation in Athens in the fifth century BCE did not hinder her cultural development. Far from it: this was a period of immense creativity in all branches of the arts. Architecture and sculpture flourished at the hands of the renowned Pheidias and his pupils, who were responsible for such wonders as the Athena Parthenos statue inside the Parthenon on the acropolis and the marble sculptures which formed part of the east and west pediments of that temple (the so-called Elgin Marbles). Literature also flourished, and it was in this atmosphere that drama grew out of ritual performances originally intended to honour Dionysus, the god of wine, ecstasy, revelry and (later, i.e. in our period) the theatre.

The exact relationship between drama and religion (specifically, drama and Dionysiac ritual) is difficult to discern. Fundamentally, it makes sense that the god who enables mortals to change state through intoxication also enables them to change state when they become a character in the theatre. For modern readers and spectators, how drama and religion are related is less important than the simple recognition of the existence of such a relationship in Sophocles' day. For although we might agree with the Greeks that theatre has both an educational and an entertainment function, the involvement of religious elements is rather alien to contemporary society.

Athens had three main drama festivals, all of which were in honour of the god Dionysus:

- The City (or 'Great') Dionysia (the greatest festival) took place each year in March/April. This was the beginning of the sailing season, which meant that visitors from the rest of the Greek world could attend.
- The Lenaia (primarily a comedy festival) was held in January, and therefore only Athenians were able to attend.
- The Rural Dionysia (a provincial version of the City Dionysia) was held in various localities around Attica in December.

We do not know at which festival *Ajax* was first performed, but the City Dionysia is the most likely contender, not least because it was the major tragedy festival.

The City Dionysia

Tragedy was probably instituted as part of the City Dionysia by the tyrant Peisistratus in the 530s BCE, but the earliest tragedy that survives, Aeschylus' *Persae*, was produced in 472. The festival constituted a public holiday: the law courts were closed, and prisoners were released for the day to attend the performances. It was attended by both Athenian citizens (possibly women as well as men) and visitors from all over Greece. It was therefore an important propaganda event for the (relatively new) democratic government, and Athens thoroughly exploited this opportunity to advertise her democratic credentials through her organization of the festival, the opening ceremonies and the subject matter of the plays presented. As with religion, the exact relationship between democracy and drama is hard to pin down, but (as many scholars have noted) it can be no coincidence that drama and the democracy both started to flourish at around the same time.

Indeed, democratic principles infused every aspect of the festival. It was organized by an *archon*, one of Athens' elected magistrates. The chorus and actors were all Athenian male citizens. The chorus (in terms of accommodation, training and costumes) was funded by a *choregos*, a wealthy citizen who performed this public service as a form of taxation. Moreover, at some point towards the end of the fifth century or during the fourth century (so probably after the *Ajax* was first performed), the Theoric Fund was established to pay for poorer citizens to attend; they had hitherto been hindered by the entry fee of two obols per day.

Despite the highly democratic nature of the festival, it was also heavily competitive. The plays were performed as part of a competition, and playwrights, choregoi and actors were all competing for public favour.

Structure of the festival

The structure of the festival changed over time, but the following represents a reasonably likely sequence of events for the second half of the fifth century BCE.

A few days before the festival, the playwrights and their casts offered some kind of pre-show presentation known as the *proagon*. The festival itself started with an elaborate procession of a statue of Dionysus through the streets of Athens. This was followed by sacrifices to the god, dithyrambic (choral) competitions in which each tribe presented two choruses to sing and dance a dithyramb, and a feast.

Day two was the most obviously 'democratic' day of the festival. A religious ceremony took place in the Theatre of Dionysus (see below on this building). This consisted of a sacrifice and the pouring of libations to the gods by Athens' ten *strategoi*. It was followed by a parade of all of the tribute which Athens had collected from her allies in the Delian League over the course of the preceding year. This tribute was carried into the *orchestra* so that everyone, including foreigners, could marvel at the city's power and greatness. The tribute parade was followed by a reading of the names of all those who had benefited the *polis* (city-state) over the course of the year, and the honours which had been bestowed on them were announced. Finally there was another parade, this time of all those male orphans whose fathers had died in the service of the polis. Such orphans were reared at state expense, and thus were expected to repay the state when the time should come. Indeed, some scholars argue that this reciprocity was enacted in the ceremony itself when those orphans who were of age (i.e. 18) were presented with hoplite armour so that they could go out and fight on behalf of the polis as their fathers had done before them. As Goldhill has noted, it seems likely that the audience of *Ajax* will have been reminded of this part of the procession (if indeed it was in existence in the 440s: scholars are divided) when they see Ajax bequeathing his shield to his son, Eurysaces (lines 574–576), whose name means 'broad-shield'. Perhaps as a counterpoint to these serious democratic procedures, the day ended with a comedy contest in which five playwrights would each present a single play.

The tragedy competition took place over three days. Each playwright presented three tragedies and one satyr play. A satyr play was a sort of tragicomedy, a play on a mythological theme which was somehow connected with the tragedies, but which used a greater number of comic elements such as drunkenness, sexual humour and a chorus of satyrs (satyrs were mythological creatures with the ears and tail of a horse, the legs of a human, and an exaggerated and permanent erection). As with the previous day's comedies, this perhaps served to lighten the mood after the heavy stuff. After all this (i.e. at the end of day five), the judges were required to choose a winner. A list of potential judges was submitted by each tribe but, as we would expect in such a democratic contest, the final selection of judges was by lot (i.e. random) in order to avoid corruption.

The theatre and theatrical conventions

The Theatre of Dionysus was rather different from the sorts of theatres with which most of us are familiar (i.e. proscenium-arch, etc.). It sat at the bottom of the acropolis, Athens' sacred citadel (yet another indication of the strong link between drama and religion), and the area for seating was cut out of the lower part of that hill. In the fifth century, the audience sat on wooden benches. It is very difficult to work out the maximum capacity of the theatre, but estimates range from 4,000 to 15,000 and beyond; most scholars argue for a figure between 4,000–7,000, but even this is a considerably greater number than can be crammed into a modern theatre – only five West End theatres can hold more than 2,000 audience members. The atmosphere must have been more like that of a contemporary major sporting event. The theatre was open-air, and thus playwrights had to use dialogue to indicate whether it was night or day (as we see in the speech of the watchman at the start of Aeschylus' *Agamemnon*).

The audience sat round a (perhaps) circular area used for acting and choral dancing and known as the *orchestra*. An altar to Dionysus stood in the middle of this. Behind it, where we would expect a stage and a backdrop, was a *skene* or stage-building (the word literally means 'tent') which usually represented the house or palace of the family whose destiny was to be overturned by the events of the tragedy. At the start of the *Ajax*, it represents Ajax's hut at the eastern end of the Greek camp at Troy. The skene may or may not have been decorated (scholars' opinions are divided) and it had a door for entries into and out of the hut (or palace, if another play). We do not know whether there was a raised stage in front of the skene in this period, but either way it seems likely that actors mostly used the area directly in front of the skene for acting, moving out into the orchestra as and when required. Either side of the skene were two *eisodoi*, or entry paths, one of which generally indicated the route into the city and the other of which indicated a way out into the countryside. In *Ajax*, one eisodos represents the route to the rest of the Greek camp, whilst the other leads to the 'untrodden place' out in the wilderness where Ajax will end his life and where the second half of the play is set.

An actor's basic costume consisted of a long-sleeved tunic and flat-soled boots. Depending on the character and the play, some actors had nothing else, but others would also be required to wear a cloak and other items (a breastplate, a hat, etc.) and to carry props (weapons, suppliant branches, etc.). All actors wore masks to indicate which character they were playing. Scholars used to think that the masks also contained some sort of amplificatory device, but this theory has recently been discounted. It seems likely that good vocal projection, the use of highly stylized gestures and an imaginative use of the space available were the essential ways in which actors would convey their message.

The cast was all-male, and by the time of *Ajax* there were three main actors in any production. The use of masks meant that the same actor could play more than one character: in *Ajax,* the actor playing Ajax probably also played either Agamemnon or Teucer (the former suggesting an interesting overlap between these two enemies, the latter emphasising the relationship between brothers). The masks also allowed one character to be played by two different actors if necessary: it seems likely that the actor playing Tecmessa in the first half of the play will have played Agamemnon or Menelaus in the second half, leaving a mute actor to play Tecmessa from line 1168 onwards. Mute actors were also used for the attendants and for Eurysaces, and this was common practice at the time.

The chorus

The chorus is the aspect of Greek drama that often feels the most alien to modern readers. By contrast, choruses of various sorts were very prevalent in Athenian society: choral competitions were held throughout the year, and choruses performed at important occasions such as weddings.

The chorus was also all-male and consisted of 12 and later 15 members (the ancient *Life of Sophocles* states that Sophocles himself was the playwright who expanded it). The chorus members came in after the prologue, entering via the eisodoi, and singing their *parodos* (entry song). After this their main function was to sing a *stasimon* (choral ode) at the end of each episode, but they might also engage in (spoken or sung) dialogue with one or more of the actors. We see this in the *Ajax* when the chorus engages in a lamenting exchange with Tecmessa over the discovery of Ajax's body (line 879ff).

Scholars have identified various different functions of the chorus within tragedy:

- The chorus is often sympathetic towards one of the characters. In *Ajax*, it consists of soldiers and sailors from Salamis (Ajax's birthplace). These men are Ajax's fighting crew who have followed him here to Troy. They are very loyal towards him.

- It also acts as a representation of a community, and therefore it can be seen to reflect and/or guide what the audience response towards the events might be. For example, in their entry song we see the chorus (due to their partial understanding of the situation) expressing disbelief at the idea that Ajax is the one who has harmed the cattle and sheep. This perhaps reflects one possible audience response to the situation.

- The chorus sometimes asks for news, mirroring the audience's need for the same information, and enabling them to acquire it. We see our chorus doing this in the parodos.

- At times, it acts as a mediator between central characters who are engaging in an *agon* (or rhetorical debate). In these instances, the chorus generally provides a 'middle way', advocating moderation rather than the excess which is so characteristic of the genre. An example would be the chorus leader's warning to Menelaus at lines 1091–1092 to avoid any potentially hypocritical or hubristic actions or the wish he expresses at 1264–1265 that both Teucer and Menelaus would act with moderation and good sense.

- The chorus will often use a first-person singular pronoun to indicate its collective status, and the idea that it is acting almost as another character in the drama. Sometimes, as frequently in this play, the chorus leader will speak on his own.

- Choral odes (*stasima*, the songs sung by the chorus in between the 'episodes', or scenes) act as a 'curtain' between scenes, giving actors the chance to change costume/mask, etc. They also allow for the passage of time.

- The chorus sometimes uses a choral ode to summarise the events or mood of a previous scene. We see this in the first stasimon (line 596ff): the chorus' sense of despondency reflects the sad mood of Ajax in the previous episode.

- The chorus can be used to provide entertainment and light relief between scenes. The original meaning of the word *choros* is 'dance', and the chorus sang their choral odes to elaborate metres whilst dancing around the orchestra.

- However, light relief is not always the aim. Sometimes, choral odes add to a foreboding tone already established by the preceding episode, and the chorus is just as capable of building up tension and suspense as it is of dissipating it. We see this, for example, in the first stasimon.

There are also certain things which convention dictates that a chorus should not do (although it should be noted that these were not 'rules' as such – playwrights were not bound by them):

- Interfere/intervene in the action of the play.
- Leave the orchestra after its initial entry song.

Sophocles' use of the chorus in *Ajax* sometimes bends or breaks these conventions, an indication of his interest in theatrical innovation and experimentation:

- The chorus exits after line 814 to search for Ajax, on Tecmessa's instructions. This is very unusual: there are only four other known instances in Greek tragedy. It is necessary here in order that Ajax might be alone for his suicide. NB: this is also the point at which there is a suspected scene change.
- At this point, the chorus also divides, with one half exiting via each eisodos, so that they might search for him on both the eastern and western sides of the ships. This means that the chorus which returns at line 866 is still split in two. Such a division is again very unusual, although not unknown (for example, it occurs in Euripides).
- The chorus re-enters in two halves at line 866ff and delivers a second parodos (this time probably in a mixture of song and speech), known as an *epiparodos,* in which its members lament their failure to find Ajax. The two choruses also engage in a dialogue regarding the geographical extent of their search. As many scholars have noted, this second entry song (again, very unusual) see below, p. 364) mirrors Odysseus' search in the prologue, and thus indicates that the second part of the play is beginning, and that the focus is now the burial of Ajax.

'Special effects'

There was little available to ancient dramatists in the way of 'special effects'. However, three devices were readily available and widely used by both tragedians and, in particular, by comedians (who often used them to parody or mock their use in tragedy):

Ekkyklema

This was a platform that was wheeled out of the skene to reveal an interior tableau, thereby allowing the audience to see what was going on inside the house. This would otherwise not have been possible without a scene change. The *ekkyklema* was often used to reveal a corpse or corpses; Sophocles uses it to reveal the corpse of

Eurydice in *Antigone*. In *Ajax*, he uses it at line 348 to reveal an even grimmer scene: the mad Ajax surrounded by slaughtered sheep which he believes to be his Greek comrades.

Mechane

The *mechane* was a wooden crane, operated by pulleys, which could be used to lift actors onto the top of the skene. It was thus frequently used for divine characters. Some scholars believe that it was used to raise Athena at the start of this play (although it must be noted that this view is rare).

Theologeion

This was a small platform or upper balcony from which a god would speak. The term theologeion is sometimes used simply to refer to the top of the skene. Jebb believes that Athena speaks to Odysseus from the theologeion in the prologue (thereby ensuring that she is visible to the audience, but not to Odysseus, who states that he cannot see her – lines 14–15; note that this would also provide a very striking visual representation of the metaphorical distance which exists between gods and men). If this is the case, it is possible that Athena is raised up to the theologeion using the mechane, but it is also possible that she reaches the top of the skene using the ladder generally used by mortals who are going to speak from a height. Other scholars (e.g. Finglass) believe that Athena enters via an eisodos and remains 'onstage' throughout, though still unseen by Odysseus.

Tragedy: the genre

We only have the works of three tragedians from classical Athens. Various ancient sources have furnished us with the names of other tragedians and their works, but they exist only as names and fragments.

Tragedy as a genre follows a very clear pattern, recorded by the fourth-century philosopher and polymath Aristotle in his *Poetics*. It must be remembered that Aristotle was writing after the time of our three great tragedians: he was neither a tragedian nor the author of a handbook for budding writers, but simply a keen observer of the genre. Sophocles certainly conforms to the patterns identified by Aristotle (probably because he was the tragedian whom Aristotle admired the most!) and exceptions to Aristotle's observations tend to be found most frequently amongst the works of Euripides (e.g. *Trojan Women* or *Alcestis*).

Some key tragic conventions include:

- **No violence onstage,** because the play was being performed at a religious festival. This causes great problems for our play: it is very unclear exactly what happens at line 865 after Ajax has delivered the final words of his suicide speech. Some scholars have argued that he goes off and the audience is to imagine his suicide, but this raises the question of how to get his body back 'onstage'. Others have argued that he falls onto his sword behind a makeshift grove near the edge of the orchestra.

- **Unity of time, place, action**: according to some of the early interpreters of Aristotle's *Poetics,* a tragedy should take place within the space of a single day and in one place. Furthermore, it should have a single unified plot, with minimal subplots. (NB: Aristotle himself focused only on the latter.) Although we will want to be cautious in using these critical observations as a benchmark against which to measure each play, it should be noted that whilst *Ajax* conforms to the unity of time, it (probably) doesn't conform to the unity of place (see above on the likelihood of a scene change). Moreover, some scholars would argue that it doesn't conform to unity of action either, as it is in two parts.

- Due to the lack of scene changes and the prohibition against violence onstage, the **messenger speech** became a prominent feature of tragedy. This was a highly elaborate and vivid piece of rhetoric in which the messenger described an important event which had occurred in another location, sometimes the violent death of a character. In *Ajax,* the messenger appears in the third episode to deliver the vital information from the prophet Calchas that Ajax must be kept inside his hut while daylight lasts. In addition, Tecmessa's speech (284ff) in which she describes Ajax's state of mind inside the hut is very like a messenger speech, but it is not of course delivered by a messenger.

- **The use of myth**: although Ajax was one of the eponymous heroes of the Athenians, the action of the play is set several centuries before its first performance (during the Trojan War) and in the Greek camp at Troy. Indeed, the plots of all extant tragedies, with the exception of Aeschylus' *Persae,* were based on events from the distant (mythological) past, rather than contemporary events, and they were generally not set in Athens. Such a 'distancing' effect allowed authors to debate contemporary issues but at a safe temporal and geographical distance from the everyday experiences of the audience members.

- In such a highly competitive society, it is unsurprising that the **agon**, or 'contest', became such an important part of Greek tragedy. This was a formal rhetorical debate between two characters, which generally took the form of a *rhesis* (monologue) delivered by each, after which the argument would often descend into *stichomythia.* This play contains a double agon, one between Menelaus and Teucer and one between Agamemnon and Teucer, but the subject matter (whether or not Ajax deserves to be buried) is the same in each. The strong relationship between tragedy and democracy, a system of government which was heavily dependent on the ability of citizens to argue or defend a point of view in both the Assembly and the law court (and on the ability of other citizens to judge such debates wherever they took place), is evident in the agon. Sophocles' audiences will have fully understood the value of the techniques employed by Teucer and the sons of Atreus, and they may even have expected to learn techniques from such onstage debate.

The background story: Ajax in earlier Greek literature and thought

Sophocles' original audience will have known the basic outline of the Ajax story:

- He was a great fighter at Troy.
- He had a huge shield, and was famous for his defensive abilities. Indeed, he protected the ships from being burnt by the Trojans.
- He exchanged arms with Hector after a duel.
- He was part of the embassy sent to try to persuade Achilles to return to the fighting.
- When Achilles died, Ajax carried his body back to the camp.
- But Achilles' arms were given to Odysseus rather than Ajax.
- As a result of this, Ajax committed suicide.
- The shade of Ajax turned away from Odysseus when the latter descended into the Underworld.

By the time of Sophocles, the Ajax story had already been tackled many times by writers of epic, lyric and tragedy and by vase painters and sculptors. It is useful to compare these versions in order to see which parts of Sophocles' treatment are original and how he generates meaning from the interplay between his own and other versions of the Ajax myth.

Epic

There is a strong relationship between Sophocles' *Ajax* and the Homeric epics. Many of the characters in our play, including Ajax himself, appear in the *Iliad* and *Odyssey*:

- In the *Iliad*, Ajax is a superb fighter. He has a huge shield (which he will bequeath to his son in this play), a sign of his ability to defend himself against any attacker. In *Iliad* book 7, Ajax fights a duel with Hector which concludes with the exchange of arms: Ajax hands over his sword-belt and Hector hands over his sword, the very sword which Ajax will later use to commit suicide. True Homeric heroes are supposed to be adept at speaking as well as fighting ("speaker of words and doer of deeds"), and Ajax displays his intelligence and oratorical abilities in book 9 when he acts as a member of the embassy sent to Achilles.
- In the *Odyssey*, Ajax has already committed suicide after the Judgement of the Arms, and Odysseus meets his shade in the Underworld (book 11, lines 541–567). Ajax is set apart from the ghosts of all the other men who have died at Troy, and refuses to speak to Odysseus. He is still very angry with him. At the end of the passage, Odysseus hints at the possibility of some kind of reconciliation (he says that they might have spoken, but that he, Odysseus, had other people whom he wanted to speak to). This seems very relevant to the ending of our play (see below).

Ajax also appears in several poems within the so-called 'epic cycle', a collection of non-Homeric poems which deal with various events before, during and after the Trojan War, and which survive only in fragments and summary form:

- Two of these poems, the *Aethiopis* and the *Little Iliad*, deal with the Judgement of Arms and Ajax's suicide at dawn.
- In the *Little Iliad*, the decision as to who deserves the arms of Achilles is made on the basis of a conversation between two Trojan maidens (overheard by the Greeks) in which one girl, "by the foresight of Athena", suggests that Odysseus' fighting was more impressive than Ajax's action of carrying the body of Achilles out of the battlefield.

Thus, Ajax's abilities as a warrior, the Judgement of Arms and his subsequent suicide were all features of the tradition before it reached Sophocles. The prominence of Ajax within the epic tradition is perhaps unsurprising, given his known heroic qualities. Moreover, this tradition has at least to some degree affected the language of Sophocles' play. For example, the simile in which Ajax is compared to a vulture and the Trojans to a flock of birds (164–171) is reminiscent of the sort of imagery found in the Homeric epics.

Lyric

The early fifth-century Theban poet Pindar mentions the suicide of Ajax in three of his odes. In all three versions, Pindar suggests that Ajax was the better man: he should have won the contest but didn't, and thus he killed himself out of anger. This had been hinted at in the *Little Iliad* (which mentioned Athena's involvement in the Judgement), but Pindar's assertion of Ajax's superior worth is bolder.

Tragedy

Aeschylus dealt with the story of Ajax in a trilogy, the *Judgement of Arms*, the *Thracian Women* and the *Salaminian Women*, all of which survive only in fragment form. They seem to depict the same basic storyline as that found in the Homeric epics and lyric poetry: Thetis sets up a contest for the arms of Achilles (*Judgement of Arms*); Ajax subsequently commits suicide (*Thracian Women*), leaving his brother Teucer to return home to Salamis without him (*Salaminian Women*).

Art

Ajax was a popular subject in archaic and classical Greek art. The following scenes are common:

- Ajax and Achilles playing dice, or another game, during a break from the fighting.
- The Judgement of Arms (much Athenian red-figure pottery shows the voting).

- Ajax' suicide:
  - Ajax pierced through by a sword.
  - Ajax preparing the sword. The Exekias painter's interpretation of this scene on a black-figure *amphora* is worth seeing. It very effectively conveys Ajax's solitude and isolation.
- Ajax's corpse.

Originality in the Sophoclean version

Sophocles makes heavy use of all previous versions of the myth, and he retains the basic storyline. However, he deviates from it in several important ways, all of which are dealt with in detail by Patrick Finglass in his commentary. Here follows a summary of the most important differences and a few important similarities, with the disclaimer that some of it is rather conjectural given the fragmentary nature of what survives of the epic cycle:

- Like his great literary predecessor Homer, Sophocles chooses to start mid-way through the story (rather than, for example, at the start of the Trojan War). When the play begins, Achilles is dead and the arms have already been awarded to Odysseus.
- Athena's involvement in Ajax's downfall, although mentioned in previous sources (e.g. the *Little Iliad*), is much greater in Sophocles' version: rather than simply acting in support of Odysseus, she is actively hostile towards Ajax.
- Sophocles possibly invented Ajax's attempt to kill the Greeks who have dishonoured him. In all previous versions that survive, he kills himself due to the dishonour of not being awarded the arms, rather than his failure to get revenge and the disgrace of having killed animals by mistake.
- The idea that Ajax cannot be buried is also (probably) a Sophoclean invention, although in the *Little Iliad*, Agamemnon refuses to allow Ajax to be cremated (the usual practice) and so he has to be buried instead.

In all versions of the story, Ajax subscribes to the 'heroic code', a value system which governs the lives of Homeric heroes such as Achilles, Hector, et al. This system is very heavily focused on how a hero is perceived by others:

- Heroes seek *timé* ('honour'), which can be measured by the spoils of war they receive and the esteem in which they are held by their compatriots.
- They also seek *kleos* (eternal glory). *Kleos* negates their deaths, as their actions in battle gain them a sort of surrogate immortality. Ultimately, they will be remembered.
- Heroes greatly fear the laughter of their enemies. They feel *aidos* ('shame') if they do something wrong.
- They also subscribe to the well-known Greek ethical principal, that one should 'help friends (*philoi*) and harm enemies (*echthroi*)'.

The relationship between the heroic code and the actions of Ajax and others within this play has been the subject of some debate. Some scholars, such as Garvie, believe that Ajax's killing of the Atreidae is justified by the heroic code: the Atreidae (his 'friends') have dishonoured him by awarding the arms to Odysseus. If we follow this line of reasoning, Ajax kills himself because he has failed to take revenge on his enemies and has instead humiliated himself (by slaughtering the sheep). However, others, such as Finglass, do not think that the killing of the Atreidae can be justified by the code. Finglass notes that even Achilles chooses not to kill Agamemnon in *Iliad* book 1. It is up to the reader to decide which view she prefers.

Synopsis and structure

The play begins with a prologue (1–133) in which we learn of Ajax's actions in trying to kill the Greek chiefs during the night and of Athena's involvement in turning him against the cattle instead. After the parodos (opening choral song [134–200], during which the chorus of Salaminian sailors enter the orchestra) we move into a series of episodes separated by choral odes (or *stasima*). The first part of the first episode (201–347) involves a discussion between Tecmessa and the chorus in which she informs them of Ajax's delusional state. A brief *kommos* (lyrical song of lamentation: 348–429) divides the episode into two. In its second half (430–595), Ajax and Tecmessa each deliver a long speech (or *rhesis*). Ajax concludes that his only way out of his current situation is death. Tecmessa tries to persuade him to change his mind, and the debate descends into a stichomythic exchange. Much pathos is generated by the arrival of their son, Eurysaces. However, the episode ends on a sour note with Ajax's cruel dismissal of Tecmessa and her pleas. The chorus then deliver their first stasimon (596–645), a sad ode in which they contrast the security of their homeland (Salamis) with their misery at Troy.

The (much calmer) second episode (646–692) is dominated entirely by Ajax's so-called 'deception speech', a speech whose ambiguous language seems, on one level at least, to suggest that he has changed his mind about what he must do next (see p. 433 for discussion). Crucially, he leaves via an *eisodos* at the end of this episode: he does not re-enter the hut. The second stasimon follows (693–718). It is a joyful ode: the chorus are delighted that he has changed his mind.

The third episode (719–865) again splits into two parts. The first part (719–814) begins with the arrival of a messenger, who brings news for Ajax. He is horrified when he hears that Ajax has left the hut. He repeats the instructions of Teucer (upon hearing predictions of the prophet Calchas), that Ajax should remain inside. Tecmessa arrives and hears this story. She encourages the chorus to hunt for Ajax. The chorus then divides and leaves the orchestra in order to look for him. The second part of the episode then begins (815–865), after a likely scene change (see pp. 356 and 435 for discussion of this). It is dominated by Ajax's soliloquy in which all his earlier bitterness and resentment once again come to the fore. He curses the Atreidae and the Greek army, and the speech is followed by his suicide.

The most unusual aspect of the structure of this play is that this death comes so early: one would expect the suicide of the tragic hero to be the climax, but 555 lines still remain. Most scholars argue that the play essentially splits into two halves, with the second half focused on the question of whether or not Ajax should be buried, a question of vital significance to those Athenians in the audience who worshipped him as part of the hero-cult rituals which were such an important part of ancient Greek religion.

The second half of the play begins with an epiparodos (second parodos: 866–973), signalling the return of the chorus to the orchestra, and a kommos. Tecmessa is the first to find Ajax's body. She and the chorus are distraught. (NB: many scholars have noted the parallels between first and second parodos: a hunt for Ajax; the theme of recent bloodshed, etc.) Tecmessa speaks her last line at 973; after leaving to fetch Eurysaces, she returns (at 1168ff) and remains (in the form of a mute actor) 'onstage' for the rest of the play. The fourth episode (974–1184) begins with the arrival of Teucer, who laments Ajax's death, and who will now essentially take Tecmessa's place as Ajax's defender and chief mourner. Teucer wishes to bury Ajax's body but is prevented from doing so by the arrival of the Greek chief Menelaus, who states that Ajax must remain unburied. An agon (or 'contest/debate') then takes place between Teucer and Menelaus. The latter storms out and the chorus sing the third stasimon (1185–1222) in which they express their immense desire to be back in Salamis. The *Exodos* (1223–1420) contains another agon to balance that of the fourth episode: this time, the argument is between Odysseus and Agamemnon. Odysseus comes in to save the day; he persuades Agamemnon that Ajax should indeed be buried. Both Agamemnon and Odysseus exit, leaving the chorus, Teucer and Eurysaces to begin funeral rites for Ajax, probably with a silent Tecmessa still onstage.

Language and style

Sophocles' popularity in antiquity is often attributed to his creation of a 'middle way' between the archaic poetry of Aeschylus and the down-to-earth psychological realism of Euripides. This is of course an over-simplification. However, he does seem to have been responsible for a number of changes and innovations within the genre, if we are to believe our sources. Aristotle tells us that Sophocles introduced the third actor (some sources suggest that until this point there had only been two main actors, but it must be noted that this whole theory is very controversial) and invented the art of scene painting. Moreover, his writing style is distinctive, and several recurring features of his writing (including key themes) appear in this play:

- A focus on the loneliness of the tragic hero.
- An exploration of the Greek maxim 'help friends and harm enemies', and of the limitations of this maxim (i.e. what happens when friends become enemies?).
- A focus on the themes of honour and duty.
- Dramatic use of a recurring prop/motif (here, the sword of Hector).

This play also includes some innovations which are not found elsewhere in Sophocles' plays. Firstly, as Finglass has noted, it contains more entrances and exits than any of his other works. Even more unusually, most scholars believe that it contains a scene change, one of only two which can be identified in the tragedies which survive (the other appears in Aeschylus' *Eumenides,* when the scene changes from Delphi to Athens). After Ajax delivers his so-called 'deception speech', in which he states in highly ambiguous language that he will go to find an 'untrodden place' (χῶρον . . . ἀστιβῆ) in which he will 'bury' or 'conceal' (κρύψω) his sword, he leaves to find this lonely spot for his deed. It seems most likely that the audience was required to imagine the next scene (815ff), in which Ajax commits suicide, as taking place in the 'untrodden' place of which Ajax spoke.

This scene change signals further potential innovations. Assuming such a change takes place, it seems likely that the chorus leaves the orchestra after line 814 (in order to search for Ajax and bring him back to the camp, as per the instructions of Tecmessa), thereby breaking the convention that a chorus should stay 'onstage' for the whole play after its initial entry (see p. 348). Furthermore, when the chorus does return into the orchestra, it probably returns in two halves, as suggested by the sort of dialogue which we find from line 872 onwards. Such a splitting of the chorus is unparalleled in extant tragedy, but it serves a useful purpose in that it conveys the sense that Ajax's friends have searched everywhere for him. It also provides an essential structural function within the play: as noted above, the chorus' re-entry could be termed a second entry song, signalling the start of the second half of the play in which there is a new focus, namely Ajax' burial.

One possible conclusion to draw from all this is that Sophocles was keen on challenging and disrupting theatrical conventions. But when taken together with his use of the ekkyklema to reveal to a horrified audience the mad Ajax sitting around the bodies of the animals he has slaughtered, these innovations suggest that he was very interested in the possibilities generated by the theatrical potential of movement and space, or (in contemporary jargon) in stagecraft and dramaturgy. We can perhaps see why if we consider the size of the audience and the (probable) lack of any reliable means of vocal projection. Masks, the use of space within the orchestra, dramatic entrances and exits, and heavily stylized gestures will all have been essential tools for a playwright wishing to capture and maintain the attention of, and convey his story to, those sitting on the back seats.

Stylistic devices

Below are a few examples of stylistic devices which Sophocles frequently employs. Try to look out for your own examples when reading through the Greek.

- Repetition of a word or an idea for emphasis. In lines 55–56 Sophocles repeats the idea of hacking/cutting (ἔκειρε/ ῥαχίζων).
- Polyptoton (the repetition of the same word but in a different case), e.g. lines 293: γύναι, γυναιξί.
- Figura etymologica or use of cognate forms, i.e. use of different words derived from the same root, e.g. 679: ὅ τ᾽ ἐχθρὸς ἡμῖν . . . ἐχθαρτέος – 'my enemy must be hated . . .'.

- Alliteration to draw attention to a key word or phrase, or to convey a particular mood. In line 528, the harsh alliteration of τ and θ underlines Ajax's dictatorial tone.

- Imagery, including the use of similes and metaphors, e.g. the simile in which Athena compares Odysseus to a Spartan hound, lines 7–8: εὖ δέ σ᾽ ἐκφέρει/ κυνὸς Λακαίνης ὥς τις εὔρινος βάσις; or the metaphorical use of γυμνόν ('naked') to mean 'without prizes' in line 463.

- Homeric resonances, such as the use of epithets (line 19, Αἴαντι τῷ σακεσφόρῳ – 'Ajax the shield-bearer'), the frequency of similes in the opening section of the play, and the use of terms which are particularly relevant to the heroic code which forms such a core part of the characterisation of the heroes in Homer (e.g. αἰσχρόν – 'shameful/ disgraceful' – line 473). Extensive allusions to *Iliad* 6 are also prominent (see the Commentary Notes for more details).

- Contrast, e.g. between Ajax's daring and boldness (line 46, τόλμαις, θράσει) and the means by which he attacks the cattle (line 47, νύκτωρ, δόλιος – 'at night, craftily). On a larger scale, the joyful mood of the second stasimon contrasts greatly with the despondency of the first.

- Chiasmus (ABBA structure), often used draw out the contrast between two words or phrases (particularly the internal, i.e. 'B' pair). A good example can be found in lines 132–133: **τοὺς** δὲ **σώφρονας** θεοὶ φιλοῦσι καὶ στυγοῦσι **τοὺς κακούς** ('the gods love those who are moderate and hate those who are wicked').

- Juxtaposition of words for contrast, e.g. line 664 ἐχθρῶν ἄδωρα δῶρα – 'the gifts of enemies are no gifts'. This often involves an oxymoron too.

- Collocation (placement side-by-side, but without contrast) of important words or ideas, e.g. line 60, where two main verbs are juxtaposed: ὤτρυνον, εἰσέβαλλον ('I urged him on, I hurled him . . .').

- Paradox, e.g. line 52, τῆς ἀνηκέστου χαρᾶς = 'incurable/fatal/desperate joy'.

- Emphatic placement of key words at the start of the line, e.g. lines 59–60: ἐγὼ δὲ φοιτῶντ᾽ ἄνδρα μανιάσιν νόσοις/ὤτρυνον: 'As the man roamed in his mad illness, it was I who urged him on'. The enjambement adds further emphasis to the verb ὤτρυνον.

- Pleonasm (the use of more words than are necessary to convey meaning; an English example would be 'I see with my own eyes'), e.g. line 858 κοὔποτ᾽ αὖθις ὕστερον = 'and never again later'.

- Disrupted word order (hyperbaton), such as separation of nouns and their adjectives for emphasis, e.g. line 123: ὁθούνεκ᾽ ἄτῃ συγκατέζευκται κακῇ – 'because he has been yoked to an **evil ruin**'.

- Historic present, used to create a sense of vividness and immediacy, e.g. line 288, κἀγὼ 'πιπλήσσω καὶ λέγω, 'and I rebuked him and said'.

- Wordplay, e.g. lines 105 (δέσποινα, δεσμώτης) and 106 (θακεῖ· θανεῖν). We must remember that this text was meant to be performed out loud, and such devices are pleasing to the ear even if they serve no other purpose.

- The absence of connecting words (e.g. 115, χρῶ χειρί, φείδου μηδὲν ὧνπερ ἐννοεῖς: 'use your hand, spare none of what you intend'), known as asyndeton. It can have many effects. In this example, it perhaps gives the imperatives an added weight and sense of urgency. It can also be used to suggest an abrupt transition or an increase in pace (e.g. see line 62).

- Rhetorical questions, e.g. lines 119–120, τούτου τίς ἄν σοι τἀνδρὸς ἢ προνούστερος/ἢ δρᾶν ἀμείνων ηὑρέθη τὰ καίρια; = 'who, I ask you, could've been found (who was) more prudent than this man and better at doing what was right?' (see also line 518). In such questions, the answer is strongly implied by the format of the question (and therefore does not need to be stated).

- Tricolon, a very effective way of delivering three parallel phrases/clauses, e.g. the list of animals killed by Ajax given in lines 296–297: ἔσω δ᾽ ἐσῆλθε **συνδέτους** ἄγων ὁμοῦ/**ταύρους, κύνας βοτῆρας, εὔερόν τ᾽ ἄγραν** ('he went inside, taking with him **the bound bulls, the herdsmen's dogs,** and **the fleecy prey**').

Themes

The themes of the play are mostly revealed through the words and actions of the protagonist and through his interactions with those around him. Key themes include:

- madness and sanity – i.e. the 'madness' visited upon Ajax by Athena, his mad rage about the Judgement of the Arms, etc.

- excess (of the tragic hero) – Ajax's excessive pride/arrogance (*hubris*) leads to his downfall, as Athena warns in lines 127–133. Most tragic heroes are excessive, but Ajax's capacity for excess would exceed the expectations of the most committed theatre-goer of the fifth century!

- isolation – Sophoclean tragic heroes are often isolated. Ajax is isolated from those around him even when they are there; he fails to listen properly to the pleas of Tecmessa, and instead dismisses her with sharp orders. (We see this in the section from 430–582). Such isolation culminates in his lonely suicide, an action from which even the chorus is absent.

- burial – the second part of the play is devoted entirely to the theme of whether or not Ajax should be buried, an issue of great importance to the Athenians watching the play (see below under hero-cult). Note that burial was a necessary part of the transition to the afterlife, and not being buried was the great fear of every Homeric hero.

- *sophrosyne*/moderation/good sense – Ajax's inability to think rationally and with moderation is one of many factors which leads to his downfall, something which he does eventually recognize (677). Odysseus, however, shows a lot of *sophrosyne*. His is the voice of reason in the second part of the play, and indeed he is able to see Ajax's positive qualities despite the latter's behaviour towards him.

- heroism/manhood/honour – this theme is introduced in the prologue, and remains live throughout the play. Ajax is obsessed with honour. One of many examples would be lines 434–440, where we see him contrasting his own dishonour with the honour enjoyed by his father.
- father–son relationships – Telamon/Ajax (as in the above example: 434–440) and Ajax/Eurysaces. Family relationships more generally (Ajax/Teucer, etc.) are important within the play.
- reciprocity/'helping friends and harming enemies' – the words φιλός and ἐχθρός are used many times throughout the course of the play, not least by Ajax. Indeed, the theme occurs as early as the second line. The Atreidae and Odysseus were Ajax's friends. Due to the Judgement of the Arms and his attack on them, they become his enemies. Moreover, Hector was Ajax's enemy, but gifted him a sword, thereby (to some extent) becoming a friend. As in other plays (*Antigone* to name but one), Sophocles poses the question of what happens when a friend becomes an enemy. Which part of the maxim should be followed?
- the effects of war (especially on innocents) – Tecmessa's fears about her own treatment after Ajax's death (496ff) is a good example of this.
- deception – see the introduction to the deception speech (p. 433).
- hero-cult/hero-worship – Ajax was one of the eponymous heroes of the ten tribes. Members of the audience will have worshipped at his tomb. It is important that Ajax is buried, and his character rehabilitated, if they are to continue to make offerings to him. (NB: this is not an explicit theme within the play, but is likely to have been on the mind of the audience.)

As you read through the text, make a list of key quotations relevant to each theme. Many important lines have been indicated in the Commentary Notes.

Metre

Greek drama was written in verse – that is to say, it is poetry, not prose. As in much English poetry, Greek verse works on the basis of stressed (often called 'long') and unstressed (often called 'short') syllables. An understanding of this system is crucial to a full appreciation of Sophocles' artistry, and in particular to a recognition of the fundamental differences between his achievement and that of a prose writer such as Herodotus or Thucydides.

Iambic trimeter

Almost the entirety of the sections prescribed for AS and A level are written in iambic trimeter, the standard metre for spoken dialogue in Greek tragedy. The choral odes use a variety of different and generally more complicated metres; these odes were sung to the accompaniment of music and dancing. The effect must have been spectacular, and indeed some scholars have compared Greek tragic performances to modern-day opera.

Iambic trimeter consists of three *metra* (each iambic *metron* = two feet of iambs: ∪ –), hence the name <u>tri</u>meter. The basic pattern of each metron is: × – ∪ – (the first syllable is marked as *anceps*, i.e. it can be long or short). The basic pattern is as follows: × – ∪ – / × – ∪ – / × – ∪ ×. Note that the final syllable of the line can also be either long or short.

Here is an example of a scanned line:

$$\text{–} \quad \text{–} \quad ∪ \quad \text{–} \quad / \quad \text{–} \quad \text{–} \quad ∪ \quad \text{–} \quad / \quad \text{–} \quad \text{–} \quad ∪ \quad ×$$
πεῖράν τιν᾽ ἐχθρῶν ἁρπάσαι θηρώμενον:

(line 2)

The Greeks also considered one long syllable to be metrically equivalent to two short syllables, and thus a long syllable can be 'resolved' into two shorts. On this basis, several other combinations are possible within each metron (although resolution in the last metron of the three is very rare).

A *caesura* indicates a break or pause in the line that generally corresponds with a break in sense. In practical terms, a caesura in iambic trimeter is always a break between words in the second metron (coming either after the first or third syllable of that metron) and it should be marked whenever you are scanning a line (see below on scansion). Thus each line of iambic trimeter divides into two (or more) parts, which not only ensures that the actor is able to maintain momentum until the end of the line, but also can be used to draw out a contrast between the two parts (although note that two equal halves are avoided: the caesura rarely comes after the second syllable of the second metron).

Long and short syllables and scansion

Whereas metre refers to the ideal pattern laid out above (which for iambic trimeter means three iambic metra), scansion is the process of marking out the reality for each line, i.e. deciding which syllables are long and which are short. In order to do this, we need to know which syllables were considered by the Greeks to be naturally long or short (often determined by the natural length of the vowel) and which could, for the purposes of scansion – be either.

The following syllables are always long:

- Those containing vowels which are long by nature (i.e. η, ω).
- Those containing diphthongs (two or more vowels which together form one sound, e.g. ει/αι/ευ).
- Contracted syllables.
- Those containing vowels with a circumflex accent.

The following syllables become long:

- Those containing short vowels which are followed by a double consonant, i.e. ζ, ξ or ψ.
- Those containing short vowels which are followed by two consonants (in the same or in different words), unless they form a combination of a plosive

(π, β, φ, τ, δ, θ, κ, γ, χ) and a liquid (λ, ϱ) or nasal (μ, ν) <u>in the same word</u>, in which case the preceding syllable can be short or long.

The vowels ε and ο are always short, but note that α, ι and υ have both long and short variants. A syllable containing a short vowel followed by one consonant (or none) is short.

Here is a simple process for scanning a line of iambic trimeter:

1   Count the number of syllables in the line. If there are 12, there are no resolutions, If there are 13 or 14, then there are one or two resolved feet.

2   Mark in the syllables which are naturally long or short (see above).

3   Work out whether the rest of the syllables are long or short. Do this by a process of elimination, bearing in mind the rules laid about above. The key to spotting resolutions is to find where two short syllables can come together in the first two metra.

4   Mark in the principal caesura. This will occur in the second metron (after the first or third syllable).

Elision

Note that, unlike in Latin, you don't need to worry about marking in elisions, i.e. the places where a short vowel at the end of a word disappears due to the fact that the next word starts with a vowel. These will already have been indicated in the text by the use of an apostrophe (e.g. line 2 has τιν᾽ ἐχθρῶν for τινα ἐχθρῶν). It should be noted that Greek poetry also makes extensive use of prodelision, i.e. where the vowel at the start of a word is lost due to contact with a vowel at the end of the preceding word (e.g. 535 ἐγὼ ᾽φύλαξα for ἐγὼ ἐφύλαξα).

Further Reading

Athens in the fifth century

For a general introduction to Athenian culture, see:
   Osborne, Robin. *The World of Athens: An Introduction to Classical Athenian Culture.* CUP 2008, 2nd edition.

For an overview of the political situation in Athens in the fifth century BCE:
   Carey, Christopher. *Democracy in Classical Athens.* Bloomsbury Academic 2017.

For an alternative interpretation of Athens' use of the Delian League, in which the author suggests that Athens' heavy-handed treatment of her subject states was in fact economically motivated, and that her use of the League in general was a continuation of her economic policy, read:
   Kallet, Lisa. 'Thucydides and the origins of the Athenian economic *arche*', *Journal of Hellenic Studies* Vol. 133 (2013), 43–60.

Tragedy and the theatre

For a general introduction to Greek tragedy and its context:
> Swift, Laura. *Greek Tragedy: Themes and Contexts*. Bloomsbury Academic 2016.

The following volume contains many useful articles about all aspects of Greek tragedy:
> Easterling, P. E. (ed.). *Cambridge Companion to Greek Tragedy*. CUP 1997.

Simon Goldhill's seminal article on civil ideology and the Great (or City) Dionysia is a good place to start for those interested in the 'democratic' aspects of this festival:
> Goldhill, Simon. 'The Great Dionysia and civic ideology', *Journal of Hellenic Studies* 107 (1987), 58–76.

On the staging of Greek tragedy in general (and of Ajax in particular), see:
> Taplin, Oliver. *Greek Tragedy in Action*. Routledge 2014, 2nd edition.

For an innovative analysis of the language of Sophocles and of the genre of tragedy in general, see:
> Goldhill, Simon. *Sophocles and the Language of Tragedy*. OUP 2012.

For a rather different approach to the analysis and discussion of tragic language, see:
> Rutherford, Richard. *Greek Tragic Style: Form, Language and Interpretation*. CUP 2012.

Translations

The following contains an accurate translation, a useful introduction and a set of accessible notes:
> Sophocles: Electra *and Other Plays*. Penguin 2008. Translated and edited by David Raeburn, with an introduction by Pat Easterling.

Commentaries

Every commentary written in the twentieth and twenty-first centuries makes extensive use of the monumental edition of the Victorian scholar Richard Jebb. You may wish to consult the most recent edition:
> Jebb, R. C. *Sophocles: Plays* – Ajax. Bristol Classical Press 2004. (With an introduction by Peter Wilson; General editor: P.E. Easterling.)

However, it is rather difficult to use for those new to Greek verse (and – I add with caution – a little outdated in its views). More accessible (yet still very scholarly) is the commentary of Patrick Finglass, which is also very attentive to recent scholarship on Sophocles in general and *Ajax* in particular:
> Finglass, P. J. *Sophocles* Ajax. CUP 2011.

Another translation and very accessible commentary, worth reading not least for the contextual information it provides, can be found here:
> *Sophocles* Ajax. Aris and Phillips Ltd., 1998. Edited with introduction, translation and commentary by A. F. Garvie.

Critical interpretations

The following monograph provides an excellent overview of the context behind the play and includes a thorough scene-by-scene analysis:

Hesk, Jon. *Sophocles: Ajax.* Duckworth, 2003.

Other interesting observations can be found here:

Winnington-Ingram, R. P. *Sophocles: An Interpretation.* CUP 1980. Chapters 1–3 are the most relevant.

This recent collection of essays covers all of the key themes of the play:

Stuttard, David (ed.). *Looking at* Ajax. Bloomsbury 2019.

This book provides an argument against the (widely-accepted) theory that a scene change occurs at line 815 (NB: many scholars, not least Finglass, have debunked Scullion's ideas):

Scullion, Scott. *Three Studies in Athenian Dramaturgy.* B.G. Teubner 1994.

The following examines the unity (or lack thereof) of the play:

Tyrrell, William. 'The Unity of Sophocles' *Ajax*', *Arethusa,* Vol. 18, no. 2 (1985), 155–185.

Text

Ἀθήνα	ἀεὶ μέν, ὦ παῖ Λαρτίου, δέδορκά σε
	πεῖράν τιν᾽ ἐχθρῶν ἁρπάσαι θηρώμενον·
	καὶ νῦν ἐπὶ σκηναῖς σε ναυτικαῖς ὁρῶ
	Αἴαντος, ἔνθα τάξιν ἐσχάτην ἔχει,
	πάλαι κυνηγετοῦντα καὶ μετρούμενον	5
	ἴχνη τὰ κείνου νεοχάραχθ᾽, ὅπως ἴδης
	εἴτ᾽ ἔνδον εἴτ᾽ οὐκ ἔνδον. εὖ δέ σ᾽ ἐκφέρει
	κυνὸς Λακαίνης ὥς τις εὔρινος βάσις.
	ἔνδον γὰρ ἁνὴρ ἄρτι τυγχάνει, κάρα
	στάζων ἱδρῶτι καὶ χέρας ξιφοκτόνους.	10
	καί σ᾽ οὐδὲν εἴσω τῆσδε παπταίνειν πύλης
	ἔτ᾽ ἔργον ἐστίν, ἐννέπειν δ᾽ ὅτου χάριν
	σπουδὴν ἔθου τήνδ᾽, ὡς παρ᾽ εἰδυίας μάθης.

Ὀδυσσεύς	ὦ φθέγμ᾽ Ἀθάνας, φιλτάτης ἐμοὶ θεῶν,
	ὡς εὐμαθές σου, κἂν ἄποπτος ᾖς ὅμως,	15
	φώνημ᾽ ἀκούω καὶ ξυναρπάζω φρενὶ
	χαλκοστόμου κώδωνος ὡς Τυρσηνικῆς.
	καὶ νῦν ἐπέγνως εὖ μ᾽ ἐπ᾽ ἀνδρὶ δυσμενεῖ
	βάσιν κυκλοῦντ᾽, Αἴαντι τῷ σακεσφόρῳ·
	κεῖνον γάρ, οὐδέν᾽ ἄλλον, ἰχνεύω πάλαι.	20
	νυκτὸς γὰρ ἡμᾶς τῆσδε πρᾶγος ἄσκοπον
	ἔχει περάνας, εἴπερ εἴργασται τάδε·
	ἴσμεν γὰρ οὐδὲν τρανές, ἀλλ᾽ ἀλώμεθα·
	κἀγὼ ᾽θελοντὴς τῷδ᾽ ὑπεζύγην πόνῳ.
	ἐφθαρμένας γὰρ ἀρτίως εὑρίσκομεν	25
	λείας ἁπάσας καὶ κατηναρισμένας
	ἐκ χειρὸς αὐτοῖς ποιμνίων ἐπιστάταις.
	τήνδ᾽ οὖν ἐκείνῳ πᾶς τις αἰτίαν νέμει.
	καί μοί τις ὀπτὴρ αὐτὸν εἰσιδὼν μόνον
	πηδῶντα πεδία σὺν νεορράντῳ ξίφει	30
	φράζει τε κἀδήλωσεν· εὐθέως δ᾽ ἐγὼ
	κατ᾽ ἴχνος ᾄσσω, καὶ τὰ μὲν σημαίνομαι,
	τὰ δ᾽ ἐκπέπληγμαι κοὐκ ἔχω μαθεῖν ὅτου.
	καιρὸν δ᾽ ἐφήκεις· πάντα γὰρ τά τ᾽ οὖν πάρος

	τά τ᾽ εἰσέπειτα σῇ κυβερνῶμαι χερί.	35
Ἀθήνα	ἔγνων, Ὀδυσσεῦ, καὶ πάλαι φύλαξ ἔβην τῇ σῇ πρόθυμος εἰς ὁδὸν κυναγία.	
Ὀδυσσεύς	ἦ καί, φίλη δέσποινα, πρὸς καιρὸν πονῶ;	
Ἀθήνα	ὡς ἔστιν ἀνδρὸς τοῦδε τἄργα ταῦτά σοι.	
Ὀδυσσεύς	καὶ πρὸς τί δυσλόγιστον ὧδ᾽ ᾖξεν χέρα;	40
Ἀθήνα	χόλῳ βαρυνθεὶς τῶν Ἀχιλλείων ὅπλων.	
Ὀδυσσεύς	τί δῆτα ποίμναις τήνδ᾽ ἐπεμπίπτει βάσιν;	
Ἀθήνα	δοκῶν ἐν ὑμῖν χεῖρα χραίνεσθαι φόνῳ.	
Ὀδυσσεύς	ἦ καὶ τὸ βούλευμ᾽ ὡς ἐπ᾽ Ἀργείοις τόδ᾽ ἦν;	
Ἀθήνα	κἂν ἐξεπράξατ᾽, εἰ κατημέλησ᾽ ἐγώ.	45
Ὀδυσσεύς	ποίαισι τόλμαις ταῖσδε καὶ φρενῶν θράσει;	
Ἀθήνα	νύκτωρ ἐφ᾽ ὑμᾶς δόλιος ὁρμᾶται μόνος.	
Ὀδυσσεύς	ἦ καὶ παρέστη κἀπὶ τέρμ᾽ ἀφίκετο;	
Ἀθήνα	καὶ δὴ ᾽πὶ δισσαῖς ἦν στρατηγίσιν πύλαις.	
Ὀδυσσεύς	καὶ πῶς ἐπέσχε χεῖρα μαιμῶσαν φόνου;	50
Ἀθήνα	ἐγώ σφ᾽ ἀπείργω, δυσφόρους ἐπ᾽ ὄμμασι γνώμας βαλοῦσα, τῆς ἀνηκέστου χαρᾶς, καὶ πρός τε ποίμνας ἐκτρέπω σύμμικτά τε λείας ἄδαστα βουκόλων φρουρήματα· ἔνθ᾽ εἰσπεσὼν ἔκειρε πολύκερων φόνον κύκλῳ ῥαχίζων· κἀδόκει μὲν ἔσθ᾽ ὅτε δισσοὺς Ἀτρείδας αὐτόχειρ κτείνειν ἔχων, ὅτ᾽ ἄλλοτ᾽ ἄλλον ἐμπίτνων στρατηλατῶν. ἐγὼ δὲ φοιτῶντ᾽ ἄνδρα μανιάσιν νόσοις ὤτρυνον, εἰσέβαλλον εἰς ἕρκη κακά. κἄπειτ᾽ ἐπειδὴ τοῦδ᾽ ἐλώφησεν πόνου, τοὺς ζῶντας αὖ δεσμοῖσι συνδήσας βοῶν ποίμνας τε πάσας εἰς δόμους κομίζεται, ὡς ἄνδρας, οὐχ ὡς εὔκερων ἄγραν ἔχων, καὶ νῦν κατ᾽ οἴκους συνδέτους αἰκίζεται. δείξω δὲ καὶ σοὶ τήνδε περιφανῆ νόσον,	55 60 65

ὡς πᾶσιν Ἀργείοισιν εἰσιδὼν θροῇς.
θαρσῶν δὲ μίμνε μηδὲ συμφορὰν δέχου
τὸν ἄνδρ᾽· ἐγὼ γὰρ ὀμμάτων ἀποστρόφους
αὐγὰς ἀπείρξω σὴν πρόσοψιν εἰσιδεῖν.   70
οὗτος, σὲ τὸν τὰς αἰχμαλωτίδας χέρας
δεσμοῖς ἀπευθύνοντα προσμολεῖν καλῶ·
Αἴαντα φωνῶ· στεῖχε δωμάτων πάρος.

Ὀδυσσεύς   τί δρᾷς, Ἀθάνα; μηδαμῶς σφ᾽ ἔξω κάλει.

Ἀθήνα   οὐ σῖγ᾽ ἀνέξη μηδὲ δειλίαν ἀρῇ;   75

Ὀδυσσεύς   μὴ πρὸς θεῶν, ἀλλ᾽ ἔνδον ἀρκείτω μένων.

Ἀθήνα   τί μὴ γένηται; πρόσθεν οὐκ ἀνὴρ ὅδ᾽ ἦν;

Ὀδυσσεύς   ἐχθρός γε τῷδε τἀνδρὶ καὶ τανῦν ἔτι.

Ἀθήνα   οὔκουν γέλως ἥδιστος εἰς ἐχθροὺς γελᾶν;

Ὀδυσσεύς   ἐμοὶ μὲν ἀρκεῖ τοῦτον ἐν δόμοις μένειν.   80

Ἀθήνα   μεμηνότ᾽ ἄνδρα περιφανῶς ὀκνεῖς ἰδεῖν;

Ὀδυσσεύς   φρονοῦντα γάρ νιν οὐκ ἂν ἐξέστην ὄκνῳ.

Ἀθήνα   ἀλλ᾽ οὐδὲ νῦν σε μὴ παρόντ᾽ ἴδῃ πέλας.

Ὀδυσσεύς   πῶς, εἴπερ ὀφθαλμοῖς γε τοῖς αὐτοῖς ὁρᾷ;

Ἀθήνα   ἐγὼ σκοτώσω βλέφαρα καὶ δεδορκότα.   85

Ὀδυσσεύς   γένοιτο μεντἂν πᾶν θεοῦ τεχνωμένου.

Ἀθήνα   σίγα νυν ἑστὼς καὶ μέν᾽ ὡς κυρεῖς ἔχων.

Ὀδυσσεύς   μένοιμ᾽ ἄν· ἤθελον δ᾽ ἂν ἐκτὸς ὢν τυχεῖν.

Ἀθήνα   ὦ οὗτος, Αἴας, δεύτερόν σε προσκαλῶ.
             τί βαιὸν οὕτως ἐντρέπη τῆς συμμάχου;   90

Αἴας   ὦ χαῖρ᾽ Ἀθάνα, χαῖρε Διογενὲς τέκνον,
             ὡς εὖ παρέστης· καί σε παγχρύσοις ἐγὼ
             στέψω λαφύροις τῆσδε τῆς ἄγρας χάριν.

Ἀθήνα   καλῶς ἔλεξας· ἀλλ᾽ ἐκεῖνό μοι φράσον,
             ἔβαψας ἔγχος εὖ πρὸς Ἀργείων στρατῷ;   95

Αἴας	κόμπος πάρεστι κοὐκ ἀπαρνοῦμαι τὸ μή.	
Ἀθήνα	ἦ καὶ πρὸς Ἀτρείδαισιν ἤχμασας χέρα;	
Αἴας	ὥστ᾽ οὔποτ᾽ Αἴανθ᾽ οἵδ᾽ ἀτιμάσουσ᾽ ἔτι.	
Ἀθήνα	τεθνᾶσιν ἄνδρες, ὡς τὸ σὸν ξυνῆκ᾽ ἐγώ.	
Αἴας	θανόντες ἤδη τἄμ᾽ ἀφαιρείσθων ὅπλα.	100
Ἀθήνα	εἶεν, τί γὰρ δὴ παῖς ὁ τοῦ Λαερτίου, ποῦ σοι τύχης ἕστηκεν; ἢ πέφευγέ σε;	
Αἴας	ἦ τοὐπίτριπτον κίναδος ἐξήρου μ᾽ ὅπου;	
Ἀθήνα	ἔγωγ᾽· Ὀδυσσέα τὸν σὸν ἐνστάτην λέγω.	
Αἴας	ἥδιστος, ὦ δέσποινα, δεσμώτης ἔσω θακεῖ· θανεῖν γὰρ αὐτὸν οὔ τί πω θέλω.	105
Ἀθήνα	πρὶν ἂν τί δράσῃς ἢ τί κερδάνῃς πλέον;	
Αἴας	πρὶν ἂν δεθεὶς πρὸς κίον᾽ ἑρκείου στέγης –	
Ἀθήνα	τί δῆτα τὸν δύστηνον ἐργάσῃ κακόν;	
Αἴας	μάστιγι πρῶτον νῶτα φοινιχθεὶς θάνῃ.	110
Ἀθήνα	μὴ δῆτα τὸν δύστηνον ὧδέ γ᾽ αἰκίσῃ.	
Αἴας	χαίρειν, Ἀθάνα, τἄλλ᾽ ἐγώ σ᾽ ἐφίεμαι· κεῖνος δὲ τίσει τήνδε κοὐκ ἄλλην δίκην.	
Ἀθήνα	σὺ δ᾽ οὖν, ἐπειδὴ τέρψις ἥδε σοι τὸ δρᾶν, χρῶ χειρί, φείδου μηδὲν ὧνπερ ἐννοεῖς.	115
Αἴας	χωρῶ πρὸς ἔργον· σοὶ δὲ τοῦτ᾽ ἐφίεμαι, τοιάνδ᾽ ἀεί μοι σύμμαχον παρεστάναι.	
Ἀθήνα	ὁρᾷς, Ὀδυσσεῦ, τὴν θεῶν ἰσχὺν ὅση; τούτου τίς ἄν σοι τἀνδρὸς ἢ προνούστερος ἢ δρᾶν ἀμείνων ηὑρέθη τὰ καίρια;	120
Ὀδυσσεύς	ἐγὼ μὲν οὐδέν᾽ οἶδ᾽· ἐποικτίρω δέ νιν δύστηνον ἔμπας, καίπερ ὄντα δυσμενῆ, ὁθούνεκ᾽ ἄτῃ συγκατέζευκται κακῇ, οὐδὲν τὸ τούτου μᾶλλον ἢ τοὐμὸν σκοπῶν·	

ὁρῶ γὰρ ἡμᾶς οὐδὲν ὄντας ἄλλο πλὴν   125
εἴδωλ᾽ ὅσοιπερ ζῶμεν ἢ κούφην σκιάν.

Ἀθήνα   τοιαῦτα τοίνυν εἰσορῶν ὑπέρκοπον
μηδέν ποτ᾽ εἴπῃς αὐτὸς εἰς θεοὺς ἔπος,
μηδ᾽ ὄγκον ἄρῃ μηδέν᾽, εἴ τινος πλέον
ἢ χειρὶ βρίθεις ἢ μακροῦ πλούτου βάθει.   130
ὡς ἡμέρα κλίνει τε κἀνάγει πάλιν
ἅπαντα τἀνθρώπεια· τοὺς δὲ σώφρονας
θεοὶ φιλοῦσι καὶ στυγοῦσι τοὺς κακούς.

134–200: *The chorus (of Salaminian sailors) enters. They sing their parodos (or choral entry song) in which they show respect for and loyalty towards Ajax, and speculate about the rumour that Ajax is responsible for the attack on the animals. They beg him to come out of the hut in order to clear his name.*

201–284: *Tecmessa (Ajax's concubine) comes out of the hut. The chorus question her about Ajax's situation, and she informs them that he was indeed responsible for the attack, as he had been gripped by madness. She goes on to explain that things are now worse because he is coming back to sanity. The chorus leader asks her how the trouble began.*

Τέκμησσα   ἅπαν μαθήσῃ τοὔργον ὡς κοινωνὸς ὤν.   284
κεῖνος γὰρ ἄκρας νυκτός, ἡνίχ᾽ ἕσπεροι   285
λαμπτῆρες οὐκέτ᾽ ᾖθον, ἄμφηκες λαβὼν
ἐμαίετ᾽ ἔγχος ἐξόδους ἕρπειν κενάς.
κἀγὼ 'πιπλήσσω καὶ λέγω· "τί χρῆμα δρᾷς,
Αἴας; τί τήνδ᾽ ἄκλητος οὔθ᾽ ὑπ᾽ ἀγγέλων
κληθεὶς ἀφορμᾷς πεῖραν οὔτε τοῦ κλύων   290
σάλπιγγος; ἀλλὰ νῦν γε πᾶς εὕδει στρατός".
ὁ δ᾽ εἶπε πρός με βαί᾽, ἀεὶ δ᾽ ὑμνούμενα·
"γύναι, γυναιξὶ κόσμον ἡ σιγὴ φέρει".
κἀγὼ μαθοῦσ᾽ ἔληξ᾽, ὁ δ᾽ ἐσσύθη μόνος.
καὶ τὰς ἐκεῖ μὲν οὐκ ἔχω λέγειν πάθας·   295
ἔσω δ᾽ ἐσῆλθε συνδέτους ἄγων ὁμοῦ
ταύρους, κύνας βοτῆρας, εὔερόν τ᾽ ἄγραν.
καὶ τοὺς μὲν ηὐχένιζε, τοὺς δ᾽ ἄνω τρέπων
ἔσφαζε κἀρράχιζε, τοὺς δὲ δεσμίους
ᾐκίζεθ᾽ ὥστε φῶτας ἐν ποίμναις πίτνων.   300
τέλος δ᾽ ἀπᾴξας διὰ θυρῶν σκιᾷ τινι
λόγους ἀνέσπα, τοὺς μὲν Ἀτρειδῶν κάτα,
τοὺς δ᾽ ἀμφ᾽ Ὀδυσσεῖ, συντιθεὶς γέλων πολύν,
ὅσην κατ᾽ αὐτῶν ὕβριν ἐκτείσαιτ᾽ ἰών·
κἄπειτ᾽ ἐπᾴξας αὖθις ἐς δόμους πάλιν   305
ἔμφρων μόλις πως ξὺν χρόνῳ καθίσταται,

καὶ πλῆρες ἄτης ὡς διοπτεύει στέγος,
παίσας κάρα 'θώϋξεν· ἐν δ᾽ ἐρειπίοις
νεκρῶν ἐρειφθεὶς ἕζετ᾽ ἀρνείου φόνου,
κόμην ἀπρὶξ ὄνυξι συλλαβὼν χερί.   310
καὶ τὸν μὲν ἧστο πλεῖστον ἄφθογγος χρόνον·
ἔπειτ᾽ ἐμοὶ τὰ δείν᾽ ἐπηπείλησ᾽ ἔπη,
εἰ μὴ φανοίην πᾶν τὸ συντυχὸν πάθος,
κἀνήρετ᾽ ἐν τῷ πράγματος κυροῖ ποτέ.
κἀγώ, φίλοι, δείσασα τοὐξειργασμένον   315
ἔλεξα πᾶν ὅσονπερ ἐξηπιστάμην.
ὁ δ᾽ εὐθὺς ἐξῴμωξεν οἰμωγὰς λυγράς,
ἃς οὔποτ᾽ αὐτοῦ πρόσθεν εἰσήκουσ᾽ ἐγώ·
πρὸς γὰρ κακοῦ τε καὶ βαρυψύχου γόους
τοιούσδ᾽ ἀεί ποτ᾽ ἀνδρὸς ἐξηγεῖτ᾽ ἔχειν·   320
ἀλλ᾽ ἀψόφητος ὀξέων κωκυμάτων
ὑπεστέναζε ταῦρος ὣς βρυχώμενος.
νῦν δ᾽ ἐν τοιᾷδε κείμενος κακῇ τύχῃ
ἄσιτος ἀνήρ, ἄποτος, ἐν μέσοις βοτοῖς
σιδηροκμῆσιν ἥσυχος θακεῖ πεσών·   325
καὶ δῆλός ἐστιν ὥς τι δρασείων κακόν.
τοιαῦτα γάρ πως καὶ λέγει κὠδύρεται.
ἀλλ᾽, ὦ φίλοι, τούτων γὰρ οὕνεκ᾽ ἐστάλην,
ἀρήξατ᾽ εἰσελθόντες, εἰ δύνασθέ τι·
φίλων γὰρ οἱ τοιοίδε νικῶνται λόγοις.   330

Χορός   Τέκμησσα, δεινά, παῖ Τελεύταντος, λέγεις
                ἡμῖν, τὸν ἄνδρα διαπεφοιβάσθαι κακοῖς.

Αἴας   ἰώ μοί μοι.

Τέκμησσα   τάχ᾽, ὡς ἔοικε, μᾶλλον· ἢ οὐκ ἠκούσατε
                Αἴαντος οἵαν τήνδε θωΰσσει βοήν;   335

Αἴας   ἰώ μοί μοι.

Χορός   ἁνὴρ ἔοικεν ἢ νοσεῖν ἢ τοῖς πάλαι
                νοσήμασιν ξυνοῦσι λυπεῖσθαι παρών.

Αἴας   ἰὼ παῖ παῖ.

Τέκμησσα   ὤμοι τάλαιν᾽· Εὐρύσακες, ἀμφὶ σοὶ βοᾷ.   340
                τί ποτε μενοινᾷ; ποῦ ποτ᾽ εἶ; τάλαιν᾽ ἐγώ.

Αἴας   Τεῦκρον καλῶ. ποῦ Τεῦκρος; ἦ τὸν εἰσαεὶ
                ληλατήσει χρόνον; ἐγὼ δ᾽ ἀπόλλυμαι.

Χορός	ἀνὴϱ φϱονεῖν ἔοικεν. ἀλλ᾽ ἀνοίγετε.	
	τάχ᾽ ἄν τιν᾽ αἰδῶ κἀπ᾽ ἐμοὶ βλέψας λάβοι.	345

Τέκμησσα	ἰδού, διοίγω· πϱοσβλέπειν δ᾽ ἔξεστί σοι
	τὰ τοῦδε πϱάγη, καὐτὸς ὡς ἔχων κυϱεῖ.

348–429: The ekkyklema is wheeled out through the door of the skene to reveal Ajax sitting amongst the animals he has killed. He engages in a song of lamentation (with the chorus and Tecmessa replying) during which he begs the chorus to kill him, and curses the Atreidae and Odysseus.

Αἴας
αἰαῖ· τίς ἄν ποτ᾽ ᾤεθ᾽ ὧδ᾽ ἐπώνυμον   430
τοὐμὸν ξυνοίσειν ὄνομα τοῖς ἐμοῖς κακοῖς;
νῦν γὰρ πάρεστι καὶ δὶς αἰάζειν ἐμοὶ
καὶ τρίς· τοιούτοις γὰρ κακοῖς ἐντυγχάνω·
ὅτου πατὴρ μὲν τῆσδ᾽ ἀπ᾽ Ἰδαίας χθονὸς
τὰ πρῶτα καλλιστεῖ᾽ ἀριστεύσας στρατοῦ   435
πρὸς οἶκον ἦλθε πᾶσαν εὔκλειαν φέρων·
ἐγὼ δ᾽ ὁ κείνου παῖς, τὸν αὐτὸν ἐς τόπον
Τροίας ἐπελθὼν οὐκ ἐλάσσονι σθένει
οὐδ᾽ ἔργα μείω χειρὸς ἀρκέσας ἐμῆς,
ἄτιμος Ἀργείοισιν ὧδ᾽ ἀπόλλυμαι.   440
καίτοι τοσοῦτόν γ᾽ ἐξεπίστασθαι δοκῶ·
εἰ ζῶν Ἀχιλλεὺς τῶν ὅπλων τῶν ὧν πέρι
κρίνειν ἔμελλε κράτος ἀριστείας τινί,
οὐκ ἄν τις αὔτ᾽ ἔμαρψεν ἄλλος ἀντ᾽ ἐμοῦ.
νῦν δ᾽ αὔτ᾽ Ἀτρεῖδαι φωτὶ παντουργῷ φρένας   445
ἔπραξαν, ἀνδρὸς τοῦδ᾽ ἀπώσαντες κράτη.
κεἰ μὴ τόδ᾽ ὄμμα καὶ φρένες διάστροφοι
γνώμης ἀπῇξαν τῆς ἐμῆς, οὐκ ἄν ποτε
δίκην κατ᾽ ἄλλου φωτὸς ὧδ᾽ ἐψήφισαν.
νῦν δ᾽ ἡ Διὸς γοργῶπις ἀδάματος θεὰ   450
ἤδη μ᾽ ἐπ᾽ αὐτοῖς χεῖρ᾽ ἐπευθύνοντ᾽ ἐμὴν
ἔσφηλεν, ἐμβαλοῦσα λυσσώδη νόσον,
ὥστ᾽ ἐν τοιοῖσδε χεῖρας αἱμάξαι βοτοῖς·
κεῖνοι δ᾽ ἐπεγγελῶσιν ἐκπεφευγότες,
ἐμοῦ μὲν οὐχ ἑκόντος· εἰ δέ τις θεῶν   455
βλάπτοι, φύγοι τἂν χὠ κακὸς τὸν κρείσσονα.
καὶ νῦν τί χρὴ δρᾶν; ὅστις ἐμφανῶς θεοῖς
ἐχθαίρομαι, μισεῖ δέ μ᾽ Ἑλλήνων στρατός,
ἔχθει δὲ Τροία πᾶσα καὶ πεδία τάδε.
πότερα πρὸς οἴκους, ναυλόχους λιπὼν ἕδρας   460
μόνους τ᾽ Ἀτρείδας, πέλαγος Αἰγαῖον περῶ;
καὶ ποῖον ὄμμα πατρὶ δηλώσω φανεὶς
Τελαμῶνι; πῶς με τλήσεταί ποτ᾽ εἰσιδεῖν
γυμνὸν φανέντα τῶν ἀριστείων ἄτερ,
ὧν αὐτὸς ἔσχε στέφανον εὐκλείας μέγαν;   465
οὐκ ἔστι τοὔργον τλητόν. ἀλλὰ δῆτ᾽ ἰὼν
πρὸς ἔρυμα Τρώων, ξυμπεσὼν μόνος μόνοις
καὶ δρῶν τι χρηστόν, εἶτα λοίσθιον θάνω;
ἀλλ᾽ ὧδέ γ᾽ Ἀτρείδας ἂν εὐφράναιμί που.
οὐκ ἔστι ταῦτα. πεῖρά τις ζητητέα   470

A Level

τοιάδ᾿ ἀφ᾿ ἧς γέροντι δηλώσω πατρὶ
μή τοι φύσιν γ᾿ ἄσπλαγχνος ἐκ κείνου γεγώς.
αἰσχρὸν γὰρ ἄνδρα τοῦ μακροῦ χρῄζειν βίου,
κακοῖσιν ὅστις μηδὲν ἐξαλλάσσεται.
τί γὰρ παρ᾿ ἦμαρ ἡμέρα τέρπειν ἔχει   475
προσθεῖσα κἀναθεῖσα τοῦ γε κατθανεῖν;
οὐκ ἂν πριαίμην οὐδενὸς λόγου βροτὸν
ὅστις κεναῖσιν ἐλπίσιν θερμαίνεται·
ἀλλ᾿ ἢ καλῶς ζῆν ἢ καλῶς τεθνηκέναι
τὸν εὐγενῆ χρή. πάντ᾿ ἀκήκοας λόγον.   480

Χορός　　οὐδεὶς ἐρεῖ ποθ᾿ ὡς ὑπόβλητον λόγον,
Αἴας, ἔλεξας, ἀλλὰ τῆς σαυτοῦ φρενός·
παῦσαί γε μέντοι καὶ δὸς ἀνδράσιν φίλοις
γνώμης κρατῆσαι, τάσδε φροντίδας μεθείς.

Τέκμησσα　　ὦ δέσποτ᾿ Αἴας, τῆς ἀναγκαίας τύχης   485
οὐκ ἔστιν οὐδὲν μεῖζον ἀνθρώποις κακόν.
ἐγὼ δ᾿ ἐλευθέρου μὲν ἐξέφυν πατρός,
εἴπερ τινὸς σθένοντος ἐν πλούτῳ Φρυγῶν·
νῦν δ᾿ εἰμὶ δούλη· θεοῖς γὰρ ὧδ᾿ ἔδοξέ που
καὶ σῇ μάλιστα χειρί. τοιγαροῦν, ἐπεὶ   490
τὸ σὸν λέχος ξυνῆλθον, εὖ φρονῶ τὰ σά,
καί σ᾿ ἀντιάζω πρός τ᾿ ἐφεστίου Διὸς
εὐνῆς τε τῆς σῆς, ᾗ συνηλλάχθης ἐμοί,
μή μ᾿ ἀξιώσῃς βάξιν ἀλγεινὴν λαβεῖν
τῶν σῶν ὑπ᾿ ἐχθρῶν, χειρίαν ἐφείς τινι.   495
ἦ γὰρ θάνῃς σὺ καὶ τελευτήσας ἀφῇς,
ταύτῃ νόμιζε κἀμὲ τῇ τόθ᾿ ἡμέρᾳ
βίᾳ ξυναρπασθεῖσαν Ἀργείων ὕπο
ξὺν παιδὶ τῷ σῷ δουλίαν ἕξειν τροφήν.
καί τις πικρὸν πρόσφθεγμα δεσποτῶν ἐρεῖ   500
λόγοις ἰάπτων· "ἴδετε τὴν ὁμευνέτιν
Αἴαντος, ὃς μέγιστον ἴσχυσεν στρατοῦ,
οἵας λατρείας ἀνθ᾿ ὅσου ζήλου τρέφει."
τοιαῦτ᾿ ἐρεῖ τις· κἀμὲ μὲν δαίμων ἐλᾷ,
σοὶ δ᾿ αἰσχρὰ τἄπη ταῦτα καὶ τῷ σῷ γένει.   505
ἀλλ᾿ αἴδεσαι μὲν πατέρα τὸν σὸν ἐν λυγρῷ
γήρᾳ προλείπων, αἴδεσαι δὲ μητέρα
πολλῶν ἐτῶν κληροῦχον, ἥ σε πολλάκις
θεοῖς ἀρᾶται ζῶντα πρὸς δόμους μολεῖν·
οἴκτιρε δ᾿, ὦναξ, παῖδα τὸν σόν, εἰ νέας   510
τροφῆς στερηθεὶς σοῦ διοίσεται μόνος
ὑπ᾿ ὀρφανιστῶν μὴ φίλων, ὅσον κακὸν
κείνῳ τε κἀμοὶ τοῦθ᾿, ὅταν θάνῃς, νεμεῖς.
ἐμοὶ γὰρ οὐκέτ᾿ ἔστιν εἰς ὅ τι βλέπω
πλὴν σοῦ. σὺ γάρ μοι πατρίδ᾿ ᾔστωσας δόρει,   515

καὶ μητέρ᾽ ἄλλη μοῖρα τὸν φύσαντά τε
καθεῖλεν Ἅιδου θανασίμους οἰκήτορας.
τίς δῆτ᾽ ἐμοὶ γένοιτ᾽ ἂν ἀντὶ σοῦ πατρίς;
τίς πλοῦτος; ἐν σοὶ πᾶσ᾽ ἔγωγε σῴζομαι.
ἀλλ᾽ ἴσχε κἀμοῦ μνῆστιν· ἀνδρί τοι χρεὼν   520
μνήμην προσεῖναι, τερπνὸν εἴ τί που πάθοι.
χάρις χάριν γάρ ἐστιν ἡ τίκτουσ᾽ ἀεί·
ὅτου δ᾽ ἀπορρεῖ μνῆστις εὖ πεπονθότος,
οὐκ ἂν γένοιτ᾽ ἔθ᾽ οὗτος εὐγενὴς ἀνήρ.

Χορός   Αἴας, ἔχειν σ᾽ ἂν οἶκτον ὡς κἀγὼ φρενὶ   525
           θέλοιμ᾽ ἄν· αἰνοίης γὰρ ἂν τὰ τῆσδ᾽ ἔπη.

Αἴας   καὶ κάρτ᾽ ἐπαίνου τεύξεται πρὸς γοῦν ἐμοῦ,
         ἐὰν μόνον τὸ ταχθὲν εὖ τολμᾷ τελεῖν.

Τέκμησσα   ἀλλ᾽ ὦ φίλ᾽ Αἴας, πάντ᾽ ἔγωγε πείσομαι.

Αἴας   κόμιζέ νύν μοι παῖδα τὸν ἐμόν, ὡς ἴδω.   530

Τέκμησσα   καὶ μὴν φόβοισί γ᾽ αὐτὸν ἐξελυσάμην.

Αἴας   ἐν τοῖσδε τοῖς κακοῖσιν; ἢ τί μοι λέγεις;

Τέκμησσα   μὴ σοί γέ που δύστηνος ἀντήσας θάνοι.

Αἴας   πρέπον γέ τἂν ἦν δαίμονος τοὐμοῦ τόδε.

Τέκμησσα   ἀλλ᾽ οὖν ἐγὼ ᾽φύλαξα τοῦτό γ᾽ ἀρκέσαι.   535

Αἴας   ἐπήνεσ᾽ ἔργον καὶ πρόνοιαν ἣν ἔθου.

Τέκμησσα   τί δῆτ᾽ ἂν ὡς ἐκ τῶνδ᾽ ἂν ὠφελοῖμί σε;

Αἴας   δός μοι προσειπεῖν αὐτὸν ἐμφανῆ τ᾽ ἰδεῖν.

Τέκμησσα   καὶ μὴν πέλας γε προσπόλοις φυλάσσεται.

Αἴας   τί δῆτα μέλλει μὴ οὐ παρουσίαν ἔχειν;   540

Τέκμησσα   ὦ παῖ, πατὴρ καλεῖ σε. δεῦρο προσπόλων
           ἄγ᾽ αὐτὸν ὅσπερ χερσὶν εὐθύνων κυρεῖς.

Αἴας   ἕρποντι φωνεῖς ἢ λελειμμένῳ λόγων;

Τέκμησσα   καὶ δὴ κομίζει προσπόλων ὅδ᾽ ἐγγύθεν.

Αἴας   αἶρ᾽ αὐτόν, αἶρε δεῦρο· ταρβήσει γὰρ οὖ   545

**A
Level**

νεοσφαγῆ που τόνδε προσλεύσσων φόνον,
εἴπερ δικαίως ἔστ᾽ ἐμὸς τὰ πατρόθεν.
ἀλλ᾽ αὐτίκ᾽ ὠμοῖς αὐτὸν ἐν νόμοις πατρὸς
δεῖ πωλοδαμνεῖν κἀξομοιοῦσθαι φύσιν.
ὦ παῖ, γένοιο πατρὸς εὐτυχέστερος,   550
τὰ δ᾽ ἄλλ᾽ ὅμοιος· καὶ γένοι᾽ ἂν οὐ κακός.
καίτοι σε καὶ νῦν τοῦτό γε ζηλοῦν ἔχω,
ὁθούνεκ᾽ οὐδὲν τῶνδ᾽ ἐπαισθάνει κακῶν·
ἐν τῷ φρονεῖν γὰρ μηδὲν ἥδιστος βίος,   554
[τὸ μὴ φρονεῖν γὰρ κάρτ᾽ ἀνώδυνον κακόν]   554ᵇ
ἕως τὸ χαίρειν καὶ τὸ λυπεῖσθαι μάθῃς.   555
ὅταν δ᾽ ἵκῃ πρὸς τοῦτο, δεῖ σ᾽ ὅπως πατρὸς
δείξεις ἐν ἐχθροῖς, οἷος ἐξ οἵου 'τράφης.
τέως δὲ κούφοις πνεύμασιν βόσκου, νέαν
ψυχὴν ἀτάλλων, μητρὶ τῇδε χαρμονήν.
οὔτοι σ᾽ Ἀχαιῶν, οἶδα, μή τις ὑβρίσῃ   560
στυγναῖσι λώβαις, οὐδὲ χωρὶς ὄντ᾽ ἐμοῦ.
τοῖον πυλωρὸν φύλακα Τεῦκρον ἀμφί σοι
λείψω τροφῆς ἄοκνον ἔμπα, κεἰ τανῦν
τηλωπὸς οἰχνεῖ, δυσμενῶν θήραν ἔχων.
ἀλλ᾽, ἄνδρες ἀσπιστῆρες, ἐνάλιος λεώς,   565
ὑμῖν τε κοινὴν τήνδ᾽ ἐπισκήπτω χάριν,
κείνῳ τ᾽ ἐμὴν ἀγγείλατ᾽ ἐντολήν, ὅπως
τὸν παῖδα τόνδε πρὸς δόμους ἐμοὺς ἄγων
Τελαμῶνι δείξει μητρί τ᾽, Ἐριβοίᾳ λέγω,
ὥς σφιν γένηται γηροβοσκὸς εἰσαεί,   570
[μέχρις οὗ μυχοὺς κίχωσι τοῦ κάτω θεοῦ,]
καὶ τἀμὰ τεύχη μήτ᾽ ἀγωνάρχαι τινὲς
θήσουσ᾽ Ἀχαιοῖς μήθ᾽ ὁ λυμεὼν ἐμός.
ἀλλ᾽ αὐτό μοι σύ, παῖ, λαβὼν τοὐπώνυμον,
Εὐρύσακες, ἴσχε διὰ πολυρράφου στρέφων   575
πόρπακος, ἑπτάβοιον ἄρρηκτον σάκος·
τὰ δ᾽ ἄλλα τεύχη κοίν᾽ ἐμοὶ τεθάψεται.
ἀλλ᾽ ὡς τάχος τὸν παῖδα τόνδ᾽ ἤδη δέχου
καὶ δῶμα πάκτου, μηδ᾽ ἐπισκήνους γόους
δάκρυε· κάρτα τοι φιλοίκτιστον γυνή.   580
πύκαζε θᾶσσον· οὐ πρὸς ἰατροῦ σοφοῦ
θρηνεῖν ἐπῳδὰς πρὸς τομῶντι πήματι.

583–645: *A short and rapid exchange between Tecmessa and Ajax, in which she begs him not to leave (a plea which is ignored), ends this episode. It is followed by the first stasimon (standing choral ode) in which the chorus members contrast the security of their homeland with their (present) misery at Troy.*

Αἴας   ἅπανθ᾽ ὁ μακρὸς κἀναρίθμητος χρόνος   646
                 φύει τ᾽ ἄδηλα καὶ φανέντα κρύπτεται·
                 κοὐκ ἔστ᾽ ἄελπτον οὐδέν, ἀλλ᾽ ἁλίσκεται

A
Level

χὠ δεινὸς ὅρκος χαὶ περισκελεῖς φρένες.
κἀγὼ γάρ, ὃς τὰ δείν᾿ ἐκαρτέρουν τότε   650
βαφῇ σίδηρος ὥς, ἐθηλύνθην στόμα
πρὸς τῆσδε τῆς γυναικός· οἰκτίρω δέ νιν
χήραν παρ᾿ ἐχθροῖς παῖδά τ᾿ ὀρφανὸν λιπεῖν.
ἀλλ᾿ εἶμι πρός τε λουτρὰ καὶ παρακτίους
λειμῶνας, ὡς ἂν λύμαθ᾿ ἁγνίσας ἐμὰ   655
μῆνιν βαρεῖαν ἐξαλέξωμαι θεᾶς·
μολών τε χῶρον ἔνθ᾿ ἂν ἀστιβῆ κίχω,
κρύψω τόδ᾿ ἔγχος τοὐμόν, ἔχθιστον βελῶν,
γαίας ὀρύξας ἔνθα μή τις ὄψεται·
ἀλλ᾿ αὐτὸ Νὺξ Ἅιδης τε σῳζόντων κάτω.   660
ἐγὼ γὰρ ἐξ οὗ χειρὶ τοῦτ᾿ ἐδεξάμην
παρ᾿ Ἕκτορος δώρημα δυσμενεστάτου,
οὔπω τι κεδνὸν ἔσχον Ἀργείων πάρα.
ἀλλ᾿ ἔστ᾿ ἀληθὴς ἡ βροτῶν παροιμία,
ἐχθρῶν ἄδωρα δῶρα κοὐκ ὀνήσιμα.   665
τοιγὰρ τὸ λοιπὸν εἰσόμεσθα μὲν θεοῖς
εἴκειν, μαθησόμεσθα δ᾿ Ἀτρείδας σέβειν.
ἄρχοντές εἰσιν, ὥσθ᾿ ὑπεικτέον. τί μήν;
καὶ γὰρ τὰ δεινὰ καὶ τὰ καρτερώτατα
τιμαῖς ὑπείκει· τοῦτο μὲν νιφοστιβεῖς   670
χειμῶνες ἐκχωροῦσιν εὐκάρπῳ θέρει·
ἐξίσταται δὲ νυκτὸς αἰανὴς κύκλος
τῇ λευκοπώλῳ φέγγος ἡμέρᾳ φλέγειν·
δεινῶν τ᾿ ἄημα πνευμάτων ἐκοίμισε
στένοντα πόντον· ἐν δ᾿ ὁ παγκρατὴς Ὕπνος   675
λύει πεδήσας, οὐδ᾿ ἀεὶ λαβὼν ἔχει.
ἡμεῖς δὲ πῶς οὐ γνωσόμεσθα σωφρονεῖν;
ἔγωγ᾿· ἐπίσταμαι γὰρ ἀρτίως ὅτι
ὅ τ᾿ ἐχθρὸς ἡμῖν ἐς τοσόνδ᾿ ἐχθαρτέος,
ὡς καὶ φιλήσων αὖθις, ἔς τε τὸν φίλον   680
τοσαῦθ᾿ ὑπουργῶν ὠφελεῖν βουλήσομαι,
ὡς αἰὲν οὐ μενοῦντα· τοῖς πολλοῖσι γὰρ
βροτῶν ἄπιστός ἐσθ᾿ ἑταιρείας λιμήν.
ἀλλ᾿ ἀμφὶ μὲν τούτοισιν εὖ σχήσει· σὺ δὲ
ἔσω θεοῖς ἐλθοῦσα διὰ τέλους, γύναι,   685
εὔχου τελεῖσθαι τοὐμὸν ὧν ἐρᾷ κέαρ.
ὑμεῖς δ᾿, ἑταῖροι, ταὐτὰ τῇδέ μοι τάδε
τιμᾶτε, Τεύκρῳ τ᾿, ἢν μόλῃ, σημήνατε
μέλειν μὲν ἡμῶν, εὐνοεῖν δ᾿ ὑμῖν ἅμα.
ἐγὼ γὰρ εἶμ᾿ ἐκεῖσ᾿ ὅποι πορευτέον·   690
ὑμεῖς δ᾿ ἃ φράζω δρᾶτε, καὶ τάχ᾿ ἄν μ᾿ ἴσως
πύθοισθε, κεἰ νῦν δυστυχῶ, σεσωμένον.

693–747: The chorus sing the second stasimon (standing choral ode), a song filled with joy at the apparent change in Ajax's intentions. The third episode then begins

A Level

(719ff) with the arrival of a messenger. He has come to tell Ajax that Teucer has just arrived. On hearing that Ajax has gone, he bursts into exclamations of horror: he states that Teucer had instructed that Ajax should remain in the tent, and makes mention of a prophecy of Calchas.

Ἄγγελος	τοσοῦτον οἶδα καὶ παρὼν ἐτύγχανον.	748
	ἐκ γὰρ συνέδρου καὶ τυραννικοῦ κύκλου	
	Κάλχας μεταστὰς οἶος Ἀτρειδῶν δίχα,	750
	εἰς χεῖρα Τεύκρου δεξιὰν φιλοφρόνως	
	θεὶς εἶπε κἀπέσκηψε, παντοίᾳ τέχνῃ	
	εἶρξαι κατ᾽ ἦμαρ τοὐμφανὲς τὸ νῦν τόδε	
	Αἴανθ᾽ ὑπὸ σκηναῖσι μηδ᾽ ἀφέντ᾽ ἐᾶν,	
	εἰ ζῶντ᾽ ἐκεῖνον εἰσιδεῖν θέλοι ποτέ.	755
	ἐλᾷ γὰρ αὐτὸν τῇδε θἠμέρᾳ μόνῃ	
	δίας Ἀθάνας μῆνις, ὡς ἔφη λέγων.	
	τὰ γὰρ περισσὰ κἀνόνητα σώματα	
	πίπτειν βαρείαις πρὸς θεῶν δυσπραξίαις	
	ἔφασχ᾽ ὁ μάντις, ὅστις ἀνθρώπου φύσιν	760
	βλαστὼν ἔπειτα μὴ κατ᾽ ἄνθρωπον φρονῇ.	
	κεῖνος δ᾽ ἀπ᾽ οἴκων εὐθὺς ἐξορμώμενος	
	ἄνους καλῶς λέγοντος ηὑρέθη πατρός.	
	ὁ μὲν γὰρ αὐτὸν ἐννέπει· "τέκνον, δόρει	
	βούλου κρατεῖν μέν, σὺν θεῷ δ᾽ ἀεὶ κρατεῖν".	765
	ὁ δ᾽ ὑψικόμπως κἀφρόνως ἠμείψατο·	
	"πάτερ, θεοῖς μὲν κἂν ὁ μηδὲν ὢν ὁμοῦ	
	κράτος κατακτήσαιτ᾽· ἐγὼ δὲ καὶ δίχα	
	κείνων πέποιθα τοῦτ᾽ ἐπισπάσειν κλέος."	
	τοσόνδ᾽ ἐκόμπει μῦθον. εἶτα δεύτερον	770
	δίας Ἀθάνας, ἡνίκ᾽ ὀτρύνουσά νιν	
	ηὐδᾶτ᾽ ἐπ᾽ ἐχθροῖς χεῖρα φοινίαν τρέπειν,	
	τότ᾽ ἀντιφωνεῖ δεινὸν ἄρρητόν τ᾽ ἔπος·	
	"ἄνασσα, τοῖς ἄλλοισιν Ἀργείων πέλας	
	ἵστω, καθ᾽ ἡμᾶς δ᾽ οὔποτ᾽ ἐκρήξει μάχη".	775
	τοιοῖσδέ τοι λόγοισιν ἀστεργῆ θεᾶς	
	ἐκτήσατ᾽ ὀργήν, οὐ κατ᾽ ἄνθρωπον φρονῶν.	
	ἀλλ᾽ εἴπερ ἔστι τῇδε θἠμέρᾳ, τάχ᾽ ἂν	
	γενοίμεθ᾽ αὐτοῦ σὺν θεῷ σωτήριοι.	
	τοσαῦθ᾽ ὁ μάντις εἶφ᾽· ὁ δ᾽ εὐθὺς ἐξ ἕδρας	780
	πέμπει με σοὶ φέροντα τάσδ᾽ ἐπιστολὰς	
	Τεῦκρος φυλάσσειν. εἰ δ᾽ ἀπεστερήμεθα,	
	οὐκ ἔστιν ἀνὴρ κεῖνος, εἰ Κάλχας σοφός.	

784–814: *Tecmessa arrives and the chorus repeat the messenger's story. She encourages them to hunt for Ajax. They divide into two groups and leave the orchestra.*

Αἴας
 ὁ μὲν σφαγεὺς ἔστηκεν ᾗ τομώτατος   815
 γένοιτ᾽ ἄν, εἴ τῳ καὶ λογίζεσθαι σχολή·
 δῶρον μὲν ἀνδρὸς Ἕκτορος ξένων ἐμοὶ
 μάλιστα μισηθέντος ἐχθίστου θ᾽ ὁρᾶν·
 πέπηγε δ᾽ ἐν γῇ πολεμίᾳ τῇ Τρῳάδι,
 σιδηροβρῶτι θηγάνῃ νεηκονής·   820
 ἔπηξα δ᾽ αὐτὸν εὖ περιστείλας ἐγώ,
 εὐνούστατον τῷδ᾽ ἀνδρὶ διὰ τάχους θανεῖν.
 οὕτω μὲν εὐσκευοῦμεν· ἐκ δὲ τῶνδέ μοι
 σὺ πρῶτος, ὦ Ζεῦ, καὶ γὰρ εἰκός, ἄρκεσον.
 αἰτήσομαι δέ σ᾽ οὐ μακρὸν γέρας λαβεῖν.   825
 πέμψον τιν᾽ ἡμῖν ἄγγελον, κακὴν φάτιν
 Τεύκρῳ φέροντα, πρῶτος ὥς με βαστάσῃ
 πεπτῶτα τῷδε περὶ νεορράντῳ ξίφει,
 καὶ μὴ πρὸς ἐχθρῶν του κατοπτευθεὶς πάρος
 ῥιφθῶ κυσὶν πρόβλητος οἰωνοῖς θ᾽ ἕλωρ.   830
 τοσαῦτά σ᾽, ὦ Ζεῦ, προστρέπω, καλῶ δ᾽ ἅμα
 πομπαῖον Ἑρμῆν χθόνιον εὖ με κοιμίσαι,
 ξὺν ἀσφαδάστῳ καὶ ταχεῖ πηδήματι
 πλευρὰν διαρρήξαντα τῷδε φασγάνῳ.
 καλῶ δ᾽ ἀρωγοὺς τὰς ἀεί τε παρθένους   835
 ἀεί θ᾽ ὁρώσας πάντα τὰν βροτοῖς πάθη,
 σεμνὰς Ἐρινῦς τανύποδας, μαθεῖν ἐμὲ
 πρὸς τῶν Ἀτρειδῶν ὡς διόλλυμαι τάλας,
 [καί σφας κακοὺς κάκιστα καὶ πανωλέθρους
 ξυναρπάσειαν, ὥσπερ εἰσορῶσ᾽ ἐμὲ   840
 αὐτοσφαγῆ πίπτοντα· τὼς αὐτοσφαγεῖς
 πρὸς τῶν φιλίστων ἐκγόνων ὀλοίατο.]
 ἴτ᾽, ὦ ταχεῖαι ποίνιμοί τ᾽ Ἐρινύες,
 γεύεσθε, μὴ φείδεσθε πανδήμου στρατοῦ·
 σὺ δ᾽, ὦ τὸν αἰπὺν οὐρανὸν διφρηλατῶν 845
 Ἥλιε, πατρῴαν τὴν ἐμὴν ὅταν χθόνα
 ἴδῃς, ἐπισχὼν χρυσόνωτον ἡνίαν
 ἄγγειλον ἄτας τὰς ἐμὰς μόρον τ᾽ ἐμὸν
 γέροντι πατρὶ τῇ τε δυστήνῳ τροφῷ.
 ἦ που τάλαινα, τήνδ᾽ ὅταν κλύῃ φάτιν,   850
 ἥσει μέγαν κωκυτὸν ἐν πάσῃ πόλῃ.
 ἀλλ᾽ οὐδὲν ἔργον ταῦτα θρηνεῖσθαι μάτην,
 ἀλλ᾽ ἀρκτέον τὸ πρᾶγμα σὺν τάχει τινί.
 [ὦ Θάνατε Θάνατε, νῦν μ᾽ ἐπίσκεψαι μολών.
 καίτοι σὲ μὲν κἀκεῖ προσαυδήσω ξυνών.   855

A Level

σὲ δ᾽, ὦ φαεννῆς ἡμέρας τὸ νῦν σέλας,
καὶ τὸν διφρευτὴν Ἥλιον προσεννέπω,
πανύστατον δὴ κοὔποτ᾽ αὖθις ὕστερον.]
ὦ φέγγος, ὦ γῆς ἱερὸν οἰκείας πέδον
Σαλαμῖνος, ὦ πατρῷον ἑστίας βάθρον   860
κλειναί τ᾽ Ἀθῆναι καὶ τὸ σύντροφον γένος
κρῆναί τε ποταμοί θ᾽ οἵδε, καὶ τὰ Τρωϊκὰ
πεδία προσαυδῶ, χαίρετ᾽, ὦ τροφῆς ἐμοί·
τοῦθ᾽ ὑμῖν Αἴας τοὔπος ὕστατον θροεῖ,
τὰ δ᾽ ἄλλ᾽ ἐν Ἅιδου τοῖς κάτω μυθήσομαι.   865

Commentary Notes

1–133: Prologue

The purpose of a prologue is to set up the main issue(s) at stake, and to provide the audience with necessary background information. Although six of Sophocles' seven surviving tragedies begin with a dialogue, *Ajax* is the only one in which one of the participants is divine.

Odysseus is trying to find out who is responsible for a horrific attack made in the night on the Greek cattle and sheep, and is scanning footsteps. He has got as far as Ajax's hut. Athena appears (although she is invisible to Odysseus, as shown by lines 14–17, but visible to us) and reveals to him that Ajax is indeed responsible for the slaughter. She adds that he had wanted to take revenge on the Greek chiefs for failing to award him the arms of Achilles, but that she sent him mad and turned him instead against the animals, which he believes to be the Greeks. Athena then summons Ajax (much to the concern of Odysseus) and delivers a moral in which she encourages Odysseus to practise *sophrosyne*, 'moderation', a key theme of the play.

It is through Athena's interactions with Odysseus and then with Ajax that some key themes and elements of characterization are introduced. The delusional madness and physical strength of Ajax contrast him with the resourceful, logically-minded Odysseus, who plays the role of a detective in this scene. Odysseus' status as Athena's favourite is also confirmed, as is the hostility between Ajax and Odysseus. In some sense, therefore, these characters appear to have stepped straight out of the pages of the Homeric epics. However, Ajax's madness is possibly a Sophoclean innovation; if so, it is a very striking one, as is the pity that Odysseus shows towards his enemy at lines 121–126 (see on line 2). Odysseus' attitude here foreshadows his involvement in the burial and elevation to heroic status of Ajax in the final scene.

Stage directions for Greek tragedies mostly don't survive, and thus we have to use references embedded within the text (and common sense) in order to reconstruct the stagecraft. Lines 3–4 indicate that the *skene* (stage-building) represents Ajax's hut at the eastern end of the Greek camp at Troy. But other key questions still remain unanswered, such as where Athena stood in relation to Odysseus, and whether or not she was raised on the *mechane* (the crane often used to raise gods and goddesses above the height of the skene) or even on top of the skene itself (see introduction p. 349).

1–33

Odysseus enters via an eisodos and scans the footprints that lead into Ajax's hut. Athena delivers a short monologue (a rhesis) in which she establishes key aspects of his characterization and asks what he is doing. Odysseus answers with his own rhesis, full of reverence for and gratitude towards his patron goddess, in which he explains his progress thus far.

1–2

ἀεὶ μέν, ὦ παῖ Λαρτίου, δέδορκά σε/πεῖράν τιν᾽ ἐχθρῶν ἁρπάσαι θηρώμενον: this is a difficult opening line. The most likely translation is: 'I always see you, son of Laertes, hunting to seize some opportunity against your enemies'. θηρώμενον governs the aorist infinitive ἁρπάσαι, which in turn governs the object πεῖράν τιν᾽. ἐχθρῶν is an objective genitive, that is to say a genitive which is the direct object of an action contained within another noun.

1

ὦ παῖ Λαρτίου: 'son of Laertes', i.e. Odysseus.

2

τιν᾽: unlike in Latin, elision (i.e. the loss of a short vowel at the end of a word if the next one starts with a vowel) in Greek poetry is always indicated by the editor. τιν᾽ = τινα.

θηρώμενον: 'hunting'. Hunting imagery is very prominent in the prologue (see also lines 5, κυνηγετοῦντα, and 6, ἴχνη τὰ κείνου νεοχάραχθ᾽, and the simile in lines 7–8). Irony is generated by the fact that Ajax, the hunter of the Greek chiefs/animals, has become the hunted. There is also a sense of foreboding: the net is closing in on Ajax and on the worldview which he represents.

ἐχθρῶν: this introduces a core ethical principle of Greek thought, that one should 'help friends and harm enemies'. Athena and Ajax both take this principle for granted. Odysseus' attitude is more complicated, however, and his ability to pity an enemy is striking.

3

καὶ νῦν … ὁρῶ: a contrasting response to the opening formula ἀεὶ μὲν … δέδορκά (one might have expected νῦν δέ). We are reminded that Odysseus' intelligence and cunning are not new, nor is Athena's interest in and support for him.

3–4

ἐπὶ σκηναῖς … ναυτικαῖς … /Αἴαντος, ἔνθα τάξιν ἐσχάτην ἔχει: 'at the hut of Ajax by the ships, where he holds the furthest position'. σκηναῖς … ναυτικαῖς is (probably) an example of what is often called the poetic plural, i.e. the use, for stylistic effect or metrical reasons, of a plural noun with a singular meaning or reference. Note that Athena has to explain what the skene represents and where the hut is, as there are no programme notes or surtitles to indicate this to the audience.

AS

The superlative adjective ἐσχάτην and the noun τάξιν (which also has the meaning of 'battle-line') remind us of Ajax's importance as a warrior (and the phrase as a whole also points to his social isolation): the two ends of the camp are likely to be the most vulnerable to attack. Indeed, Achilles' hut was at the other end.

5

κυνηγετοῦντα: this participle is cognate with (i.e. related to) the noun for dog (κύων) and therefore anticipates the comparison between Odysseus and a hound which is found below (lines 7–8).

The language once again suggests Odysseus' resourcefulness, intelligence and tenacity (πάλαι, μετρούμενον).

6

κείνου: an alternative (poetic) form of ἐκείνου, referring to Ajax.

νεοχάραχθ': if elision occurs but the second word begins with a vowel with a rough breathing, the aspiration of the breathing is transferred onto the final consonant of the first word. It therefore assumes an aspirated form, if such a form exists. So, νεοχάραχτα ('newly-printed') becomes, through elision, νεοχάραχτ' and then νεοχάραχθ'.

ὅπως ἴδης: ὅπως can be used to introduce a purpose clause. ἴδης is aorist subjunctive of the verb 'to see'.

7–8

εὖ δέ σ' ἐκφέρει/κυνὸς Λακαίνης ὥς τις εὔρινος βάσις: the grammatical case of εὔρινος ('keen-scented') is unclear. If it is genitive masculine singular, agreeing with κυνός, we get: 'your course, like that [lit. 'one'] of a keen-scented Laconian hound, brings you well to your goal'.

Laconian (i.e. Spartan) dogs were famous for their advanced sense of smell, and the comparison generated by the simile is appropriate.

ἐκφέρει: here has the meaning of 'carry forward to fulfilment' (the sense of completion is indicated by the prefix ἐκ-).

9

ἁνήρ: = ὁ ἀνήρ. The process by which two vowels merge to form one vowel (or diphthong) is known as crasis. Note that the rough breathing of the article remains when the merge takes place.

9–10

κάρα/στάζων ἱδρῶτι καὶ χέρας ξιφοκτόνους: 'shedding sweat from his head and his sword-killing hands'. στάζω ('I shed, drop, let fall') is here followed by accusatives of respect (κάρα ... καὶ χέρας ξιφοκτόνους), lit. 'dripping with sweat with respect to his head and sword-killing hands'. Several commentators have suggested that Ajax should be dripping with blood as well as sweat.

10

ξιφοκτόνους: 'sword-killing'. This is the first reference in the play to Ajax's sword, an item teeming with significance and symbolic value. In book 7 of the *Iliad*, it

AS

was given to Ajax by his 'enemy' Hector after their duel. It symbolizes, of course, Ajax's exceptional abilities as a warrior. But in this play its associations are much darker: Ajax has used this sword to slaughter innocent animals. The shame caused by this event, and by his inability to get revenge on his enemies, will lead him to suicide, a deed which he will commit using this very sword.

11–12

οὐδὲν ... /ἔτ᾽ ἔργον ἐστίν: 'there is no further need', followed by the infinitive construction with σε as the accusative subject of the infinitive παπταίνειν. The same phrase (in the positive) needs to be supplied again in the next clause with ἐννέπειν δ᾽: 'but there is need that you should say . . .'.

12

ὅτου: = οὕτινος. These shorter alternative forms of the indefinite relative pronoun ὅστις are common in poetry.

χάριν: + gen. = 'for the sake of', therefore ὅτου χάριν = 'why' (lit. 'for the sake of what').

ἔθου: 2nd person singular aorist middle of τίθημι. The phrase σπουδὴν τίθεμαι is a periphrasis meaning 'I make an effort/take the trouble'.

13

ὡς ... μάθῃς: ὡς here introduces a purpose clause.

παρ᾽ εἰδυίας: 'from one who knows', i.e. Athena herself.

14

The formality and flattery of this opening line is underlined by the alliteration of θ/τ and φ.

15

κἂν: = καὶ ἐάν (by crasis), which introduces a generalizing indefinite (conditional) clause (subjunctive + ἄν).

ἄποπτος: some scholars translate this as 'out of sight', others as 'seen at a distance'. Although the ending of this adjective looks masculine, it is in fact feminine (he is addressing Athena). Compound adjectives in Greek, including those starting with an alpha privative, have the same ending for masculine and feminine (-ος) and different ending for neuter (-ον). They are thus called two-termination adjectives. See also χαλκοστόμου in line 17.

ὅμως: some editors prefer to put the comma before rather than after this word.

Odysseus' language in lines 14–16 (φθέγμ᾽, κἂν ἄποπτος ἦς) indicates that he cannot see Athena (or, at best, that he can only see her dimly). This touches on two key themes. The first is that of sight and blindness, which is important when we consider the effect of the delusional madness and blindness inflicted on Ajax by the goddess. The other is the gulf between the divine and the mortal (already noted): although Athena is his patron, Odysseus is not granted the privilege of seeing her.

17

χαλκοστόμου κώδωνος ὡς Τυρσηνικῆς: 'like that [i.e. the voice] of a bronze-mouthed Etruscan trumpet'. There is a legend that Athena invented the trumpet for the Etruscans.

The frequency of similes in the opening of the play is perhaps a little reminiscent of Homeric epic (although it should be noted that they are not extended in the way that Homer's similes are).

18

ἐπέγνως: 2nd person singular aorist of ἐπιγίγνωσκω, followed here by an indirect statement (participle construction, used after verbs of knowing and perceiving).

18–19

ἐπ᾽ ἀνδρὶ δυσμενεῖ/ ... Αἴαντι τῷ σακεσφόρῳ: 'against a hostile man ... Ajax the shield-bearer'. These two phrases are in apposition.

The world of Homeric epic is also evoked by the use of the epithet (adjective or adjectival phrase) σακεσφόρῳ. The epithet introduces yet another object of immense symbolic significance, this time Ajax's shield. Like the sword, his shield represents Ajax's abilities as a warrior (especially as a defensive one). Moreover, his son, Eurysaces, has the word in his name (which means 'broad-shield'). However, such a shield (it is described in *Iliad* 7 as 'a shield of bronze with seven folds of ox-hide') was out of date even in Homer's day. This has significance for the discussion about the outdated values which Ajax possibly represents.

20

ἰχνεύω πάλαι: note this use of the present, where English would use a true perfect tense (see below), to emphasize that the tracking is ongoing.

21

νυκτὸς ... τῆσδε: genitive of time within which.

πρᾶγος: poetic version of πρᾶγμα.

22

ἔχει περάνας: 'he has accomplished'. This is called the periphrastic perfect tense, formed with ἔχει followed by an aorist participle. The perfect tense indicates that an action has been done and remains done, i.e. the action continues to affect the present. Ajax has accomplished these things and they remain done now. Note that the verb περαίνω takes a double accusative (ἡμᾶς ... πρᾶγος ἄσκοπον).

εἴπερ: the -περ suffix strengthens the word to which it is attached – 'if indeed'. Note the use of a condition, which introduces a note of caution continued in the next line.

23

ἀλώμεθα: the verb ἀλάομαι is used of both physical and metaphorical or mental wandering.

AS

24

κἀγώ: = καὶ ἐγώ (by crasis).

'Θελοντής: = ἐθελοντής ('volunteer'). The process whereby the first vowel of a word loses its vowel due to contact with a preceding word which ends in a vowel is called prodelision.

ὑπεζύγην: lit. = 'I was yoked to', therefore 'I submitted to'. Note that the yoking metaphor suggests necessity or compulsion. When taken with the noun 'Θελοντής, this generates something of a paradox.

25

εὑρίσκομεν: 1st person plural present indicative active. The present tense has been used to give a sense of vividness and immediacy to the action of finding.

ἐφθαρμένας: a perfect passive participle (from φθείρω), as is **κατηναρισμένας** (from κατεναρίζω = I kill outright). Note the wide separation of these participles from each other and the noun with which they are in agreement, which perhaps serves to emphasize them, and the use again of the perfect tense to indicate a past action leading to a present state (they were killed and so they are now dead).

λείας: lit. 'plunder', which here means 'stolen/plundered animals'.

27

ἐκ χειρός: i.e. they were not killed by other animals. The implication is, of course, that Ajax is the one responsible.

αὐτοῖς ποιμνίων ἐπιστάταις: 'along with the very overseers of the herds', i.e. the shepherds. This is a comitative dative, otherwise known as a dative of accompaniment. τὸ ποίημνιον = 'flock of sheep', but here it must include cattle too.

28

πᾶς τις: 'everyone'.

29

τις ὀπτήρ: 'an eyewitness'. The word order is unusual – in prose, we would expect the indefinite pronoun τις to come after its noun.

μόνον: a traditional characteristic of the Sophoclean tragic hero.

30

πηδῶντα πεδία: 'leaping across the plain'. πηδάω takes an accusative of extent of space travelled, with no preposition needed. (NB: this is the spatial equivalent to the accusative of duration of time which was learnt at GCSE.) Note also the striking alliteration, the vivid image generated by the verb, and the poetic plural of πεδία.

σὺν νεορράντῳ ξίφει: σύν + dative, meaning 'with', is common in poetry.

31

κἀδήλωσεν: = καὶ ἐδήλωσεν. Note the unusual juxtaposition of an historic present (φράζει) and an aorist (ἐδήλωσεν).

AS

32

κατ᾽ ἴχνος ᾄσσω: 'I dart/rush on his track' – hunting imagery resumes.

τὰ μὲν ... τὰ δ᾽: most commentators supply ἴχνη with each article. However, Finglass translates **τὰ μέν** as 'some features of the situation'.

33

ἐκπέπληγμαι: lit. = 'I have been struck off course', therefore, 'I am driven out of my senses' (1st person singular perfect passive of ἐκπλήσσω: again, the perfect has been used, but to indicate/describe a present state). The accusative **τὰ δ᾽** must therefore be taken as an accusative of respect: 'regarding the other (signs), I am at a loss'.

ἔχω μαθεῖν: ἔχω + infinitive = 'I am able to . . .' is a common idiom.

ὅτου = οὗτινος (see line 12) = 'whose (they are)'. The verb 'to be' needs to be supplied in this subordinate clause (as often in poetry).

34

Odysseus' reverent tone in this and the following line is striking.

καιρόν: this is being used adverbially ('at the right time').

ἐφήκεις: 'you have arrived', i.e. 'you are here'.

πάντα γὰρ τά τ᾽ οὖν πάρος/τά τ᾽ εἰσέπειτα: note the common use of a neuter plural article with an adverb/adverbial clause to mean 'things . . .' (here, 'all things in the past' and 'all things in the future'). Note also the simple but effective stylistic device of placing the important idea first in the clause – Athena always has been, and always will be, Odysseus' guide.

35

σῇ κυβερνῶμαι χερί: 'I am guided by your hand'. Sailing metaphors such as this (κυβερνάω = I steer a ship) are very common in ancient Greek poetry of all periods.

36–50

It is very common in tragedy for a conversation which starts with a rhesis delivered by each main character to then move into a section of stichomythia (single line dialogue). The change adds both pace and tension to the scene, and here (as often) enables a quick-fire exchange of questions (from Odysseus) and answers (from Athena) to take place.

36–37

πάλαι φύλαξ ἔβην/τῇ σῇ πρόθυμος εἰς ὁδὸν κυναγίᾳ: 'a while ago I set out on the road as a guardian, eager for your hunt'. Word order makes this tricky. Athena's choice of vocabulary shows her affection for Odysseus (πάλαι, φύλαξ, πρόθυμος).

38

ἦ καί: this combination adds eagerness to his question: 'am I really . . .?'.

πρὸς καιρόν: 'to advantage', 'to profit' or perhaps 'to good effect'.

39

ὡς: translate ὡς as 'that' and add an imperative (ἴσθι) – 'know that . . .'. Athena provides reassurance, and it wouldn't be inappropriate to start a translation of this line with 'yes'.

σοι: an example of an ethic dative, which shows that the person in the dative has an interest in the matter at hand ('as far as you are concerned'). We might be tempted here to follow Stanford in translating it as 'as you suspected', or 'let me tell you'.

40

καὶ πρὸς τί δυσλόγιστον ὧδ' ᾖξεν χέρα: a difficult line to translate. The verb ᾖξεν (3rd person singular aorist from ἄσσω) is here transitive = 'I set in motion'. The next difficulty is the translation of the adjective δυσλόγιστον ('unimaginable, incalculable'). There are two options:

- Take δυσλόγιστον with τί: 'and to what unimaginable purpose did he thus set his hand in motion?'

- Take δυσλόγιστον with χέρα, assuming that it should be transferred from the hand to the violence: 'and to what purpose did he thus set his hand in motion for such an unimaginable act of violence?' (lit. '. . . did he thus set his unimaginable hand in motion . . .').

41

This line contains the first reference to the Judgement of the Arms. τῶν Ἀχιλλείων ὅπλων is a genitive of cause with χόλῳ: '(weighed down) with anger because of . . .'.

42

τήνδ' . . . βάσιν: this is what is known as an internal accusative, i.e. an accusative that names, modifies or describes the action of the verb. It is very common in Greek, and often can be used to add intensity to a plainer verb. In effect, an internal accusative forms a unit with the verb: 'why, then, did he fall with such an onslaught/in this way upon the flocks?'

43

ἐν ὑμῖν . . . φόνῳ: 'in your blood'. ἐν ὑμῖν is unusual: we would expect ὑμῶν.

44

ἦ καί: an indication of surprise or astonishment which shows the severity of Ajax's offence in trying to attack the Greek army. Translating ὡς is difficult. Jebb suggests that it 'marks the intention of Ajax (which was frustrated)'.

45

ἐξεπράξατ': = ἐξεπράξατο. As before, the ἐξ/ἐκ prefix suggests completion. Note Athena's pride in her achievements, perhaps increased by the inversion of protasis (if-clause) and apodosis (main clause) and by the use of the personal pronoun ἐγώ.

46

ποίαισι τόλμαις ταῖσδε: lit. 'with what kinds of darings these?' (i.e. 'what was this daring?'), a poetic plural with ταῖσδε pointing back to the plan revealed in line 44.

As often in stichomythia, the style is elliptical, that is to say a lot has been missed out, and the sense of the line can only be completed by reference to the lines immediately preceding: 'with what kind of daring [just referred to], with what boldness of mind <u>did he act</u>?'

τόλμαις and **θράσει** are known as modal datives. They indicate the circumstances attending an event.

47

δόλιος: as often, Greek uses an adjective where English would use an adverb.

48

παρέστη: 3rd person singular intransitive aorist of παρίστημι. Translate 'he came up close', or similar.

κἀπί: = καὶ ἐπί (by crasis).

49

καὶ δή: should here be translated as 'already'.

'πί: = ἐπί (by prodelision)

δισσαῖς στρατηγίσιν πύλαις: lit. 'the twofold gates of the generals', i.e. Agamemnon and Menelaus. This is what is known as a transferred epithet, i.e. the epithet (**δισσαῖς**) refers grammatically to the gates, but in sense to the generals: 'the gates of the two generals'.

50

The participle **μαιμῶσαν** generates a striking image of Ajax's hand 'quivering with eagerness'.

Note that **φόνου** could depend on either **μαιμῶσαν** ('restrain his hand eager for slaughter') or **ἐπέσχε** ('restrain his eager hand from slaughter'). Note also that the noun φόνος can mean both 'slaughter' and 'that which is shed as a result of slaughter', i.e. 'blood'.

51–73

The stichomythia comes to an end and Athena delivers another rhesis, in which she describes her role in diverting Ajax's slaughter away from the Greek chiefs towards the animals.

51

σφε: = αὐτόν.

ἀπείργω: = to keep X (acc.) away from Y (gen.).

The personal pronoun ἐγώ is not needed, and therefore emphatic. Athena is very proud of what she has achieved (see also line 45).

51–52

ἐγώ σφ᾽ ἀπείργω . . . / . . . τῆς ἀνηκέστου χαρᾶς: take these two clauses together – 'I held him back from his incurable joy'. Note the various different possible translations of ἀνηκέστου ('incurable', 'fatal', 'desperate') and therefore the (potential) paradox generated by the phrase ἀνηκέστου χαρᾶς.

δυσφόρους . . . /γνώμας: δυσφόρους is two termination (see line 15). Note the separation of noun and adjective (hyperbaton), which emphasizes the adjective and therefore the destructive quality of the madness sent by Athena on Ajax.

53–54

ποίμνας: = flocks of sheep.

σύμμικτά τε/λείας ἄδαστα βουκόλων φρουρήματα: lit. 'and the intermingled, undivided watches of herdsmen (consisting) of spoil', i.e. 'and the mixed beasts of spoil guarded by herdsmen, as yet undivided'.

φρούρημα (here) doesn't mean 'a guard' but 'something guarded'. ἄδαστα refers to the fact that this Trojan spoil has not yet been divided between the Greek victors.

55

ἔκειρε πολύκερων φόνον: lit. 'he was cutting down a many-horned slaughter', i.e. 'he dealt death among many horned beasts by hacking them'. πολύκερων is accusative masculine singular of the adjective πολύκερως (contracted from πολύκεραος), agreeing with φόνον. κείρω = 'cut down', so κείρω φόνον = 'cause death by cutting'.

56

κύκλῳ ῥαχίζων: 'cutting through their spines all around him (lit. 'in a circle')'. ῥαχίζω is a technical term, used of cutting through spines in sacrifice. But Ajax's actions here are far from the ritual purity associated with Greek religion: indeed, they constitute a perversion of a true sacrificial ritual. Note the repetition of the idea of hacking/cutting (ἔκειρε, ῥαχίζων) and the repeated use of the harsh consonant sound κ/χ in lines 55 and 56.

56–58

ἔσθ᾽ ὅτε . . . ὅτ᾽: essentially, ἔσθ᾽ ὅτε ('sometimes') has been repeated, but with ἔσθ᾽ omitted second time round (so translate ὅτ᾽ as 'at other times'). The phrase ἄλλοτ᾽ ἄλλον means 'now one (of the generals), now another (of the generals) . . .', suggesting the large number of other generals targeted.

57

Ἀτρείδας: 'sons of Atreus' (i.e. Agamemnon and Menelaus).

αὐτόχειρ: 'by his own hand'. Although the context is different, this perhaps foreshadows Ajax's eventual suicide.

ἔχων: 'as he gripped them' or 'as he held them fast'. The idea is that the two generals are within his power.

AS

58

ἄλλοτ᾿ ἄλλον: this is an idiom; it helps to drive home the point that at one time he thought he was killing one of the generals, but at another time he thought he was killing another one. NB: this phrase does not refer to the Atreidae (who were dealt with in line 57), but to the other Greek generals.

ἄλλον: dependent on the infinitive **κτείνειν** which needs to be supplied again.

ἐμπίτνων: a poetic form of ἐμπίπτων. The use of the present participle implies repeated attacks.

στρατηλάτης: = στρατηγός.

59–60

ἐγὼ ... /ὤτρυνον: note again how the language reflects Athena's pride in the part she has played in Ajax's downfall – each of the key words is placed first in the line, with the verb emphasized even further by enjambement. Note also the asyndeton of the two verbs coming at the start of the line in 60.

μανιάσιν νόσοις: 'with fits of madness'. This phrase could go with either the main verb **ὤτρυνον** or the participle **φοιτῶντ᾿**.

60

εἰσέβαλλον εἰς ἕρκη κακά: 'I threw him into the harmful nets'. Hunting imagery returns, this time with Athena rather than Odysseus as the hunter.

61

κἄπειτ᾿: = καὶ ἔπειτα

ἐπειδὴ ... ἐλώφησεν: 'when he had taken a rest (from this toil)'. The pluperfect tense performs a different function in English compared with Greek (in Latin/English it is used to establish relative time in the past, whereas in Greek it indicates a past action leading to a past state). Therefore, Greek tends to use the aorist when we would use a pluperfect.

62–63

τοὺς ζῶντας αὖ δεσμοῖσι συνδήσας βοῶν/ποίμνας τε πάσας εἰς δόμους κομίζεται: lit. 'having bound in chains in their turn the living ones of the oxen and all the flocks [of sheep], he brought them into the house'. Note that the genitive **βοῶν** is dependent on **τοὺς ζῶντας**. It is an example of a partitive genitive, in which the noun in the genitive expresses the whole, of which a part is being indicated (e.g. a slice of cake).

δόμους: a poetic plural. Note the use of 'house' (**δόμους**) to refer to Ajax's hut; this recurs throughout the play.

64

ὡς ἄνδρας, οὐχ ὡς εὔκερων ἄγραν ἔχων: 'as if he had men, not fair-horned prey' (the second ὡς doesn't need to be translated). εὔκερως (accusative singular –ων) is an adjective (contracted from εὐκέραος) meaning 'with beautiful horns' or just 'horned'.

ἄγραν: a technical term for 'prey' or 'plunder gained from a hunt'.

AS

65

κατ᾽ οἴκους: 'in his house', another poetic plural. Prepositions take on a wide range of meanings in poetry. **αἰκίζεται** is a true present tense – he is tormenting them right now (made clear also by **νῦν**).

συνδέτους: 'bound'. There is a tragic irony in all these references to the binding of animals (see also line 62, **δεσμοῖσι συνδήσας**, and note that these words all share a root: **δεσμοῖσι συν<u>δή</u>σας/συν<u>δέ</u>τους**). Ajax thinks that by binding these 'Greeks' he is placing himself in control of this situation. But he too is a prisoner, bound by the madness of Athena (and, even before her intervention, by the madness of his uncontrollable rage against the Greeks).

66

καὶ σοί: '(to) you too' (Athena has already seen it).
περιφανῆ: 'in full view'.

67

ὡς ... θροῇς: purpose clause. **θροῇς** = 2nd person singular present subjunctive of θροέω (= 'I cry aloud', 'proclaim').
Ἀργείοισιν: 'Argives' = 'Greeks'.

68

θαρσῶν δὲ μίμνε: 'be bold, stand fast'. Where English would use two imperatives, Greek will often use a participle followed by an imperative.

68–69

μηδὲ συμφορὰν δέχου/τὸν ἄνδρ᾽: lit. 'do not receive the man as a disaster', i.e. 'do not expect the arrival of this man to be a calamity'.

69–70

ἀποστρόφους ... ἀπείρξω: treat the adjective **ἀποστρόφους** as though it were a participle: 'by turning away the lights of his eyes, I shall prevent them ...'

70

ἀπείρξω: note that ἀπείργω can also mean I prevent X (acc.) from doing Y (inf.).
σὴν πρόσοψιν: we would expect the definite article with a possessive adjective (τὴν σὴν πρόσοψιν), but such rules as this are frequently abandoned in poetry.

71

οὗτος: Athena calls Ajax. This is quite an abrupt address.

71–72

οὗτος, σὲ τὸν τὰς αἰχμαλωτίδας χέρας/δεσμοῖς ἀπευθύνοντα προσμολεῖν καλῶ: the word order of the Greek here is potentially confusing, but in fact it makes good sense if the accusative remains at the start of your English translation: 'you there, the one who is binding back the hands of prisoners in chains, I am calling you to approach'. ἀπευθύνω usually means 'I make straight/restore/guide/

AS

direct'. Finglass notes that this is a metaphor: the notion of restoring/directing/straightening is being used to refer to punishment.

αἰχμαλωτίδας: αἰχμαλωτίς, -ίδος is a feminine noun (= 'female captive'), but is here being used as an adjective in agreement with τὰς χέρας.

72

προσμολεῖν: aorist infinitive from προσβλώσκω, which has the same meaning as προσέρχομαι ('I go to, approach').

73

Αἴαντα φωνῶ: lit. 'I address Ajax', so perhaps 'Ajax, it's you I'm speaking to'.

δωμάτων: δῶμα is a poetic word for 'house', 'household' or 'hall', again used here of the hut.

74–88

We expect Ajax to emerge at this point, but he doesn't. Suspense is therefore maintained throughout the section of stichomythia which follows, not least because of Odysseus' (very apparent) fear. This fear adds much tension and contrasts greatly with his earlier, very confident self-presentation.

Odysseus' fear can be interpreted in a number of ways. Is he a coward? Or, as Garvie suggests, is the fear 'a measure of Ajax' greatness'? After all, the Ajax whom Odysseus remembers was a fierce warrior and – after the Judgement of the Arms – his sworn enemy.

This section balances that at lines 36–50. Both consist of questions and answers, but this time Athena is for the most part the one doing the questioning.

74

μηδαμῶς σφ᾽ ἔξω κάλει: lit. 'do not call him outside in any way at all'. μηδαμῶς introduces a very strong prohibition.

σφ᾽: = σφε = αὐτόν.

75

οὐ σῖγ᾽ ἀνέξῃ μηδὲ δειλίαν ἀρῇ; : difficult because of the negatives – 'won't you hold out in silence and not acquire (an accusation of) cowardice?' The two future tenses are effectively orders, and could be translated as such ('Hold out in silence, and don't earn a reputation for cowardice!').

σῖγ᾽: = σῖγα ('silently, secretly').

ἀνέξῃ: ἀνέχομαι has a range of meanings, including 'hold out', 'hold one's temper', 'keep one's ground', etc.

ἀρῇ: 2nd person future indicative of ἄρνυμαι ('I acquire, obtain').

76

μὴ πρὸς θεῶν: note the lack of an imperative after μή ('stop it, in the name of the gods', or perhaps 'no, I beg you in the name of the gods'). This sort of minimalist style is characteristic of stichomythia.

AS

ἀρκείτω: 3rd person singular present imperative active. These do not exist in English, and are probably best translated 'let him . . .', or similar. ἀρκέω here means 'I am enough (for)', so the best translation would probably be an impersonal one: 'let it be enough for him to . . .'.

ἔνδον ἀρκείτω μένων: lit. 'let him be enough remaining within', i.e. 'be content that he stays inside'.

77

τί μὴ γένηται: 'in case what may happen?' This is probably a fearing clause (introduced by μή). The verb needs to be understood from Odysseus' concerns in the previous line: '(fearing) in case what may happen?'.

ἀνήρ: this word could mean many things – 'man', 'hero', 'man not a god', even 'mere mortal'. Each translation changes the nature of the question which Athena is asking.

78

τῷδε τἀνδρί: = τῷδε τῳ ἀνδρί.

ἐχθρός γε τῷδε τἀνδρί: 'Yes, (he was) an enemy to this man' (i.e. to me). ἐχθρός returns us to the common Greek ethical principle that one should 'help friends and harm enemies' (see line 2). Many Greek tragedians (e.g. Sophocles in the *Antigone*, Euripides in the *Medea*), far from simply accepting the principle, go on to explore the problem of what happens when a friend becomes an enemy.

Note that γε is here rendered as 'yes'.

79

οὔκουν: strongly hints at the expected response to the question – 'is it not the case that . . .?'. Unusual though Athena's statement seems to us, it is perfectly acceptable within an ancient Greek worldview (see the notes on line 2 and 78).

εἰς: here should be translated as 'at'. εἰς ἐχθροὺς γελᾶν = 'to laugh at one's enemies'.

80

Whilst Athena's invitation to laugh at an enemy is not unusual within the context, Odysseus' refusal is.

ἀρκεῖ: + dat. = 'it is enough for . . .', followed here by the infinitive construction. The verb here is being used impersonally.

Note the emphatic positioning of ἐμοὶ μέν: Odysseus is drawing a distinction between Athena's expectations of him and his own wishes (and the μέν, although not answered as expected by δέ, nevertheless suggests a contrast between himself and those who would think differently). Is he therefore rejecting the conventional moral code by his refusal to mock this ἐχθρός? Or is he in fact refusing to mock Ajax because of his fear?

δόμοις: another verse word for 'house' (again here = 'hut'), in the poetic plural (and without a definite article, even though one would be needed in prose).

81

μεμηνότ': = μεμηνότα = accusative singular masculine perfect participle of μαίνομαι ('I rage, am furious'). Again, a present state has been described by a perfect tense.

AS

82

Note that the answer to Athena's question is implied by γάǫ: 'yes, for . . .'

νιν: = αὐτόν. It is a Doric form of the pronoun.

ὄκνῳ: this noun is cognate with (related to) the verb ὀκνεῖς in line 81. Repetition of the same word (or of words derived from the same root) in adjacent lines is characteristic of stichomythic dialogue.

οὐκ ἂν ἐξέστην ὄκνῳ: 'I would not have shrunk in fear (from) . . .'. A closed condition in past time. Note that instead of a protasis, we have a participle used conditionally (φǫονοῦντα, meaning: 'if he were of sound mind'). This is fairly common in Greek.

ἐξέστην = 1st person singular (strong) aorist indicative active from ἐξίσταμαι, which (here) means 'I shrink from', 'I avoid' and is followed by an accusative (φǫονοῦντα . . . νιν).

φǫονέω here has the meaning 'to be in one's right mind', 'to be in possession of one's senses'.

83

Note the combination of οὐ(δὲ) . . . μή + aorist subjunctive (ἴδη). This expresses an emphatic negative future statement: 'he will not see . . .'. The participle (παǫόντ' = παǫόντα) has a concessive force, which underlines the paradox of the situation: 'he will not see you, *although* you will be present nearby'.

84

εἴπεǫ: see note on line 22.

85

ἐγώ: as at lines 59 and 69, Athena uses an initial position personal pronoun to highlight her power. σκοτόω = 'I darken', 'I blind'.

καὶ δεδοǫκότα: lit. 'even though seeing', i.e. 'even though they [the eyes] will be able to see'. Ajax will be able to see, because he will see Athena, but he will be blind, because he will not see Odysseus. This neat paradox both emphasizes Athena's power and helps to develop the theme of sight/blindness.

δεδοǫκότα is a perfect participle (used concessively, as is παǫόντα in line 83), accusative neuter plural, from δέǫκομαι ('I see').

86

μέντἂν: = μέντοι ἄν. Translate μέντοι (here) as 'indeed' or 'certainly'.

γένοιτο ἄν: an optative with ἄν, outside of a condition, is called a potential optative. It is often translated as 'might' or 'could'. The subject is πᾶν: 'anything could happen . . .'

θεοῦ: the masculine is used because Odysseus is making a general statement. We are reminded of the reverence shown in his earlier dialogue with Athena.

87

σίγα νυν ἑστὼς καὶ μέν' ὡς κυǫεῖς ἔχων: lit. 'so (νυν – note the lack of circumflex) be quiet, standing, and remain as you are', i.e. 'so stand in silence, and remain as you are'.

AS

κυρέω + present participle = 'I happen to be X-ing' or 'I am actually X-ing'. ἔχω + adverb = I am X (adjective). Thus ὡς κυρεῖς ἔχων is a conflation of two idioms and means 'as you actually are'.

σίγα: 2nd person singular imperative from σιγάω ('I am silent'). Not to be confused with the adverb σῖγα (line 75): the accents are different.

μέν': = μένε.

ἑστώς: nominative masculine singular of the perfect participle active of ἵστημι = 'having stood' (or 'standing'). This forms a single unit with the imperative σίγα.

88

μένοιμ' ἄν: = μένοιμι ἄν. The potential optative is here used to consent to a course which someone else desires, thus is it best translated by a future tense: 'I shall remain'.

ἤθελον δ' ἂν ἐκτὸς ὢν τυχεῖν: 'I would prefer to be outside'. This is the equivalent of the apodosis of a present closed/unfulfilled condition. τυγχάνω + present participle = 'I happen to be X-ing' (the same as κυρέω + present participle; they are both common).

ἐκτός: 'outside' – the exact meaning of this is unclear. Does he mean 'away from this place', or 'outside of (i.e. free from) danger'?

90

τί βαιὸν οὕτως ἐντρέπη τῆς συμμάχου: ἐντρέπομαι + genitive = 'show regard for/reverence for X'. βαιόν is an adverbial accusative dependent on this verb: 'why do you show so little regard for your ally?'

Athena's use of the noun τῆς συμμάχου is teasing and ironic. Whereas Odysseus had refused to mock Ajax, she is happy to do so.

91–117

Ajax comes outside his hut, presumably covered in the blood of the animals he has slaughtered and carrying the whip he used to torture them. He is still in his delusional state, and Athena playfully goads him on. Ajax cannot see Odysseus (see line 85); scholars are divided as to whether he can or cannot see Athena.

Ajax and Athena's conversation is mostly in stichomythia, but occasionally couplets are used. Finglass notes that there are similarities between this dialogue and Athena's earlier stichomythic exchange with Odysseus; these similarities only serve to highlight further the important differences between Ajax and Odysseus.

91–92

There is a certain similarity between Ajax's opening address and that of Odysseus at lines 14–17. In each instance, the tone is formal, reverent and full of praise.

Διογενὲς τέκνον: 'child of Zeus'. In fact, Athena sprang from her father's head.

92

ὡς εὖ παρέστης: 'how well you have stood by me'. Much dramatic irony, and perhaps pathos, is generated by this short statement and by the promise made in lines 92–93.

παρέστης: 2nd person singular (root) aorist active from παρίστημι. This form is used as the intransitive aorist: 'I stood beside . . .'.

92–93

σε ... /στέψω: lit. 'I shall wreathe/crown you' (he means that he will make a dedication at her statue), or perhaps, metaphorically, 'I shall honour you'.

παγχρύσοις ... /λαφύροις: note the use of the παγ- prefix by assimilation of παν- (from πᾶς, πᾶσα, πᾶν) before χ: 'with *all*-golden spoils'. Ajax is probably referring to his share of the Trojan spoils taken by the Greeks.

94

φράσον: 2nd person singular aorist imperative (φράζω).

95

ἔβαψας: βάπτω = 'I dip' or 'I dye'.

πρὸς Ἀργείων στρατῷ: 'in the army of the Argives'. As noted at line 65, the translation of prepositions in verse needs to be flexible.

96

κόμπος πάρεστι κοὐκ ἀπαρνοῦμαι τὸ μή: 'the boast is there, and I do not deny it'. μή οὐ is the usual construction after a negative verb of denial. Ajax here displays the confidence of the Homeric hero.

97

κοὐκ = καὶ οὐκ.

πρός: + dative = (here) 'against'.

ἤχμασας: 2nd person singular weak aorist active of αἰχμάζω = 'I arm X (acc.) with a spear'. χέρα is the object. The meaning is clear: lit. 'did you really arm your hand with a spear against the sons of Atreus', i.e. 'did you really turn your armed hand against the sons of Atreus?'.

98

Αἴανθ': = Αἴαντα (accusative of Αἴας). Ajax's reference to himself in the third person suggests a high self-regard. For the change from τ to θ before a rough breathing, see note on line 6.

οἵδ': = οἵδε. Nominative masculine plural form of the pronoun ὅδε, referring to the sons of Atreus.

ἀτιμάσουσ': = ἀτιμάσουσι, 3rd person plural future indicative active from ἀτιμάζω. This verb introduces the question of Ajax's honour (τιμή), an issue which lies behind almost all of the events (and indeed the backstory) of the play. It is a concern to avenge his own honour which led to Ajax's attempted slaughter of the Greeks. His humiliating failure to achieve revenge will lead him to suicide. His honour will finally be restored when he is buried at the end of the play.

The issue of Ajax's honour is not just important for plot and character development. Its resolution will have been of vital importance to an Athenian audience, as Ajax was one of the eponymous heroes of the ten new tribes under Cleisthenes' reforms (see Introduction pp. 342–3).

AS

99

τὸ σόν: supply a noun such as 'remark' or 'meaning'.

ξυνῆκ᾽: = ξυνῆκα = 1st person singular aorist indicative active of ξυνίημι = (here) 'I understand'. This is an example of what is known as the instantaneous aorist. It is used in drama to express a state of mind occurring to a speaker in the moment just passed.

100

θανόντες: note again the repetition of the same basic word (τεθνᾶσιν), but in a different form (polyptoton), common in stichomythic exchanges (see line 82).

τἄμ᾽ ... ὅπλα = τὰ ἐμὰ ὅπλα. Refers to the arms of Achilles, which he unquestioningly believes to be his by right.

ἀφαιρείσθων: 'let them take away'-3rd person plural present imperative middle of ἀφαιρέω.

101

εἶεν, τί: this question has no verb, something which could be rendered in English too: 'very well; what, then, of the son of Laertes?'

γὰρ δή: forms a single unit – 'then'.

102

ποῦ σοι τύχης ἕστηκεν: lit. 'where of fortune does he stand as far as you're concerned?', i.e. 'what situation is he in as far are you're concerned?'. τύχης is a partitive genitive with ποῦ. σοι is a dative of interest, or 'ethic dative' ('as far as you are concerned/with regard to you').

103

The use of ἦ perhaps suggests Ajax's indignation in being asked about Odysseus. Note that there is a difference between the particle ἦ with a circumflex accent (an adverb meaning 'in truth', or used to introduce a question) and the conjunction ἤ(= 'or') in line 102.

τοὐπίτριπτον κίναδος: = τὸ ἐπίτριπτον κίναδος. Both ἐπίτριπτος ('accursed') and τὸ κίναδος ('fox') are words frequently used in comedy. The description suggests Odysseus' intelligence and cunning, something highlighted earlier by Athena (see the simile in lines 7–8) and well-known to readers of the *Odyssey*. However, Ajax's comment is clearly supposed to be derogatory.

A verb needs to be supplied with ὅπου to create an indirect question: 'where he is'. Both this question word and the phrase τοὐπίτριπτον κίναδος are objects of the verb: 'did you ask me where that accursed fox is?' (lit. 'did you ask me of the accursed fox, where he is?')

104

ἔγωγ᾽: = ἔγωγε, an answer to the question: 'yes indeed, I did'. Athena didn't in fact ask where Odysseus was, but what state he was in. However, it seems that the distinction is not important for her purpose (which is to tease Ajax in the presence of Odysseus).

ἐνστάτην: 'one who stands in the way', i.e. an enemy.

AS

105

ὦ δέσποινα: Odysseus also used this word of Athena (line 38).

106

See Introduction (p. 357) for a note on the wordplay here.

οὔ τί πω: lit. 'not at all yet', i.e. 'not yet'. Ignore the accent on τί (read τι): it does not make it an interrogative in this instance; τί is effectively carrying the accent because it is followed by another enclitic (πω), which has thrown its own accent back onto it.

NB: an enclitic is a word pronounced with so little emphasis that it is shortened and forms part of the preceding word. An enclitic cannot stand on its own: it has to join another word.

θέλω: poetic for ἐθέλω.

107

πρὶν ἄν: + subjunctive = 'until'. This is an example of the indefinite construction, the normal way in Greek of expressing a future temporal clause.

πλέον: an adverb (= 'more'); an alternative is to read πλέον as the object of κερδάνης and agreeing with τί. Either way, the translation of τί κερδάνης πλέον would be 'gain what further advantage?'.

108

πρὶν ἄν δεθεὶς πρὸς κίον᾽ ἑρκείου στέγης – 'not until, having been bound to a pillar of my dwelling . . .'. Ajax doesn't get a chance to finish his statement, as Athena interrupts him.

κίον᾽: = κίονα.

ἑρκείου: ἑρκείος = 'of the courtyard' (τὸ ἕρκος = the front courtyard of a house). It is a two-termination adjective, and agrees with στέγης.

στέγης: can mean 'roof' or 'dwelling'. ἑρκείου στέγης is probably best translated as 'of my dwelling' rather than 'of my courtyard roof', which makes no sense in the context of Ajax's hut.

109

ἐργάσῃ: 2nd person singular future indicative of ἐργάζομαι. This verb takes a double accusative: 'I do X (acc.) to Y (acc.)'.

110

In this line, Ajax continues his utterance in line 108.

μάστιγι πρῶτον νῶτα φοινιχθείς: νῶτα is an accusative of respect, very common in Greek with reference to parts of the body. Lit: 'having first been reddened with respect to his back by the whip', i.e. 'his back having first been reddened by the whip'.

111

μὴ . . . αἰκίσῃ: Greek uses μή + 2nd person aorist subjunctive for a negative 2nd person command (prohibition), if it is a one-off. Otherwise, μή + present imperative would be used.

AS

δῆτα: simply strengthens the command.

ὧδέ: 'thus', strengthened by the particle γε. Athena is teasing both Ajax and Odysseus (but, of course, in different ways): rather than saying 'don't torture him', her statement implies 'don't torture him *in the particularly gruelling way you have just described*'!

112–113

Ajax refuses to do what Athena has asked, indicative of his arrogance and overconfidence (which are key aspects of the characterization of a Sophoclean tragic hero). The verb choice of ἐφίεμαι ('I order, command') is particularly significant, as perhaps is the use of ἐγώ, which mirrors Athena's own manner of speaking. Note that ἐφίεμαι here takes a direct object, even though it usually takes the dative.

112

τἄλλ': = τὰ ἄλλα. Accusative of respect: 'regarding other things, Athena, I command/ permit you to rejoice . . .'. 'Rejoice' (χαίρειν) here seems to mean 'to have your own way'.

114

ἐπειδὴ τέρψις ἥδε σοι τὸ δρᾶν: the demonstrative pronoun τόδε (which is the subject) has as usual been attracted into the gender of τέρψις (the complement) to give ἥδε. The verbal noun (gerund) τὸ δρᾶν is epexegetic (explanatory) of τέρψις. Finally, we need to supply the verb 'to be': 'since this is your pleasure, namely to do it . . .'.

115

χρῶ ... φείδου: 2nd person singular present imperatives from middle verbs (χράομαι + dative = I use, φείδομαι + genitive = I spare). The asyndeton perhaps adds weight and a sense of encouragement or even urgency.

φείδου μηδὲν ὧνπερ ἐννοεῖς: = φείδου μηδὲν ἐκείνων ἃ ἐννοεῖς. The relative pronoun has been attracted into the case of the antecedent (to create ὧνπερ), and the antecedent (ἐκείνων) has then disappeared. This is fairly common in relative clauses in verse and prose.

116

χωρῶ: wordplay with χρῶ in the line above (but note that they are not from the same root, and mean different things: χωρέω = I go).

116–117

Ajax's commanding tone is even more blatant in these lines than in 112–113. In addition, he returns to the deluded belief that Athena is his ally (see lines 90 and 92). This not only generates much dramatic irony, but also further develops the theme of 'helping *friends*, harming enemies'.

τοιάνδ': = τοιάνδε ('such'), agreeing with the noun σύμμαχον which is here feminine (it is what is known as common gender, i.e. it can be either masculine or feminine). Note that τοιάνδε is here accusative whereas we would have expected a dative (following on from **σοί**): this is because the idea of the subject of an infinitive being accusative is so dominant, the dative has been changed.

This whole phrase greatly increases the irony of the situation: Athena will indeed continue to be 'such an ally', i.e. a hostile one.

παρεστάναι: 'to stand beside' – perfect (as ever, representing a present state) infinitive active of παρίστημι.

118

Ajax leaves immediately after delivering his lines at 116–117. The prologue will therefore end as it began, with Athena and Odysseus in conversation.

ὁρᾷς … ὅση: again, a verb needs to be supplied for this indirect question. This line is a good example of how the flexibility of Greek word order can be used to great rhetorical effect. Each word builds up to the climax of **ὅση**: 'do you see, Odysseus, the strength of the gods, how great it is?'.

119

τούτου … τἀνδρός: = τούτου τοῦ ἀνδρός. Genitive of comparison after **προνούστερος** and **ἀμείνων**.

προνούστερος: comparative form of πρόνους, an adjective meaning 'of good mind', 'sensible', 'prudent'.

σοι: ethic dative – perhaps 'as far as you're concerned', or 'I ask you'.

120

δρᾶν ἀμείνων: 'better at doing'. The infinitive defines the meaning of the adjective (it is epexegetic).

τὰ καίρια: the adjective καίριος = 'timely', therefore **τὰ καίρια** = 'the timely things', i.e. 'what is right/appropriate'.

Athena is not so much praising Ajax in these two lines, as lamenting his former greatness in order to add weight to the moral lesson she is about to deliver to her protégé.

τίς ἄν/ … ηὑρέθη: 'who could have been found'.

121

οὐδέν`: = οὐδένα

ἐποικτίρω: Odysseus' reaction here has been interpreted in many ways (none of which are – any longer – motivated by fear of Ajax). Is he (as suggested at line 80) rejecting the ethical principle that one should harm enemies? This seems unlikely, given the fact that he describes Ajax as an **ἐχθρός** at line 78 and a **δυσμενῆ** at 122. Most convincing is the suggestion that Odysseus subscribes fully to the principle, yet here shows some humanity and an ability to understand that all great men – including he himself – could fall if they were to incur the wrath of the gods. This notion would find support in the *Odyssey* where, at 22.411ff, Odysseus rebukes his mother Eurycleia for gloating over the dead suitors. Whatever its significance, the pity shown by Odysseus here is striking.

νιν: = αὐτόν (see line 82).

AS

122

δύστηνον ... δυσμενῆ: As far as Odysseus is concerned, Ajax is both 'wretched' (an object of pity) and also 'an enemy'. The fact that the line is framed by these two compound adjectives, each of which begins with the prefix δυσ-, perhaps highlights the oddity of showing pity for an enemy. This is stressed further by the use of ἔμπας ('all the same'), and **καίπερ** + participle ('although ...').

123

ὁθούνεκ' = ὅτου ἕνεκα = 'because'.

ἄτη συγκατέζευκται κακῇ: 'he has been yoked to an evil ruin', a striking metaphor for Ajax's mental imprisonment.

συγκαταζεύγνυμι elsewhere means 'yoke together in marriage'. Its meaning here is of course much darker, and the two prefixes in this double compound (συγ=συν-, and κατα-), strengthen the underlying tones of subordination and inescapability (lit. he has been yoked 'down' 'together'). **ἄτη** ('ruin', 'delusion') is the technical term for the madness visited upon Ajax by Athena.

124

τοὐμόν = τὸ ἐμόν.

τὸ τούτου ... τοὐμόν: a noun needs to be supplied with the neuter article: 'his lot ... my lot'. Both are direct objects of **σκοπῶν**, with **οὐδέν** functioning as a strengthened form of the negative. A literal translation would therefore be: 'considering not at all this man's lot rather than my own'. Finglass has 'as I consider not so much his condition but my own'.

As all the major commentators note, this sentiment seems selfish to us, but it is a common explanation for compassion in Greek literature. In book 24 of the *Iliad*, when the enemies Priam and Achilles share a moment of grief, Priam weeps for his son Hector and Achilles weeps because Priam reminds him of his own father. Each man is in fact each weeping for his own loss, not for the loss of the other.

125–126

A 'gnomic' statement, common in tragedy (but more often delivered by the chorus), which expresses wisdom or morality which is universally applicable. Odysseus has been moved to such philosophical speculation by Ajax's fall from greatness.

The word order is confusing, and could be reordered thus for the purposes of translation:

ὁρῶ γὰρ ἡμᾶς ὅσοιπερ ζῶμεν ὄντας οὐδὲν ἄλλο πλὴν εἴδωλ᾽ ἢ κούφην σκιάν.

ἡμᾶς ... / ... ὅσοιπερ ζῶμεν: lit. 'we, as many as are alive', i.e. 'all we who live'.

εἴδωλ': = εἴδωλα.

κούφην σκιάν: could be translated as a plural.

127–133

Athena delivers the moral of the story: *hubris* (excessive pride, arrogance and self-confidence) has led to Ajax's downfall, and Odysseus should guard against it lest he should suffer the same fate.

127–128

ὑπέρκοπον/μηδέν ποτ᾽ εἴπῃς αὐτὸς εἰς θεοὺς ἔπος: 'do not yourself ever speak an arrogant word against the gods' (lit 'speak no arrogant word . . .'). μηδὲν . . . εἴπῃς is an extension of μή + aorist subjunctive for a prohibition (see line 83). αὐτός indicates that she is making an explicit comparison between Odysseus and Ajax.

129

ἄρῃ: 2nd person singular aorist subjunctive middle (with μηδ᾽) from αἴρω = (here) 'I take on, assume'.

μηδ᾽ . . . μηδέν᾽: μηδ᾽ = μηδέ and μηδέν᾽ = μηδένα. We have here a double negative, but as the first is a simple negative, they do not cancel each other out. Instead, the second negative strengthens the first: 'do not take on *any* pride *at all*'. ὄγκον literally means 'bulk' or 'mass' (therefore comes to mean 'pride' or 'dignity').

τινος: genitive of comparison with πλέον.

130

βρίθεις: 2nd person singular present indicative active of βρίθω = (lit.) 'I am heavy', (metaphorically) 'I am powerful' or 'I outweigh'.

πλέον . . . /βρίθεις: 'if you more powerful', 'if you are stronger/mightier'. The datives χειρί and (μακροῦ πλούτου) βάθει define the two potential spheres of might (physical strength/depth of great wealth).

131–132

Lines 131–132 highlight two themes of key importance: first, the idea of a single day (the events of a Greek tragedy were generally supposed to take place within 24 hours); second, the idea of fickleness of fortune (an idea which recurs elsewhere in Greek literature, e.g. Herodotus).

131

κἀνάγει: = καὶ ἀνάγει.

132

τἀνθρώπεια: = τὰ ἀνθρώπεια = 'things to do with humans' (i.e. 'human affairs').

132–133

Note the chiastic word order, which draws out the contrast between the gods' treatment of each group: τοὺς δὲ σώφρονας θεοὶ φιλοῦσι καὶ στυγοῦσι τοὺς κακούς.

τοὺς . . . σώφρονας: = 'those who are σώφρων', i.e. of sound mind/reasonable/ moderate'. Athena's final piece of advice to Odysseus is to act with *sophrosyne*, moderation, in order to avoid the wrath of the gods. The advice to avoid excess (of anything, including wealth, emotion, etc.) is a piece of traditional Greek wisdom. It appears in much Greek literature of the archaic and classical periods, not least tragedy, and the inscription μηδὲν ἄγαν ('(do) nothing in excess') was carved into the pronaos of the famous temple at Delphi.

τοὺς κακούς: lit. 'those who are wicked', a contrast with τοὺς . . . σώφρονας.

AS

134–283: *Ajax and Odysseus exit, and the chorus of sailors from Salamis (Ajax's companions at Troy) enter via the eisodoi and sing their parodos (choral entry song). They clearly hold Ajax in high regard. They are loyal towards him and state that they are unsure as to whether or not to believe the rumour about his attack on the cattle, due not least to Odysseus' involvement in the spreading of it. Furthermore, they state that if Ajax is indeed responsible, a god must have sent him mad. They express a desire for him to come out of his hut in order to settle the affair.*

Ajax does not come out. Instead, Tecmessa does. She is Ajax's concubine; she is a prisoner of war and therefore also his slave. She engages in a dialogue with the chorus (summarized below). Initially, both parties chant to musical accompaniment, a technique used to heighten the emotion, but from line 221 Tecmessa chants while the chorus sings. This sort of lyrical song of lamentation is called a kommos.

Tecmessa states that Ajax is sick and delusional, confirms that he was responsible for the attack on the animals, and describes in graphic detail his treatment of some of them. She reveals that he is now coming out of his madness, and suggests that his state of mind will therefore be worse. The chorus leader asks how Ajax's troubles began, leading to Tecmessa's explanation (lines 284–330). This takes the form of a messenger speech, that is to say a speech which reports off-stage events, often things which have taken place inside the skene or in another location. This vivid description of an off-stage action or conversation is one of many ways in which tragedians break out of the temporal and geographical limitations of the genre in order to maintain the interest of their audience.

284

μαθήσῃ: 2nd person singular future tense. Even though the whole chorus remains in the orchestra after the parodos, the chorus leader has stepped forward as a representative (this is common in tragedy).

τοὔργον: = τὸ ἔργον.

ὡς κοινωνὸς ὤν: she does not, of course, mean that the chorus leader was in any way an accomplice in Ajax's deed. She is making a more general statement about the bond between Ajax and his men.

285

ἄκρας νυκτός: ἄκρος = 'at the furthest point of/at the peak of', therefore probably 'at dead of night' (as advocated by Jebb and Stanford). Finglass disagrees and says it means 'at the beginning of the night', i.e. after evening is over (and the evening lamps are out).

ἡνίχ': = ἡνίχα = 'at the time when'.

286

ᾖθον: a rare intransitive use of αἴθω = (here) 'I burn, blaze'.

ἄμφηκες: this epithet adds weight to a highly significant object.

287

ἐμαίετ': = ἐμαίετο. 3rd person singular imperfect of μαίομαι = I seek to do X [+ infinitive].

ἐξόδους ... κενάς: poetic plural – 'an empty expedition'.

ἕρπειν: usually 'to move slowly', but here it just means 'to go'. Treat ἐξόδους as an internal accusative (see line 42; in fact it is very nearly a cognate accusative, as the meaning of the accusative is very close to that of the verb), so the whole phrase = 'to go on an empty expedition'.

288

'πιπλήσσω: = ἐπιπλήσσω (by prodelision) – 'I strike' or 'I rebuke'. Note the sense of immediacy evoked by the historic presents: 'πιπλήσσω καὶ λέγω.

τί χρῆμα δρᾷς: lit. 'what thing are you doing?', i.e. 'what are you doing?'. Scholars have suggested that this expression is colloquial. Tecmessa speaks to Ajax in a familiar and confident manner (implied also by (ἐ)πιπλήσσω). She is not afraid to tell him off and to question his actions.

289–291

These lines are full of indications that Ajax is embarking on a mission which has not been sanctioned by his superiors, e.g. the adjective ἄκλητος; the parallel clauses: οὔθ᾽ ὑπ᾽ ἀγγέλων κληθείς and οὔτε τοῦ κλύων/σάλπιγγος; and ἀλλὰ νῦν γε πᾶς εὕδει στρατός, with its emphatic use of πᾶς and νῦν.

The verb ἀφορμᾷς ('you start [on]') is intransitive, and is here followed by an internal accusative (τήνδ᾽ ... πεῖραν).

τοῦ = a poetic/abbreviated form of τινός (indefinite pronoun).

κλύων: here followed by a genitive of the thing heard (which is parallel to the genitive of person heard as you hear noise *from* the trumpet).

292

βαί᾽: = βαιά – accusative neuter plural of βαιός ('little, small') = 'a few things'.

ἀεὶ δ᾽ ὑμνούμενα: ὑμνέω = 'sing, recite, repeat', so this phrase (referring back to βαία) = 'always repeated/recited'.

293

γύναι, γυναιξί: the polyptoton perhaps emphasizes Tecmessa's subordinate status.

κόσμον ... φέρει: 'is an adornment for', i.e. 'befits'.

This is another example of a gnomic statement (see lines 125–6), that is to say, a universal truth. Although the statement appears harsh, it was a commonly-held view in archaic and classical Greece. Pericles says something similar in his Funeral Oration ('A woman's reputation is highest when men say little about her, whether it be good or evil'); moreover, Hector is very dismissive of Andromache when she tries to offer military advice in *Iliad* book 6.

294

μαθοῦσ᾽: = μαθοῦσα.

ἔληξ᾽: = ἔληξα, 1st sg. aorist of λήγω = 'I leave off, cease' (here, 'cease speaking'). Despite her bold start, Tecmessa knows that further argument would be futile. Is this indicative of her subordinate status as a slave, or as a woman? Or does it tell us something about her intimate knowledge of his emotional temperament?

ἐσσύθη: σέυομαι = 'I run, rush, depart'.

AS

295

τὰς ἐκεῖ ... πάθας: lit. 'his sufferings there', so 'what he suffered there'. **ἐκεῖ** refers to outside the hut, i.e. on his expedition.

οὐκ ἔχω λέγειν: see note on line 33.

296

ἐσῆλθε: = εἰσῆλθε.

297

κύνας βοτῆρας: = 'herdsmen's dogs'. The noun βοτήρ (= 'herdsman') is effectively being used adjectivally (see note on αἰχμαλωτίδας, line 71).

εὔερόν τ᾽ ἄγραν: 'and the fleecy prey'.

298

The tricolon of animals (296–297) is balanced by a tricolon of ways in which they are treated (298–300). Tecmessa uses very violent verbs, all of which create a vivid image of the method of slaughter and/or of torture employed.

ηὐχένιζε: αὐχενίζω = 'I cut the throat (αὐχήν) of ...'

299

ἄνω τρέπων: 'turning them upwards'; we would say 'turning them on their backs'.

ἔσφαζε: σφάζω can mean 'slaughter' or more specifically 'cut the throat' (as in the sacrifice of an animal).

κἀρράχιζε: = καὶ ἐρράχιζε, the same verb used by Athena in line 56.

300

ᾐκίζεθ᾽: = ᾐκίζετο (for the consequences of elision here, see note on line 6). αἰκίζομαι ('I maltreat, torture') was also used by Athena (line 111).

ὥστε: here = ὡς/ὥσπερ, introducing a comparison ('as if').

ἐν ποίμναις πίτνων: πίτνων is poetic for πίπτων; lit. 'falling on the flocks', i.e. 'in his attack on the flocks'.

301–304

Tecmessa describes what she saw when Ajax conversed with Athena. There is much dramatic irony when she describes Athena as σκιᾷ τινι, 'some shadow (or other)'.

302

λόγους ἀνέσπα: ἀνασπάω λόγους is a metaphor (often found in comedy) meaning 'I draw forth/drag out/spout out words'. The exact meaning is not clear: was Ajax speaking in a long, drawn-out manner? Was he using an elevated tone? Was his delivery chaotic? What is clear is that he was speaking in an unusual and disturbed way.

Ἀτρειδῶν κάτα: 'against the sons of Atreus'.

303

ἀμφ᾽ Ὀδυσσεῖ: 'about Odysseus', a mostly poetic use of this preposition.

συντιθείς: present participle = (lit.) 'combining'. This probably means that the laughter accompanies/is combined with his criticisms of the Atreidae and Odysseus.

303–304

συντιθεὶς γέλων πολύν, /ὅσην κατ᾽ αὐτῶν ὕβριν ἐκτείσαιτ᾽ ἰών: 'adding much laughter (at) how much harm he had inflicted on them on his expedition' (ἰών lit. = 'going'). The meanings of ὕβρις – a recurring theme of this genre – are many and varied: 'violence', 'outrage', 'insolence'.

304

ἐκτείσαιτ᾽: ἐκτείσαιτο (3rd person singular aorist optative middle). This verb is optative because of the indirect question in historic sequence, introduced by ὅσην and loosely following λόγους ἀνέσπα and συντιθείς. ἐκτίνω = (in the middle) 'I take revenge'.

305

κἄπειτ᾽: = καὶ ἔπειτα.
ἐς: = εἰς

306

ἔμφρων μόλις πως ξὺν χρόνῳ καθίσταται: a difficult line – 'in time [ξὺν χρόνῳ] with some difficulty [μόλις πως] he comes into (the state of) [καθίσταται] the right frame of mind [ἔμφρων]', i.e. 'in time, with some difficulty, he became sane'. πως is being used to modify the adverb μόλις.

307

ὡς: + indicative = 'when'.
ἄτης: a very important thematic word. It is the technical term for the 'madness' or 'ruin' inflicted on a tragic figure as a consequence of something he has done. Here it refers to the dead animals all around him; translate as 'destruction'.
διοπτεύει: the verb suggests careful or accurate watching.
στέγος: 'roof', therefore – by extension – 'hut'.

308

'Θώϋξεν: = ἐθώϋξεν (by prodelision) = 'he made a cry'. The two dots above the upsilon indicate that the second vowel in this pair has its own independent sound, i.e. ωυ is not a diphthong. Such a sign is called a diaeresis.
ἐρειφθείς: ἐρείπω in the passive can mean 'I fall'.

308–309

ἐν δ᾽ ἐρειπίοις/νεκρῶν: ἐρείπιον = 'a wreckage', therefore 'in a wreckage of corpses' (ἐρειπίοις = plural for singular).
Note that ἐρειφθείς and ἐρειπίοις are from the same basic root (the forms are cognate; another term for this device is *figura etymologica*). It is difficult to bring this out in an English translation. Jebb goes for 'he fell down, a wreck amid the wrecks of the slaughtered sheep', a translation which effectively conveys the idea that Ajax has been reduced to the same state as the animals he has killed.

AS

309

ἀρνείου φόνου: lit. 'of slaughter to do with the sheep', i.e. 'of slaughtered sheep'. The genitive is dependent on νεκρῶν.

310

ἀπρίξ: = 'tightly'. This adverb suggests the intensity of Ajax's grip, a notion which is reinforced by the verb prefix συν and by the idea of gripping ὄνυξι ('with the nails' – according to many commentators, this suggests that the hair is being torn).

ὄνυξι ... χερί: lit. 'with his nails ... with his hand', i.e. he gripped his hair 'in his hands, with his nails'. χερί is singular for plural (the opposite of poetic plural).

Ajax's actions here and in line 307–308 (banging his head, pulling out hair, etc.) constitute – within an ancient Greek context – the standard actions of someone in mourning. Perhaps he is mourning his loss of honour.

311

τὸν ... πλεῖστον ... χρόνον: 'for a very long time'.

ἧστο: 3rd person singular pluperfect (from ἧμαι = 'I sit'), but with an imperfect meaning – 'he was sitting'.

312

ἐμοὶ τὰ δείν᾽ ἐπηπείλησ᾽ ἔπη: (δείν᾽ = δείνα, ἐπηπείλησ᾽ = ἐπηπείλησε), lit. 'he threatened terrible words to me', i.e. 'he threatened me with those terrible words'. We are not told the content of τὰ δείνα ἔπη (a phrase which effectively constitutes the apodosis which is lacking from the condition in the next line), but the vagueness of the threat perhaps makes it worse: our imaginations are compelled to fill in the gap.

313

εἰ μὴ φανοίην: 'if I didn't tell (him) . . .', lit. 'if I didn't reveal . . .'.

φανοίην: future optative of φαίνω. Its future indicative active is φανέω, therefore it has formed its future optative in the same way as the present optative of a contracted verb of the φιλέω type. A *future* optative is needed because this is reporting what in direct speech would have been a future indicative ('if you will not tell me . . .') in a future open conditional expressing a threat. An *optative* is used because this reported condition is in historic sequence.

συντυχόν: an aorist participle (from συντυγχάνω) agreeing with τὸ ... πάθος – lit. 'the whole befallen happening', i.e. 'the whole disaster which had occurred'.

314

Some scholars have deleted this line, on the grounds that it adds nothing to what has been said in the preceding lines. Moreover, it involves Ajax asking something which presents him in a much weaker light than the threats of the preceding lines.

κἀνήρετ᾽: = καὶ ἀνήρετο, 3rd person singular aorist of ἀνέρομαι (= 'I enquire, question').

ἐν τῷ πράγματος ... ποτέ: lit. 'in what of a situation' (partitive genitive), i.e. 'in what sort of situation'. ποτέ often emphasizes an interrogative (here the interrogative is τῷ = τίνι).

AS

κυϱοῖ: 3rd person singular present optative active of κυϱέω = 'I happen (to be)'. The optative can be used as an alternative to the indicative in indirect questions (historic sequence only).

315

τοὐξειϱγασμένον: τὸ ἐξειϱγασμένον = 'the thing having been accomplished'.

ἐξειϱγασμένον = perfect participle, neuter accusative singular, of ἐξεϱγάζομαι = I bring *to completion* (suggested by the prefix – see line 7). Again, the perfect implies a present state which can't be undone.

315–316

It is best to translate **τοὐξειϱγασμένον … πᾶν** as the object of the main verb **ἔλεξα**: 'I told him everything which had been done'.

316

ὅσονπεϱ: 'as far as', 'as much as'. The relative clause qualifies the extent of Tecmessa's knowledge.

ἐξηπιστάμην: ἐξεπίσταμαι: 'I know thoroughly' (note the intensifying prefix).

317

ἐξῴμωξεν: 3rd person singular aorist active indicative from ἐξοιμώζω = 'I say οἴμοι intensely', i.e. 'I wail aloud'. This is the third use of a compound with the prefix ἐξ in as many lines. Garvie notes that it is characteristic of a Sophoclean emotional climax.

οἰμωγάς: a cognate accusative. This is like an internal accusative, except that the noun and the verb come from the same root ('he cried cries'). This intensifies the image of lamentation.

318–322

These lines form a short digression in which Tecmessa recalls Ajax's past behaviour and contrasts it with his present lamentations.

319

πϱός: + genitive. Translate as 'in the nature of', 'characteristic of'.

βαϱύψυχου: a very rare adjective meaning 'heavy of soul', 'spiritless'. **βαϱυψύχου** and **κακοῦ** agree with **ἀνδϱός** in the next line.

320

ποτ': = ποτέ, intensifying ἀεί.

ἐξηγεῖτ': = ἐξηγεῖτο, 3rd person singular imperfect indicative of ἐξηγέομαι = (here) 'explain, teach'.

The commentators have noted that there are three ways in which **ἔχειν** can be fitted into a translation:

AS

- Treat ἔχειν (+ prepositional phrase) as an intransitive verb, equivalent in meaning to εἶναι (Jebb and Garvie): 'for he always used to teach that such cries *were* characteristic of a cowardly and dejected man'.

- Take γόους/τοιούσδ᾽ ('such cries') as the object of ἔχειν (and supply εἶναι as required later on): 'for he always used to teach that *to have* [i.e. 'indulge in'] such cries (was) characteristic of a cowardly and dejected man'.

- Treat ἔχειν as epexegetic (explanatory): 'for he always used to teach that such cries were characteristic of a cowardly and dejected man *to have*'.

321

ἀψόφητος: + genitive = 'without the sound of'.

322

ὑπεστέναζε: 'he would utter low moans'. The idea of 'low' moans, or groaning 'deeply', suggested by the prefix ὑπο, contrasts Ajax with the ὀξέων κωκυμάτων ('shrill cries') of others. His moans used to have a sense of dignity, in Tecmessa's eyes at least.

ταῦρος ὣς βρυχώμενος: 'like a bellowing bull' (don't be caught out by the delayed position of ὥς). The use of a simile comparing a hero to an animal is very reminiscent of Homeric epic. The specific comparison with a bull, coming as it does from a devoted concubine, may be intended to suggest masculinity.

323

νῦν δ᾽: returns us to the present.

324

ἄσιτος . . . ἄποτος: 'without food . . . without drink' – although they are intended primarily to show Ajax's disturbed mental state (and perhaps even suggest a death wish), the use of two alpha-privative adjectives also helps to generate an image of Ajax's isolation. This is perhaps strengthened by ἥσυχος in the next line.

ἀνήρ: see line 9.

324–325

ἐν μέσοις βοτοῖς/σιδηροκμῆσιν: 'in the middle of beasts slain by the sword'.

ἥσυχος: this adjective could mean 'quiet' (here, as often with adjectives in Greek, translated as an adverb, 'quietly'), or could mean 'at rest' (see below on 327).

326

καὶ δῆλός ἐστιν ὥς τι δρασείων κακόν: lit. 'and he is clear as intending some evil', i.e. 'and it is clear that he intends (to carry out) some evil deed' (δρασείω = 'I have a mind to do, intend').

τι . . . κακόν: Tecmessa is vague, which adds to the tension and fear of the chorus and audience, although the whole tone of the passage would suggest that 'some form of harm to himself' is what is meant.

327

Some editors have deleted this line, because it contradicts the assertion in 325 that Ajax is sitting *quietly*. Garvie disagrees: 'that Ajax is sitting quietly need not mean that he is making no sound'. Or indeed, ἥσυχος in 325 could simply mean that Ajax is sitting *at rest* (to contrast with his previous state).

Unaccented πως often means 'in some way' but here it can be translated 'I suppose'.

κὠδύρεται: = καὶ ὀδύρεται (by crasis).

328

ὦ φίλοι: this is the second time that Tecmessa has addressed the chorus in this way (see line 315). On both occasions, she is trying to gain the chorus' sympathy and to keep them on side. Here, she is also desperately appealing to them to come in to help.

ἐστάλην: 1st person singular aorist passive from στέλλω (which means 'I send' in the active, and can mean 'I set out' or 'I come out' in the middle/passive).

τούτων . . . οὕνεκ': 'for these reasons', i.e. the ones implied by her next statement.

329

ἀρήξατ': = ἀρήξατε (2nd person plural aorist imperative from ἀρήγω = 'I help').

ἀρήξατ' εἰσελθόντες: 'come in, help' (see line 68). Of course, theatrical conventions dictate that the chorus should not leave the orchestra after their initial entry; and even if some playwrights do bend *that* particular 'rule' (as Sophocles will do at line 814), there is no known play in which a chorus enters the *skene*. Sophocles neatly gets round this issue in the simplest and most dramatically effective way possible: he reveals the inside of the *skene* to the chorus (and audience).

εἰ δύνασθέ τι: 'if you have any power'. τι is an adverbial (i.e. internal) accusative.

330

φίλων: a very important thematic motif (see Introduction pp. 353, 355 and 359).

οἱ τοιοίδε: lit. 'those such as this', therefore 'men of his kind'.

332

διαπεφοιβάσθαι: perfect infinitive passive of διαφοιβάζω ('I drive mad').

333–334

ἰώ μοί μοι: a highly emotive off-stage cry (note that this utterance interrupts the iambic trimeters), which effectively builds up tension as we wait to see the 'sane' Ajax.

334

τάχ': τάχα = soon, quickly.

ἔοικε: = 'it seems'

μᾶλλον: supply a verb – '(he will be) worse', or similar.

334–335

ἢ οὐκ ἠκούσατε/ Αἴαντος οἵαν τήνδε θωΰσσει βοήν: this is a little tricky – 'or did you not hear from Ajax what sort of cry this was he uttered?', i.e. 'didn't you hear what sort of cry Ajax shouted?'. ἢ οὐκ is scanned as one long syllable, i.e. two originally separate vowel sounds are pronounced and scanned as one. This is called synizesis and generally occurs in order to preserve the metrical pattern.

335

θωΰσσει: on the diaresis, see line 308 (and note the use of the same verb: θωΰσσω = 'I make a noise').

337

τοῖς πάλαι/νοσήμασιν ξυνοῦσι λυπεῖσθαι: 'to be grieving for the ills/sickness which recently afflicted him'. As well as 'long ago', πάλαι can mean 'recently (in the past)'. σύνειμι = 'I am with, I am joined with'.

παρών: lit. 'being present'. Other translators have offered 'as he sits there' or 'in their midst' (i.e. in the midst of the sickness).

339

ἰὼ παῖ παῖ: previously, Ajax mourned his own state (lines 333, 336). Now he mourns the fate of a son whose father is such a disgrace.

340

ὤμοι τάλαιν᾽: (τάλαιν᾽ = τάλαινα) 'alas, wretched woman' – a very common tragic utterance.

340

ἀμφὶ σοί: 'concerning you' (see also line 303).

341

μενοινᾷ: μενοινάω = 'I desire eagerly'.

The use of short questions aimed in turn at Ajax and Eurysaces suggests a sense of urgency.

342

ἦ: the interrogative particle (see 103).

εἰσαεί: (with τὸν ... χρόνον) = 'forever'.

343

λεηλατήσει: 3rd sg. future of λεηλατέω = 'I plunder, drive away booty' (especially cattle).

ἀπόλλυμαι: 'I die, perish, am lost' (middle of ἀπόλλυμι).

344

ἀνοίγετε: 2nd pl. imperative (from ἀνοίγω) = 'open (the doors)!'. The chorus is presumably addressing Tecmessa and her attendants, hence the plural.

345

τάχ᾽: τάχα here = 'perhaps'.

κἀπ' ἐμοί = καὶ ἐπὶ ἐμοί = 'even with respect to me', or perhaps 'towards me too', going with αἰδῶ.

ἄν τιν' αἰδῶ ... λάβοι: 'he might feel some shame'. Sight of the chorus might return Ajax to normality (i.e. cause him to feel that sense of shame which he ought to feel as a result of his recent actions, but from which he is currently being shielded by his madness).

346

ἰδού, διοίγω: 'behold, I am opening it!'. This indicates the appearance of the *ekkyklema* (see Introduction pp. 348–9).

347

καὐτός = καὶ αὐτός.

ὡς ἔχων κυρεῖ: 'how he fares' (see on line 87).

AS

348–429: The ekkyklema is wheeled out through the door of the skene to reveal Ajax sitting with the animals he has killed. Oliver Taplin has suggested that Ajax remains seated, perhaps until after our next section (i.e. until line 595, when the ekkyklema is removed), as if he were to leave the ekkyklema, that would equate to leaving the hut. Tecmessa, Ajax and the chorus now embark on a kommos (lyrical song of lamentation, as at line 221), which effectively serves as a transition between the two halves of the first episode. Tecmessa and the chorus (probably just the chorus leader) speak their lines in iambic trimeter, and Ajax sings his. This split delivery is highly effective in creating a contrast between the more emotional Ajax and everyone else, and in generating both tension and pathos.

Ajax laments his situation, using highly loaded language which suggests his shame and degradation/humiliation; he begs the chorus to kill him. The chorus leader initially addresses Tecmessa, and comments on the action. He then directly appeals to Ajax, begging him to take advice and accept that past deeds cannot be undone. During the course of his lamentations, Ajax curses Odysseus and the Atreidae and calls on Zeus, the Underworld and on the countryside around Troy. Several scholars have noted that we see Ajax becoming more and more isolated from those around him as the kommos progresses. Indeed, his inability to listen to the advice of others is striking, as is his insistent desire for revenge.

The kommos also provides us with further insight into the relationship between Ajax and Tecmessa: he is dismissive of her (line 369) yet she remains utterly dependent on him (393–394).

430–582

This section begins with a balanced pair of long speeches, in which we see a conflict between Homeric values (represented by Ajax) and a more rational, fifth-century view (represented by Tecmessa). Such a rhetorical debate in tragedy is known as an *agon* (see Introduction p. 350). Ajax, now speaking in iambic trimeter, ignores both Tecmessa and the chorus, and dwells solely on his humiliation. He goes through his options and concludes that his only way out is death. The ever-loyal Tecmessa then replies. She tries to persuade him to change his mind, comforts him and reminds him of his obligations towards his family and his friends. Ajax cruelly dismisses her pleas. The debate then switches to a stichomythic exchange in which he asks to see his son. Eurysaces – an obvious focus for pathos – is carried on by an attendant. Ajax addresses his son, and then Tecmessa, in a moving speech (lines 545–582) which is modelled on the exchange between Hector, Andromache and Astyanax in *Iliad* book 6; a comparison of these texts serves to highlight the core differences between Ajax and Hector.

430

αἰαῖ: 'alas', a standard cry in Greek literature. Ajax goes on to note the close etymological link between this cry and his name (430–431). The metaphor is extended and thus could be termed a conceit. Ajax is not trying to be humorous; the Greeks believed in the relationship between one's name and one's nature or situation. Other examples include 'Oedipus' (swollen foot).

ᾤεθ᾽: = ᾤετο: 3rd sg. imperfect from οἴομαι (I think, forebode).

A
Level

τίς ἄν ποτ᾽ ᾤεθ᾽: 'who would ever have thought . . .', followed by an indirect
   statement (infinitive construction).

The indicative + ἄν is used for the apodosis (main clause) of a contrary-to-fact/
   unfulfilled conditional in past time. An aorist indicative would be more usual for
   past time, but the imperfect is sometimes used for the past when referring to a
   continual or habitual state, as here. (NB: the usual use of the imperfect tense in
   this sort of condition is to indicate a present habitual state.) The protasis ('if-
   clause') has not been expressed.

ἐπώνυμον: = (here) 'significantly named' or 'aptly named'. Stanford has
   'descriptively'. See on line 431.

431

τοὐμόν = τὸ ἐμόν.

ξυνοίσειν: future infinitive from ξυμφέρω, which has an intransitive meaning here
   ('I correspond with/agree with'). Jebb suggests that it should be translated with
   ὧδ᾽ ἐπώνυμον to mean 'would agree so significantly with . . .'. Finglass has
   'would thus correspond to . . .'.

Note the use of figura etymologica (ἐπώνυμον, ὄνομα) to drive the point home
   (see line 308–309).

432

πάρεστι . . . ἐμοί: 'it is possible for me'.

αἰάζειν: = 'to say αἰαῖ', i.e. 'to cry, wail, groan'.

433

Some scholars have deleted this line, on the grounds that καὶ δὶς . . . καὶ τρίς ('both
   twice and thrice') is weak, as is the use of γάρ in two successive sentences.
   Moreover, ὅτου (434) would follow more easily directly after ἐμοί (432).

ἐντυγχάνω: + dat. = 'I meet with, light upon'.

434–440

Ajax now contrasts his own dishonour with the honour enjoyed by his father. Both
Ajax and Teucer fear Telamon's disapproval, and Ajax's own words to his son (see
below) suggest that he wishes Eurysaces to have a similar fear of his own father.

434

ὅτου: = οὗτινος = masculine genitive singular of the relative pronoun ὅστις. ὅστις
   (rather than the expected ὅς) can be used after a definite antecedent, especially
   when a reason or cause is being suggested. Ajax is referring to himself: 'I whose
   father . . .'.

435

τὰ πρῶτα καλλιστεῖ᾽: τὸ καλλιστεῖον = 'an offering of what is fairest', i.e. 'a
   prize' (here in the poetic plural); so τὰ πρῶτα καλλιστεῖα . . . στρατοῦ = 'the
   fairest prize in/of the army'. This refers to Hesione, daughter of king Laomedon,

A
Level

whom Heracles awarded to Telamon as a result of the latter's sacking of Troy a
generation earlier.

ἀριστεύω = 'I am the best (ἄριστος)'. It is here followed by an internal accusative:
'I win X as the sign of my ἀριστεία (excellence)'. So τὰ πρῶτα καλλιστεῖ'
ἀριστεύσας στρατοῦ = 'having won the fairest prize of the army'.

437

κείνου: = ἐκείνου (see line 6).

438

ἐπελθών: note the prefix, which suggests that he came 'against' the Trojans.

σθένει: τὸ σθένος = 'might/strength', or perhaps (here) 'a force of men'.

439

ἀρκέσας: ἀρκέω + acc. (here) = 'I perform/achieve', a very rare use of a verb which
  almost always means 'I ward off, defend/suffice'.

ἔργα μείω: 'lesser deeds' – μείω is an irregular comparative, here in a contracted
  form (accusative neuter plural).

440

ἄτιμος Ἀργείοισιν: 'dishonoured by the Greeks'. ἄτιμος is a very loaded term
  within the world of the Homeric hero. Ἀργείοισιν is here being used like a dative
  of the agent after ἄτιμος.

441

τοσοῦτόν γ': '(I think I know) this at least', a reference to the following statement
  (γ' = γε).

442–444

An unfulfilled condition in past time. It makes use of an imperfect indicative (ἔμελλε)
  rather than the expected aorist in the protasis (see on 430), and an aorist
  (ἔμαρψεν) + ἄν in the apodosis.

442

ζῶν: present participle (masc. nom. sg.) from ζάω.

ὧν: = 'his own', so (πέρι) τῶν ὅπλων τῶν ὧν = '(concerning) the arms, the ones
  which are his own'.

Lines 442–443 are tricky: 'If Achilles, while he were alive (ζῶν), had been going to
  award (κρίνειν ἔμελλε) the prize (κράτος) for excellence (ἀριστείας)
  concerning his own arms (τῶν ὅπλων τῶν ὧν πέρι) to anyone (τινί) . . .'

The noun ἀριστεία is a very significant term within the Homeric world. It refers to
  a sequence of great deeds achieved by a hero.

444

οὐκ . . . τις . . . ἄλλος: 'no-one else'.

αὔτ': = αὔτα (refers to the arms).

ἄν . . . ἔμαρψεν: 'would have taken hold . . .'.

**A
Level**

445

As often, **νῦν** returns us from the hypothetical to reality (it happens at 450 too).

παντουργῷ: παντουργός = πάνουργος = 'wicked'.

φρένας: accusative of respect (and poetic plural) – '(wicked) with respect to/in his mind/heart'.

446

ἔπραξαν: 'they have handed them over', an unusual meaning of πράττω. Note also that a true perfect translation in English is what is required by sense, even though the Greek has an aorist.

ἀνδρὸς τοῦδ': Ajax is referring to himself.

κράτη: = (here) 'victories, mighty deeds'.

ἀπώσαντες: = aorist participle (masc. nom. pl.) of ἀπωθέω = 'I thrust aside'.

There is within these lines (and line 449 too) a suggestion that the Atreidae rigged the vote. This is yet another sign of the degradation of Ajax's mental state.

447

κεἰ: = καὶ εἰ, introducing yet another unfulfilled condition in past time: Ajax dwells on what could/should have been.

τόδ' ὄμμα: = (τόδ' = τόδε) 'this eye', i.e. 'my eyes'.

φρένες: 'mind' (poetic plural).

διάστροφοι: 'twisted, distorted'. The adjective could refer to both nouns (ὄμμα/φρένες). It is here being used predicatively rather than attributively.

448

ἀπῇξαν: 3rd pl. aorist from ἀπαίσσω ('I swerve away from' + genitive).

γνώμης ... τῆς ἐμῆς: 'my intention', i.e. to kill the Atreidae and Odysseus.

448–449

οὐκ ἄν ποτε/δίκην ... ὧδ' ἐψήφισαν: 'they would never have voted such a judgement . . .'.

(δίκην ψηφίζω = 'decide by vote').

449

κατ': κατά + genitive = (here) 'against (another man)'. Ajax means that had he managed to kill the Atreidae, they would never again have had an opportunity to cheat someone as they cheated him.

450

γοργῶπις: 'Gorgon-eyed', i.e. 'grim-eyed'.

ἀδάματος: an adjective which means both 'invincible' and 'virgin'.

Note that Athena and her epithets take up an entire line: Ajax wishes to emphasize her power.

451

ἐπ' αὐτοῖς χεῖρ' ἐπευθύνοντ' ἐμήν: 'just as I was directing my hand against them'. ἐπευθύνοντα, from ἐπευθύνω (I guide, direct) agrees with **μ'** (= με).

A Level

452

λυσσώδη νόσον: 'a plague/disease of madness'.

453

ὥστ᾽ ἐν τοιοῖσδε χεῖρας αἱμάξαι βοτοῖς: 'with the result that I stained my hands among beasts such as these', a result clause with an infinitive rather than an indicative.

455

ἐμοῦ μὲν οὐχ ἑκόντος: 'against my will'. μέν emphasizes ἐμοῦ and contrasts strongly with (δέ) τις θεῶν in the next sentence.

455–456

εἰ δέ τις θεῶν/βλάπτοι, φύγοι τἂν χὡ κακὸς τὸν κρείσσονα: 'but if one of the gods does harm, then even a coward can flee from a stronger man', i.e. if a god is on their side, even 'base' men (such as Odysseus) will be victorious over strong men (such as Ajax). In grammatical terms, this is a future remote conditional clause, with optatives in both the protasis and the apodosis. But a translation using 'would' and 'could' does not seem appropriate for what is clearly a gnomic statement (see on 125–6 and 293).

τἂν = τοι ἄν.

χὡ κακός = καὶ ὁ κακός: 'even a coward' (referring to Odysseus). χὡ as crasis for καὶ ὁ is relatively common in poetry.

Ajax in his single-mindedness fails to see that perhaps those who judged the contest had different ideas about what constitutes 'noble deeds', i.e. a set of criteria against which Odysseus comes out above Ajax. Indeed, this conflict between 'old' and the 'new' value systems is at the heart of the tragedy.

457

ὅστις: 'who' (see 434). Ajax is referring to himself: 'I who am hated . . .'. It is again used with a note of causation, as in 434.

Ajax now moves into a section of contemplation: he goes through his options, retaining concerns of shame and pride in the forefront of his mind as he does so.

459

ἔχθει: the subject is both Τροία πᾶσα and the neuter plural πεδία τάδε ('these plains'). ἔχθω = 'I hate'. Ajax's sense of isolation is striking; he believes that he is hated by gods, men and even Troy itself and its surroundings. He forgets (or ignores) the fact that he has the support of his concubine and the chorus.

460

πότερα: = πότερον, which usually introduces a question with two alternatives. However, here Ajax doesn't move on to the second question for quite a while: he gets fixated on what would happen if he were to return home. The next option is introduced by ἀλλὰ δῆτ᾽ in 466.

460–461

λιπών: governs two objects (ναυλόχους . . . ἕδρας and μόνους τ᾽ Ἀτρείδας) – 'leaving the stations which afford safe anchorage and (leaving) the Atreidae alone'. ἕδρας refers to stations for ships; ναυλόχους is a two-termination adjective meaning 'affording anchorage'. Note Ajax's arrogant belief that, without him, the Atreidae will be 'alone' (i.e. without help).

πρὸς οἴκους ... / ... πέλαγος Αἰγαῖον περῶ: 'Am I to cross the Aegean sea towards home?'. περῶ is subjunctive (περάω = 'I pass a barrier/boundary') because this is a deliberative question.

462

φανείς: 'having appeared', i.e. 'when I arrive' – aorist passive participle from φαίνω.

ποῖον ὄμμα ... δηλώσω: lit. 'what sort of face shall I show ...?', i.e. 'how will I show my face ...?'

The repeated references to shame in lines 462–465 emphasize its importance within Ajax's value system. There is a sense of urgency in his questioning.

463

πῶς ... τλήσεταί: 'how will he endure ...?' or 'how will he bring himself ...?'. τλήσεταί is a (middle) future from τλάω (I endure).

γυμνόν: a strong metaphor ('naked' = 'without prizes') which adds to our understanding of the shame which Ajax feels.

τῶν ἀριστείων: ἀριστεία lit. = 'excellence/prowess', and therefore by extension can be used to refer to the prizes awarded for acts of excellence. Ajax is of course thinking of the καλλιστεῖα referred to in 435.

465

ὧν αὐτὸς ἔσχε στέφανον εὐκλείας μέγαν: 'of which he himself held a great crown of glory'.

466

οὐκ ἔστι τοὔργον τλητόν: 'the deed is not to be endured' (τοὔργον = το ἔργον).

467

ἔρυμα: 'safeguard/defence', i.e. 'the wall' (of Troy).

ξυμπεσὼν μόνος μόνοις: the juxtaposition and polyptoton help to highlight Ajax's isolation. It is difficult to convey this in translation: 'joining battle, just me against just them'. It is possible, as Garvie notes, that Ajax is expecting a series of duels. Or we could join Finglass in seeing Ajax's belief that he would be able single-handedly to take on the Trojans as suggesting 'Ajax's conception of his status as a warrior'.

ξυμπίπτω = 'fall together', i.e. 'join battle with', 'attack'.

468

τι χρηστόν: 'some good deed'.

λοίσθιον: used here as an adverb = 'at the last', 'finally'.

θάνω: another deliberative subjunctive, this time aorist.

469

ἂν εὐφράναιμί: (aorist) optative with ἄν = 'I would/might gladden/cheer/give pleasure to ...'. This is a potential optative (see line 86).

A Level

που: as indicated by the lack of accent, this is not a question word (**ποῦ**) but an adverb, meaning 'perhaps' or 'somehow'.

470

οὐκ ἔστι ταῦτα: this short clause echoes line 466. Ajax is rapidly running out of options. But we might question how much he really wishes to accept any way out other than the one on which he seems already to have decided.

πεῖρά τις ζητητέα: 'some enterprise is to be sought'. **ζητητέα** is a passive verbal adjective (a gerundive), meaning 'needing to be sought'. Further examples can be found at 668 and 853.

471

τοιάδ᾽ ἀφ᾽ ἧς: (= τοιάδε ἀπο ἧς) lit. 'such as this, from which', i.e. 'whereby'. This relative pronoun is followed by a purpose clause with a future indicative.

472

μή τοι φύσιν γ᾽ ἄσπλαγχνος: '(that I, his son, am) not indeed a coward by nature'. **μή τοι ... γε** (taken together) = 'at any rate not'. **ἄσπλαγχνος** = 'without bowels', 'without heart', i.e. 'cowardly', 'a coward'. **φύσιν** is an accusative of respect ('in nature').

473

αἰσχρὸν γάρ: supply ἔστι – 'for it is shameful for . . . (+ accusative)'. **αἰσχρόν** is another very loaded term within the Homeric code.

χρῄζειν: = 'to want' (+ genitive).

474

κακοῖσιν ὅστις μηδὲν ἐξαλλάσσεται: 'whoever/if he finds no change in his troubles/misfortunes'. **ἐξαλλάσσω** = 'I change utterly'; the middle use here means 'see a change with respect to one's own circumstances'. **μηδέν** is an adverbial accusative, modifying the verb. **κακοῖσιν** is a locative dative – 'in the midst of his troubles'.

Lines 473–474 constitute another gnomic statement, that it is shameful to cling on to life if it isn't getting any better.

475

τί γὰρ παρ᾽ ἦμαρ ἡμέρα τέρπειν ἔχει: lit. 'for how (**τί**) is each successive day (**παρ᾽ ἦμαρ ἡμέρα**) able (**ἔχει**) to please (**τέρπειν**)?', so 'for what pleasure does each successive day have . . .?' or 'for what pleasure is there in each successive day . . .?'. Note that ἔχω + infinitive = 'I am able to'.

παρ᾽ ἦμαρ ἡμέρα: (**παρ᾽** = παρά) 'day by day', i.e. 'each successive day'. **το ἦμαρ** = ἡ ἡμέρα. παρά + accusative = 'beside, along'.

476

προσθεῖσα κἀναθεῖσα τοῦ γε κατθανεῖν: 'pushing (each man) towards death and pulling (him) from it'.

This line is corrupt, hence the confusion in both grammar and meaning. The general sense seems to be that a longer life is not necessarily a better life. But whilst the idea of each day moving men closer to death is in keeping with Ajax's previous sentiments, the inclusion of the antithesis is not. Jebb reads a boardgame metaphor, in which pieces are moved forwards or backwards. This reading has many problems. But if it is right, the shuffling backwards and forwards might imply the pointlessness of such an empty existence.

The subject of the participles **προσθεῖσα** (προστίθημι = 'I hand over, deliver' or perhaps 'I push towards', usually + dative) and **κἀναθεῖσα** (= καὶ ἀναθεῖσα; ἀνατίθημι = [here] 'I put/move back') is **ἡμέρα** (παρ᾽ ἦμαρ). **τοῦ . . . κατθανεῖν** is a genitive of separation after ἀνατίθημι.

477

λόγου: (here) = 'value, estimate, price'. **λόγου** is a genitive of value after the metaphorical **οὐκ ἂν πριαίμην** – 'I would not buy . . .' (another potential optative).

In lines 477–480, Ajax delivers a universal statement which in many ways epitomizes his Homeric worldview.

478

ὅστις . . . θερμαίνεται: another metaphor, 'who is warmed/comforted by'. **ὅστις** means 'of the sort who . . .'.

479

ἢ καλῶς ζῆν ἢ καλῶς τεθνηκέναι: 'to live well or to be dead well'. Garvie notes that the use of a perfect infinitive in **τεθνηκέναι** suggests that Ajax is thinking 'not so much of the manner of his death as of his reputation after he is dead' (once again, we see the perfect in Greek describing a past action leading to a present state).

480

πάντ᾽ ἀκήκοας λόγον: (**πάντ᾽** = πάντα) 'you have heard everything I have to say'. Ajax is trying to prevent any further discussion, because his mind has already been made up.

481

The chorus frequently acts as a (generally neutral) commentator in an *agon*.

ποθ᾽: = ποτέ = 'ever'.

ὑπόβλητον λόγον: 'a false speech', i.e. a speech in which Ajax was not true to himself.

482

ἀλλὰ τῆς σαυτοῦ φρενός: supply a verb – 'but (it was) from your own mind'. In poetry, the genitive (by itself) can mean 'from'.

483

παῦσαί: 2nd singular aorist imperative middle – 'cease!'.

δός: 2nd singular aorist imperative active – lit. 'give', i.e. 'allow' (+ dative of the person).

A Level

484

κρατῆσαι: aorist infinitive of κρατέω (+ genitive = 'I prevail', 'I rule over').
γνώμης: 'judgement/will/intention'.
μεθείς: aorist participle (nom. sg.) from μεθίημι = 'I let go'.

485–524

Tecmessa tries to persuade Ajax to change his mind, reminding him of what they have shared and pointing out the likely effect of Ajax's suicide on his father, mother, child and concubine. The speech is full of rhetorical devices designed to appeal to Ajax's emotions. Moreover, it contains many allusions to the meeting between Hector, Andromache and Astyanax in *Iliad* 6 in which Hector says goodbye to his wife and son before leaving Troy to rejoin the fight. Such a comparison between Hector and Ajax paints the latter in a rather negative light.

485

ὦ δέσποτ' Αἶας: the use of **δέσποτα** instantly reminds us of Tecmessa's status as a slave. The sentiment expressed in the following lines continues this theme.

486

οὐκ ἔστιν οὐδέν μεῖζον ἀνθρώποις κακόν: 'there is no greater evil for men'. In Greek, if two negatives are used of which the first is a simple negative (**οὐκ ... οὐδέν**), they reinforce rather than cancel each other out.

487

ἐξέφυν: 1st singular aorist (intransitive) indicative active from ἐκφύω = 'I beget/ produce'. This aorist literally means 'I was born/grew up', therefore 'I am'.

487–488

ἐγὼ δ' ἐλευθέρου μὲν ἐξέφυν πατρός, εἴπερ τινὸς σθένοντος ἐν πλούτῳ Φρυγῶν: 'I was born/am the daughter of a free father, mighty in wealth, if indeed any of the Phrygians (was)'. The point is that the Phrygians (the name of one of the peoples living in Asia Minor, i.e. in the area around Troy) were generally wealthy, and her father was one of the wealthiest of the lot! Note that the genitive from the main clause (**ἐλευθέρου ... πατρός**) has been continued within the if-clause.

σθένοντος ἐν πλούτῳ: = 'strong in wealth' (**σθένοντος** = present participle of σθένω: 'I have strength').

489

που: 'I suppose'. This particle introduces a note of caution.

490

τοιγαροῦν: 'therefore' – a rare particle (it is a strengthened form of the particle τοιγάρ).

A Level

491

ξυνῆλθον: ξυν-/συνέρχομαι often means 'I come together, meet'. Here it means 'I come to' or perhaps 'I join in/share' (+ direct object). Note that ξυν is a dialectical form of συν (very common in tragedy).

εὖ φρονῶ τὰ σά: 'I am well-disposed with respect to your affairs', i.e. 'I wish you well'. Tecmessa affirms her loyalty and devotion. Note that Greek uses the present but we would use the perfect in English ('I have been well-disposed towards you'), as the action is ongoing.

The basic meaning of φρονέω = 'I am minded'. The use of neuter plural article + adjective in Greek is very common (**τὰ σά** = 'your affairs', an accusative of respect).

492

σ' ἀντιάζω: (σ' = σε) 'I supplicate/beg you'. Supplication is usually described in Greek literature as placing one's hand on the knees or chin of the person being supplicated. There is no direct suggestion that Tecmessa is performing those actions here (and it is indeed often stated directly), but she is certainly placing him under a lot of pressure simply by using this verb.

πρός: + genitive = 'in the name of'.

ἐφεστίου Διός: Zeus in the guise of god of the hearth (the most sacred part of the house), i.e. protector of the household and its members.

εὐνῆς τε τῆς σῆς, ᾗ συνηλλάχθης ἐμοί: 'and by your bed, where you had intercourse with me'. This literal translation does not quite convey the tone of Tecmessa's appeal. She is reminding him of the place where they shared their most intimate moments of love.

ᾗ is the dative feminine singular of the relative pronoun, used as an adverb to mean 'where'.

συναλλάσσω in the passive = 'have intercourse with'.

494

μὴ ... ἀξιώσῃς: 'do not think it right ...' + acc. + infinitive (for μή + aorist subjunctive, see 83).

μ' ... βάξιν ἀλγεινὴν λαβεῖν: (μ' = με) '... that I should suffer painful words' (lit. 'that I should take a painful utterance').

495

χειρίαν ἐφείς τινι: 'having left me in the power of one of them' (referring to the enemies). χείριος is a poetic adjective meaning 'in the hands/under the power of', and agrees with με in 494. ἐφείς is aorist active participle of ἐφίημι = 'I send to/I hand over'.

496

ᾗ: dative feminine singular of the relative pronoun, whose antecedent is **ταύτῃ ... τῇ ... ἡμέρᾳ** in the next line.

θάνῃς σὺ καὶ τελευτήσας ἀφῇς: 'you die and, having died, abandon (me)'. **θάνῃς** and **ἀφῇς** are 2nd singular aorist subjunctives: the subjunctive is used because this is an indefinite construction in future time (although here without the usual ἄν). τελευτάω (intransitive) = 'I finish, come to an end, die'.

A
Level

497

ταύτῃ ... τῇ τόθ᾽ ἡμέρᾳ: 'on this very day'. τόθ᾽ = τότε.

497–499

νόμιζε κἀμὲ ... δουλίαν ἕξειν τροφήν: 'consider that I too shall have a slave's way of life' (νόμιζε + infinitive construction). κἀμέ = καὶ ἐμέ.

498

ξυναρπασθεῖσαν: = 'having been dragged off' (referring to herself).

Whereas in *Iliad* 6 it was Hector who feared what might happen to Andromache after his death, here it is Tecmessa herself who, through Ajax's single-minded self-obsession, is compelled to express such fears. Ajax's inability to show any compassion or sensitivity perhaps suggests he is to be viewed (within this play) as an example of the most extreme form of Homeric hero.

500

τις ... δεσποτῶν: 'one of my masters'. Tecmessa imagines (in vivid direct speech – just as Hector does in *Iliad* 6) the sorts of taunts which might be thrown at her by her new masters.

λόγοις ἰάπτων: 'wounding (me) with words'. ἰάπτω = 'I hurl/wound', a military metaphor.

501

ὁμευνέτιν: 'bed partner' (fem. acc. sg.).

502

ἴσχυσε: 3rd sg. aorist of ἰσχύω (= 'I am strong'); the aorist indicates a completed time period (i.e. he is strong no longer). μέγιστον is here being used adverbially. στρατοῦ is a partitive genitive with the superlative.

503

οἵας λατρείας ἀνθ᾽ ὅσου ζήλου τρέφει: (ἀνθ᾽ = ἀντί) 'what kind of menial tasks/services she performs, instead of such great honour/privilege'. Stanford translates τρέφει as 'cherishes'. ἀνθ᾽ ὅσου ζήλου literally means 'in exchange for what (a great) enviable state'.

504

τοιαῦτ᾽: = τοιαῦτα = 'such things'

κἀμέ: see 497.

δαίμων: here means 'my fate/destiny'.

ἐλᾷ: 3rd sg. (poetic) future of ἐλαύνω = 'I drive'; translate here as 'drive to extremities, persecute, pursue'.

505

Tecmessa is trying to encourage Ajax to live by suggesting that her treatment after his death will bring shame (αἰσχρά) on his son and his name. In the parallel passage in the *Iliad* (6.459-463), it is Hector who voices such a concern, and the concern is for Andromache.

τἄπη: = τὰ ἔπη.

506–513
Tecmessa now movingly dwells on each member of the family in turn.

506–507
ἀλλ' αἴδεσαι μὲν πατέρα τὸν σὸν ἐν λυγρῷ/γήρᾳ προλείπων: 'but have respect for your father whom you are abandoning in mournful old age'. **αἰδέομαι** (which is from the same root as the noun **αἰδώς**) = 'I revere, feel respect for'.

508
πολλῶν ἐτῶν κληροῦχον: 'whose allotted portion is many years' (referring to his mother). Literally, the Greek says that she is a holder of a portion/allotment (κλῆρος) of many years (**πολλῶν ἐτῶν**).

509
ἀρᾶται: 'prays', here followed by the infinitive construction (**μολεῖν** = aorist infinitive of βλώσκω = 'I go/come') with an accusative subject (**σε**).

510
ὦναξ: = ὦ ἄναξ
οἴκτιρε: (2nd sg. imperative) governs two objects – **παῖδα τὸν σόν** and **ὅσον ... νεμεῖς**. The latter expands on the former. Compare English: 'I know you, who you are'.

501–511
νέας ... /τροφῆς: 'care suitable for the young'.

511
σοῦ διοίσεται μόνος: 'he will pass his life apart from you'; **διοίσεται** = future of διαφέρομαι = 'I go through life, live'.

512
ὑπ' ὀρφανιστῶν μὴ φίλων: (**ὑπ'** = ὑπό) 'under the influence of unfriendly guardians'. **μὴ φίλων** is an example of litotes (an understatement in which something is stressed ·by the negation of its opposite: 'not friendly' = 'very unfriendly'). It seems likely that the word ὀρφανιστής ('orphan-carer') would have resonated with a fifth-century Athenian audience. After all, the opening celebrations of the City Dionysia included a procession of the orphans of those who had died fighting for the state. These orphans were raised by the state and would go on to serve the *polis* as their fathers had done before them (see Introduction p. 345).

512–513
ὅσον κακὸν/κείνῳ τε κἀμοὶ τοῦθ', ὅταν θάνῃς, νεμεῖς: νεμεῖς is future. Literally: 'how great this evil you will dispense for both me and him when you die'.

**A
Level**

κἀμοί: = καὶ ἐμοί

ὅταν θάνῃς: lit. 'when you die' (subjunctive + ἄν = indefinite construction as used in a future temporal clause).

τοῦθ': = τοῦτο

514

ἐμοὶ γὰρ οὐκέτ' ἔστιν εἰς ὅ τι βλέπω: (**οὐκέτ':** = οὐκέτι) 'since for me there is no longer anything to which I (can) look', i.e. for aid and assistance. **ἐμοί** is a possessive dative here.

515

μοι: dative of disadvantage.

ἤστωσας: 2nd sg. aorist indicative of ἀιστόω (= 'I annihilate').

516

τὸν φύσαντα: 'the one who begot me', i.e. 'my father'. **φύσαντα** = masc. acc. sg. aorist participle from φύω ('I produce, beget'). Definite article + participle = relative clause.

517

καθεῖλεν: 3rd sg. aorist from καθαιρέω = 'I take down, lay low'.

Ἅιδου θανασίμους οἰκήτορας: this predicative phrase describes **μητέρ'** (= μητέρα) and **τὸν φύσαντα** – 'another fate laid low my mother and father so as to become dead inhabitants of Hades'.

As part of her plea, Tecmessa reminds Ajax that she has nothing left without him, and that he is partly to blame for this.

518–519

The pathos of the speech is increased by the introduction of these short rhetorical questions. To Tecmessa, Ajax is both homeland (**πατρίς**) and wealth (**πλοῦτος**): any homeland and wealth which she had before the arrival of the Greeks has now gone, and she could not hope for better than he could provide anyway.

519

ἐν σοὶ πᾶσ' ἔγωγε σῴζομαι: lit. 'for I at least am entirely saved in you' (**πᾶσ'** = πᾶσα), i.e. 'for my whole safety is in your hands'.

520

κἀμοῦ: = καὶ ἐμοῦ.

ἴσχε: 'have'. ἴσχω is a form of ἔχω, and is sometimes used interchangeably with it in poetry.

520

χρεών: supply ἐστι. χρεών ἐστι + acc. = 'it is necessary', a metrically useful equivalent of χρή in iambic poetry.

520–521

ἀνδρὶ . . . /μνήμην προσεῖναι: '(it is necessary) for a man to remember' (lit. 'it is necessary for memory to be attached to a man').

A
Level

τερπνὸν εἴ τί που πάθοι: 'if he perhaps experiences something pleasurable', potentially a reference to sexual pleasure. The accent has been thrown onto τί by the following enclitic (που = 'possibly, perhaps, I suppose'): therefore, it should be translated as the indefinite. πάθοι is optative because this is a generalizing statement.

522

χάρις χάριν γάρ ἐστιν ἡ τίκτουσ᾽ ἀεί: 'for kindness is the thing which always begets kindness'.

Finglass notes that 'χάρις is a key word in the vocabulary of reciprocity', a theme which is highlighted by the use of polyptoton (χάρις χάριν – see 58) and collocation (a term referring to the juxtaposition of words which are not contrasting).

523

ὅτου δ᾽ ἀπορρεῖ μνῆστις εὖ πεπονθότος: lit. 'but from whom having experienced good things the memory falls away', i.e. 'if anyone allows his recollection of good things to fall away . . .'. For the genitive without a preposition, see on line 482. Note that the antecedent of ὅτου is οὗτος in line 524.

524

οὐκ ἂν γένοιτ᾽ ἔθ᾽ οὗτος εὐγενὴς ἀνήρ: (γένοιτ᾽ ἔθ᾽ = γένοιτο ἔτι) 'this man would no longer be noble'.

These closing lines (520–524) contain some significant ideas. Tecmessa is essentially saying that nobility is not achieved through selfish actions carried out due to loss of τιμή. True nobility requires reciprocity, and one good deed (such as her kindness towards him) deserves another.

525–526

ἔχειν σ᾽ ἂν οἶκτον ὡς κἀγὼ φρενὶ /θέλοιμ᾽ ἄν: (σ᾽= σε, κἀγώ = καὶ ἐγώ, θέλοιμ᾽= θέλοιμι) 'I wish that you too had pity in your mind'. The optative of a verb of wishing + infinitive = a polite request. ὡς κἀγώ means 'as I do too'.

526

αἰνοίης γὰρ ἄν: 'for you would praise' – this is the apodosis of a future remote condition. The protasis has been replaced with the wish above.

τῆσδ᾽: = τῆσδε, referring to Tecmessa.

527

καὶ κάρτ᾽: = καὶ κάρτα = 'surely', 'yes indeed'.

τεύξεται: τυγχάνω + gen. = 'I obtain, get'.

528

ἐὰν μόνον . . . εὖ τολμᾷ: Finglass translates this as 'if she can only bring herself . . .'.

τὸ ταχθέν: lit. 'the thing having been ordered', i.e. 'her instructions', or 'what I order her to do'.

Ajax says that Tecmessa will indeed gain praise, but only on condition that she does what she is told. The dictatorial tone (emphasized also by the harsh

A Level

alliteration of τ and θ) contrasts strongly with the politeness of the chorus in lines
525–526.

529

πάντ' ἔγωγε πείσομαι: 'I at least shall obey in every way'. πάντα is an internal
accusative.

We have now moved into a section of stichomythia, which increases the pace (after
two long speeches) and raises the emotional temperature of the piece.

530

νύν: = 'then, so'. This is the enclitic form of the word, carrying an accent here only
because of the following enclitic μοι. It is not 'now', which is **νῦν**.

531

καὶ μήν: 'and yet', introducing a new point in a dialogue.

φόβοισί: 'due to my fear' – a causal dative.

αὐτὸν ἐξελυσάμην: 'I released him', i.e. sent him away from the tent. Tecmessa is
deliberately vague, and this prompts Ajax's blunt questioning (532) and her direct
response (533).

533

μὴ ... θάνοι: negative purpose clause – 'lest he should die'.

σοι ... ἀντήσας: 'having met you'. ἀντάω + dative = I meet.

534

πρέπον γέ τἂν ἦν δαίμονος τοὐμοῦ τόδε: 'this at any rate would have been
worthy of my fortune', i.e. of what he is now suffering. A grim line.

πρέπον: + genitive (here) = 'worthy of'. **τἂν** = τοι ἄν. ἄν + the imperfect of
εἰμί is used in the apodosis of a past closed conditional. γέ τοι = γοῦν = 'at any
rate'.

535

ἀλλ' οὖν: (**ἀλλ'** = ἀλλά) 'well at any rate'.

'φύλαξα τοῦτό γ' ἀρκέσαι: (**γ'** = γε) 'I kept watch/took precautions to ward off
that at least'. **'φύλαξα** = ἐφύλαξα by prodelision.

536

ἐπήνεσ': = ἐπήνεσα. This is an instantaneous aorist used idiomatically in Greek of
an event which takes place just a moment before the time of speaking; English
uses the present. See line 99.

πρόνοιαν ἣν ἔθου: 'the foresight which you demonstrated'.

537

τί δῆτ' ἂν ... ἂν ὠφελοῖμί σε: (**δῆτ'** = δῆτα) 'how then could I help you?'. A
potential optative with a second (redundant) ἄν.

ὡς ἐκ τῶνδ': (**τῶνδ'** = τῶνδε) lit. 'as from these things', i.e. 'as things stand now'.

**A
Level**

538

δός μοι: 'allow me'.

ἐμφανῆ τ᾽ ἰδεῖν: (τ᾽ = τε) 'and to see him clearly', i.e. 'face to face'.

539

καὶ μήν: 'yes'. Here, this phrase indicates agreement (note that this use is different to that found in 531).

προσπόλοις: '(he is being guarded) by attendants'; dative of the agent (rarely used with the present).

540

τί δῆτα μέλλει μὴ οὐ παρουσίαν ἔχειν: lit. 'why, then, is he hesitating/delaying to have a presence', i.e. 'why, then, is his arrival delayed?'.

παρουσίαν ἔχειν = παρεῖναι = 'be present'. μὴ οὐ should not be translated: it is what normally happens in Greek after a verb of hindering/delaying in a question expecting some sort of negative answer.

541

At this point, Eurysaces begins to be carried onstage along one of the *eisodoi*. Children are often a focus of pathos in Greek tragedy (e.g. Euripides' *Medea*).

541–542

προσπόλων/ ... ὅσπερ χερσὶν εὐθύνων κυρεῖς: lit. 'whichever of you servants happens to be/actually is (κυρεῖς) guiding him (εὐθύνων) with your hands (χερσίν)'. Jebb translates the phrase as 'whosoever of you is guiding his steps'.

543

ἕρποντι φωνεῖς ἢ λελειμμένῳ λόγων: 'do you speak to someone who is coming or to someone who has not heard your words?'. λείπομαι (passive) + genitive can mean 'I am wanting/lacking in', or perhaps 'I am left behind/fall short of'. Ajax is impatient.

544

ἐγγύθεν: 'from nearby'.

545–582

In contrast to his first speech, and perhaps in response to Tecmessa's speech, Ajax now deals with his family obligations, but not in the way in which she had intended – he still plans to commit suicide. There are many similarities between this passage and Hector's exchange with his son Astyanax in *Iliad* 6. In some respects, Ajax comes off worse, but it is not clear-cut: Hector also acts clumsily when dealing with his son.

546

νεοσφαγῆ ... τόνδε ... φόνον: 'this fresh-slaughtered death/blood'.

**A
Level**

547

εἴπερ δικαίως ἔστ᾽ ἐμὸς τὰ πατρόθεν: **τὰ πατρόθεν** (neuter plural article + adverb) is both pleonastic and a little awkward. The whole phrase literally means 'if he is justly mine, with regard to the from-the-father things' (!). An idiomatic translation might be 'if indeed he is truly mine, born with me as father'.

Many scholars have commented on the fact that whereas Hector removed the helmet which was causing his son distress (*Iliad* 6.466-470), Ajax expects his son to look on the slaughter all around, almost as a test of his true paternity: he sees his son purely as 'an extension of himself' (the phrase of R.P. Winnington-Ingram). Others have argued that Ajax is a better fighter than Hector (and therefore his comments are perhaps more justified), and that Hector is just as obtuse in *Iliad* 6.

548

αὐτίκ᾽: = αὐτίκα, a significant adverb, for it indicates the speed with which Ajax wishes his son to be 'broken in' or 'initiated'. The contrast with Hector (who expressed a wish that his son *grow up* to be a good fighter) is clear.

ὠμοῖς . . . ἐν νόμοις πατρός: 'in the crude ways/customs of his father'.

549

πωλοδαμνεῖν: = 'to train/break in', a metaphor from breaking in horses (πῶλος = foal). The object is αὐτόν.

κἀξομοιοῦσθαι φύσιν: 'and to be made like his father in nature'. **κἀξομοιοῦσθαι** = καὶ ἐξομοιοῦσθαι. ἐξομοιόω = 'I make X like'. The infinitive here is passive, and αὐτόν needs to be resupplied as its subject. φύσιν is an accusative of respect.

550

γένοιο: an optative in a main clause here indicates a wish – 'may you be'.

551

τὰ δ᾽ ἄλλ᾽: = τὰ δ᾽ ἄλλα = 'with respect to other things' (accusative of respect).

γένοι᾽ ἂν οὐ: 'you would not be', a potential optative which could be translated as a future: 'you will not be' (γένοι᾽ = γένοιο).

Whereas Hector prays that Astyanax might be better than his father, Ajax prays that Eurysaces might be like him in everything except his misfortune.

552

σε . . . τοῦτό γε ζηλοῦν ἔχω: 'I can envy you this'. ἔχω + infinitive can mean 'I am able to', 'I may' (we have seen this several times, e.g. 475). **τοῦτό** is an accusative of respect.

553

ὁθούνεκ᾽: = ὁθούνεκα = 'because'.

554

ἐν τῷ φρονεῖν . . . μηδέν: lit. 'in the understanding nothing', i.e. 'when one understands nothing' or 'when you understand nothing' (it is a gnomic, i.e. generalizing statement: see line 293). **τῷ φρονεῖν** (article + infinitive) is a verbal noun (gerund). There are three more in the next two lines.

A Level

554b

This line is bracketed because many editors think that is was not in Sophocles' original text. It certainly seems to add nothing to the sentiment expressed in the preceding line.

555

ἕως ... μάθῃς: 'until you understand/learn/experience'. ἕως + subjunctive = 'until', referring to an uncertain event in future time (indefinite construction, but here without ἄν). The gerunds (τὸ χαίρειν καὶ τὸ λυπεῖσθαι) could be translated as abstract nouns ('joy and grief').

556

ὅταν δ᾽ ἵκῃ πρὸς τοῦτο: 'when you reach this'. ἵκῃ = 2nd sg. aorist subjunctive from ἱκνέομαι ('I arrive'). This is the indefinite construction in future time (subjunctive + ἄν). τοῦτο refers to the stage of life mentioned in line 555.

556–557

δεῖ σ᾽ ὅπως ... /δείξεις: 'it is necessary that you show' (σ᾽ = σε). δεῖ here governs a clause (+ acc. + ὅπως + future indicative) rather than an infinitive. δείξεις is 2nd sg. future of δείκνυμι.

δεῖ σ᾽ ὅπως πατρός /δείξεις ἐν ἐχθροῖς, οἷος ἐξ οἵου ᾽τράφης: it is unclear whether πατρός goes with ἐν ἐχθροῖς or οἷος ἐξ οἵου. Both position and sense would suggest the former: 'it is necessary that you show amidst your father's enemies what kind of man you are and from what stock you were born'. ᾽τράφης: = ἐτράφης. τρέφομαι here = 'I am born'.

Ajax continues to emphasize the idea that his son is an extension of himself. He presumably means in these lines (556–557) that Eurysaces should take revenge on his father's enemies.

558

βόσκου: 'nourish', 'feed' – 2nd singular middle imperative from βόσκω. Its object is νέαν/ψυχήν and the whole phrase goes with κούφοις πνεύμασιν: 'feed your young soul on the light breezes'.

559

ἀτάλλων: 'being carefree'. ἀτάλλω = 'I am innocent/carefree/childlike'. Here a participle is used where we would in English use another imperative – 'and be free from care'.

χαρμονήν: in apposition to the whole sentence.

560

ὑβρίσῃ: 3rd singular aorist subjunctive. οὐ μή + aorist subjunctive is an idiomatic way of doing a prediction. It is very emphatic, and is made more so by the use of οὔτοι ('indeed not' – a strong initial negative) rather than just οὐ. Translate the whole phrase as a future.

οἶδα: Ajax is very confident that his reputation for greatness will protect Eurysaces even after he (Ajax) has died: a further sign of his arrogance, perhaps?

**A
Level**

561

οὐδέ: (here) = 'even'.

ὄντ᾽: = ὄντα, agreeing with σ᾽ (= σε) in the line above.

562

φύλακα: in apposition with τοῖον πυλωρόν – 'such a warder (I shall leave) as a guard (for you)'. Also in apposition is the identity of the guard (Τεῦκρον) and an adjective describing him (ἄοκνον).

563

ἔμπα: an adverb which emphasizes κεἰ (= καὶ εἰ) to mean 'even if in fact'.

The genitive τροφῆς defines the sphere of Teucer's unhesitatingness: 'unhesitating in his care'.

τανῦν: = νῦν.

564

τηλωπὸς οἰχνεῖ: lit. 'he goes far away', so perhaps 'he travels far off'.

θήραν ἔχων: 'having a hunt', or 'involved in/busy with a hunt'.

565

Ajax now addresses the chorus of Salaminian sailors.

ἐνάλιος λεώς: 'men/people of the sea'; λεώς is voc. sg.

ἐπισκήπτω: here means 'I impose'.

κοινήν: lit. 'common' (referring to the χάριν); it should be translated with ὑμῖν. The whole phrase means '(I impose this favour) on you too', i.e. 'on you as well as on Teucer'.

τήνδ᾽ ... χάριν: 'this favour/service'.

567

ὅπως: 'that ...' – introduces the content of the command.

569

Ἐριβοίᾳ λέγω: 'I mean to Eriboea'. Ajax is clarifying that Eurysaces should be shown to his own mother, not to Teucer's.

570

ὡς ... γένηται: ὡς (+ subjunctive) introduces a purpose clause – 'so that he might be ...'.

γηροβοσκός: lit. 'nourishing in old age'. This adjective might better be translated as a noun: '(so that he might provide) support in old age (for them)'.

εἰσαεί: 'forever'.

571

μέχρις οὗ: + subjunctive = 'until'.

Many scholars believe this line to be spurious, added at some point to limit the reference of εἰσαεί in the previous line. It is metrically strange too.

A Level

572–573

καὶ ... μήτ' ... /θήσουσ': this is a further command dependent on ὅπως in 567.

ἀγωνάρχαι: a rare word meaning 'judges of a contest'. Ajax is of course thinking of the contest for the arms of Achilles which started all of this off. He wants to ensure that nothing similar happens here.

573

θήσουσ': = θήσουσι (3rd future active of τίθημι) = (here) 'they will place X before' (+ dative).

ὁ λυμεὼν ἐμός: 'my destroyer', i.e. Odysseus.

Several scholars believe there to be a gap in this line, not least because of a grammatical error: ὁ λυμεὼν ἐμός (ἐμός should be sandwiched between the article and the noun, or the article should be repeated).

574

αὐτὸ ... τοὐπώνυμον: = αὐτὸ ... τὸ ἐπώνυμον = 'the very thing which gives a name (to you)', i.e. the shield. Just as Ajax's name seems appropriate to him in his anguish (see on line 430), so Eurysaces' name (= 'broad-shield') also holds the key to his destiny – in Ajax's mind, at least.

μοι: an ethic dative going with the imperative.

574–575

λαβὼν ... / ... ἴσχε: 'take ... and hold fast ...'. As we have seen many times in this text, Greek often uses a participle (sometimes aorist) followed by an imperative where English would use two imperatives. Ajax now addresses Eurysaces directly.

575

διὰ πολυρράφου ... /πόρπακος: διά here (unusually) indicates the means by which something is to be done: '(turning it) by its well-stitched strap'. This refers to a strap of leather on the inside of the shield.

576

ἑπτάβοιος: 'of seven hides' (ἑπτά = seven; βοεία = ox-hides). This famous shield was mentioned in the *Iliad* too.

577

κοίν' ἐμοί: translate κοίνα adverbially – 'together with me'.

τεθάψεται: a future perfect (passive) to indicate the completeness/finality of the action which will take place in the future. Translate as a simple future: 'will be buried'. Note the singular verb, as the subject is neuter plural.

Ajax expresses a wish that his own weapons should not form the basis of a contest after his death. Eurysaces is to have the shield (to continue his father's work), and the rest will be buried with him. This perhaps reflects the fact that his whole identity revolves around his experience as a Homeric warrior. It could also simply

A
Level

suggest that his anger over what happened to Achilles' arms is still very much alive.

578

ὡς τάχος: = ὡς τάχιστα.

These instructions are for Tecmessa. The use of ἀλλά + three imperatives creates a sense of urgency.

579

πάκτου: 'close' – 2nd singular active imperative of an omicron-contracted verb (πακτόω).

579–580

μηδ᾽ ἐπισκήνους γόους/δάκρυε: lit. 'do not weep (μηδ᾽ . . . δάκρυε) weepings (γόους) in front of the tent (ἐπισκήνους)'. The repetition of meaning in verb and noun (which is very similar to a cognate and internal accusative) adds to the force of the command. The distinction between public and private spaces and actions is often a theme in Greek tragedy (e.g. *Antigone*), and Ajax asserts that a woman's grief should be a private affair.

580

κάρτα φιλοίκτιστον: 'very much prone to pity'. The neuter form of the adjective has been used even though it is the complement of γυνή. This is another of Ajax's gnomic statements about the nature of women (see 293).

581

πύκαζε θᾶσσον: 'close (the doors of the house) quickly'. θᾶσσον is here an adverb meaning 'sooner', and therefore (with an imperative) 'straightaway'.

πρός: + genitive (here) = 'in the nature of', 'characteristic of' (see 319).

582

πρὸς τομῶντι πήματι: 'over a wound which needs cutting' (πρός + dative [here] = 'over'; τομάω = 'I need cutting').

A second gnomic statement: words are of no use when surgery is required. This stark metaphor makes it clear that suicide is still his intention.

583–645: this episode ends with a short and rapid exchange between Tecmessa and Ajax in which she begs him not to leave her and her son and he once again shuts her down. He withdraws indoors, and the ekkyklema is (presumably) wheeled inside. It is uncertain whether or not Tecmessa also leaves the stage at this point (possibly by another entrance to the skene) or whether she remains onstage with Eurysaces (indeed, all three may leave and then return together at 646 – we simply do not know - but clearly his family do need to be onstage from 646: see below). The chorus then sing and dance the first stasimon (standing choral ode), a very poetic and sad ode in which they contrast the security of their homeland (Salamis) with their misery at Troy. They express deep concerns for Ajax and how his parents will react to the news of what has happened.

A Level

646–692

This marks the beginning of the so-called 'deception speech'. It takes up the whole episode and is one of the most important (and heavily disputed) passages in the play. Our interpretation of it is likely to affect our overall assessment of Ajax's character.

Ajax returns through the *skene* to the acting area/orchestra (in which Eurysaces, the chorus and probably Tecmessa are still standing), carrying Hector's sword, and in a calm mood. The latter is a surprise given the anger and desperation with which he spoke at the end of the last episode. He delivers a rational speech, full of poetic language and imagery, in which he states (amongst other things) that stubbornness can be overcome, that Tecmessa has changed him (and that he pities her), that he will 'bury' his sword by the shore, that in the future he will know how to yield to the gods, and that enemies will one day become friends. But this moment of gentleness is the calm before the storm. Ajax's next appearance (at 815) sees a return to the anger and fury we saw earlier, and he goes on to commit suicide.

Most scholars interpret this speech as an exercise in deception: Ajax is, they say, trying to convince his friends and family that he does not intend to commit suicide, in order that they might give him the space to carry out the deed; he is using linguistic ambiguity in order to achieve this. A significant minority argue that Ajax is not being deceptive or manipulative, but is simply misunderstood by those around him. After all, his core message – that he has come to a new understanding of his situation and of the world around him – is true even though he still wishes to commit suicide. Indeed, he does not directly state that he will not kill himself, and many of his utterances (e.g. the idea that he must 'yield' to the gods) could be interpreted as indicating suicide.

There are many other possible interpretations of this speech. However one reads it, it is likely to come as a shock to an audience which (due to its knowledge of the Ajax myth) is expecting an Ajax full of resentment and fury. This episode is one of many ways in which Sophocles plays with the received version of the myth and surprises us. Nevertheless, we know that Ajax must die and thus much dramatic irony is generated by the reaction of Tecmessa and the chorus to Ajax's words.

646
ἅπανθ᾽: = ἅπαντα. Take with ἄδηλα: 'everything hidden'.
κἀναρίθμητος: = καὶ ἀναρίθμητος.

647
καὶ φανέντα κρύπτεται: 'and, once it has been revealed, hides it (again)'. κρύπτεται is middle, with χρόνος still the subject. The theme is that of change over time.

648
κοὐκ ἔστ᾽ . . . οὐδέν: 'and nothing is . . .' (κοὐκ = καὶ οὐκ, ἔστ᾽= ἔστι). On double negatives in which the first is a simple negative, see 129.

A Level

ἁλίσκεται: 'is overcome'. It has two subjects (line 649) but has been attracted into the number of the nearest one.

649

χὦ ... χαὶ = καὶ ὁ ... καὶ αἱ (see 456).

χὦ δεινὸς ὅρκος: 'the dread oath'. Ajax has not actually sworn an oath to commit suicide, but he must be referring to his (previously) unwavering intention so to do.

χαὶ περισκελεῖς φρένες: = 'and stubborn wills'.

650

ὃς τὰ δείν' ἐκαρτέρουν: it is best to translate τὰ δείνα as an adverb, e.g. 'I who was so/dreadfully obstinate', 'I who was obstinate in that terrible way', or similar. Finglass has 'I who . . . was mightily steadfast'.

τότε: 'once', or 'back then'.

651

βαφῇ σίδηρος ὥς: move ὥς to the start of the phrase – 'as iron in the dipping'. This simile comes from the world of metalworking: when hot iron is dipped in water, it hardens.

ἐθηλύνθην: 1st sg. aorist passive of θηλύνω (= 'I make womanish', therefore, in the passive, 'I am made soft'). Finglass translates it as 'I have been feminised'. Another option is 'I have been softened'. Ajax clearly thinks that pity is a feminine quality (see below).

στόμα: acc. of respect.

οἰκτίρω δὲ/ . . . λιπεῖν: 'I feel pity at leaving her' (νιν = αὐτήν).

παρ' ἐχθροῖς: (παρ' = παρά) 'among my enemies'.

654

εἶμι: 'I shall go' (rather than 'I am', which is εἰμί: note that the accents are different).

τε: translate as if this comes after λουτρά.

655–656

λύμαθ' ἁγνίσας ἐμά: 'having washed away my dirt'. λύμαθ' = λύματα = dirt washed off during the washing process. It has both a literal sense and a metaphorical one here (blood and dirt from his attack on the animals/the stain on his honour).

ὡς ἄν . . . ἐξαλέξωμαι: a purpose clause – 'so that I may ward off . . .'. (ἐξαλέξωμαι = 1st singular aorist subjunctive middle of ἐξαλέξω = 'I ward off').

On the face it of it, it seems that Ajax wishes to undergo some form of ritual purification in order to ward off the anger of Athena. But the language is ambiguous. As Finglass notes, 'washing a corpse is also an essential preparation for burial'.

657

μολών τε χῶρον ἔνθ' ἂν ἀστιβῆ κίχω: 'going wherever I can find an untrodden place'. κίχω = 1st singular aorist subjunctive active of κιχάνω (ἔνθ' ἂν . . . κίχω = indefinite construction in primary sequence). ἔνθ' = ἔνθα.

A Level

658

κρύψω: note the ambiguity – 'hiding' the sword could of course refer to suicide. However, the next line, in which he talks about digging a hole in the ground, slightly confuses that interpretation.

ἔγχος: here = 'sword' (it more often means 'spear').

659

γαίας ... ἔνθα: lit. 'where of the ground' (γαίας is a partitive genitive), i.e. '(I shall dig) a hole in the ground where . . .'. μή is used for the negative here as this relative clause, introduced by ἔνθα with a future indicative (ὄψεται), expresses purpose (for which μή is the correct negative).

660

σῳζόντων: this is a 3rd person plural imperative (present active): 'let (Night and Hades) keep (it) safe . . .'.

661

ἐξ οὗ: 'from the time when', 'ever since'.

662

A reminder that Hector gifted this sword to Ajax after their duel in *Iliad* 7 (lines 303–305).

663

τι κεδνόν: 'anything good'.

664

οὔπω: some scholars translate as 'never' or 'not at all', rather than the usual 'not yet'. Others prefer the usual translation.

ἐχθρῶν ἄδωρα δῶρα κοὐκ ὀνήσιμα: (κοὐκ = καὶ οὐκ) 'the gifts of enemies are not gifts, and are not beneficial/useful' (or 'and they have no use/benefit'). The oxymoron is underlined by juxtaposition and use of cognate forms: ἄδωρα δῶρα. This line, with its suggestion that friends and enemies may never truly be reconciled, might give us a hint as to Ajax's underlying intentions.

666

τοιγάρ: 'therefore'.

τὸ λοιπόν: 'in the future', 'henceforth'.

666–667

εἰσόμεσθα μὲν θεοῖς/εἴκειν: 'we will know how to yield to the gods'. This and the following statement (about revering the Atreidae) are ambiguous and thus can be used to argue for or against the idea that Ajax is being deliberately deceptive.

A Level

668

ὥσθ᾽ ὑπεικτέον: (ὥσθ᾽ = ὥστε) 'with the result that one needs to submit', a result clause without the signpost word. ὑπεικτέον is a gerundive of obligation, being used impersonally in the neuter.

τί μήν: lit. 'what else?', i.e. 'of course'.

669

καὶ γὰρ τὰ δεινὰ καὶ τὰ καρτερώτατα: 'for even terrible and the most mighty things . . .'. The use of the neuter plural indicates that this statement has a truly universal application. It applies as much to the elemental forces of nature as it does to mankind, as the next lines will show.

670

τιμαῖς: '(yield) to dignity/high office', or perhaps '(yield) to people in authority'.

τοῦτο μέν: Leave τοῦτο untranslated. τοῦτο μὲν . . . τοῦτο δέ sometimes appears in tragedy when examples are being given. Here we have a slight variation: τοῦτο μὲν . . . δέ.

671

ἐκχωροῦσιν: 'give way (to)'.

672

ἐξίσταται: 3rd singular middle – 'makes way (for)'.

αἰανής: 'eternal', or 'grim'. The adjective can mean either, and its particular meaning here is unclear. I would tentatively suggest the latter, as night isn't eternal.

673

τῇ λευκοπώλῳ . . . ἡμέρᾳ: 'for day with its white horses'. Probably a reference to the sun god Helios, here depicted as carried in a chariot by white horses.

φέγγος . . . φλέγειν: 'to kindle light'.

674

ἐκοίμισε: 3rd singular aorist of κοιμίζω (= 'I put to sleep', 'calm'). The use of an aorist in a gnomic statement is common; in English it is best translated as a present tense.

675

ἐν δ᾽: (δ᾽ = δέ) lit. 'and among (them)', 'like the rest' i.e. 'like the other powers of nature, (Sleep) . . .'.

676

λύει πεδήσας: lit. 'having bound, releases', i.e. 'releases what he has bound'.

οὐδ᾽ ἀεὶ λαβὼν ἔχει: (οὐδ᾽ = οὐδέ) 'and, having taken it, he doesn't hold on to it forever'. The adverb should be translated with the main verb.

677

ἡμεῖς: Finglass suggests that Ajax is referring to himself, but in the poetic plural. Others take it to be a true plural ('we humans') which is then made specific in the next line with the use of ἔγωγ᾽.

A Level

σωφρονεῖν: 'to be prudent', 'to be sensible', 'to have sophrosyne'. Up to this point, Ajax has shown very little (if any) ability to be rational and moderate. But the sentiment expressed here should not surprise us: his realization that sophrosyne is what the world requires is one of the driving forces behind his decision that suicide is the only way out.

678

ἔγωγ᾽: (= ἔγωγε) a single word affirmative answer – 'yes, I will learn'.

679–680

ὅ τ᾽ ἐχθρὸς ἡμῖν ἐς τοσόνδ᾽ ἐχθαρτέος,/ ὡς καὶ φιλήσων αὖθις: lit. 'my enemy (ὅ τε ἐχθρὸς ἡμῖν) must be hated (ἐχθαρτέος) [so much] as (ἐς τοσόνδε ... ὡς) one who will later (αὖθις) also (καί) be a friend (φιλήσων)'.

One of the key themes of the play comes to the fore here. This is a traditional piece of ancient Greek wisdom, thought to derive from Bias of Priene (one of the Seven Sages). The saying splits into two halves: a more positive one (the notion that enemies may become friends), with which Ajax begins, and the other side of the coin (that friends might also become enemies: see below on 680-682). Note the figura etymologica in ἐχθρὸς ... ἐχθαρτέος.

680–682

ἔς τε τὸν φίλον/ τοσαῦθ᾽ ὑπουργῶν ὠφελεῖν βουλήσομαι, /ὡς αἰὲν οὐ μενοῦντα: 'but regarding a friend (ἔς τε τὸν φίλον), I will want (βουλήσομαι) to assist and help him (ὑπουργῶν ὠφελεῖν) this much (τοσαῦθ᾽), as (ὡς) one who will not always (αἰὲν οὐ) remain thus (μενοῦντα)'. τοσαῦθ᾽ = τοσαῦτα (here used as an adverbial accusative). Ajax is of course referring to the Atreidae.

682–683

Ajax now dwells further on the negative half of the maxim, i.e. that friendship is false for most men.

ἑταιρείας λιμήν: 'the harbour of friendship'. Nautical metaphors are very common in Greek poetry.

684

A vague and ambiguous statement; it puts Tecmessa and the chorus at ease, but generates a vast amount of dramatic irony for the audience or the reader, who know what Ajax really means when he says εὖ σχήσει.

ἀμφί + dat. = 'concerning'. εὖ σχήσει: 'it will turn out well' (σχήσω is a future from ἔχω). ἔχω + adverb = 'to be X' (a very common usage: see 87).

684–686

σὺ δὲ/ ... γύναι: Ajax moves out of his pensive state and addresses Tecmessa (and then the chorus). He is no gentler in his tone with his concubine than in previous interactions: note that he continues to give orders, he still does not use her name, and that by moving her inside the tent he is essentially putting her back in (what he considers to be) her proper zone. His character has not changed all that much, despite the seeming magnitude of his philosophical and psychological insights.

A Level

διὰ τέλους: 'fully', 'in all fullness'. There is figura etymologica here (τέλους ...
   τελεῖσθαι).

ἐρᾷ: ἐράω: + 'I love/desire' + genitive (ὧν). The antecedent of the relative pronoun
   has been omitted (as often in Greek).

τοὐμὸν ... κέαρ: 'my heart'.

It seems likely that Tecmessa and Eurysaces will leave via the *skene* at this point,
rather than waiting until the end of the speech.

687–688

ταὐτὰ τῇδέ μοι τάδε/τιμᾶτε: 'honour (τιμᾶτε) these same things (ταὐτὰ ...
   τάδε – note the crasis in ταὐτά) as this woman (τῇδέ) for me (μοι – ethic
   dative)'. Note the alliteration of dentals (θ/τ) in lines 687–688.

688

ἢν μόλῃ: 'if he comes'. ἢν = ἐάν. μόλῃ = 3rd person singular aorist subjunctive
   from βλώσκω.

Τεύκρῳ...σημήνατε: 'tell/explain to Teucer ...'.

689

μέλειν: here, μέλω = 'take care of' (+ gen: ἡμῶν = both 'us' more generally, and
   'me', referring to Ajax's body).

εὐνοεῖν δ' ὑμῖν ἄμα: (δ' = δέ) 'and at the same time to show goodwill towards you'.

690

ἐγὼ γὰρ εἶμ' ἐκεῖσ' ὅποι πορευτέον: 'for I will go (εἶμ' = εἶμι) there/to the place
   (ἐκεῖσ' = ἐκεῖσε) where (ὅποι) I must travel (πορευτέον)'. Another ambiguous
   statement which adds dramatic tension to the piece (cf. 684).

691–692

ἄν μ' ... /πύθοισθε σεσωμένον: (μ' = με) 'you might hear that I have been saved'
   (potential optative introducing indirect statement). σεσωσμένον = perfect
   participle masc. acc. sing. from σῴζω.

τάχα and ἴσως are often used idiomatically together to mean 'perhaps'. κεἰ =
   καὶ εἰ.

*693–747: Ajax heads off to the wasteland beyond the camp (hence he uses the
eisodos which leads away from the city). The chorus break into the second stasimon
(693–718). This choral ode contrasts greatly with the first, filled as it is with joy at
the apparent change in Ajax's intentions. They call on the gods (Pan, Apollo, Ares
and Zeus) to join them in their happy state, and the mood is one of great religious
excitement.*

   *The third episode (719–865) begins with the arrival of a messenger. We probably
expect him to announce the death of Ajax, but once again Sophocles prolongs the
dramatic tension by frustrating our expectations. The messenger comes from the
camp. (NB Ajax had left via the other exit.) He has come to tell Ajax that Teucer has
just arrived back from an expedition, that he was insulted by the Greeks (who also
tried to attack him physically), and that the elders managed to calm the situation. On*

**A
Level**

hearing that Ajax is not inside the tent but has departed, the messenger bursts into exclamations of horror (ἰοὺ ἰού) and states that he is 'too late': Teucer instructed that Ajax should remain inside the tent. To the chorus' statement that Ajax has gone 'having turned to more profitable thoughts', the messenger replies with derision: 'these words are full of great stupidity, if indeed Calchas (the prophet of the Greek army at Troy) is sensible in his prophecy'. The chorus respond with a question: 'What sort of prophecy? What does he know concerning this matter?' (line 747), and thus begins the next section.

**A
Level**

748–783

In this section, the messenger responds in detail to the question asked by the chorus in line 747. He is the first messenger we have met, but not the first messenger speech we have heard (Tecmessa's explanation at line 284ff took this form). Messenger speeches give the audience the opportunity to learn of events far distant (in both temporal and geographical terms) from those set before them, and are generally very descriptive (see Introduction p. 350).

748

τοσοῦτον: 'so much/thus much/this much'.

παρὼν ἐτύγχανον: 'I was there'. τυγχάνω + participle = 'I happen to be X-ing' or 'I am actually X-ing'.

749–750

ἐκ γὰρ συνέδρου καὶ τυραννικοῦ κύκλου/Κάλχας μεταστάς: lit. 'For Calchas, departing from the sitting-in-council and royal circle . . .', i.e. 'leaving the circle of leaders in council, Calchas . . .'.

μεταστάς is the participle of μετέστην, the active (in form) but intransitive aorist of μεθίσταμαι = I change my position/depart.

750–751

Calchas withdraws from the Atreidae and the other members of the council (**οἷος Ἀτρειδῶν δίχα**) in order to give Teucer some advice. He clearly has kind intentions towards Teucer and his brother (**φιλοφρόνως** = in a friendly manner).

752

κἀπέσκηψε: = καὶ ἐπέσκηψε ('and he commanded him [i.e. Teucer]').

παντοίᾳ τέχνῃ: lit. 'by all possible cunning/manner', i.e. 'by any means possible' (παντοῖος lit. = 'of all sorts').

753

εἷρξαι: aorist infinitive active from εἴργω = 'I shut in'.

κατ᾽ ἦμαρ τοὐμφανὲς τὸ νῦν τόδε: lit. 'by day, the visible one, this one now' (**κατ᾽** = κατά, **τοὐμφανές** = τὸ ἐμφανές), i.e. 'during this day which is now visible'.

754

ὑπό: + dative = under (so, 'in the tent').

μηδ᾽ ἀφέντ᾽ ἐᾶν: 'and not to let him out'. ἀφέντ᾽ = ἀφέντα: aorist active participle, masc. acc. sg., from ἀφίημι (= 'I send forth, discharge'). **μηδ᾽** = μηδέ.

755

εἰ . . . θέλοι: a future open condition, but within indirect speech in historic sequence (i.e. the messenger is reporting Calchas' future open condition). As a result, ἐάν + subjunctive in the protasis has become εἰ + optative.

ζῶντ᾽: = ζῶντα.

756

ἐλᾷ = 3rd singular future indicative active of ἐλαύνω (= 'I persecute/plague').

θἠμέρᾳ: = τῇ ἡμέρᾳ (by crasis).

757

ὡς ἔφη λέγων: 'as he said speaking', i.e. 'as he said in his speech'.

758

περισσὰ κἀνόνητα: = περισσὰ καὶ ἀνόνητα = 'excessive and unprofitable', i.e. 'unprofitably excessive', referring to the σώματα (which can mean 'people' or 'lives' as well as 'bodies'). The core tragic theme of excess, especially excessive pride or arrogance, is thus restated.

760

ἔφασχ᾽: = ἔφασκε (which is followed by an indirect statement, infinitive construction).

760–761

ὅστις ἀνθρώπου φύσιν/βλαστών: lit. 'whoever born with respect to nature of man', i.e. 'whoever is mortal in nature'. βλαστών = masc. nom. sg. aorist participle from βλαστάνω = 'I am born/come to light'. φύσιν = accusative of respect. This clause is loosely in apposition with σώματα in 758.

ὅστις . . ./μὴ . . . φρονῇ: 'whoever does not think'. Indefinite construction using the subjunctive, but here without the expected ἄν.

761

κατ᾽ ἄνθρωπον: (κατ᾽ = κατά) 'according to man', i.e. 'as man should'. Note that Calchas is repeating what Athena said at 127–133.

762

εὐθὺς ἐξορμώμενος: 'just when he was setting out'. ἐξορμάομαι = 'I set out/start out'.

763

ἄνους καλῶς λέγοντος ηὑρέθη πατρός: 'he was found to be foolish, despite his father speaking wise words'. The genitive absolute (καλῶς λέγοντος . . . πατρός) has a concessive force, highlighted by the juxtaposition of ἄνους καλῶς.

764

ἐννέπει: 'addressed him' (historic present). The use of direct speech here gives some variety to the messenger's account (and of course it makes this particular section vivid). It also perhaps stresses the importance of Telamon's words, and of Ajax's failure to heed them.

765

βούλου: 2nd person singular present middle imperative. A father giving advice to his son before the latter heads off to war is a familiar scene in Greek art and literature. Peleus' advice to Achilles in *Iliad* 9 (lines 9.254-258) is the most famous example.

σὺν θεῷ: 'with the help of a god', i.e. any god/the gods generally.

766

ὑψικόμπως κἀφρόνως: = ὑψικόμπως καὶ ἀφρόνως = 'boastfully and foolishly'. The alpha-privative adverb suggests that he was 'without mind', i.e. 'out of his mind'.

ἠμείψατο: 'he replied' (3rd sg. aorist middle of ἀμείβω, a verb which is very common in Homer).

767–768

κἂν ὁ μηδὲν ὢν ... / κράτος κατακτήσαιτ': 'even a nobody might obtain success'. **κἂν** = καὶ ἄν. **κατακτήσαιτο** = 3rd sg. aorist middle optative from κατακτάομαι = I obtain. **ὁ μηδὲν ὢν** = 'he who is nothing'.

Note that **θεοῖς** and **ὁμοῦ** go together (despite their separation): 'together with the gods'.

769

πέποιθα: 'I trust', 'I am confident that . . .'. **πέποιθα** is 1st person singular perfect active indicative from πείθω. In poetry (and very occasionally in prose), the perfect of πείθω can be used intransitively to mean 'I trust'.

ἐπισπάσειν: future infinitive of ἐπισπάω (= 'I win/acquire').

κλέος: 'glory', a very loaded term which refers to the surrogate immortality (achieved through deeds on the battlefield) which is the goal of each Homeric hero (see Introduction p. 353). Finglass notes that Ajax's words are clearly a direct response to those of his father (**κράτος** picks up **κρατεῖν**; **σὺν θεῷ** becomes **δίχα/κείνων**). He is clearly rejecting Telamon's advice.

770

τοσόνδ' ἐκόμπει μῦθον: lit. 'he boasted such a big story'. Both Jebb and Finglass translate **τοσόνδε** as 'so proud' (i.e. referring not to size, but to the manner in which he boasted).

εἶτα δεύτερον: 'then, on another occasion'. This occasion is more damning, as Ajax directly refuses divine aid in battle.

771

δίας Ἀθάνας: this could be taken as a genitive of respect, and therefore translated as 'regarding divine Athena'. Alternatively, one could read it as being governed by the preposition in **ἀντιφωνεῖ** (773) although, as Finglass notes, this seems rather forced.

ἡνίκ': = ἡνίκα = 'when'.

νιν: = αὐτόν (see line 82).

ηὐδᾶτ': = ηὐδᾶτο (3rd person singular imperfect indicative middle from αὐδάω = 'I speak').

772

ἐπ' ἐχθροῖς: here, ἐπί + dative = against.

χεῖρα φοινίαν: 'blood-stained hand'.

773
ἄρρητόν: 'not to be spoken' or 'unspeakable'.
ἔπος: 'utterance' or 'speech'.
πέλας: + dative = near.
ἴστω: 'stand' – 2nd person singular present middle imperative from ἴστημι.

775
καθ᾽ ἡμᾶς: = κατὰ ἡμᾶς – lit. 'near us', i.e. 'near me' (poetic plural). A looser
   translation such as 'where I'm standing' would also work well.
οὔποτ᾽: = οὔποτε
ἐκρήξει: (battle) will break forth = 3rd singular future indicative of ἐκρήγνυμι (= 'I
   break out/forth').

776–777
ἀστεργῆ . . . / . . . ὀργήν: 'anger not to be desired', or 'implacable anger'.

777
ἐκτήσατ᾽: = ἐκτήσατο.
κατ᾽ ἄνθρωπον: see 761.

778
ἔστι: = 'he is (still) alive'.
θἠμέρᾳ: see 756.

778–779
τάχ᾽ ἂν/γενοίμεθ᾽ αὐτοῦ . . . σωτήριοι: 'Perhaps we might become his saviours',
   i.e. 'perhaps we might be able to save him'. (τάχ᾽ = τάχα, γενοίμεθ᾽ = γενοίμεθα)

779
σὺν θεῷ: 'with the help of [the] god' (see 765). The religious devotion of the speaker
   contrasts strongly with the impiety of Ajax.

780
τοσαῦθ᾽: = τοσαῦτα = 'so much' (or, following Jebb and Finglass, 'thus far').
εἶφ᾽: = εἶπε

780–782
ὁ δ᾽ εὐθὺς ἐξ ἕδρας/πέμπει με . . . /Τεῦκρος: 'Teucer from his seat immediately sent
   me . . .'. The phrase εὐθὺς ἐξ ἕδρας emphasizes the speed and urgency with which
   Teucer acts (he doesn't even have time to rise), as does the historic present πέμπει.

781–782
σοὶ φέροντα τάσδ᾽ ἐπιστολὰς/ . . . φυλάσσειν: (τάσδ᾽ = τάσδε) 'carrying these
   letters for you to observe', or perhaps better is 'bearing these instructions for you
   to follow'.

AS

782

εἰ δ' ἀπεστερήμεθα: 'if we have been deprived (of the opportunity to observe these commands)'. ἀπεστερήμεθα = 1st plural perfect passive from ἀποστερέω (= 'I deprive').

783

οὐκ ἔστιν ἀνὴρ κεῖνος: 'that man is not alive' or 'that man is no more' (for ἀνήρ, see line 9).

784–814: Tecmessa arrives, and the chorus repeat the messenger's story; as expected, she reacts strongly. She encourages the chorus to hunt for Ajax, and they divide into two groups, something which is very rare in tragedy. Even more unusual is that the chorus leaves the orchestra (each half departing via a different eisodos), thus breaking the convention that the chorus should remain onstage for the whole play (see Introduction p. 349). This is motivated by dramatic necessity: Ajax must be alone for his suicide speech. So, we must assume that Tecmessa also goes off to look for Ajax. The Messenger probably leaves to find Teucer (which had, after all, been the original reason for his arrival).

815–865

The second part of the third episode is dominated entirely by Ajax's soliloquy, a speech which in the words of Oliver Taplin is both 'a prologue to the second part of the play and the conclusion of the first'. Scholars are very divided over the issue of exactly where Ajax is supposed to be at this point in the play. Most scholars (Jebb/Stanford/Finglass) agree that there must be a scene change. Jebb states: 'A change of scene is now supposed to take place, from the ground in front of the tent of Ajax to a lonely spot on the sea-shore, with trees or bushes'. This would, of course, be very unusual – only one extant tragedy, the *Eumenides*, has a definite change of scene. Moreover, as Jebb himself notes, it is difficult to see how such this would be managed or conveyed to the audience. But despite these objections, it is difficult to see how the transition to the suicide speech could've been managed without a change of scene of some kind, and perhaps the exit of the chorus might be sufficient to indicate that we are now somewhere else.

The tone of Ajax's soliloquy is very different from that of lines 646–692. His former bitterness and resentment have returned. He blames Agamemnon and Menelaus for his death, and asks for the Greek army to be destroyed. He also speaks ill of Hector, the man who had gifted him the sword with which he is to end his life. More interesting than what he does say is what he does not: he makes no mention of Athena; furthermore, he does not directly mention Tecmessa or Eurysaces. It is clear that his previous speech was indeed to a large extent a deception, even if it is true that he has come to a greater understanding of the world (and his own inability to exist within it).

815

ὁ . . . σφαγεύς: lit. 'the slaughterer/slayer' (a sacrificial term here applied to the sword).
ᾗ: 'where' (see 492).

816

εἴ τῳ καὶ λογίζεσθαι σχολή: 'if a man has leisure even to make calculations'. Supply the verb 'to be'. τῳ = τινι. Finglass comments: 'His contempt for mere deliberation (λογίζεσθαι) and idleness (σχολή) suits a man of action'.

817

ἐμοί: 'to me', 'as far as I'm concerned' – probably a dative of agent after μισηθέντος (aorist passive participle from μισέω), which is possible after an aorist passive.

A Level

818

μισηθέντος: 'hated'; take this with **μάλιστα:** 'most hated'. This phrase is qualified by **ξένων:** whilst as far as Ajax is concerned, Hector is the most hated/hateful of guest-friends, he is not the person Ajax hates the most. That is reserved for the Atreidae.

ἐχθίστου θ' ὁρᾶν: (θ' = τε) 'and the most hateful to see'.

Note the contrast between the spirit in which the gift was given by Hector (i.e. as a symbol of the ending of hostilities between the two men) and Ajax's present attitude: for Ajax, an enemy will always remain an enemy.

819

πέπηγε: 'it is fixed' – 3rd singular perfect indicative active (intransitive) from πήγνυμι.

ἐν γῇ πολεμίᾳ τῇ Τρῳάδι: 'in the hostile land of Troy'. Ajax's (to a degree self-imposed) isolation is highlighted.

820

σιδηροβρῶτι θηγάνῃ νεηκονής: 'recently sharpened by an iron-eating whetstone'. A whetstone is a stone used to sharpen tools and weapons. Note the use of a three-word trimeter, which allows Ajax to dwell on the sword.

821

ἔπηξα: 'I fixed/planted (it)' – 1st singular aorist indicative active (transitive this time!) of πήγνυμι.

εὖ περιστείλας: 'having secured it well'. **περιστείλας** = aorist participle from περιστέλλω.

822

διὰ τάχους: 'quickly'.

θανεῖν: Jebb suggests that this should be translated as a result clause, but with ὥστε omitted.

τῷδ' ἀνδρί: 'to/for this man'. Ajax is referring to himself (translate 'to/for me'). Garvie notes that this is 'a common way of referring to oneself, but here perhaps marking Ajax' final assertion of his status as a hero'.

823

εὐσκευοῦμεν: 'I am well equipped', i.e. for suicide. Plural for singular.

Ajax now prays to Zeus. Garvie emphasises that this 'should not be taken ... to show that he has learnt *sophrosyne*', not least because he doesn't pray to Athena (the goddess whom he directly offended).

ἐκ δὲ τῶνδέ: 'After this' or 'next'.

824

ἄρκεσον: 2nd sg. aorist imperative from ἀρκέω (here) = 'I assist' (+ dative - **μοι**).

καὶ γὰρ εἰκός: 'as indeed is fitting'.

825

αἰτήσομαι δέ σ' οὐ μακρὸν γέρας λαβεῖν: (σ' = σε) 'I shall ask to obtain no great prize from you'. **αἰτήσομαι** takes a double accusative ('I [shall] ask X for

Y') and **λαβεῖν** is an epexegetic (i.e. explanatory) infinitive. Note that **οὐ** is to be taken very closely with **μακρόν** – i.e. the request will not be a great one. However, as noted by Garvie and Finglass, although the request might seem small, it will in fact not be granted easily. This problem will dominate the second half of the play.

826
ἡμῖν: 'for me' - ethic dative.

827
πρῶτος ὥς με βαστάσῃ: 'so that he might be the first to raise me' (purpose clause). **βαστάσῃ** = 3rd singular aorist subjunctive active from **βαστάζω**.

828
τῷδε περὶ νεορράντῳ ξίφει: 'on this newly-sprinkled sword' (**περί** + dative = 'on' [here]).

829–830
καὶ μὴ ... κατοπτευθεὶς ... /ῥιφθῶ: 'in order that I might not be observed ... and thrown' (lit. 'lest, having been observed, I might be thrown'). **ῥιφθῶ** is 1st singular aorist subjunctive passive from **ῥίπτω**.
του: τινος, with **πρός** + genitive = (here) 'by one of'.

830
κυσὶν πρόβλητος οἰωνοῖς θ᾽ ἕλωρ: (**θ᾽** = τε) 'as prey, cast to the dogs and the birds'. **ἕλωρ** ('prey') is a very epic word. It is every Homeric hero's greatest fear that he might remain unburied on the battlefield and end up as prey for dogs and birds.

831
τοσαῦτά σ᾽, ὦ Ζεῦ, προστρέπω: (**θ᾽** = τε) lit. 'such things, Zeus, I supplicate you', i.e. 'I make such supplication to you, Zeus'. **τοσαῦτά** is an internal accusative.

832
πομπαῖον Ἑρμῆν χθόνιον: 'Hermes who escorts (souls) under the earth'.

833
ξὺν ἀσφαδάστῳ καὶ ταχεῖ πηδήματι: 'with a leap which is free from struggle and swift'.
πλευρὰν διαρρήξαντα: 'having broken through my ribs', or perhaps 'as I break through/when I have broken through my ribs'. **διαρρήξαντα** aorist participle (acc. masc. sg., agreeing with **με**) from διαρρήγνυμι = 'I break through'. **πλευράν** is technically singular, but a plural translation works best in English.

835
καλῶ δ᾽ ἀρωγούς: (**δ᾽** = δέ) 'and I call as my helpers ...'.

836
πάντα τὰν βροτοῖς πάθη: 'all the sufferings amongst mortals' (**τὰν** = τὰ ἐν).

**A
Level**

837

σεμνὰς Ἐρινῦς τανύποδας: 'the revered, far-striding Erinyes'. The Erinyes (otherwise known as the Eumenides or the Furies) were goddesses of revenge. Note that Ἐρινῦς here is accusative plural. Garvie translates τανύποδας as 'with their long strides', and notes that it 'suggests the swift and relentless pursuit of the victim'.

837–838

μαθεῖν ἐμὲ/πρὸς τῶν Ἀτρειδῶν ὡς διόλλυμαι τάλας: 'to learn how, wretched as I am, I am destroyed at the hands of the Atreidae'. ἐμέ is an anticipatory accusative and does not need to be translated.

839–842

All commentators agree that these lines are problematic, and that at least some of them are spurious (i.e. fake), for a variety of reasons, not least the lack of attestation of any tradition of the Atreidae being killed by their sons, and the fact that φιλίστων (842) is not a classical form. One scholar, Wesseling, deletes all four lines; Jebb and Finglass would delete just the last two.

840

ξυναρπάσειαν: 3rd plural aorist optative active, used here for a wish – 'may they seize'.

840–841

ὥσπερ εἰσορῶσ' ἐμὲ/αὐτοσφαγῆ πίπτοντα: 'just as they see (εἰσορῶσ' = εἰσορῶσι) me falling, slain by myself (αὐτοσφαγῆ)'.

841

τώς: 'so/in this way' (adverb).

842

φιλίστων: 'dearest' – irregular superlative, genitive plural.

ὀλοίατο: another optative (3rd pl. aor. opt. mid. of ὄλλυμαι) used for a wish – 'may they perish'.

843

ἴτ᾽: = ἴτε = 'come' (2nd plural imperative active).

844

γεύεσθε ... πανδήμου στρατοῦ: 'taste ... the entire army'. γεύομαι + gen. = 'I taste'. This verb creates a very striking image, and one which is fairly common in Greek literature – the Furies are traditionally bloodsuckers. Ajax's curse is made even more forceful by the use of two imperatives in asyndeton. Note that his desire for revenge now extends beyond the Atreidae to the entire army.

845

τὸν αἰπὺν οὐρανὸν διφρηλατῶν: 'driving your chariot across high heaven' (τὸν αἰπὺν οὐρανόν = accusative of distance travelled). Ajax turns aside to address Helios (the Sun-god) and to ask him to bear a message.

A Level

847

ἐπισχὼν χρυσόνωτον ἡνίαν: 'as you check your golden reins', i.e. in order to make an announcement (see 848).

848

ἄγγειλον ἄτας τὰς ἐμάς: 'announce my ruin'. ἄγγειλον = 2nd singular aorist imperative active. ἄτας = poetic plural.

849

τῇ τε δυστήνῳ τροφῷ: lit. 'and to my unlucky rearer', i.e. 'and to the unlucky woman who reared me', a way of saying 'my unlucky mother'.

850

ἦ που: 'indeed, I suppose'. ἦ is an affirmative particle, and που modifies it slightly.
ἤσει: 'she will raise' – 3rd sg. fut. indic. active of ἵημι. The image of Eriboea's lamentation recalls that of Hecabe and the other Trojan women on hearing of the death of Hector in the *Iliad*.

852

ἀλλ᾽ οὐδὲν ἔργον: (ἀλλ᾽ =ἀλλά) 'but there is no point in . . .'.

853

τὸ πρᾶγμα ἀρκτέον: 'the deed must be begun'. ἀρκτέον = gerundive (passive verbal adjective) from ἀρκέω.

854–858

These lines have also been suspected and deleted by several scholars, generally on the grounds of a lack of continuity between this passage and what comes before it. Finglass summarises the argument: 'As a whole, the passage causes an unacceptable delay after 852–853. The trite invocations also contrast with the distinctive and moving vocatives which follow.'

854

ὦ Θάνατε Θάνατε: 'O Death, Death!'. Those disagreeing with Finglass (see note above) might argue that these particular repeated vocatives are as effective as those which come later, not least because the repetition has a certain urgency about it.
νῦν μ᾽ ἐπίσκεψαι μολών: 'come now and look upon me'. ἐπίσκεψαι = 2nd sg. aorist middle imperative from ἐπισκοπέομαι (= 'I look upon'). μ᾽ = με.

855

καίτοι σὲ μὲν κἀκεῖ προσαυδήσω ξυνών: 'and yet I shall meet you and converse with you there too' (κἀκεῖ = καὶ ἐκεῖ). ξυνών = present participle from ξύνειμι (lit. 'I am with').

856

τὸ νῦν σέλας: lit. 'the now brightness', i.e. 'present light', or perhaps 'the light which I see now'.

A Level

858

πανύστατον: 'for the very last time' (adverb, intensified by **δή**).

κοὔποτ᾽ αὖθις ὕστερον: 'and never again later' (**κοὔποτ᾽** = καὶ οὔποτε). Note the pleonasm.

As part of the argument that these lines should be deleted, Finglass notes: 'Since Ajax has only just declared that he wishes to end his life without delay, it is incredible that he should utter a three-line invocation of the Sun so shortly after he has addressed it for five'.

859–865

As we reach the climax of the speech, Ajax movingly bids farewell to his surroundings (and in particular the places with which he has been associated): the light of the sun, his native land of Salamis, his home, Athens and the plain of Troy. The list is varied in grammatical terms, beginning as it does with vocatives, which are followed by nominatives connected by **τε/καί**.

860

βάθρον: 'foundation' or 'seat'.

861

τὸ σύντροφον γένος: lit. 'the brought-up-together race', i.e. 'the race which is kindred with mine', referring to the ancestral relationship between the Athenians and the Salaminians.

863

ὦ τροφῆς ἐμοί: 'you who have nourished me'. **τροφῆς** = vocative plural of τροφεύς, -έως, m. (= 'one who brings up'). **ἐμοί** = possessive.

864

τοῦθ᾽: = τοῦτο

τοὔπος: = το ἔπος

865

τὰ δ᾽ ἄλλ᾽: = τὰ δ᾽ ἄλλα (supply ἔπη)

ἐν Ἅιδου τοῖς κάτω: 'to those down below in (lit. 'of') Hades'.

866ff: Ajax's suicide.

Scholars are divided regarding what happens directly after this speech. One possibility is that Ajax kills himself in full view of the audience. Others argue that this would break the convention that violence is not to be shown onstage in Greek tragedy, and cite that there is no example of such an onstage death happening anywhere within the plays which have survived. Moreover, it confuses the issue of why the chorus is not able to find Ajax when they enter the stage at 866.

However, regarding the latter point, it is possible that the chorus members are simply looking at another part of the orchestra/acting area, rather than the area in which Ajax's corpse is lying. Moreover, we do need to remember that Sophocles was an innovator, and so the fact that (as far as we know) something wasn't done before him doesn't mean that he didn't do it. Therefore, there is a strong argument to be made that Ajax does kill himself onstage. This would be both dramatically effective and useful in practical terms, because (as noted) his body needs to be onstage for it to be found by the chorus. The principle alternative views are as follows:

- *Jebb suggests that during the scene change, something representing a copse or a bush has been placed at the edge of the orchestra, and that Ajax falls behind this. Given the size and layout of the Theatre of Dionysus, this is an unsatisfactory conclusion. It would work on a (present-day) proscenium stage, but not in a fifth-century Athenian theatrical setup.*

- *Other scholars have suggested that Ajax kills himself on the ekkyklema, which is then wheeled inside in order to shield the body. But again this is unsatisfactory, not least because the ekkyklema is supposed to reveal a scene from inside a house/palace (or, here, a tent). Moreover, it still (potentially) requires Ajax to kill himself in front of the audience, and therefore is not a better solution than that advanced above.*

A
Level

Vocabulary

An asterisk * denotes a word in OCR's Defined Vocabulary List for AS.

*ἀγαθός, -ή, όν	good	*αἴρω	I raise, lift, take on, assume
*ἀγγέλλω (aor. ἤγγειλα)	I announce	ἀιστόω	I annihilate
*ἄγγελος, -ου, m.	messenger	*αἰσχρός, -ά, -όν	disgraceful, ugly, shameful
ἁγνίζω	I wash, cleanse, purify	*αἰτέω	I ask for
ἄγρα, -ας, f.	prey	*αἰτία, -ας, f.	blame
*ἄγω	I lead, bring	αἰχμάζω	I arm X (acc.) with a spear
ἀγωνάρχης, -ου, m.	judge of a contest		
ἀδάματος, -ον	invincible; virgin	αἰχμαλωτίς, -ίδος	captive (adj.)
ἄδαστος, -ον	undivided	ἄκλητος, -ον	uncalled, unbidden
ἄδηλος, -ον	unseen, invisible	*ἀκούω + acc. of thing, gen. of person	I hear, listen to
ἄδωρος, -ον	'not being gifts', without gifts		
*ἀεί	always	*ἄκρος, -α, -ον	top, farthest point, end (of)
ἄελπτος, -ον	unexpected, beyond expectation	ἀλάομαι	I am perplexed/at a loss
ἄημα, -ατος, n.	blow, blast	ἀλγεινός, ή, όν	painful
*Ἀθῆναι, -ων, f.pl.	Athens	*ἀληθής, -ές	real, true
Ἀθήνη (poetic Ἀθάνη), -ης, f.	Athena	ἁλίσκομαι	I am overcome, captured
αἰαῖ	alas! [a cry]	*ἀλλά	but
αἰάζειν	to cry, wail, groan (lit. 'to say αἰαῖ')	*ἄλλος, -η, -ο	other, another
αἰανής, -ές	eternal; grim	ἄλλοτε	at another time (if repeated: at one time ... at another)
Αἴας, Αἴαντος, m.	Ajax		
Αἰγαῖος, -α, ον	of the Aegean (sea)		
*αἰδέομαι	I respect, revere	*ἅμα	at the same time
Ἅιδης, -ου, m.	Hades (the underworld/god of the underworld)	ἀμείβομαι (aor. ἠμείψαμην)	I answer
αἰδώς, οῦς, f.	shame	ἀμείνων, -ον	better (comparative of ἀγαθός)
αἰέν	always		
αἴθω	I burn	ἀμφήκης, -ες	two-edged
αἰκίζω	I mistreat, torture (same meaning in act/mid)	ἀμφί + dat.	about, concerning; for
		*ἄν	would, could (used in conditions, potential optative and the indefinite construction)
αἱμάσσω	I stain with blood		
αἰνέω	I praise, approve of		
αἰπύς, -εῖα, -ύ	high		

ἀναγκαῖος, -α, -ον — of necessity

ἀνάγω — I raise, lift up

ἄναξ, ἄνακτος, m. — lord, master

ἀναρίθμητος, -ον — not to be counted, countless

ἀνασπάω — I spout out (+ λόγους = I spout out words)

ἄνασσα, -ης, f. — lady (fem. of ἄναξ)

ἀνατίθημι — I move X back from

ἀνέρομαι — I enquire, question

ἀνέχομαι — I hold out, hold my temper

ἀνήκεστος, -ον — incurable, fatal; irresistible

*ἀνήρ, ἀνδρός, m. — man, husband

ἀνθρώπειος, -α, -ον — human, of/to do with humans

ἀνοίγνυμι — I open

ἀνόνητος, -ον — unprofitable

ἄνοος, -ον — without mind/sense, foolish

ἀντάω + dat. — I meet

*ἀντί + gen. — instead of, in place of

ἀντιάζω — I supplicate, beg

ἀντιφωνέω — I reply, answer in reply

ἄνω — upwards

ἀνώδυνος, -ον — free from pain

*ἀξιόω — I think fit/think it right

ἄοκνος, -ον — unhesitating

ἀπαίσσω (aor. ἀπῇξα) — I leap/swerve away from (+ gen.)

ἀπαρνέομαι — I deny utterly

*ἅπας, -ασα, -αν — the whole, all, every

ἀπάσσω — I leap/dart off

ἀπείργω — I keep X (acc.) away from Y (gen.); prevent X (acc.) from Y (infinitive)

ἀπευθύνω — I bind back

ἄπιστος, -ον — faithless, without faith

*ἀπό + gen. — from, by

*ἀπόλλυμι — I lose, destroy; (middle) I perish

ἀπορρέω — I fall away

*ἀποστερέω — I deprive X (acc.) of Y (gen.)

ἀπόστροφος, -ον — turned away, averted

ἄποπτος, -ον — invisible, dimly seen

ἄποτος, -ον — without drink

ἀπρίξ — tightly

ἀπωθέω (aor. ἀπέωσα) — I thrust aside, reject

ἀράομαι — I pray to

Ἀργεῖος, -α -ον — from Argos, Argive; Greek

ἀρήγω — I help

ἀριστεία, -ας, f. — excellence, prize for excellence

ἀριστεύω — I win

ἀρκέω (aor. ἤρκεσα) — (intransitive) I am enough; (transitive) I achieve; I ward off, keep off; I assist

ἀρνείος, -α, -ον — of a lamb/sheep

ἄρνυμαι — I acquire, obtain

*ἁρπάζω — I seize, snatch away

ἄρρηκτος, -ον — unbreakable

ἄρρητός, -όν — unspeakable, not to be spoken

*ἄρτι — recently

ἀρτίως — recently

*ἄρχων, -οντος, m. — ruler, leader

ἀρωγός, -οῦ, m. — helper

ἄσιτος, -ον — without food

ἄσκοπος, -ον — unimaginable, incomprehensible

ἀσπιστήρ, -ῆρος, m. — one who bears a shield

ἄσπλαγχνος, -ον — cowardly (lit. 'without stomach')

ἄσσω (aor. ἦξα) — I dart (intransitive); I set in motion (transitive)

ἀστεργής, -ές — implacable, unyielding

ἀστιβής, -ές — untrodden

ἀσφάδαστος, -ον — without struggle

ἀτάλλω — I am carefree

ἄτερ + gen. — without

ἄτη, -ης, f. — ruin, delusion

ἀτιμάζω — I dishonour

ἄτιμος, -ον — dishonoured

Ἀτρείδης, -ου, m. — son of Atreus (Agamemnon or Menelaus)

*αὖ — in turn

αὐδάω — I speak/tell

*αὖθις — again

*αὐτίκα — at once

αὐτόχειρ, -χειρος — by one's own hand

*αὐτός, -ή, -ό — himself; same; him, her, it, them (in oblique cases)

αὐτοσφαγής, -ές — self-slain, slain by myself

αὐχενίζω — I cut the throat of

ἀφαιρέω — I take away

ἄφθογγος, -ον — speechless

ἀφίημι — I send forth, discharge, let out

*ἀφικνέομαι — I arrive

ἀφορμάω — I start (intransitive)

ἀφρόνως — foolishly

Ἀχαιοί, -ῶν, m.pl. — Achaeans, Greeks

Ἀχίλλειος, -α, -ον — of Achilles

Ἀχιλλεύς, Ἀχιλλέως, m. — Achilles

ἀψόφητος, -ον + gen. — without the sound of

βάθος, -ους, n.	depth	*γυνή, γυναικός, f.	woman, wife
βάθρον, -ου, n.	foundation, seat		
*βαίνω (aor. ἔβην)	I go	δαίμων, -ονος, m.	fate, destiny, fortune
βαιός, ά, όν	little, small	*δακρύω	I weep, cry
*βάλλω	I throw	*δέ	and, but
βάπτω	I dip, dye	*δεῖ (+ acc.)	it is necessary
βαρύνω	I weigh down	δείδω (aor. ἔδεισα)	I fear
*βαρύς, -εῖα, -ύ	heavy, grievous	*δείκνυμι (fut. δείξω)	I show, present
βαρύψυχος, -ον	heavy of soul, spiritless	δειλία, -ας, f.	cowardice
βάσις, -εως, f.	step, course	*δεινός, -ή, -όν	terrible, clever, strange
βαστάζω	I raise, lift up	*δεξιά, -ᾶς, f.	right hand
βάξις, -εως, f.	saying, report/rumour	δέρκομαι (pf.	I see clearly
βαφή, -ῆς, f.	dipping (of iron into	δέδορκά)	
	water)	δεσμίος, -α, -ον	bound
βέλος, -ους, n.	weapon, missile	*δεσμός, -οῦ, m.	bond, chain
*βία, -ας, f.	force, strength	*δεσμώτης, -ου, m.	prisoner
*βίος, -ου, m.	life	*δεσπότης, -ου, m.	master
*βλάπτω	I harm, damage	*δέσποινα, -ης, f.	mistress
βλαστάνω (aor. pple.	I am born, come to light	*δεῦρο	here/to here
βλαστών)		δεύτερος, α, ον	next, second
*βλέπω	I look	δεύτερον	later, on a second
βλέφαρα, -ων, n.pl.	eyes, eyelids		occasion
βλώσκω (aor. ἔμολον)	I go, come	*δέχομαι	I receive, welcome
*βοάω	I shout, cry	δέω	I bind, tie
*βοή, -ῆς, f.	shout	*δή	indeed [emphasises
βόσκω	I nourish, feed		preceding word]
βοτήρ, -ῆρος, m.	herdsman	*δῆτα	then
βοτόν, -οῦ, n.	beast	*δῆλος, -η, -ον	clear
βούλευμα, -ατος, n.	plan, resolution	*δηλόω	I show, point out
βουκόλος, -ου, m.	herdsman	*διά + gen.	through; by
*βούλομαι (fut.	I wish	διαρρήγνυμι	I break through
βουλήσομαι)		διάστροφος, -ον	twisted, distorted
βοῦς, βοός, m./f.	ox	διαφέρομαι	I go through life, live
βρίθω	I am heavy, powerful	διαφοιβάζω (pf.	I drive X mad
βροτός, -οῦ, m.	mortal	inf. pass.	
βρυχάομαι	I roar, bellow	διαπεφοιβάσθαι)	
		*δίδωμι	I give; grant, allow
*γάρ	for	*δίκαιος	just, fair
*γε	at any rate, at least, even	*δίκαιος, -α, -ον	justly, fairly
*γελάω	I laugh	*δίκη, -ης, f.	justice; penalty,
γέλως, -ωτος, m.	laughter		judgement
*γένος, -ους, n	family, race	Διογενής, -ές	sprung from Zeus
γέρας, -ως, n.	prize, reward, favour	διοίγω	I open
*γέρων, -οντος, m.	old man	διόλλυμαι	I perish utterly, am
γεύομαι + gen.	I taste		utterly destroyed
*γῆ, γῆς, f.	land, earth	διοπτεύω	I look (into), see
γῆρας, -ως, n.	old age	δῖος, -α, -ον	divine, heavenly
γηροβοσκός, -όν	nourishing in old age	δίς	twice
*γίγνομαι	I become, happen, occur	δισσός, -η, -ον	twofold, double
*γιγνώσκω (fut.	I (get to) know, realise,	διφρευτής, -οῦ, m.	charioteer
γνώσομαι)	understand	διφρηλατέω	I drive a chariot
*γνώμη, -ης, f.	fantasy; judgement,	δίχα + gen.	apart from
	intention	*δοκέω	I seem; I think
γόος, -ου, m.	weeping, cry, lament	*δοκεῖ (+ dat.)	it seems good (to x)
γοργῶπις, -ιδος	Gorgon-eyed, grim-eyed	δόμος, –ου, m.	house
*γυμνός, -ή, -όν	naked, unarmed	δόρυ, -ατος, n.	spear

δόλιος, -α, -ον — crafty, deceitful
δόρυ, δορός, n. — spear
δός — give/allow (+ dat.)
    [= aor. imp. 2nd sg. of δίδωμι]
δούλιος, -α, -ον — of slavery, servile
*δούλη, -ης, f. — slave
*δράω — I do
*δύναμαι — I can, have power
δυσλόγιστος, -ον — unimaginable, incalculable
δυσμενής, -ές — hostile, enemy
δυσπραξία, -ας, f. — misfortune
δύστηνος, -ον — wretched
δυστυχέω — I am unfortunate, unlucky
δυσφόρος, -ον — hard to bear, intolerable
δῶμα, -ατος, n. — house
δώρημα, -ατος, n. — gift
*δῶρον, -ου, n. — gift, present

*ἐάν/ἤν — if (introducing a future open condition)
ἐγγύθεν — from nearby
ἔγχος, -ους, n. — sword
*ἐγώ — I
*ἔγωγε — I
ἕδρα, -ας, f. — seat, station
ἕζομαι — I sit
ἐθελοντής, -οῦ, m. — volunteer
*ἐθέλω — I am willing, wish
*εἰ — if (εἴπερ = if indeed)
εἴδωλον, -ου, n. — image, likeness, phantom
εἰδώς, -υῖα, ός — knowing (pres ppl of οἶδα)
εἶεν — very well then
εἰκός ἐστι — it is fitting
εἴκω — I give way to, yield
*εἶμι (pres. pple. ἰών) — I shall go
*εἰμί — I am
εἴργω — I shut in
*εἰς + acc. — into, to
εἰσαεί — forever
εἰσακούω — I hear, listen to
εἰσέπειτα — in the future
εἰσέρχομαι (aor. εἰσῆλθον/ἐσῆλθον) — I go/come in
εἰσοράω — I look at, perceive, behold
εἰσπίπτω — I fall upon/into, attack
εἴσω + gen. — inside, within
εἶτα — then, afterwards
*εἴτε ... εἴτε ... — whether ... or ...

*ἐκ or ἐξ + gen. — out of; from; by
ἔκγονος, -ου, n. — offspring
*ἐκεῖ — there
*ἐκεῖσε — to there, to that place
*ἐκεῖνος, -η, -ο — that
ἐκλύομαι — I release
ἐκπράσσω — I bring about, achieve
ἐκπλήσσω (pf. pass. ἐκπέπληγμαι) — I strike out of, drive away (passive: I am thrown off course)
ἐκρήγνυμι (fut. ἐκρήξω) — I break out, breath forth
ἐκτίνομαι — (middle) I take revenge
ἐκτός — outside
Ἕκτωρ, -ορος, m. — Hector
ἐκτρέπω — I turn aside
*ἐκφεύγω — I escape
ἐκφέρω — I carry X forward to fulfilment, bring X to a goal
ἐκφύω (aor. ἐξέφυν) — I beget, produce (aorist: I am born, I am)
ἐκχωρέω + dat. — I make way for, give way to
*ἑκών, -οῦσα, -όν — willing
ἐλάσσων, -ον — smaller, weaker (comparative of ὀλίγος)
*ἐλαύνω (fut. ἐλαω) — I drive/pursue, persecute
*ἐλεύθερος, -α, -ον — free
*Ἕλλην, -ηνος, m. — Greek
ἐλπίς, -ίδος, f. — hope
ἕλωρ, n. (no genitive) — prey, spoil
*ἐμός, -ή, όν — my
ἐμβάλλω — I throw in
ἔμπα (ς) — all the same, nevertheless, in any case
ἐμπίτνω — I fall upon
ἐμφανής, -ές — visible, clear, manifest
ἐμφανῶς — visibly, openly
ἔμφρων, -ον — in one's mind/senses
*ἐν + dat. — in, on; among
ἐνάλιος, -α, -ον — of the sea
ἔνδον — within, inside
*ἕνεκα + gen. — on account of, for the sake of
*ἔνθα — where; there
ἐννέπω — I speak, say
*ἐννοέω — I consider, think of, intend
ἐνστάτης, -ου, m. — enemy
ἐντολή, -ῆς, f. — instruction, order
ἐντρέπω — (+ gen.) show regard for/reverence for X
*ἐντυγχάνω + dat. — I meet with, light upon

ἐξαλέξω — I ward off

ἐξαλλάσσομαι — (middle) I see a change in my circumstances

ἐξεπίσταμαι — I know thoroughly

ἐξεργάζομαι — I accomplish, bring to completion

ἐξέρομαι (aor. ἐξηρόμην) — I inquire, ask

*ἔξεστι + dat. — it is allowed, is possible, X (dat.) can

ἐξηγέομαι — I explain, teach

ἐξίσταμαι (strong aor. ἐξέστην) — I shrink from, avoid; I make way for

ἔξοδος, -ου, f. — mission, expedition

ἐξοιμώζω (aor. ἐξῴμωξα) — I wail aloud

ἐξομοιόω — I make X like (passive: I am made like)

ἐξορμάομαι — I set out, start out

ἔξω — outside

*ἐξ οὗ — since the time when

ἔοικε(ν) — it seems

*ἐπαινέω (aor. ἐπῄνεσα) — I praise, approve

ἔπαινος, -ου, m. — approval, praise

ἐπαισθάνομαι — I perceive

ἐπαπειλέω — I threaten

ἐπάσσω — I rush at

ἐπεγγελάω — I laugh at, exult over

*ἐπεί — since, when

*ἐπειδή — when

*ἔπειτα — then, afterwards

ἐπεμπίπτω — I fall upon

ἐπέρχομαι — I approach/attack, proceed against

ἐπευθύνω — I guide, direct

ἐπέχω — I restrain

*ἐπί + acc. — against, onto, on, at

*ἐπί + dat. — on; by; against; with respect to, towards

ἐπιγιγνώσκω (aor. ἐπέγνων) — I discover, observe

ἐπιπλήσσω — I rebuke

ἐπίσκηνος, ον — in front of the tent (i.e. 'public')

ἐπισκήπτω — I impose, command

ἐπισκοπέομαι (aor. ἐπεσκεψάμην) — I look upon

*ἐπίσταμαι — I understand, know (how to)

ἐπιστάτης, -ου, m — overseer

*ἐπιστολή, -ῆς, f. — letter

ἐπίσχω — I hold, restrain, check

ἐπίτριπτος, -ον — accursed

ἐποικτίρω — I pity, have compassion for

ἔπος, -ους, n. — word, speech, saying

ἑπτάβοιος, -ον — of seven hides

ἐπῳδή, -ῆς, f. — incantation, spell

ἐπώνυμος, -ον — significantly named, aptly named

ἐράω + gen. — I love, desire

*ἐργάζομαι — I work, do

*ἔργον, -ου, n. — deed; need

ἐρείπιον, -ου, n. — wreckage, fallen ruin

ἐρείπομαι (aor. pass. pple. ἐρειφθείς) — (passive): I am thrown down, fall down

Ἐρίβοια, -ας, f. — Eriboea (Ajax's mother)

Ἐρινύς, -ύος, f. — the Erinys (an avenging deity)

ἑρκεῖος, -ον — of the courtyard

ἕρκος, -ους, n. — net

Ἑρμῆς, -οῦ, m. — Hermes

ἕρπω — I go, come

ἔρυμα, -ατος, n. — safeguard, defence

*ἔρχομαι (aor. ἦλθον) — I go, come

ἐρῶ — I will say

ἐς (= εἰς) — into

ἔσθ᾽ ὅτε ... (ἔσθ᾽) ὅτε ... — sometimes ... at other times ...

ἕσπερος, -ον — (of) evening

ἑστία, -ας, f. — hearth

*ἔσχατος, -ή, -όν — last, furthest

ἔσω — inside

ἑταιρεία, -ας, f. — friendship, comradeship

*ἑταῖρος, -ου, m. — companion

*ἔτι — still, yet

*ἔτος, -ους, n — year

*εὖ — well

*εὐγενής, -ές — noble, well-born

εὕδω — I sleep

εὐερός, -ον — fleecy

εὐθύνω — I direct, guide

εὐθέως (= εὐθύς) — at once, immediately

εὔκαρπος, -ον — fruitful, rich in fruit

εὔκερως, -ον — horned, with beautiful horns

εὔκλεια, -ας, f. — glory, good repute

εὐμαθής, -ές — easy to understand, intelligible

εὐνή, -ῆς, f. — marriage-bed

εὐνοέω + dat. — I am well-inclined/favourable towards

εὔνους, -ουν — kind, friendly, well-disposed

εὔρινος, -ον — keen-scented

*εὑρίσκω — I find

Εὐρύσακης, -ες, m. — Eurysaces

εὐσκευέω — I am well-equipped

*εὐτυχής. -ές — fortunate, lucky

εὐφραίνω (aor. εὔφρανα) — I cheer, gladden

*εὔχομαι — I pray

ἐφεστίος, -ον — of the hearth/household

ἐφήκω — I have arrived

ἐφίεμαι — I order, command

ἐφίημι — I send to, hand over

ἐχθαίρω — I hate, detest (passive: I am hated)

ἐχθαρτέος, -α, -ον — to be hated (verbal adjective)

*ἐχθρός, -ου, m. — enemy; [as 2-1-2 adj.] hostile (sup. ἔχθιστος)

ἔχθω — I hate

*ἔχω (aor. ἔσχον, fut. ἕξω/σχήσω) — I have, hold; + infinitive = I am able to

*ἕως — until

*ζάω — I live

*Ζεύς, Διός, m. — Zeus

ζῆλος, -ου, m. — envy/enviable state

ζηλόω — I am jealous of, envy

*ζητέω (gerundive ζητητέος, -α, -ον) — I seek

*ἤ — or

*ἤ . . . ἤ . . . — either . . . or . . .

ἦ — indeed [interrogative particle]

ᾗ — where (dat. fem. sg. of rel. pron., used as an adverb)

*ἤδη — (by) now, already

*ἡδύς, ἡδεῖα, ἡδύ (sup. ἥδιστος) — pleasant, sweet

*Ἥλιος, -ου, m. — the Sun (personified, i.e. the sun god)

ἧμαι (ἧστο = 3rd sg. pluperfect) — I sit

ἦμαρ, -ατος, n. — day

*ἥμεις — we

*ἡμέρα, -ας, f. — day

ἤν — if (= ἐάν, introducing a future open condition)

ἡνία, -ας, f. — reins, bridle

ἡνίκα — at the time when

ἥσυχος, -ον — silent, quiet, at rest

θακέω — I sit

θανάσιμος, -ον — dead

*Θάνατος, -ου, m. — Death (personified as a god)

*θάπτω — I bury

*θαρσέω — I am confident/bold

θάσσων, -ον — quicker, sooner (comparative of ταχύς)

*θεά, -ᾶς, f. — goddess

θέλω — I want, wish

*θεός, -ου, m. — god

θερμαίνω — I warm

*θέρος, -ους, n. — summer

θηγάνη, -ης, f. — whetstone

θηλύνω — I soften, feminise (transitive)

θήρα, -ας, f. — hunt, hunting wild beasts

θηράω — I hunt, chase

θνήσκω (aor. ἔθανον, pf. τεθνήκα) — I die

θράσος, -ους, n. — daring, courage, over-boldness

θρηνέω — I wail, sing

θροέω — I cry aloud, proclaim

*θύρα, -ας, f. — door

θωύσσω — I cry, make a noise

ἰάπτω — I wound, assault

*ἰατρός, οῦ, m. — doctor

Ἰδαῖος, -α, -ον — of Ida

ἰδού — behold!

ἱδρώς, -ῶτος, m. — sweat

*ἱερός, -ά, -όν — holy, sacred

*ἵημι (fut. ἥσω) — I send, hurl, raise

ἱκνέομαι — I arrive, reach

ἰσχύς, -ύος, f. — strength

*ἴσως — perhaps

*ἵστημι (pf. act. ἕστηκα; pf. pple. act. ἑστώς) — I make to stand

*ἵσταμαι — I stand

ἰσχύω — I am strong

ἴσχω — I have, hold

ἰχνεύω — I track

ἴχνος, -ους, n. — track, footstep

ἰώ — [a cry]

καθαιρέω (aor. καθεῖλον) — I take down, lay low

*καθίσταμαι — I come/get (into the state of . . .)

*καί — and, even, also, actually

*καίπερ — although

καίριος, -α, -ον — timely

*καιρός, -οῦ, m. — right time, opportunity; advantage, profit

*καίτοι — and yet

*κακός, -ή, -όν — bad, cowardly, wicked (sup. κάκιστος)

*καλέω (aor. pass. ἐκλήθην) — I call, summon

Κάλχας, -αντος, m. Calchas
καλλιστεῖον, -ου, n. prize
*καλός, -ή, -όν fine, beautiful, handsome
κάρα, n. (no gen.) head
κάρτα surely, certainly, very, extremely
καρτερέω I am steadfast, obstinate, stubborn
καρτερός, -ά, -όν strong, mighty
*κατά + acc. according to; by; in (the house); near
κατά + gen. against
καταθνήσκω I die
κατακτάομαι I obtain
καταμελέω I neglect
κατεναρίζω (pf. pple. pass. κατηναρισμένος) I kill outright
κατοπτεύω I spy out, observe
κάτω below
κέαρ, n. (no gen.) heart
κεδνός, -ή, -όν good, valuable
*κεῖμαι I lie
κεῖνος, -η, -ο (= ἐκεῖνος, -η, -ο) that
κείρω I cut (down)
*κενός, -ή, όν empty
κερδαίνω I gain, derive profit
κίναδος, -οὺς, n. fox
κιχάνω I reach, hit, find
κίων, -ονος, m./f. pillar, column
κλεινός, -ή, -όν famous, renowned
κλέος, n. (no genitive) glory
κληροῦχος, -ου, m./f. someone who has an allotted portion
κλίνω I lay low
κλύω I hear
κοιμίζω I put to sleep, lull, calm
*κοινός, -ή, -όν common
κοινωνός, -οῦ, m./f. partner, companion
κόμη, -ης, f. hair
*κομίζω I bring; convey
κομπέω I boast
κόμπος, -ου, m. boast
κόσμος, -ου, m. adornment
κοῦφος, -η, -ον light
*κρατέω I control, rule over (+ gen); I am strong, powerful, prevail
*κράτος, -ους, n. victory; might, force; prize
κρείσσων, -ον stronger, mightier (comparative)
κρήνη, -ης, f. well, spring, fountain
*κρίνω I judge, award (a prize)
*κρύπτω I hide (something: transitive)

*κτάομαι I obtain, get
κτείνω I kill, slay
κυβερνάω I steer, guide
*κύκλος, -ου, m. circle
κυκλόω I move in a circle
κώκυμα, -ατος, n. shriek, wail, cry
κυναγία, -ας, f. hunt, chase
κυνηγετέω I hunt
κυρέω I happen, happen to be (+ participle)
κύων, κυνός, m. dog
κώδων, -ωνος, f. trumpet
κωκυτός, -οῦ, m. lamentation, wail

Λαέρτης, -ου, m. Laertes
Λάκαινα, -ης, f. Spartan
*λαμβάνω (aor. ἔλαβον) I take, capture
λαμπτήρ, -ῆρος, m. watch-fire, lamp
λαός, -οῦ, m. man
λατρεία, -ας, f. service
λάφυρα, -ων, n. pl. spoils (taken in war)
*λέγω (aor. ἔλεξα) I say, tell, speak
λεία, -ας, f. plunder; flocks and herds
λειμών, -ῶνος, m. meadow
*λείπω I leave (behind); (passive + genitive) I am lacking in/I fall short of
λεηλατέω I plunder, drive away booty (e.g. cattle)
λευκόπωλος, -ον with white horses
λέχος, -ους, n. bed
λήγω (aor. ἔληξα) I cease
*λιμήν, -ενος, m. harbour
λογίζομαι I calculate, make a calculation
*λόγος, -ου, m. word
*τὸ λοιπόν in the future
λοίσθιον in the end, finally
λουτρόν, -οῦ, n. bathing place
λυγρός, ά, όν mournful, wretched
λῦμα, -ατος, n. dirt, defilement
λυμεών, -ῶνος, m. destroyer, corrupter
*λυπέομαι (passive) I am grieved/distressed
λυσσώδης, -ες of madness
*λύω I loose, untie, set free
λώβη, -ης, f. outrage, dishonour, violence
λωφάω I take a rest from (+ gen.)

μαιμάω I am eager
μαίνομαι (pf. pple. μεμηνώς) I rage, am furious

μαίομαι	(+ infinitive) I seek to do X	νέμω (fut. νεμῶ)	I deal out, dispense
*μακρός, -ά -όν	long; great	νεόρραντος, ον	newly-sprinkled, freshly-dripping
*μάλιστα	very much, especially	*νέος, -α, -ον	young, new, recent
*μᾶλλον	more, rather; worse	νεοσφαγής, -ές	newly-slaughtered
*μανθάνω (aor. ἔμαθον)	I learn, understand	νεοχάρακτος, -ον	newly-imprinted
		*νικάω	I conquer, win
μανιάς, άδος	mad, frantic, raving	νιν	him/her (= Doric form of αὐτόν/-ήν)
*μάντις, -εως, m.	prophet		
μάρπτω	I take hold of, seize	νιφοστιβής, -ές	snowy, piled with snow
μάστιξ, -ιγος, f.	whip	*νομίζω	I consider, believe, think
*μάτην	in vain	*νόμος, -ου, m.	law, custom
*μάχη, -ης, f.	fight, battle	*νοσέω	I am ill
*μέγας, μεγάλη, μέγα	great, big	νόσημα, -ατος, n.	disease, illness
		*νόσος, -ου, f.	illness, disease
μεθίημι (aor. pple. μεθείς)	I let go	*νῦν	now
		νύκτωρ	at night
μεθίσταμαι (intr. aor. pple. μεταστάς)	I change my position, depart	*νύξ, νυκτός, f.	night
		νῶτα, -ων, n.pl.	back
μείων, -ον	lesser, less (comparative)		
*μέλλω	I intend, am going to; I hesitate	*ξένος, -ου, m.	stranger, foreigner
		ξιφοκτόνος, -ον	sword-killing
μέλω + gen.	I take care of	*ξίφος, -οῦς, n.	sword
*... μέν ... δέ	on the one hand ... on the other ...	ξυμπίπτω + dat.	I join battle with, attack
		ξυμφέρω (fut. inf. ξυνοίσειν) + dat.	I correspond with, agree with
μενοινάω	I desire eagerly		
*μέντοι	however; certainly	ξύν + dat.	with
*μένω	I remain, await	ξυναρπάζω	I grasp, snatch and carry off
*μέσος, -η, -ον	middle		
μετρέω	I measure	ξύνειμι + dat.	I am with/meet with
*μέχρι(ς) (οὐ)	until	ξυνέρχομαι + dat.	I join with/come to
*μή	not	ξυνίημι (pf. ξυνῆκα)	I understand
*μηδαμῶς	in no way		
*μηδέ	and not, nor, not even	*ὁ, ἡ, τό	the
*μηδείς, -μία, -έν	no-one, nothing	ὄγκος, -ου, m.	pride
μήν	truly; yet	*ὅδε, ἥδε, τόδε	this
μῆνις, -ιος, f.	anger	ὀδύρομαι	I lament, bewail
μίμνω	I remain, stand fast	*ὁδός, -οῦ, f.	road, journey, path, way
*μισέω	I hate	Ὀδυσσεύς, -έως, m.	Odysseus
μνήμη, -ης, f.	remembrance, memory	ὁθούνεκα	because
μνῆστις, -ιος, f.	thought, recollection	*οἶδα (fut. εἴσομαι)	I know
μοῖρα, -ας, f.	fate, lot, destiny	οἰκεῖος, -α, -ον	native, belonging to one's home
μολεῖν/μολών	[aorist inf./pple. of βλώσκω]		
		οἰκήτωρ, -ορος, m.	inhabitant
*μόλις	scarcely, with difficulty	*οἶκος, -ου, m.	house, home
*μόνον	only	*οἰκτείρω	I pity
*μόνος, -η, -ον	alone	οἶκτος, -ου, m.	pity, compassion
μόρος, -ου, m.	fate, destiny	οἰμωγή, -ῆς, f.	wailing, lamentation
μυθέομαι	I speak	οἴομαι	I think
*μῦθος, -ου m.	story	οἶος, -α, -ον	alone, lonely
μυχός, -οῦ, m.	innermost part, recess	*οἷος, -α, -ον	such (as), of what sort
		οἰχνέω	I go, come
ναυλόχος, -ον	affording safe anchorage of ships, nautical	οἰωνός, -οῦ, m.	bird of prey
ναυτικός, -ή, -όν		ὀκνέω	I shrink from
νηηκονής, -ές	recently-sharpened	ὄκνος, -ου, m.	fear, alarm
*νεκρός, -οῦ, m.	corpse		

ὄλλυμαι (aor. ὠλόμην)	I perish	*οὕτω(ς)	thus; so
ὁμευνέτις, -ιδος, f.	bed partner	*ὀφθαλμός, -οῦ, m.	eye
ὄμμα, -ατος, n.	eye; face		
*ὅμοιος, -α, -ον	similar, like	παγκρατής, -ές	all-powerful
ὁμοῦ	together, along with	παγχρύσεος, -ον	all-golden
*ὅμως	nevertheless	πάθη, -ης, f.	happening, event
ὀνήσιμος, -ον	useful, beneficial	πάθος, -ους, n.	happening, event; misfortune, suffering
*ὄνομα, -ατος n.	name		
ὄνυξ, -υχος, m.	nails	*παῖς, παιδός, m./f.	boy, girl, child, son, daughter
*ὀξύς, -εῖα, -ύ	sharp, shrill, bitter	παίω	I strike
*ὅπλα, -ων, n.pl.	arms, armour, weapons	πακτόω	I close, fasten
ὀπτήρ, -ῆρος, m.	eye-witness	*πάλαι	formerly, in the past; for a long time; recently
*ὅποι	to where? (to) where (indirect interrogative or indefinite)	*πάλιν	back, again
		πάνδημος, -ον	the whole body of
ὅπου	where	παντοῖος, -α, -ον	of all sorts
*ὅπως	that; so that (introduces purpose clause); [also introduces a clause expressing obligation]	παντουργός, -ον	wicked
		πανύστατον	for the very last time
		πανώλεθρος, -ον	utterly destroyed/ wretched
*ὁράω (fut. ὄψομαι, aor. εἶδον)	I see	*παρά + acc.	beside, along
*ὀργή, -ῆς, f.	anger	*παρά + gen.	from (a person)
*ὅρκος , -ου, m.	oath	*παρά + dat.	among, beside
*ὁρμάομαι	I set out	παράκτιος, -α, -ον	by the shore, on the sea-side
ὀρύσσω	I dig	*πάρειμι	I am present
ὀρφανιστής, -οῦ, m.	orphan-carer	*πάρεστι + dat.	it is possible for X (dat.)
ὀρφανός, -οῦ, m.	orphan	*παρθένος, -ου, f.	virgin
*ὅς, ἥ, ὅ	who, which	παροιμία, -ας, f.	saying, proverb
*ὅσος, -η, ον	how big/as much (as), as big (as); 'what a'; pl: 'as many as'	παρίστημι (intr. aor. παρέστην; perf. inf. act. παρεστάναι)	I cause to stand beside; pass (+ strong aorist): I stand beside
*ὅστις, ἥτις, ὅ τι	who/what, whoever/ whatever	πάρος	(adv.) formerly, beforehand; (prep. + gen.) in front of, before
*ὅταν	when, whenever		
*ὅτι	that		
ὅτου ἕνεκα	because	παρουσία, -ας, f.	presence
ὀτρύνω	I urge, encourage	*πᾶς, -ᾶσα, -ᾶν	the whole, every, all
*οὗ	where (relative)	παπταίνω	I glance, peer
*οὐ/οὐκ/οὐχ/οὐχί	not	*πάσχω (aor. ἔπαθον)	I suffer, experience
*οὐδέ	and not, nor, not even		
*οὐδείς, -μία, -έν	no one, nothing	*πατήρ, πατρός, m.	father
*οὔποτε	never	*πατρίς -ίδος, f.	fatherland
*οὐκέτι	no longer	πατρόθεν	from the father
*οὔκουν	not	*πατρῷος, -α, -ον	of a father
*οὖν	and so, therefore	πεδάω	I bind
οὕνεκα + gen.	on account of, because of	*πεδίον, -ου, n.	plain
		πέδον, -ου, n.	ground, earth
οὔπω	not yet	*πείθω (pf. πέποιθα)	I persuade; (in the perfect) I trust
*οὐρανός, -ου, m.	sky, heaven		
*οὔτε ... οὔτε	neither ... nor	*πείθομαι (fut. πείσομαι) + dat.	I obey
οὔτοι	indeed not		
*οὗτος, αὕτη, τοῦτο	this	πεῖρα, -ας, f	opportunity, attempt, expedition

πέλαγος, -ους, n.	sea
πέλας (adv. or prep. + dat.)	near
*πέμπω	I send
-περ	[strengthening suffix]
περαίνω	I finish, accomplish (+ double accusative)
περάω	I cross (i.e. pass a boundary)
*περί	(+ gen.) about, concerning; (+ dat.) on
περισκελής, -ές	unflinching, very stubborn
περισσός, -ή, -όν	excessive (in number)
περιστέλλω	I wrap, cover, secure
περιφανής, -ές	in full view, manifestly
πήγνυμι (aor. ἔπηξα, pf. πέπηγα)	I stick in, stand fixed in (intransitive); I fix, plant (transitive)
*πηδάω	I leap
πήδημα, -ατος, n.	leap
πῆμα, -ατος, n.	wound
πικρός, ά, όν	bitter
*πίπτω	I fall
πίτνω (= πίπτω)	I fall
πλεῖστος, -η, -ον	most, largest, greatest (superlative of πολύς)
πλείων, -ον	more (comparative of πολύς)
πλευρά, -ᾶς, f.	rib
*πλήν + gen.	except
πλήρης, -ες	full (of + gen.)
πλοῦτος, -ου, m.	wealth, riches
πνεῦμα, ατος, n.	breeze, wind
ποίμνη, -ης, f.	flock
ποίνιμος, -ον	avenging
ποίμνιον, -ου, n.	flock
*ποῖος, -α, -ον	of what sort
*πολέμιος, -α, -ον	enemy, hostile
*πόλις, -εως, f.	city-state, city
*πολλάκις	often
πολύκερως, -ωτος	many-horned
πολύρραφος, -ον	well-stitched
*πολύς, πολλή, πολύ	much (pl. many)
πομπαῖος, -α, -ον	escorting souls (an epithet of Hermes)
*πονέω	I toil, suffer
*πόνος, -ου, m.	task, toil
πόντος, -ου, m.	sea
*πορεύομαι	I march, travel
πορευτέον	one must travel (verbal adjective)
πόρπαξ, -ακος, m.	handle or strap of a shield
*ποταμός, -οῦ, m.	river
*ποτε	ever, at some time
πότερα	= πότερον [introduces a question with two alternatives]
*ποῦ;	where?
*που	I suppose, perhaps
*πρᾶγμα, -ατος, n.	thing, matter, situation
πρᾶγος, -οῦς, n.	deed, act
*πράσσω	I do, make; I hand over to/procure for
πρέπον ἐστι + gen.	it is worthy of
πρίαμαι	I buy
*πρίν	before, until
πρόβλητος, -ον	thrown forth
*πρόθυμος, -ον	eager, ready, willing
προλείπω	I abandon, desert
πρόνοια, -ας, f.	foresight, prudence
πρόνους, -ουν	sensible, prudent
*πρός	(+ acc.) to, towards, against; (+ gen.) in the name of, by, at the hands of, from, in the nature of/ characteristic of; (+ dat.) in, against, over
προσαυδάω	I speak to, address
προσβλέπω	I look at
προσβλώσκω (aor. inf. προσμολεῖν)	I approach
προσειπεῖν	to speak to
προσειπεῖν (inf.)	I speak to, address
*πρόσθεν	before
προσίημι (aor. inf. προσεῖναι)	I attach myself to
προσκαλέω	I call on, summon
προσλεύσσω	I look on
πρόσοψις, -εως, f.	face
πρόσπολος, -ου, m.	servant, attendant
προστίθημι	I hand over, deliver, push towards
προστρέπω	I supplicate
πρόσφθεγμα, -ατος, n.	salutation, address, saying
πρῶτος, -η, -ον	first
*πρῶτον	first
πυκάζω	I close, shut
*πύλη –ης, f.	gate, door
πυλωρός, -οῦ, m.	gate-keeper, warder
*πυνθάνομαι (aor. ἐπυθόμην)	I ascertain, learn, ask
πω	yet
πωλοδαμνέω	I train, break in
*πῶς;	how?
*πως	in some way; I suppose
ῥαχίζω	I cut through the spine, cut in two
*ῥίπτω	I throw

σακεσφόρος, -ον — shield-bearing
σάκος, -ους, n. — shield
Σαλαμίς, -ῖνος, f. — Salamis
σάλπιγξ, -ιγγος, f. — war trumpet
σαυτοῦ (= σεαυτοῦ) — of you
*σεαυτόν — yourself
σέβω — I honour, respect
σέλας, -αος, n. — light, brightness
σεμνός, -ή, -όν — revered, holy
σεύομαι (aor. ἐσσύθην) — I run, rush
*σημαίνω — I show, declare, give orders to; (in the middle:) I interpret, note down.
σθένος, -ους, n. — might, strength; force (of men)
σθένω — I have strength
σῖγα — silently
*σιγή, -ῆς, f. — silence
σιδηροβρώς, -ῶτος — iron-eating
σιδηροκμής, -ῆτος — slain by iron/the sword
σίδηρος, -ου, m. — iron
σκιά, ᾶς, f. — shadow
*σκηνή, -ης, f. — tent, hut
*σκοπέω — I look at, examine
σκοτόω — I darken, blind
*σός, σή, σόν — your
*σοφός, -ή, -όν — clever, wise
σπουδή, -ης, f. — effort
στάζω — I shed, drop (+ acc. of thing affected + dat. of thing shed)
στέγη, -ης, f. — roof
στέγος, -ους — house, hut
στείχω — I come, go
*στέλλομαι — (mid./pass.:) I set out, come out
στένω — I moan, groan
στερέω — I deprive X (acc.) of Y (gen.)
στέφανος, -ου, m. — crown (of victory)
στέφω — I wreathe, I honour
*στόμα, -ατος, n. — mouth
στρατηγίς, -ιδος — of the general
στρατηλάτης, -ου, m. — general, commander
*στρατός, -οῦ, m. — army
στρέφω — I turn, twist
στυγέω — I hate
στυγνός, ή, όν — hateful
*σύ — you (sg.)
συγκαταζεύγνυμι — I yoke (together)
συλλαμβάνω — I gather, grasp
*σύμμαχος, -ου, m./f. — ally
σύμμικτος, -ον — intermingled

*συμφορά, -ᾶς, f. — disaster, event, misfortune
σύν + dat. — with
συναλλάσσομαι + dat. — (passive:) I have intercourse with
σύνδετος, -ον — bound
συνδέω — I bind
σύνεδρος, -ον — sitting with in council (referring to people)
σύνειμι + dat. — I am joined with
συντίθημι — I combine
σύντροφος, -ον — brought up together (with me), i.e. kindred
συντυγχάνω — I happen, befall
σφαγεύς, -έως, m. — slayer; sword
σφάζω — I slaughter, cut the throat (of)
σφάλλω (aor. ἔσφηλα) — I cause to fall, overthrow, frustrate
*σφᾶς (dat. σφίν) — them
σφε — them (= αὐτούς)
σχολή, -ῆς, f. — leisure
*σῴζω — I save; (passive:) I am saved, get away safely
*σῶμα, -ατος, n. — body
σωτήριος, -ον — saving, delivering (of persons: people who save)
σωφρονέω — I am of sound mind, I am sensible/moderate
*σώφρων, -ονος — sensible, sober, moderate
τάλας, τάλαινα, τάλαν — wretched
τανῦν — now
τανύπους, -ποδος — far-striding
*τάξις, -εως, f — arrangement, (battle) order/battle line
ταρβέω — I am frightened, alarmed
*τάσσω (aor. pass. ἐτάχθην) — I order, command
ταῦρος, -ου, m. — bull
*τάχα — quickly, soon; perhaps
ταχ' ἄν — perhaps
τάχος, -ους, n. — speed, swiftness (διὰ τάχους = quickly)
*ταχύς, -εῖα, -ύ — quick, swift, fast
*τε — and
*τε . . . τε — both . . . and . . .
*τε . . . καί — both . . . and . . .
Τέκμησσα, -ης, f. — Tecmessa
τέκνον, -ου, n. — child
Τελαμών, -ῶνος, m. — Telamon (Ajax's father)
τελέω — I fulfil, accomplish
Τελεύτας, m. (no gen.) — Teleutas
*τελευτάω — I die
*τέλος — at last, finally

τέλος, -ους, n.	completion (διὰ τέλους = 'fully')	Τρωικός, -ή, -όν	Trojan
*τέμνω	I cut	*τυγχάνω (fut. τεύξομαι)	I happen, am at (a place); I happen to be (+ participle); I get (+ genitive)
τέρμα, -ατος, n.	goal		
τερπνός, -ή, όν	pleasurable, pleasant		
τέρπω	I delight, gladden	τυραννικός, -ή, -όν	of/for a royal
τέρψις, -εως, f.	joy, pleasure	Τυρσηνικός, -ή, -όν	Etruscan
Τεῦκρος, -ου, m.	Teucer (Ajax's brother)	*τύχη, -ης, f.	chance, luck, fortune (good or bad)
τεῦχος, -ους, n.	weapon, arms		
τεχνάομαι	I contrive	τώς	so, in this way
*τέχνη, -ης, f.	contrivance, cunning		
τέως	meanwhile	*ὑβρίζω	I assault, maltreat
τηλωπός, -όν	far off, far away	ὕβρις, -εως, f.	violence, outrage, insolence
*τίθημι (aor. mid. ἐθέμην, fut. θήσω)	I put, place, set before; make		
		*ὑμεῖς	you (pl)
τίκτω	I beget, bring forth	ὑμνέω	I repeat, recite
*τιμάω	I honour, respect	ὑπείκω	I yield, give way
*τιμή, -ῆς, f.	honour, dignity	ὑπεικτέον	one must yield (verbal adj.)
τίνω (fut. τείσω)	I pay (a price, a debt, etc).		
		ὑπέρκοπος, -ον	arrogant
*τίς; τί;	who? what?	*ὕπνος, -ου, m.	sleep
τί;	why? how?	*ὑπό	(+ gen.) by; (+ dat.) under, within
*τις, τι	a, a certain, some		
τλάω (fut. τλήσομαι)	I endure, dare	ὑπόβλητος, -ον	counterfeit, false
τλητός, -ή, -όν	to be endured	ὑποζεύγνυμι (aor. pass. ὑπεζύγην)	in passive: I submit to
*τοι	indeed, certainly		
τοιγάρ	therefore	ὑποστενάζω	I utter low moans
τοιγαροῦν	therefore	ὑπουργέω + dat.	I help, assist
τοίνυν	therefore	ὕστατος, -η, -ον	last
τοιόσδε, -άδε, όνδε	such [as this]	*ὕστερον	later
*τοιοῦτος, -αύτη, -οῦτο	such	ὑψικόμπως	boastfully
*τόλμα, -ης, f.	daring	φαεννός, -ή, -όν	bright, shining
*τολμάω	I dare	*φαίνομαι	I appear
τομάω	I need cutting	φαίνω (aor. pass. ἐφάνην)	I reveal
τομός, -ή, -όν	cutting, sharp		
*τόπος, -ου, m.	place	φάσγανον, -ου, n.	sword
*τοσοῦτος, -αύτη, -οῦτο	so much, so great (pl.: so many)	φάσκω	I say, declare
		φάτις, f. (no genitive)	news, report
τοσόσδε, -ήδε, -όνδε	so much, so great (pl.: so many)	φέγγος, -ους, n.	light
		φείδομαι + gen.	I spare
*τότε	at that time, then	*φέρω (fut. οἴσομαι)	I carry, bear, endure
τρανής, -ές	clear, distinct	*φεύγω	I flee, run away
*τρέπω	I turn, direct	*φημί	I say
τρέφω (aor. pass. ἐτράφην)	I cherish; passive: I am born	φθέγμα, -ατος, n.	voice
		φθείρω (perf. pple. pass. ἐφθαρμένος)	I destroy
τρίς	thrice		
Τροία, -ας, f.	Troy	*φιλέω	I love, like
τροφεύς, -έως, m.	nourisher, one who brings up	φιλοίκτιστος, -ον	pity-loving, inclined to pity
τροφή, -ῆς, f.	way of life; care, support, nourishment	φίλος, -η, -ον (poetic superlative φίλτατος, -η, -ον)	dear, friendly
τροφός, -ου, f.	mother		
Τρωάς, -άδος, f.	Troy	φιλοφρόνως	in a friendly manner
Τρῶες, -ων, m.	the Trojans		

φλέγω — I blaze forth, shine forth

*φόβος, -ου, m. — fear

φοίνιος, -α, -ον — bloody

φοινίσσω (aor. pass. pple. φοινιχθείς) — I redden, make red

φοιτάω — I roam about, go back and forth

φόνος, -ου, m. — slaughter; blood

φωνέω — I call, speak to

φράζω — I tell, declare

φρήν, φρένος, f. — mind, heart, purpose, will

φρονέω — I am in my right mind; I think

φροντίς, -ίδος, f. — thought

φρούρημα, -ατος, n. — that which is watched/guarded

*φύλαξ, φύλακος, m. — guard

*φυλάσσω — I guard, take precautions

φύσις, -εως, f. — nature

φύω (aor. ἐφύσα) — I produce, beget, bring forth

φώνημα, -ατος, n. — voice, sound, utterance

φώς, φωτός, m. — man

*χαίρω — I rejoice; imperative: 'hello/hail'; 'goodbye'

χαλκόστομος, -ον — with mouth of bronze

χαρά, -ας, f. — joy

χάριν + gen. — for the sake of; in thanks for

χάρις, χάριτος, f. — kindness, favour, service

χαρμονή, -ῆς, f. — source of joy

*χειμών, -ῶνος, m. — winter

*χείρ, χειρός, f. (poetic χέρος etc.) — hand

χείριος, α, ον — in the hands of, under the control of

χήρα, -ας, f. — widow

χθόνιος, -α, -ον — under the earth

χθών, χθονός, f. — land

χόλος, -ου, m. — anger

χραίνω — I stain

*χράομαι + dat. — I use, treat

χρεών ἐστι — it is necessary

*χρή — it is necessary

χρήζω + gen. — I want, lack

*χρῆμα, -ατος, n. — thing

χρηστός, -ή, -όν — good, useful

*χρόνος, -ου, m. — time

χρυσόνωτος, -ον — studded with gold

*χωρέω — I go

χωρίς + gen. — without, apart from

χῶρος, -ου, m. — place

ψηφίζω — I vote

ψυχή, -ής, f. — soul

ὦ — O (+ vocative)

*ὧδε — thus

ὤμοι — alas! [cry of grief]

ὠμός, ή, όν — harsh, savage, cruel

ὤν — his own

*ὡς — as/since; when; as, as if, like; that; so that (introducing a purpose clause); how as . . . as possible

*ὡς + superlative adverb

*ὥσπερ — just as

*ὥστε — with the result that, so that (result); as if

*ὠφελέω — I benefit, help

Aristophanes, *Clouds*

Introduction, Commentary Notes and
Vocabulary by Jo Lashly

A Level: 1–242

Introduction

Aristophanes – A life in drama

All dates are BCE.

The little we know about Aristophanes comes either from his own plays or references to him in other contemporary literature. We know that he was born *c.* 450 and was a member of the *deme* (a locality with its own political system) of Cydathenaeum, which was in the centre of Athens. His father was Philippus, and his sons all became playwrights. We know that he wrote more than forty plays, of which eleven are extant, and there are around a thousand fragments attributed to him. It is believed that he died about 385, because his last play was produced (by his son, Ararus) in 386. Aristophanes' first play, *Banqueters*, now lost, was produced in 427 by Callistratus. Although it was customary for playwrights to produce their own plays, we know, from the lists of plays presented, that he did not produce his earlier works, and because in the *parabases* of *Knights* (424), *Clouds* (423) and *Wasps* (422) he comments on this, referring in *Clouds* (lines 530–531) to his plays as though they were his children whom he had to give up to be raised by another. There could have been many reasons for this, but the training and organization of twenty-four chorus members may well have felt too big a job, or he may have wished to concentrate on directing the play itself. We do know that *Knights* was the first play he produced himself and that it won first prize in the Lenaea (see below on 'The dramatic festivals'). We also learn from the play lists that his first play, *Banqueters,* won second prize at the City Dionysia, and his second, *Babylonians* (426), is said to have got him into legal trouble with the politician Cleon, who allegedly took him to court for ridiculing the Athenian people at the City Dionysia. According to the scholia (annotations by ancient commentators), the case was dismissed and in *Acharnians* (425) which won first prize at the Lenaea he states that Cleon could not, on this occasion, accuse him of slandering the City in the presence of foreigners, as this festival was held before the opening of the sailing season when foreigners would not be present.

The topical nature of Old Comedy meant that Aristophanes often (e.g. *Acharnians, Clouds, Peace, Lysistrata,*) focused on, or made reference to, the ongoing war between Athens and Sparta (the Peloponnesian War, which began in 431) and that he satirized, often cruelly, leading Athenian citizens. This means that a basic understanding of historical context and a knowledge of the major characters is often helpful to students of his plays, although it is perfectly possible to find them funny without this, since as Halliwell writes, 'there is always a large helping of unrestrained exuberance, irreverence and indecency'. The genius of Aristophanes' comedy is that there is something for everyone (unless you are easily offended).

Clouds was first produced in 423 at the City Dionysia and came third, beaten by Cratinus' *Pytine* (first) and Ameipsias' *Konnos* (second). The failure clearly annoyed Aristophanes and he began a revision of the text. Some biting comments in the *parabasis* (lines 524–525) of the text we have reveal this annoyance, particularly when he comments that he had thought the audience sophisticated enough to understand this 'cleverest of all [his] plays'. The version we have seems never to have been produced, although it may have been circulated amongst friends, and it is sometimes called *Clouds II*. In this parabasis (see notes below on the structure of *Clouds*), Aristophanes claims that he 'left the theatre defeated by vulgar rivals' and refers to the *Marikas* of Eupolis (a rival playwright) which was produced at the Lenaea in 421; other references to Hyperbolus, a politician who was ostracized around in or shortly after 417, place this revision not later than 416.

Not many details about Aristophanes himself can be gleaned from the plays apart from the fact that he seems to have been bald: a 'gleaming forehead' is mentioned in *Knights* by the chorus (line 550) and repeated in *Clouds* (line 545) and *Peace* (lines 771–774). It is dangerous to infer the political views of a playwright from the drama that he writes, and even more so when that drama is presented to the public in a competition, but it is clear from the way Aristophanes presents the democratic system under which he had been born, as not entirely perfect, that he is not blind to its failings and he is not afraid to attack every class, age group or profession for their part in it. Clues to his view may be found in the words of the chorus of *Clouds* which at first make them seem to be representative of new religious views, but later (line 1461) reveal that they have behaved in this way towards Strepsiades, because they wish him to fear the gods, a view more suggestive of traditional religion. However, in the *agon* between Right and Wrong, Right, despite being dismissive of his opponent's defence of modern education, in the end (line 1104) gives in and joins Wrong. We are left wondering whether Aristophanes was putting forward views he believed in or whether he was simply going for laughs. Perhaps however, Aristophanes' view of the purpose of drama may be seen in the parabasis of *Acharnians* (lines 656–658) and again in *Frogs* (line 687), where he uses διδάσκειν to describe his plays suggesting that their purpose is more than simply to entertain, and his anger, as seen in the parabases of *Acharnians* and *Clouds*, at Cleon's response to *Babylonians*, as well as losing with 'the cleverest of all [his] plays', would tend to support the view that he, as a playwright, is seeking to educate his audience. The fact that we have eleven full plays of his, while his competitors' plays are fragmentary would seem to suggest that his audience, and the judges, also appreciated this by voting his work first on several occasions, or at the very least they found them funny.

The dramatic festivals

There were two main dramatic festivals in Athens: the Lenaea, which was held over four days from the twelfth of the month of *Gamelion* (roughly the end of our January), and the Great (or City) Dionysia which was held over five days from about the tenth of the month of *Elaphebolion* (roughly late March). Both the Dionysia and the Lenaea admitted tragedy and comedy, although it seems that comedy at the Lenaea began *c.* 440 and tragedy in 432; at the Dionysia, comedy was performed from the 480s. Tragedy had a longer history at the Dionysia, most probably from the mid-sixth century during Pisistratus' development of the festival of Dionysus Eleuthereus, and certainly from the later reorganization by Cleisthenes at the end of that century. A dramatic festival was not just a series of plays but was a religious occasion involving a procession and religious rites. In the case of the Great Dionysia, there was also the display of the annual tribute from the allies (subjects) of the Athenian empire. From the time of Aristophanes, it is fair to assume that both festivals took place at the theatre of Dionysus on the southern flank of the Acropolis, but the theatre that we see today with its stone seats is a later version of the one that Aristophanes would have known. His theatre would have had seats cut out of the turf, or perhaps wooden ones; the stone seats date from the later fourth century. The *orchestra*, in which the chorus sang and danced in the fifth century may have been rectilinear, only later becoming semi-circular, and a rectangular building (*skene*) provided a backdrop for the stage and with room for costume changes and scenery stores. The four-day Lenaea was smaller than the Dionysia with citizens and metics (resident immigrants) in the audience, which would account for Aristophanes' comments in *Acharnians* (lines 504–507), where he says that no foreigners are present to hear his criticisms of the City. The longer Dionysia was held after the sailing season had begun, so foreigners would have been in the audience which was the reason for Cleon's attempted prosecution of Aristophanes after *Babylonians*. It is not known exactly how the days were organized, but it seems that the first day of the Dionysia was given over to a procession which brought the wooden statue of Dionysus, god of theatre, from Eleutherae, through the city gate by which he was believed to have entered Athens originally. On the same day there seem to have been dithyrambic contests (hymns sung and danced in honour of Dionysus). Over a thousand citizen men and boys would have taken part in these, which means that the audience for the subsequent plays would have included spectators who had not only experience in taking part in choruses, but who were familiar with the stories that were being performed. The final four days of the Dionysia were given over to the performance of plays, but also would have included various civic displays such as the ten generals (*strategoi*) pouring libations, the recitation of the names of all those who had been officially honoured for benefitting the city, the display of tribute from the states in the Athenian empire and the parade of 'war orphans' (boys who had lost their fathers in war against Athens' enemies). These boys were raised at state expense and given special seats in the theatre.

To take part in the competition the playwrights submitted a draft outline of their play (comedy) or plays (tragedy) to the relevant archon (state official) during the summer preceding the festival; this was known as 'asking for a chorus'. The archon would choose which three tragedians and which five comic writers would get to stage their dramas. The archons had no particular expertise in drama, as they were primarily concerned with overseeing religious occasions and presiding over courts, but they would doubtless have known who the most popular playwrights were and would have had an eye to pleasing the audience. At this point, the successful playwrights were each allocated a *choregos*; these men were wealthy citizens, or metics, who were obliged to fund choruses (metics were liable for this at the Lenaea only) or, as a *trierarchos,* to pay for the fitting of a warship as part of their civic responsibilities (*leitourgiai*). This responsibility was heavy; a comic chorus was composed of twenty-four Athenian citizens who had to be financially supported, there was a chorus-trainer to find, the provision of rehearsal space, costumes (often elaborate to represent the animals or characters for whom the play was named), masks, music and an after-show party. In his speech *A Defence against a Charge of Bribery* 1–5, Lysias claims that, as *choregos* for Cephisodorus he spent 1,600 drachmas (one drachma was the cost of a day's labour for a skilled craftsman). The winning *choregos* was awarded an ivy wreath and could erect a small monument to acknowledge his personal triumph. The playwright was allotted actors who were paid from the public purse and the director (*didaskalos*) was normally (though not always) the playwright himself. On the day of the competition the order of plays was decided by lot and the presiding archon also chose the judges by lot. The judges were drawn from the ten tribes and did not have any qualification other than being Athenian citizens. The way that the plays were distributed amongst the days is not certain, but there appear to have been five comedies, possibly on the second day and before the tragedies. During the Peloponnesian War, perhaps because of a shortage of citizens to take part in the choruses, it is believed that the number of comedies was reduced to three, either held on one day or tagged on to the end of each day. This would mean that audiences saw three tragedies, one satyr play and a comedy – a long day – and may be the explanation of a comment in *Birds* (lines 785–789), where the chorus leader talks about the advantages of having wings so that audience members could fly home for lunch, escape a boring tragedy and still be back in time for the comedy.

The audience was composed of citizens and metics, with perhaps a few women and slaves at the back. There were also a lot of young boys and, at the Dionysia, many foreign visitors. There was space for approximately 8,000 seats with the rest crowded onto the hillside behind. Festivals were an important state occasion and were very popular. The cost of entry was 2 obols (a day's pay for a manual labourer), but later in the mid-fourth century there was the Theoric Fund which allowed the poorest citizens to attend theatrical performances. Inside the theatre, the audience sat in specific areas (*kerkides*), perhaps marked out for the ten tribes, metics and foreigners. The central block was marked out for the Council, and ambassadors, dignitaries and judges sat in the front rows. The seats were raked and built into the side of a hill, so the view of the performance would have been unimpeded. The *skene* at the back of the stage area seems to have included a double door, and possibly two more, from which characters could come and go. The stage machinery consisted of a crane (*mechane*) onto which actors were strapped and lifted up above the skene, either to represent gods or, as in the case of *Peace*, to show Trygaeus' journey to Olympus on a dung beetle. Scenes inside a building could be shown by means of a platform (*ekkyklema*) which seems to have been wheeled out through the double door in the skene. The opening scenes of *Clouds*, showing the father and son sleeping, could perhaps have used this piece of machinery, although they might just as easily be lying wrapped in blankets on the stage. It was most certainly used for the scene inside the Reflectory where the students are revealed at their strange studies. All actors were male, and masks were used to portray the various characters. 'Portrait masks' may have been used to represent well-known characters and Aelian, writing some 600 years after Socrates' death in *c.* CE 200 (*Varia Historia* 2.13), tells us that Socrates stood up in the audience, during the performance of *Clouds*, to show those who did not know him what he actually looked like (though it is also said that the mask of the actor playing Socrates was a good likeness). The fact that actors wore distinctive costumes and masks makes it easier for us to understand how a play could be performed by three (four for comedy) actors only, as the full body-covering and mask meant that there was less confusion if an actor left and came back on stage as a different character. The comic chorus was distinct from the tragic one which seems to have worn long flowing robes and vase paintings depict comic characters in shorter tunic-like costumes with over-sized, stitched leather phalluses. Depictions of lavish costumes seen in vase paintings (Gela Painter, black-figure oinochoe *c.* 480 showing chorus members dressed as birds) and for productions such as *Clouds, Wasps* and *Birds* suggest a degree of spectacle such as Aristotle later included in his key ingredients for a successful dramatic production.

Metre

The section set for A Level (lines 1–242) is most of the prologue of the play and is entirely in iambic trimeters, the metre that sounds most like ordinary speech, with lines divided into three '*metra*' or patterns of syllables each containing a pair of iambs. Choruses sang in lyric metres which were accompanied by music and dance. The *aulos* or double pipe seems to have been the usual instrument. (See Further Reading below for a link to a reconstruction of the music of ancient theatre.) The chorus' songs make use of a greater range of metres and are often presented in matching, or answering, pairs (*strophe* and *antistrophe*). The rhythms would be matched to the action on stage, so a series of short syllables might be used for rapid movement with longer syllables for speech.

How accurate was the portrayal of Socrates in *Clouds*?

Socrates (*c.* 470–399) was an Athenian citizen and philosopher who is seen as one of the founders of philosophy in the Western world. He left no writings and the only accounts we have of him are from his pupils. The most famous of these is Plato, who wrote many dialogues about Socrates' method of questioning (*elenchus*) by which he caused his interlocutor to reassess his understanding of (typically) some moral concept. Another well-known student, Xenophon, also wrote a series of Socratic dialogues known as the *Memorabilia*, and an *Apology of Socrates to the Jury*. Both wrote a *Symposium* (a fictional account of a drinking party), in which Socrates appears. According to Plato's *Apology* (19c), an account of Socrates' trial by an Athenian court for 'corrupting the youth of Athens' and for impiety (not believing in the gods of the state), Aristophanes' portrayal of Socrates in *Clouds* was used as evidence that people were influenced against him. Socrates' subsequent conviction might suggest that Aristophanes was felt to be partially responsible for his death. *Clouds* was seen by around 8,000 Athenian citizens twenty-four years before the trial in 399, so perhaps some of those in the jury of Socrates' trial might have recalled it, but it is hard to believe that this could have been a major element in the guilty verdict so long afterwards. However in his *Symposium* (written no earlier than 385 and describing an event that purportedly occurred in 416), Plato seems to go out of his way to refute the accusation that Socrates was a corrupter of youth, so perhaps Plato believed there was a connection, or at least wished to ascribe some blame. Aristophanes also appeared in this work of Plato, where there appears to be no bad feeling between him and Socrates; and Xenophon in his *Symposium* of the late 360s (describing an event seemingly held in 422), presented Socrates as a genial character who enjoyed sensual pleasures, not the austere, threadbare figure of *Clouds* and Ameipsias' lost play *Konnos*. In neither of these works did Socrates appear to be one of the 'Sophists', i.e. men who were broadly defined as itinerant teachers of higher education, travelling widely to give popular lectures and specializing in instruction in a wide range of topics including techniques of persuasion and argument. Furthermore, in Plato's *Apology* (19d), Socrates denies he is a professional teacher who receives payment for his time, which seems to have been one of the criteria, at least for Socrates, of a Sophist. We must remember, however, that Plato was a pupil of Socrates, and Xenophon was also a member of his circle in the late 400s, so impartiality is an issue. The case against Socrates in 399 was probably brought because of his known association with men who had been involved in the oligarchic government set up at the end of the Peloponnesian War, the Thirty. Critias, leader of their most extreme faction, had been a student of Socrates' and this would not have endeared him to many Athenians. However, Socrates certainly had a sense of moral duty, and was not afraid to speak out when he saw something he thought was wrong. This was shown when, as chairman of the assembly's presiding committee, at the trial of the generals who had failed (because of a storm) to recover the dead after the victory in the sea-battle at Arginusae in 406, he was the only one to speak against trying them en bloc, an action which was illegal under Athenian law (*Apology* 32b-c). He also stood up against the Thirty in 404 when he refused to arrest an innocent citizen, Leon of Salamis, who had been condemned to death (*Apology* 32c-d). This, and Socrates' tendency to insist on critically examining every opinion, no matter how widely accepted, made him suspect and unpopular with some people, particularly those in power. In the uncertainty of life after the end of the Peloponnesian War, this is more likely to have been the cause of the prosecution.

If Plato and Xenophon were correct in their presentation of Socrates as a convivial man, why does *Clouds*, twenty-four years before the trial, present Socrates as a dishonest, overly austere, and rather other-worldly figure running a school where students learn how to make the weaker argument the stronger? Firstly, this was a comedy, and entered in a competition that the playwright wished to win, and secondly Socrates would have been a useful representative of intellectual thought as he would have been a familiar figure around the *agora* (market-place), whereas the Sophists tended to come from outside Athens. The real Socrates would have been about forty-five years old in 423. He had fought at Potidaea in 432 where he had saved the life of the aristocratic and maverick Alcibiades, and the year before the production of *Clouds* he had fought at the battle of Delium, so he must have been physically tough. He is not presented as such in *Clouds*, but there does seem to be a degree of truth in the presentation of him as careless of physical comfort. In Ameipsias' *Konnos*, which beat *Clouds* into third place in 423, references are made to Socrates' thin cloak and habit of going shoeless. In the opening of Plato's *Symposium* Apollodorus, a guest at the party, comments on Socrates being bathed and wearing shoes, which he describes as ὀλιγάκις (a rare event), so perhaps there was accuracy in that part of Aristophanes' presentation. A. M. Bowie believes that Socrates' austere lifestyle may have branded him as a member of the cult of Pythagoras whose followers were known for their asceticism. It is hard to know what to believe in a dramatic or literary presentation such as *Clouds* or the *Symposia* of Plato and Xenophon, but it is most likely that Aristophanes chose a representative of intellectualism of whom the majority of the audience would have heard, and would also know by sight, whereas most Sophists would have been visitors to Athens, and therefore would not have been well enough known to ordinary people to be effective targets of satire. There is no reason to suppose that the portrayal was entirely true to life, but there must have been enough accuracy in the caricature to make it recognizable. There are elements, which can be pinpointed, showing a lack of accuracy in the portrayal of Socrates. He himself never headed a school in Athens from which he taught his methods of dialectic (establishing the truth through reasoned argument), in fact he was well-known for talking to 'students', or anyone that was prepared to converse with him, in the agora. Furthermore, he was not known for pursuing the kind of research that the student shows Strepsiades (lines 143ff); he says as much in Plato's *Apology*, though in *Phaedo* (96a–99d) he admits that as a young man he had some interest in natural science. In *Clouds* (line 275ff), Socrates introduces his new pupil, Strepsiades, to the cloud chorus who initially seem to be new deities, claiming later that the traditional gods are all nonsense (φλύαρος, line 365), however by the end of the play they are revealed to be guardians of traditional values. Which was Socrates' own view? Does it matter in the context of a play?

In his lifetime, Socrates seems to have been a relatively frequent figure on the stage: apart from the two plays in the Dionysia of 423, he was also referred to in *Birds* (414) and *Frogs* (405), where he was variously described as unwashed (line 1555) and idling his time away (lines 1491–1499), and later in the *Symposium* of Xenophon, as well as being immortalized in the dialogues of Plato. By 423 Socrates must have been a familiar enough figure around Athens for the ordinary theatre-goer to be able to recognize the references to his method of questioning, and the basics of scientific research might also have been relatively well-known. We learn from *Phaedo* (96a–99d) that Socrates, early in his career, was interested in reasons or causes, and that he associated with Prodicus, who was one of the earliest to be described as a Sophist. So, with his broad range of interests and immediately recognizable public image, Socrates would have been a convenient figure and the ideal representative of philosophy and intellectual pursuits.

Is Aristophanes funny?

Aristophanes flourished in the period we call Old Comedy, which ran from about the mid-fifth century to the early fourth century. Comic drama at this time was characterized by jokes and satire on contemporary political issues, individuals and vulgarity; for Aristophanes it seemed a winning combination. For modern audiences however the political references can be quite daunting and even for Athens, Old Comedy seemed to have run its course by the early part of the fourth century. At this point, comic drama began to make the transition into a form where political satire was avoided in favour of comedy based on more generic, social situations, laying the foundations for New Comedy in which stock characters played out situations that were closer to reality and the role of the chorus dwindled. We have nothing left of Middle Comedy, but the influence of Menander on New Comedy in the later fourth century was great. His plays influenced Plautus and Terence in the Roman world, and through them Shakespeare, Jonson, Congreve and Molière.

Aristophanes' humour thrived on biting political satire, sexual innuendo and scatological humour, along with exuberant choruses, slapstick routines and outrageous mythological references (cf. *Wasps* where Philocleon attempts to escape from his house by hiding under a donkey as Odysseus hid under a ram to escape from the Cyclops), as well as choruses dressed in elaborate costumes and lively musical numbers. The political satire can be off-putting for the modern viewer who is unversed in the politics of fifth-century Athens, but there are plenty of other ways to find amusement, such as the slapstick at the end of *Clouds* where the frustrated Strepsiades burns down the Reflectory, or the visual humour of Socrates appearing on stage in a basket hanging in the air in the same play. There is also verbal humour with Aristophanes' own coinages of unusually long compound words and verbal tricks picked up from listening to politicians and prominent citizens which allow the audience to recognize who is being parodied. We need only think of modern impressionists on popular shows such as *Dead Ringers* who are able parody a celebrity from a few catchphrases to see that this is still a rich source of humour. There is also paratragedy, where characters on stage quote or refer to specific tragedies or tragic situations usually where the situation is much less serious than in the tragedy being quoted. An example of this is the scene in *Thesmophoriazusae* where Euripides' kinsman, disguised as a woman to infiltrate a woman-only festival, threatens to sacrifice a wine-skin itself disguised as a baby. The scene refers to Euripides' now lost play of 438, *Telephus*. Clearly Aristophanes himself was very well-versed in the tragic genre but, to a degree, the humour also relies on the knowledge and understanding of the audience for the full effect. Again, one can see that this is still possible with comedians making reference to television shows or genres that are familiar to large numbers of people. There would have been less variety available to Athenians of the fifth century but the audience at a comedy would probably have been much the same as that at a tragedy, so it was likely that a good proportion of the audience would have recognized direct quotation, specific situations or at the very least the type of reference being made. However, the humour that most people think of when discussing Aristophanes is the direct attack he makes on political figures or institutions and the scatological humour that runs through every play. Prominent figures such as Cleon receive personal and political ridicule which would probably lead to court cases these days: we know that Cleon tried to haul Aristophanes through the courts after comments made in *Babylonians* in 426 (see above), although, interestingly, the charge was ridiculing the Athenian people rather than the personal attacks on Cleon himself. These seem to have been accepted as part and parcel of the comic genre at the time. It is not necessary for the modern audience to have an encyclopaedic knowledge of fifth-century Athenian politics to enjoy these comments, although it can help, as it is still possible to find the humour by looking at these characters as generic types – the arrogant buffoon, the coward who drops his shield in battle, the glutton, the drunkard, etc. Scatological humour is also important in Old Comedy, with some people believing that it makes the plays juvenile and vulgar, while others simply enjoy the laughs. The humour contained in plays such as *Peace* (421) which opens with slaves kneading dung for their master's dung beetle which will later carry him up to visit the gods, or the scene in *Lysistrata* (411) where Myrrhine leads on her sex-starved husband, or in *Clouds* where Socrates likens the process by which clouds make thunder to the effect that broth at the Panathenia has on the digestive system, is easily accessible. One final type of humour used by Aristophanes, which might be considered less acceptable in modern times, is gaining laughs by ridiculing people who are 'not like us', which (as Edith Hall says) is a way of building identity and common feeling in the audience. There are numerous jokes about barbarians (i.e. non-Greeks), women and effeminate men, even philosophers, all designed to create a fellow-feeling against the 'other', and to create a bond between the members of the audience. Whilst we can distance ourselves by explaining that fifth-century Athens was a different time and a different culture, we must still find a way to talk sensibly about such differences while seeing the inherent racism, sexism, homophobia and xenophobia apparent in the performances. However we view the plays of Aristophanes, they were clearly thought funny by their original audiences, and more importantly the judges, and they have continued to be performed and enjoyed for two millennia.

Structure and summary

Comedy, like tragedy, has a structure which most plays seem to follow but which could be varied to suit the plot. This section summarizes the plot of the play with the structure. The section set for A Level, lines 1–242 is the majority of the **prologue** (i.e. the whole of the first scene up to the entrance of the Chorus at 275).

1–24 These lines are spoken by the protagonist and introduce the audience to the main themes of the play. This is sometimes presented as a soliloquy and sometimes as a dialogue, or a mixture of the two. It is spoken in iambic trimeters.

The scene at the beginning is of two men lying asleep, probably on the floor of the stage in front of the *skene* building, although it may have been shown by means of the *ekkyklema* (see 'The dramatic festivals' above). The opening lines of *Clouds* do not immediately give us any indication of the subject matter of what is to follow, but it is similar to *Acharnians* in that we have a grumpy old man whom we might suppose to be a country-dweller of no great wealth. He refers to his inability to punish lazy slaves because of the war (when they had more opportunity to run away and join the opposing side), and there is a complaint about the young man, whom we soon learn to be his son, sleeping without a care in the world. It swiftly becomes clear that the problems which are keeping the old man awake are nothing to do with the war, but are debts incurred by this horse-mad son.

25–78 As the old man goes through his accounts, the son stirs, complaining that his father is keeping him awake, before rolling over to sleep again. The old man launches into his recent family history and explains how he made a marriage which seems to have been rather above his social station, to a well-connected city woman who wished to bring up her son in the style to which her wealthy relatives were accustomed: this meant keeping horses. She even insisted that he should have ἵππος in his name. The old man, whose name we later learn is Strepsiades (from στρέφω 'I dodge' or 'twist'), has a plan.

79–130 The old man wakes his son and tries to persuade him to enter the Reflectory (φροντιστήριον), which, with the suspension of disbelief that we are familiar with today, is located next door to Strepsiades' house, or may even have been the same door representing both. This is the school where he wishes his son to learn how to argue and win arguments so that he can put off his creditors. Strepsiades indicates a door in the skene which represents the Reflectory. The son, Pheidippides, is not prepared to become a student, mainly because he is worried about losing his tanned complexion by staying inside and studying. He does not want to be laughed at by his friends in the cavalry, young men who have the leisure to spend time at the gymnasium.

131–221 A student opens the door; this is the cue for several set-ups, probably using the *ekkyklema* to wheel out a tableau of what is happening inside the Reflectory. The humour here is directed at both the weird scientific investigations being pursued by the students but also at Strepsiades himself when he shows that he has not seen a map before, or when he misunderstands what the students are looking for under the earth. Strepsiades' literal-minded explanation to his son of the kind of people who live in the Reflectory has already shown us the lack of sophistication which we might expect from a countryman in a comedy. The broad range of studies which are described to Strepsiades by the student is meant to be representative of all branches of intellectual enquiry, and Aristophanes weaves in topical points about the Athenian jury system and the Spartans captured at Pylos.

222–274 Socrates' entrance in a basket hanging from the *mechane* is suitably absurd. He is considering things in the sky and therefore has to be elevated above the restraining and contaminating earth. We have already been told that Socrates has been performing experiments, and the Reflectory seems to be a place where students can learn a wide variety of things – cosmology, astronomy, meteorology, geometry, geography, zoology and philosophical theology – as well as rhetoric. Socrates seems to be a representative of all of these disciplines. When he speaks to Socrates, Strepsiades clearly asks to be taught rhetoric but Socrates sidesteps the request to discuss the gods, which prepares the way for the entrance of the Cloud chorus. In preparation for his admission to the Reflectory, Strepsiades must go through a parody of a religious ritual: he sits on a couch and is given a wreath to wear while Socrates sprinkles him with flour in the same way that, in a sacrifice, animals had grain sprinkled on them. The scene is typical of Aristophanes' reference to Athenian life in his plays. The use of the chorus of Initiates in *Frogs* is another example.

275–290 *Parodos* – the chorus of clouds seems to be above the *skene* at this point and does not enter the *orchestra* until line 326 – this perhaps symbolizes their divine nature, as this is where gods traditionally appeared in tragedy. Aristophanes refers to the side entrance of the orchestra as the *eisodos,* sometimes called the *parodos,* the name by which the entrance of a chorus came to be known. The Chorus sings the *strophe* and *antistrophe* (alternate stanzas) while they are approaching the *orchestra.* There is a change to lyric metre here, which is the standard metre for choruses in both tragedy and comedy. Strepsiades is awestruck by the figures summoned by Socrates' prayers and asks how they can be deities since he thought they were mist and steam; at this point we begin to see how the old man's perceptions are being subtly shifted. Socrates now persuades Strepsiades that these are goddesses who can change their form, giving the playwright an opportunity to make fun of important Athenian citizens by claiming that the clouds shapeshift according to whom they see when they look down on Athens from the sky.

291–297 There is a brief section of reaction to the *strophe* by Strepsiades and Socrates, suggesting that another piece of theatrical machinery, the *bronteion*, has been used here to imitate thunder.

298–313 The *antistrophe*, or answering section of the *parodos*, is now sung by the Chorus as it approaches the orchestra.

314–411 Socrates explains to Strepsiades who the Chorus are, and Aristophanes uses the opportunity for some more satire of well-known Athenian citizens. The Chorus addresses Socrates as the only mortal to whom it will speak, and he refers to the chorus members as the only deities. There is a section of vulgar, and possibly visual, comedy as Socrates explains to Strepsiades how rain and thunder appear using the analogy of flatulence after eating broth at the Panathenaea. The Chorus Leader approaches Strepsiades.

412–456 The Chorus Leader warns Strepsiades that his education will not be easy. He initially misunderstands his desire to speak well, assuming that Strepsiades wishes to speak in the Assembly (*ekklesia*), but on learning why he wants to study the art of speaking he is equally happy to assist the old man in his desire to argue his way out of debt.

457–475 A short passage of lyric dialogue occurs between Strepsiades and the Chorus as they imagine what his life will be like with this new skill of speaking well.

476–509 Strepsiades' initiation into the Reflectory begins, and he is tricked into removing his cloak which is presumably scooped up by Socrates as they go inside.

510–626 *Parabasis* – this is the section of the play where the Chorus Leader steps forward to address the audience and speak for the playwright. The *parabasis* begins with a complaint that the first version of *Clouds* did not win the City Dionysia even though it was a clever play. The Chorus Leader (as the playwright) promises that he has not employed the usual comic tricks of the trade to gain laughs and notably that he has not included people waving torches – an interesting claim given the ending of the play as we have it. There are references to rival playwrights and to Cleon, including one to him being elected general (*strategos*) in 424 against Aristophanes' advice. Cleon was killed at Amphipolis in 422 so this may be part of the original *parabasis* from before the revision.

627–888 Socrates re-emerges from the Reflectory complaining that Strepsiades is unable to learn anything, but begins to try to teach him about metre, rhythm and grammar – unsuccessfully. Socrates leaves, and the Chorus encourage Strepsiades. Socrates re-enters and the comedy becomes more vulgar with puns and gestures of an obscene nature from Strepsiades until Socrates, despairing of teaching the old man anything, moves away to the edge of the stage. Strepsiades decides to go back to his own house and drag his son along to learn, however unwillingly. Socrates agrees to accept Pheidippides as a pupil, but leaves the stage declaring that he must learn from the Arguments themselves.

889–1114 *Agon* – this is the set-piece contest between two opposing parties, in this case, the personified Right and the Wrong Arguments. Each party will state its case and, by the convention of a play, the party speaking second wins. The participants speak in a recitative style which is in a variety of metres – anapaestic or iambic tetrameters. There is a short introductory section with the two Arguments staking their claims. At 949 the Chorus introduces the *agon* proper and Right Argument begins his speech, arguing that the kind of education that young men used to receive was the reason that Athenians were strong enough, through hours spent at the gymnasium, to defeat the Persians at Marathon (490). Wrong Argument then puts his case; he uses examples from mythology and literature to show that his form of education is better, e.g. Heracles did not take cold baths and Homer approved of people spending time talking in the agora. He then addresses Strepsiades, asking whether he still wishes his son to be taught by him: he does, and the reluctant Pheidippides is led into the Reflectory.

1115 – 1130 Second *parabasis* – the Chorus addresses the judges. They remain in character and promise to reward the judges if they vote this play first prize, they indicate that there will be vengeance if they do not.

1131–1213 Dramatic convention allows time to pass during the *parabasis* and Strepsiades returns to collect his son from the Reflectory; he is delighted when Socrates emerges to tell him that Pheidippides is now fully trained and able to argue his way out of any lawsuit. After a triumphant song from Strepsiades and a brief display of Pheidippides' arguing skills, the father and son go into their house.

1214–1320 In this section we see the arrival of Strepsiades' creditors to claim their money. The old man tells the first creditor that now his son has learnt how to argue and win a case, he will not be paying him back, despite having sworn an oath. The first creditor leaves threatening legal action and the second creditor appears, injured after a chariot-racing accident. Strepsiades refuses to pay him and begins to use a horsewhip on him. It is ironic that after sending Pheidippides to learn from the Wrong Argument, it is Strepsiades, the failed student, who is getting rid of the creditors. The old man goes inside, and the Chorus sings a lyric song which foreshadows Strepsiades' fate.

1321–1511 In this final scene of the play, Strepsiades comes hurtling out of his house, pursued by his son Pheidippides. He is clearly in distress and is calling on his neighbours for help. It seems there has been a violent scene between the father and son inside and Pheidippides is preparing to argue that he is right to beat his father.

At lines 1345–1451, there is a second *agon* which mirrors that of the Right and Wrong Argument. The Chorus introduces this with a brief strophe and refers directly to itself, claiming that it needs to hear the details of the argument. At 1353, Strepsiades begins his story. We hear that a fight broke out over dinner when Pheidippides refused to recite the poetry of Aeschylus, preferring the more contemporary Euripides.

Dinner parties and celebration sequences were a common way to finish comedies (e.g. *Wasps*) but this is a subversion of that type of ending. For Strepsiades it seems all to have gone wrong. The protagonist, who often wins out in an Aristophanes play, is here being punished for his own misdemeanours and must face the consequences of his actions. The Chorus Leader introduces the opposing side of the agon, which is Pheidippides' argument, and Strepsiades admits defeat.

1452–1464 Strepsiades turns to the Chorus and blames it for his defeat. It responds that he has no one to blame but himself, and that it just helped him on his way to teach him to fear the gods. The supposedly radical Clouds turn out to be guardians of the traditional gods after all.

1464–1510 Strepsiades has failed to persuade Pheidippides to join him in revenge on Socrates and Chaerephon, his right-hand man in the Reflectory. (Chaerephon was a keen student of Socrates, best known for being the one to hear from the Delphic Oracle that Socrates was the wisest of men.) Pheidippides is now thoroughly sophistic in his outlook and returns inside. Strepsiades turns to the Herm (stone figure placed outside Greek houses as a boundary marker), and here a stage property, for advice. Allegedly urged on by it, he calls a slave to bring a mattock and a ladder with which he begins to dismantle the roof of the Reflectory. The play ends, not with a song and a dance, or a party, but with Strepsiades, now triumphant, on the roof, throwing a burning torch into the building while Socrates and his students run for their lives.

Further Reading

The two most useful commentaries on *Clouds* are:
> *Aristophanes Clouds ed. K. J. Dover (OUP 1968), abridged student edition. OUP 1970.*
> *Clouds, Alan H. Sommerstein. Aris & Phillips Classical Texts 1982.*

Other books of general interest are:
> *Aristophanes Frogs and Other Plays. Trans. Steven Halliwell. Oxford World's Classics 2015.*
> *Bowie, A. M. Aristophanes, Myth, Ritual and Comedy. CUP 1993.*
> *Cartledge, Paul. Aristophanes and his Theatre of the Absurd. Bloomsbury reprinted 2013.*
> *D'Angour, Armand. Socrates in Love: The Making of a Philosopher. Bloomsbury 2019.*
> *Dover, Kenneth J. Aristophanic Comedy. University of California Press 1972.*
> *MacDowell, Douglas M. Aristophanes and Athens. OUP 1995.*
> *Robson, James. Aristophanes: An Introduction. Duckworth 2009.*

The Classical Association magazine, *Omnibus*, has numerous articles aimed directly at A-level students. The entire archive can be found at: https://archive.org/details/omnibusmagazine Articles of particular note are:
> *'Good and bad comedy in Aristophanes'; Clouds – James Robson (Issue 60).*
> *'Flying scholars and the rise of flatulence: the scientific fantasy of Aristophanes'*
>   *Clouds' – Phillip Sidney Horky (Issue 69).*

For a reconstruction of the music likely to have been heard accompanying tragedy or comedy see Armand D'Angour's 'Rediscovering Ancient Greek Music' at: youtube.com/watch?v= 4hOK7bU0S1Y&t=411s

Text

ΣΤΡΕΨΙΑΔΗΣ
    ἰοὺ ἰού·
    ὦ Ζεῦ βασιλεῦ, τὸ χρῆμα τῶν νυκτῶν ὅσον·
    ἀπέραντον. οὐδέποθ᾽ ἡμέρα γενήσεται;
    καὶ μὴν πάλαι γ᾽ ἀλεκτρυόνος ἤκουσ᾽ ἐγώ·
    οἱ δ᾽ οἰκέται ῥέγκουσιν · ἀλλ᾽ οὐκ ἂν πρὸ τοῦ.   5
    ἀπόλοιο δῆτ᾽, ὦ πόλεμε, πολλῶν οὕνεκα,
    ὅτ᾽ οὐδὲ κολάσ᾽ ἔξεστί μοι τοὺς οἰκέτας.
    ἀλλ᾽ οὐδ᾽ ὁ χρηστὸς οὑτοσὶ νεανίας
    ἐγείρεται τῆς νυκτός, ἀλλὰ πέρδεται
    ἐν πέντε σισύραις ἐγκεκορδυλημένος.   10
    ἀλλ᾽, εἰ δοκεῖ, ῥέγκωμεν ἐγκεκαλυμμένοι.
    ἀλλ᾽ οὐ δύναμαι δείλαιος εὕδειν δακνόμενος
    ὑπὸ τῆς δαπάνης καὶ τῆς φάτνης καὶ τῶν χρεῶν
    διὰ τουτονὶ τὸν υἱόν. ὁ δὲ κόμην ἔχων
    ἱππάζεταί τε καὶ ξυνωρικεύεται,   15
    ὀνειροπολεῖ θ᾽ ἵππους· ἐγὼ δ᾽ ἀπόλλυμαι
    ὁρῶν ἄγουσαν τὴν σελήνην εἰκάδας·
    οἱ γὰρ τόκοι χωροῦσιν. ἅπτε, παῖ, λύχνον,
    κἄκφερε τὸ γραμματεῖον, ἵν᾽ ἀναγνῶ λαβὼν
    ὁπόσοις ὀφείλω καὶ λογίσωμαι τοὺς τόκους.   20
    φέρ᾽ ἴδω, τί ὀφείλω; δώδεκα μνᾶς Πασίᾳ.
    τοῦ δώδεκα μνᾶς Πασίᾳ; τί ἐχρησάμην;
    ὅτ᾽ ἐπριάμην τὸν κοππατίαν. οἴμοι τάλας,
    εἴθ᾽ ἐξεκόπην πρότερον τὸν ὀφθαλμὸν λίθῳ.

ΦΕΙΔΙΠΠΙΔΗΣ
    Φίλων ἀδικεῖς· ἔλαυνε τὸν σαυτοῦ δρόμον.   25
Στ.   τοῦτ᾽ ἔστι τουτὶ τὸ κακὸν ὅ μ᾽ ἀπολώλεκεν·
    ὀνειροπολεῖ γὰρ καὶ καθεύδων ἱππικήν.
Φε.   πόσους δρόμους ἐλᾷ τὰ πολεμιστήρια;
Στ.   ἐμὲ μὲν σὺ πολλοὺς τὸν πατέρ᾽ ἐλαύνεις δρόμους.
    ἀτὰρ τί χρέος ἔβα με μετὰ τὸν Πασίαν;   30
    τρεῖς μναῖ διφρίσκου καὶ τροχοῖν Ἀμυνίᾳ.

Φε. ἄπαγε τὸν ἵππον ἐξαλίσας οἴκαδε.
Στ. ἀλλ᾽, ὦ μέλ᾽, ἐξήλικας ἐμέ γ᾽ ἐκ τῶν ἐμῶν,
ὅτε καὶ δίκας ὤφληκα χἄτεροι τόκου
ἐνεχυράσεσθαί φασιν.
Φε.   ἐτεόν, ὦ πάτερ,   35

τί δυσκολαίνεις καὶ στρέφει τὴν νύχθ᾽ ὅλην;
Στ. δάκνει μέ τις δήμαρχος ἐκ τῶν στρωμάτων.
Φε. ἔασον, ὦ δαιμόνιε, καταδαρθεῖν τί με.
Στ. σὺ δ᾽ οὖν κάθευδε· τὰ δὲ χρέα ταῦτ᾽ ἴσθ᾽ ὅτι
εἰς τὴν κεφαλὴν ἅπαντα τὴν σὴν τρέψεται.   40
φεῦ.
εἴθ᾽ ὤφελ᾽ ἡ προμνήστρι᾽ ἀπολέσθαι κακῶς,
ἥτις με γῆμ᾽ ἐπῆρε τὴν σὴν μητέρα·
ἐμοὶ γὰρ ἦν ἄγροικος ἥδιστος βίος,
εὐρωτιῶν, ἀκόρητος, εἰκῇ κείμενος,
βρύων μελίτταις καὶ προβάτοις καὶ στεμφύλοις.   45
ἔπειτ᾽ ἔγημα Μεγακλέους τοῦ Μεγακλέους
ἀδελφιδῆν ἄγροικος ὢν ἐξ ἄστεως,
σεμνήν, τρυφῶσαν, ἐγκεκοισυρωμένην.
ταύτην ὅτ᾽ ἐγάμουν, συγκατεκλινόμην ἐγὼ
ὄζων τρυγός, τρασιᾶς, ἐρίων, περιουσίας,   50
ἡ δ᾽ αὖ μύρου, κρόκου, καταγλωττισμάτων,
δαπάνης, λαφυγμοῦ, Κωλιάδος, Γενετυλλίδος.
οὐ μὴν ἐρῶ γ᾽ ὡς ἀργὸς ἦν, ἀλλ᾽ ἐσπάθα,
ἐγὼ δ᾽ ἂν αὐτῇ θοἰμάτιον δεικνὺς τοδὶ
πρόφασιν ἔφασκον, "ὦ γύναι, λίαν σπαθᾷς."   55

ΟΙΚΕΤΗΣ
ἔλαιον ἡμῖν οὐκ ἔνεστ᾽ ἐν τῷ λύχνῳ.
Στ. οἴμοι. τί γάρ μοι τὸν πότην ἧπτες λύχνον;
δεῦρ᾽ ἔλθ᾽, ἵνα κλάῃς.
Οἰ.   διὰ τί δῆτα κλαύσομαι;
Στ. ὅτι τῶν παχειῶν ἐνετίθεις θρυαλλίδων.
μετὰ ταῦθ᾽, ὅπως νῶν ἐγένεθ᾽ υἱὸς οὑτοσί,   60
ἐμοί τε δὴ καὶ τῇ γυναικὶ τἀγαθῇ,
περὶ τοὐνόματος δὴ 'ντεῦθεν ἐλοιδορούμεθα·
ἡ μὲν γὰρ ἵππον προσετίθει πρὸς τοὔνομα,
Ξάνθιππον ἢ Χάιριππον ἢ Καλλιππίδην,
ἐγὼ δὲ τοῦ πάππου 'τιθέμην Φειδωνίδην.   65
τέως μὲν οὖν ἐκρινόμεθ᾽· εἶτα τῷ χρόνῳ
κοινῇ ξυνέβημεν κἀθέμεθα Φειδιππίδην.
τοῦτον τὸν υἱὸν λαμβάνουσ᾽ ἐκορίζετο,
"ὅταν σὺ μέγας ὢν ἅρμ᾽ ἐλαύνῃς πρὸς πόλιν,
ὥσπερ Μεγακλέης, ξυστίδ᾽ ἔχων." ἐγὼ δ᾽ ἔφην,   70
"ὅταν μὲν οὖν τὰς αἶγας ἐκ τοῦ φελλέως,
ὥσπερ ὁ πατήρ σου, διφθέραν ἐνημμένος."

ἀλλ᾽ οὐκ ἐπείθετο τοῖς ἐμοῖς οὐδὲν λόγοις,
ἀλλ᾽ ἵππερόν μοι κατέχεεν τῶν χρημάτων.
νῦν οὖν ὅλην τὴν νύκτα φροντίζων ὁδοῦ 75
μίαν ηὗρον ἀτραπὸν δαιμονίως ὑπερφυᾶ,
ἣν ἢν ἀναπείσω τουτονί, σωθήσομαι.
ἀλλ᾽ ἐξεγεῖραι πρῶτον αὐτὸν βούλομαι.
πῶς δῆτ᾽ ἂν ἥδιστ᾽ αὐτὸν ἐπεγείραιμι; πῶς;
Φειδιππίδη, Φειδιππίδιον.

Φε. τί, ὦ πάτερ; 80
Στ. κύσον με καὶ τὴν χεῖρα δὸς τὴν δεξιάν.
Φε. ἰδού. τί ἔστιν;
Στ. εἰπέ μοι, φιλεῖς ἐμέ;
Φε. νὴ τὸν Ποσειδῶ τουτονὶ τὸν ἵππιον.
Στ. μή 'μοί γε τοῦτον μηδαμῶς τὸν ἵππιον·
οὗτος γὰρ ὁ θεὸς αἴτιός μοι τῶν κακῶν. 85
ἀλλ᾽ εἴπερ ἐκ τῆς καρδίας μ᾽ ὄντως φιλεῖς,
ὦ παῖ, πιθοῦ.
Φε. τί οὖν πίθωμαι δῆτά σοι;
Στ. ἔκστρεψον ὡς τάχιστα τοὺς σαυτοῦ τρόπους,
καὶ μάνθαν᾽ ἐλθὼν ἂν ἐγὼ παραινέσω.
Φε. λέγε δή, τί κελεύεις;
Στ. καί τι πείσει;
Φε. πείσομαι 90
νὴ τὸν Διόνυσον.
Στ. δεῦρό νυν ἀπόβλεπε.
ὁρᾷς τὸ θύριον τοῦτο καὶ τᾠκίδιον;
Φε. ὁρῶ. τί οὖν τοῦτ᾽ ἐστὶν ἐτεόν ὦ πάτερ;
Στ. ψυχῶν σοφῶν τοῦτ᾽ ἐστὶ φροντιστήριον.
ἐνταῦθ᾽ ἐνοικοῦσ᾽ ἄνδρες, οἳ τὸν οὐρανὸν 95
λέγοντες ἀναπείθουσιν ὡς ἔστιν πνιγεύς,
κἄστιν περὶ ἡμᾶς οὗτος, ἡμεῖς δ᾽ ἄνθρακες.
οὗτοι διδάσκουσ᾽, ἀργύριον ἤν τις διδῷ,
λέγοντα νικᾶν καὶ δίκαια κἄδικα.
Φε. εἰσὶν δὲ τίνες;
Στ. οὐκ οἶδ᾽ ἀκριβῶς τοὔνομα· 100
μεριμνοφροντισταὶ καλοί τε κἀγαθοί.
Φε. αἰβοῖ, πονηροί γ᾽, οἶδα. τοὺς ἀλαζόνας,
τοὺς ὠχριῶντας, τοὺς ἀνυποδήτους λέγεις,
ὧν ὁ κακοδαίμων Σωκράτης καὶ Χαιρεφῶν.
Στ. ἢ ἤ, σιώπα· μηδὲν εἴπῃς νήπιον. 105
ἀλλ᾽ εἴ τι κήδει τῶν πατρῴων ἀλφίτων,
τούτων γενοῦ μοι, σχασάμενος τὴν ἱππικήν.
Φε. οὐκ ἂν μὰ τὸν Διόνυσον εἰ δοίης γέ μοι
τοὺς Φασιανοὺς οὓς τρέφει Λεωγόρας.
Στ. ἴθ᾽, ἀντιβολῶ σ᾽, ὦ φίλτατ᾽ ἀνθρώπων ἐμοὶ, 110
ἐλθὼν διδάσκου.
Φε. καὶ τί σοι μαθήσομαι;

Στ. εἶναι παρ᾽ αὐτοῖς φασὶν ἄμφω τὼ λόγω,
     τὸν κρείττον᾽, ὅστις ἐστί, καὶ τὸν ἥττονα.
     τούτοιν τὸν ἕτερον τοῖν λόγοιν, τὸν ἥττονα,
     νικᾶν λέγοντά φασι τἀδικώτερα.   115
     ἢν οὖν μάθῃς μοι τὸν ἄδικον τοῦτον λόγον,
     ἃ νῦν ὀφείλω διὰ σέ, τούτων τῶν χρεῶν
     οὐκ ἂν ἀποδοίην οὐδ᾽ ἂν ὀβολὸν οὐδενί.
Φε. οὐκ ἂν πιθοίμην· οὐ γὰρ ἂν τλαίην ἰδεῖν
     τοὺς ἱππέας τὸ χρῶμα διακεκναισμένος.   120
Στ. οὐκ ἄρα μὰ τὴν Δήμητρα τῶν γ᾽ ἐμῶν ἔδει,
     οὔτ᾽ αὐτὸς οὔθ᾽ ὁ ζύγιος οὔθ᾽ ὁ σαμφόρας·
     ἀλλ᾽ ἐξελῶ σ᾽ ἐς κόρακας ἐκ τῆς οἰκίας.
Φε. ἀλλ᾽ οὐ περιόψεταί μ᾽ ὁ θεῖος Μεγακλέης
     ἄνιππον. ἀλλ᾽ εἴσειμι, σοῦ δ᾽ οὐ φροντιῶ.   125
Στ. ἀλλ᾽ οὐδ᾽ ἐγὼ μέντοι πεσών γε κείσομαι,
     ἀλλ᾽ εὐξάμενος τοῖσιν θεοῖς διδάξομαι
     αὐτὸς βαδίζων εἰς τὸ φροντιστήριον.
     πῶς οὖν γέρων ὢν κἀπιλήσμων καὶ βραδὺς
     λόγων ἀκριβῶν σχινδαλάμους μαθήσομαι;   130
     ἰτητέον. τί ταῦτ᾽ ἔχων στραγγεύομαι,
     ἀλλ᾽ οὐχὶ κόπτω τὴν θύραν; παῖ, παιδίον.

     ΜΑΘΗΤΗΣ
     βάλλ᾽ ἐς κόρακας· τίς ἐσθ᾽ ὁ κόψας τὴν θύραν;
Στ. Φείδωνος υἱὸς Στρεψιάδης Κικυννόθεν.
Μα. ἀμαθής γε νὴ Δί᾽, ὅστις οὑτωσὶ σφόδρα   135
     ἀπεριμερίμνως τὴν θύραν λελάκτικας,
     καὶ φροντίδ᾽ ἐξήμβλωκας ἐξηυρημένην.
Στ. σύγγνωθί μοι· τηλοῦ γὰρ οἰκῶ τῶν ἀγρῶν.
     ἀλλ᾽ εἰπέ μοι τὸ πρᾶγμα τοὐξημβλωμένον.
Μα. ἀλλ᾽ οὐ θέμις πλὴν τοῖς μαθηταῖσιν λέγειν.   140
Στ. λέγε νυν ἐμοὶ θαρρῶν· ἐγὼ γὰρ οὑτοσὶ
     ἥκω μαθητὴς ἐς τὸ φροντιστήριον.
Μα. λέξω. νομίσαι δὲ ταῦτα χρὴ μυστήρια.
     ἀνήρετ᾽ ἄρτι Χαιρεφῶντα Σωκράτης
     ψύλλαν ὁπόσους ἅλλοιτο τοὺς αὑτῆς πόδας·   145
     δακοῦσα γὰρ τοῦ Χαιρεφῶντος τὴν ὀφρῦν
     ἐπὶ τὴν κεφαλὴν τὴν Σωκράτους ἀφήλατο.
Στ. πῶς δῆτα διεμέτρησε;
Μα.   δεξιώτατα.
     κηρὸν διατήξας, εἶτα τὴν ψύλλαν λαβὼν
     ἐνέβαψεν εἰς τὸν κηρὸν αὐτῆς τὼ πόδε,   150
     κᾆτα ψυχείσῃ περιέφυσαν Περσικαί.
     ταύτας ὑπολύσας ἀνεμέτρει τὸ χωρίον.
Στ. ὦ Ζεῦ βασιλεῦ, τῆς λεπτότητος τῶν φρενῶν.
Μα. τί δῆτ᾽ ἄν, ἕτερον εἰ πύθοιο Σωκράτους
     φρόντισμα;

Στ.   ποῖον; ἀντιβολῶ, κάτειπέ μοι.   155
Μα. ἀνήρετ᾽ αὐτὸν Χαιρεφῶν ὁ Σφήττιος
ὁπότερα τὴν γνώμην ἔχοι, τὰς ἐμπίδας
κατὰ τὸ στόμ᾽ ᾄδειν ἢ κατὰ τοὐρροπύγιον.
Στ. Τί δῆτ᾽ ἐκεῖνος εἶπε περὶ τῆς ἐμπίδος;
Μα. ἔφασκεν εἶναι τοὔντερον τῆς ἐμπίδος   160

στενόν· διὰ λεπτοῦ δ᾽ ὄντος αὐτοῦ τὴν πνοὴν
βίᾳ βαδίζειν εὐθὺ τοὐρροπυγίου·
ἔπειτα κοῖλον πρὸς στενῷ προσκείμενον
τὸν πρωκτὸν ἠχεῖν ὑπὸ βίας τοῦ πνεύματος.
Στ. σάλπιγξ ὁ πρωκτός ἐστιν ἄρα τῶν ἐμπίδων.   165
ὦ τρισμακάριος τοῦ διεντερεύματος.
ἦ ῥᾳδίως φεύγων ἂν ἀποφύγοι δίκην
ὅστις δίοιδε τοὔντερον τῆς ἐμπίδος.
Μα. πρῴην δέ γε γνώμην μεγάλην ἀφῃρέθη
ὑπ᾽ ἀσκαλαβώτου.
Στ.   τίνα τρόπον; κάτειπέ μοι.   170
Μα. ζητοῦντος αὐτοῦ τῆς σελήνης τὰς ὁδοὺς
καὶ τὰς περιφοράς, εἶτ᾽ ἄνω κεχηνότος
ἀπὸ τῆς ὀροφῆς νύκτωρ γαλεώτης κατέχεσεν.
Στ. ἤσθην γαλεώτῃ καταχέσαντι Σωκράτους.
Μα. ἐχθὲς δέ γ᾽ ἡμῖν δεῖπνον οὐκ ἦν ἑσπέρας.   175
Στ. εἶεν· τί οὖν πρὸς τἄλφιτ᾽ ἐπαλαμήσατο;
Μα. κατὰ τῆς τραπέζης καταπάσας λεπτὴν τέφραν
κάμψας ὀβελίσκον, εἶτα διαβήτην λαβὼν
ἐκ τῆς παλαίστρας θοἰμάτιον ὑφείλετο.
Στ. τί δῆτ᾽ ἐκεῖνον τὸν Θαλῆν θαυμάζομεν;   180
ἄνοιγ᾽ ἄνοιγ᾽ ἀνύσας τὸ φροντιστήριον,
καὶ δεῖξον ὡς τάχιστά μοι τὸν Σωκράτη.
μαθητιῶ γάρ· ἀλλ᾽ ἄνοιγε τὴν θύραν.
ὦ Ἡράκλεις, ταυτὶ ποδαπὰ τὰ θηρία;
Μα. τί ἐθαύμασας; τῷ σοι δοκοῦσιν εἰκέναι;   185
Στ. τοῖς ἐκ Πύλου ληφθεῖσι, τοῖς Λακωνικοῖς.
ἀτὰρ τί ποτ᾽ ἐς τὴν γῆν βλέπουσιν οὑτοί;
Μα. ζητοῦσιν οὗτοι τὰ κατὰ γῆς.
Στ.   βολβοὺς ἄρα
ζητοῦσι. μή νυν τοῦτό γ᾽ ἔτι φροντίζετε·
ἐγὼ γὰρ οἶδ᾽ ἵν᾽ εἰσὶ μεγάλοι καὶ καλοί.   190
τί γὰρ οἵδε δρῶσιν οἱ σφόδρ᾽ ἐγκεκυφότες;
Μα. οὗτοι δ᾽ ἐρεβοδιφῶσιν ὑπὸ τὸν Τάρταρον.
Στ. τί δῆθ᾽ ὁ πρωκτὸς ἐς τὸν οὐρανὸν βλέπει;
Μα. αὐτὸς καθ᾽ αὑτὸν ἀστρονομεῖν διδάσκεται.
ἀλλ᾽ εἴσιθ᾽, ἵνα μὴ ᾽κεῖνος ὑμῖν ἐπιτύχῃ   195
Στ. μήπω γε, μήπω γ᾽· ἀλλ᾽ ἐπιμεινάντων, ἵνα
αὐτοῖσι κοινώσω τι πραγμάτιον ἐμόν.
Μα. ἀλλ᾽ οὐχ οἷόν τ᾽ αὐτοῖσι πρὸς τὸν ἀέρα

ἔξω διατρίβειν πολὺν ἄγαν ἐστὶν χρόνον.
Στ. πρὸς τῶν θεῶν, τί γὰρ τάδ᾽ ἐστίν; εἰπέ μοι. 200
Μα. ἀστρονομία μὲν αὑτηί.
Στ.   τουτὶ δὲ τί;
Μα. γεωμετρία.
Στ.   τοῦτ᾽ οὖν τί ἐστι χρήσιμον;
Μα. γῆν ἀναμετρεῖσθαι.
Στ.   πότερα τὴν κληρουχικήν;
Μα. οὔκ, ἀλλὰ τὴν σύμπασαν.
Στ.   ἀστεῖον λέγεις.
τὸ γὰρ σόφισμα δημοτικὸν καὶ χρήσιμον. 205
Μα. αὕτη δέ σοι γῆς περίοδος πάσης. ὁρᾷς;
αἵδε μὲν Ἀθῆναι.
Στ.   τί σὺ λέγεις; οὐ πείθομαι,
ἐπεὶ δικαστὰς οὐχ ὁρῶ καθημένους.
Μα. ὡς τοῦτ᾽ ἀληθῶς Ἀττικὴ τὸ χωρίον.
Στ. καὶ ποῦ Κικυννῆς εἰσίν, οὑμοὶ δημόται; 210
Μα. ἐνταῦθ᾽ ἔνεισιν. ἡ δέ γ᾽ Εὔβοι᾽, ὡς ὁρᾷς,
ἡδὶ παρατέταται μακρὰ πόρρω πάνυ.
Στ. οἶδ᾽· ὑπὸ γὰρ ἡμῶν παρετάθη καὶ Περικλέους.
ἀλλ᾽ ἡ Λακεδαίμων ποῦ ᾽σθ᾽;
Μα.   ὅπου ᾽στίν; αὑτηί.
Στ. ὡς ἐγγὺς ἡμῶν. τοῦτο μεταφροντίζετε, 215
ταύτην ἀφ᾽ ἡμῶν ἀπαγαγεῖν πόρρω πάνυ.
Μα. ἀλλ᾽ οὐχ οἷόν τε.
Στ.   νὴ Δί᾽ οἰμώξεσθ᾽ ἄρα.
Φέρε, τίς γὰρ οὗτος οὑπὶ τῆς κρεμάθρας ἀνήρ;
Μα. αὐτός.
Στ.   τίς αὐτός;
Μα.   Σωκράτης.
Στ.   ὦ Σώκρατες.
ἴθ᾽ οὗτος, ἀναβόησον αὐτόν μοι μέγα. 220
Μα. αὐτὸς μὲν οὖν σὺ κάλεσον· οὐ γάρ μοι σχολή.
Στ. ὦ Σώκρατες,
ὦ Σωκρατίδιον.

ΣΩΚΡΑΤΗΣ
   τί με καλεῖς, ὦφήμερε;
Στ. πρῶτον μὲν ὅ τι δρᾷς, ἀντιβολῶ, κάτειπέ μοι.
Σω. ἀεροβατῶ καὶ περιφρονῶ τὸν ἥλιον. 225

Στ. ἔπειτ᾽ ἀπὸ ταρροῦ τοὺς θεοὺς ὑπερφρονεῖς,
ἀλλ᾽ οὐκ ἀπὸ τῆς γῆς, εἴπερ;
Σω.   οὐ γὰρ ἄν ποτε
ἐξηῦρον ὀρθῶς τὰ μετέωρα πράγματα,
εἰ μὴ κρεμάσας τὸ νόημα καὶ τὴν φροντίδα,
λεπτὴν καταμείξας ἐς τὸν ὅμοιον ἀέρα. 230

εἰ δ᾽ ὢν χαμαὶ τἄνω κάτωθεν ἐσκόπουν,
οὐκ ἄν ποθ᾽ ηὗρον· οὐ γὰρ ἀλλ᾽ ἡ γῆ βίᾳ
ἕλκει πρὸς αὑτὴν τὴν ἰκμάδα τῆς φροντίδος.
πάσχει δὲ ταὐτὸ τοῦτο καὶ τὰ κάρδαμα.
Στ.   πῶς φής;   235
ἡ φροντὶς ἕλκει τὴν ἰκμάδ᾽ εἰς τὰ κάρδαμα;
ἴθι νυν κατάβηθ᾽, ὦ Σωκρατίδιον, ὡς ἐμέ,
ἵνα με διδάξῃς ὧνπερ ἕνεκ᾽ ἐλήλυθα.

Σω.   ἦλθες δὲ κατὰ τί;
Στ.   βουλόμενος μαθεῖν λέγειν.   240
ὑπὸ γὰρ τόκων χρήστων τε δυσκολωτάτων
ἄγομαι, φέρομαι, τὰ χρήματ᾽ ἐνεχυράζομαι.
Σω.   πόθεν δ᾽ ὑπόχρεως σαυτὸν ἔλαθες γενόμενος;

Commentary Notes

The play opens with two men asleep on the stage. The younger man is sleeping soundly, the other, an old man, is more wakeful and in the opening monologue he explains this insomnia. The old man is Strepsiades, as we learn in 134; the other is his son, Pheidippides.

1–2

ἰοὺ ἰού / ὦ Ζεῦ βασιλεῦ τὸ χρῆμα τῶν νυκτῶν ὅσον: the opening cry is one of distress. Aristophanes leaves ὅσον (how great) to the end (hyperbaton), beginning the next line with ἀπέραντον (agreeing with τὸ χρῆμα), thereby intensifying the distress felt by the speaker.

4

καὶ μὴν πάλαι γ᾽ ἀλεκτρυόνος ἤκουσ᾽ ἐγώ: 'and yet'. ἀλεκτρυόνος: genitive as the source of the sound after ἀκούω. Cockerels conventionally crow at dawn.

5

ἀλλ᾽ οὐκ ἂν πρὸ τοῦ: 'but they would not [have snored like this] in the past'. ἂν goes with an unexpressed aorist indicative of ῥέγκω. τοῦ, the definite article, is used in its original sense as a demonstrative. This is a reference to disaffected slaves who had been running away to the hostile neighbouring city states of Boeotia and Megara. The Peace of Nicias (421) between the Athenians and the Spartans, negotiated two years after the original production of *Clouds*, included a clause that neither side should receive deserters from the other, 'whether free men or slaves' (Thuc. 4.118.7); or perhaps it is just a nostalgic view of the past from an old man.

6

ἀπόλοιο δῆτ᾽ ὦ πόλεμε πολλῶν οὕνεκα: ἀπόλοιο, aorist middle optative of ἀπόλλυμι, expressing a wish. The repetition of the plosive π helps to make this line sound petulant.

7

ὅτ᾽ οὐδὲ κολάσ᾽ ἔξεστί μοι τοὺς οἰκέτας: ὅτ᾽ is elided ὅτε (when). Strepsiades laments the fact that he cannot punish his slaves for fear of them running away.

8

ὁ χρηστὸς οὑτοσὶ νεανίας: the use of χρηστὸς is heavily sarcastic. οὑτοσὶ suggests that Strepsiades is pointing, i.e. this one here.

9–10

ἀλλὰ πέρδεται / ἐν πέντε σισύραις ἐγκεκορδυλημένος: comedy often associates farting with sleeping, and with not having a care in the world. ἐγκεκορδυλημένος perfect middle participle of ἐγκορδυλέω: 'having wrapped himself up'. Greek uses the middle to express actions that are reflexive.

11

ἀλλ᾽ εἰ δοκεῖ ῥέγκωμεν ἐγκεκαλυμμένοι: The idiom εἰ δοκεῖ suggests moral good: 'if it seems good'. ῥέγκωμεν is the present subjunctive of ῥέγκω used jussively (as an order). ἐγκεκαλυμμένοι is perfect middle participle of ἐγκαλύπτω, again showing the reflexive use of the middle.

12

δακνόμενος: '(I am) being bitten . . .' but what follows is rather surprising, cf. line 37.

14–15

ὁ δὲ κόμην ἔχων ... ὀνειροπολεῖ θ᾽ ἵππους: long hair was characteristic of young men who were in the cavalry (cf. 120). A συνωρίς is a pair of horses, here used to describe a two-horse chariot. The boy associates with aristocratic young men and in doing so eats into his father's income.

17

ὁρῶν ἄγουσαν τὴν σελήνην εἰκάδας: interest on loans was due at the end of the month, and the months were aligned with the moon; as the moon waxed therefore, the time for paying off interest approached. As the twenties (εἰκάδας cf. εἴκοσι) of each month approached, debtors began to worry, and line 18 confirms this. Interest was calculated monthly and may have ranged from 10 per cent to 36 per cent per annum.

18–20

οἱ γὰρ τόκοι χωροῦσιν: τόκος here means 'interest', 'for the interest is advancing'.

παῖ: Strepsiades addresses a slave from his household, probably standing at the side of the stage.

κἄκφερε = καὶ ἔκφερε, (crasis). Strepsiades uses the word (ἐκφέρω), which is appropriate for bringing something outside rather than from one room to another; an example of comedy explicitly referring to dramatic conventions which are in fact unrealistic.

τὸ γραμματεῖον: most probably a set of waxed tablets from which the message could be erased when the debts were paid off.

ἀναγνῶ: aorist active subjunctive of ἀναγιγνώσκω.

21

φέρ᾽ ἴδω: 'Now, let me see'. ἴδω: aorist active subjunctive. A μνᾶ was worth 100 drachmas, (one drachma = 6 obols, 3 obols was the amount paid to Athenian jurymen under Cleon who raised it from 2 obols in the mid-420s. A skilled workman received a drachma a day according to the Erechtheum building accounts). Twelve minae therefore is well over a year's pay.

22

τοῦ δώδεκα μνᾶς Πασίᾳ: τοῦ: an alternative genitive of τί, so 'on account of what do I owe . . .', i.e. 'why twelve minae to Pasias?'

23

τὸν κοππατίαν: a horse branded with the obsolete letter *koppa* (Q), the source of our letter Q, and found on Corinthian coins. This symbol meant that the horse was a thoroughbred.

24

ἐξεκόπην: 1st person aorist passive of ἐκκόπτω. Note the pun on κοππατίας.

26

ἀπολώλεκεν: perfect active of ἀπόλλυμι (ἀπόλωλα is used for perfect middle). Strepsiades explains how he has got into debt. The repetition of τοῦτ᾽ . . . τουτὶ reinforces Strepsiades' annoyance.

27

καὶ καθεύδων: here καὶ means 'even'. 'Even lying down to sleep . . .'.

28

τὰ πολεμιστήρια: 'war-chariots' were a type of racing chariot, probably with two men, like the ones formerly used in battle, and which were now used in races at festivals such as the Panathenaea. Note the singular of the verb (ἐλᾷ) with a neuter plural subject.

29

ἐμὲ μὲν σὺ πολλοὺς τὸν πατέρ᾽ ἐλαύνεις δρόμους: 'at any rate you are driving your father around many racecourses'. Note the similarity to the English idiom 'driving someone around the bend.' With the personal or demonstrative pronoun μὲν often means 'at any rate' and does not imply a contrast.

30

ἀτὰρ τί χρέος ἔβα με: a quotation from an unnamed Euripides play (Fragment 1011). '. . . what sad debt befell me?' The incorporation of quotes from tragedies was a common element of Aristophanes' comedy and is known as paratragedy. The poetic language is melodramatic and plays on the two senses of χρέος: in everyday language 'thing,' but in poetry 'debt'.

31

τροχοῖν Ἀμυνίᾳ: τροχοῖν is genitive dual. Ἀμυνίας: a variant manuscript (V) gives Ἀμεινίᾳ (Ameinias) which may have been a topical reference to an archon of 423/422.

32

ἄπαγε τὸν ἵππον ἐξαλίσας οἴκαδε: ἐξαλίσας: aorist active participle of ἐξαλίνδω. 'Lead the horse home when you have rolled him.' Pheidippides wants his horse to roll in the dust to dry off the sweat. οἴκαδε: homewards cf. *domum* in Latin, -δε, as a suffix implies motion towards.

33

... ἐξήλικας ἐμέ γ᾽ ἐκ τῶν ἐμῶν: 'You have rolled me out of my own possessions'. ἐξήλικας is the perfect active of ἐξαλίνδω. γ(ε) emphasizes the pronoun.

34

ὅτε καὶ δίκας ὤφληκα: ὅτε (for now). ὤφληκα: perfect active of ὀφλισκάνω: 'for now I have become a debtor'.

35

χἄτεροι τόκου / ἐνεχυράσεσθαί φασιν. ἐτεὸν ὦ πάτερ: χἄτεροι = καὶ ἕτεροι. ἐνεχυράσεσθαί: future middle infinitive of ἐνεχυράζω .... 'and the others say that they will take securities for my debt'. τόκου is genitive after ἐνεχυράζω. Line 35 is distributed between the two speakers, which is known as antilabe and is used in tragedy also, though less commonly. ἐτεὸν here is used adverbially: 'really!' Presumably the young man is exasperated that his father has woken him up with his complaints.

37

δάκνει μέ τις δήμαρχος ἐκ τῶν στρωμάτων: 'a magistrate from the bedspreads is biting me'. A *demarchos* was the magistrate in charge of a *deme*. He was responsible for producing the official list of members of the *deme* and, possibly, also for ensuring that debtors paid their creditors, cf. line 12 for a similar joke.

38

ἔασον ὦ δαιμόνιε καταδαρθεῖν τί με: 'allow me to get some sleep, you fool!' ἔασον: aorist active imperative of ἐάω. τί is not an interrogative here, but has (misleadingly) acquired an accent because it is followed by another unaccented enclitic word. Here it is used as an internal accusative.

41

εἴθ᾽ ὤφελ᾽ ἡ προμνήστρι᾽ ἀπολέσθαι κακῶς: εἴθ᾽ ὤφελ᾽: 'would that the matchmaker had perished miserably' has a tragic feel (Euripides' *Medea* opens εἴθ᾽ ὤφελ᾽ ... 'would that ...'). προμνήστρια: a matchmaker was a common figure in societies where mixing of the sexes was limited, at least in prosperous families.

43–47

Strepsiades describes his life pre-marriage as one of rustic simplicity and peacefulness. The origins of comic heroes (e.g. Dicaeopolis in *Acharnians*) and the way they look back wistfully at peace is perhaps related to the origins of comedy at the festivals of Dionysus which took place in the country after the grape vintage. Μεγακλέους: the name Megacles comes from the Alcmaeonid family, who had been prominent citizens and statesmen in Athens from the seventh century BCE (Herodotus I.60ff). Aristophanes is using a name that has aristocratic overtones rather than referring to a specific person.

48

σεμνὴν τρυφῶσαν ἐγκεκοισυρωμένην: σεμνὴν usually refers to gods, but here as applied to a woman, means 'haughty' or perhaps 'stuck-up'. ἐγκεκοισυρωμένην: perfect middle participle of ἐγκοισυρόομαι, 'as luxurious as Coesyra'. Coesyra was the mother of Megacles, who was secretary to the treasurers of Athena in 428/427 BCE. Her name was a byword for self-indulgent luxury.

51

κρόκου: on special occasions Athenian women wore saffron-dyed dresses; this was not everyday attire for a countryman's wife.

52

Κωλιάδος Γενετυλλίδος: Aphrodite Colias had a temple near Athens and Genetullis was a goddess of love and midwifery who was also termed 'harlot' by the Athenians. The old man was clearly bowled over by this high-class wife, at least initially.

53

οὐ μὴν ἐρῶ γ᾽ ὡς ἀργὸς ἦν, ἀλλ᾽ ἐσπάθα: 'I won't say she was lazy, but quite the reverse, she was energetic in weaving' (with a possible secondary meaning of 'in sexual intercourse'). Weaving was a common occupation for Greek women (cf. Penelope in the *Odyssey*) and often exemplified moral behaviour.

54

ἐγὼ δ᾽ ἂν αὐτῇ θοἰμάτιον δεικνὺς τοδὶ: δεικνὺς: present active participle of δείκνυμι '. . . showing this cloak to her'. Strepsiades is holding up a tattered cloak as evidence of his wife's weaving; the irony is that its state is at odds with her tight packing of the threads.

55

λίαν σπαθᾷς: 'you are weaving excessively'. Strepsiades states that his wife packs the threads too tightly on her loom, i.e. using more than necessary. Her style of weaving therefore becomes a metaphor for her general extravagance.

57

τὸν πότην . . . . λύχνον: 'the thirsty lamp' i.e. the one that uses a lot of oil and is therefore more expensive. ἧπτες: imperfect active, suggesting that the slave has done this before. See also the use of the imperfect of ἐνετίθεις in line 59. The annual destruction of the Attic olive groves by the Spartans in the early years of the Peloponnesian War would have made oil for lamps more expensive, but Strepsiades would doubtless have complained anyway.

58

διὰ τί δῆτα κλαύσομαι: κλαύσομαι: future middle of κλαίω. Note the distribution of the line between two speakers.

59

ἐνετίθεις: 2nd person singular imperfect active of ἐντίθημι, reinforcing that it was not the first time the slave had done this.

θρυαλλίς: plantain, a fibrous plant used to make wicks. The thicker the wick the more oil a lamp uses to burn (see 57).

It appears that the slave leaves swiftly to go into the house at this point as he does not speak again.

60

ὅπως νῷν: νῷν, dual dative. This is explained by ἐμοί and γυναικὶ in 61. υἱὸς οὑτοσί indicates a gesture towards the sleeping young man (see 8 for the form of οὑτοσί).

62

δὴ 'ντεῦθεν ἐλοιδορούμεθα: 'from then on we argued with one another'. ἐλοιδορούμεθα: imperfect active of λοιδορέω 'I rail at'. In the middle voice this means to argue with another person.

63–67

ἡ μὲν γὰρ ἵππον προσετίθει πρὸς τοὔνομα: Strepsiades' wife wished to give her son a name with ἱππ in it. προσετίθει, 'τιθέμην and ἐκρινόμεθ(α) are all imperfect suggesting a long drawn out 'discussion'. The giving of a name was, as it is now, important as the wife wanted her son's name to be an indication of what he was going to become: a horseman. In 67 we hear that there was a compromise, and the boy was named after the old man's father, Pheidonides, which was common practice, but with a modification to make Φειδιππίδης.

69–72

ὅταν ... διφθέραν ἐνημμένος: ἐλαύνῃς: present active subjunctive in an indefinite clause: 'when you are driving to the city'. Strepsiades' wife was indoctrinating the young Pheidippides. His mother could be referring to her hopes for her son's future participation in the Panathenaic Festival or ὥσπερ Μεγακλέης, hoping that he would follow in the footsteps of her relative (46–47) Megacles who won the chariot-race at Olympia in 436. ξυστίδ' ἔχων: the xystis was the saffron coloured robe worn by charioteers. Parental aspirations for their son are emphasized by a series of contrasted phrases: πρὸς πόλιν and ἐκ τοῦ φελλέως, ὥσπερ Μεγακλέης and ὁ πατήρ σου, ξυστίδ' ἔχων and διφθέραν ἐνημμένος.

73

οὐκ ... οὐδὲν: the double negative intensifies the phrase rather than negating it.

74

ἀλλ᾽ ἵππερόν μοι κατέχεεν τῶν χρημάτων: ἵππερός means horse-fever, by analogy with ἴκτ-ερος (jaundice).

75–76

ὁδοῦ / μίαν ηὗρον ἀτραπὸν: ὁδοῦ: a way out. The genitive is partitive after ἀτραπὸν (f).

77

ἢν ἢν ἀναπείσω τουτονί: 'and if I persuade him of this'. ἢν is a relative pronoun looking back to ἀτραπὸν. ἢν = ἐάν. ἀναπείσω: aorist active subjunctive. ἀναπείθειν is used when persuading someone against their own inclinations.
σωθήσομαι: future passive of σῴζω.

79

ἐπεγείραιμι: (ἐπεγείρω) aorist active optative in a deliberative question. The old man's anxiety is emphasized by the repetition of πῶς.

80

Φειδιππίδη Φειδιππίδιον: we imagine a wheedling voice here as Strepsiades tries to wake up his son. The diminutive is particularly effective and is characteristic of the old man as he uses it later when he speaks to Socrates. Note the antilabe as Pheidippides wakes up straightaway and replies to his father.

81

τὴν χεῖρα δὸς τὴν δεξιάν: the giving of the right hand was a common sign of affection and good faith.

82

ἰδού. τί ἔστιν; εἰπέ μοι, φιλεῖς ἐμέ: ἰδού: 'there you are'. Presumably we are to imagine that Pheidippes sits up at this point. φιλεῖς has a wide range of meanings to do with love and attraction but here is used of the strong bond between parent and child.

83

νὴ τὸν Ποσειδῶ τουτονὶ τὸν ἵππιον: νὴ: a particle denoting a strong exclamation usually with a divinity in the accusative. Pheidippides swears by Poseidon whose special care, apart from the sea and earthquakes, was horses. There was a treasury for Poseidon Hippios on the Acropolis. τουτονὶ indicates that Pheidippides is gesturing to a statue of Poseidon standing at the door of the house.

84

μὴ 'μοί γε τοῦτον μηδαμῶς: an imperative, λέγε needs to be supplied here. The double negative emphasizes the force of Strepsiades' response, since Pheidippides' choice of oath highlights the problem.

86

ὄντως: really, truly. Adverb from the present participle of εἰμί I am.

87

ὦ παῖ πιθοῦ / τί οὖν πίθωμαι δῆτά σοι: πιθοῦ is aorist middle imperative, and πίθωμαι aorist middle subjunctive for a deliberative question. Pheidippides is suspicious of his father's intentions.

88

ἔκστρεψον: Dover emends to ἔκτρεψον on the grounds that ἔκστρέφειν means to turn clothes inside out, whereas ἔκτρέπειν means to turn aside from a path or course of action, which is suggested by τρόπους. The theme of 'twisting' is continued (cf. 36).

89

καὶ μάνθαν᾽ ἐλθὼν ἂν ἐγὼ παραινέσω: ἄν = crasis for ἃ ἄν, 'whatever'.

90–91

νὴ τὸν Διόνυσον / δεῦρό νυν ἀπόβλεπε: Pheidippides now swears by Dionysus, god of wine, that he will obey his father. δεῦρό, 'to here', is used with verbs of motion and indicates that the father and son are moving across the stage. Stage directions in Greek plays were not written, or have not survived, so they must be inferred from the clues in the dialogue.

92

θύριον . . . τὠκίδιον: τὠκίδιον = τὸ οἰκίδιον: the old man is probably indicating the double door on the stage building. Both door and the house are indicated with diminutives, perhaps to make them sound less threatening. Strepsiades has a fondness for diminutives when he speaks to his son, or when he wants to get his own way.

94

ψυχῶν σοφῶν τοῦτ᾽ ἐστὶ φροντιστήριον: 'this is the Reflectory of wise souls'. φροντιστήριον is a coinage which first appears in *Clouds*, along with φροντιστής (a person who thinks deeply, *Clouds* 266); and the -ήριον ending indicates a place where something is done, cf. δικαστής (jury member) and δικαστήριον (court-house), βουλή (council) and βουλευτήριον (place where the council meets).

95–97

We hear about the theories worked on by the inhabitants of the Reflectory. Hippon (a fifth-century BCE philosopher) allegedly put forward the theory that the sky was shaped like an upturned bowl (πνιγεύς) which acted as an oven. ἄνθρακες (charcoal) was first placed under the πνιγεύς to heat it and then placed around the outside of the cover while dough was baked inside. The philosophers' model of the universe refers to the latter stage, where the people are under the dome and the food is raised up on a trivet. Strepsiades is doing his best to remember what he has heard. The inclusion of theories such as this, and later ones, when the student attempts to instruct the old man, are evidence that such ideas might have been at least vaguely known by Athenians. Even if they were not, the way that the old man relates them is enough to make them funny.

98–99

οὗτοι διδάσκουσ᾽, ἀργύριον ἤν τις διδῷ / λέγοντα νικᾶν καὶ δίκαια κἄδικα: these are ideas key to the understanding of *Clouds*: 'if someone pays them money, these people teach you to win, whether you speak justly or unjustly'. The historical Socrates was adamant that he did not require payment and was therefore not a Sophist (see Introduction).

101

μεριμνοφροντισταὶ καλοί τε κἀγαθοί: μεριμνοφροντισταὶ: 'minute philosophers' i.e. philosophers who think in a detailed way. καλοί τε κἀγαθοί: a stock phrase to denote excellent men, usually implying wealthy and aristocratic as well. They are the opposite of the πονηροί which is what Pheidippides calls them in 102. The kind of activities pursued by the inhabitants of the Reflectory are not normally those which mark a man out as καλός τε κἀγαθός, and the placement of this phrase immediately after the preceding (coined) word highlights this oxymoron.

102–104

τοὺς ἀλαζόνας / τοὺς ὠχριῶντας τοὺς ἀνυποδήτους λέγεις: ἀλαζόνας: imposters. ὠχριῶντας comes from ὠχριάω, 'I am pale'. Intellectuals were caricatured as pale since they spent all their time inside rather than working in the fields or taking part in athletic activities. Socrates, however, had been a soldier and spent his time in the agora. ἀνυποδήτους: Socrates was famous for going barefoot (see Introduction).

104

Σωκράτης καὶ Χαιρεφῶν: Pheidippides names two of the inhabitants of the house. Socrates is the more famous, but Chaerephon was a real person, and a friend of Socrates' from his youth. It was he who received the oracle from Delphi, mentioned in *Apology* (21a-c). He was referred to by the comic poets as 'sallow' (Aristophanes *Wasps* 1413, Eupolis fr. 239).

105

μηδὲν εἴπῃς: εἴπῃς: aorist subjunctive jussive.

106

ἀλλ᾽ εἴ τι κήδει τῶν πατρῴων ἀλφίτων: κήδει, 2nd person singular present middle of κήδω + genitive. ἀλφίτων: literally barley meal but here it is metaphorical for livelihood.

107

τούτων γενοῦ μοι: 'become one of these men for me, please'. μοι: ethic dative, indicating personal interest in the action.

σχασάμενος τὴν ἱππικήν: σχασάμενος (from σχάζω) here meaning 'give up'. The old man is keen for his wayward son to join the Reflectory and learn the art of arguing to save him from his creditors, and more immediately to give up his hobby and avoid him incurring any more expense.

108–109

οὐκ ἂν μὰ τὸν Διόνυσον, εἰ δοίης γέ μοι /τοὺς φασιανοὺς οὓς τρέφει Λεωγόρας: '. . . not even if you were to give me . . .' δοίης: aorist active optative of δίδωμι. This is the equivalent of 'I wouldn't do it for all the tea in China'. φασιανούς: the pheasants mentioned here may have been bred more for show than for eating. Leogoras was a wealthy citizen of Athens. Note that the name is left until the end of the line for maximum effect.

110–111

ἀντιβολῶ σ᾽ ὦ φίλτατ᾽ ἀνθρώπων ἐμοὶ / ἐλθὼν διδάσκου: ἀντιβολῶ: here, I entreat or beg. ὦ φίλτατ᾽ ἀνθρώπων ἐμοὶ: this high-flown phrase sounds like paratragedy cf. e.g. Sophocles *Electra* 1126. διδάσκου: present middle imperative, 'get yourself taught'. Contrast the use of the passive of διδάσκω in 127, διδάξομαι: 'I shall be taught'.

112–113

εἶναι παρ᾽ αὐτοῖς φασιν ἄμφω τὼ λόγω, / τὸν κρείττον᾽, ὅστις ἐστί, καὶ τὸν ἥττονα: ἄμφω τὼ λόγω: dual masculine accusative. The two arguments, τὸν κρείττον[α] (better) and τὸν ἥττονα (worse) are referred to as such by the Arguments themselves, although the old man does call the worse argument ἄδικος(115) and ἀδικώτατον (657). The best translation is Right and Wrong as it combines the appropriate moral, legal and intellectual overtones.

119

οὐκ ἂν πιθοίμην: aorist middle optative 'I would not obey'.

120

τὸ χρῶμα διακεκναισμένος: διακεκναισμένος: perfect passive participle of διακναίω, 'having had all the colour scraped from' [the skin], i.e. to be pale like the inhabitants of the Reflectory, cf. 103.

121

οὐκ ἄρα μὰ τὴν Δήμητρα τῶν γ᾽ ἐμῶν ἔδει: ἔδει: 2nd person future middle of ἐσθίω (ἔδομαι). τῶν γ᾽ ἐμῶν: partitive genitive (cf. 33), '[any] of my food'.

122

οὔτ᾽ αὐτὸς οὔθ᾽ ὁ ζύγιος οὔθ᾽ ὁ σαμφόρας: ζύγιος: a horse that draws a chariot, specifically one of the two in the middle of a four-horse team. σαμφόρας: a horse branded with the Dorian letter σάν (M) cf. 23. Pheidippides appears to have quite a range of expensive bloodstock available to him.

123

ἀλλ᾽ ἐξελῶ σ᾽ ἐς κόρακας ἐκ τῆς οἰκίας: ἐξελῶ: future active of ἐξελαύνω. ἐς κόρακας: a colloquial expression literally meaning 'Go to the crows!' but we might translate 'Go to hell!'. It originally implies 'die, and may your body be eaten by carrion birds.'

124–125

ἀλλ᾽ οὐ περιόψεταί μ᾽ ὁ θεῖος Μεγακλέης / ἄνιππον: θεῖος: here meaning uncle (great-uncle) Μεγακλέης cf. 46, 70. περιόψεται: future middle of περιοράω 'he will not stand by and watch' (as in allow). ἄνιππον: without a horse. The privative α needs a ν before the vowel. The mention of Megacles is a threat from Pheidippides as he flounces off into the house.

126

ἀλλ᾽ οὐδ᾽ ἐγὼ μέντοι πεσών γε κείσομαι: μέντοι: 'whatever you say!' πεσών: the old man imagines himself beaten in a fight, but has no intention of taking it lying down, literally.

127–128

ἀλλ᾽ εὐξάμενος τοῖσιν θεοῖς διδάξομαι / αὐτὸς βαδίζων ἐς τὸ φροντιστήριον: ἀλλ᾽ εὐξάμενος τοῖσιν θεοῖς: 'Then, I'll pray to the gods.' Strepsiades does not actually pray, the phrase itself counts as the prayer. This was termed 'performative utterance' by J. L. Austin. Presumably the prayer is for the gods' blessing on his studies. The emphatic αὐτὸς reinforces Strepsiades' action.

129–130

πῶς οὖν γέρων ὢν κἀπιλήσμων καὶ βραδὺς: κἀπιλήσμων = καὶ ἐπιλήσμων (crasis): 'so how shall I, being an old man, forgetful and slow …' One of the attributes that a student at the Reflectory would need would be a good memory. λόγων ἀκριβῶν σχινδαλάμους: 'the splinters (of wood) of precise arguments.' The phrase refers to the triviality of the arguments rather than their difficulty. It does not seem that Strepsiades has a very high opinion of those who are about to be his teachers.

131–132

ἰτητέον. τί ταῦτ᾽ ἔχων στραγγεύομαι / ἀλλ᾽ οὐχὶ κόπτω τὴν θύραν: ἰτητέον = ἰτέον impersonal gerundive of εἶμι, I shall go meaning 'I must go!' τί ταῦτ᾽ ἔχων στραγγεύομαι: 'understanding these things (i.e. the situation), why am I delaying rather than knocking at the door?' The old man is screwing up his courage.

133

βάλλ᾽ ἐς κόρακας: a longer version of 123, literally meaning 'throw yourself to the crows.'

134

Φείδωνος υἱὸς Στρεψιάδης Κικυννόθεν: Strepsiades proves that he is an Athenian citizen. This is the first time we hear the old man's name. He gives his father's name, Pheidon (chosen for the pun on φείδομαι to be sparing), his own name, Cicynna, the deme from which he came (see Introduction). Demes could be large such as Acharnae, or small such as Cicynna seems to have been. It is not known exactly where it was but may have been to the south-east of the city near Mount Hymettus. From the text of *Clouds* we can imagine that it was a suburb of Athens and rural. Realism is ignored as Strepsiades' house appears to be next door to the Reflectory, although it is possible that the set of double doors in the skene stands for both doors. – θεν: the suffix expresses motion from a place.

135–137

ἀμαθής γε νὴ Δί᾽ ὅστις οὑτωσὶ ... ἐξηυρημένην: ἀμαθής, the student is not impressed with Strepsiades' intellect. οὑτωσὶ: see line 8. λελάκτικας: 2nd person perfect active indicative of λακτίζω: I kick. ἐξήμβλωκας: 2nd person perfect active indicative of ἐξαμβλόω: 'you have made a thought miscarry'. We can assume comic exaggeration of the effect of the knock on the ridiculously hypersensitive and pompous student.

138

σύγγνωθί μοι: τηλοῦ γὰρ οἰκῶ τῶν ἀγρῶν: σύγγνωθι: aorist active imperative of συγγιγνώσκω. τηλοῦ γὰρ οἰκῶ τῶν ἀγρῶν: the scholiast says this line is a parody of Euripides (fr. 884). The use of tragedy makes the exchange funnier as the student's hyperbolic reaction and Strepsiades' unknowingly literary response complement each other. There is also the problem of Strepsiades' house being next door to the Reflectory (see 134). It seems for the purposes of the play the actual distance between Athens and Cicynna is ignored.

139

τοὐξημβλωμένον: crasis for τό ἐξημβλωμένον (ἐξαμβλόω). Strepsiades is very polite to the rather pompous student, either because he is easily impressed, or he wishes to ingratiate himself.

140

ἀλλ᾽ οὐ θέμις πλὴν τοῖς μαθηταῖσιν λέγειν: οὐ θέμις is particularly used of situations where secrets must not be told to uninitiated people. The student is likening the members of the Reflectory to members of a mystery cult (see Introduction).

141

λέγε νυν ἐμοὶ θαρρῶν, ἐγὼ γὰρ οὑτοσὶ / ἥκω μαθητὴς ἐς τὸ φροντιστήριον: θαρρῶν: from θαρρέω [Attic for θαρσέω]. οὑτοσὶ: emphasizes ἐγώ, 'That's why I am here, I have come as a student to the Reflectory.'

143

λέξω. νομίσαι δὲ ταῦτα χρὴ μυστήρια: νομίσαι aorist active infinitive following χρή. μυστήρια: the student continues to liken study in the Reflectory to being an initiate in a mystery cult. Mystery cults were a branch of Greek religion that involved rites and emblems which were not seen by those outside the membership of the group and in order to join, one had to undergo an initiation ceremony. Well-known mystery cults were the cult of Kore at Eleusis, or the rituals of the Great Mother, through to Roman worship of Mithras and Isis.

144–145

ἀνήρετ᾽ ἄρτι Χαιρεφῶντα Σωκράτης / ψύλλαν ὁπόσους ἄλλοιτο τοὺς αὑτῆς πόδας: 'Socrates asked Chaerephon how many of its own feet a flea might jump.' ἀνήρετ[ο] ... ψύλλαν ὁπόσους = ἀνήρετ[ο] ...: ὁπόσους ψύλλα is normal, but in this sentence the verb has two accusatives Χαιρεφῶντα and ψύλλαν, which, as Dover notes, is unusual. ἄλλοιτο: present middle optative of ἄλλομαι in an indirect question in historic sequence.

146–147

τοῦ Χαιρεφῶντος τὴν ὀφρῦν / ἐπὶ τὴν κεφαλὴν τὴν Σωκράτους ἀφήλατο: a scholiast writes that Chaerephon had bushy eyebrows and Socrates had a bald head: these ideas are likely to have come from the present passage.

149–150

εἶτα τὴν ψύλλαν λαβὼν / ἐνέβαψεν ἐς τὸν κηρὸν αὐτῆς τὼ πόδε: τὼ πόδε: accusative dual of πούς. Aristophanes writes as though a flea, which has six legs, uses only two for jumping, and he may have considered the other four as arms. Although inaccurate, we have to remember that this is comedy.

151–152

κᾆτα = καὶ εἶτα: 'and then'. ψυχείσῃ: feminine dative aorist passive participle of ψύχω referring grammatically to the flea, although the reference is clearly to the wax. Περσικαί: Persian boots, a common form of women's soft footwear. The experiment itself is obviously impossible, but as a piece of scientific parody it works well enough to impress Strepsiades.

153

... τῆς λεπτότητος τῶν φρενῶν: genitive of exclamation. Exclamations come from strong emotion, and verbs of emotion often take the genitive case. 'What subtlety of mind!'

154

τί δῆτ᾽ ἂν ἕτερον εἰ πύθοιο Σωκράτους / φρόντισμα: τί δῆτ᾽ ἂν ... εἰ: (supply 'If you are so impressed with that') 'what if you learnt ...' πύθοιο: aorist optative of πυνθάνομαι in a remote condition, 'if you were to learn ....'

156

Χαιρεφῶν ὁ Σφήττιος: Sphettos was a *deme*, much larger than Cicynna (see note on 134). It was about eight miles south-east of Athens, slightly east of Mount Hymettus. It is uncertain whether this was really the *deme* of Chaerephon, but Dover suggests it may be to make a pun on σφήξ 'wasp' to introduce the story about the gnat.

158

ἢ κατὰ τοὐρροπύγιον: crasis τοὐρροπύγιον = τὸ ὀρροπύγιον: left to the end for comic effect. Old Comedy revolves around jokes to do with bodily functions and this fits nicely into that genre.

160–161

ἔφασκεν εἶναι τοὔντερον τῆς ἐμπίδος / στενόν: crasis τοὔντερον for τὸ ἔντερον.

162

βίᾳ βαδίζειν εὐθὺ τοὐρροπυγίου: εὐθύ adverb of place from εὐθύς, used with the genitive, 'straight through'. Both elements of the answer (160 ff.) depend on ἔφασκεν with the accusative and infinitive construction.

165

σάλπιγξ ὁ πρωκτός ἐστιν ἄρα τῶν ἐμπίδων: the comparison to a σάλπιγξ is a hyperbolic way of describing the sound made by such a small creature. Significantly it is the first word in the sentence and placed next to πρωκτός (bathos). ἄρα here is used to show that Strepsiades, at last showing some sense, is drawing a conclusion.

166

ὦ τρισμακάριος τοῦ διεντερεύματος: διεντερεύματος: 'sharp-sightedness', making a pun with its apparent literal meaning of looking through animal entrails at a sacrifice, or of a fishmonger gutting fish. An Aristophanic coinage?

167–168

ἢ ῥᾳδίως φεύγων ἂν ἀποφύγοι δίκην /ὅστις δίοιδε τοὔντερον τῆς ἐμπίδος: Strepsiades uses φεύγων in the legal sense of being a defendant. Use of ἀπο as a prefix reinforces the idea of acquittal in court, as in 'a defendant who knew about the intestines of a gnat, would easily be acquitted.' Strepsiades shows simple enthusiasm for the theory which would be sarcasm from a more sophisticated student. His ludicrous leap of logic is a complete non sequitur.

169–170

πρώην δέ γε γνώμην μεγάλην ἀφῃρέθη / ὑπ' ἀσκαλαβώτου: ἀφῃρέθη: 3rd person singular aorist passive of ἀφαιρέω.

171

ζητοῦντος αὐτοῦ: genitive absolute with present participle, 'while he was searching for . . .'.

172–173

εἶτ' ἄνω κεχηνότος / ἀπὸ τῆς ὀροφῆς νύκτωρ γαλεώτης κατέχεσεν: κεχηνότος: genitive perfect active participle of χάσκω 'I gape' (i.e. with open mouth). νύκτωρ: adv. by night. κατέχεσεν: 3rd person singular aorist καταχέζω, here means 'shat', and takes the genitive.

174

ἥσθην γαλεώτη . . .: ἥσθην: aorist passive of ἥδομαι which takes the dative. Translate as 'I am pleased'.

176

εἶεν: τί οὖν πρὸς τἄλφιτ᾽ ἐπαλαμήσατο: εἶεν: exclamation, 'well!' τἄλφιτ᾽ crasis for τὰ ἄλφιτα barley meal (see note on 106).

178–179

εἶτα διαβήτην λαβὼν / ἐκ τῆς παλαίστρας θοἰμάτιον ὑφείλετο: διαβήτην: the primary meaning here is 'compasses' as Socrates is apparently about to demonstrate geometry. The alternative meaning is 'bestrider' or 'one who spreads his legs' which is derived from the look of a pair of compasses and from the verb διαβαίνω: 'I walk with a wide stride'. Sommerstein supports this by reference to θοἰμάτιον 'the cloak' of someone previously mentioned or assumed to be known, and by the use of this verb in other Aristophanes plays, e.g. *Knights* (77–78), *Wasps* (688) and *Lysistrata* (60). The joke lies in the swift move from intellectual pursuits (geometry) and the ignoring of physical needs (there was no food for dinner), to criminality and sexual satisfaction. The gymnasium was a hot-spot for theft of clothes which was one of the reasons a slave accompanied the athlete. θοἰμάτιον: crasis for τὸ ἱμάτιον, cloak.

180

τί δῆτ᾽ ἐκεῖνον τὸν Θαλῆν θαυμάζομεν: Thales of Miletus (early sixth century BCE) was the founding father of Greek philosophy. Strepsiades enthusiastically exclaims that Socrates should replace Thales, which is a high compliment.

181

ἄνοιγ᾽ ἄνοιγ᾽: Strepsiades is very keen to begin his studies, as is shown by the urgent repetition.

184

ὦ Ἡράκλεις ταυτὶ ποδαπὰ τὰ θηρία: from Strepsiades' reaction we can assume that the inside of the Reflectory is now revealed. The *ekkyklema* was almost certainly used for this (see Introduction). What Strepsiades sees so surprises him that he calls on Heracles, a strong hero who could protect him physically, and a very commonly used oath. Inside are τὰ θηρία, 'creatures'. These are the pale and feeble students (ὠχριῶντας 103) that Pheidippides was so keen to avoid.

186

τοῖς ἐκ Πύλου ληφθεῖσι τοῖς Λακωνικοῖς: τοῖς: the dative is still governed by δοκοῦσιν εἰκέναι in line 185. This is common in quick-fire dialogue where one speaker uses constructions or ideas which have been introduced by the other in a rapid delivery of lines or half lines. τοῖς Λακωνικοῖς: the Laconians, or Spartans, captured at Sphacteria near Pylos in 425 BCE. A Spartan force occupying the island of Sphacteria, adjoining Pylos in the western Peloponnese, had been defeated in 425, by Cleon and Demosthenes, who had taken prisoner about 292 Spartans, just under half of whom were from the ruling caste (Spartiates or Homoioi). Spartans usually never surrendered, so Athenian morale was raised by their capture. They would have been pale because they have been imprisoned for two years at the time of the production of *Clouds*. They were released in 421 BCE after the Peace of Nicias, which suggests this line was from the original version of *Clouds* (see Introduction). ληφθεῖσι: dative plural is aorist passive participle from λαμβάνω.

187

ἀτὰρ τί ποτ᾽ ἐς τὴν γῆν βλέπουσιν οὑτοιί: ἐς τὴν γῆν: they are looking intently at the ground, an attitude associated with grief by the Greeks and would add to Strepsiades' identification of them as captured Spartans.

188

ζητοῦσιν οὗτοι τὰ κατὰ γῆς. βολβοὺς ἄρα: Strepsiades naively interrupts with βολβοὺς ἄρα (antilabe), which is both in emphatic position and an example of bathos. He interprets everything as a simple farmer. Plato (*Republic* 372c) states that βολβοί and λάχανα were staples in an agrarian diet. These plants were gathered not cultivated, so Strepsiades says he knows of a good place to find them.

190

ἐγὼ γὰρ οἶδ᾽ ἵν᾽ εἰσὶ μεγάλοι καὶ καλοί. ἵν᾽ εἰσί: ἵνα: the normal meaning with the indicative, as here, is 'where'. Strepsiades, misunderstanding completely, offers to show the students where to find the βολβοί that he believes they are searching for. As Silk comments, 'for [Strepsiades] the earth is a practical source of edibles not a cavern of mysteries.'

191

τί γὰρ οἵδε δρῶσιν οἱ σφόδρ᾽ ἐγκεκυφότες: ἐγκεκυφότες: perfect active participle of ἐγκύπτω, 'I stoop to the ground'. This group of men is much more bent double than the last, and Strepsiades' surprise is shown by γὰρ: 'Why then . . .?'

192

οὗτοι δ᾽ ἐρεβοδιφῶσιν ὑπὸ τὸν Τάρταρον: ἐρεβοδιφῶσι: from ἐρεβοδιφάω which appears to be an Aristophanic coinage. 'These men are groping about in Erebus beneath Tartarus.' In Homer, Erebus is the kingdom of Hades, but the students are delving even below that, to Tartarus.

194

αὐτὸς καθ᾽ αὑτὸν ἀστρονομεῖν διδάσκεται: αὐτὸς καθ᾽ αὑτὸν with διδάσκεται (middle): to emphasize the strangeness: 'It is teaching <u>itself</u> astronomy'. αὑτὸν = ἑαυτον. Note the bathos as the focus switches from eyes to πρωκτός.

195

ἀλλ᾽ εἴσιθ᾽, ἵνα μὴ 'κεῖνος ὑμῖν ἐπιτύχη: plural imperative from εἴσειμι: I shall enter. The student is addressing the group rather than just Strepsiades. He is not concerned about being outside himself, nor about Strepsiades, who is not yet a member of the Reflectory, as he says ὑμῖν as opposed to ἡμῖν.

196–197

μήπω γε μήπω γ': ἀλλ' ἐπιμεινάντων, ἵνα / αὐτοῖσι κοινώσω τι πραγμάτιον ἐμόν: μήπω γε μήπω γ': 'Not yet, not yet', Strepsiades is very keen for the students to stay (cf. line 181). ἐπιμεινάντων: 3rd person plural aorist active imperative of ἐπιμένω. Πραγμάτιον: Strepsiades uses a diminutive to describe his situation, perhaps as a ruse to get them to listen: 'my little problem' (see notes on lines 80 and 92).

198

ἀλλ' οὐχ οἷόν τ' αὐτοῖσι πρὸς τὸν ἀέρα: 'it is not possible for them to be out in the air'. It is repeated that the group of students should not be outside (see note on 195). This would explain the pale complexions that Pheidippides despised so much.

200

πρὸς τῶν θεῶν τί γὰρ τάδ' ἐστίν; εἰπέ μοι: πρὸς τῶν θεῶν: the genitive follows πρὸς where there is a supplication (cf. also 153). As in 191, γὰρ here expresses surprise. τάδ[ε]: Strepsiades begins to look at the equipment which is lying on the stage (or possibly the *ekkyklema*).

202

γεωμετρία: literally earth-measuring. Presumably Strepsiades is indicating rulers, compasses, etc. His lack of understanding of the mathematical purpose of geometry is shown by the next question, which sets up the joke.

203

πότερα τὴν κληρουχικήν: πότερα τὴν κληρουχικήν: a cleruchy (κλῆρος, allotted portion) was a settlement of Athenian citizens on land confiscated often after a revolt. It was an effective way of providing land for Athenian citizens and ensuring the subjugation of rebellious states. The way that Strepsiades jumps in completing the metrical line, demonstrates his desire to display knowledge, which is ironic as he clearly does not understand what he is being shown. He is clearly far more literal-minded than the student imagined, but again he shows the farmer's perspective.

204

οὔκ, ἀλλὰ τὴν σύμπασαν / ἀστεῖον λέγεις: τὴν σύμπασαν supply γῆν. ἀστεῖον: adjective suggesting the thing said is 'of the town' and therefore clever. Compare the meanings of 'urbane' and 'rustic' in English.

205

τὸ γὰρ σόφισμα δημοτικὸν καὶ χρήσιμον: σόφισμα: a clever device or skill. δημοτικὸν: Strepsiades shows his lack of understanding as he believes that geometry is a democratic way of redistributing all the land in the world to

Athenian citizens thereby allowing the poorest citizen to become economically independent (Dover), which seems quite a sensible view for an Athenian, and a likely one for a poor countryman. Sommerstein comments that Strepsiades sees it almost as magical.

206

αὕτη δέ σοι γῆς περίοδος πάσης. ὁρᾷς: γῆς περίοδος: a map. Anaximander (*c.* 610–540) is credited with the earliest Greek map. Such examples were probably much more diagrammatic than modern-day maps and would not have been much help in finding particular features such as fresh water. Herodotus (*Histories* 1.49.1) tells of Aristagoras *c.* 499 using a map engraved on a bronze board (χάλκεον πίνακα) to persuade the Spartan king, Cleomenes, to join the Ionian Revolt. This may have been the map produced by Hecataeus of Miletus (sixth/fifth century BCE).

208

ἐπεὶ δικαστὰς οὐχ ὁρῶ καθημένους: δικαστάς: jurors. The Athenians of the fifth century were proud of their jury system with jurors drawn from across the *phylai* (tribes) sitting in large juries of sometimes 501. There were many complaints that the Athenians were over fond of their courts and, as the empire grew, they became more insistent on trying cases both domestic and imperial at Athens. This, and the size of the juries, gave much material to the satirists. (See Aristophanes' *Wasps* which hilariously satirizes the jury system, and being produced in 422, a year after the production of *Clouds* may have already been in Aristophanes' mind as the subject for his next play.) In fact, so keen were they on their legal system that jury-courts became the hallmark of Athens. We are invited to laugh at Strepsiades' failure to understand the limitations of a map, as well as laughing at the litigiousness of the Athenians. Note that the humour turns against Strepsiades here. Up to now, we have largely been laughing at the pretentiousness of the students, but now we more explicitly laugh at Strepsiades' ignorance.

209

ὡς τοῦτ᾽ ἀληθῶς Ἀττικὴ τὸ χωρίον: 'This really is the land of Attica!' Strepsiades' delight is clear.

210

καὶ ποῦ Κικυννῆς εἰσὶν οὑμοὶ δημόται: καὶ ποῦ expresses surprise and possibly suspicion on the part of Strepsiades who clearly does not understand the limitations of a map, specifically the concept of scale (as we soon see), but is touchingly thrilled to see his own locality. Κίκυννα is his *deme* (134). οὑμοί = οἱ and ἐμοί. δημόται are Strepsiades' fellow demesmen.

212

ἡδὶ παρατέταται μακρὰ πόρρω πάνυ: the island of Euboea is long and thin and lies along the coast of Attica and Boeotia hence the παρα of παρατέταται: 3rd person singular perfect middle of παρατείνω. μακρά refers to the length of the island. πόρρω πάνυ: emphasizes how long the island is. ἡδί: indicates that the student is pointing.

213

ὑπὸ γὰρ ἡμῶν παρετάθη καὶ Περικλέους: 'It was stretched out (i.e. knocked out in a metaphorical sense) by Pericles and us.' Strepsiades refers to the Euboean revolt of 446 BCE which was put down by the Athenians by Pericles, the great fifth-century Athenian statesmen and member of the Alcmaeonid family, as their leader. Strepsiades means he was involved in, or is at least taking some credit for, it as part of the Athenian citizen-body. There was no standing army at this time and when the Athenian assembly (ekklesia) voted to go to war, it was the very citizens who voted who took part.

214

ἀλλ᾽ ἡ Λακεδαίμων ποῦ 'σθ᾽ / ὅπου 'στίν; αὑτηί: Λακεδαίμων: Sparta. The Spartans (referred to as Laconians in 186) were also known as Lacedaimonians. ὅπου 'σθ᾽ = ποῦ ἐστιν. The student completes the line presumably in a tone of surprise at Strepsiades' stupidity. αὑτηί: he points to the map.

215–216

ὡς ἐγγὺς ἡμῶν: 'How close to us!' Strepsiades reveals his lack of understanding of cartography and of scale, by suggesting that Sparta can be moved further away from Athens. In 423, the war between Athens and Sparta had been going on for eight years.

217

νὴ Δί᾽ οἰμώξεσθ᾽ ἄρα: 'By Zeus, you will be wailing for yourselves!' (i.e. you'll regret it) οἰμώξεσθ᾽: 2nd person plural future middle of οἰμώζω. Sommerstein points out that although it is not the Socratic students' fault that geography cannot be altered, Strepsiades has a tendency to react angrily when he does not get his way (see lines 57–59).

218

φέρε τίς γὰρ οὗτος οὑπὶ τῆς κρεμάθρας ἀνήρ: φέρε: 'Hang on!' Strepsiades' attention is caught by a strange sight. οὑπὶ is a crasis of ὁ ἐπί followed by the genitive: 'the man on the hook'. Fortunately for the student, Socrates appears, swung into view above the stage by the mechane (see Introduction) which was used in tragedy to show gods appearing physically above mortals. Here as in other comedies (cf. Aristophanes' *Peace*, where the hero rides to Olympus on a dung beetle) it has the amusing purpose of providing a suitably eccentric entrance or mode of transport. Socrates appears on a κρεμάθρα, a rope on a hook, although the scholiast calls it a basket or fowl-perch (perhaps it was a trapeze?).

219

αὐτός / τίς αὐτός; / Σωκράτης / ὦ Σώκρατες: one line distributed between two characters, each with two comments, balanced with the student first saying αὐτός: 'It is he, himself!' Sommerstein tells us that this pronoun is commonly used to denote the master of a house, and by Pythagorean philosophers to denote the founder of their school. Strepsiades completes the line with an invocation, ὦ Σώκρατες. The repetition of vocabulary and the way that the speakers cut in increases the drama of the line.

220

ἴθ᾿ οὗτος, ἀναβόησον αὐτόν μοι μέγα: ἀναβόησον: 2nd person singular aorist active imperative of ἀναβοάω. μέγα is used adverbially, 'loudly'.

221

αὐτὸς μὲν οὖν σὺ κάλεσον: οὐ γάρ μοι σχολή: κάλεσον: 2nd person singular aorist active imperative of καλέω. μοι: dative of possession, 'I have no time' (lit. there is no time for me).

222

ὦ Σώκρατες: this invocation makes up the line. It is one iambic *metron* long and has a precedent in *Acharnians* (line 407).

223

ὦ Σωκρατίδιον: the diminutive reminds us of the wheedling voice of Strepsiades earlier in the play (80 and 132). ὦφήμερε: 'O creature of a day'. Socrates speaks in highly poetic language. He is physically looking down on Strepsiades from the *mechane* as a god would look down from Olympus, and he is also addressing Strepsiades as a god would a mortal. The use of 'creature of a day' virtually amounts to claiming that he himself is immortal.

225

ἀεροβατῶ καὶ περιφρονῶ τὸν ἥλιον: ἀεροβατῶ: 'I walk on air'. An Aristophanic coinage. περιφρονῶ: 'I am thinking about . . .' is contrasted with ὑπερφρονέω: 'I look down upon/ despise' in line 226 (cf. the reference in *Apology* 19c to this passage).

226

ἔπειτ᾿ ἀπὸ ταρροῦ τοὺς θεοὺς ὑπερφρονεῖς: ἀπὸ ταρροῦ: the ancient interpretation of this was that a ταρρός was a perch, although a wicker basket seems more likely. τοὺς θεοὺς ὑπερφρονεῖς: 'you are looking down on the gods' (see note on 225).

227

ἀλλ᾿ οὐκ ἀπὸ τῆς γῆς, εἴπερ: περ strengthens εἴ. 'But [can you not do this] from the ground, if that is really so?'

228–230

ἐξηῦρον ὀρθῶς . . . ἐς τὸν ὅμοιον ἀέρα: τὰ μετέωρα πράγματα: 'higher matters' and, by association, astronomical phenomena. Socrates is using the kind of terms that philosophers might be expected to use. It does not matter whether they are accurate or fully understood by the audience, because the joke works as a caricature of a philosopher. Aristophanes' humour here, as in line 188, lies in the metaphor being made literal and visual, e.g. 'high-thinking' must be done up in the air. Socrates was not known for his interest in astronomy (in fact he moved philosophy away from the 'scientific' interests of the pre-Socratics to moral philosophy and epistemology), but many features of Aristophanes' Socrates are not Socratic (e.g. charging his students). Sommerstein notes that the ideas here are a garbled parody of the doctrines of Diogenes of Apollonia, who believed that for intelligent thought to take place the air, which constitutes the soul and mind, must be 'pure and dry'. Socrates talks of 'having hung up his mind' (εἰ μὴ κρεμάσας τὸ νόημα) as one would to dry clothes, and to do that he must also 'hang up' his body, hence he needs to be lifted into the air. τὴν φροντίδα / λεπτὴν καταμείξας ἐς τὸν ὅμοιον ἀέρα: Diogenes' belief that the soul consisted of air was because air was composed of much small particles than anything else, therefore to think effectively the philosopher must let his mind be as much like air as possible.

231–233

εἰ δ᾽ ὢν χαμαὶ ... τῆς φροντίδος: χαμαὶ: on the ground (cf. Latin *humi*). τἄνω: crasis for τά ἄνω κάτωθεν (for suffix -θεν see 134). Aristophanes is parodying Diogenes' theory that moisture was a hindrance to clear thinking, so lifting oneself up above the moist earth was necessary to attain clear perception.

234

πάσχει δὲ ταὐτὸ τοῦτο καὶ τὰ κάρδαμα: κάρδαμα, watercress. The delay of κάρδαμα to the end of the line emphasizes the joke and the anticlimax after the high-flown philosophical language. Socrates seems, for a moment, to have adopted Strepsiades' common-sense approach, which sets up the joke for the next line.

235

πῶς φής; 'How do you mean?' This line is extra metrical (outside the metre of the line), perhaps reinforcing Strepsiades' confusion at Socrates' words.

236

ἡ φροντὶς ἕλκει τὴν ἰκμάδ᾽ ἐς τὰ κάρδαμα: Strepsiades latches onto something he can relate to (κάρδαμα), but the humour is in his misunderstanding. Aristophanes is concerned only with making Socrates speak like a philosopher or scientist; he does not need to be making any sense, even to Strepsiades. Aristophanes has made Socrates into a generalized sophist or trendy intellectual.

237–238

ἴθι νυν κατάβηθ᾽ ... ἐλήλυθα: ὦ Σωκρατίδιον: see note on 80.

239

ἦλθες δὲ κατὰ τί;/ βουλόμενος μαθεῖν λέγειν: Socrates' question is phrased formally and Strepsiades jumps in, keen to be heard.

240–241

ὑπὸ γὰρ τόκων χρήστων τε δυσκολωτάτων / ἄγομαι φέρομαι / τὰ χρήματ᾽ ἐνεχυράζομαι: δυσκολωτάτων: superlative, 'ill-tempered'. Both τόκων and χρήστων δυσκολωτάτων depend on ὑπὸ, by (with genitive), itself depending on the passive verbs ἄγομαι and φέρομαι: 'I am being attacked and carried off ...' which effectively personifies the debts in a zeugma (a literary device joining two words which appear grammatically similar but are logically different). ἄγειν καὶ φέρειν is used in *Iliad* 5, 484 so Strepsiades is exaggerating his situation. τὰ χρήματ᾽ ἐνεχυράζομαι: 'I am being plundered of the goods taken as pledges.' In line 35 this was seen as a possibility, now it is said to be actually happening.

242

πόθεν δ᾽ ὑπόχρεως σαυτὸν ἔλαθες γενόμενος: 'How can it be that you yourself did not notice you were in debt?' λανθάνω: I escape the notice of . . .' takes a participle in this case the aorist participle of γίγνομαι.

Vocabulary

While there is no Defined Vocabulary List for A Level, words in the OCR Defined Vocabulary List for AS are marked with * so that students can quickly see the vocabulary with which they should be particularly familiar.

*ἀγαθός -ή -όν — good
*ἄγαν — too much
ἄγροικος -ον — rustic, in/of the country
*ἀγρός -οῦ m — field
*ἄγω — I lead, bring
ἀδελφιδῆ -ῆς f — niece, a sibling's daughter
*ἀδικέω — I do wrong, cheat
* ἄδικος -ον (comp: ἀδικώτερος) — unjust
ᾄδω — I sing
ἀεροβατέω — I walk on air
ἀήρ ἀέρος m — air
*Ἀθῆναι -ῶν f pl — Athens
αἰβοῖ — yuck! (an exclamation of disgust)
αἴξ αἰγός m/f — goat
*αἴτιος -α -ον — the cause of, to blame for + gen
ἀκόρητος -ον — unswept
*ἀκούω — I hear, listen to
ἀκριβής -ές — accurate, precise
ἀλαζών -όνος m — imposter, charlatan
*ἀλλά — but
ἀλεκτρυών -όνος m — cockerel
ἀληθῶς — truly
ἅλλομαι (3 sg. pres. mid. opt.: ἅλλοιτο) — I leap, spring
ἄλφιτα -ων n — barley
ἀμαθής -ές — ignorant, stupid
ἄμφω — both (dual nom)
* ἄν — makes indefinite e.g. would, could
ἀναβοάω (2 sg. aor. act. imp.: ἀναβόησον) — I shout, cry out loud

*ἀναγιγνώσκω (aor. subj.: ἀναγνῶ) — I read, get to know
ἀναμετρέω — I measure carefully
ἀναπείθω (fut.: ἀναπείσω) — I convince, persuade
ἀνέρομαι (aor. mid: ἀνηρόμην) — I ask
*ἀνήρ ἀνδρός m — man
ἄνθραξ -ακος m — charcoal
*ἄνθρωπος -ου m — man, human being
ἄνιππος -ον — without a horse
ἀνοίγω (imp.: ἄνοιγε) — I open
ἀντιβολέω — I meet, take part in
ἀνυπόδητος -ον — barefoot
ἀνύω (aor.: ἤνυσα) — I make haste, hurry
ἄνω — upwards, up above
ἀπάγω — I lead away
*ἅπας ἅπασα ἅπαν — whole, all together
ἀπέραντος -ον — countless, infinite
ἀπεριμερίμνως — thoughtlessly
*ἀπό + gen. — away from
ἀποβλέπω — I look, I look at
ἀποδίδωμι (aor. act. opt.: ἀποδοίην) — I pay off, pay back
ἀπόλλυμαι mid. see ἀπόλλυμι below — I perish
*ἀπόλλυμι (perf: ἀπολώλεκα, 2 sg. aor. mid. opt.: ἀπόλοιο) — I destroy
ἀποφεύγω (aor. opt.: ἀποφύγοι) — I flee, run away and succeed in getting off
ἅπτω — I fasten, bind / I light, kindle
*ἄρα — then
ἀργός -ή -όν — idle

*ἀργύριον -ου n — a small coin, money
*ἅρμα -ατος n — chariot
*ἅρτι — just now
ἀσκαλαβώτης -ου m — lizard
ἀστεῖος -α -ον — of the town, polite, sophisticated
ἀστρονομέω — I study astronomy
ἀστρονομία -ας f — astronomy
*ἅστυ -εως n — town, city
ἀτάρ — but, nevertheless
ἀτραπός -οῦ f — short cut
Ἀττικός -ή -όν — Attic, Athenian
*αὖ — again, in turn
*αὐτός -ή -ό — self; same; him, her, it, them
ἀφαιρέω — I take away
ἀφάλλομαι (3 sg. aor.: ἀφήλατο) — I jump off

*βαδίζω — I walk
*βαίνω (aor.: ἔβην) — I go
*βάλλω (aor.: ἔβαλον) — I throw, (idiomatically: away with you!)
*βασιλεύς -έως m — king
*βία -ας f — force, bodily strength
*βίος -ου m — life
*βλέπω (see ἀποβλέπω) — I look at, observe, see
βολβός -οῦ m — bulb, onion
*βούλομαι — I want, wish, am willing
*βραδύς -εῖα -ύ — slow
βρύω — I teem, have abundance of

γαλεώτης -ου m — gecko, type of lizard
*γαμέω (aor.: ἔγημα) — I marry
*γάρ — for
*γε — at least, at any rate
Γενετυλλίς -ίδος f — Genetyllis (a goddess of childbirth)
*γέρων -οντος m — old man
γεωμετρία -ας f — earth-measuring
*γῆ γῆς f — earth
*γίγνομαι (fut.: γενήσομαι; aor.: ἐγενόμην) — I become
*γνώμη -ης f — opinion
γραμματεῖον -ου n — writing tablet
*γυνή γυναικός f — woman, wife

δαιμόνιον -ου n — divinity, supernatural power
δαιμόνιος -α -ον — miraculous, marvellous
δάκνω (aor.: ἔδακον) — I bite

δαπάνη -ης f — expense, extravagance
*δείκνυμι (pres. act. part.: δεικνύς; aor. imp.: δεῖξον) — I bring to light, show
δείλαιος -α -ον — wretched, sorry
*δεῖπνον -ου n — meal, dinner
*δεξιός -ά -όν f δεξιώτατα adv — on the right, (metaphorically: shrewd, clever)
*δεῦρο — to here
*δή — indeed
δήμαρχος -ου m — deme official
Δημήτηρ -τρος f — Demeter
δημότης -ου m — demesman, member of a deme
δημοτικός -ή -όν — democratic, of the people
*δῆτα — certainly, of course; then, in that case
Δία (acc.) — see Ζεύς
*διά + acc. — because of
*διά + gen. — through
διαβήτης -ου m — pair of compasses
διακναίω (perf. mid./ pass. part.: διακεκναισμένος) — I scrape off
διαμετρέω — I measure
διατήκω (aor.: διετήξα) — I melt, soften by heating (as of wax)
διατρίβω — I spend (time)
*διδάσκω — I teach (mid: I get myself taught)
*δίδωμι (pres. subj.: διδῷ; aor. opt.: δοίης; aor. imp.: δός) — I give
διεντέρευμα -ατος n — looking through entrails
*δίκαιος -α -ον — just, right, well-ordered
δικαστής -οῦ m — juryman
*δίκη -ης f — custom, lawsuit
δίοιδα — I know well
Διόνυσος -ου m — Dionysus, god of wine and theatre
διφθέρα -ας f — piece of leather
διφρίσκος -ου m — chariot
*δοκεῖ + dat. — it seems good to X
δοκέω — I think, suppose, imagine, seem
*δράω — I do, accomplish
*δρόμος -ου m — race, racecourse, lane
*δύναμαι + infin. . — I am able
δυσκολαίνω — I am bad-tempered, peevish
δύσκολος -ον (superl.: δυσκολωτάτος) — hard to please, discontented
δώδεκα — twelve

*ἐάω (aor. imp.: ἔασον) — I allow

*ἐγγύς + gen. or as adv — near

ἐγείρω — I awaken, rouse (mid: I wake up)

ἐγκαλύπτω (perf. mid. part.: ἐγκεκαλυμμένοι) — I veil, wrap up

ἐγκοισυρόομαι (perf. mid. part.: ἐγκεκοισυρωμένην) — I live like Coesyra

ἐγκορδυλέω (perf. mid. part.: ἐγκεκορδυλημένος) — I wrap up in blankets

ἐγκύπτω (perf. act. part.: ἐγκεκυφότες) — I stoop and peep

*ἐγώ — I (1 sg. pronoun)

εἶεν — well!

εἰκάς -άδος f — twentieth day of the month

εἰκῆ adv. — carelessly

*εἰμί — I am

*εἶμι (imp.: ἴθι) — I shall go

εἴπερ — if really, if indeed

*εἰς (ἐς) + acc. — into

εἰς μία ἕν — one (numeral)

εἴσειμι — I enter, go in

εἶτα — then, next

ἐκ + gen. — from, out of

*ἐκεῖνος -η -ο — that

ἐκκόπτω — I knock out

ἐκστρέφω — I turn inside out

ἐκφέρω — I carry out

ἔλαιον -ου n — olive oil (used for a lamp)

*ἐλαύνω (fut.: ἐλάω) — I drive

*ἕλκω — I drag

ἐμβάπτω — I dip in

*ἐμός -ή -όν — my

ἐμπίς -ίδος f — gnat, mosquito

ἐν + dat. — in/on

ἐνάπτω (perf. pass. part.: ἐνημμένος) — I bind, tie on (pass: I wear)

ἔνειμι — I am present in

ἕνεκα (with gen. preceding) — on account of

ἐνεχυράζω (fut. mid. infin.: ἐνεχυράσεσθαί) — I take a pledge from

ἐνοικέω — I dwell in

*ἐνταῦθα — here, there, then

ἔντερον -ου n — intestines

*ἐντεῦθεν — then

ἐντίθημι (2 sg. Imperf.: ἐνετίθεις) — I put in place

ἐξαλίνδω (aor. part.: ἐξαλίσας; perf. ἐξήλικα) — I roll out (here: I allow my horse to roll)

ἐξαμβλόω (2 sg. perf: ἐξήμβλωκας; perf. pass. part.: ἐξημβλωμενος) — I make to miscarry

ἐξεγείρω — I awaken, rouse (see ἐγείρω above)

ἐξελαύνω (fut.:ἐξελῶ) — I drive out

*ἔξεστι + dat. + infi — It is allowed, is possible for X to do Y

ἐξευρίσκω (perf. part.: ἐξηυρημένην) — I find out, discover

ἔξω — out

ἔοικα (infin.: εἰκέναι) — I am like, similar to

ἐπαίρω (aor.: ἐπῆρα) — I persuade

ἐπεγείρω — I awaken, rouse from sleep

ἐπεί — when, since

*ἔπειτα — then, next

ἐπί + acc. — to, against

ἐπί + gen. — in, on

ἐπί + dat. — on, on condition of

ἐπιλήσμων -ονος — forgetful

ἐπιμένω (3 pl. aor. imp.: ἐπιμεινάντων) — I stay on, linger

ἐπιτυγχάνω (aor.: ἐπέτυχον) — I happen upon, meet with

ἐρεβοδιφάω — I look about in the darkness of the Underworld

ἔριον -ου n — wool

*ἔρχομαι (aor.: ἦλθον; perf: ἐλήλυθα) — I go, I come

*ἐσθίω (2 sg. fut.: ἔδει) — I eat

*ἑσπέρα -ας f — evening

ἐτεόν adv. — really, truly

*ἕτερος -α -ον — another

Εὔβοια -ας f — Euboea, long, thin island off the east coast of Attica

εὕδω — I sleep

εὐθύ + gen. — straight through to

*εὑρίσκω (aor.: ηὗρον) — I find

εὐρωτιάω — I am mouldy, 'unwashed'

*εὔχομαι (aor.: εὐξάμην) — I pray

ἐφήμερος -ου m — creature of a day

ἐχθές — yesterday

*ἔχω — I have

*Ζεύς Διός m — Zeus, father of gods and men

*ζητέω — I seek, look for

ζύγιος -ου m — yoke-horse i.e. one that can be yoked to pull a chariot

ἤ — exclamation expressing disapproval, here: shh! shh!

ἤν (= ἐάν) — If . . .

*ἤδομαι (aor.: ἥσθην) — I am pleased

*ἡδύς -εῖα -ύ (superl.: ἥδιστος) — pleasant

*ἥκω — I have come

*ἥλιος -ου m — sun

*ἡμεῖς — we (1 pl pronoun)

*ἡμέρα -ας f — day

Ἡρακλῆς -οῦ m — Heracles, son of Zeus and Alcmene

ἥττων ἧττον — weaker, worse

ἠχέω — I resound

Θαλῆς Θάλεω m — Thales, one of the founders of Western philosophy

*θαρρέω — I am confident

*θαυμάζω — I wonder (at), admire, am amazed

θεῖος -ου m — uncle

θέμις -ιστος f — right by custom

*θεός –οῦ m — god

*θεράπων -οντος m — servant

*θηρίον -ου n — wild beast

θρυαλλίς -ίδος f — wick (of a lamp)

*θύρα -ας f — door

θύριον -ου n — little door

ἰδού (aor. mid. imp.: ὁράω) — look!

ἰκμάς -άδος f — moisture

ἱμάτιον -ου n — cloak

ἵνα adv. — where

*ἵνα conj. — in order that

ἰού — a cry of sorrow, joy or surprise

ἱππάζομαι — I drive horses (in a chariot)

ἵππερος -ου m — horse-fever

*ἱππεύς -έως m — one who fights from a chariot

ἱππική -ῆς f — horse-riding

ἵππιος -α -ον — of horses

*ἵππος -ου m — horse

ἰτητέον = ἰτέον (neut. gerundive of εἶμι I shall go) — I must go

*καθεύδω — I lie down to sleep, sleep

κάθημαι — I sit

κακοδαίμων -ονος m — possessed by an evil spirit, wretched

*κακός -ή -όν (adv: κακῶς) — bad

*καλέω — I call

*καλός -ή -όν — fine, beautiful

κάμπτω (aor.: ἔκαμψα) — I bend, curve

κάρδαμον -ου n — watercress

καρδία -ας f — heart

*κατά + acc. — down, through

*κατά + gen. — down upon; under

καταβαίνω (aor. imp.: κατάβηθι) — I come/go down

καταγλώττισμα -ατος n — a deep kiss

καταδαρθάνω (aor.: κατέδαρθον) — I fall asleep

καταμίγνυμι (aor. part.: καταμείξας) — I mix, mingle

καταπάσσω — I sprinkle

καταχέζω (aor. part.: καταχέσας) — I shit on

καταχέω — I pour X over Y

κάτειπέ (aor.) — tell me (imp)

κάτωθεν — from below

*κεῖμαι (fut.: κείσομαι) — I am lying down

*κελεύω — I order, urge on

*κεφαλή -ῆς f — head

κήδομαι + gen. — I am concerned, care for

κηρός -οῦ m — beeswax

Κικύννα -ας f — Cicynna (an Attic deme)

κλαίω (fut.: κλαύσομαι) — I weep (middle: I weep for myself)

κληρουχικός -ή -όν — of/for a cleruchy (Athenian settlement)

κοῖλος -η -ον — hollow

κοινός -ή -όν — common, shared, (κοινῇ = by common consent)

κοινόω — I share

*κολάζω — I punish, chastise

κόμη -ης f — hair

κοππατίας -ου m — branded with the letter 'koppa'

*κόπτω (aor.: ἔκοψα) — I strike, knock at

κόραξ -ακος m — raven (idiomatically: 'ἐς κόρακας' 'go to hell!')

κορίζομαι — I caress, fondle

κρείττων -ον — stronger, better

κρεμάθρα -ας f — hanging basket

κρεμάννυμι (aor. act. part.: κρεμάσας) — I hang (from a rope)

*κρίνω — I decide, judge (mid: dispute)

κρόκος -ου m — saffron

κυνέω (aor. imp.: κύσον) — I kiss

Κωλιάς -άδος f — Colias (a cult title of Aphrodite from the site of a temple)

Λακεδαίμων -ονος m — Sparta

λακτίζω (2 sg. perf: λελάκτικας) — I kick

Λακωνικός -ή -όν — Laconian, from Sparta

*λαμβάνω (aor.: ἔλαβον, aor. pass: ἐλήφθην) — I take, capture

*λανθάνω + participle (aor.: ἔλαθον) — I escape the notice of

λαφυγμός -οῦ m — greed, gluttony

*λέγω (aor.: εἶπον, fut.: ἐρῶ) — I say, speak

λεπτός -ή -όν — thin, narrow

λεπτότης -ητος f — subtlety

Λεωγόρας -ου m — Leogoras, a man known for his luxurious lifestyle

λίαν — too much, excessively

*λίθος -ου m — stone

λογίζομαι — I count, reckon up

*λόγος -ου m (λόγοιν gen./dat. dual) — word, argument

λοιδορέω — I abuse, rebuke, quarrel; mid: argue

λύχνος -ου m — lamp

μά + acc. e.g. of divinity — no, by . . . . (exclamation in negative)

μαθητής -οῦ m — student, learner

μαθητιάω — I am eager to become a student

*μακρός -ά -όν — long

*μανθάνω (fut.: μαθήσομαι; aor.: ἔμαθον) — I learn, study

Μεγακλῆς -ους m — Megacles, member of an aristocratic family and possibly uncle of Pheidippides

*μέγας μεγάλη μέγα — big, grown up

μέλε (voc) — mate, (familiar address)

μέλιττα -ης f — honey-bee

μέντοι — however, certainly

μεριμνοφροντιστής -οῦ m — 'minute philosopher' (i.e. one who can think through a problem in minute detail)

*μετά + acc. — after

*μετά + gen. — with

μετέωρος -ον — raised on high, in the air

*μή — don't . . . (negative used with imperative)

*μηδαμῶς adv. — not at all

*μηδείς μηδεμία μηδέν — no one, nothing

μήν — certainly, surely

μήπω — not yet

*μήτηρ μητρός f — mother

μνᾶ μνᾶς f — mina, a sum of money

μύρον -ου n — myrrh, perfume

μυστήριον -ου n — mystery rite, holy secret

*νεανίας -ου m — young man

νή + acc. of e.g. divinity — yes, by . . . . (strong affirmation)

νήπιος -η -ον — childish, infantile

*νικάω — I win

νόημα -ατος n — thought

*νομίζω (aor.: ἐνόμισα) — I treat as

νύκτωρ — by night

*νῦν — now

*νύξ νυκτός f — night

νώ (nom./acc. dual of ἐγώ; gen./dat. dual νῷν) — we two

ξυνωρικεύομαι (also συνωρικεύομαι) — I drive a pair (of horses)

ξυστίς -ίδος f — long robe (worn by charioteer after victory)

ὀβελίσκος -ου m — small skewer, spit

ὀβολός -οῦ m — obol (small coin)

*ὅδε ἥδε τόδε — this

*ὁδός -οῦ f — road, way, path

ὄζω + gen. of source of smell — I smell of

*οἶδα — I know

*οἴκαδε — homewards

οἰκέτης -ου m — household slave

*οἰκία -ας f — house

οἰκίδιον -ου n — small house

*οἰκέω — I live

οἴμοι — alas!

οἰμώζω (fut.: οἰμώξομαι) — I wail, lament

*οἷος οἵα οἷον — such as, of the sort that

ὅλος -η -ον — whole, entire

*ὅμοιος -α -ον — of the same kind, like, resembling

ὀνειροπολέω — I dream

*ὄνομα -ατος n — name

ὄντως (adv. from εἰμί) — really, truly

ὁπόσος -η -ον — as big as, pl as many as

ὁπότερος -α -ον ... ἤ — which of two ... or ...

ὅπου — where

*ὅπως — how; when

*ὁράω (aor.: εἶδον) — I see

ὀρθῶς — correctly

ὀρροπύγιον -ου n — rump, rear end, tail

*ὅσος -η -ον — how great, what a big ...!

ὀροφή -ῆς f — roof (of a house)

*ὅς ἥ ὅ — who, which

*ὅστις ἥτις ὅτι — (the one) who, which, whoever, whatever

*ὅταν — when, whenever

*οὐδέ — and not, not even

*οὐδείς οὐδεμία οὐδέν — no one, nothing

*οὐδέποτε — never

*οὖν — therefore

οὕνεκα (= οὗ ἕνεκα) — because of which ...

*οὐρανός -οῦ m — heaven, sky

οὔτε ... οὔτε — not, neither ... nor

*οὗτος αὕτη τοῦτο (gen./dat. dual: τούτοιν) — this (man, woman, thing)

*οὕτως — in this way

ὀφείλω + infin. (aor.: ὤφελον; perf: ὠφείληκα) — I owe, am in debt

*ὀφθαλμός -οῦ m — eye

ὀφλισκάνω (perf: ὤφληκα) — I incur (a debt), bring upon myself

ὀφρῦς -ύος f — eye-brow

*παῖς παιδός m/f (voc: παι; dim: παιδιον) — child

*πάλαι — long ago

παλαίστρα -ας f — wrestling ground, exercise area

παλαμάομαι — I contrive

πάνυ — very much, entirely

πάππος -ου m — grandfather

*παρά + dat. — beside, with (παρ᾽ αὐτοῖς: at their house)

παραινέω — I advise, exhort

παρατείνω (aor. pass.: παρετάθην; perf. pass.: παρατέταμαι) — I stretch out beside

*πᾶς πᾶσα πᾶν — all, whole, entire

*πάσχω — I experience, suffer

*πατήρ πατρός m — father

πατρῷος -α -ον — of a father

παχύς -εῖα -ύ — thick

*πείθομαι + dat. (fut.: πείσομαι; imp.: πιθοῦ; subj.: πίθωμαι; aor. opt.: πιθοίμην) — I obey

*πείθω — I persuade

πέντε — five

πέρδομαι — I break wind, fart

*περί + gen. — about, concerning

Περικλῆς -έους m — Pericles, Athenian statesman and general

περίοδος -ου f — map

περιοράω (fut.: περιόψομαι) — I stand by and watch, tolerate

περιουσία -ας f — extravagance, abundance

περιφορά -ᾶς f — circuit, revolution

περιφρονέω — I think about

περιφύω (aor.: περιέφυσα) — I make to grow around

Περσικός -ή -όν — Persian, here in fem pl. fancy slippers

*πίπτω (aor.: ἔπεσον) — I fall

*πλήν + gen. or as adv. — except

πνεῦμα -ατος n — wind, blast

πνιγεύς -έως m — baking-cover

πνοή πνοῆς f — wind, blast

ποδαπός -ή -όν — from what country?

*πόθεν — from where? how can that be?

*ποῖος -α -ον — what sort of?

πολεμιστήρια -ων — n pl. war-chariots

*πόλεμος -ου m — war

*πόλις -εως f — city

*πολύς πολλή πολύ — much, pl many

πονηρός -ά -όν — useless, good-for-nothing

πόρρω — to/for a long distance

Ποσειδῶν -ῶνος m — Poseidon, god of the sea, earthquakes and horses

*πόσος -η -ον — how much, pl. how many?

ποτε — intensifies a question (τί ποτ᾽ what in the world ...)

*πότερος -α -ον — which of two?

πότης -ου m — drinker (adj: thirsty)

*ποῦ — where?

*πούς πόδος m (nom./ acc. dual: πόδε) — foot

*πρᾶγμα -ατος n — thing, matter, business

πρίαμαι — I buy

*πρό + gen. — before

πρόβατον -ου n — sheep

προμνήστρια -ας f — matchmaker

*πρός + acc. — to, towards

*πρός + dat. — close to, next to

πρόσκειμαι — I lie near, lie next to

προστίθημι — I add to

*πρότερον — before, formerly

πρόφασις -εως f — reason, evidence

πρῴην — lately, just now

πρωκτός -οῦ m — arse

*πρῶτον — first, at first

πρῶτος -η -ον — first

Πύλος -ου m — Pylos (town in the western Peloponnese)

*πυνθάνομαι (2 sg. aor. opt.: πύθοιο) — I learn

*πῶς — how

ῥᾳδίως — easily

ῥέγκω — I snore

σάλπιγξ -ιγγος f — war-trumpet

σαμφόρας -ου m — horse branded with the old letter 'san'

*σαυτοῦ σεαυτῆς m/f — of yourself, your own

σελήνη -ης f — moon

σεμνός -ή -όν — holy, haughty

σισύρα -ας f — goat's hair cloak

σιωπάω — I keep quiet

*σκοπέω — I look at

*σός σή σόν — your (sg)

σόφισμα -ατος n — clever device

*σοφός -ή -όν — wise

σπαθάω — I work the loom hard (metaphor for extravagance)

στέμφυλον -ου m — olive-cake (mass of olives left after the oil has been pressed out)

*στενός -ή -όν — narrow

*στόμα -ατος n — mouth

στραγγεύομαι — I loiter, delay

στρέφω — I turn around (mid: I twist, turn myself around)

Στρεψιάδης -ους m — Strepsiades

στρώματα -ων n pl — bedclothes

*σύ — you (sg)

συγγιγνώσκω + dat. (aor. imp.: σύγγνωθι) — I pardon, forgive

συγκατακλίνομαι — I lie in bed with

συμβαίνω (aor.: ξυνέβην) — I come together, come to an agreement

σύμπας σύμπασα σύμπαν — altogether, all at once

Σφήττιος -ου m — man from the deme of Sphettius

*σφόδρα — very much, vehemently, violently

σχάζομαι (aor.: ἐσχασάμην) — I let go, give up

σχινδάλαμος -ου m — splinter

σχολή -ῆς f — leisure, rest

*σῴζω (fut. pass: σωθήσομαι) — I save

Σωκράτης -ους m — Socrates, Athenian philosopher and master of the Reflectory

τάλας τάλαινα τάλαν — miserable, wretched

ταρρός -οῦ m — wicker basket

Τάρταρος -ου m — the Underworld

*ταχύς -εῖα -ύ (superl. adv.: τάχιστα; ὡς τάχιστα as quickly as possible) — swift, fast

τέφρα -ας f — ashes

τέως — for a while

τηλοῦ — far away

*τίθημι (impf. mid: ἐτιθέμεθα) — I place mid: I agree upon

τίς τί — who? what? (τί also why?)

τλάω — I endure, bear

τόκος -ου m — lit offspring, here interest (on a loan)

τράπεζα -ης f — table

τρασιά -ᾶς f — dried fig

τρεῖς m/f τρία n — three

*τρέπω — I turn

τρέφω — I rear

τρισμακάριος -α -ον — thrice-blest

*τρόπος -ου m — way, manner, habit

τροχός -οῦ m (gen./ dat. dual: τροχοῖν) — wheel

τρύξ -υγος f — unfermented wine, must

τρυφάω — I live luxuriously

*υἱός -οῦ m — son

ὑπερφρονέω — I think myself superior to, look down on

ὑπερφυής -ές | extraordinary
*ὑπό + acc. | under
*ὑπό + gen. | by, at the hands of
ὑπολύω | I take off, remove
ὑπόχρεως -ων | in debt
ὑφαίρομαι (aor.: | I steal
   ὑφειλομην) |

φάσκω | I say, declare
φάτνη -ης f | manger
Φειδιππίδης -ους m | Pheidippides, son of
   | Strepsiades
Φείδων -ωνος m | Pheidon, Strepsiades'
   | father
φελλεύς -έως m | stony ground
*φέρω (idiom: φέρε | I carry, bear, endure
   come, . . .) |
φεῦ | alas!
*φεύγω | I run away, defend (a
   | lawsuit)
*φημί | I say
*φιλέω | I love
*φίλος -η -ον (superl.: | dear
   φίλτατος) |
φρήν φρένος f | mind
φροντίζω + gen. (fut.: | I consider, care about
   φροντιῶ) |
φροντίς -ίδος f | thought, idea
φρόντισμα -ατος n | thought, idea, invention
φροντιστήριον -ου n | place for thinking,
   | 'Reflectory', Thinking
   | -shop

Πυλος -ου m/f | Pylos, town on the
   | western
   | Peloponnese

Χαιρεφῶν -ῶντος m | Chaerephon, Socrates'
   | student
χαμαί | on the ground
χάσκω (perf. part.: | I gaze up open-mouthed
   κεχήνως) |
*χείρ χείρος f | hand
χράομαι + dat. (aor. | I use, deal with, do
   mid: ἐχρησάμην) | business with
χρέος -ους n | debt
*χρή + infin. | it is necessary
*χρῆμα -ατος n | thing, business, problem,
   | pl money, property
*χρήσιμος -η -ον | useful
χρήστης -ου m | creditor
*χρόνος -ου m | time
χρῶμα -ατος n | colour, sun-tan
χωρίον -ου n | place, distance

ψύλλα -ης f | flea
ψύχω (aor. pass. part.: | I make cool
   ψύχεις) |
ψυχή -ῆς f | soul

*ὡς + acc. | to, towards
*ὡς adv. | thus
*ὥσπερ | like as, just as
ὠχριάω | I am pale